HISTORY OF
United States Naval Operations
IN WORLD WAR II

★

VOLUME ONE

The Battle of the Atlantic

September 1939–*May* 1943

HISTORY OF UNITED STATES NAVAL OPERATIONS

IN WORLD WAR II

By Samuel Eliot Morison

Photo by Steichen

Admiral Ernest J. King USN

Commander in Chief United States Fleet

Taken at the Admiral's Washington headquarters, October 1943

HISTORY OF UNITED STATES NAVAL OPERATIONS IN WORLD WAR II

VOLUME I

The Battle of the Atlantic

September 1939–*May* 1943

BY SAMUEL ELIOT MORISON

WITH AN INTRODUCTION ON

The United States Navy Between World Wars

by Commodore Dudley Wright Knox USN

With Illustrations

CASTLE BOOKS

This edition published by arrangement with
Little, Brown and Company, (Inc.).

This edition published in 2001 by Castle Books
A division of Book Sales, Inc.
114 Northfield Avenue, Edison, NJ 08837

Printed in the United States of America

HISTORY OF UNITED STATES NAVAL OPERATIONS IN WORLD WAR II

***The* BATTLE OF THE ATLANTIC**
1939 - 1943
VOL. I

ISBN: 0-7858-1302-0

To

The Memory of

FRANKLIN DELANO ROOSEVELT

1882–1945

President of the United States

Commander in Chief of the Army and Navy

4 March 1933–12 April 1945

O this may march through endless time, immortal,
if one but tell it well. If so it be,
across the fruitful earth and o'er the sea,
shoots a bright beam of noble deeds, unquenchable.

— PINDAR, *Isthmian Ode*, iv. 40–43

Foreword

EARLY IN 1942, Samuel Eliot Morison, Jonathan Trumbull Professor of American History in Harvard University, suggested to President Roosevelt the desirability of preparing for the American people a full, accurate, and early record of the activities of the Navy in World War II; he volunteered his services in the preparation of such a record. The proposal met with the approval of Secretary Knox, and Dr. Morison was commissioned in the Naval Reserve with the sole duty of preparing a "History of United States Naval Operations in World War II."

All naval activities, afloat and ashore, were directed to make available to Captain Morison such records as he might desire to consult. The complete work, of which this volume is a part, is the result. Captain Morison has been afforded access to official documents, with full authority to discuss them with all naval personnel concerned. He has visited the various theaters of war on combat ships and has taken part in several amphibious operations and surface engagements with the enemy. The Navy Department has done everything possible to enable him to make his research exhaustive and to afford him firsthand impressions.

This work, however, is in no sense an official history. The form, style and character of the narrative are the author's own. The opinions expressed and the conclusions reached are those of Dr. Morison, and of him alone. He has been subject to no restrictions other than those imposed by the necessity of safeguarding information which might endanger national security.

It is believed that the original purpose has been well served and the work is a stirring account of the Navy's operations in World War II.

James Forrestal

THE SECRETARY OF THE NAVY
Washington

Preface

MY PURPOSE in writing this work was to tell the world what the United States Navy accomplished in the greatest of all naval wars, and how it was done. The story, in the main, is one of fighting; that is what the Navy is for and what its entire effort was directed toward. I have devoted just enough space to strategic discussions, planning, organization and logistics to explain the end product – the naval operations. And when other armed services of the United States and her allies participated, I have brought them in too, although not in so great detail.

The Navy plans various works to cover other phases of the war. Rear Admiral W. R. Carter USN (Ret.), who commanded Service Squadron 10 during the war, has written the history of naval logistics afloat in the Pacific, published in 1953 as *Beans, Bullets and Black Oil;* and he is now at work on a history of American naval logistics in the Atlantic. Rear Admiral J. A. Furer USN (Ret.), who served as Coördinator of Naval Research during the war, is now preparing a history of the Navy Department's administrative experiences during World War II.

Believing that too many histories are written from the outside looking in, I or one of my assistants visited almost every theater of naval warfare and took part in as many operations as possible. In addition, an intensive research has been made in the naval archives of the United States and of allied and enemy powers; and oral evidence has been obtained from very many participants.

No history written during or shortly after the event it describes can pretend to be completely objective or even reasonably definitive. Facts that I know not will come to light; others that I discarded will be brought out and incorporated in new patterns of interpretation. Nevertheless, I believe that more is to be gained by writing in contact with the events, when most of the participants are alive, than by waiting until the ships are broken up and the sailors have departed to wherever brave fighting men go. Historians in years to come may shoot this book full of holes; but they can never recapture the feeling of desperate urgency in our planning and preparations, of the excitement of battle, of exultation over a difficult operation successfully concluded, of sorrow for shipmates who did not live to enjoy the victory.

Feeling and seeing the thing are not the only advantage that a participant has. The historian should recreate the past for his readers, no matter how much time separates him from them, or from the events described. Perspective is an aid in giving events their true setting. Yet there is a roundness that one can only obtain on shipboard, seeing the events as they unroll, and later, "shooting the breeze" with shipmates and sailors of other ships. This saves one from the delusion common to historians, that they could have conducted the operation better. So could the admiral or general, if he had had possession of the facts and factors available to the historian. Seamen who write action reports seldom take the trouble to analyze their own minds and explain why they did thus and so; hence the historian often assumes that they knew far more than they did, and regards their estimates of the situation or their decisions as mistaken when, in view of facts in hand or legitimately apprehended, they may have been sound and wise. Also, historians are apt to overlook the tremendous influence of luck in all warfare, especially naval warfare. Twelve inches' difference in the course of a torpedo, a few yards' deflection in the fall of a salvo, may make the difference between victory and defeat. Historians with military experience will always be more tolerant of failure or lack of success than those without it, because they well know how slight a factor beyond his control may make or break a military commander.

On the other hand, if I confined myself to personal impressions and oral testimony this work would not be history. As rigorous a study of the written documents has been made as if this were a war of the last century. But official reports are not impeccable, and my own observations, as well as the oral testimony of others, have been of great assistance in reconciling contradictory statements, and clearing up inconsistencies. At the same time documentary evidence has caused many of my own immediate impressions and tentative conclusions to be given the "deep six." In other words, a seaman's eye has been applied to the technique of a professional historian, but the seaman has also learned to discount the evidence of his eye.

The Introduction to this volume, numbered I of the series, was kindly undertaken by Commodore Dudley W. Knox USN (Ret.), the senior historian of the United States Navy. Therein he has described both the development and the vicissitudes of the United States Navy during the twenty years between the two World Wars.

The entire History of Naval Operations, as published, consists of the following volumes: –

I. THE BATTLE OF THE ATLANTIC, SEPTEMBER 1939–MAY 1943. (1st edition, 1947; new and revised edition, 1954.)
II. OPERATIONS IN NORTH AFRICAN WATERS, October 1942–June 1943. (1st edition, 1947; new and revised edition, 1954.)
III. THE RISING SUN IN THE PACIFIC, 1931–April 1942. (1st edition, 1948; revised edition, 1954.)
IV. CORAL SEA, MIDWAY AND SUBMARINE ACTIONS, May–August, 1942. (1st edition, 1949; revised edition, 1954.)
V. THE STRUGGLE FOR GUADALCANAL, August 1942–February 1943. (1st edition, 1949; revised edition, 1954.)
VI. BREAKING THE BISMARCKS BARRIER, 22 July 1942–1 May 1944. (1st edition, 1950; revised edition, 1954.)
VII. ALEUTIANS, GILBERTS AND MARSHALLS, June 1942–April 1944 (1st edition, 1951.)
VIII. NEW GUINEA AND THE MARIANAS, 1944. (1st edition, 1953.)
IX. SICILY, SALERNO AND ANZIO, 1943–1944. (1st edition, 1954.)
X. THE BATTLE OF THE ATLANTIC WON, MAY 1943–MAY 1945.
XI. THE INVASION OF FRANCE AND GERMANY, 1944–1945.

The Battle of the Atlantic attempts to include all United States naval operations in that Ocean, from pole to pole; and in the Caribbean, Gulf of Mexico, Barents Sea and Atlantic territorial waters. The story will be continued from the middle of 1943 to the end of the war in Volume X.

The United States Navy participated in no fleet actions in the Atlantic. Apart from the *Bismarck* battle and a few minor engagements in the Barents Sea there were none in that area during the period covered by this volume. The Battle of the Atlantic was, by and large, a fight for the protection of shipping, supply and troop transport waged by the United States Atlantic Fleet and Allied Navies against Axis submarines, supporting aircraft and a few surface ships. It was essentially a war of maintaining communications with our own forces in Europe and Africa and with our overseas Allies, including Russia; an offensive development of the original policy of hemispheric defense against an Axis approach to the New World.

Only Roosevelt and Churchill, of the heads of state concerned in the war, seem to have appreciated the transcendent importance of ocean communications. In all former wars, trade was the primary reason for "keeping 'em sailing"; and as Mahan proved, that nation won who could both trade and fight. In World War II this axiom was still true over a wider periphery, but private trading for profit declined to a vanishing point. The amount and kind of commerce among the Allies was determined exclusively by military considerations – the "war effort." All shipping not used for troop transport and supply was employed in transporting immense quantities of strategic materials from widely separated islands and continents in order to forge the weapons, equip the men and build the planes, ships and armored vehicles necessary to wage a modern war. Britain virtually abandoned her traditional trade routes in order to become a military workshop, staging point and bridgehead; America followed suit, converting factories of consumer goods to war industry plants. Neither could do less to win; for armies can no longer live off an invaded country or reach a decision with infantry weapons alone. Their standard of living has gone up with that of the world at large; soldiers, sailors and aviators have to be supplied with food, drink, tobacco, clothing and special equipment in great quantity and variety. At the same time, the adoption of automatic weapons and mechanized equipment has vastly increased the shipping space necessary to keep an army supplied with ordnance, ammunition and a variety of land and amphibious vehicles. Even Russia, fighting a desperate war of defense on land, could only make her manpower effective against Germany if supplied by sea with armor and equipment from the workshops of the United Kingdom and the United States.

Germany had the advantage of a long head start in war preparations. Her land communications were vulnerable only from the air. Hitler had built up such enormous stockpiles before 1939, German scientists had worked out so many formulas for synthetic oil, rubber and the like, and the German armies as they overran western Europe acquired so much more food and matériel, that Hitler believed he could defy the tightest sea blockade. So he could up to a certain point; but that point came after the fall of France "called the New World into existence to redress the balance of the Old." Then the Germans had reason to regret their Fuehrer's flouting of sea power and ignorance of naval strategy. Unable to reach out across the seas to obtain more strategic supplies – except for a thin trickle from the Far East in blockade-runners and submarines – they concentrated their entire naval effort on cutting the lifelines of their enemies.

Thus the Battle of the Atlantic was second to none in its influence on the outcome of the war. Yet the history of it is exceedingly difficult to relate in an acceptable literary form. For Anti-Submarine Warfare is an extremely complicated, diverse and technical subject, somewhat repetitious in its operational details. To simplify it by merely relating a series of the more spectacular fights between escorts and U-boats would be a grave distortion of the truth. So, in order to give the reader some idea of the difficulties involved in defeating the Axis submarines, I have had to go behind naval operations in the narrow sense, and describe some of the training schools, technical devices and scientific research that helped to make brave men and gallant ships effective. Many anti-submarine operations, moreover, were conducted jointly with the United States Army Air Force, or combined with the British and Canadian Navies and Air Forces, including attached units of the French and Polish Navies.[1] In a history of the United States Navy it is not possible to devote the space to the exploits of sister services and Allies that they would deserve in a general history of the war; yet, again, it would distort the picture if nothing were said about their participation, which was essential to victory.

During the emergency of 1942–1943 a number of auxiliary and amateur forces, such as the Civil Air Patrol and Coastal Picket Patrol, were created for the protection of shipping. As these represented a sincere effort on the part of civilians to help the Navy and the cause, a chapter has been devoted to them.

Although the United States Navy began indirect participation in the Atlantic struggle several months in advance of the formally declared war by Germany, the British and Canadians fought the lonely battle for almost two years. Hence I have begun this volume by describing the convoy system established in the fall of 1939 by the naval authorities in Ottawa and London. And as escort-of-convoy was the first belligerent service assumed by the United States Navy, that was the first subject that I pursued after receiving my commission in May 1942.

[1] The operations of the United States Coast Guard are, however, included with those of the Navy, because President Roosevelt, as authorized by Act of Congress, directed the Coast Guard to "operate as a part of the Navy, subject to the orders of the Secretary of the Navy," on 1 Nov. 1941. It was turned back to the Treasury Department by executive order of President Truman effective 1 Jan. 1946.

In order to obtain the necessary background of experience, I was ordered to temporary duty on the staff of Captain John B. Heffernan, commanding Destroyer Squadron 13, and sailed in his flagship, U.S.S. *Buck*, to the United Kingdom and back in July 1942 with Task Force 37 escorting Convoy AT–17. Captain Heffernan gave me most valuable indoctrination in modern naval warfare and escort-of-convoy duty. I then caught up with anti-submarine history by obtaining temporary duty with the Anti-Submarine Warfare Unit of the Atlantic Fleet at Boston, then under the direction of Commander Thomas L. Lewis. The same subject was pursued at Eastern Sea Frontier Headquarters, and in the Convoy and Routing and Anti-Submarine Warfare Sections of the Navy Department. After making fairly satisfactory progress, I felt obliged to depart for Africa in October 1942. Writing the history of Operation "Torch" and a subsequent tour of temporary duty in the Pacific prevented my returning to the Atlantic battle before the summer of 1943.

By that time the peak of German success had passed, and the whole set-up of anti-submarine warfare had changed, with the creation of the Tenth Fleet. I therefore returned to the Pacific while my assistant, Ensign Henry Salomon Jr., USNR, proceeded to Bermuda, the West Indies and Brazil to gather information on the war in the Caribbean and South Atlantic. We both returned to the United States early in 1944, and devoted the next few months to completing the first draft of this volume. During that stage of the work, Captain P. R. Heineman, commanding the Anti-Submarine Warfare Unit Atlantic Fleet, and Commander C. E. Ames USNR, in the Convoy and Routing Section Tenth Fleet, were particularly helpful. Additional information was obtained from time to time on visits to Headquarters Operational Training Command Atlantic Fleet, Subchaser School at Miami, Sound Schools at Key West and San Diego, Headquarters Gulf, Eastern and Caribbean Sea Frontiers. And I acquired more experience of convoy duty and anti-submarine warfare in November–December 1944 while crossing by the southern route with Convoy UGS–61 as a temporary member of the staff of the escort commander, Captain W. A. P. Martin, in U. S. Coast Guard Cutter *Campbell.*

Although personally I have seldom passed a dull moment at sea, whether in peace or in war, in sail or in steam, it must be admitted that for most sailors and aviators the Holmesian dictum "war is an organized bore" has a particular application to this Battle of the Atlantic. It could not be otherwise when by far the greater part of anti-submarine warfare consisted in searching and waiting for a fight that very rarely took place; yet every escort or patrol ship was supposed to be completely alert from the time she passed the sea buoy until she returned to harbor. Visual lookouts became weary with reporting floating boxes and bottles as periscopes; deck officers became exasperated with the vagaries of merchant seamen; they in turn got "gold braid" in their hair; and the monotonous, never-ending "ping"-ing of the echo-ranging sound gear had the cumulative effect of a jungle tom-tom. Officers and bluejackets in escort vessels, coastguardsmen on their frigid offshore and Greenland patrols, aviators searching the sea lanes for submarines or survivors, experienced excruciating boredom, despite the need of constant alertness; and if no action materialized for weeks on end, as often happened, a feeling of frustration made the monotony almost unbearable for young men. One cannot write a history of things that do not happen. So I wish to emphasize here the ninety-and-nine moments of devoted, continuous vigilance on the part of ships, planes and men, as against the one moment of action (always welcome, often joyful, but sometimes tragic) that makes the stuff of operational history.

During visits to London in 1942, 1944 and 1951, I made fruitful connections with Captain A. C. Dewar RN and his successor Vice Admiral Roger M. Bellairs RN, who headed the Historical Section of the Admiralty. We have continued to exchange information ever since. I have also received much assistance from the historical staff of the Royal Canadian Navy under Dr. Gilbert Tucker.

The German Admiralty Records were seized by United States armed forces shortly after the surrender of Germany and taken to

London, where they have been studied and, to some extent, translated by British and American military men. Copies of these were made available to me early in 1946, when Lieutenant Commander Henry D. Reck USNR of my staff, in addition to his other duties, applied himself to analyzing and abstracting the relevant portions of the German records.

Since 1950, the study of these German records has been resumed by Lieutenant Philip K. Lundeberg USNR, at the same time that he prepared the groundwork for Volume X, in which the Battle of the Atlantic will be continued to its victorious conclusion.

German submarine logs are not uniformly reliable. Most of those consulted appear to have been written up after return to base from rough notes, memory and guesswork, and from knowledge received ashore; bluff and bravado characterize many. On the other hand, the War Diary of the German Submarine Command is on the whole a realistic and reliable source, in which submarine movements and losses are accurately recorded. By comparing these with the known facts of our own and Allied attacks on submarines, it is possible to reach a reasonably accurate score of kills, but not of damage. The Navy's Press Release of 27 June 1946, "German, Japanese and Italian Submarine Losses in World War II," is probably as accurate a list as we shall ever have.

Mr. Reck and Mr. Salomon were my assistants in preparing this volume. Lieutenant J. Willard Hurst USNR collected material for me on the North Russia convoys, the Merchant Marine and the Naval Armed Guards. The charts were executed by Elinor M. Ball, Specialist Wave 1st Class. The checking and some of the typing were done by Chief Yeoman Donald R. Martin USNR; the rest of the typing by Antha E. Card, Wave Yeoman 1st Class, and Harry E. Foster, Yeoman 2nd Class. At least a score of officers of the United States and Royal Navies who had special knowledge of the events or movements described have read the whole or parts of the text and provided many corrections and elucidations. I am particularly grateful to two Directors of Naval History, Rear Admirals Vincent R. Murphy and John B. Heffernan; to Commodore Dudley W.

Knox, their predecessor, and to several members of his staff, notably Captain John W. McElroy USNR and Commander Walter M. Whitehill USNR, as well as the efficient Naval Archivist, Miss Loretta I. MacCrindle.

Captain McElroy, after several active tours of sea duty in World War II and the Korean War, undertook in 1952 to prepare this revised edition. He weighed and checked the large number of corrections and suggestions for improvement that had flowed in since the first edition was published, and supplied other corrections and improvements from his own knowledge.

In retrospect, the person I feel most grateful to is the late President Franklin D. Roosevelt. For he appreciated the value of a history of this sort, as soon as I had called the need of it to his attention; he commissioned me to undertake it, and even during the war found time to talk with me on the subject. My admiration for the quality of his leadership of our armed forces has, if anything, increased with the lapse of years. So I have dedicated this revised Volume I, and the series, to his memory.

SAMUEL E. MORISON

HARVARD UNIVERSITY
1947 and 1953

Contents

List of Illustrations

(All photographs not otherwise described are Official United States Navy)

List of Charts

Drawn by Elinor M. Ball, Sp(X)1c W-USNR
Following the sources listed under each title

Introduction

The United States Navy Between World Wars

BY COMMODORE DUDLEY W. KNOX USN (Ret.)

THE colossal American Navy of World War II, with its incredible complexity and superlative combat effectiveness, was a product of many factors. The spirit of our people, the mighty efforts of industry, the virility and skill of our political leadership, our rapid advances in science and its applications to warfare, were among the chief elements which brought complete and surprisingly speedy victory on a vast scale.

Another cardinal factor, obviously, was the general state of the Navy itself at the President's declaration of limited emergency in September 1939. There lay the foundation stones upon which the broad and towering structure was to be so quickly raised. Personnel was to be suddenly expanded more than thirty times and ships and other equipment in even greater proportion. By far the larger part of the increase came under the high pressure of warfare while vigorous and competent foes were inflicting severe losses. Essential supplements of combat were the throes of organization, administration, planning and training as well as logistics in mountainous proportions.

The parent stock of personnel was fortunate in having roots deeply embedded in traditions of a high order. Readiness, efficiency, vigor and determined action were heritages transmitted through many generations of gallant and capable officers; conspicuous among them being Paul Jones, Barry, Truxton, Preble, the Porters, the Perrys, Farragut, Dewey and Sampson. The Naval Academy had long been an important influence upon the capabilities, spirit and cohesion of the general body of officers. In later years the Naval War College, founded by Admiral Luce and supported by Mahan, had effectively indoctrinated and trained senior officers in the essential art of higher command. Application of War College teaching afloat was led by Sims. Nor should the sterling worth of the warrant and petty officers be forgotten. In 1939 the service was fortunate in having passed through an era of long average service among the lower ratings, which were a vital base for the great pyramid of wartime expansion.

With respect to ships, planes and materiel in general the Navy had maintained superior standards of upkeep and operating efficiency, and of design corresponding to age. In 1939–1940 there was a substantial shortage in numbers of both ships and planes as well as of personnel, as measured by the need of taking the early brunt of a war on two oceans. Many battleships were of obsolete type. Our outlying Pacific bases were critically inadequate in number and facilities. These serious deficiencies were not the result of apathy or want of vision within the Navy itself but were largely due to three influences at work after World War I: (1) inequities in the international treaties limiting naval armaments; (2) persistent propaganda and lobbying against the Navy, led by many high-purposed organizations and individuals and causing public prejudice; (3) the crusade, led by Brigadier General William Mitchell, U. S. Army, to supplant sea power by air power. Discussion of these three adverse influences will follow. An examination will also be made of certain constructive developments after 1918, such as those relating to naval aviation and amphibious techniques, which added much to the power of our Navy in 1939–1940, despite its deficiencies in numbers.

Captain Morison's preëminence as a maritime scholar and historian is well known. He has also long been a proficient seaman and navigator. To this unusual background he has more recently added substantial combat and other naval experience in several great campaigns. Altogether the unique combination of qualifications fits him exceptionally well for the difficult task of writing an operational history of American naval forces in the vastest war of all time. Our Navy and public are extremely fortunate in having him, above all others, to undertake it. His work is comprehensive and authoritative, and done in a style of great charm as well. This brief introduction to the monumental product of Captain Morison is intended merely to outline the more important developments affecting our naval strength prior to World War II.

1. *International Limitation of Naval Armaments*[1]

In 1916, under the ardent sponsorship of President Wilson, Congress authorized a great naval building program to extend over a period of years. Sixteen capital ships (battleships and battle cruisers) besides other craft were provided for and the actual construction of some of them was begun. When the United States entered World War I, the acute crisis of the German submarine campaign called urgently for destroyers and other anti-submarine types. In order to turn these out rapidly and in quantity, work on building capital ships was halted. The British and ourselves together already possessed sufficient capital ships for the current war. Moreover, the delay in our construction would afford opportunity to revise designs so as the better to incorporate lessons learned from war experience.

In December 1918, soon after the Armistice, the President recommended to Congress the resumption of this great naval building program of 1916. Consternation was immediate throughout Britain, whose traditional naval supremacy was seriously jeopardized. They had been through a long, hard war which had not only worn out many vessels of the fleet but also had undermined finances so as to forbid replacements on any scale comparable to America's program. When our Secretary of the Navy Daniels visited Paris early in 1919, during the Versailles Peace Conference, British Cabinet members urged upon him that we should suspend construction of our new capital ships. President Wilson would not consider such a proposal.

[1] Principal sources: the official "Report of the American Delegation," Senate Documents, 67th Congress 2nd Session, IX 3–90. Dudley W. Knox *The Eclipse of American Sea Power* (1922).

He was still wedded to his doctrine that America should have "incomparably the most adequate Navy in the world."[2] This policy continued throughout his administration and our ship construction work went forward.

During the succeeding Harding administration this policy was substantially altered in favor of naval limitation agreements among the principal naval powers. An international conference on this question met at Washington in November 1921, under the presidency of the American Secretary of State, Charles Evans Hughes. His opening proposals were astonishingly generous to other countries at the expense of the United States. We were "To scrap all capital ships now under construction. This includes six battle cruisers and seven battleships on the ways and in course of building, and two battleships launched. The total number of new capital ships thus to be scrapped is fifteen. The total tonnage of the new capital ships when completed would be 618,000 tons."[3]

Here was a magnificent potential of sea power upon which we had already spent upwards of $300,000,000, tossed overboard in a magnanimous gesture for international good will and peace, neither of which was subsequently realized. It was not merely the number and tonnage of the ships that counted. Their modernity was of great importance, especially with regard to their protection against high-angle gunfire, aërial bombs, torpedoes and mines. Their design was much superior in these and other respects to the residue of capital ships with which we had to start World War II. In 1921 no other nation had a comparable building program with which to match the sacrifice. Japan came nearest with three battleships and four battle cruisers of design inferior to ours. Mr. Hughes called upon her to scrap these, as well as to forgo the laying down of other projected ships. Britain was asked to scrap four battle cruisers under construction and abandon plans for new battleships not yet started. All nations had a considerable number of old capital ships rapidly becoming obsolete. Of these Mr. Hughes proposed that the

[2] Address at St. Louis 3 Feb. 1916.
[3] Secretary Hughes's opening address 12 Nov. 1921 p. 8.

decks be cleared and that no new capital ships be started for ten years.

After all scrapping of old and new tonnage was completed there would be left 500,650 tons of capital ships for the United States, 604,450 tons for Britain and 299,700 tons for Japan. Allowing for age, power and other variables in individual ships this was calculated to be in a ratio of about 5–5–3 in strength, which was to be the proportion for replacements after the ten-year holiday. The final treaty followed these original proposals respecting capital ships, with minor changes. Japan wished to retain the nearly completed battleship *Mutsu*. We and the British concurred in return for retention by the United States Navy of two similarly unfinished battleships of the *West Virginia* class, and for the British right to build two new battleships at an early date. In all these modifications equivalent old tonnage was to be scrapped, and although the allowed total tonnage was slightly increased the 5–5–3 ratio was preserved. Also, it should be observed, the ships earmarked for scrapping from the American building program were those of superior design – the ones which would have been of most value in World War II. Our sacrifice in new tonnage was not matched even approximately by any other power.

There was little difficulty in reaching agreement limiting aircraft carriers on a 5–5–3 basis, with allowances somewhat in excess of the comparatively small existing tonnage in this type. The class was then only in an experimental stage. Fortunately, we gained the right to so convert two large battle cruisers, then under construction, that otherwise would have been scrapped. These were the *Lexington* and *Saratoga*, which proved themselves invaluable in World War II.

Another grave inequity to the United States that emerged from the Conference was its failure to limit naval combat auxiliary vessels – of which cruisers are the principal type although destroyers, submarines and other craft are also important.[4] This failure to limit

[4] The term "naval auxiliaries" was commonly used in the negotiations and treaties to denote strictly *combat* vessels auxiliary to capital ships, and would thus

combat auxiliaries in 1921–1922 in reality defeated the main object of the Conference: to stop competitive naval building, which was assumed to be a principal cause of wars. The failure was also the origin of our great handicap in cruiser strength during the early years of World War II.

Mr. Hughes's original proposal included the limitation not only of capital ships but also of combat auxiliaries, as cardinal predicates. Both were major elements of total strength. Therefore with respect to both classes there was to be "renunciation of building programs, of scrapping of existing ships and of establishing an agreed ratio of naval strength."[5] Otherwise the general structure of limitation obviously would be badly out of balance. The ratio for combat auxiliaries was to be the same as for capital ships: 5–5–3.

The main obstacle to agreement on combat auxiliaries lay in the very great preponderance of British cruisers, which they were unwilling to sacrifice in return for the proposed American sacrifice of capital ship superiority. In addressing the conference Mr. Balfour, as head of the British Delegation, eulogized the plan respecting capital ships and eagerly accepted it. When it came to combat auxiliaries, however, he saw the case differently. He was quite willing to accept parity with the United States in those combat auxiliaries which are normally attached closely to the capital ships in fleet operations or battle. But there was great stress upon the "hard, brutal necessities of plain and obvious facts" rendering it imperative that Britain control her sea lanes. Inferentially, although so obscured in skillful oratory that the point was then completely missed by most persons, Britain could not afford to give up her relative superiority in cruisers.

Considerably later in the protracted negotiations the French insisted upon a rather large quota of submarines. Britain had been

---

include cruisers, destroyers, submarines and lesser types designed especially for combat. The term as here used should not be confused with later practice to consider "auxiliaries" as meaning only the vessels provided for servicing the fleet, such as oilers, tenders, supply ships, transports, hospital ships, etc.

[5] "Report of the American Delegation" p. 17.

advocating the complete abolition of the type. When the French would not recede the British countered with a refusal to accept any limitation whatever upon naval combat auxiliaries, because of their value against submarines. Thus Britain kept her great preponderance of cruiser strength and we were left with no commensurate concession to our generous commitment to sacrifice our large superiority of capital ships.

Our naval strength with which to fight World War II was also seriously impaired by a third great inequity born by the Washington Conference of 1921–1922. Japan would not assent to the 5–5–3 ratio of tonnage without an agreement maintaining the *status quo* regarding the fortification and facilities of naval bases in the Pacific – excepting only Hawaii, Japan proper and certain British possessions very distant from Japan. This virtually doubled the value of Japanese tonnage quotas for naval and air operations in the Orient and throughout a large section of the vast Pacific Ocean. It rendered effective defense of Guam and the Philippines practically impossible and left Alaska very vulnerable. The blood, material and treasure that we expended during World War II to capture positions for naval and air bases, including the recapture of Guam and the Philippines, are fresh in our memory. These grueling and costly experiences leave little need to dwell herein upon our diplomatic folly respecting naval bases at the Washington Conference.

The original Hughes plan for limiting naval armaments "was a proposal of sacrifices, and the American Government, in making the proposal, at once stated the sacrifices which it was ready to make and upon the basis of which alone it asked commensurate sacrifices from others," so said the American Delegation in its final official report.[6] As events proved, when Uncle Sam stopped playing Santa Claus, reindeer took on another color.

Had the Conference succeeded in a main objective of stopping competitive naval building, a case in justification of our single-handed sacrifices might have been made out. But the ink was

6 "Report" p. 17.

scarcely dry on the treaties before Japan embarked upon a large building program of cruisers and other combat naval auxiliaries. Britain felt it necessary to meet this threat and soon France as well as Italy joined the competition on a large scale. In effect they were all spending on combat auxiliaries the money saved from the holiday in capital ship construction.

These developments progressively impaired the relative naval strength of the United States, which resolutely refrained from joining the arms race. On grounds that we should set a good example, the mobilized pacifists and other politically powerful groups prevented Congress from making appropriations for a balancing American naval tonnage. After several abortive diplomatic efforts to stem the naval building tide abroad, under the sponsorship of President Coolidge, we finally negotiated a treaty at London in 1930 limiting cruisers, destroyers, submarines and other combat auxiliaries. But the price was a substantially lowered American ratio. Counting the American quota of total strength at 5, the British quota became about 5.2 and the Japanese about 3.25. This because the other powers would agree only to a *status quo* basis which included their recent active building, while we were setting a futile example of restraint.

Secure in her increased strength from the naval base agreement together with numerous newly built combat naval auxiliaries, Japan invaded Manchuria in 1931. This was in violation of the Nine-Power and the Four-Power Treaties which had been negotiated at Washington in 1921–1922 to give political bolstering to the Naval Limitation Treaty. Despite our repeated protests Japan continued to advance in China. In 1934 she served notice resulting in terminating all the treaties limiting naval armament, two years being required before such notice would technically become effective. Even these beacons of coming trouble did comparatively little to stir us into active naval building. Pacifist and isolationist control over such matters continued to be very firm.

2. *Pacifist Propaganda*

One could be forgiven for wondering why we were such dupes concerning naval affairs in the 1920's and later. A cardinal explanation is the flood of distorted and misleading propaganda that swept over the country. The great theme was the furtherance of world peace. This met with an irresistible ground swell of public support, based largely on natural revulsion from the then recent slaughter of war in Europe. Emotion surged over reason. Armaments were represented as the principal cause of war and their severe reduction, and even abolition, was strongly advocated as a panacea. Extremists, of whom there were many, urged this country to set an example and disarm regardless of what was done abroad.

The floodgates were opened by the Washington Conference of 1921–1922 on limitation of naval armament. Our government represented this as a great move towards world peace, which it might well have been if other countries had met us only halfway in concession, conciliation and altruism. Instead they played the old game of self-interest, understandably and perhaps justifiably. None should criticize responsible government officials for discharging their trust to look after the interests of their own people. The failure of our public to recognize this inherent basis of international conferences and agreements was a prime factor in American gullibility to the misleading propaganda against appropriate naval armament.

The American delegation to the Washington Conference apparently was unprepared to deal adequately with the important function of publicity. At any rate, the wav of handling the function was revealed soon afterwards by Mr. Wickham Steed, Editor of *The Times* of London, in a speech in Montreal. There he said: –

> The American delegates refused to give out any news during the Conference. They left this whole matter with the British publicity agent, Lord Riddell, and I am not giving away any state secrets when I say that when Lord Riddell left Washington there was general lamentation among the American and other correspondents, who wondered

where they would proceed to get the real news. That may have been Quixotic on the part of the Americans, but rather than be under any suspicion of using their press to turn public opinion against nations with whom they may have had differences, they did this, and the American delegates were absolutely and honourably silent.[7]

Who could blame the British for capitalizing on such an opportunity? That the "real news" was well colored in their own interest is amply clear from the all but hysterical acclaim of the American public. To no material degree did our people understand that (1) we had made an enormous sacrifice of capital ship strength and money; (2) the British had unreasonably declined to make the commensurate and balancing sacrifice of cruiser strength that Mr. Hughes had asked of them; (3) the Japanese had nearly doubled the potential value of their Navy against us through the restrictions on naval bases, without greatly affecting British interests.

The great high-purposed but misled pacifistic propaganda machine was soon in high gear and developed plenty of power for at least fifteen years. It received fresh impetus from the Kellogg-Briand Pact of 1928 renouncing war as an instrument of national policy. There was never any sane appraisal of the unquestionably high value of armaments as a preserver of peace, when properly used. Religious and other emotional fervor mounted to absurd heights; to the point where prominent Protestant clergymen or other spokesmen maintained that even advocacy of armaments was sinful. How this was reconciled with the fact that most churches had ardently supported World War I and were to do the same in World War II has never been explained to this "miserable sinner," who happens himself to be an Episcopalian, formally confirmed.

A typical example of a general attitude of the churches is given by the following extracts from Pastoral Letters adopted for the guidance of Episcopal congregations by General Conventions of the Bishops of my own Church: –

[7] D. W. Knox *Eclipse of American Sea Power* (1922), quoting *Congressional Record* 22 Mar. 1922 p. 4712.

The most hopeful step towards world peace ever taken is the agreement . . . to abandon war as an instrument of national policy. Yet the powers most active in promoting that agreement have shown a persistent disregard of its logical inferences and continue to put their trust in armed preparedness. We covet for our country the courage to lead along the pathway of world peace, by doing its utmost even at the cost of risk and sacrifice to achieve immediate, substantial reduction of armaments. [1931.]

The only armed force, whether on land or sea, which is justifiable, is a constabulary designed to regulate and safeguard those interests that have to do with the prosecution of an orderly social economic life. . . . The Christian Church . . . refuses to respond to that form of cheap patriotism that has as its slogan "In times of peace prepare for war." It regards as wicked the waste of the nation's wealth in the building of vast armament and the maintenance of greatly augmented forces on land and sea. [1934.]

Practically all other Protestant sects adopted similar policies and propagandized the country in many widely read church publications. The numerous Methodists were extremely active and articulate politically. Their large Washington headquarters building in the shadow of the Capitol dome was convenient for exerting pressure on members of Congress.

At the top levels the Protestant churches mobilized their offensive against armaments in an organization called the Federal Council of Churches of Christ in America. The president of this Council was "an Englishman by birth and education, who came to this country when about thirty-one years old; . . . This is the organization which led the successful movement through nation-wide propaganda to defeat the Coolidge program for large new construction of cruisers and other naval auxiliaries, following the breakdown of the 1927 Geneva Naval Conference." [8]

The churches were far from playing a lone hand in the great game of undermining the relative power of the American Navy. They were enthusiastically supported by virtually the entire press, in the beginning. This continued for some years and tapered off but

[8] D. W. Knox "The Navy and Public Indoctrination" *U. S. Naval Institute Proceedings* LV 485 (June 1929).

very gradually. Not until World War II began to loom on the horizon did any substantial section of the American press turn in favor of national armament.

With a few notable exceptions the same pattern at first characterized the educational system of the country, with its powerful influence on public opinion. The League of Nations, the limitation treaties and the Kellogg Pact appealed strongly to the academic world as justifying a belief that there would be no more war. During the 1920's schools and colleges were free fields for the swarm of British lecturers, and sounding boards for the plethora of articles in our leading journals by Britishers on peace and naval topics. Naturally they were bent on the maintenance of the naval primacy of their country despite the guise of idealism. Our student bodies became rampant with pacifism, together with a disturbing proportion of their teachers, especially among women.

The tide turned when the Japanese invaded Manchuria in 1931. Then premises began to be more carefully verified and clarified, logic was weighed against emotional fervor, and conclusions began to bear a reasonable relation to reality. But the flood tide of rational support to naval preparedness by academicians ran slowly until the cloud of coming war in Europe became clearly visible.

Through all this controversy the feeble voices of American naval officers, the only competent domestic advisers on many technical points, were completely drowned out, or else held up to scorn and ridicule as warmongering. It was obvious to professionals that our legions of well-meaning lay propagandists for peace were unwittingly relying indirectly upon the advice of foreign technicians, justifiably working in the interest of their own countries. Those who thus contributed to this serious weakening of the American Navy must have been conscience-stricken in 1939–1941. Then it became crystal clear that in modern times a strong American Navy is not a menace but a safeguard to British security.

In any event the effect upon naval appropriations in the 1920's and later was devastating, since well-meaning churchmen, pacifists and all their allies were extremely active politically, both in election campaigns and in the halls of Congress. Thus the naval strength with which we entered World War II was seriously reduced below what was demanded by a sane naval policy; it was well below what was urgently needed to defend American interests, and Allied interests as well.

Probably another somber result was the actual promotion of war rather than peace. That at least is the opinion of the board of civilians who recently assisted in the "U. S. Strategic Bombing Survey," which included a careful examination and study of Japanese evidence obtainable from documents and important witnesses. Their comprehensive report contains the following comment: –

> Larger overall appropriations to the armed forces, beginning at the time of Japanese occupation of Manchuria (1931), when the threat to peace in the Far East became evident, might have made war unnecessary and would have paid for itself many times over in reduced casualties and expenditures had war still been unavoidable.

Ardor for righteousness must be amply tinctured with rational judgment if constructive results are to be achieved.

3. *The "Billy Mitchell" Crusade*

Brigadier General William Mitchell, United States Army, spearheaded an active movement against the Navy in Congress and the press during the 1920's and after. Its coincidence in time with the great "disarmament by example" propaganda augmented the effectiveness of both, towards weakening our naval forces available at the onset of World War II. The pacifists opposed augmenting the Navy even to treaty strength on the absurd premise that war would thus be promoted. Mitchell advocated the abolition of the Navy, except submarines, on the false assumption that it had become useless with the advent of air power.

He had organized and commanded a large Army Air Force in France during World War I, and returned home with an all but fanatical conviction that air power alone was destined to have supreme control of warfare over both land and sea. His major premises are readily found in his published works, from which the following quotations are taken: –

> Land power has become a holding agent which occupies a place conquered by air power. Sea power in its old rôle of defending a coastline has ceased to exist.
>
> The seas cannot be controlled through the agency of ships when such invincible enemies exist as aircraft and submarines . . .
>
> Air power has completely superseded sea power or land power as our first line of defense.
>
> Effectiveness [of anti-air guns] is constantly diminishing [and] never can improve much.
>
> If a naval war were attempted against Japan, for instance, the Japanese submarines and aircraft would sink the enemy fleet long before it came anywhere near their coast.
>
> Airplane carriers are useless instruments of war against first-class Powers.[9]

> Today the principal weapon in the sea is the submarine.
>
> The best defense against submarines is other submarines.
>
> At this time . . . it is practical to do away entirely with the surface battleship, the airplane carrier . . .
>
> The surface ship as an element of war is disappearing.
>
> An attempt to transport large bodies of troops, munitions and supplies across a great stretch of ocean, by seacraft, as was done during the World War [I] from the United States to Europe, would be an impossibility.
>
> A superior air power will dominate all sea areas when they act from land bases and no seacraft, whether carrying aircraft or not, is able to contest their aërial supremacy.
>
> In the future the mere threat of bombing a town by an air force will cause it to be evacuated.[10]

Every one of these statements proved to be completely fallacious in the crucible of actual warfare on a grand scale in 1939–1945. Much similar doctrine by the General could be quoted from 1921 onward, in speeches and in such leading journals as the *Review of Reviews*, *Saturday Evening Post*, *World's Work*, *National Geo-*

[9] "Building a Futile Navy" *Atlantic Monthly* CXLII (Sept. 1928) pp. 408–413.
[10] *Winged Defense* (1925) pp. xvi, 5, 6, 11–12, 121, 136.

graphic, and so on. A group of able journalists and broadcasters with negligible technical knowledge followed Mitchell's lead and covered the country for a long period of years with propaganda that influenced many persons and adversely affected naval appropriations which were needful in preparations for World War II.

Had General Mitchell's military and naval knowledge and experience been greater, his fanaticism for air as a virtual substitute for ground and sea power would have been more convincing. He was ignorant of naval affairs. His field service on the ground in warfare was very limited, except as an observer. As to aviation experience, I am unable to find any record of his having been in combat with a hostile plane, although he was unquestionably a fine pilot and commander of land aviation forces.

Such a record scarcely qualified Mitchell as an oracle on how aviation was to affect future ground fighting, and certainly he was wholly incompetent to estimate the aviation-naval probabilities. There were many naval aviators at that time who had qualified as pilots several years before him and who were also seamen and professional naval officers. Moreover, the Navy had operated a large group of land-bombing planes against the Germans in World War I. Competent naval men were seriously at work on the problem of integrating air power with sea power when Mitchell undertook his fallacious propaganda.

In 1921 a series of bombing and other tests were made against several of our obsolete battleships and some ex-German vessels, required to be sunk under the terms of allocation to us. The Navy had planned these exercises in practically their final form by December 1920, and invited the Army Air Service to participate in them.[11] Some of these tests were made exclusively by the Navy, others by the Navy and Army jointly but under naval jurisdiction, and still others by the Army Air Service alone against ships delivered to it by the Navy.

As a result of these aviation experiments the Joint Board (Army and Navy) reported "that it has become imperative as a matter of

[11] Report of the Secretary of the Navy for 1921 p. 7.

national defense to provide for the maximum possible development of aviation . . . in the Navy." It recommended aircraft carriers of the maximum size and speed. The Navy Department then adopted the policy of supplying the fleet "with an adequate aviation force that will be an integral part of it." [12] Here was sound decision flowing from careful analysis of experiments by professionally competent officers.

As a result of the same experiments, Mitchell took the opposite tack, propagandized on a national scale for the virtual substitution of air power in the place of sea power and lobbied extensively in Congress to that end. His father having been a Senator, "Billy" had many powerful political friends. The mere fact that a number of ships had been sunk by aviation became the cardinal predicate in his whole effective propaganda movement. Other truths equally if not more important were ignored or distorted. Among these may be mentioned the obsolete design of the targets, their extremely poor condition as to watertight integrity, the absence of crews on board to effect damage control, their immobility, and the want of any defensive gunfire or planes which permitted bombing from a low altitude impossible in actual warfare. In those tests conducted by the Army alone no attempt was made to examine the results of hits. Bombing was simply continued until the vessel was sunk, and thus all evidence of what caused the sinking was destroyed. The Navy's tests, on the other hand, were on a scientific basis, a specially appointed board of technical observers making a careful inspection of the damage after each hit registered before the final sinking. And on tests held jointly the Army planes ruthlessly ignored previous agreements and emergency signals that had been arranged to permit inspection between hits. Valuable information was thus lost.

The Navy's voice in rebuttal of Mitchell's propaganda went virtually unheard. Common sense should have been enough. The business of sinking ships had been a specialty of navies for centuries. Naval personnel were best capable of applying any weapon effectively to that end, whether guns, torpedoes, mines, depth charges,

[12] Report of the Secretary of the Navy, p. 7.

rams or aërial bombs were employed, singly or in combination, as was amply demonstrated in World War II.

On the whole Mitchell's crusade against the Navy was unsoundly based and was conducted by persons wholly incompetent to evaluate the probabilities as to the impact of aviation on naval power. Nevertheless, the propaganda was very skillful and effective. It had followed the general pattern of proverbial crusading whose technique requires that sensational attack be leveled against someone or something. The Navy was Mitchell's most convenient target. His aim and volume of fire were excellent. Unquestionably, he substantially weakened the Navy which was destined to begin World War II.

4. *Development of Fleet Aviation*

Despite the pacifists, General Mitchell, wholesale scrapping of capital ships and sharply reduced appropriations, the Navy's vigor of spirit and enterprise remained unimpaired. The most important constructive development between the two World Wars was that of integrating naval aviation with the Fleet. This had started almost with the inception of aviation but its progress was necessarily slow owing to the need of experimental work and the imperfections of early aircraft. With the call to war in 1917 all naval aviation effort was turned to immediate war aid. A detachment of naval aviation was the first American military force to land in France, except for an Army medical unit. Thereafter a large organization was rapidly built up and operated from shore stations in France and Britain. It was exceedingly active in all forms of wartime aviation, even including a strong bombing group which attacked German submarine bases in Belgium.

The Armistice had scarcely been signed before the Navy again turned diligently to the task of putting aviation afloat. Within two weeks Admiral Mayo, Commander in Chief of the Atlantic Fleet, made strong and very comprehensive recommendations to that end. "In view of the great advantage given to a fleet by an efficient air service" he urged that our Navy "be provided with an air service sufficient in all respects for reconnaissance, spotting, carrying torpedoes, anti-submarine patrols and escort duty." Among many detailed needs specified he included not less than two airplane carriers with planes "for reconnaissance and for torpedo carrying."

The General Board at once began a thorough study of the whole question and, in May 1919, made a preliminary report that "The development of fleet aviation is of paramount importance and must be undertaken immediately if the United States is to take its proper place as a naval power." In June the Board defined the basic policy: –

> To insure air supremacy, to enable the United States Navy to meet on at least equal terms any possible enemy, and to put the United States in its proper place as a naval power, fleet aviation must be developed to the fullest possible extent. Aircraft must become an essential arm of the fleet. A naval air service must be established, capable of accompanying and operating with the fleet in all waters of the globe.

Even before the General Board's conclusions a detachment of planes was sent to Guantanamo in January 1919 for exercises with the Fleet. They made enemy bombing attacks, scouted for and intercepted the Fleet at sea, directed submarines into position for attack, and made trial take-offs from a turret platform on a battleship. Later on the catapult was developed for such take-offs from shipboard. Early in May three naval seaplanes flew to Halifax as a first stop to span the Atlantic, via Azores and Lisbon. Many naval vessels stood by along the route. Two of the planes made forced landings and had to taxi on water part of the way. *NC–4*, piloted by Lieutenant Albert C. Read, made the whole distance by air, thus becoming the first airplane to fly across the Atlantic Ocean.

The next few years witnessed naval aviation development along several lines; largely experimental because of the pioneer nature of implementing the broad policies of integrating sea and air power. Kite balloons were tried and rejected. Rigid airships had a long, thorough and expensive trial also, but were finally abandoned as too delicate for naval use. Various types of vessels were improvised as tenders for seaplanes, to give them mobile bases. The first vessel designed and constructed for this purpose was the U.S.S. *Wright*, and she proved to be exceedingly useful over a long period of years. Similarly, the first carrier was the *Langley*, converted from a collier and fitted with a flying deck. She had a long and honorable career after 1921. Also arrangements were made to place aircraft on battleships, and later on cruisers. A considerable number of indispensable shore seaplane bases were provided.

These early adolescent years had severe growing pains. Mitchell's sustained attacks in the press and on Capitol Hill were a constant thorn in the flesh. A series of interminable Congressional hearings, apparently instigated by Mitchell, took an inordinate amount of effort and time. There were also sharp controversies within the Navy on the rôle and importance of aviation, on types of carriers and aircraft, on the question of a separate corps for aviation personnel and many other matters. The creation of the Bureau of Aeronautics in the Navy Department in July 1921 was a stabilizing factor, bringing to a focus the development as a whole, although many important aspects still remained under the cognizance of other bureaus. In 1925, the Morrow Board, appointed by the President to study aviation questions from a national viewpoint, made an exceedingly comprehensive and carefully prepared report. It generally sustained the Navy's contentions of several years, especially as to keeping naval aviation under the Navy. The great prestige of the board largely allayed the controversial ferment that had grown to be chronic and seriously hindering. The creation of an Assistant Secretary of the Navy for Aeronautics in 1926 was also very helpful.

Among the greater steps towards integrating aviation with the Fleet was the inclusion in 1921 of aircraft and carriers in war games at the Naval War College. Here the future high command afloat was educated and trained in the conduct of war and the games converted many skeptics into enthusiasts over the potentially high value of aviation in sea warfare. An invaluable supplement to such academic training was the annual practice of holding fleet exercises on a grand scale, simulating war conditions by specific strategical and tactical problems. These practical fleet exercises at sea were the major factor in the evolution of integrating air and sea power.

Naval aviation had its baptism in the great annual fleet problems, in the rôle of an infant, but with rather astonishing results. In 1923, the Fleet essayed an attack on the Panama Canal to test its defenses, which included Army aviation and naval ships. In the attacking force was the battleship *Oklahoma* fitted with a catapult and carrying one plane. She theoretically represented a carrier and her plane was a "constructive" substitute for a squadron of naval planes. The lone plane was launched at sea a long distance away and, entirely undetected, dropped ten miniature bombs on Gatun spillway before any anti-aircraft guns began shooting or any defending Army planes took off from the ground. In 1925, the pioneer carrier *Langley* was able to participate in the fleet problem. Her utility so impressed the Fleet Commander that he urgently recommended rushing to completion the big carriers *Saratoga* and *Lexington* then under construction. He also wanted development of planes of greater durability, dependability and radius, as well as better catapults and recovery gear aboard cruisers and battleships.

The large, new and fast carriers *Saratoga* and *Lexington* were ready to participate in fleet maneuvers for the first time in 1929. They made an impressive confirmation of the vulnerability of the Canal to air attack from sea. Much more was learned in carrier tactics, in methods of protecting them with other naval vessels, etc. The succeeding ten years of great fleet problems held annually over a vast expanse of ocean were invaluable as grand dress rehearsals for war. Various forms of fleet attack against land positions and of purely naval campaigns of fleet against fleet, with naval aviation components always present, were worked out.

Successively each problem brought the steady evolution of integration – the relation of ships to their air arm and as well the part of aviation in the merger. Both the ships and the aviation learned potent lessons while developing the power and efficiency with which they were jointly to meet the grueling tasks and win the hard victories of World War II.

Among the more important milestones of evolution were: (1) the demand for smaller individual carriers to spread the risk of loss; (2) the insistent demand for more carriers that led to the addition of *Ranger*, *Yorktown* and *Enterprise* to the Fleet; (3) the demand for escort carriers for spotting, landings support, fleet coverage and anti-submarine work; (4) the lesser importance of aircraft tenders and of battleship and cruiser planes; (5) the urgent development of anti-aircraft ordnance; (6) the urgent demand for planes of greater speed, range and striking power; (7) the development of dive-bombing against rapidly moving targets; (8) the development of carrier tactics in fleet operations; (9) the evolution of the carrier task force with attendant battleships, cruisers and destroyers; (10) the advent of the fast carrier task force having great range, mobility and striking power and the ability to refuel at sea.

All these and more came from the extensive annual maneuvers, until naval aviation in fleet work reached nearly full maturity, so far as was possible without actual war experience as a crowning guide.

It is worthy of special note that in the 1938 fleet problem the carrier *Saratoga* launched a successful, surprise attack on Pearl Harbor, from a position one hundred miles away, using the same tactics employed by the Japanese in December 1941. Also should be mentioned the active participation of Marine Corps aviation, more particularly in work related to amphibious warfare.

5. *Development of Amphibious Warfare*

Mother Ocean herself seemed to spawn myriads of prehistoric monsters for the amphibious phase of World War II. In scarcely more than three years upwards of three million men received this specialized training and went out to combat in world-wide theaters.

This vast development stemmed from our incomparable Marine Corps – an organization of exceptional esprit, discipline, efficiency and combat ardor, whose web-footed missions and techniques of long standing provided an indispensable model upon which to expand. But the conditions of World War I had turned the Corps away from amphibious thinking, to which it did not seriously return until 1924, when an expeditionary force from Quantico held practice landings on Culebra Island. Other similar maneuvers followed both in the Atlantic and the Pacific.

In 1933, the Fleet Marine Force was established and a series of annual fleet landing exercises was begun. They dealt with problems of transportation of troops in naval vessels, of ship-to-shore movements, of assault landings, of naval gunfire support, of aviation support, and of development of suitable landing craft. In 1938 our splendid Army and Coast Guard sent units to participate in this specialized advance training; thus renewing their traditional partnership with the Navy for war. In 1939, with a new war in the offing, the Army undertook its own independent training of a division, with Navy and Marine Corps guidance.

Unlike naval aviation, amphibious development was far from full-fledged at the onset of war. The greatest prewar impetus came from President Roosevelt's instructions in mid-1940 to prepare to take Martinique. More transports were provided; the important matter of combat loading was gone into; the development of landing craft was activated; and greater numbers of specialized troops were trained. In February 1941, Fleet Landing Exercise Number 7 was held under the personal command of Admiral Ernest J. King, then Commander in Chief of the Atlantic Fleet. A large naval force supported a practice landing at Culebra of three Marine combat teams, two Army combat teams and three reinforced Marine companies. The troops were commanded by Major General Holland Smith USMC. In August 1941, another similar exercise in large force was held at New River, North Carolina. Meanwhile a sizable part of the troops trained in amphibious operations had been sent to Iceland to relieve the British garrison there.

The first large exercise in the Pacific was held in 1937 in the San Diego-San Clemente area, and was featured by battleships bombarding the target area on San Clemente Island with live ammunition. Experimentation with new types and designs of landing craft had begun in 1936. During 1940–1941 most of the basic landing craft types were tested, including the American LCVP and LCM and the British LCT. Steps were taken to establish a permanent amphibious force in the Pacific, including conversion of several merchant ships to transports, and landing exercises continued. However, the main activity was in the Atlantic because of the larger forces concentrated there, incidental to the neutrality patrol.

The art of modern amphibious warfare had been advanced immeasurably by all this preparation and hard training. Yet when war broke it was far from ready to meet the mammoth tasks which were soon to be undertaken. At best the foundation had been laid for an amazing evolution which progressed rapidly from intelligent application of grueling combat lessons. In October 1941, on the eve of war, Admiral King summarized the state of amphibious readiness "to make clear and to emphasize that the Atlantic Amphibious Force is not in condition to be relied upon for the successful conduct of active operations and to urge that immediate steps be taken to remedy the shortcomings herein set forth."

His principal recommendations were (1) to set up an effective organization analogous to a corps; (2) to equip the troops adequately; (3) to provide transports adequate in number, capacity and equipment, including cargo vessels fitted to carry and to handle landing boats, tank lighters, and alligator tanks as well as heavy impedimenta including anti-aircraft guns, howitzers, trucks, tractors and transportation vehicles; (4) to hold realistic rehearsals when the foregoing conditions had been met. Fate ordained that most of the rehearsals were to be more than full-dress; that combat itself should furnish the principal training. Vast credit is due to those gallant and sturdy souls who developed the art in such rugged fashion.

6. *General Progress*

More so than with any other comparable agency, the American Navy has been characterized by incessant activity; by a synthesis of the academic with the practical; by imaginative leadership in professional matters; as well as by devotion to duty and zeal in serving public interests with high purpose and uncompromising loyalty.

The fleet exercises previously mentioned were but the crowning dome of a great structure of annual training, built upwards through progressive levels and segments of organization, from the most elementary foundations of individual skill and character. Through it all ran the cohesive mortar of discipline of the better sort, having due regard for self-respect. Except for discipline, leading to instant obedience, battles cannot be won nor lives and property well safeguarded when sudden emergency in its numerous forms must be met.

A factor of primary importance in World War II was the extraordinary mobility of our Fleet and its auxiliary forces. The enemy was often surprised and seriously embarrassed by the rapidity of our "strikes" and also by the great range of our Fleet and its uncanny ability to sustain operations far from base for long periods. These advantages grew out of our normal dearth of naval bases and our persistent habit of frequent exercises at sea, many of very long range. In comparison, other Navies maneuvered seldom and over short distances, largely because of restricted fuel supplies but also from having a greater luxury of bases. Hence their tendency was to stay tied to bases while ours was to cruise without benefit of adequate shore facilities.

After World War I naval thought turned principally to problems of warfare in the Pacific, with its vast distances and the deficiency of naval bases. Increasingly the Fleet's mobility and capacity for self-maintenance were improved. A Fleet Train, later designated as the Base Force, was organized. This was the ancestor of the famous Service Squadron 10 in World War II. The Fleet Train comprised oilers, cargo ships, transports, repair ships, ammunition ships, hospital ships and the like, all capable of accompanying and serving the Fleet in any locality. In addition, there were destroyer tenders, submarine tenders and aircraft tenders, designed to serve as mobile bases for groups of such small craft. Through subsidies it was arranged that many new merchant ships were built with characteristics making them suitable for ready conversion to use as naval auxiliaries in war. Another notable development was the steady advance in the difficult techniques of fueling at sea. Upon this general background was built the great mobility of our Fleet in World War II, together with its relative independence of base facilities on land.

All such operational matters were dovetailed with strategic and tactical study and training at the Naval War College, where some seventy senior officers were graduated annually. Theory evolved there was tried out afloat and conversely fleet experience was made available to the academic group. A similar synthesis also existed in the realm of materiel. The technical bureaus of the Navy Department that were responsible for the design and production of ships, machinery, weapons and equipment kept constant touch with actual performance in service.

The tonnage restrictions on the size of navies and on the sizes of several types of vessels that were effected by the international treaties of limitation led to emphasis on the importance of quality and light weight. It was a challenge which our designers and technicians met speedily and with great credit. Large economies in weight were gained by the use of light metals, from the adoption of welding instead of riveting for ship-plating, from increased pressures and temperatures in motive power, and the like. The design of the new cruisers and destroyers, as well as of much machinery, was very superior. Our naval planes, guns, torpedoes and mines were greatly improved and new fire-control apparatus, so vital in combat, became superlatively good.

The 1933 building program, including destroyers, cruisers and aircraft carriers, was a large and important undertaking. Between that date and 1940 the *Atlanta* class cruisers, bristling with anti-aircraft guns, were designed. Several types of fleet auxiliaries, including the new fleet minesweepers, were transferred from the drawing boards to the building ways. All battleships of the *North Carolina*, *South Dakota* and *Iowa* classes were designed in these prewar years, beginning in 1935. They were characterized by 16-inch main batteries, thicker armored decks for protection from air bombing, heavy fragment protection around important control stations, modern 5-inch anti-aircraft guns in twin mounts, and the forerunners (found by battle experience to be entirely inadequate) of the present types and numbers of close-range anti-aircraft weapons. They were also given good torpedo protection and excellent speed and steering qualities for the rapid maneuvering required in modern naval warfare.

Immediately upon the outbreak of war in Europe, the technical bureaus launched very comprehensive surveys of warship requirements under advisement by the General Board. The suspension of naval limitation treaties, as a result of the war, was a primary factor in the new program. The problem was no longer one of designing the best ship of a limited size, but one of selecting the most desirable combination of basic characteristics, including size, as one of the variables in the problem. With the aid of previous evolution and experience, designs were undertaken for new types of destroyers, cruisers and aircraft carriers. By 7 December 1941, contract plans had been completed for the *Fletcher* class destroyers, the 6-inch *Cleveland* class cruisers, the 8-inch *Baltimore* class cruisers, the *Essex* class aircraft carriers, the first class of destroyer escort vessels, the *Alaska* class large cruisers, and various auxiliaries including minecraft. All these embodied many fundamental characteristics later shown to be highly important in combat – short-range and long-range anti-aircraft guns, fragment protection for personnel, good armor, improved subdivision and watertight integrity to resist underwater attack. In order even to approach all the demands of modern warfare, an increase in size of every type was inescapable. Some of the requirements were: more ammunition for the increased number of guns, more crews to man the gun-mounts, more fuel oil for increased cruising radius, more machinery to give desired speed – all leading to an increased tonnage in order to carry the added weight with sufficient reserve buoyancy and afford the stability which gave a reasonable power of survival after damage.

Modern designs of main propulsion steam-driven plants using high-pressure, high-temperature steam had been introduced during the prewar period and had reached such a state of development in reliability that our new ships were able to steam enormous distances without Navy Yard overhauls of machinery – in some cases reaching incredible records and in many cases well over 100,000 miles within a single year. Extensive research and refinement in propeller design also began to pay large dividends. Tremendous improvements and developments in the diesel engine industry had made available another flexible and reliable source of propulsive power which was to be utilized to the staggering total of 35,000,000 shaft horsepower during the war in a Navy total shaft horsepower of some 90,000,000.

A basic influence on the general development of materiel was the system of experimental laboratories and testing stations that were maintained by various bureaus. They were staffed with technicians and scientists who coördinated their work with practical results in service. Among such establishments were ship-model basins, wind tunnels, powder, gun, torpedo, mine and aircraft factories, ordnance proving grounds, as well as engineering testing and experimental stations. A Naval Research Laboratory was established in 1928 for general, overall scientific aid on high levels. Its success in radio and radar was outstanding but it was helpful in a multitude of other fields as well. There was close collaboration with such federal agencies as the Bureau of Standards, the Army Chemical Warfare Service, the National Research Council, and also with the vast research activities of private industry. All of this together laid the foundations for the phenomenal wartime success of the Navy in quickly mobilizing the immense scientific resources of the country and utilizing them for operational applications. Thus the scientific world made exceptional and invaluable contributions to victory.

The evolution and adoption of principles and methods of unified command in the field, covering joint Navy and Army operations, were among the greater peacetime contributions towards the winning of World War II, so speedily and decisively. Supplementing this was the almost equally important plan to coördinate the general conduct of the war, through the agency of a joint board comprising the Chiefs of Staff. These organizational and administrative devices were to prove themselves immensely superior to the corresponding methods of the Germans and the Japanese – who were seriously hampered by lack of unified commands as well as by deficient coördination at the top-level headquarters.

The American methods grew out of staff and War College studies by both the Army and the Navy. These were followed by the recreation in 1919 of the Joint Board, which promulgated instructions in 1920 for unified command in the field on the basis of paramount interest. This meant that the chief command of any particular operation or theater would be taken by either Army or Navy, depending in each case upon which service had the primary interest therein. These 1920 instructions were substantially the basis of unified field command as practised in World War II. Moreover the 1919 Joint Board itself was developed into the Joint Chiefs of Staff, the agency in Washington which so brilliantly coördinated the conduct of all American forces in World War II.

7. *Comparisons of Naval Strength*

The following tabular statistics of naval tonnage will indicate the rapid deterioration of the American total strength, relative to other powers, from the beginning of the limitation treaties in 1922 to the outbreak of war late in 1941.

TONNAGE OF COMPLETED SHIPS IN 1922 AFTER SCRAPPING BY TREATY

(In Thousands of Tons)

	U. S.	BR. EMP.	JAPAN	FRANCE	ITALY
Capital Ships	526	559	301	221	182
Carriers	13	88	15	25	—
Cruisers	183	393	142	142	85
Destroyers	363	245	65	36	33
Submarines	49	76	24	31	18
Totals	1134	1361	547	455	318

COMPLETED TONNAGE AT END OF LIMITATION TREATIES IN 1936, EXCLUDING SHIPS OBSOLETE FROM AGE

(In Thousands of Tons)

	U. S.	BR. EMP.	JAPAN	FRANCE	ITALY
Capital Ships	464	475	312	186	87
Carriers	81	115	68	22	—
Cruisers	249	359	242	147	172
Destroyers	216	191	96	115	97
Submarines	68	52	66	78	55
Totals	1078	1192	784	548	411

COMPLETED TONNAGE IN 1941, EXCLUDING SHIPS OBSOLETE FROM AGE

(In Thousands of Tons)

	U. S.	BR. EMP.	JAPAN	FRANCE	ITALY
Capital Ships	534	443	357	177	164
Carriers	135	161	178	22	—
Cruisers	329	471	299	150	119
Destroyers	237	268	154	114	101
Submarines	117	55	107	61	84
Totals	1352	1398	1095	524	468

Particularly noteworthy is the great relative rise of Japan's Navy. During this twenty-year period it gained about 61 per cent in relativity. In 1922, its total tonnage was only 50 per cent of American strength, but Mr. Hughes then proposed to give Japan a 60 per cent quota. The treaty of 1922 allowed her 60 per cent in capital ship tonnage, besides the further great advantage incident to the agreed restrictions on naval bases.

By 1936, when the treaties expired, Japan's total tonnage had risen to 73 per cent of the corresponding strength of the United States. This rapid augmentation resulted from the feverish Japanese activity in building naval combat auxiliaries (upon which there was no limit until 1930) while we at the same time held down our own new construction to small proportions. The unnatural, if not unholy alliance between pacifists and air crusaders was the main cause of our restraint.

Even after the limitation treaties expired we were tardy in starting and long in completing new ships, while many older vessels were becoming obsolete from age. On the eve of war in 1941 Japan's total tonnage of modern and completed ships had risen to 81 per cent of ours. Since we had to fight in the Atlantic as well as in the Pacific, and because of our great inferiority in overseas bases, the Japanese Navy was then substantially superior to ours for operations in the central and western Pacific Ocean.

The Battle of the Atlantic

September 1939–*May* 1943

Officers' ranks and bluejackets' ratings are those contemporaneous with the event. Officers named will be presumed to be of the United States Navy unless otherwise stated; Naval Reservists are designated USNR.

Other service abbreviations, following an officer's name, are: —

RCN, Royal Canadian Navy.
RN, Royal Navy; RNVR, Royal Navy Volunteer Reserve.
USCG, United States Coast Guard; USCGR, Reserve of same.
USMC, United States Marine Corps; USMCR, Reserve of same.
USA, United States Army.

In footnote references, only the titles of printed or multigraphed books, pamphlets and periodicals have been italicized. Other documents, including the Action Reports and War Diaries of ships and naval commands, are in Roman type.

Some of the common abbreviations used in this volume are as follows: —

A.A.F. — Army Air Force or Forces
Cinclant — Commander in Chief, Atlantic Fleet
Cincwa — Commander in Chief, Western Approaches (to U.K.)
Cominch — Commander in Chief, United States Fleet
C.O. — Commanding Officer
H.M.C.S. — His Majesty's Canadian Ship (Royal Canadian Navy)
H.M.S. — His Majesty's Ship
Momp — Mid-ocean meeting point
N.A.S. — Naval Air Station
N.O.B. — Naval Operating Base
O.N.I. — Office of Naval Intelligence
Opnav — Chief of Naval Operations U. S. Navy
R.A.F. — Royal Air Force
S.S. — Steamship (Merchant Marine)
U.S.C.G.C. — United States Coast Guard Cutter
U.S.S. — United States Ship (Navy)

CHAPTER I

The Naval Antagonists

1939–1940

1. *The Nazi Navy and Naval Policy*[1]

THE BRITISH Nation and Empire depend for their freedom and existence on the maintenance of ocean communication. By the same token it is a primary object of their enemies to disrupt these communications, cut the lifelines of the Empire and blockade the British Isles. Down to the War of 1914–1918 surface supremacy in the narrow seas and on the broad oceans kept Britain safe and free. By 1917 Germany had developed the striking power of the submarine warship to a pitch of effectiveness that came very near to beating down the British capacity to hold out; but in so doing she brought into the war the United States and other nations that wished to stay neutral. During that war, in order to cope with the submarine menace and with fast armed raiders which dashed destructively into the sea lanes, the United States and Royal Navies invented various anti-submarine devices and techniques, and revived the old system of convoys, which had been little used in naval warfare since days of sail.

Military men are often accused of planning every new war in terms of the last one. Now, the pattern of World War II in the Atlantic turned out to be very similar to that of World War I; yet nobody planned it that way. Hitler had endeavored to build

[1] This section is based largely on German sources: (1) Karl Doenitz "Essay on the War at Sea" 24 Sept. 1945, prepared for the United Nations after surrender, translation communicated by Commander U. S. Naval Forces Europe 31 Oct. 1945; (2) Admiral Walter Gladisch and Vice Admiral Kurt Assmann "Report to Office of British Commander in Chief Germany" 10 Feb. 1946; (3) Assmann's Diary of conferences between Hitler, Raeder and Doenitz, translated by the British Naval Intelligence Division as "Report on the German Naval War Effort."

up a high-seas fleet and neglected U-boats; while Britain, France and the United States were far better prepared to deal with a surface than with an underwater navy. Until the German Admiralty records were examined, almost everyone in the United States and Great Britain thought that the U-boat campaign had been prepared long in advance. Nothing could be further from the truth. Submarine warfare was unwanted and unexpected by Hitler, unprepared for by the German Navy; when adopted perforce it was improvised until well on into 1943 when all German naval effort and a large share of production were concentrated on making it a success.

In September 1939 the German Fleet was divided into three commands under Grand Admiral Erich Raeder, Commander in Chief Navy[2]: Armored Ships (Battleships and Battle Cruisers),[3] Scouting Forces (cruisers, destroyers, torpedo boats and minesweepers),[4] and Submarines, under Commodore Karl Doenitz. At that time the German Navy had only 57 U-boats actually in service, 30 of which were the so-called 250-tonners. The rest were mostly 500- or 750-tonners, types which did most of the damage in World War II. Germany was then producing only 2 to 4 new underwater craft per month.[5] "The war was in one sense lost before it began," said Doenitz bitterly when questioned on 9 June 1945, because "Germany was never prepared for a naval war against England. . . . A realistic policy would have given Germany a thousand U-boats at the beginning."[6]

[2] Promoted *Grossadmiral* 1 Apr. 1939—which corresponds to Fleet Admiral in the United States Navy.

[3] Battleships (old) *Schleswig-Holstein, Schlesien*; Pocket Battleships *Admiral Graf Spee, Admiral Scheer, Lützow* (ex-*Deutschland*); Battle Cruisers *Scharnhorst, Gneisenau.*

[4] Cruisers (8-inch) *Admiral Hipper, Bluecher;* cruisers (6-inch) *Koenigsberg, Karlsruhe, Köln, Emden, Leipzig, Nürnberg;* destroyers (5-inch), 16 of the *Maass* class, 6 of the *Roeder* class; 20 torpedo boats; 8 escort boats; 32 minesweepers; 40 motor minesweepers; 20 E-boats.

[5] U. S. Strategic Bombing Survey, *German Submarine Industry Report* (1946), Exhibit B1. The 500-tonners were Types VIIA and VIIB; the 750-tonner, Type IXA. Type II (250-ton) not used outside North Sea (Dr. Rohwer).

[6] "Essay on the War at Sea" translated by the British Naval Intelligence Division, Appendix II Interrogation para. 4.

Doenitz was naïf to assume that England would have stood idly by while Germany built up her U-boat force to four figures; but it was true enough that the German Navy was unprepared for a submarine war. And Adolf Hitler was to blame.

Fortunately for the Allied Nations, the Fuehrer had slight appreciation of the significance of sea power and only faint glimmerings of naval strategy. He was *landsinnig* (land-minded), obsessed with a geopolitical theory very similar to that of the *blocus continental* through which Napoleon had hoped to strangle England. If he could bring the European "Heartland" under his dominion or influence, the maritime powers would be stalemated. If then they refused to make peace on her terms, Germany would build a powerful high-seas fleet to beat them. In contrast to the predominantly naval attitudes of his mightiest opponents, Roosevelt and Churchill, Hitler was almost wholly preoccupied with thoughts of glorious continental victories as the one means necessary to achieve world domination. He was air-minded – Goering saw to that – but his efforts to build up a strong Luftwaffe in the prewar years slowed the development of other armed forces.

Mussolini, who brought Italy into the war in June 1940, had a modern well-rounded Navy; but as Churchill once remarked, it was apparently built to run rather than to fight. Italian naval strategy, when not dictated by Hitler, conformed to the ancient "fleet in being" concept – a force to be conserved as a threat rather than to be expended as a weapon.

Hitler, moreover, hoped to avert war with England, at least until 1944.[7] He repeatedly told his admirals that the German Navy was not going to fight England. His strategy was to keep England neutral until the European "Heartland" was reduced to obedience, when she would be unable to do anything about it. Still less did Hitler want war with the United States. With the aid of our pacifists and fascist sympathizers he counted on cajoling us into keep-

[7] Raeder's "Reflections on the Outbreak of War 3 Sept. 1939" in *Fuehrer Conferences on Matters Dealing with the German Navy, 1939* (1946).

ing neutral until England had been brought to book, when he would be able to dictate to the New World the conditions under which it could live. Shortly after the fall of France in 1940 he commenced studying ways and means of occupying Atlantic islands like Iceland and the Azores, with a view to intimidating America, or for use as bases if the American republics proved recalcitrant.

Thus, in September 1939 there was even less hope than in 1914 of the German Navy's winning command of even the narrow seas. When England surprised Hitler by refusing to stand by while Poland was gobbled up, the German Navy was up against it. To risk its few capital ships in fleet actions would be suicidal, and the number of U-boats was inadequate for a war on shipping and communications. Admiral Raeder accordingly informed his Fuehrer that the German Navy's mission would be confined to defense of coastal waters and to attacks on enemy shipping. He counseled Hitler in January 1940 that "a concentration on the sea and air war against England is urgently necessary," and privately he complained of "the current tendency to concentrate on continental aspects" of the war.[8]

Neither Hitler nor Raeder was willing to accept the logic of this situation and stop all construction of capital ships. But they did immediately step up the production of submarines from 4 per month to between 20 and 25. Plans were approved by which 300 submarines (most of them 500- and 750-tonners) would be in operation by 1942 and more than 900 by the end of 1943. This program was not fulfilled; and even if it had, that would have been insufficient.

The number of shipyards concentrating on submarines was increased from 3 to 16, but accelerated methods were not adopted until the summer of 1943. "Speed in hull and machinery assembly was aided by the widespread use of welding. The larger yards reduced the construction period for the 500-ton class (Type VIIC) to 36–40 weeks, excluding trials, while the minimum for

[8] Assmann Diary in "Report on the German Naval War Effort" p. 6 ff.

the 740-ton class (Type IXD) was 40–44 weeks. Yards less well equipped took 12 to 16 weeks longer for these classes." [9]

As for the German air arm, Marshal Goering was then Hitler's white-haired boy and his Luftwaffe got almost all that it wanted,[10] without even asking for anything that naval strategy required of an air force. The German Navy had no air arm of its own,[11] and the Luftwaffe concentrated on tactical bombing – by Stukas and the like – as an adjunct to Army operations. It had little or no training in bombing moving objects like ships. During the early weeks of the war, before the Royal Navy had developed an efficient anti-aircraft fire, German bombers caught and sank several combat ships and a number of merchant vessels in the narrow seas. But they never developed much proficiency in that art until 1942, against the convoys to North Russia.

In totalitarian governments like those of the Axis, personalities counted even more than in the democracies. At first only one naval officer was in the German high command, of which Hitler was the head and chief. All the rest were Army and Air Force officers. Yet this was what Raeder, an "empire builder," wished. His experience in World War I convinced him that the German Navy was too much tied up with other branches of the armed forces. "He therefore zealously set about making the Navy a self-sufficient organism with all reins of administration firmly in his own hands." [12] Already 63 years old in 1939, he was highly intelligent and a good organizer, but a solitary, close-mouthed individual, inept at dealing with other men and disliking debate and controversy. He usually gave orders without previous consultation, yet was subservient to Hitler, the one man over him. Hitler at first had a high regard for Raeder, which the Admiral failed

[9] "Submarine Building Policy and Program, 1933–1939" p. 4. An essay in "Monograph on Germany, Section 902–100," on file in O.N.I.; Doenitz Essay.

[10] There was a German saying during the war, "We are fighting with the Prussian Army, the Imperial Navy and the National Socialist Air Force."

[11] Excepting the few planes carried on battleships and cruisers. The German Navy had plans for aircraft carriers, but the only one under construction was so frequently bombed by the R.A.F. that it was never completed.

[12] Gladisch and Assmann p. 201.

to exploit by making himself accessible; he held himself aloof from the Fuehrer as much as possible, and so had no opportunity to "educate" Hitler on naval strategy. A middle-class German who had absorbed aristocratic attitudes under the imperial régime, Raeder was singularly unfitted to deal with a Johnny-come-lately like Marshal Goering, on whose favor and coöperation he depended for air support, since virtually no naval air arm existed.

Rear Admiral Karl Doenitz, in command of submarines,[13] proved to be one of the most able, daring and versatile flag officers on either side of the entire war. Forty-seven years old when the war began, he "was esteemed a strong man and enjoyed the passionate devotion of the younger officers' corps."[14] He had the drive and ruthlessness that appealed to Hitler and which Raeder lacked; but until January 1943 when he relieved Raeder as Commander in Chief of the Fleet, he had no direct access to the Fuehrer.

From the opening day of the war, Germany disregarded her treaty obligations respecting submarines. Article 22 of the London Naval Treaty of 1930, which the United States and Great Britain ratified promptly and to which the Third Reich formally adhered on 23 November 1936, is perfectly explicit: –

> In their action with regard to merchant ships, submarines must conform to the rules of International Law to which surface vessels are subject.
>
> In particular, except in the case of persistent refusal to stop on being duly summoned, or of active resistance to visit or search, a warship, whether surface vessel or submarine, *may not sink or render incapable of navigation a merchant vessel without having first placed passengers, crew and ship's papers in a place of safety.* For this purpose the ship's boats are not regarded as a place of safety unless the safety of the passengers and crew is assured, in the existing sea and weather conditions, by the proximity of land, or the presence of another vessel which is in a position to take them on board.[15]

[13] Promoted from Commodore to Rear Admiral 1 Oct. 1939, but still three ranks below Raeder.

[14] Gladisch and Assmann p. 206.

[15] *Proceedings of London Naval Conference of 1930* (1931) p. 218; date of German adhesion to same from Department of State.

As a corollary, merchant ships were not allowed to be armed, and neither Great Britain nor any other country did so arm them before war was declared. The treaty, as respected submarines, was violated by Germany in a spectacular manner on the very first day of the war. On 4 September 1939, twelve hours after war was declared, *U-30* torpedoed without warning, 200 miles off the coast of Donegal, the unarmed, unescorted British passenger steamer *Athenia*. She went down with the loss of 112 lives, including women and children. The British Admiralty naturally took this attack as evidence that Doenitz had no intention of respecting the treaty, and gave notice that British merchant vessels would be armed in self-defense. Hitler's government, with characteristic impudence and mendacity, declared that the British had sunk the *Athenia* themselves in order to involve the United States in the war, and that their countermeasures constituted a violation of international law which justified the U-boats in sinking at sight. After the defeat of Germany, Admiral Doenitz ruefully admitted the lie,[16] but claimed that the sinking of *Athenia* was a mistake. He could not, however, show that the mistaken U-boat commander had been disciplined.

On 23 September 1939 Hitler agreed to a request of Admiral Raeder to "sink at sight" enemy merchant vessels not passenger ships on the assumption that they would be armed; but gave orders that "neutrals should be especially well treated." Raeder took the exception as to passenger ships to apply only if they were fully lighted, which, naturally, after the loss of *Athenia*, they never were. Neutral vessels, especially those of the "friendly" neutrals such as Italy, Japan, Russia and Spain, were to be respected; but on the suggestion of Raeder the Fuehrer consented to a step-by-step "intensification" of the submarine warfare, to the point where, by the end of 1939, all ships except fully lighted ones of the four

[16] "The Trial of Admiral Doenitz" *O.N.I. Review* Oct. 1946 p. 29, which is based on Nuremberg Trial Court Proceedings. Doenitz does not, however, refer to the *Athenia* in his Essay. He seems to have shared the Nazi ideology that international law was a one-way affair, to be invoked or disregarded by Germany according to her interest.

"friendlies" could be sunk at sight when within the war zones prohibited to American merchantmen by the American neutrality laws. Our war zone legislation was taken by the Germans to mean, as indeed it was, a determination of the United States to avoid trouble.[17]

This somewhat cautious if deceptive step-by-step intensification went on until after the fall of France, when Hitler felt sufficiently secure to consult only German interest as to what ships were to be sunk and what to be spared. No holds were barred. At the Nuremberg trials it was brought out that Doenitz had even issued orders to his U-boats to machine-gun survivors of torpedoed vessels, so that they could not ship over again.[18] It is to the credit of his officers that many of them could not stomach a practice so contrary to humanity and the ancient customs of the sea, and disregarded Doenitz's barbarous command more often than not.

After losing the Battle for Britain and especially after taking on the United States, the German war lords realized that their continental strategy was a failure; that they could only win by rupturing Allied sea communications, preferably before an invasion of the "Heartland." And so the Battle of the Atlantic resolved itself into a mighty contest between the Allied powers who were seeking to transport, equip, build up and supply armed forces for the invasion of the European Continent, and the Axis submarines and planes that were trying to prevent it. If Hitler had planned that sort of war, he might well have won; for his U-boats came appreciably close to doing so in spite of his topsy-turvy continental strategy.

The Japanese leaders were equally blind, in 1941, to their own weakness and to American strength; but they at least tried to knock out Anglo-American sea power in the Pacific before making further conquests.

[17] "Fuehrer Conferences" (records of conferences between Hitler, Raeder and others, captured at the end of the war). The display of ordinary running lights was not to be taken as evidence of a neutral flag.

[18] *O.N.I. Review* Oct. 1946 p. 29.

2. *The Royal Navies*

The British Navy, as Commodore Knox has pointed out, was of approximately equal strength to the United States Navy in capital ships, and superior in cruisers. Nevertheless, it was as ill prepared to cope with the U-boats and Luftwaffe as the German Navy was to wage a war on shipping. A special unit of the Navy had been studying and experimenting in anti-submarine methods and gear for several years, to our common benefit; but at the outbreak of hostilities the Fleet included few vessels suitable for escort-of-convoy other than destroyers, of which it was very short. The United States Navy, with even greater warning, was even less well provided with escort vessels in December 1941, and had no group or unit specially devoted to the study of anti-submarine warfare. Naval officers on both sides of the Atlantic commonly blame this unpreparedness on the naval limitation treaties, but actually each country might have built up a better-rounded fleet within the treaty framework, had it been willing to pay the cost. Both England and America might have been better provided with the smaller ships from destroyers down, and with naval ordnance. But in each country it was considered wiser to spend the severely limited naval budgets on big ships that took a long time to build, rather than on small ones that could be constructed fairly quickly; and both Navies were optimistic about their ability to improvise an anti-submarine fleet if necessary. The Royal Navy had practically no mines on hand in 1939 for defense of coastal waters against submarines and was unable to provide more than 23 per cent of merchantmen with cannon and gun crews until the middle of 1941. Sins of omission on the part of the United States were equally great, as we shall see in due time.[19]

[19] Note what Admiral Sir William James RN said on 5 Jan. 1944, for it is almost equally applicable to the United States Navy.

"I was on the Board of the Admiralty before the war and it was always a question of trying to do the best we could with what money was available, and the plan arrived at . . . with regard to Coastal Craft was that we should go for proto-

In the matter of air power, the Royal Navy was as badly off as the German Navy. It had been deprived of its air arm during the peace. The Royal Air Force had the planes, but was not equipped to fight submarines. Yet a typical British compromise was worked out. The R.A.F. set up the Coastal Bomber Command of 19 squadrons and about 220 planes, practically a separate air force. With the aid of twenty-five years' development in naval aviation technique and equipment freely and promptly communicated by the United States Navy, this command was intensively trained to protect shipping and hunt U-boats. Conversely, in 1941 a large group of United States naval aviators, assigned to duty as observers with the Coastal Command, learned invaluable lessons in the air aspects of anti-submarine warfare. On 15 April 1941, the Coastal Bomber Command was placed under Admiralty operational control, which made it for practical purposes a land-based air arm of the Royal Navy. In conjunction with the patrol craft, armed trawlers, destroyers and other combat ships, the planes of the Coastal Bomber Command, operating on interior lines from numerous bases in Great Britain and Northern Ireland, succeeded in driving submarines out of the Western Approaches to the United Kingdom, but not until the spring of 1941.[20]

The Royal Navy lost no time in organizing trade convoys. Mindful of the depredations of German raiders in Caribbean waters in 1914–1915, it began making up transatlantic convoys at Kingston, Jamaica, in early September 1939. Since no attacks developed, the port of origin was soon shifted to Halifax, whence merchant shipping was escorted eastward by the Royal Canadian Navy.

Too much praise cannot be given to that gallant, efficient force

---

types. There were three reasons for that. One was that the type was in the process of development: it was no good giving an order for say a hundred of a certain type when next year something very far in advance might be produced. Another was the manning problem: you cannot in peacetime keep a large number of Coastal Craft in commission; they wear out very quickly . . . and we could not really find the personnel for them. The third reason was we felt that they were the one type of craft that could be built quickly, and that what money we had ought to be put into ships that took a long time to build – destroyers and cruisers." *Journal* Royal United Service Institution LXXXIX 56 (Feb. 1944).

[20] See appended series of charts.

of our nearest neighbor. The Royal Canadian Navy, starting almost from scratch in 1939, expanded so rapidly by construction and purchase that by May 1942 it comprised some 300 vessels and 31,000 officers and men.[21]

This Navy included no capital ships, but specialized in two types of escort vessel developed by the Royal Navy – the corvette and the frigate. Eighteen of the former and two of the latter were built for or purchased by the United States Navy, which reclassified the corvettes as patrol gunboats.[22] The corvettes were well armed with one 4-inch gun, machine guns and depth charges, and equipped with asdic (a listening and echo-ranging sound gear). They carried no torpedo tubes. Powerful enough to deal with any submarine, they were more quickly maneuverable than destroyers – an immense benefit in anti-submarine warfare; but their 16-knot speed left much to be desired. Corvettes were among the most seaworthy ships in the world. They fairly bounced over the waves, and seldom sustained storm damage; but this buoyancy made them most uncomfortable, and a severe strain on their crews.

Corvettes had not been designed as ocean escorts, for which purpose the frigate, a larger, faster, more heavily armed and much more comfortable type which the Royal Navy brought into operation in the spring of 1942, was more suitable. Canadian-built frigates began to appear in the spring of 1943. Until many new destroyers were ready for operation these corvettes and frigates were the busiest and most reliable escorts for transatlantic convoys between North America and the United Kingdom.

3. *The Neutrality Patrol of the Atlantic Squadron*

At the outbreak of war in Europe, 3 September 1939, Franklin D. Roosevelt was in his seventh year as President of the United States;

[21] Cdr. Lincoln Lothrop USNR "The Royal Canadian Navy" *U. S. Naval Institute Proceedings* LXVIII 1239 (Sept. 1942).

[22] These ex-Canadian corvette PGs may be recognized by names of qualities, such as *Action*, *Restless*, *Tenacity*, and should not be confused with PGs such as *Vixen* and *Plymouth* which are converted yachts, or *Charleston* and *Erie* which were built as gunboats in 1936.

Charles A. Edison, acting Secretary of the Navy (Secretary Swanson having died in July); Admiral Harold R. Stark, Chief of Naval Operations and Admiral James O. Richardson, Commander in Chief of the Fleet. The predominant strength of the United States Navy was deployed in the Pacific, as had been the case for over ten years; but a partial deployment eastward had begun with the formation of the Atlantic Squadron in January 1939. In September this squadron, commanded by Rear Admiral Alfred W. Johnson, comprised four old battleships (*New York*, *Texas*, *Arkansas* and *Wyoming*) under Admiral Johnson's immediate command; one division of heavy cruisers (*San Francisco*, *Tuscaloosa*, *Quincy* and *Vincennes*), commanded by Rear Admiral A. C. Pickens; Captain W. Greenman's Destroyer Squadron 10 and aircraft carrier *Ranger*, together with her own planes and those of carrier *Wasp*, which was not yet in commission.[23] Herein was the nucleus of the great Atlantic Fleet United States Navy, of which Admiral Ernest J. King became Commander in Chief on 1 February 1941, the day of its organization.[24]

The first impact of the European War on the United States Navy was an order from President Roosevelt on 5 September 1939 to organize a Neutrality Patrol. The avowed object of this patrol was to report and track any belligerent air, surface or underwater naval forces approaching the coasts of the United States or the West Indies. The fundamental purpose was to emphasize the readiness of the United States Navy to defend the Western Hemisphere. At the Conference of Foreign Ministers of the American Republics, which opened at Panama on 25 September 1939, Mr. Sumner Welles presented the plan for this patrol and asked that it be given Pan-American sanction. After considerable debate, and a few reservations, this was accorded. The Act of Panama issued by the conference on 2 October 1939 declared it to be the united policy of the Americas to keep the European War from the New World,

[23] Also, all the patrol craft, patrol squadrons and train then in the Atlantic.

[24] From 1 Nov. 1940 to 1 Feb. 1941, the Atlantic Squadron was designated Patrol Force United States Fleet.

and warned the belligerents against conducting warlike operations within a line approximately down long. 60° W to lat. 20° N, thence to a point about 600 miles south of Fogo, Cape Verde Islands, and thence southwesterly, roughly parallel to the South American coast.[25]

As no American power except the United States possessed more than a handful of combat ships capable of performing such a patrol, the burden of it fell on the United States Navy. Admiral Johnson began assigning vessels to the Neutrality Patrol in September, the day after the Navy Department passed the word. By the 12th it was organized. Eight units covered offshore waters from Newfoundland to the Guianas: Patrol "Zero" extended from Placentia Bay and Halifax south to lat. 40° N; Patrol "1" ran along a northwest-southeast line off Georges Shoal; Patrol "2" covered a triangle from Newport to lat. 43°05′ N, long. 65°30′ W and lat. 37°50′ N, long. 70°20′ W; Patrol "3" covered the waters between Chesapeake Lightship, lat. 37°50′ N, long. 70°20′ W, and lat. 34°10′ N, long. 73°05′ W; Patrol "9" cruised within 300 miles of the coast between Newport and Cape Hatteras; Patrol "6" covered the Florida Straits, Yucatan Channel and adjacent waters; Patrols "7" and "8" operated at their commanders' discretion in the eastern Caribbean south of lat. 23°10′ N.[26] The four battleships and the *Ranger* at Hampton Roads constituted a reserve group.[27]

[25] In detail, from Quoddy Head east to long. 60° W, thence south to lat. 20° N, thence to lat. 05° N, long. 24° W, thence to lat. 58° S, long. 57° W (Atlantic Fleet Operation Plan 7–41, 1 Sept. 1941).

[26] Commanders and their forces were: –

"Zero" – Capt. L. E. Denfeld, Desdiv 18 (*Davis, Jouett, Benham, Ellet*);
"1" – Lt. Cdr. T. C. Evans, *Hamilton* and *Leary;*
"2" – Cdr. S. N. Moore, *Hopkins, Goff,* Patron 54, and *Owl;*
"3" – Capt. W. G. Greenman, *Decatur, Barry, Reuben James, Manley,* Patrons 52 and 53;
"9" – Capt. P. H. Bastedo, *Quincy* and *Vincennes;*
"6" – Lt. Cdr. H. R. Parker, *Babbitt* and *Claxton;*
"7" and "8" – Rear Admiral A. C. Pickens, *San Francisco, Tuscaloosa, Truxtun, Simpson,* Patron 33, *Lapwing, Broome, Borie,* Patron 51, *Gannet* and *Thrush.* (Commander Atlantic Squadron Operation Order 20–39.)

[27] Shore-based naval air detachments were also under this command.

The patrol areas were modified from time to time and forces were changed as the Navy built up strength in the Atlantic. With the assistance of the Coast Guard, a continuous patrol area approximately 200 miles off shore from the Grand Banks through the Bahamas and Lesser Antilles to Trinidad was set up in October.[28] In January 1940 a Striking Group under Rear Admiral A. C. Pickens with cruisers and destroyers, based at Norfolk and in the Caribbean, began patrolling the triangle Norfolk–Bermuda–St. Thomas.[29] Subsequent to the acquisition of bases in Bermuda, three PBY-2s of Patrol Squadron 54 were based there, beginning November 1940, to conduct an air patrol around the islands.[30]

One other force of the United States Navy was in European waters at the outbreak of war. This was Squadron 40-T, originally organized in September 1936 to evacuate Americans from Spain during the civil war. On 1 September 1939 this squadron, commanded by Rear Admiral Charles E. Courtney, comprised light cruiser *Trenton*, destroyers *Badger* and *Jacob Jones*, and an occasional auxiliary vessel. Based at Lisbon, it "continued to operate in the western Mediterranean for the purpose of cultivating friendly relations and protecting American interests" until 22 October 1940, when it was disbanded "due to the conditions prevailing in certain parts of Europe." [31]

[28] Commander Atlantic Squadron Operation Order 24–39, 16 October. The Grand Banks Patrol was discontinued 29 Jan. 1940.

[29] Op. Order 1–40, 1 Jan. 1940.

[30] Commander Bermuda Patrol Operation Order 1–40, 18 Nov. 1940.

[31] Report of the Secretary of the Navy for 1941. By that time U.S.S. *Dickerson* and *Herbert* had relieved the two destroyers.

CHAPTER II

Transatlantic Convoys under Anglo-Canadian Escort[1]

September 1939 – December 1940

1. *Convoy Definitions*

A CONVOY is the supply train and reinforcement column of the sea. A group of merchant vessels or troop transports, highly vulnerable to surface or submarine attack when alone, steam in company escorted by warships of types able to ward off the anticipated attack: battleships, cruisers and carriers to deal with enemy warships, raiders or aircraft; destroyers and smaller vessels to handle submarines. In 1917–1918 the convoy system was brought to a high state of efficiency. More than any other factor it defeated the German unrestricted submarine warfare and enabled American troops and supplies that turned the tide toward victory to be safely transported to Europe.

Before proceeding further, it will be well to define a few terms. A *convoy* includes all the ships, whether combat, auxiliary, merchant, or troop transport, which travel together as a unit. The same word is also used in a more restricted sense, as covering only the noncombatant ships whose protection is the prime reason for the convoy. The *escort* includes all warships charged with protecting the convoy from the enemy. The *screen* includes only those

[1] The principal source for this Chapter is the British Admiralty's ms. War Diary of Atlantic Convoys, compiled by Cdr. W. B. Rowbothom RN (Ret.) and communicated to the writer at London in July 1942.

vessels of the escort, such as destroyers and corvettes, which are fitted with sound and other gear for anti-submarine warfare. The remainder of the escort, cruisers or battleships, are there primarily to protect the convoy against enemy surface ships, especially raiders, and to assist the anti-aircraft protection.

The *escort commander*, generally the commander of a destroyer squadron in merchant convoys, or the rear admiral commanding a battleship or cruiser division in a troop convoy, is responsible for the safety of the entire convoy from all kinds of attack, and therefore in overall command. The *convoy commodore*, on the other hand, sails in a merchant ship or transport, and is responsible for the internal discipline of the convoy proper. In transatlantic convoys of which the majority of ships were British the convoy commodore was generally a retired flag officer of the Royal Navy; in American convoys he was more often a captain in the Naval Reserve who had had considerable merchant marine experience.

From the outset of the war in 1939, the Royal Canadian Navy coöperated with the British Admiralty. Detailed plans for convoy and escort duty were ready. Naval control staffs were set up at Montreal, Quebec, Halifax, Sydney and St. Johns, Newfoundland, and the first of many hundreds of "HX" (Halifax–United Kingdom) convoys sailed 16 September 1939. From the beginning a distinction was made between slow and fast convoys, the first supposedly capable of an average speed of advance of 7½ knots, and the latter composed of faster vessels, 9½ to 10 knots.[2] They departed together from Halifax every eight days, thus arriving alternately in the Western Approaches to the United Kingdom every three or four days. Escorts out of Halifax were composed, whenever possible, of one battleship or one cruiser of the Royal Navy, and two Canadian destroyers. The battleship (or cruiser),

[2] In practice it was found impossible to maintain these average speeds. In the memorandum on Convoy Operations issued 20 June 1942 by Rear Admiral M. K. Metcalf (Director of the Convoy and Routing Division of Cominch) he says, "The average speed for SC and ONS convoys is 6½ knots, while the average speed of HX and ON convoys is 9 knots."

at about longitude 20° W, turned over the convoy to another escort group that came out from Britain, usually with a westbound convoy that the Canadian-based escort group took over and conducted to Halifax.

Merchant skippers, as in the last war, at first preferred to chance it alone rather than obey the exacting requirements of convoy, and only accepted them willingly when the going became tough. Initially there was much damage by collision, especially in the heavy fogs that hung off the Nova Scotia coast in most seasons of the year. Considerable difficulty was also experienced in meeting the Britain-based escort at the "mid-ocean meeting point," which was newly designated by the Admiralty for each convoy. As long as France remained in the war, the bulk of these transatlantic convoys were routed to London, except when congestion in the Downs made it necessary to divert them to West of England ports.

2. *The Transatlantic Convoys*

The typical transatlantic convoy of 1939–1941 consisted of 45 to 60 merchant ships steaming in nine to twelve columns, with 1000 yards between columns and 600 yards between ships. A nine-column convoy would, therefore, present a frontage of four nautical miles and a depth of one and a half miles or more, depending on the number of ships. The use of battleships and heavy cruisers in escorting merchant convoys was given up by the Royal Navy early in the war, because the feared German raiders seldom materialized, and capital ships provided no defense against submarines. For that purpose, fast and quickly turning destroyers and corvettes, equipped with sound gear and depth charges as well as guns, were essential. These formed the screen, each unit having a definite segment of a circle on the periphery of the convoy which it patrolled by day, if the weather was clear; at night or in thick weather it kept station, closing occasionally with the nearest merchantman to establish position. Each convoy was

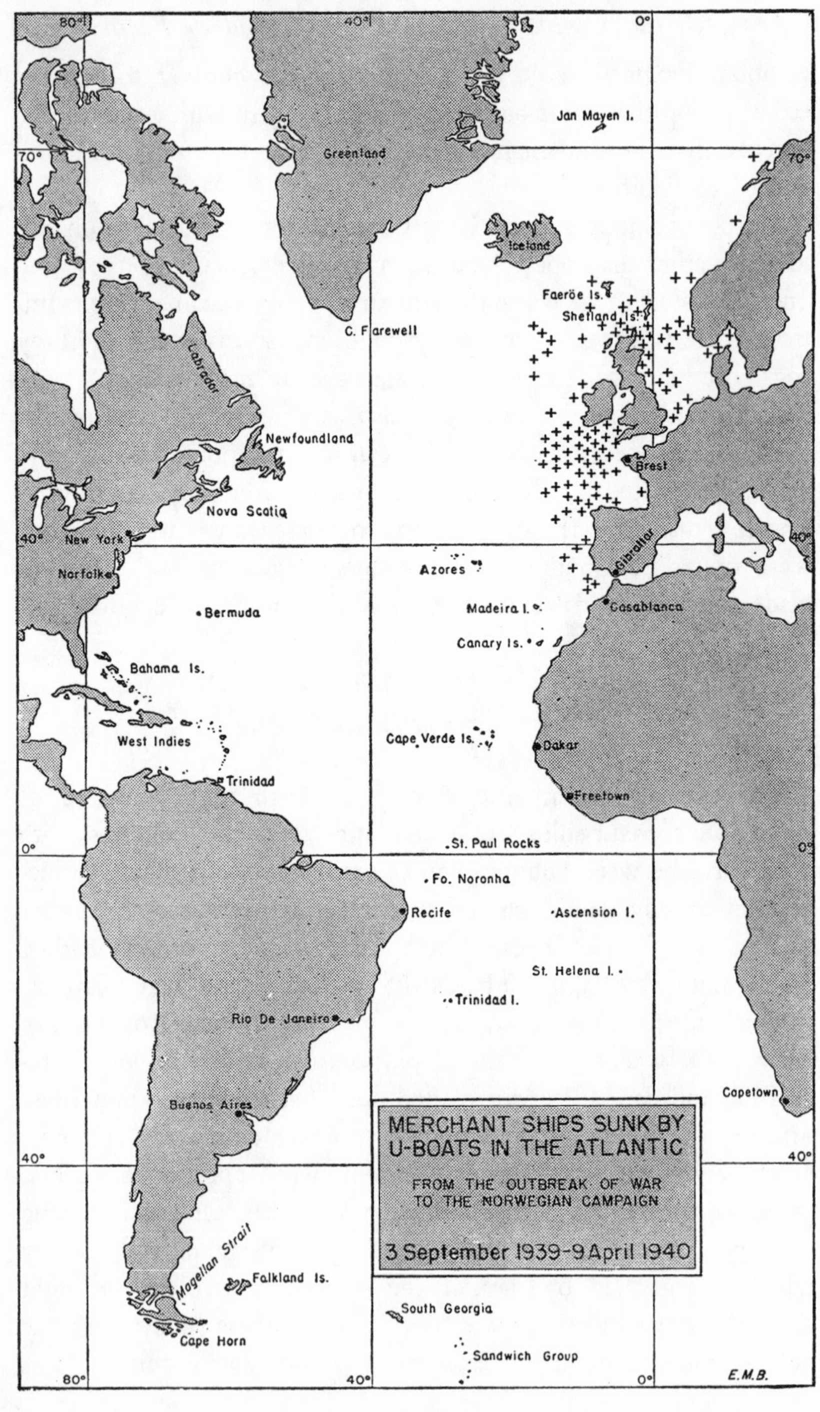

MERCHANT SHIPS SUNK BY U-BOATS IN THE ATLANTIC
FROM THE OUTBREAK OF WAR TO THE NORWEGIAN CAMPAIGN
3 September 1939-9 April 1940
80°
40°
0°
70°
Greenland
Jan Mayen I.
Iceland
Faeröe Is.
Shetland Is.
C. Farewell
Labrador
Newfoundland
Nova Scotia
New York
Norfolk
Brest
Gibraltar
Azores
Madeira I.
Casablanca
Canary Is.
Bermuda
Bahama Is.
West Indies
Trinidad
Cape Verde Is.
Dakar
Freetown
St. Paul Rocks
Fo. Noronha
Recife
Ascension I.
St. Helena I.
Trinidad I.
Rio De Janeiro
Buenos Aires
Capetown
Magellan Strait
Falkland Is.
South Georgia
Cape Horn
Sandwich Group
E.M.B.

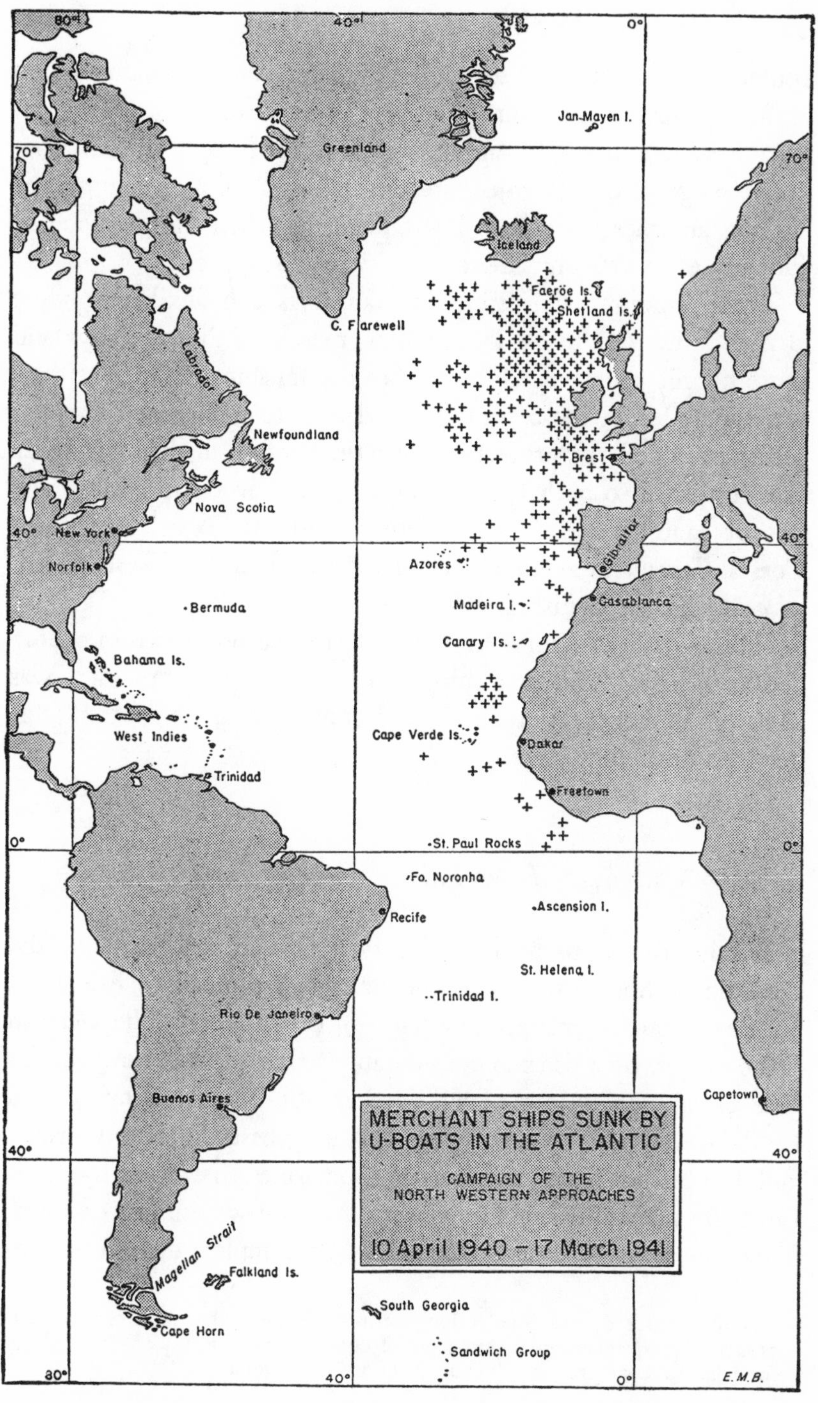
MERCHANT SHIPS SUNK BY U-BOATS IN THE ATLANTIC
CAMPAIGN OF THE NORTH WESTERN APPROACHES
10 April 1940 – 17 March 1941
Greenland
Jan Mayen I.
Iceland
Faeröe Is.
Shetland Is.
C. Farewell
Labrador
Newfoundland
Nova Scotia
New York
Norfolk
Bermuda
Bahama Is.
West Indies
Trinidad
Brest
Gibraltar
Azores
Madeira I.
Casablanca
Canary Is.
Cape Verde Is.
Dakar
Freetown
St. Paul Rocks
Fo. Noronha
Recife
Ascension I.
St. Helena I.
Trinidad I.
Rio De Janeiro
Buenos Aires
Capetown
Magellan Strait
Falkland Is.
South Georgia
Cape Horn
Sandwich Group
80°
70°
40°
0°
E.M.B.

routed by the Admiralty through designated ocean positions before it sailed; the escort commander was given discretion whether to steer evasive courses, to zigzag,[3] or to steam straight ahead. Slow convoys generally steamed steadily along, only zigzagging or making an emergency turn if attacked, or when the presence of submarines in the immediate vicinity was suspected.

Troop convoys, consisting of transports and auxiliaries, were always faster (12 to 15 knots) than merchant ship convoys and more heavily escorted. One or more capital ships or light cruisers were included in these convoys, and a more numerous destroyer screen provided. Air protection from the Royal Canadian Air Force was furnished to both kinds of convoy for several hundred miles out of Halifax, weather permitting; and the Royal Air Force Coastal Command afforded a similar coverage in the Western Approaches to the British Isles.

Halifax–United Kingdom convoys suffered no loss from enemy action in 1939. The first ship to be torpedoed, a straggler, was sunk on 14 February 1940. Losses continued to be few and far between until June 1940.

3. *Effect of the Fall of France, June 1940*

Britain seemed to be in a fair way to win the Battle of the Atlantic without effective challenge, when the fall of France in June 1940 put an entirely new face on the situation. The German U-boat fleet, by this time considerably enlarged, was now able to base on French outposts such as Brest, St.-Nazaire, Lorient and La Pallice. Merely by setting up operating bases in these Norman and Breton ports, the number of submarines that could be continuously maintained in the western Atlantic was almost doubled. Since one man – Admiral Doenitz – had complete charge of sub-

[3] While evasive courses involve long periods of time and wide diversions, zigzags involve frequently repeated changes of course, according to plans worked out beforehand so as to provide a minimum of wasted motion.

marine operations with only Admiral Raeder between him and Hitler, the offense enjoyed a unity of direction that the defense never acquired. Doenitz established his headquarters at Brest (later at Lorient), and St.-Nazaire became the chief operating and repair base for the U-boats. German-built submarines had their trial trips and training cruises in the Baltic and a final shakedown in the North Sea, whose eastern coasts were now under German control. They then slipped out between the Faeroes and Iceland, and after their first war cruise returned to the French outports. By studying the underwater sound equipment that fell into their hands from captured French ships, the German high command worked out new attack techniques, especially that of night attack on a convoy. All this added up to a deadly submarine efficiency. Hitler's "New Order" in western Europe was signaled by the sinking of seven ships from three different HX convoys, between 14 and 17 June 1940; and in July several other convoys were badly mauled at night without ever catching sight of the enemy.

The British were hard put to it to meet this new strategic situation. Many destroyers had been lost when covering the evacuation of Dunkirk; other escort vessels were undergoing extensive overhauls owing to their hard usage in the unsuccessful attempt to defend Norway. The summer of 1940 was the U-boats' greatest harvest season of the war. Although the total destruction that they wrought was far less than in 1942, the average tonnage sunk per submarine was almost ten times as great.[4]

Shipping losses and lack of escorts forced England to adopt a new convoy plan. Eastbound transatlantic convoys were now met by the British escort at about long. 17° W, and split in two at about 8° W. One section proceeded through the Minches and Pentland Firth to the East Coast of Britain; the other through the North Channel, protected by airplanes based on Northern Ireland and Scotland, to Glasgow and Liverpool. The Germans took about two months to catch on. Convoy HX–65 lost seven ships by U-boat and bomber attacks in the Western Approaches and along

[4] Doenitz Essay, Secs. 53–58.

the East Coast during the last week of August; it was the first convoy that sustained losses by air attack.

About the same time, owing to congestion in Halifax Harbor and Chedabucto Bay, it was decided to escort only the faster merchant vessels from that point. The slower ships made their way independently to Sydney, Cape Breton Island, and were there organized into convoys designated SC. The first of these was attacked by a U-boat which sank one ship together with the sole escort, H.M.S. *Penzance*. On 20–22 September 1940, Convoy HX–72 lost eleven ships by U-boat attack, and two were damaged. Losses continued to be heavy through the autumn and winter months, when British sloops-of-war, which had served as efficient escorts, had to be withdrawn on account of heavy weather. On 5 November 1940, Convoy HX–94, escorted by the armed merchant cruiser H.M.S. *Jervis Bay*, was attacked by the German "pocket battleship" *Scheer* in lat. 52°48′ N, long. 32°15′ W. *Scheer* opened fire at 17,000 yards. While the convoy scattered like chickens pursued by a hawk, the escort steamed bravely forth and engaged an enemy greatly her superior in fire power. *Jervis Bay* was sunk together with Captain E. S. F. Fegen and most of his officers and men; but they saved most of the convoy by their courage.[5] Six ships out of 38 were lost, five by the *Scheer* and one by aircraft. Convoy HX–90 was attacked five times within 24 hours on December 1 and 2, losing ten ships (six of them stragglers), together with H.M.S. *Forfar*.

In these successful onslaughts during the last of 1940, the U-boats began to move out into the mid-Atlantic and employ a new and deadly attack technique.[6] Hitherto, submarines operated individually, submerged before approaching a convoy in order to sight their target from the periscope, and by preference chose morning or evening twilight when ships were silhouetted against the sky. But British escort vessels were equipped with a listening and echo-

[5] Office of Chief of Naval Operations Information Bulletin No. 1, *Anti-Submarine Warfare 1940* (a mimeographed reprint of the Admiralty Anti-Submarine Report for that period).

[6] Doenitz Essay, Secs. 61–63.

ranging sound gear (asdic) which enabled them to obtain both range and bearing of a submerged U-boat and attack it with depth charges. Aggressive tactics by British escorts and bombing by the R.A.F. Coastal Command were more often than not thwarting the U-boats in the narrow seas. And on the high seas, their difficulty was to find the convoys. To meet these two conditions – good sound gear and want of air reconnaissance – Admiral Doenitz devised a new method of attack, *Die Rudeltaktik*, which we call "the wolf-pack." The principle of it, he said himself, was that of "being as strong as possible in the right place at the right time."

Die Rudeltaktik was a surface tactic, particularly successful with a slow convoy. The U-boats were sent out fanwise in well-dispersed groups, generally of about eight or nine, but sometimes up to twenty. Their movements were closely controlled by radio from Doenitz's command post at Lorient. The submarine which first made sight or sound contact on a convoy reported its course and disposition to Doenitz, who, knowing exactly where each "wolf" was located, issued the orders homing in for the kill every member of the pack within reach. The U-boat that made contact shadowed the convoy by day, keeping at the extreme distance from which smoke or masts were visible, so that it could estimate where the targets would be found at night. When the pack made its night rendezvous, Doenitz shifted tactical command to the senior officer present. Under cover of darkness the boats approached on the surface, fired their torpedoes, submerged to escape counterattack; and, when things quieted down, resurfaced and maneuvered into position for a fresh attack. Unless the convoy managed to elude the pack by a radical change of course, or the escorts dispersed it by well-directed aggression, the ships might be shadowed for several days and attacked for several nights on end. Several other factors favored the enemy. He had discarded his magnetic torpedo fuze, which often failed to detonate, in favor of an impact fuze. He now had plenty of the new Type VIIC U-boat, a 500-tonner carrying 14 torpedoes, with a high action radius for its size, a small turning circle and sufficient surface speed to outrun corvettes and other slow escorts.[7] And on the United Kingdom–Gibraltar shipping route, his U-boats were helped to find targets by air reconnaissance out of Bordeaux.[8]

Obviously, if no answer could be found to the wolf-pack, Britain was doomed.

One new defensive weapon of great promise was radar, the new device for detecting vessels on the surface; but radar was no use without more destroyers and other escorts to install it on, and destroyers were precisely what the Royal Navy lacked. It had lost a large number in the evacuation of Dunkirk. The remainder were being kept at sea in winter weather for such long periods that crews became exhausted and the vessels wore out. It is said that as much as 70 per cent of the British destroyer fleet was laid up for repairs in January 1941. Only the gallant corvettes carried on.

If America's first substantial aid to the Battle of the Atlantic was to offer her experience in naval aviation technique, the second was to provide the Royal Navy with fifty destroyers to combat the wolf-packs. But before that deal was consummated, Congress had provided for a vast increase in the United States Navy.

[7] Type VIIC U-boat, which we called the 500-tonner and Doenitz the 517-tonner, actually displaced 708 tons surfaced. It was 220 ft. long, 20.3 ft. beam, had average diving limit of 66 fathoms, maximum speed 17.7 knots surfaced, 7.6 knots submerged, had 4 bow tubes and one stern tube, and carried 14 torpedoes. At cruising speed of 10 knots Type VIIC had an endurance radius of 8500 miles without fueling. Details from U-boat Chart prepared by O.N.I. Operational Intelligence Division.

[8] Doenitz Essay, Secs. 14, 22, 64, 65–68. Doenitz however adverts to much the same difficulties in submarine-aircraft coöperation that we later experienced in escort-aircraft coöperation, and deplores the want of a German naval air arm which compelled him to beg for aircraft reconnaissance from Goering. One would suppose that communication difficulties would have made manipulation of wolf-packs from France difficult, but Doenitz's chief complaint was that he wasted boats on reconnaissance that should have been performed by aircraft so that on occasions only three U-boats out of a large pack were in position to attack.

CHAPTER III

"Short of War" Policy[1]

June 1940 – March 1941

1. *The "Two-Ocean Navy"*

PRESIDENT ROOSEVELT, considerably in advance of public opinion, apprehended the threat to American security contained in the German seizure of the Atlantic Coast of France, and the strong possibility of a German invasion of Great Britain. For three centuries the British Navy could always be depended upon to prevent any power dominant on the European Continent from obtaining control of the Western Ocean sea lanes. In expectation that Britain could do it again, the United States Navy since 1922 had been largely concentrated in the Pacific, to watch Japan. Now we were faced with a possible pincer movement from across both oceans.

The naval expansion bill that had been discussed since the fall of 1939, increasing by about 25 per cent the new carrier, cruiser and submarine tonnage already authorized by the Act of 17 May 1938, was approved on 14 June 1940.[2] Exactly three days later Admiral Harold R. Stark, Chief of Naval Operations, asked the Congress for four billion dollars to begin building a "two-ocean Navy." And in a little more than one month a bill to that effect – providing for 1,325,000 tons of new construction in battleships, battle cruisers, carriers, cruisers, destroyers and submarines; the

[1] The principal facts of diplomatic history in this chapter are taken from the Department of State's publication *Peace and War, United States Foreign Policy 1931–1941* (the 1943 edition with documents).

[2] 76th Cong. 3rd Sess., Chap. 364, 14 June 1940. New tonnage authorized, 167,000. Already authorized in Act of 1938, 659,480 tons.

purchase or conversion of 100,000 tons of auxiliary vessels; and $50,000,000 worth of patrol, escort and miscellaneous craft – was approved by President Roosevelt.[3] By peacetime methods of construction, six years would be required to build that two-ocean Navy. Would Hitler, if he got control of Britain and of every shipyard in Europe, be so considerate as to hold his hand that length of time? Would Japan wait?

Peacetime methods could be, and were, stepped up by increased equipment in naval and other shipyards, double and triple shifts, and the like. But, as Admiral Stark said, "dollars cannot buy yesterday."[4] For two years at least the Americas would be exceedingly vulnerable in the event of a German victory in Europe. To meet this emergency, President Roosevelt adopted the political strategy of helping England and (after June 1941) Russia to withstand Germany, and of keeping Japan quiet by diplomacy. The Atlantic phase of this policy meant violating the laws of neutrality. Neither Germany nor Japan had respected neutrality, but Americans were loath to discard the concept, deeply rooted in the national tradition and recently buttressed by a legislative structure. Congress voted money for a two-ocean Navy as a hedge against war, and most Americans regarded a wall of ships in the blueprint stage as sufficient protection. Fortunately events carried the country along with the President until the attack on Pearl Harbor made further persuasion unnecessary.

In every phase of this "short of war" policy, the Navy was involved; in some of them it conducted operations indistinguishable from war. Never before has the Navy so well justified its function as the nation's first line of defense. Behind the screen that it furnished, the new draft Army of the United States was being trained and factories being converted to war production. At the same time,

[3] 76th Cong. 3rd Sess., Chap. 644, 19 July 1940. It was this act that provided four out of six of the *Iowa* class battleships, the *Essex* class carriers, the battle cruisers *Alaska* and *Guam*, the *Baltimore* class heavy cruisers, most of the *Cleveland* class light cruisers, most of the *Atlanta* class anti-aircraft cruisers, the first of the *Fletcher* class 2100-ton destroyers, and most of the *Bristol* class of 1700-ton destroyers.

[4] Address "Background at Chatham House" 21 July 1942.

the Navy itself was being expanded, strengthened and tempered.

On 15 June 1940, the very day after approving the new Navy bill, President Roosevelt signed another set of documents that proved to be of vital importance in winning the war. These were the letters appointing a group of eminent civilian scientists – including Vannevar Bush, President of the Carnegie Institution of Washington; James Bryant Conant, President of Harvard University; Karl T. Compton, President of the Massachusetts Institute of Technology; Frank B. Jewett, President of the National Academy of Sciences – together with Rear Admiral J. A. Furer, Navy Coordinator of Research and Development, members of the new National Defense Research Committee. Dr. Bush had been working on the mobilization of American scientists for war since late 1939, but it took the fall of France to bring matters to a head. From this N.D.R.C. stemmed most of the essential civilian research done for the Army and Navy during the "short of war" period and the war itself.[5]

At the same time President Roosevelt, in order to emphasize the dangerous situation of the country, strengthen his administration, and obtain Republican support for preparedness, appointed two leading Republicans Secretary of the Navy and Secretary of War. Frank Knox,[6] who relieved Secretary Edison on 11 July 1940, quickly acquired a thorough grasp of naval business and became one of the best secretaries the Navy ever had. The office of Under Secretary of the Navy was created and first filled by Knox's future successor, James V. Forrestal, on 22 August. Henry

[5] James Phinney Baxter 3rd *Scientists Against Time* (1946) Chap. I. The Navy already had Research Laboratories at Anacostia, the David Taylor Experimental Model Basin, and other facilities of the sort; but it was anticipated that all these facilities, being swamped by routine testing, would have little time for fundamental research.

[6] His full name was William Franklin Knox. Born in Boston in 1874, he fought in the Rough Riders in the Spanish-American War, and as a colonel of field artillery in World War I. A prominent newspaperman, first in New England and next in Chicago, he was candidate for Vice President on the Republican ticket in 1936. He died suddenly, when still Secretary of the Navy, 28 April 1944. Lewis Compton, Assistant Secretary of the Navy under Mr. Edison, was relieved on 24 Feb. 1941 by Ralph A. Bard; Artemus L. Gates became the first Assistant Secretary of the Navy for Air on 5 Sept. 1941.

L. Stimson, the elder statesman who had been Secretary of War in the cabinet of President Taft, Governor General of the Philippines, and Secretary of State in the cabinet of President Hoover, became Secretary of War again in July 1940. At his urgent recommendation, Congress passed the Selective Training and Service Act on 16 September. This was the first occasion that the United States adopted compulsory military training in time of peace.

During the summer and fall of that year, President Roosevelt initiated several important steps in high-level strategy in the Atlantic: including the vital Destroyers and Naval Bases deal, Lend-Lease, and staff conversations with the British.

2. *Martinique and Neutrality Patrol*

The fall of France brought up the disquieting question of what was to become of French territory in America – the islands of St. Pierre and Miquelon off Newfoundland; Martinique, Guadeloupe and several smaller islands in the West Indies; French Guiana on the continent. Strategically located as they were, the possibility that Pétain would be forced to cede some or all of them to Germany had to be faced. One month earlier a somewhat similar problem had been created when the fall of the Netherlands left the Dutch West Indies, including the important oil-refining islands of Curaçao and Aruba, out on a limb. But the Royal Netherlands government in exile continued the war against Germany, and was ready to defend its American possessions with all the assistance that the United States could spare; while the Vichy government asserted its neutrality and somewhat truculently declined American offers to protect the islands.

In Fort de France, Martinique, best harbor in the Lesser Antilles, lay the French aircraft carrier *Béarn*, cruiser *Émile Bertin*, gunboat *Barfleur*, and six new tankers. Guadeloupe sheltered the old training cruiser *Jeanne d'Arc*. All were under the command of Rear Admiral Robert, appointed in 1939 High Commissioner for the French Antilles. Also immobilized at Martinique were 112 American-built planes which the *Béarn* was about to transport to France, and a large sum in gold bullion. Marshal Pétain promptly assured the United States government that there would be no transfer of American territory or of these instruments of war to Germany; yet the fear that he would be forced to do so, or that Admiral Robert would service U-boats or attempt some sort of monkey business, created grave anxiety at Washington.

One way to handle the situation would have been to break with Vichy, recognize the "Fighting French" government of General de Gaulle in London as the government of France, and turn over French possessions in America to them, as De Gaulle himself wished. Apart from general considerations of policy, which required that we continue to deal with Vichy,[7] any such course would have entailed several inconveniences. Admiral Robert would not have yielded Martinique without a fight, which at that time Washington was determined not to start. And if the United States Navy and Marine Corps had crashed into the French Antilles, as they were ready to do when given the word, the susceptibilities of other American republics whose good will and coöperation President Roosevelt was assiduously cultivating would have been aroused. It would not have been well to revive the cry of *imperialismo yanqui* at a time when all the Americas had to stick together lest they be blitzed and nazified separately.

It was therefore conceived to be essential that any policy toward French and other European possessions in the New World be a Pan-American and not a United States policy. Accordingly the whole subject was thrashed out at the Havana Conference of American Republics in June 1940. The final resolutions of this conference, dated 30 June, declared that the transfer of American territory from one non-American power to another would not be tolerated, and provided an Inter-American Commission for Ter-

[7] These are entered into at some length in Vol. II Chap. I. For the Martinique business I have relied largely on W. L. Langer *Our Vichy Gamble* (1947).

ritorial Administration to take over and administer any European colony in America whose transfer was threatened. The Neutrality Patrol, already set up by the United States Navy with Pan-American backing in the fall of 1939, was again approved.

President Roosevelt met Mr. Mackenzie King, Prime Minister of Canada, in August 1940. Both men were accompanied by military and naval advisers to discuss their respective parts in hemisphere defense. A United States-Canadian Mutual Defense Pact was promptly signed, assuring the Navy the use of facilities in the Maritime Provinces.

The Chief of Naval Operations sent Rear Admiral John W. Greenslade to Fort de France in August 1940 to see what could be done about the Martinique situation. Admiral Robert received him very cavalierly, and promised nothing. After the Pétain-Hitler conversations at Montoire in October, which aroused the liveliest apprehension of a deal that would affect American interests, Admiral Greenslade paid a second call on the French admiral. This time he used language that a sailor understood; threatened to patrol Martinique with an aircraft carrier, whose commander would be instructed to sink any French ship that attempted to sortie. Robert then made a "gentleman's agreement" to give Washington four days' notice of any intended ship movements, to receive a United States naval observer at Fort de France, and to allow United States ships and planes to enter Martinique territorial limits. In return, we undertook to supply the French islands with food, paid for from blocked French funds in the United States.

Although Admiral Robert was true to his word, despite our inability (owing to shipping shortages) to keep the islands properly provisioned,[8] the United States could not afford to take any chances. Watching the French Antilles was the mission of one of the neutrality patrols, based at San Juan, Puerto Rico. This patrol was conducted for many months only by Destroyer Squadron 2,

[8] Information from Admiral Raymond A. Spruance, who at that time was Commandant Tenth Naval District (San Juan) and in overall command of the patrol.

commanded by Captain Walden L. Ainsworth in U.S.S. *Moffett*, and by Patrol Squadron 51, twelve PBYs under Commander W. J. Mullins, based at San Juan.[9] Gros Islet Bay, the leased British base on St. Lucia, became an advanced post for observing Martinique. The Navy looked with covetous eyes on Fort de France as the best naval and air base between Puerto Rico and Trinidad. It had a plan ready for an assault with the Fleet Marine Force in case Admiral Robert gave any provocation. He gave none, beyond allowing his official radio to broadcast the Nazi line. So sleeping dogs, grounded planes and anchored ships were allowed to lie.[10]

3. *The Destroyer-Naval Base Deal with Britain*

The practical policy for the United States while building a two-ocean Navy was to do everything in its power to prevent the British Isles being conquered by Germany. That policy seems obvious enough now, but at the time it ran counter to traditional currents of American opinion, and to the same quasi-pacifism that had kept the peacetime Navy down. Few Americans would even contemplate a formal entry into the war against the totalitarian Axis; President Roosevelt still and for some time to come believed that the Nazi menace could be averted by measures "short of war." That limitation was in fact a political necessity in a democratic and peace-loving country, whether the President believed in it or not.

While one of Britain's immediate needs was more destroyers, the United States wanted more naval bases to implement the defense of the Panama Canal and the Atlantic Coast. President Roosevelt, Secretary Knox and Mr. Winston Churchill decided on the famous

[9] In January 1941, this patrol was augmented by two more PBY squadrons, based on San Juan and Guantanamo. The Caribbean Patrol organized 18 April 1941 patrolled an ocean area east of long. 60° W (which passes between Trinidad and Barbados) and south of lat. 20° N.

[10] In May 1943 an amphibious force was trained at Guantanamo and Puerto Rico to occupy the French Antilles, but the operation was never launched because Admiral Robert was relieved by a Free French high commissioner 14 July.

destroyer-naval base deal in principle on 24 July 1940, and it was formally agreed to on 2 September. Britain ceded to the United States sovereign rights for 99 years over sites for naval, military and air bases in the Bahamas, Jamaica, Antigua, St. Lucia, Trinidad and British Guiana, in exchange for 50 four-stack destroyers built during or shortly after the last war.[11]

"Great excitement in Berlin," noted Count Ciano in his Diary on 4 September when news of the deal reached Germany. British naval crews took over the first eight destroyers at Halifax on 9 September 1940, three days after the Luftwaffe's all-out air assault on London commenced. On the 22nd, Ribbentrop told Ciano that Hitler contemplated breaking diplomatic relations with the United States, and Mussolini chimed in with his usual "me too!" The German admirals were eager to retaliate by sending U-boats into American waters. Wisely, however, Hitler decided against either course. The air attack on England was not nearly so successful as he had expected; Germany had no amphibious force capable of breaking through the Channel defenses; and it was no time to provoke the United States.

The destroyer-naval base deal did, however, influence German naval policy. On 6 September 1940 Admiral Raeder obtained Hitler's consent for the "strictest execution" of submarine and air warfare against British shipping and land targets. This meant that all previously agreed restrictions on submarine warfare would be scrapped, and that some Americans were likely to be "accidentally" killed. At the same time, Hitler was planning to seize some of the Atlantic islands from Iceland to the Cape Verdes, partly as advance bases for submarines and partly (as respects the Azores) as "a jumping-off point for the Luftwaffe against the United States, in order to pin down the latter's anti-aircraft defenses." Goering was ready to provide air transportation for the capture of islands by paratroopers, but Raeder warned his Fuehrer that the German Navy

[11] The Argentia (Newfoundland) and Bermuda bases were granted to the United States at the same time, but as a free gift, not as part of the destroyer deal.

had not the means to furnish proper surface cover or logistic support. The Royal Navy was far too strong.

Thus, in the fall of 1940, Hitler, hitherto the spoiled child of victory, received two serious setbacks. The Luftwaffe was so decimated by the R.A.F. that the planned invasion of England had to be postponed, and the realities of sea power made any further extension of German might in the direction of the United States impossible, unless by U-boats. And they could not be used within the prohibited zone of the Americas, except at the cost of bringing in the United States, which Hitler could not then afford to do. Both Doenitz and Assmann testify that the "Pan-American safety zone," which some American patriots derided as weak and inadequate, was a real "hindrance to naval operations." Hitler gave strict orders that until his planned invasion of Russia commenced, "there should be avoidance of any incident with the United States," and Doenitz declares that he had to order his submarines not to attack destroyers or smaller warships, since such vessels could not be positively identified as British, and might therefore be American. The U-boat commander complained bitterly that he was not allowed to concentrate his submarines on the convoy bottlenecks off Halifax and Cape Race, because of these political considerations.[12]

This destroyer-naval base deal of 1940 was the first definite reaction by the Roosevelt Administration to a precarious situation which the American people in general were not yet willing to face. Preconceptions from another era, hatred of war, suspicion of European propaganda and other trends of thought that were the more difficult to combat because they were sincere and kindly, prevented public opinion from demanding anything forthright or drastic in their own defense, such as cutting off war supplies from Japan, or backing Britain to the limit. Consequently, President Roosevelt could only bolster up a tottering though defiant Britain insofar as such action increased American defensive strength. Ad-

[12] Doenitz Essay, Sec. 71. Obviously, however, his orders did not apply to the narrow seas or the eastern Atlantic where any destroyer encountered might be presumed not to be American.

miral Assmann's postwar revelations of discussions in the German high command prove that Franklin D. Roosevelt, with his uncanny perception and sense of timing, had gauged the situation correctly. His estimate that Hitler would overlook considerable direct aid to England rather than declare war on the United States was absolutely right. The arrogant Nazi government chose to accept the destroyer deal, lend-lease and partial convoying because it knew very well that the United States at war would be far more formidable than the United States "short of war." [13] And the time gained by us for preparation was of inestimable value.

Deliveries of destroyers continued as fast as the "four-pipers," many of them laid up for the last twenty years, could be made ready for sea. And by 10 April 1941 the United States had delivered to the Royal Navy, over and above the fifty destroyers, ten "Lake" class Coast Guard cutters, 250 feet long and well fitted for escort-of-convoy.

During the U-boat blitz off our Atlantic Coast early in 1942, one of the high-ranking admirals in Washington wrote to Stark saying he wished we had those fifty destroyers and ten cutters. To which the former Chief of Naval Operations replied that owing to the "deal" those vessels had been working for us about a year longer than otherwise they would have done. Moreover, although ships were expendable, the bases received in exchange were not.

4. *Lend-Lease*

As sixty escorts were insufficient to save Britain, so unconstructed bases and a blueprint two-ocean Navy were not enough to defend America. In November 1940, after his election to a third term, President Roosevelt went for a vacation on his favorite element. On board U.S.S. *Tuscaloosa* he and his confidential adviser Mr. Harry Hopkins worked over the lend-lease plan for financial

[13] It was also a principle of Nazi foreign policy to soothe and placate countries that Germany was not yet ready to strike, and when so ready, suddenly to "get tough," which baffled and confused the government and people.

Secretary Knox and Admiral King on board U.S.S. *Augusta*, September 1941

ir View of Bermuda, 26 September 1942. U. S. Naval Operating Base is on the white ninsula; British Naval Base and dockyard on long peninsula at left. U.S.A.A.F. Kindley Field is the white area near top of picture

N.O.B. Bermuda

Submarine base and airfield, St. Thomas, Virgin Islands, June 1942

Naval Air Station, St. Lucia, May 1942

United States Naval Stations

and material aid to Britain. By existing neutrality legislation, it was illegal for American merchant ships to trade with belligerents, for private investors to lend money to them, or for private firms to extend credit to any warring governments. Whatever supplies Britain or Canada procured in the United States had to be paid for with cash, and carried in their own ships. The President, refreshed by his sea voyage, presented the lend-lease formula at a press conference on 17 December 1940. The plan was briefly this. The United States, by enlisting private enterprise and building new government plants, would embark on an all-out military and naval defense program, but lend or lease as much production (including food) as could be spared to Great Britain and other countries that were fighting the Axis. The preliminary agreement with Great Britain, signed at Washington 23 February 1941, purposely left vague the method of repayment, mindful of how the war-debt question had bedeviled Anglo-American relations since 1919. But this agreement, unlike the destroyer deal, required Congressional sanction and appropriation.

Mr. Henry Morgenthau, Secretary of the Treasury, testified before a Congressional committee on 17 December 1940 that Britain was "scraping the bottom of the barrel." She still had certain financial holdings in America, but it was not to our interest that these should be liquidated. After a protracted debate, House Bill Number 1776 passed Congress by substantial majorities and became the first Lend-Lease Act on 11 March 1941. "This decision," said the President on 15 March, "is the end of any attempt at appeasement in our land; the end of urging us to get along with the dictators; the end of compromise with tyranny and the forces of oppression." [14]

Unfortunately it was not quite that; certainly not, respecting Japan. But the Nazis had to "take it." Assmann's entry for 9 July 1941 is particularly significant as the discussion started with Raeder expressing the fear lest Iceland pass into Allied hands.

Raeder points out that this will have strongest effect in damaging German war effort in the Atlantic, and asks for new directives for the

[14] *Roosevelt's Foreign Policy, 1933–1941* (1942) p. 343.

Navy. Hitler replies that "it is vitally important to put off America's entry into the war for another one or two months. Hence avoidance of all incidents with the United States and no change from previous directives. As before, only merchant ships may be attacked without warning in the prohibited area, but American ships are as far as possible to be excluded from this." Raeder points out that mistakes are possible, and the commanding officers of U-boats cannot be held responsible.[15] Hitler concurs. Raeder fears that the United States or England will now also attack Northwest Africa, whose decisive importance in the war is again stressed by him.

Hitler's conviction that a decision against Russia would be reached in September 1941 determined his cautious strategy in the Atlantic war. "There must be no incidents with the U.S.A. before mid-October." [16] But Russia held firm.

5. *Staff Conversations and Basic Strategic Decisions,*[17] *August 1940–March 1941*

a. Admiral Stark and Exploratory Conversations

At the time of the American declaration of war on Germany in April 1917, the United States Navy had no plan for coöperation with the British and French Navies in the common fight. Typical of the situation was Admiral Sims's departure for England in the last week of March, with no instructions, but this admonition from the Chief of Naval Operations: "Don't let the British pull the wool over your eyes. It is none of our business pulling their chestnuts out of the fire. We would as soon fight the British as the Germans." [18]

At the time war was declared in 1917, the commodore of Tor-

[15] Several such "mistakes" were made – S.S. *Lehigh* sinking on 19 Oct. 1941, and those of S.S. *ZamZam* and *Robin Moor,* hereinafter noted.

[16] Assmann Diary.

[17] This section is based largely on the documents reproduced in *Pearl Harbor Attack* Hearings before Joint Committee on the Investigation, Part 15; also on conversations with President Roosevelt and Admiral Ghormley. I am deeply indebted to Admiral Ghormley, Cdr. Tracy B. Kittredge USNR and Lt. Cdr. P. A. Van der Poel USNR for help in interpreting the reports, which for this period are very slim.

[18] Elting E. Morison *Admiral Sims* (1942) p. 338.

pedo Flotilla Asiatic Fleet, composed of ancient 400-ton torpedo boats, was Lieutenant Commander Harold R. Stark. These boats, badly needed in the Mediterranean and English Channel, were brought around against the southwest monsoon, without casualties and in excellent time, by their commander. That mission well completed, Mr. Stark was drafted by Admiral Sims to be his flag secretary in London. There he learned the secret of how to get on with the Royal Navy – to cultivate personal friendships with its officers, always shoot straight, and take no back wind from anyone. After World War I was over, he exercised various important commands, culminating in that of Chief of Naval Operations on 1 August 1939.[19]

Admiral Stark was determined that the situation of 1917 should not recur. General George C. Marshall, his opposite number in the Army, and President Roosevelt, his Commander in Chief, were of the same mind. So were the Secretaries of State, War and Navy. All still hoped to keep the war away from America. But they remembered how Woodrow Wilson, who hated war, was forced into it; they could not count on escaping this time. Moreover, the situation after the fall of France was unprecedented and urgent. Mussolini's Navy was now available to Hitler and at any time the French Fleet might come in too. The command of the Atlantic, hitherto shared by Britain and America, was sharply challenged.

That, in brief, is why those responsible for safeguarding American interests decided, in June 1940, that plans for a full, armed coöperation with the British Commonwealth must be prepared without further delay. A recent and terrible example of failure to

[19] Harold Raynsford Stark, born Wilkes-Barre, Pa., 1880, Naval Academy '03. Future naval historians may be puzzled at the identity of the person who wrote important letters to King and other high-ranking officers during the war, signed simply "Betty." That was the nickname given to plebe Stark in 1899 because the papers at the time were full of a celebration commemorating Betty Stark, wife of General Stark of Bennington fame. Between the two World Wars, H. R. Stark served as exec. of U.S.S. *West Virginia*, Inspector of Ordnance, Chief of Staff to Commander Destroyer Squadrons Battle Fleet, aide to Secretaries Adams and Swanson, C.O. *West Virginia*, Chief of BuOrd 1934; Com Crudiv 3 1937; C.N.O. 1939; Com U. S. Naval Forces Europe 1942–45; ret. as Admiral 1946. See *Sat. Eve. Post* 5 Aug. 1944.

make such arrangements was before them. The King of the Belgians had been so scrupulously neutral that his Army staff were not allowed to confer with French staff officers on what should be done in case Germany invaded his country. So when the Germans did just that, it was too late to concert war plans with France; Belgium was overrun and the King was forced to surrender his country within a few days.

President Roosevelt did not intend to allow any American republic to be caught like that. Accordingly, on 12 July 1940, Admiral Stark ordered Rear Admiral Robert L. Ghormley, Assistant Chief of Naval Operations, to visit London in the capacity of Special Naval Observer for "exploratory conversations" with the British Chiefs of Staff. He was accompanied by Major General D. C. Emmons of the Army Air Force, and by Major General George V. Strong USA, Assistant Chief of Staff to General Marshall, who in the meantime began similar conversations with a ranking British general in Washington.

Admiral Ghormley and the two generals arrived in London 15 August,[20] one week after the great air blitz on England began. Their first object was to report to the President whether England could hold out; for this was the period of her greatest danger, when she stood alone against the Nazi fury. Senator Pickering's toast of 1810 – "The world's last hope – Britain's fast-anchored Isle!" – had again become a reality. The British Chiefs of Staff showed the Americans their plan for continuing the war; and the Royal Air Force demonstrated with its radar-directed Spitfires that the air blitz could be defeated. September 15 was the day of the great fall turkey shoot, when the R.A.F. shot down 56 German bombers. Strong and Emmons, who returned to Washington shortly after, reported to General Marshall that the "fast-anchored Isle" was not likely to go adrift.[21]

[20] They crossed on a British merchant ship which carried a cargo of small arms and ammunition. The officer who met them said that these were the first new rifles received by the British Army since Dunkirk.

[21] General Marshall sent to London Brigadier General Sherwood A. Chaney USA (Ret.) as his personal representative in Oct. 1940.

Admiral Ghormley conferred almost daily with a special committee of the Admiralty, headed by Admiral Sir Sydney Bailey. He was impressed with the frankness of the British. They made no concealment of their weakness, but were ready and eager to give the United States Navy the benefit of their strength, which came from actual war experience. As Ghormley put it in a dispatch only a few days after the conferences began, he was obtaining information fresh from the laboratory of war, of priceless value to national defense.

Satisfied that England could and would hold out, Ghormley's next object was to ascertain where and how American naval and military strength could best be brought to bear, in conjunction with armed forces of the British Empire, if and when the United States were forced into war with Germany or Japan or both. British ideas in their general scope appeared to be harmonious with those expressed by President Roosevelt, Secretary Knox and Admiral Stark to Admiral Ghormley before he sailed: prosecute the war against the Axis; try to keep Japan quiet. This encouraged our Special Naval Observer to amplify the discussions and arrange a mutual exchange of military and technical information. Divergence of views developed respecting Singapore; but in regard to the Atlantic, where the obvious tasks for the United States naval participation would be escort-of-convoy and anti-submarine warfare, there was complete harmony. A full report of these conferences, and estimate of the situation, was sent by Ghormley to Stark in October.

Admiral Stark, with his pink complexion, benevolent countenance, rimless spectacles and thick shock of white hair, looked more like a bishop than a sailor. Gentle in manner and unobtrusive in personality, he had one of the best brains in the Navy; and, what was equally important, he possessed in a high degree the Washingtonian capacity for selecting from a welter of conflicting opinions the right course to follow. Although unmethodical in habits of work, and slow to make up his mind, he expressed himself with perfect clarity when it was made up, and acted with energy and decision. He was a born diplomat, too. Frequently appearing before Congressional committees to ask for more funds for the Navy, he used to be asked whether he was dealing with the British, to which he used to reply, "If we ever get into this war – you know that is a possibility – and we are not ready, you will be the first to ask why in the world we were not." [22]

As Admiral Ghormley's accounts of the staff conversations arrived from London, and as the reports of naval observers and intelligence officers flowed in from various parts of the world, Admiral Stark gave them deep thought and discussed their implications with high government officials and ranking officers of the armed forces. An important Memorandum on National Policy that he placed on the desk of Secretary Knox on 12 November 1940 expressed his matured opinion on the high strategy that his country should adopt for its own security: –

> Our major national objectives in the immediate future might be stated as preservation of the territorial, economic, and ideological integrity of the United States, plus that of the remainder of the Western Hemisphere; the prevention of the disruption of the British Empire, with all that such a consummation implies; and the diminution of the offensive military power of Japan, with a view to the retention of our economic and political interests in the Far East.

Stark's assessment of the Japanese threat thirteen months before the attack on Pearl Harbor was impressively astute, and this part of the summary was the point of departure for all subsequent naval war planning in the Pacific.[23] Beating Japan, he pointed out, would require a mighty effort and involve severe losses of ships and men. But if the United States could avoid involvement in the Pacific, and if the British did not capitulate, the problem in the Atlantic would be less difficult. Coastal defense of the Western Hemisphere on the Atlantic side must come first, and even this might involve combined operations with the Royal Navy. In any case, "purely naval assistance would not . . . *assure* final victory for Great Britain," because that country did not possess the man power to launch an invasion

[22] Admiral Stark "Background at Chatham House" 21 July 1942.
[23] To be considered in Volume III of this work.

of the Axis-held Continent. America would eventually have "to send large air and land forces to Europe or Africa, or both, and to participate strongly in this land offensive. The naval task of transporting an army abroad would be large."

The United States, despite strong desire for peace, might "at any moment become involved in war." It was therefore imperative for the American people to have "a national policy with mutually supporting diplomatic and military aspects" to protect the national interest. The Navy could not plan properly until it obtained political guidance on the following questions from the President and Secretary of State: –

1. Shall our principal military effort be directed toward hemisphere defense, and include chiefly those activities within the Western Hemisphere which contribute directly to security against attack in either or both oceans? . . .

2. Shall we prepare for a full offensive against Japan, premised on assistance from the British and Dutch forces in the Far East, and remain on the strict defensive in the Atlantic? . . .

3. Shall we plan for sending the strongest possible military assistance both to the British in Europe, and to the British, Dutch and Chinese in the Far East? . . .

4. Shall we direct our efforts toward an eventual strong offensive in the Atlantic as an ally of the British, and a defensive in the Pacific? . . .

Admiral Stark favored (1) hemisphere defense, as the first objective. This required a vigorous increase in the strength of the United States Army and Navy. When and if full-fledged war seemed unavoidable, he believed that (4) offensive strategy in the Atlantic, defensive in the Pacific, would be the right course.[24] This, as we shall see, became the basic strategic concept of the war. Yet, even hemisphere defense, with a neutrality patrol extending 1500 miles off shore, required an agreement with the Royal Navy. Consequently Stark, in his Memorandum of 12 November 1940,

[24] Admiral Turner's War Plans Committee of Opnav, which included Cdr. Forrest Sherman and Capt. Harry Hill, submitted a memorandum on 12 Nov. 1940 recommending (4) as the basic strategy, not only for "short of war" but in the event of war with Japan and Germany.

strongly urged that the President authorize Army and Navy representatives immediately to enter upon an exhaustive series of secret staff conversations with the British, from which definite plans and agreements to promote unity of effort against the Axis and Japan could emerge.

Secretaries Hull, Knox and Stimson fully agreed. President Roosevelt, it is believed, had reached this conclusion a month earlier, but wished to take no further step until after the election. Admiral Stark accordingly instructed Admiral Ghormley, whose exploratory conversations in London had reached the limit of their usefulness, to make arrangements with the British for serious staff conversations to begin at Washington early in the new year. Stark set the stage for these conversations himself. Regarding British ideas of American naval deployment in the Pacific as inacceptable,[25] he instructed Ghormley to inform the Admiralty that anyone they sent to Washington "should have instructions to discuss concepts based on equality of considerations for both the United States and British Commonwealth, and to explore realistically the various fields of war coöperation."

Admiral of the Fleet Sir Dudley Pound, First Sea Lord, answered this himself, assuring the Chief of Naval Operations that the ideas already expressed by the Admiralty were not to be regarded as "an unalterable basis" of discussion. He admitted that staff conversations in which each side fought for a preconceived plan would accomplish no good. Royal Navy representatives would be free to discuss the entire field of global strategy in the hope of reaching a joint plan which would best serve the common interest.

Already Admiral Stark had ordered the War Plans Division of his office to draft preliminary plans for naval participation if and when the United States became involved in war with the Axis. In December 1940 Captain Harry W. Hill and Commander Forrest P. Sherman of this Division submitted to their colleagues a plan for transatlantic escort-of-convoy, assuming that in the event of war

25 Owing largely to British preoccupation with the defense of Singapore. More of this in Volume III.

the United States Navy would share responsibility for the protection of transoceanic shipping, and establish advanced bases in the United Kingdom. This report was accepted by the War Plans Division, whose director, Rear Admiral Richmond K. Turner, informed Admiral Stark on 17 January 1941 that the Navy could be made ready to escort convoys from North America to Scotland by 1 April, and advised him that plans for such service be immediately prepared.

b. The Basic Strategic Concept of the War

On 29 January 1941 there opened in Washington a series of secret staff conversations, lasting two months, between representatives of the Chief of Naval Operations and the Army Chief of Staff, and a United Kingdom delegation representing the British Chiefs of Staff.[26] Rear Admiral R. L. Ghormley, Rear Admiral Richmond K. Turner, Captain A. G. Kirk, Captain DeWitt Ramsey and Lieutenant Colonel O. T. Pfeiffer USMC represented the United States Navy; Major General S. D. Embick, Brigadier Generals Sherman Miles and L. T. Gerow, and Colonel J. T. McNarney represented the Army. Rear Admiral R. M. Bellairs RN, Rear Admiral V. H. Danckwerts RN, Major General E. L. Morris, Air Vice-Marshal J. C. Slessor and Captain A. W. Clark represented the British armed forces.[27]

The purposes of this staff conference were: (*a*) to determine the best methods by which the United States and Great Britain could defeat Germany and her allies "should the United States be compelled to resort to war"; (*b*) to coördinate plans for the employment of American and British forces in that event; (*c*) to reach agreements concerning major lines of military strategy, principal areas of responsibility, and determination of command arrangements, if and when the United States came in. Conferences were

26 Report of U. S.-British Staff Conversations (ABC-1, 27 Mar. 1941). *Pearl Harbor Attack*, Part 15 pp. 1485–1550.

27 Representatives of Canada, Australia and New Zealand were in the British delegation but not present at joint meetings.

held daily, either in plenary session or in committees, from 29 January to 27 March 1941.

The conclusion, known as "ABC–1 Staff Agreement," [28] dated 27 March 1941, constituted the basis for Anglo-American coöperation during the war. It envisaged, first, a "short of war" collaboration on the basis of lend-lease in the Atlantic, and of dissuading the Japanese from further aggression in the Pacific; and, second, a full-fledged war coöperation when and if Axis aggression forced the United States into war. Simultaneously, the Canadian representatives in Washington concluded an "ABC–22 Staff Agreement" for joint Canadian-United States defense, which was integrated with ABC–1.[29]

Fundamental to these staff agreements was the basic strategic conception of World War II, of beating Hitler first. Already agreed upon in conversations between Admiral Stark, General Marshall, the Secretaries of State, War and Navy, and the President in November 1940, this conception is best stated in the United States Joint Army and Navy Basic War Plan, drafted in May 1941.[30] "Since Germany is the predominant member of the Axis powers, the Atlantic and European war is considered to be the decisive theater. The principal United States military effort will be exerted in that theater, and operations of United States forces in other theaters will be conducted in such a manner as to facilitate that effort." [31]

Here then was the basic and vital decision, based on an estimate of the then global situation, and on a correct anticipation of the future. The fundamental factors in this situation were these: (1) The entire Pacific area was still in an uneasy state of peace. The Japanese were not actually fighting any nation but China, and both the Department of State and the Foreign Office still hoped to dissuade the war lords of Japan from further aggression, whether

[28] *Pearl Harbor Attack,* Part 15 pp. 1485–1550.

[29] Same, pp. 1585–1593.

[30] Same, pp. 1426–1428.

[31] Paraphrase of the plan by Admiral Stark in his statement before Joint Congressional Committee on Investigation of the Pearl Harbor Attack, 31 Dec. 1945, para. 21.

against the United States or against British, Dutch, or French possessions in the Far East. For it was obviously the interest of the United States as well as of Great Britain to prevent Japan from actively supporting the Axis. (2) Germany, Italy and their satellites were at war with Great Britain and it was becoming very probable that Hitler would soon swing on Russia. American assistance should be applied at the point of contact, both to prevent Germany from acquiring complete hegemony in the Atlantic and Middle Eastern theaters, and to defeat her at the earliest possible moment. Germany was then and looked to be a more formidable enemy to free institutions and free nations in the Western Hemisphere than Japan. And it was rightly feared that if war in the West were unduly prolonged, German scientists would invent secret weapons that would prove irresistible.[32]

Whether this decision would have been the same had it been reached after the Pearl Harbor attack, may be questioned. Had there been no basic agreement and war plan, emotion and public opinion might then have dictated a concentration of American armed forces against Japan, as all fascist sympathizers in the United States vociferously advocated. But by that time United States naval forces had been so deployed that no responsible military authority could have advised a turnover. In December 1941 the United States Navy was prepared to close its teeth on the European Axis; retirement from the Atlantic at that juncture would have brought German victory dangerously near accomplishment, while effecting little good against Japan. To defeat Japan or even to make useful progress toward victory, we had to train many more divisions of troops, build scores of ships, hundreds of landing craft and thousands of planes, and put into effect a vast logistics program. Any wholesale transference of the then very limited American military power[33]

[32] "There was no time to lose in eliminating German science from the war. There was no comparable peril from Japanese science." Statement by Secretary of War Robert P. Patterson in 1946, quoted in Baxter *Scientists Against Time* p. 26.

[33] It must not be forgotten how long it took to train the new draft Army, to give the Regular Army modern equipment, to build planes and train pilots. At the Staff Conferences in February, the U. S. Army delegates said that on 1 Sept.

from the Atlantic to the Pacific in December 1941 would not have advanced victory over Japan by more than a few days.

The main subjects of the ABC–1 Staff Agreement were as follows: –

(1) Collaboration in Planning. (*a*) While the United States was still neutral, informal staff conversations would continue both in Washington and in London. (*b*) If and when the United States entered the war, a body known as the Supreme War Council (in January 1942 renamed Combined Chiefs of Staff) would be formed to conduct top-level planning for the Allied nations.

(2) Strategic Defense Policies. Each country agreed to the other's fundamental security – (*a*) for Britain, the security of the United Kingdom as a base of future operations against Germany; (*b*) for the United States, security of the Western Hemisphere against any Axis attempt on North, Central or South America. It followed that the security of sea communications and the maintenance of Anglo-American command of the Atlantic were indispensable.

(3) General Strategic Concepts. (*a*) Rigorous enforcement of the blockade against the Axis. (*b*) Extension of the air offensive against Germany. (*c*) Concentration of naval striking power in the Mediterranean, to eliminate Italy from the war. (*d*) Commando raids on Axis-held coasts, pending a big offensive. (*e*) Aid and encouragement of neutrals to resist Axis pressure. (*f*) Introduction of psychological warfare. (*g*) Concentration of United States and British troops in the British Isles to prepare for an invasion of the Continent. (*h*) Capture of Mediterranean or other bases from which one or more invasions of Europe could be launched at the appropriate moment.

(4) Principles of Command. (*a*) Each power to be charged with strategic direction of all Allied forces in specific areas of responsi-

---

1941 they would have a *maximum* of 4 infantry and 2 armored divisions in a state of combat readiness, and on 1 Dec., 8 squadrons of B-17s, 4 of B-25s, 4 of B-26s, 4 of A-20s and 3 of P-40s or P-39s in air readiness. At the same time, Admiral Turner reported that the Fleet Marine Force consisted of 2 divisions and 7 battalions in combat readiness.

bility; but the forces of each Ally to operate under its own task force commanders, not be broken up into small units. Specifically, the United States naval air arm operating in British strategic areas to be under United States, not Royal Air Force, command.[34] (*b*) Special and separate arrangements to be made for each combined operation.

(5) Exchange of intelligence data and other information to be prompt and complete between Allies. That was a very important aspect of the plan. Moreover, since 1941 there was wholehearted coöperation and even comradeship between the officers of the two services. It had to be so in order to win.

(6) The principal United States naval task would be the protection of shipping and sea communication in the Atlantic; the Royal Navy would take care of the Mediterranean.[35] The United States naval air arm would operate offensively with the Royal Air Force, besides protecting United States naval and military bases. Every British base would be at the disposal of the United States, and vice versa.

Thus, the basic pattern of United States participation in World War II was outlined at Washington by 27 March 1941. But the greater part of this staff agreement would only come into play if and when the United States chose to enter as a belligerent. There was no agreement expressed or implied as to when or under what circumstances that would take place, if ever.

6. *Transatlantic Escort Plans and the Support Force*

The subject of immediate moment in the ABC–1 Staff Agreement, one which did not depend on a declaration of war by the

[34] In a series of jingles produced by the British delegation to lighten the close of the conference appears this: –

> The U. K. delegation have had the luck to learn a
> Great deal of naval strategy from Admiral Kelly Turner.
> No piteous entreaties or objurgations harsh'll
> Induce him to put PBYs under Air Vice-Marshal!

[35] The possibility of the U. S. Navy taking over the western Mediterranean, in case the French Fleet joined the Axis, was envisaged.

United States, was that of escort-of-convoy. One section of the agreement stated: —

> Owing to the threat to the sea communications of the United Kingdom, the principal task of the United States naval forces in the Atlantic will be the protection of shipping of the Associated Powers,[36] the center of gravity of the United States' effort being concentrated in the Northwestern Approaches to the United Kingdom.

This meant that the United States Navy would take over the prime responsibility for protecting transatlantic merchant convoys, as soon as the Atlantic Fleet was in a position to do so. Preparation for that task meant, among other things, changes in department administration, training of naval personnel and ships in escort duty and establishment of new advanced bases. Training had, of course, been going on in peacetime; but it was now greatly accelerated and intensified by the Royal Navy giving to the United States Navy benefit of its experience, and of the new devices and methods for fighting submarines that had already been evolved. Admiral Ghormley began to obtain this information at London during the summer of 1940. Particularly useful were (1) the "Very Secret" Anti-Submarine Warfare publications of the Admiralty; (2) "Mersigs," the simple system of coded flag and blinker signals for intra-convoy communication; and (3) the British Naval Control Service, a worldwide organization which routed, diverted and reported merchant ships' movements in all parts of the world not under enemy domination. This was the model for our own Convoy and Routing Section of the Office of the Chief of Naval Operations, which on 17 June 1941 issued its first instructions for the naval control of merchant shipping. Ten days later, following the torpedoing of the non-routed S.S. *Robin Moor*, they were put into effect.[37]

Above all, the responsibility now assumed by the United States

[36] Meaning the United States and Great Britain, and such Norwegian, Danish, Dutch, Polish and French shipping as had escaped the Nazis.

[37] The Port Directors' offices in the various naval districts administered these routing instructions. (*Brief History of the Office of Port Director, Third Naval District* pp. 12–13.) Before Pearl Harbor 228 merchant ships were routed by the Port Director's Office, New York.

Navy meant the organization of a force for escort-of-convoy, and suitable bases in the United Kingdom for it to operate from. Argentia, the intended base on the American side, was already under construction in January 1941.

On 17 January 1941, as we have seen, Rear Admiral Richmond K. Turner, director of the War Plans Division, informed the Chief of Naval Operations that the Navy could be ready to escort convoys from North America to Scotland on 1 April. In January, Rear Admiral Arthur LeR. Bristol Jr. was summoned from Honolulu to organize a Support Force [38] for escort duty from available units of the Atlantic Fleet, and to take charge of building up bases such as Argentia, which he made his headquarters. Admiral Bristol, an admirable choice for this important task, received his orders as Commander Support Force on 26 February 1941.

On 15 February Admiral Stark directed that the Support Force be created out of the Atlantic Fleet within three weeks. Abstracted largely from the Neutrality Patrol, it included three destroyer squadrons and four patrol squadrons of 12 Navy Catalinas or Mariners each, with suitable tenders.[39] On 1 March the Support Force was formally constituted, and on the 3rd Admiral Bristol hoisted his flag in destroyer tender *Prairie* at Norfolk.

The Patrol Force had already been given the new and appropriate designation of Atlantic Fleet on 1 February 1941, and its commander, Rear Admiral Ernest J. King, was promoted on the same date to the rank of Admiral and designated Commander in Chief Atlantic Fleet.[40]

[38] It was at first called the Northeastern Escort Force; designation changed to Support Force about Mar. 1941. This Force included the later Task Force 4, whose designation was changed to Task Force 24 on 13 Mar. 1942.

[39] Cinclant's Letter of 26 Feb. 1941 to Type Commanders. For composition of the Support Force, see Appendix V.

[40] Ernest Joseph King, b. Lorain, Ohio, 1878, Naval Academy '01, graduating fourth. After five years' duty in various ships, instructor in ordnance and gunnery at Naval Academy; engineer officer U.S.S. *New Hampshire;* flag secretary to Rear Admiral Hugo Osterhaus when C. in C. Atlantic Fleet, 1911–1912; C.O. destroyers *Cassin* and *Terry* and division commander, 1914–1916. During World War I assistant chief of staff to Admiral H. T. Mayo, C. in C. Atlantic Fleet. Head of Naval Postgraduate School, Annapolis, 1919–1921; C.O. supply ship *Bridge;* Comsubdivs 11 and 3. Comsubbase New London, 1923–1925; in charge of

About two months after Admiral King became "Cinclant," he issued a confidential memorandum which was not only characteristic of the man, but well summarizes the conditions under which his fleet had to operate.

Making the Best of What We Have[41]

1. If and when the existing emergency becomes intensified – develops into a state of war – all of us will accept cheerfully and willingly the difficulties and discomforts as well as the hazards and the dangers with which we shall then be confronted.

In the existing emergency, we are not confronted with hazards and dangers (except potentially) but we are faced with difficulties and discomforts which are inherent in the emergency. These difficulties and discomforts must be faced in the same spirit of cheerfulness and willingness with which we will face the hazards and dangers of war – if and when it comes.

These difficulties and discomforts are chiefly those involved in lack of trained seagoing *personnel*, inadequacies of *materiel*, the necessity to continue *operations* in that area which is strategically central, and the *waiting* for developments over which we have no control.

2. It must be the key idea of all hands that we will make the best of what we have.

3. *As to personnel* – we must not only train our own personnel (officers as well as men) to meet the current needs of our own ships but we must do our share in providing trained personnel to man the new ships whose coming into service will reinforce the three fleets.

As to materiel – our needs are many but there is a clear-cut distinction between what is *necessary* (urgent) and what is *desirable.* We must not only conserve and improve what we have – with the means available in the ships themselves and in the Fleet – but we must take heed of the fact that overhaul periods at navy yards longer than those required for urgent items of work not only keep our own ships "out

---

salvage of *S-51* and *S-4*. C.O. airplane tender *Wright*, 1926–1928, during which time qualified as naval aviator at Pensacola; Assistant Chief Buaer, 1928–1929, C.O. Naval Air Station Norfolk, C.O. U.S.S. *Lexington* for two years, Naval War College course, and Chief Buaer with rank Rear Admiral, 1933. Com. Aircraft of Base Force, Scouting Force and Battle Force 1936–1939; General Board; Com. Patrol Force Dec. 1940, C. in C. Atlantic Fleet with rank of Admiral, 1 Feb. 1941. C. in C. U. S. Fleet 20 Dec. 1941–Dec. 1945 (also C.N.O. from 18 Mar. 1942); Fleet Admiral 15 Dec. 1944; died 25 June 1956.

41 Atlantic Fleet Confidential Memorandum 2CM–41, 24 March 1941.

of service" but affect the availability of labor and material for new ships and for urgent items of work on other ships.

As to operations – we must not only accept the circumstances premised on strategical considerations imposed by the current international situation but also must realize that we must do all that we can with the forces available, even though they are less in numbers and in power than appear adequate to present and prospective tasks.

As to waiting – we must make the most of the time available to perfect the training of personnel, to improve the material condition of ships, to better our capacity in operation, and otherwise to make ourselves ready (physically and mentally) for the work for which the Navy exists and for which we are in the Navy.

4. I expect the officers of the Atlantic Fleet to be the leaders in what may be called the pioneering spirit – to lead in the determination that the difficulties and discomforts – personnel, materiel, operations, waiting – shall be dealt with as "enemies" to be overcome by our own efforts.

There is *work* in plenty for all hands – officers and men. *Recreation* is a field in which officers (and chief petty officers) must show their leadership, by improvising and promoting recreation on board ship, as well as seeking out and making use of such shore facilities as can be made to serve the purpose.

5. *We must all do all that we can with what we have.*

Captain Louis Denfeld, Admiral Bristol's chief of staff, accompanied by an aviator and a civil engineer, visited the British Isles in March 1941 in order to select bases from which both surface ships and aircraft of the United States Navy might operate. They arrived in the midst of the Battle of Britain, with raids by the Luftwaffe nightly. Liverpool was badly strafed twice while the American delegation was there, conferring with Commander in Chief Western Approaches ("Cincwa") Admiral Sir Percy L. H. Noble RN. As it seemed likely that the Germans might bomb us out of one pair of bases, two were selected: Gare Loch, an estuary of the Clyde, for destroyers, together with Loch Ryan at the entrance of the Firth for naval aircraft; Londonderry for destroyers with Lough Erne in County Fermanagh for aircraft.[42] The first

[42] Conversation with Rear Admiral Denfeld in 1943. He tried to obtain the use of Lough Swilly in County Donegal for the Irish base, but it could not be had;

pair were then undeveloped, but the Irish bases were already in use by the Royal Navy and Air Force. Captain Denfeld, after returning and reporting in April, was given the job of procuring the money out of lend-lease; and "after chasing Harry Hopkins around Washington and calling at the White House," [43] he induced President Roosevelt to allot $50,000,000 for installation of these bases. The contract was awarded to an American construction company which began sending over the materials in June. They had to use British ships, since it was still illegal for American vessels to enter war zones.[44]

About the first of March 1941, intensive training in anti-submarine warfare was begun by the Support Force at Norfolk and New London, using "tame" submarines for practice. Secretary Knox informed the President on 20 March that the Navy would shortly be ready to convoy merchant shipping from North America to the United Kingdom. He planned to base an initial force, consisting of 27 destroyers, four patrol squadrons of twelve Catalina planes each, and a number of minesweepers and tenders, on Lough Foyle and Lough Erne beginning about mid-September; and the movement of 15,000 troops of the United States Army to protect and service the bases was provided for.[45]

Around mid-June, however, this plan for the Support Force to convoy merchant shipping all the way across was given up in favor of the Support Force concentrating on the Argentia–Iceland sector of the transatlantic convoy route. That was the way the Admiralty and the Navy Department wanted it from the first. Such an arrangement would make for economy in administration and operation. The delay in adopting this division of responsibility

---

Mr. de Valera, in spite of a visit from Col. William J. Donovan, remained obdurate. The two naval air bases were subsequently found to be unnecessary and were turned back to the British.

[43] Cdr. E. W. Litch Report on First U. K. Bases Dec. 1941.

[44] The materiel was assembled at the Naval Air Station at Quonset, Rhode Island, which the same companies were then constructing. It was marked TAF (Temporary Aviation Facilities) for secrecy. Even naval personnel wore civilian clothes and were referred to as TAF.

[45] "Administrative History of the Atlantic Fleet" II 25.

was due to the fact that many convoys originating on the western side of the Atlantic were Canadian troop convoys, and the President believed that the Navy should not, as yet, escort combat troops. Escorting merchant ships, he felt, was a different matter, since the entire U-boat warfare on merchant ships, as conducted by Germany, was contrary to international law and treaty obligations.

In the meantime, liaison groups had been set up, both to carry on "short of war" collaboration, and to ensure that if and when the United States entered the war, machinery would be ready to make the change rapidly and smoothly. The United States Army and Navy observers in London organized their staffs and arranged in May 1941 for continuous consultation and coöperation with the British Chiefs of Staff, including their War Plans sections. It was in this manner that weighty subjects, such as the relief of the British Army of Occupation in Iceland by United States forces, were arranged.

CHAPTER IV

"Short of War" Operations

March–August 1941

1. *British Transatlantic Convoys, March–May 1941*

WHILE staff conversations went on in Washington, U-boat attacks on convoys and counterattacks by British and Canadian escorts became more intense. Convoy HX–112, consisting of 41 merchant vessels escorted by five destroyers and two corvettes, lost five ships on 16–18 March. On the other hand, five U-boats were sunk by British escorts in the area between lats. 60° to 62°30′ N and longs. 12° to 17° W in March.

Doenitz replied by concentrating further to the westward, with the object of catching convoys naked. For, owing to scarcity of escorts and difficulty in fueling, there was a considerable gap between the position where the Canadian escort peeled off and that where the British escort joined. On the night of 3–4 April, a typical wolf-pack, attacking first at latitude 58°20′ N, longitude 28°10′ W, broke up Convoy SC–26 by sinking 10 out of 22 ships, at the cost of two U-boats. The Admiralty then decided to establish an escort base in Iceland, which would enable it to close the unprotected gap.

"The situation is obviously critical in the Atlantic," wrote Admiral Stark on 4 April. "In my opinion, it is hopeless except as we take strong measures to save it. The effect on the British of sinkings with regard both to the food supply and essential material to carry on the war is getting progressively worse." Three days later he took a measure which, in view of our ticklish situation with Japan, was both strong and risky. He ordered the transfer of battleships

Idaho, Mississippi and *New Mexico*, carrier *Yorktown*, light cruisers *Philadelphia, Brooklyn, Savannah* and *Nashville*, and two destroyer squadrons (8 and 9) from the Pacific to the Atlantic Fleet. The transit was effected by the end of May.[1]

"Whoever possesses Iceland holds a pistol permanently pointed at England, America and Canada." So wrote Karl Haushofer, the Nazi geopolitical expert.

Iceland had been occupied by British Army units in May 1940, on the invitation of the local government, in order to deny it to the Nazis after they had overrun Denmark and Norway. Obviously, a German base in Iceland would have meant the end of communication by the northern route. About 1 March 1941, Hitler announced that Iceland and its surrounding waters, up to the three-mile limit off Greenland, was a war zone in which neutral ships would be sunk at sight. Admiral Stark had already pointed out the usefulness of Iceland for convoys and air bases if and when we entered the war. President Roosevelt ordered him to conduct a preliminary reconnaissance of the strategic island; this was effected by the destroyer *Niblack* (Lieutenant Commander E. R. Durgin) in April. On the 10th of that month, when closing the coast, *Niblack* picked up three boatloads of survivors from a torpedoed Netherlands freighter. Just as the last men were being pulled on board, *Niblack's* sound operator made contact on a submarine evidently approaching for attack. Commander D. L. Ryan, the division commander, ordered *Niblack* to attack with depth charges. He did, and the U-boat retired. So far as can be ascertained, this bloodless battle of 10 April 1941 was the first action of the war between United States and German armed forces.[2]

During the same month, the Royal Navy commenced basing escort groups at Hvalfjordur, about 25 miles from Reykjavik. These ships filled the mid-ocean gap between the Canada-based and Britain-based escorts; but, owing to the continued scarcity

[1] *Pearl Harbor Attack* Part 16 p. 2161 and Part 11 p. 5502.

[2] "Administrative History Atlantic Fleet" IV, "Commandant N.O.B. Iceland," pp. 7–8.

of suitable vessels, the number allotted to each convoy was now less than ever. Heavy losses continued, and at positions farther and farther west. Consequently a new system of routing convoys was adopted, and other improvements were made. An advanced Canadian base was established at St. Johns, and to the Newfoundland Escort Force, which started operating 27 May, was allotted every available corvette. Convoys were routed to the United Kingdom via Iceland, the escorts refueling at the Hvalfjordur base; they could now stay with a convoy through the Newfoundland–Iceland leg of the voyage instead of leaving this important part of the crossing unprotected.

2. *Greenland and Western Hemisphere Defense*[3]

Taking action parallel to the British occupation of Iceland, the United States tried to insure that Greenland could not be the scene of Nazi penetration. On the East Coast the Germans were known to have weather-reporting stations, highly important for Luftwaffe operations. A single cryolite mine at Ivigtut on the West Coast was one of the world's most important sources of that mineral, an essential ingredient of commercial aluminum.

The local government of Greenland asked for American protection on 3 May 1940, only three weeks after Denmark was occupied by the Germans. Rear Admiral Russell R. Waesche, Commandant of the United States Coast Guard, was promptly alerted to assign cutters for special missions to Greenland. U.S.C.G.C. *Comanche* landed the Honorable James K. Penfield, first United States diplomatic representative to Greenland, at Ivigtut in May 1940; and by the end of July, American newspapers announced an "unofficial protectorate over Greenland."

[3] *The Coast Guard at War, Greenland Patrol* (mimeographed book prepared in Historical Section Public Information Division U.S.C.G. Headquarters, 15 July 1945) is a good comprehensive account. Rex Ingraham *First Fleet* (1944) tells some of the stories; "Administrative History Atlantic Fleet" III contains additional facts.

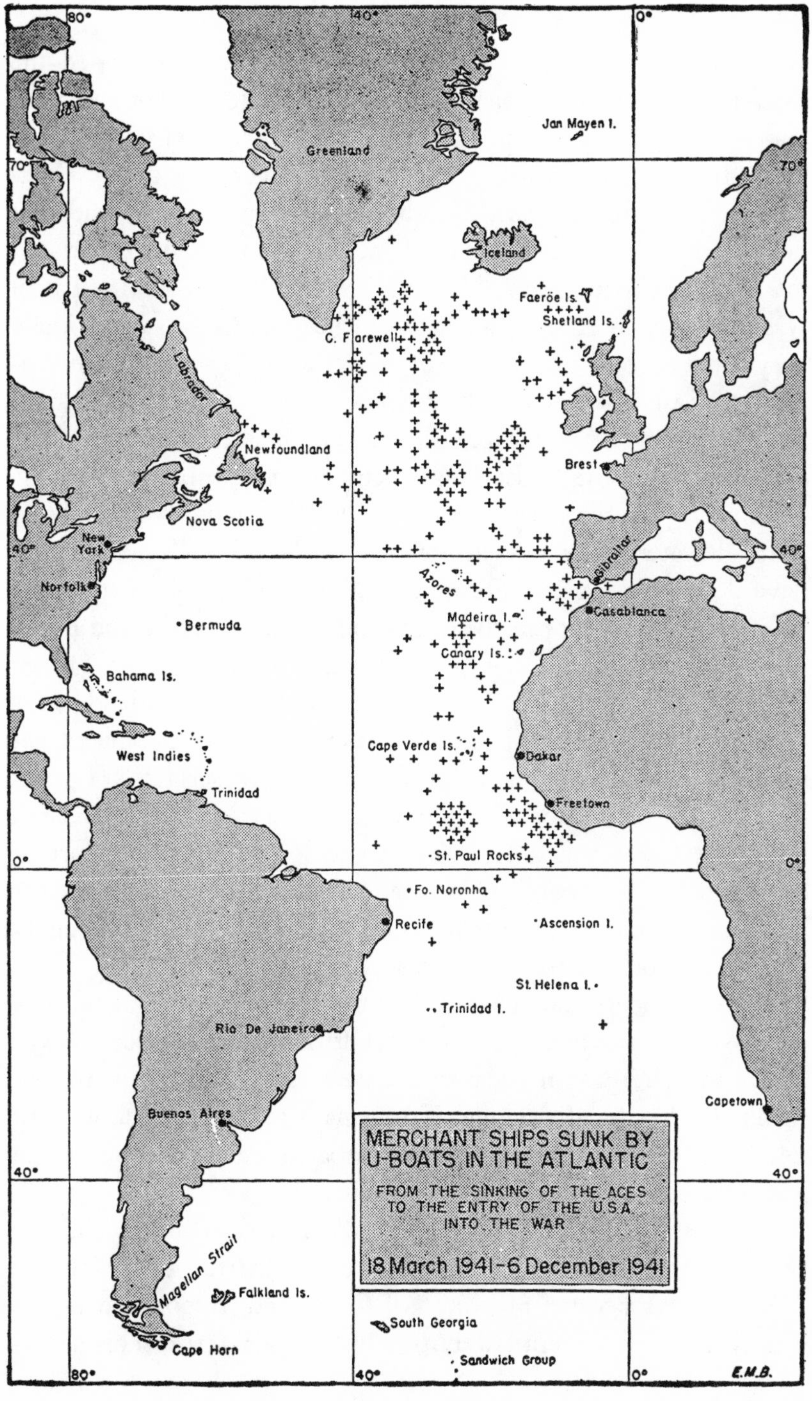

MERCHANT SHIPS SUNK BY U-BOATS IN THE ATLANTIC
FROM THE SINKING OF THE ACES TO THE ENTRY OF THE U.S.A. INTO THE WAR
18 March 1941–6 December 1941
Jan Mayen I.
Greenland
Iceland
Faeröe Is.
Shetland Is.
C. Farewell
Labrador
Newfoundland
Nova Scotia
Brest
New York
Norfolk
Gibraltar
Azores
Casablanca
Bermuda
Madeira I.
Canary Is.
Bahama Is.
West Indies
Cape Verde Is.
Dakar
Trinidad
Freetown
St. Paul Rocks
Fo. Noronha
Recife
Ascension I.
St. Helena I.
Trinidad I.
Rio De Janeiro
Capetown
Buenos Aires
Magellan Strait
Falkland Is.
South Georgia
Cape Horn
Sandwich Group
80°
40°
0°
70°
E.M.B.

For some twenty-five years the Coast Guard had carried the burden of the International Ice Patrol in waters around Greenland with specially equipped vessels, the most famous being Admiral Byrd's former flagship, the ancient auxiliary bark *Bear*. Commander Edward H. Smith USCG had made a specialty of scientific oceanography and became one of the world's foremost experts on ice, earning the nickname "Iceberg" Smith. But, as the Ice Patrol was primarily interested in shipping lanes, the Coast Guard knew very little about the shores of Greenland, especially the ice-infested East Coast where German weather men were operating. And the Germans had seized all the Danish secret charts.

During 1940 the Coast Guard lent personnel and guns to the Greenland government to guard the cryolite mine, which was so near tidewater that a few air bombs or U-boats' shells could easily have flooded it. Cutters *Duane* and *Northland* with Coast Guard planes attached surveyed the coasts and added a "Greenland Pilot" to the long list of Hydrographic Office publications.

As the great circle course from Newfoundland to Scotland passes close to Cape Farewell, this southern extremity of Greenland became an obvious staging point for the "ferry service" of lend-lease planes to England. But there were no airfields in Greenland. The East Coast was a logical place to locate weather-reporting stations, as well as search radars, radio stations and high-frequency direction-finder instruments to pick up enemy forces approaching America through Denmark Strait. Accordingly, several government departments combined to organize the South Greenland Survey Expedition which arrived at Godthaab in the cutter *Cayuga* on 31 March 1941 in order to locate and survey sites for these facilities. Shortly after, loyal Norwegians sent us the disquieting news that Germany was preparing to base an air squadron on the East Coast, and service it with U-boats.

At Washington on 9 April 1941 the Danish Minister and the Secretary of State signed an agreement by virtue of which the United States became protector of Greenland, responsible for its supply and defense until Denmark herself were free. This agree-

Benson class destroyer patrolling Grand Banks off Newfoundland, autumn 1941

U.S.C.G.C. *Amarock* at Entrance Inland Passage, Southern Greenland

Northern Patrols

Coast Guard Photo

Freighter and Coast Guard Tug at Kungnat Bay, February 1943

Coast Guard Photo

Cutter *Northland* on mission to destroy German weather-reporting station, Northern Greenland

Greenland Patrol

ment gave the United States the right to establish any facilities deemed necessary for the defense of Greenland or of America.

President Roosevelt had already declared, at the time of the Havana Pan-American Conference in July 1940, that the United States would hold itself responsible for the defense of the Western Hemisphere. Now Admiral Ernest J. King, as Commander in Chief of the Atlantic Fleet, proceeded, like Pope Alexander VI in 1493, to draw a line of demarcation between hemispheres. According to his Operation Plan No. 3 of 18 April 1941, "The Western Hemisphere extends from approximately 26° W,[4] westward to the International Date Line and, in the Atlantic, includes all of Greenland, all of the islands of the Azores, the whole of the Gulf of St. Lawrence, the Bahama Islands, the Caribbean Sea and the Gulf of Mexico.

"Entrance into the Western Hemisphere by naval ships or aircraft of belligerents other than those powers having sovereignty over territory in the Western Hemisphere is to be viewed as possibly actuated by an unfriendly interest toward shipping or territory in the Western Hemisphere."[5]

Admiral King's next operation plan, which came out three days later, repeated these stipulations, and organized the Atlantic Fleet into task forces for patrol of the North Atlantic, the Caribbean, the Gulf of Mexico and Panama Canal approaches. Task Force 11[6] was ordered to "enter the Northeast Greenland area as early in the season as conditions permit, and remain there as late in the summer as possible. Prevent establishment of military, naval and air bases, or landing of European nationals except as authorized by the Government of Greenland."

As a result of work by the South Greenland Survey Expedition and by cutter *Northland* in April and May 1941, it was decided to build landing fields at Narsarssuak at the head of the Julianehaab Fjord, at Kipisako near Ivigtut, with seaplane bases at other points;

[4] The meridian that passes about 50 miles west of Reykjavik.

[5] Navy Department Operations Files (1941).

[6] TF 11 (Cdr. Smith) was composed of U.S.C.G.C. *Northland*, U.S.C.G.C. *North Star* and U.S.S. *Bear*.

to set up a radio central and main aerological station on Akia Island near Kipisako, with secondary observing station elsewhere. Work was begun shortly, and the United States Army sent detachments for their defense. These weather, radio and radar stations proved invaluable to Allied forces. The meteorological information on the basis of which General Eisenhower set D-day for Normandy came largely from Greenland. The airfields were most useful both in ferrying planes to Europe, and getting them back after V–E day in 1945.[7]

The numerous casualties to convoys south of Greenland, and the *Bismarck* Battle of May 1941, emphasized the strategic importance of Greenland and probably hastened the formal organization of the Greenland Patrol on 1 June.[8] The commander, "Iceberg" Smith in cutter *Northland*, received orders from the Chief of

[7] As the Greenland stations were called "Bluies" in Army Code, and usually so referred to in Navy communications, this list of them (compiled by Harry E. Foster Y2c USNR) may be useful: –

Bluie East 1, Torgilsbu, the base near Cape Farewell
Bluie East 2, Ikateq on Angmagsalik Island, opposite Iceland, radio and meteorological station
Bluie East 3, Gurreholm on Scoresby Sound
Bluie East 4, Ella Island on Davy Sound, at lat. 73° N
Bluie East 5, Eskimonaes, at lat. 74° N, radio (seized by Germans 23 Mar. 1943, and when reëstablished, located at Myggbukta)
Bluie West 1, Narsarssuak, the main U. S. Army and Navy base and airfield
Bluie West 2, Kipisako
Bluie West 3, Simiutak, at mouth of Skovfjord, a HF/DF station
Bluie West 4, Faeringerhavnen, at lat. 63°40′ N
Bluie West 5, Godhavn, on South Disko Island
Bluie West 6, Thule, at lat. 76°30′ N
Bluie West 7, Grondal, protection of cryolite mine at Ivigtut
Bluie West 8, Sondrestromfjord, emergency landing field on S. Stromfjord, lat. 67° N

There was also a Navy Loran navigation station at Fredriksdal known as Navy 226. As part of the airfield steppingstones, Capt. Bob Bartlett and his famous schooner *Morrissey* sailed a party of U. S. Navy hydrographers, including Cdr. Alexander Forbes USNR, to Frobisher Bay, Baffin Island, where they made surveys for an airfield known as "Crystal 2," in June 1942. This emergency airfield was not much used.

[8] Designated TG 24.8 in Oct. 1941, and a part of Admiral Bristol's command, originally comprising only five cutters, icebreaking tug *Raritan* and U.S.S. *Bear*, this patrol was greatly augmented in 1942 by the assignment of 125-foot cutters, SCs, and six converted 110-foot fishing draggers, which were given Eskimo names such as *Aklak* and *Natsek*. The last-named was lost with all hands, probably as a result of icing, in the Gulf of St. Lawrence; her commander, Lt. (jg) Thomas S. La Farge USCG, was a noted artist.

Naval Operations to do a little of everything – the Coast Guard is used to that. He must convoy U. S. Army transports and supply ships, breaking the ice for them if necessary; discover and destroy enemy weather or radio stations in Greenland, continue the hydrographic survey, maintain communications among the several United States and Greenland government posts, bring supplies to the Eskimos and the small Danish settlements, escort the cryolite ships and perform air-sea rescue missions as required to vessels in distress and splashed planes. These duties the Coast Guard performed with exemplary fortitude and faithfulness throughout the war. Commander Smith even thought up others, such as the Northeast Greenland Sledge Patrol. That outfit on 11 September 1941 sighted the Norwegian schooner *Buskoe*, whose crew included a member of the Gestapo. She was seized by cutter *Northland* and sent into Boston. Still other duties, such as the stationing of certain cutters (and later frigates) as weather-reporting ships, were given to the Greenland Patrol from time to time.

In April of 1941 Germany crushed Yugoslavia and turned on Greece, which had recently given Mussolini's army a bad drubbing; by midsummer the Germans controlled the whole of the Balkan Peninsula and Crete. British sea power in the eastern Mediterranean was almost nullified; the Axis army in Libya, reinforced at will, now recovered earlier losses of territory, advanced eastward and threatened the Suez Canal.

Three events in the Atlantic in May 1941 considerably shortened the shortness of "short of war." A neutral passenger ship of Egyptian registry, S.S. *ZamZam*, was sunk by a German raider in the South Atlantic. About 150 of her passengers were United States citizens, forbidden by the Neutrality Acts to travel on a belligerent's ship in the war zone. S.S. *Robin Moor*, an American freighter sailing from the United States to South Africa with a general cargo, was sunk on 21 May by German U-boat *69* in the South Atlantic; her crew sailed hundreds of miles in lifeboats before being rescued. That became a common enough experience for American merchant seamen in 1942, but in 1941 the United States was not at war, and the Neutrality Act ensured that *Robin Moor* was neither carrying contraband nor destined for a war zone.

Even more ominous was the brief career of the great new German battleship *Bismarck*. In Denmark Strait on 24 May she sank with a single salvo H.M. battle cruiser *Hood*. The Royal Navy and Air Force hunted *Bismarck* down and sank her on 27 May; but she almost escaped.[9] Neither the Atlantic Fleet nor the entire United States Navy at that time had a vessel capable of trading punches on anything like equal terms with the *Bismarck* or her sister ship *Tirpitz*, who had not yet been heard from. Our latest battleship available, U.S.S. *West Virginia*, was twenty years old; *North Carolina* and *Washington*, first of the new 35,000-ton battleships with nine 16-inch guns, had not yet had their shakedown cruises.

3. *The Crisis of Midsummer, 1941*

a. Unlimited National Emergency

These recent events were the subject of President Roosevelt's National Emergency broadcast on 27 May 1941, the very day that *Bismarck* went down. "The war," he declared, "is approaching the brink of the Western Hemisphere itself. It is coming very close to home. . . . The Battle of the Atlantic now extends from the icy waters of the North Pole to the frozen continent of the Antarctic." Great numbers of merchant vessels had already been sunk by Axis raiders and submarines "actually within the waters of the Western Hemisphere." Everything pointed to an eventual attack on the American nations. In view of the sudden striking force of modern war, "it would be suicide to wait until they are in our front yard. . . . Old-fashioned common sense calls for the use of a strategy which will prevent such an enemy from gaining a foot-

[9] Coast Guard Cutters *Modoc, Northland* and *General Greene*, then engaged in rescuing survivors from a transatlantic convoy, witnessed a large part of the *Bismarck's* battle. Their observations of it are told in *Coast Guard at War, Greenland Patrol* pp. 20–32.

hold in the first place. We have, accordingly, extended our patrol in North and South Atlantic waters. We are steadily adding more and more ships and planes to that patrol." The President hinted that even Dakar, the Azores and the Cape Verdes came under the watchful scrutiny of the United States Navy, which would prevent by force any attempt of the Axis to gain a foothold on such bases as threatened the security of the Americas. At the conclusion of this address, the most important that he made in the first half of 1941, the President declared an Unlimited National Emergency.[10]

This was said on 27 May 1941. Three days later, as if to prove that the President was right, a pack of 9 U-boats located Convoy HX-126 almost due south of Cape Farewell, Greenland, and sank nine ships carrying lend-lease goods to Britain.

b. The Escort-building Program

It was also on 27 May that the first of several Iceland-routed convoys under British and Canadian escort sailed from Halifax. For about three weeks the U-boats could not locate convoys on this new route. Then, in a series of attacks extending over 24–29 June, Convoy HX-133 lost six ships, but sank two out of a pack of ten.

Admiral King already knew that available British and Canadian escorts were wholly inadequate for transatlantic convoys.[11] Now, as an emergency measure, the United States Navy undertook to build escort vessels for the British. Rear Admiral J. W. S. Dorling RN, head of the British Supply Council in North America, pointed out to Secretary Knox, on 23 June, that the extension of enemy submarine activity had increased the need for escorts, a want which could best be filled by an escort vessel of about 1500 tons.[12] British and Canadian building capacity for such vessels being only eight a month, he proposed that the United States undertake construc-

[10] *Roosevelt's Foreign Policy, 1933–1941* (1942) pp. 395–403.
[11] Combatdiv 5 to Admiral King 15 May 1941.
[12] This letter and other correspondence on the subject are on file in the office of the Munitions Assignment Board of the Combined Chiefs of Staff.

tion out of lend-lease funds. Understanding that our Bureau of Ships had an acceptable design for a 1500-ton destroyer escort, he proposed that a beginning be made by constructing one hundred of them for the Royal Navy at the rate of ten a month, together with 20 minesweepers and 14 rescue tugs. After some discussion in the higher command, Secretary Knox on 18 July 1941 approved this building program, which was started at once. At the same time or shortly after, discussions began between officers of the United States and Royal Navies about building landing and beaching craft, which subsequently played a vital part in amphibious warfare.[13] Considering that in 1941 the United States Army had no means of transporting tanks overseas, except in the hulls of cargo vessels, and that the Navy had very few landing craft capable of putting them on the beach, the value of this British fillip to our building program is obvious.

c. Azores or Iceland?

From the best intelligence we could obtain of enemy intentions, Germany was preparing the occupation of Spain and Portugal as her next aggression after the invasion of the Balkans. There were many signs and portents of it in the air. The German radio started an anti-Portuguese campaign; the United States was accused of ambition to annex the Azores; walls in Madrid were scrawled with the slogan "Sea to Sea." Dr. Salazar, deeply apprehensive, shipped a large part of the Portuguese Army to the Azores, prepared to shift the government thither after making a token defense on the mainland, and requested his ancient ally Great Britain to protect the Western Islands. Corvo lies a little over one thousand miles from Cape Race by the great-circle route. The British government, faced with losing Gibraltar and the use of Lisbon, prepared expeditions to occupy Grand Canary, the Cape Verde Islands and one of the Azores, and requested American aid in keeping Germany out of all the Azores. On 24 May 1941

[13] Memorandum of Lt. Cdr. R. S. McIver to Admiral Reeves 27 Nov. 1941.

President Roosevelt directed the Joint Chiefs of Staff to get ready an Azores occupation force of United States Marines, to be covered by the Atlantic Fleet. The units of the Corps were actually being trained for that purpose, under Major General Holland M. Smith USMC who later won fame in the Pacific, when, owing to an exchange of views between Winston Churchill and the President early in June, the occupation of the Azores was called off and that of Iceland substituted. The reason for this change of objective was entirely sound. Mr. Churchill had been convinced by his Intelligence Service that Hitler was preparing to invade Russia that month, and that General Franco had refused him a peaceful occupation of Spain. Obviously Germany would be in no position to add Spain and Portugal to her list of enemies. By the same token Iceland, already important as covering the northern transatlantic convoy route, would have additional strategic value for getting aid to Russia by way of Archangel. Great Britain undertook to obtain an official Icelandic "invitation" to the United States, and preparations were made to divert the Marines from Horta to Hvalfjordur.

d. Casco and Argentia

The tempo of world events accelerated. On 22 June 1941 Hitler invaded Russia. Shortly after, Vichy handed over military control of Indo-China to Japan, who thereby secured without a blow an advance base for an assault on Thailand, Singapore, and the Netherlands East Indies whenever it suited her convenience. It looked as if the western and the eastern partners of the Axis were planning to join hands in India. President Roosevelt replied by freezing Japanese funds in the United States on 25 July; by mustering the Philippine Army, with its Commander in Chief, General Douglas MacArthur, into United States service; and by warning Pétain that the United States might find it necessary in self-defense to occupy French possessions in the Caribbean.

That, in the opinion of many, was the moment when the United

States should have taken over the French West Indies. The President, however, advised by the Secretary of State, decided against it. His decision was justified by events, although at the time it was regretted by the Navy, and bitterly criticized by a section of public opinion as "appeasing the Axis." [14]

The Caribbean Patrol in itself was no strain on the Navy; but it now also had the responsibility for keeping Axis ships out of the North Atlantic, west of a line between Iceland and the Azores. Consequently, at least two new North Atlantic bases, an inner and an advanced one, were required. For the former, none of the existing navy yards or stations were suitable. Narragansett Bay alone had sufficient space, but was too far from the convoy routes. Casco Bay in Maine was finally selected as a destroyer base, and development for that purpose began in the summer of 1941. Base "Sail," as Casco Bay was called, afforded an excellent protected anchorage of wide extent, adjacent to deep water where gunnery practice and maneuvers could be held, and near the city of Portland as a railhead for supplies and recreation center.

As the outer and advanced base for escort-of-convoy, the Navy had already, in 1940, chosen Argentia in Newfoundland. Lying halfway up Placentia Bay, that deep fjord which almost makes an island of the Avalon Peninsula, Argentia was near the site of Plaisance, a French fortress and settlement in the seventeenth century. The logic of sea power brought Plaisance into the British Empire, for as the Privy Council remarked in the reign of Charles II, "that place will allwayes belong to him that is superior at sea." [15] As the Alcock-Brown transatlantic flight showed in 1919, Newfoundland strategically may be compared to a gigantic airplane carrier permanently moored near the fishing banks, and the Avalon Peninsula resembles a hand stretching forth into the sea lanes to help the convoys across. Argentia in 1940 was a ghost village, an extinct silver-mining settlement. Construction of the naval base

[14] See also Volume II of this work pp. 1–10.

[15] Quoted in Gerald S. Graham "Britain's Defense of Newfoundland" *Canadian Historical Review* Sept. 1942 p. 267.

by civilian contractors began in the last week of December, and a company of Marines raised the American flag there on 13 February 1941.[16] Admiral Bristol flew up for a short visit on 20 May in one of the Navy Catalinas of Patrol Squadron 52 that made Argentia its temporary base. When *Bismarck* made her sortie, destination unknown, Bristol sent his planes out to patrol a sector southwest of Cape Farewell, in the hope of locating her. Flying conditions were "zero-zero-zero," which resulted in scattering the aircraft; and *Bismarck* never entered their patrol areas.

A United States Naval Air Station and Naval Operating Base were commissioned at Argentia on 15 July 1941;[17] and on 19 September 1941 Admiral Bristol transferred headquarters Support Force thither. By August, although far from completed, this base was protected by coast and anti-aircraft artillery and by an anti-submarine net and boom.

e. The Atlantic Conference

Argentia was chosen as the meeting place for President Roosevelt and Mr. Winston Churchill on 10–15 August 1941.

The secret of this meeting was well kept. Mr. Roosevelt sailed from New London on 3 August in the presidential yacht U.S.S. *Potomac*, apparently bent on a holiday cruise along the New England coast. Off Martha's Vineyard he was transferred to U.S.S. *Augusta* which, with U.S.S. *Tuscaloosa* and a destroyer escort, laid a course for Newfoundland.[18] In Argentia Harbor they met the ill-fated H.M.S. *Prince of Wales*, strongly escorted, and bearing not only Mr. Churchill, but Mr. Harry Hopkins, fresh from his meeting with Stalin and filled with confident and accurate as-

[16] "Administrative History Atlantic Fleet" II 3–4.

[17] Same 33, 40, 42, 55.

[18] U.S.S. *Potomac*, in the meantime, was routed through the Cape Cod Canal with a histrionic touch that deceived everyone. A fireman and two bluejackets, dressed in white summer clothes and bearing a superficial resemblance to Mr. Roosevelt, Stephen Early and Gen. Watson, lolled in easy chairs on the quarter-deck and waved genially to the public that lined the banks and bridges. Even the Chief of the Secret Service did not know where the President was for several days.

surances of Russian might and determination.[19] With the Prime Minister were the British Under-Secretary for Foreign Affairs, and high-ranking admirals, generals and air marshals. With President Roosevelt were Cordell Hull, Secretary of State; Sumner Welles, Assistant Secretary of State; General George C. Marshall, Chief of Staff of the United States Army; Admiral Harold R. Stark, Chief of Naval Operations; and Admiral Ernest J. King, Commander in Chief Atlantic Fleet.

During the next few days plans and technical matters were discussed by the experts. Admiral King and Admiral Sir W. Percy Noble RN worked out plans for the United States Navy's escorting Halifax convoys halfway across the Atlantic, which the occupation of Iceland (shortly to be described) had made possible. The chiefs of the two Navies confirmed what had been agreed upon at the earlier staff conferences.

If Mr. Churchill expected to commit the United States to war, he was unsuccessful. But Mr. Roosevelt succeeded in committing the Prime Minister to a policy which would commend itself to American ways of thinking, satisfy the doubters of British sincerity, and quiet those who were asking, "What are we going to fight for?" He obtained what he wanted in the Atlantic Charter. That document shows nautical knowledge on the part of both Chiefs of State, and their grasp of the realities of sea power. Instead of the vague "freedom of the seas" of Woodrow Wilson's Fourteen Points, Roosevelt and Churchill declared that the future peace "should enable all men to traverse the high seas and oceans without hindrance," and that aggressor nations must be disarmed "pending the establishment of a wider and permanent system of general security."

19 President Roosevelt was transported from the *Augusta* to the *Prince of Wales* in U. S. destroyer *McDougal*, whose bow was level with the *Augusta's* main deck and the British battleship's stern. It was a ticklish performance. When the destroyer made a Chinese landing (bow to stern) on the *Prince*, the British crew were drawn up at attention along the rail, Mr. Churchill alone being on the fantail to receive the President. A chief boatswain's mate of *McDougal* hailed the Premier with "Hey! Will you take a line?" Mr. Churchill replied "Certainly!" and not only caught the line but hauled it most of the way in before British tars came to his assistance.

The President boards H.M.S. *Prince of Wales* from U.S.S. *McDougal*

up on deck of *Prince of Wales* following Divine Service. Standing, left to right: Harry Hopkins, Mr. Averell Harriman, Admiral King, General Marshall, Rear niral McIntire, General Sir John Dill, Captain John R. Beardall, Admiral Stark, Admiral Sir Dudley Pound

The Atlantic Conference, August 1941

St. Johns, Newfoundland

United States Naval Operating Base and Naval Air Station, Argentia, about 1 September 1941

"Newfyjohn" and Argentia

Indirectly, the meeting at Argentia had a bearing on convoy history. In order to assure the safety of their illustrious passengers, the three Navies concerned put forth their best efforts to clear the Eastern Sea Frontier (as we call our side) [20] and the Western Approaches (as the British call theirs) of hostile craft, and to evade them in mid-ocean. There were none at that time off the Atlantic Coast; and the convoys were so cleverly routed that even the fanned-out wolf-packs were unable to find them in July and August.[21] Between 22 July and 10 August 1941, nine convoys, totaling five hundred and thirty-three ships with an aggregate tonnage of about four million, sailed from Halifax and Sydney for the United Kingdom. Twenty-five of these ships turned back, owing to collisions (mostly with icebergs) or engine trouble; but not one was lost by enemy action or through any other casualty. Convoy HX–143 of 73 ships was reviewed by Mr. Churchill when returning home. Moreover, every contemporary westbound convoy crossed the ocean without loss.

Yet this Anglo-Canadian period of convoy history was not to end without casualties. On 8–11 September, Convoy SC–42, making the unusually slow speed of advance of five knots, meagerly escorted by one destroyer and three corvettes, was shadowed and repeatedly attacked by a wolf-pack of as many as twelve U-boats. About 15 ships were lost, but *U–501* and *U–207* were sunk as a result of attacks of H.M.S. *Leamington* and *Veteran* and H.M.C.S. *Moose Jaw* and *Chambly*. The submarines boldly surfaced near the convoy, and unfortunately only a minority of the merchant ships were armed. Also in the month of September, Convoys SC–41 and SC–44 between them lost five merchant ships and one escort, the Canadian corvette *Levis*.[22] These gave the Germans great satis-

[20] On 6 Feb. 1942 the designation "Naval Coastal Frontiers" was changed to "Sea Frontiers." At the same time the designation "North Atlantic Naval Coastal Frontier" was changed to "Eastern Sea Frontier." (*Organization Manual of Eastern Sea Frontier, March 1943.*) For the sake of clarity I have used the term Sea Frontier throughout, even in the period before they were so designated.

[21] So says Doenitz in his Essay Sec. 69.

[22] On 27 Aug. 1941 a Hudson plane of the Royal Air Force bombed *U–570* to the surface about 80 miles south of Iceland, and its skipper hoisted the white

faction. "The difficulty lay in the finding," said Admiral Doenitz. "Once contact was made with the convoy, the attack succeeded every time."[23]

Nevertheless, the story of this Anglo-Canadian period of transatlantic convoys is a glorious one. Thousands of merchant vessels were taken safely across by a distressingly small number of armed escorts, losing less than 2 per cent in spite of aggressive, determined attacks by new and stronger U-boats using the wolf-pack technique. For two years, summer and winter, blow high blow low, destroyers and corvettes slogged back and forth across the North Atlantic, protecting precious cargoes that enabled Britain to survive. In the meantime British scientists and naval officers working as a team had adopted certain devices, training methods and techniques in anti-submarine warfare which were equally suitable for their coming ally. Hence, when the United States Navy entered the conflict it had no feeling of sustaining a faltering fighter or supporting a dying cause; it simply joined forces in the Atlantic with the two Royal Navies, which, in addition to their duties in other parts of the world, had shown their ability to get the cargo vessels across, in spite of a ruthless and resourceful enemy.

The United States Navy had undertaken a limited partnership with the British and Canadians, and was moving toward full participation as fast as political events permitted. Possibly when we look back on this period fifty years from now, the acquisition of bases will seem the most significant accomplishment of the Roosevelt Administration before war was declared. The United States had long been deficient in the base component of sea power; this acquisition greatly multiplied the effectiveness of our ships. Look at the globe: trace the curve of outposts and naval bases starting in Iceland, passing through Greenland, Newfoundland, Bermuda, Puerto Rico, and on to Trinidad. There the curve was left hang-

---

flag, the only occasion until near the close of the war when a German submarine surrendered. Trawlers of the Royal Navy took the sub in tow, beached it on Iceland, and it was salvaged, renamed H.M.S. *Graph*, and proved to be of great value as a "guinea pig" for finding out how German submarines operated.

[23] Doenitz, Sec. 69.

ing in air; but Brazil would extend it before long to Cape San Roque and Rio de Janeiro. Here was a defense chain of vast potentialities. But for the time being, the latter part of 1941, it flattered the American defense complex and engendered a sense of false security. "That place will allwayes belong to him that is superior at sea" might have been said of every one of these bases; and "at sea" now included the airy heights and the watery depths. Bases without ships are a delusive defense. Easily, far too easily, the German U-boats penetrated these outer defenses in 1942, and took their pleasure among the American merchant fleet.

NOTE ON *Niblack* AND *Texas* INCIDENTS

The *Niblack* incident mentioned on page 57 above, in all probability was a false contact. The German Submarine Command War Diary and the logs of all German submarines in the vicinity have been checked, and none mentioned any depth-charge attack.

An unsuccessful attempt by *U–203* to attack U.S. battleship *Texas* on 20 June 1941 remained unknown to us until after the war. Shortly after midnight this U-boat sighted *Texas* on the high seas, at lat. 53° N, longitude 27° W, between Newfoundland and Greenland. The skipper quaintly recorded in his log, "Was soll das? Was will der Amerikaner hier? Ist *Texas* an England verkauft?" He pursued the battleship for 16 hours, but was unable to reach a favorable attack position because of the battleship's speed and "zickzack" course. The incident is noted in the German Submarine Command War Diary, and in *Feuhrer Conferences on Matters Relating to German Navy 1941* II p. 1 (30 June). Admiral Raeder, assuming apparently that *Texas* had seen the U-boat and fled, remarked to Hitler that this incident, as well as that of *Robin Moor*, was welcome as a "warning meant in earnest" to us; the United States to keep off the high seas; that "where the U. S. A. is concerned, firm measures are always more effective than apparent yielding." Hitler, however, gave orders that "until operation Barbarossa" (the invasion of Russia) was "well under way, he wishes to avoid any incident with the U. S. A. After a few weeks the situation will become clearer, and can be expected to have a favorable effect on the U. S. A. and Japan." Cf. above, p. 37, and below, p. 95.

CHAPTER V

The United States Navy Joins Battle

September–December 1941

1. *From Patrol to Escort Duty*

a. Occupation of Iceland; Operation Plans of July

ON 16 June 1941 Admiral Stark wrote to Admiral King, "The President has directed that United States troops relieve the British garrison in Iceland," and ordered him to alert the Marines and the ships to take them there.[1]

Ostensibly this move was made at the joint request of the Icelandic and British governments; the latter wished to use its occupation troops elsewhere and the former wanted protection, but was very much afraid of Germany and backed and filled about making a formal request. Only after considerable heat had been applied by Winston Churchill did Premier Herman Jonasson issue the invitation to the United States on 7 July 1941, just as our first occupation force was steaming into Reykjavik. Invitation, acceptance and execution had to be announced simultaneously. On the 15th, Admiral King redefined the Western Hemisphere as including Iceland, and in his Operation Plan No. 5, issued that day, announced to the Fleet the official reason for our action. "The occupation of Iceland by a power, other than one which has sovereignty over Western Hemisphere territory, would constitute a serious

[1] "Administrative History Atlantic Fleet" IV, "Commandant N.O.B. Iceland," p. 9.

threat against Greenland and the northern portion of the North American Continent . . . against all shipping in the North Atlantic, and against the steady flow of munitions to Britain."

Task Force 19, comprising twenty-five ships, was formed at Argentia, and sailed on 1 July 1941, after a delay of two days in the hope of receiving the Icelandic "invitation." Six United States Navy transports and cargo ships, carrying the 1st Brigade United States Marine Corps (reinforced) commanded by Brigadier General John Marston USMC, were the nucleus of the force, which was commanded by Rear Admiral David McDougal LeBreton in battleship *New York*. Premier Jonasson stipulated that we should send "picked troops," and he certainly got them; but nobody was more surprised than the Marines. In early June the 2nd Division of the famous Corps, based at San Diego, California, had been ordered to send its "best equipped and trained regiment, reinforced," to join the 1st Division in "amphibious maneuvers in the Caribbean," which was generally supposed to be a euphemism for the occupation of Martinique, but which the 1st Division supposed to mean the occupation of Fayal and San Miguel. The 6th Regiment, Colonel Leo D. Hermle commanding, was selected for this honor, which became the nucleus of the 1st Brigade (reinforced), with a total strength of 194 officers and 3714 men. The 6th Marines and other units traveled by transport or rail to Charleston, South Carolina, where, much to their astonishment, woolen underwear was issued; and on 22 June they were shipped north to Argentia. That's the Marines.[2]

The composition of this, the first of the United States Naval task forces to be assembled for foreign service in World War II, follows on page 76.

During the short passage from Argentia, destroyer *Hughes* recovered 14 survivors, including four American Red Cross nurses, from a torpedoed Norwegian freighter. The ships commenced zig-

[2] John L. Zimmerman (Marine Corps Historian) *The 1st Marine Brigade Iceland 1941–1942* (1946); Capt. Richard G. Hubler USMCR "Some Like It Cold" *Marine Corps Gazette* XXVIII No. 2 (Feb. 1944) p. 47.

TASK FORCE 19

Rear Admiral David McD. LeBreton, Commander, in *New York*

Rear Admiral Alexander Sharp in *Arkansas*, after November 1941

BB 34	NEW YORK	Capt. J. G. Ware
BB 33	ARKANSAS	Capt. C. F. Bryant
CL 40	BROOKLYN	Capt. E. S. Stone
CL 43	NASHVILLE	Capt. F. S. Craven

Inner Screen, Capt. J. L. Kauffman

Destroyer Squadron 7, Capt. Kauffman

DD 431	PLUNKETT	Lt. Cdr. W. A. Graham

Destroyer Division 13, Cdr. D. L. Ryan

DD 424	NIBLACK	Lt. Cdr. E. R. Durgin
DD 421	BENSON	Lt. Cdr. A. L. Pleasants
DD 423	GLEAVES	Lt. Cdr. E. H. Pierce
DD 422	MAYO	Lt. Cdr. C. D. Emory

Destroyer Division 14, Cdr. F. D. Kirtland

DD 428	CHARLES F. HUGHES	Lt. Cdr. G. L. Menocal
DD 426	LANSDALE	Lt. Cdr. John Connor
DD 427	HILARY P. JONES	Lt. Cdr. S. R. Clark

Outer Screen,[3] Cdr. J. B. Heffernan

Destroyer Division 60, Cdr. Heffernan

DD 154	ELLIS	Lt. Cdr. L. R. Lampman
DD 153	BERNADOU	Lt. Cdr. G. C. Wright
DD 144	UPSHUR	Lt. Cdr. W. K. Romoser
DD 188	LEA	Lt. Cdr. Clarence Broussard
DD 420	BUCK	Lt. Cdr. H. C. Robison

Transport Base Force, Capt. F. A. Braisted

AP 15	WILLIAM P. BIDDLE (ex-*San Francisco*)	Capt. C. D. Edgar
AP 14	FULLER (ex-*Newport News*)	Capt. P. S. Theiss
AP 12	HEYWOOD (ex-*Baltimore*)	Capt. R. J. Carstarphen
AP 524	ORIZABA [4]	Capt. C. Gulbranson
AK 18	ARCTURUS (ex-*Mormachawk*)	Cdr. Henry Hartley
AK 30	HAMUL (ex-*Doctor Lykes*)	Cdr. E. M. Tillson
AO 26	SALAMONIE (ex-*Esso Columbia*)	Cdr. T. M. Waldschmidt
AT 66	CHEROKEE	Lt. Cdr. P. L. F. Weaver

[3] Outer Screen destroyers steamed 10,000 yards ahead of the rest of the Task Force.

[4] This transport met the 1st Brigade at Charleston; the other three APs had transported the 6th Marines from the West Coast.

zagging on 5 July when nearing their destination. Next day the snow-covered dome of Snaefellsjökull rose above the horizon; an hour later a roar of laughter passed through the Task Force when fleet tug *Cherokee* in the rear made signal "Land Sighted!" During the evening of 7 July 1941, anchors were dropped in the outer roadstead of Reykjavik. Next day the Marines commenced disembarking to the skirl of bagpipes of a Scottish regiment they were to relieve.[5] Disembarkation was completed on the 12th, and the Task Force stood out to sea.

From that time to the end of the war, the defense of Iceland was a primary responsibility of the United States Army and Navy. Regular Army units under Major General Bonesteel began arriving in August 1941. In February–March 1942, since Marines were badly wanted in the Pacific, the 1st Brigade returned to the United States, where most of it was incorporated with the 2nd Marine Division.

Navy planes had visited Iceland in the spring of 1941 on observation flights, but it was not until 6 August that Patrol Squadron VP–73 of Catalinas (Lieutenant Commander James E. Leeper), and VP–74 of Mariners (Lieutenant Commander A. B. Vosseller) arrived at Reykjavik from Argentia.[6] An air base, humorously nicknamed Camp Snafu, was constructed on an open, treeless, boulder-strewn field near Reykjavik.

In the meantime the Marines had established a camp of British Nissen huts at Alafoss, about fifteen miles inland; the Navy shared the British base at Hvalfjordur (which the Marines nicknamed "Valley Forge"), about twenty-five miles from Reykjavik. That base amounted to nothing more than a protected anchorage with indifferent holding ground; but a Navy "tank farm" for storing oil was soon established on shore.

[5] They were surprised to find other Marines already on the dock, a part of the 12th Provisional Company, Maj. W. I. Jordan USMC, intended for an embassy guard in London. Embarked in the Netherlands S.S. *Maasdam*, torpedoed and sunk in an HX convoy in June, they had been picked up and taken into Reykjavik.

[6] These squadrons were part of Patrol Wing 7 under the command of Capt. H. M. Mullinnix.

Although the government of Iceland under pressure from the British had requested the United States to protect the country, the people did not accept the occupation with good grace. Intensely nationalistic and provincial in their outlook, they did not sense the need of protection. Moreover, the Nazis had been cultivating Iceland, giving free scholarships in German universities to youths and stressing the derivation of the Nazi myth from early Scandinavian mythology. Their propaganda represented the United States forces as tyrannizing over a small nation, and many Americans followed the cue. Eventually the Navy installed recreational features in its bases so that the men no longer had to seek amusement in "Rinky Dink" (Reykjavik); the people discovered the good qualities of American enlisted men; and each side decided to bear and forbear.

While the announced purpose of occupying Iceland was to deny it to Germany, there were positive reasons as well. Iceland was of primary value as an escort and air base for covering convoys. Admiral King, in the already quoted Operation Plan 5 of 15 July 1941, ordered the Atlantic Fleet to "support the defense of Iceland" and "capture or destroy vessels engaged in support of sea and air operations directed against Western Hemisphere territory, or United States or Iceland flag shipping." Lest there be any doubt about it, he expressly declared that his "interpretation" of this threat was the presence of "potentially hostile vessels . . . actually within sight or sound contact of such shipping or of its escort." Four days later, on 19 July 1941, Commander in Chief Atlantic Fleet issued Operation Plan No. 6, organizing Task Force 1, with the duty to support the defense of Iceland, "to escort convoys of United States and Iceland flag shipping, including shipping of any nationality which may join such United States or Iceland flag convoys, between United States ports and bases, and Iceland." This Task Force will "provide protection for convoys in the North Atlantic Ocean as may be required by the strategic situation."[7] Approximately eight

[7] Cinclant Operation Plan 6, 19 July 1941. Admiral King himself was CTF 1, but Admiral LeBreton and Admiral Bristol had actual command of the forces allotted.

Canadian destroyers, nineteen Canadian corvettes and three French corvettes had been allotted by Canada and General de Gaulle to coöperate with the United States Navy in this duty. With their assistance, the Navy began escort duty by conducting convoys to Iceland, while the British continued to take charge of the transatlantic route. We were, theoretically, escorting our own and the Icelanders' ships to and from Iceland; but the little clause "including shipping of any nationality which may join" allowed any others to come along if they chose; and many, of course, did so choose.

b. Attack on U.S.S. *Greer; de Facto* War Begins

Although this service was essentially a belligerent one, Admiral King's operation plans of July had to be so cautiously worded that commanders of United States ships and planes were not sure what they were expected to do if a German raider, submarine or aircraft was encountered. Were they to shoot first and let the Navy explain, or only fire if fired upon? Was it to be Concord Bridge or Lexington Green?

This anomalous situation, neither peace nor war, was brought out by the *Greer* incident. U.S.S. *Greer*, carrying the pennant of Commander G. W. Johnson and commanded by Lieutenant Commander L. H. Frost, was proceeding independently toward Iceland on 4 September 1941 in lat. 62°45′ N, long. 27°37′ W, at a speed of 17½ knots. At 0840 a British plane signaled to her that a submerged U-boat lay athwart her course some ten miles ahead. *Greer* commenced zigzagging, increased speed to twenty knots, went to general quarters, laid a course for the reported position, and on reaching it slowed to ten knots in order to allow her sound gear to operate at full efficiency. She made sound contact with the submarine and maintained it for over three hours, keeping the submerged *U-652* always on her bow but not attacking. At 1000 the British plane captain inquired whether *Greer* intended to attack, and was answered in the negative. He then dropped his depth charges more or less at random, and returned to base to refuel. At 1240 the submarine headed toward the American destroyer and launched a torpedo, which was sighted early enough to be dodged. *Greer* counterattacked with depth charges, and at 1300 the U-boat shot a second torpedo, which was also avoided. Unable to reëstablish sound contact, *Greer* discontinued the search at 1416 and resumed course for Iceland.

So, Lexington Green it was; and as in that classic incident, the side that did not shoot first burned with virtuous indignation. In a radio address delivered on 11 September, President Roosevelt characterized the attack on *Greer* as "piracy," and declared "From now on, if German or Italian vessels of war enter the waters the protection of which is necessary for American defense, they do so at their own risk."

Thus ended the embarrassing position for the United States Navy of carrying the responsibility for protecting wide expanses of the North Atlantic, without authority to shoot.

From the date of the *Greer* incident, 4 September 1941, the United States was engaged in a *de facto* naval war with Germany on the Atlantic Ocean. It was still an anomalous situation, for each antagonist was fighting with one hand tied; ours by the neutrality legislation, theirs by Hitler's restriction of the area of U-boat operations. American merchant ships could not carry goods to Britain, or even arm themselves in their own defense. It was not until 7 and 13 November 1941 that the Senate by a vote of 50 to 37, and the House by a vote of 212 to 194, passed two amendments to the Neutrality Act that freed our hands. The one act permitted the arming of merchant vessels and the other allowed them to enter war zones. American ships were now accorded the privilege of defending themselves against attack, and of convoying goods to and from ports in the British Empire. Thus was liquidated that noble experiment of attempting to prevent war by legislation. Freedom of the seas was restored to the American merchant marine by the American Congress which had denied it.

Next day, 14 November, Mr. Saburo Kurusu, special envoy of Japan, arrived in San Francisco and made a statement to the press that proved to be prophetic: "I hope to break through the line and make a touchdown." [8] Most Americans wishfully thought that his goal was peace.

The two months that elapsed between the *Greer* incident and the repeal of neutrality legislation were a distressing period for Americans who were eager to lock horns with Germany before it became too late. Many sincere persons clung to the "short of war" formula now that it had become inadequate, and indulged in the delusion that Russia and Britain were capable of winning if we gave them enough lend-lease. A strong and influential minority still wanted peace at any price. The growing group of interventionists felt that the President had let them down after his stirring addresses. But Mr. Roosevelt knew exactly what he was doing. He was making a last "short of war" effort to keep Japan out of the southwestern Pacific area; buying time with diplomacy.

c. Atlantic Patrol [9]

The second positive benefit expected from the occupation of Iceland was the protection of American coasts and shipping from German raiders. The Greenland Patrol was doing excellent work breaking up German meteorological stations, but obviously could not have stopped the *Tirpitz* coming through Denmark Strait. By an informal agreement with the British, made after consultation in Iceland, their Home Fleet undertook to prevent Axis ships debouching into the Atlantic between the Faeroes and Iceland, while that part of the United States Atlantic Fleet based on Iceland accepted responsibility for stopping up Denmark Strait.[10] And if any

[8] *N. Y. Herald Tribune*, 8, 13 and 14 Nov. 1941.

[9] Very few War Diaries or Reports exist for our naval operations at this period, and I have depended largely on conversations with officers for such facts as are found here.

[10] Admiral King's Letter of Instruction to CTG 1.5, as to coöperation with British forces, is dated 5 Dec. 1941, over a month after the agreement had been made: "The existing arrangements for joint action (coördination) between detachments of the Atlantic Fleet and of the British Home Fleet are designed to prevent the undetected passage of Axis heavy raiders into the open sea via either Denmark Strait or the waters to the southeastward of Iceland, and to deal with such raiders when detected."

German ships did break through, Admiral King agreed to put available ships of the Atlantic Fleet under temporary British command, for the purpose of hunting them down.[11]

In the reorganization of the Atlantic Fleet, dated 1 September 1941, Admiral King designated a task group, consisting of heavy cruisers *Wichita* and *Tuscaloosa*, together with two out of the three battleships, *Idaho*, *New Mexico* and *Mississippi*, Destroyer Squadron 2 (Captain W. L. Ainsworth in *Morris*), and Destroyer Division 22 (Commander J. S. Roberts in *Gwin*), as Denmark Strait Patrol.[12] Exuberantly commanded by Rear Admiral Robert C. ("Ike") Giffen in *Wichita*, this "White" Patrol, as it was called, was based on Hvalfjordur from September 1941 until well on into 1942. Most of the time it cruised to the northward of Iceland, as Denmark Strait had been mined. On 5 November 1941, when rumor had *Tirpitz, Prinz Eugen* and other German capital ships leaving Norwegian waters, Admiral Giffen dashed north to intercept them; but the Germans did not venture that far, which may have been fortunate for our older and weaker battleships.

A United States Naval Operating Base was commissioned at Iceland on 6 November 1941. Rear Admiral J. L. Kauffman became its commandant on 23 December, with the converted yacht *Williamsburg* as floating headquarters and the repair ship *Vulcan* to service naval vessels.[13] As the Navy had no small craft to spare for local patrol and defense, it was decided to retain the Royal Navy's local defense organization.

Naval Operating Base and Naval Air Station Bermuda, on the sound facing Hamilton, as well as the United States Army base on Castle Harbor near St. George, were obtained in 1940 "freely and without consideration" as far as the British government was concerned, but very grudgingly and at heavy cost, as far as the

[11] Statement to the writer by Admiral King.

[12] Cinclant Operation Plan No. 7, 1 Sept. 1941.

[13] N.O.B. Iceland War Diary. "Administrative History Atlantic Fleet" IV "Commandant N.O.B. Iceland" gives a detailed account of the development of this naval base.

Bermuda Assembly was concerned.[14] The base was commissioned 7 April 1941 with Captain Jules James as commandant; and the very next day Task Group 7.2, commanded by Rear Admiral Arthur B. Cook in carrier *Ranger* and including heavy cruisers *Tuscaloosa* and *Wichita* and destroyers *Kearny* and *Livermore*, arrived to look it over. Shortly after, a Central Atlantic Neutrality Patrol, out to long. 30° W – the then official eastern boundary of the Western Hemisphere[15] – was set up under Admiral Cook's command, and based at Bermuda. It comprised Carrier Division 3 (*Ranger*, *Wasp* and *Yorktown*; later also the *Long Island*), cruisers *Quincy* and *Vincennes*, and Destroyer Squadron 11 (Captain Morton L. Deyo in *Sampson*).[16] A very dull time of it they had; but the opportunities for gunnery practice and flight operations were excellent training for the Atlantic Fleet.

The waters between Trinidad, long. 26° W, and the hump of Brazil were patrolled from mid-June 1941 by Task Force 3, commanded by Rear Admiral Jonas H. Ingram in U.S.S. *Memphis*. This force comprised light cruisers *Milwaukee*, *Cincinnati* and *Omaha*; Destroyer Squadron 9 (*Somers*, flagship), and a few auxiliaries. The Brazilian government made Recife and Bahia freely available to our naval forces for refreshment, replenishment and upkeep,[17] and promised the use of Natal and Maceio as naval aircraft bases. In expectation that armed merchantmen of the German Navy were about to raid the South Atlantic, Admiral Ingram's force on 1 August was ordered by Cinclant to darken ship, operate

[14] Same, V, "Commandant N.O.B. Bermuda," pp. 13–14. The British government met the entire cost of land expropriation, the United States government that of construction and dredging approaches.

[15] Extended to long. 26° W on 14 June 1941.

[16] On 15 May *Wichita* and *Tuscaloosa* were added to *Quincy* and *Vincennes*; these on 15 July were relieved by Crudiv 8, *Philadelphia*, *Brooklyn*, *Savannah* and *Nashville* (Rear Admiral H. Kent Hewitt).

[17] Revision of Cinclant Operation Plan No. 7, 29 Sept. 1941. Before these privileges were accorded when there was some doubt as to the extent of Brazilian friendliness, Admiral King told Admiral Ingram he would have to "shift for himself" in the matter of provisions. Ingram replied that so long as there were plenty of ships sailing from the River Plate with provisions, his crews would never starve. "Jonas, I always knew you were a pirate!" answered Cinclant.

as in time of war, and maintain constant readiness to repel hostile attack. In October, cruiser *Memphis* and destroyers *Davis* and *Jouett* convoyed part of the way to Africa S.S. *Acadia*, carrying Pan American Airways' technicians and equipment, for the construction of air bases. When the merchant crew heard that Axis submarines were laying for them they threatened mutiny, but order was restored after replacing the master by a better disciplinarian. In early November, just as *Omaha* (Captain T. E. Chandler) and *Somers* were about to cross the Line at long. 27°44′ W, en route to Recife, they captured the German blockade runner *Odenwald*, disguised as "S.S. *Willmoto* of Philadelphia," carrying a cargo of rubber from Japan to Germany. They escorted her safely into San Juan, P.R., on 11 November 1941.[18] Captain Chandler, somewhat uncertain of the legality of this capture, but remembering the Navy's African patrol of a century ago, reported that the *Odenwald* was a suspected slave trader!

The Caribbean Patrol, still under Commandant Tenth Naval District at San Juan, consisted of destroyers *Barney* and *Blakeley*, Patrol Squadron 31 of the naval air arm with *Lapwing* as tender, three submarines that operated from St. Thomas, and a few small patrol craft.[19]

d. Navy Begins Escort Duty

Nobody outside the higher command knew in August 1941 that preparations had already been made for the United States Navy to assume responsibility for transatlantic convoys from a point off Argentia to the meridian of Iceland, in addition to the Iceland-bound convoys already provided for on 19 July. On 1 September Admiral King issued a new operation plan that provided for this duty.[20] Naval vessels in the North Atlantic were by now required specifically to operate under war conditions, and to darken ship

[18] Report of Capt. Chandler (CTG 3.6) 12 Nov. 1941; Admiral Ingram "F–3 Operations in Equatorial Area 6 Sept. to 11 Nov. 1941." JAG Journal November 1947 tells of Navy prize crew sharing in salvage money in this unusual case.

[19] War Diary CSF for 1942.

[20] Cinclant Op. Plan 7, 1 September 1941.

when east of Cape Breton Island.[21] In order to meet the objection that escort-of-convoy was essentially a combat duty, the theory was adopted that these convoys were being escorted between two United States bases for the purpose of supplying our occupation troops in Argentia and Iceland, and not to any belligerent country. The same little joker as in the previous operation plan, "shipping of any nationality which might join," allowed any number of Allied "hitch-hikers" to enjoy the benefit of United States naval protection. It was agreed between the Admiralty and the Navy Department that a United States escort group based on Argentia should take over from a Royal Canadian Navy escort at a designated Western Ocean meeting place off Newfoundland, and hand over the convoy (excepting Iceland-bound shipping) to a Royal Navy escort at an agreed mid-ocean meeting point. At this "Momp" the United States Navy escort group either picked up a westbound convoy, or peeled off to take Iceland-bound ships to Reykjavik. Thus, the United States Navy took definite responsibility for that section of the transatlantic route between the meridians of Newfoundland and Iceland.

Rear Admiral Arthur LeR. Bristol Jr., senior naval officer at Argentia and commander of the Support Force, was responsible for carrying out these dispositions. At the same time he had overall command of the naval air base at Quonset, the destroyer base at Casco Bay, and United States forces in Iceland and the United Kingdom. Admiral Bristol had an immense capacity for work, a talent for administration, and a generous, genial disposition that inspired devotion in his subordinates, and stimulated their best efforts. He was an old aviator himself, and his highly efficient staff, of which the chief was Captain Louis E. Denfeld,[22] was distinctly air-minded; the patrol planes operating from Argentia under his command were responsible for the two first kills of U-boats made

21 There had been previous instances. Cinclant Operation Plan 5-41 of 15 July 1941 included complete darkness of ships when at sea.

22 Others were Cdr. Robert B. Carney, Operations; Cdr. Edmond T. ("Slim") Wooldridge, Assistant Operations and Gunnery Officer; Lt. Cdr. Stuart H. Ingersoll, Air Operations; Cdr. Walter A. Buck, Supply Officer.

by any United States force in World War II. He was promoted Vice Admiral on 27 February 1942. Unfortunately his immense responsibilities brought on a heart attack, and he died on board his flagship at Argentia on 20 April 1942.

HX–150, the first transatlantic convoy to be assisted by the United States Navy, sailed from Halifax with a Canadian local escort on 16 September 1941. It consisted of 50 merchant ships of British and other Allied nationalities of widely varying types, from a 1500-ton freighter to the 17,000-ton liner *Empress of Asia.*[23] On 17 September at lat. 46° N, long. 55° W, about 150 miles south of Argentia, Captain Morton L. Deyo's escort group, consisting of destroyer *Ericsson*, *Eberle*, *Upshur*, *Ellis* and *Dallas*, took over from the Canadians. Rear Admiral E. Manners RN (Ret.), the convoy commodore, greeted his new escort with the cheery signal, "I am very delighted to have all of you to guard this convoy for the next few days," and throughout the voyage expressed his messages in a courtly language which was exceedingly pleasant to read when decoded, but provoked somewhat uncourtly language among our inexperienced communications personnel.[24]

Before Captain Deyo's escort group took over, three merchant vessels had already dropped out of the convoy, and every day there was some kind of breakdown, owing to the effects of poor upkeep during two years' unremitting war service. The convoy frequently had to change course in order to allow stragglers to catch up. There were no contacts with submarines; but one merchantman, S.S. *Nigaristan*, caught fire in her 'tween decks and was abandoned at sea. Her entire crew of 63 were rescued by U.S.S. *Eberle* (Lieutenant Commander Edward R. Gardner Jr. USN) on a black

[23] Report of Task Unit 4.1.1.

[24] Comconvoy to Comescort 18 Sept. 1941: "One of our tankers is a long way astern of convoy. I would be very grateful if your destroyer on the starboard side would tell her to return to Sydney if she cannot keep up with convoy at nine and one half knots." Same to same, 24 Sept. 1941: "Very many thanks for your complete list of ships. Yes, we are taking the Iceland ships. When relief escort arrives I will pass the papers to him. Will you please direct ships for Iceland to form on the port side well clear and we will take them on? I presume they have no one experienced in signals so would it not be better to put them in one column and follow the leader? Will appreciate your advice."

night in a gale of wind and heavy sea; a fine display of practical seamanship that elicited the hearty praise of Admiral Manners. *Eberle* was assigned to all tasks requiring extra fuel consumption, because, as the only modern destroyer in the group besides *Ericsson*, she was economical. Captain Deyo predicted that the "short-legged" United States destroyers – those like the old four-pipers with a high consumption or low fuel capacity – would be unsuitable for convoy duty; for, owing to their slender margin of fuel for a transatlantic crossing, they were unable to meet demands for speed above fifteen knots. Fueling at sea eased this problem, but only modern destroyers could solve it.

The effect of this disagreeable combat duty on our naval personnel was interesting. "At first," reported Captain Deyo, "the great difficulty was to keep people alert, to bring home the war. Then, when they actually found themselves escorting a convoy, they began to realize that they were 'in the picture.' . . . They remembered what they had heard. They became 'jumpy' and saw a submarine or heard one in every wave. Now, after dropping a depth charge on nothing and getting a shell stuck in a gun through too hasty loading, they are beginning to steady down and become more businesslike. This will teach them fast. Only one thing – they must get more gunnery training."

Unfortunately the Germans did not oblige by offering a target. They missed a good chance at the mid-ocean meeting point assigned south of Iceland, for a storm the previous night had so delayed the relieving British escort, the merchant ships from Iceland, and the convoy itself, approaching from three different directions, that about five hours' cruising was necessary to consummate the meeting. From this "Momp" the American escort proceeded to Reykjavik with the Iceland-bound shipping, while two British destroyers and four corvettes picked up the main convoy. On 25 September, when the operation was terminated, these messages were exchanged: –

Comconvoy to Comescort: Please accept my best congratulations on the brand of work and efficiencies of all your ships in looking after us so very well, and my very grateful thanks for all your kindly advice

ESCORT DISPOSITIONS
CONVOY HX-150
DAY STATIONS
0 2000 4000
Scale in yards

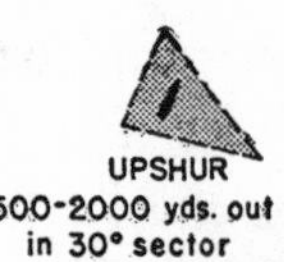

ERICSSON
1500-2000 yds. ahead
UPSHUR
500-2000 yds. out
in 30° sector
ELLIS
500-2000 yds. out
in 30° sector
C O N V O Y
DALLAS
EBERLE
500-2000 yds. out, abreast of last
or next to last ship

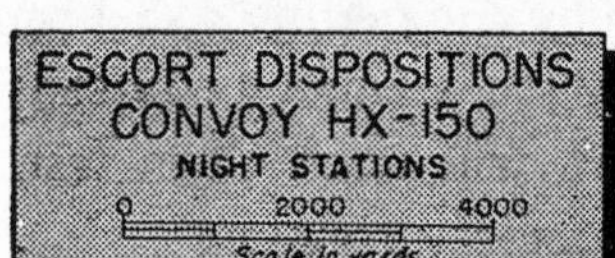

ESCORT DISPOSITIONS
CONVOY HX-150
NIGHT STATIONS
0 2000 4000
Scale in yards

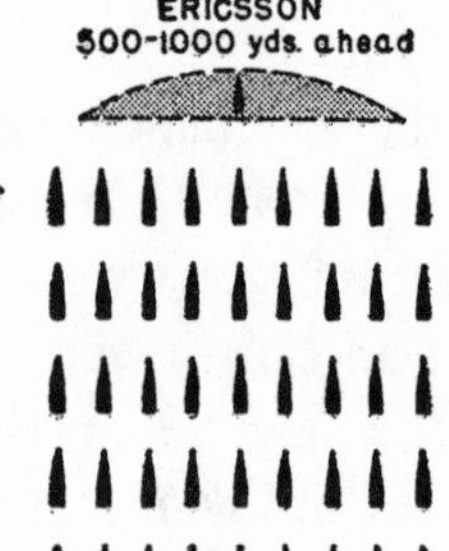

ERICSSON
500-1000 yds. ahead
UPSHUR
500-1000 yards
abeam ship 11
ELLIS
500-1000 yards
abeam ship 91
CONVOY
DALLAS
500-1000 yds. out
from rear ship
in 30° sector
EBERLE
500-1000 yds. out
from rear ship
in 30° sector
E.M.B.

and help. Wish you all success with best of luck and good hunting. If you come across Admiral Nimitz, give him my love. We were great friends some years ago out in China.

Comescort to Comconvoy: This being our first escort job your message is doubly appreciated. As in the last war I know our people afloat will see eye-to-eye. You have my admiration for handling such a varied assortment so effectively. Will give your message to Admiral Nimitz. I was in China later and knew Admiral Little and many of your people. I hope we shall meet again. Good luck.

From the viewpoint of developing escort doctrine, it is interesting to note some of the prescribed procedures in the Atlantic Fleet general instructions and in Admiral Bristol's special instructions for this convoy. Destroyers were ordered to patrol stations by day and on clear nights, but not in fog or on dark nights. They were reminded that their first duty was to protect the convoy, and cautioned against pursuing a submarine contact for more than one

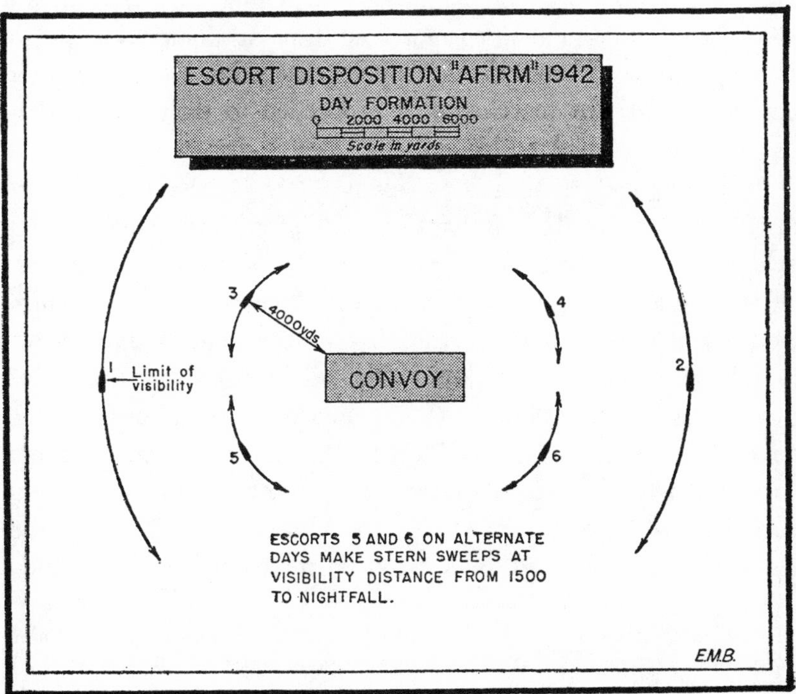

hour. At that time this was good British escort doctrine; but the success of submarine wolf-packs shortly brought about a radical change in escort disposition and procedure.

Convoy HX–150 escaped attack because no U-boats were operating on its route, owing to Hitler's prohibition as to the western part, and a fortunate diversion southward on the eastern part of the route, because of a concentration of U-boats encountered by Convoy SC–42. Another slow convoy out of Sydney, SC–44, which was dispatched by a more northerly route about the same time, took a bad beating on the night of 19–20 September. Consisting of 66 vessels in eleven columns, escorted by a Canadian destroyer and three corvettes, it lost four merchant ships and one escort, H.M.C.S. *Levis.*

The first westbound American-escorted transatlantic convoy, designated ON–18, was picked up at the "Momp" south of Iceland on 24 September 1941, by U.S.S. *Madison, Gleaves, Lansdale, Hughes* and *Simpson,* commanded by Captain F. D. Kirtland, and escorted without incident to an agreed dispersal point at lat. 43°30′ N, long. 55° W. Thence the destroyers returned to Momp for other convoys, while the merchantmen proceeded to their several destinations in North America and the West Indies.

By 10 October 1941, escort-of-convoy arrangements and procedure had been so stabilized that Commander in Chief Atlantic Fleet delegated the authority to Admiral Bristol to control and supervise all such operations in the Northwest Atlantic area.[25] Canadian escorts were placed under the flag officer commanding Newfoundland Forces, Commodore L. W. Murray RCN. It was decided (1) that the slow eastbound (SC) convoys out of Sydney would be escorted to each agreed "Momp" by Canadian destroyers and corvettes, which thereupon were promptly assigned to slow westbound (ONS) convoys; (2) that the United States Navy would escort the HX and fast ON convoys on the route Newfoundland–

[25] The designation of U. S. escort groups and patrol planes under Admiral Bristol was changed from Support Force to Task Force 4; changed to Task Force 24 on 13 Mar. 1942.

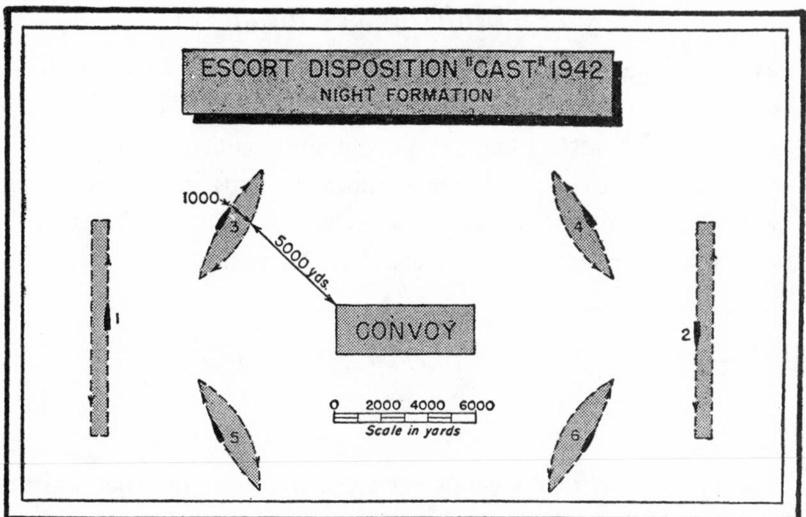

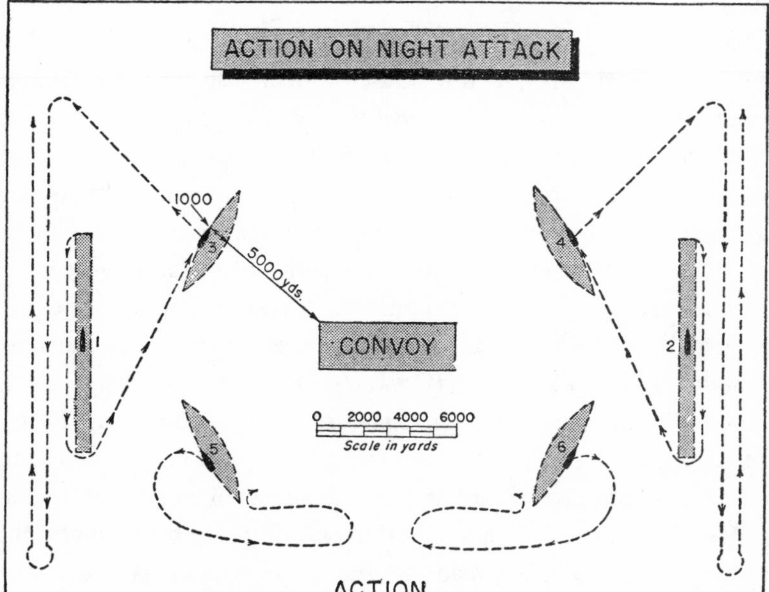

ACTION

ESCORT 1 STEAMS AHEAD TO LIMIT OF STATION, TURNS AWAY AND DOWN THROUGH STATION, THENCE (MAKING ASDIC SEARCH) TO TAKE STATION 3.

ORIGINAL ESCORT 3 STEAMS AT 20 TO 25 KNOTS TO LEFT OF BASE COURSE UNTIL ABOUT FIVE MILES FROM CONVOY, THEN TURNS LEFT, SWEEPS ON REVERSE OF BASE COURSE TO PORT QUARTER OF CONVOY, AND THEREAFTER SWEEPS ON FLANK AT HIGH SPEED UNTIL DAYLIGHT.

ESCORT 5 TURNS AWAY, SWEEPS OUTWARD AT BEST ASDIC SPEED, THEN ASTERN OF CONVOY.

ESCORTS 2, 4, AND 6 MANEUVER SIMILARLY TO 1, 3, AND 5 RESPECTIVELY.

E.M.B.

"Momp"–Iceland; and (3) that the Royal Navy would escort all convoys between the Western Approaches and "Momp," which might be as far east as long. 22° W, but always north of lat. 58° N.[26] It was agreed to increase the number of ships in United States escort units from five to six, and to make best efforts to fly naval air patrols from Argentia and Iceland all winter.

2. *First Blood for the Nazis*

a. Attack on Convoy SC–48; U.S.S. *Kearny*

In this conflict that was not yet a declared war, the enemy drew first blood, damaging one United States destroyer and sinking another.

Slow Convoy SC–48, consisting of 50 merchant ships in nine columns, sailed through the Strait of Belle Isle into the Atlantic about 10 October 1941. The weather deteriorated and eleven ships straggled, including that of the convoy commodore. On 15 October the reduced convoy, advancing at a speed of seven knots, and escorted only by four corvettes at that time,[27] ran into a concentration of submarines about 400 miles south of Iceland. Three ships were torpedoed and sunk that night. In response to an appeal for help, a division of five United States destroyers commanded by Captain L. H. Thebaud (*Plunkett*, *Livermore*, *Kearny*, *Greer*, *Decatur*) and also H.M.S. *Broadwater* and the Fighting French corvette *Lobelia*, were collected from Reykjavik and from a west-bound convoy and dispatched to the scene of action. By sunset 16 October they had taken station. During the black night that followed the wolf-pack made six successful attacks. As the escorts were stationed only 1000 to 1500 yards from the convoy, the U-boats were able to select long-range firing positions unmolested, 4000 to 5000 yards from the merchant ships, yet beyond the range of the destroyers' sound gear; not one was seen or heard. United

[26] Admiralty sources; Cinclant to CTF 4, 10 and 16 Oct. 1941.
[27] H.M.C.S. *Columbia*, a destroyer, arrived about an hour after the attack began.

"Camp Snafu" of Navy Patrol Squadron 74 near Reykjavik, 1941

Hvalfjordur Anchorage, about 1 October 1941, showing *Wichita,* two battleships of *New Mexico* class, Carrier *Wasp* and three destroyers

Iceland

From a Navy Patrol plane about ten hours after *Kearny* was torpedoed

U.S.S. *Greer*

Convoy SC–48

States destroyers were not yet equipped with radar, which might have enabled them to detect a surfaced enemy. When the first merchant ship was torpedoed, around 2200, the escorts sent up star shell and dropped depth charges indiscriminately, which added to the general confusion. In a second attack, at 2315, two more ships of inside columns were torpedoed and sunk. Then, around 0200 October 17, came three attacks in quick succession that accounted for four more. A torpedoed ship about 1200 yards from U.S.S. *Kearny* burned brilliantly, silhouetting the destroyer between her and the enemy; a corvette crossed *Kearny's* bow, causing her to stop; and before she was able to resume speed, a torpedo struck her on the starboard side, about the turn of the bilge. She suffered many casualties, but was able to turn her engines over about ten minutes after the torpedo hit and to reach Iceland under her own power, escorted by *Greer*. Blood plasma for the wounded was flown down from cruiser *Wichita* at Iceland by a Navy Catalina, and delivered on board by parachute.

On the next day, H.M.S. *Broadwater* was torpedoed by *U-101* and had to be abandoned and sunk; *Gladiolus*, detached to screen a straggler, never returned. Fundamental lessons in escort duty were expensively learned from the battle of Convoy SC–48. Destroyers had been ordered not to patrol at night or in thick weather; but it was now learned that rigid station-keeping merely invited attack. Aggressive night patrolling at distances of 2000 to 5000 yards from the convoy was now enjoined, more than double that of the earlier doctrine, in order to keep U-boats at a distance, yet make sound contacts. This procedure was much assisted by the new SG radar which enabled escorts to keep in touch with the convoy outside sighting distance. Indiscriminate depth-charging was countermanded, as more embarrassing to floating survivors than to the enemy. And certain new procedures in damage control were learned from *Kearny's* torpedoing by the *U–568*.

b. Sinking of U.S.S. *Reuben James;* Winter Escort Duty

It takes time for reports of naval disasters to come in, to be studied by staff officers and their lessons digested, and for orders to be issued to remedy faulty technique or mistaken procedure. Thus, the lessons of SC–48 were not learned in time to save *Reuben James*, the first United States naval vessel to be lost in this war,[28] on 31 October 1941. She was one of five destroyers under Commander R. E. Webb escorting HX–156, a fast convoy that was making just under nine knots. It had reached lat. 51°59′ N, long. 27°05′ W, a position about 600 miles west of Ireland. Only one of the five, U.S.S. *Niblack* which covered the rear, was equipped with radar. *Reuben James* was stationed 2000 yards on the port beam of the convoy center. Day was just breaking, the convoy was not zigzagging, and possibly not all the destroyers were patrolling their stations.[29] *Reuben James* had just commenced turning to investigate a strong direction-finder bearing when a torpedo fired by the *U–552* struck her port side. The explosion probably ignited the forward magazine, for the entire fore part of the ship was blown off as far aft as the fourth stack. The after part remained afloat for about five minutes, and as it went down several depth charges exploded, killing survivors in the water. Of the entire ship's company of about 160, only 45, including no officers, were rescued by other escorts. A vigorous sound search was made by the other four destroyers, without result; but next day a British escort group that was approaching to relieve them surprised two submarines trailing their port beam, and put them down with gunfire.

[28] Although U. S. gunboat *Panay* was sunk in the Yangtze River by Japanese aviators on 12 Dec. 1937, this outrage was so promptly disavowed by and reparation made by the Japanese government that it is not generally regarded as an event of this war. The sinking of the *Reuben James* was a deliberate act in the undeclared state of war that existed between the United States and Germany. Seven American merchant ships were sunk from a variety of war causes prior to Pearl Harbor, beginning with S.S. *City of Rayville*, which struck a mine on 8 Nov. 1940.

[29] Accounts differ as to whether *Reuben James* was not patrolling, or was doing it in such a way that the attacking submarine could anticipate her movements.

By 1 November 1941 Hitler felt sufficiently certain of conquering Russia to risk challenging the United States. Doenitz was allowed to deploy U-boats around Cape Race, in the Strait of Belle Isle, and south of Greenland. Convoy SC–52 was directed to avoid one of these concentrations by laying a course well south of Cape Race. Nevertheless it lost four ships on 3 November by enemy action, one of them in a thick fog. The convoy was then ordered to take the shortest route back to the Strait of Belle Isle, where it dispersed. No other ships were torpedoed by U-boats in the western Atlantic during November; and in December only two or three transatlantic convoys were attacked, with a loss of four ships more. The explanation was that, despite Doenitz's protests, the Naval War Staff diverted U-boats to escort or weather missions and merchant vessel concentrations in the Mediterranean. For a time, undersea warfare in the Atlantic practically ceased.

Autumn and winter escort work in the North Atlantic was arduous and exhausting for men and ships; so much so that the weather was given by Admiral King on 25 December as a principal reason for routing convoys more to the southward. That section of the North Atlantic covered by United States destroyers, between Newfoundland, Greenland and Iceland, is the roughest part of the Western Ocean. Winds of gale force, mountainous seas, biting cold, body-piercing fog and blinding snow squalls, were the rule rather than the exception; U-boats could escape this by submerging, but the escorts had to face it. Life on board a destroyer was but a few degrees less uncomfortable than on board a corvette. The continual rolling and pitching, coupled with the necessity of constant vigilance night and day, not only for enemy attack but to guard against collisions with other escort vessels and the convoy, wore men down. The so-called "rest periods" at Hvalfjordur and Argentia were rests merely from enemy attack, not from the weather; for in both ports the holding ground was bad and the weather terrible. Destroyers dragged all over these harbors in winter gales, requiring constant attention and vigorous effort in order to avoid fouling other vessels or running aground. Operation plans called for a

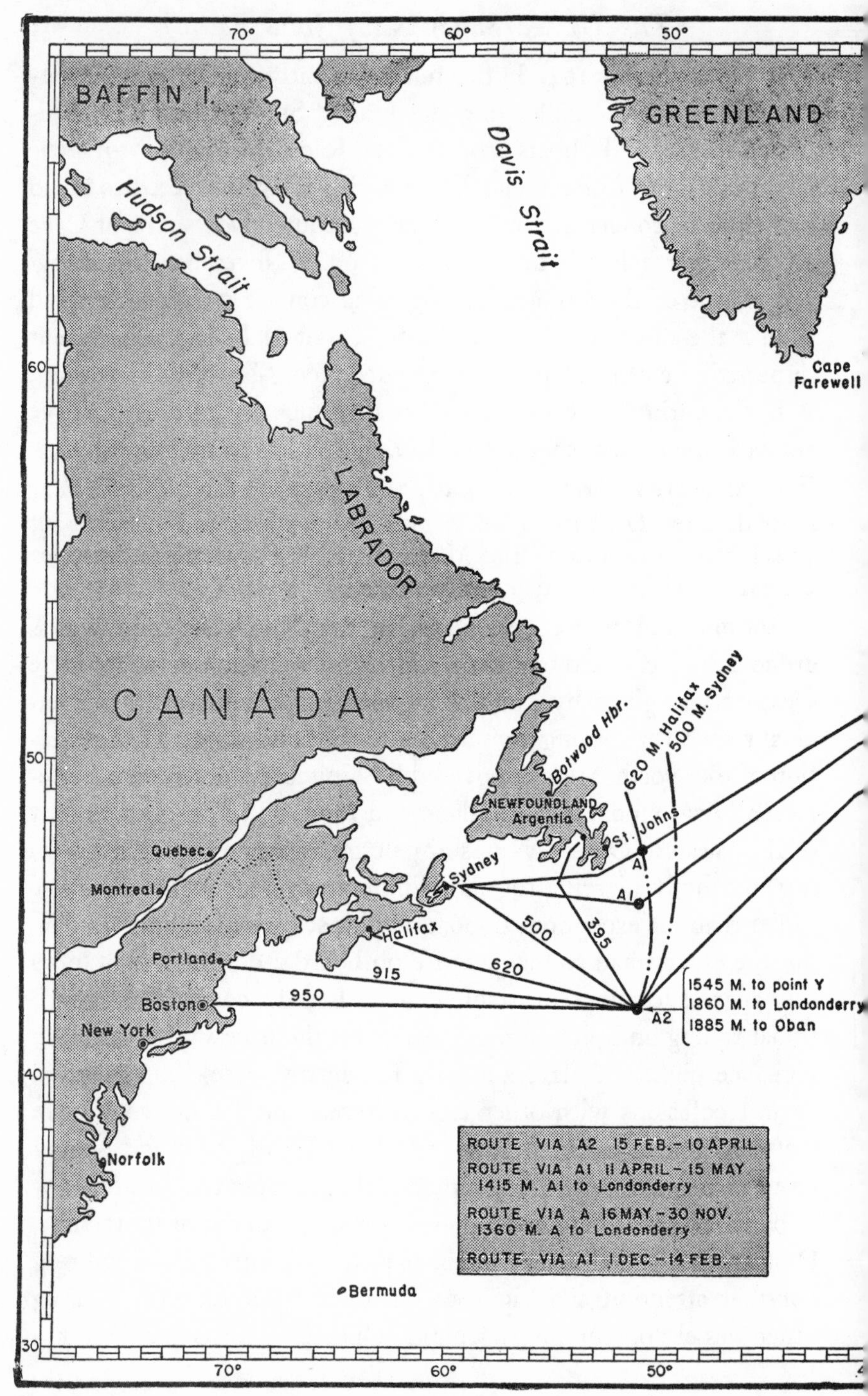

BAFFIN I.
GREENLAND
Hudson Strait
Davis Strait
Cape Farewell
LABRADOR
CANADA
Botwood Hbr.
NEWFOUNDLAND
Argentia
St. Johns
Quebec
Montreal
Sydney
Halifax
Portland
Boston
New York
Norfolk
Bermuda
620 M. Halifax
500 M. Sydney
A
A1
A2
500
395
620
915
950
1545 M. to point Y
1860 M. to Londonderry
1885 M. to Oban
ROUTE VIA A2 15 FEB.-10 APRIL
ROUTE VIA A1 11 APRIL-15 MAY
1415 M. A1 to Londonderry
ROUTE VIA A 16 MAY-30 NOV.
1360 M. A to Londonderry
ROUTE VIA A1 1 DEC-14 FEB.
70°
60°
50°
60
50
40
30

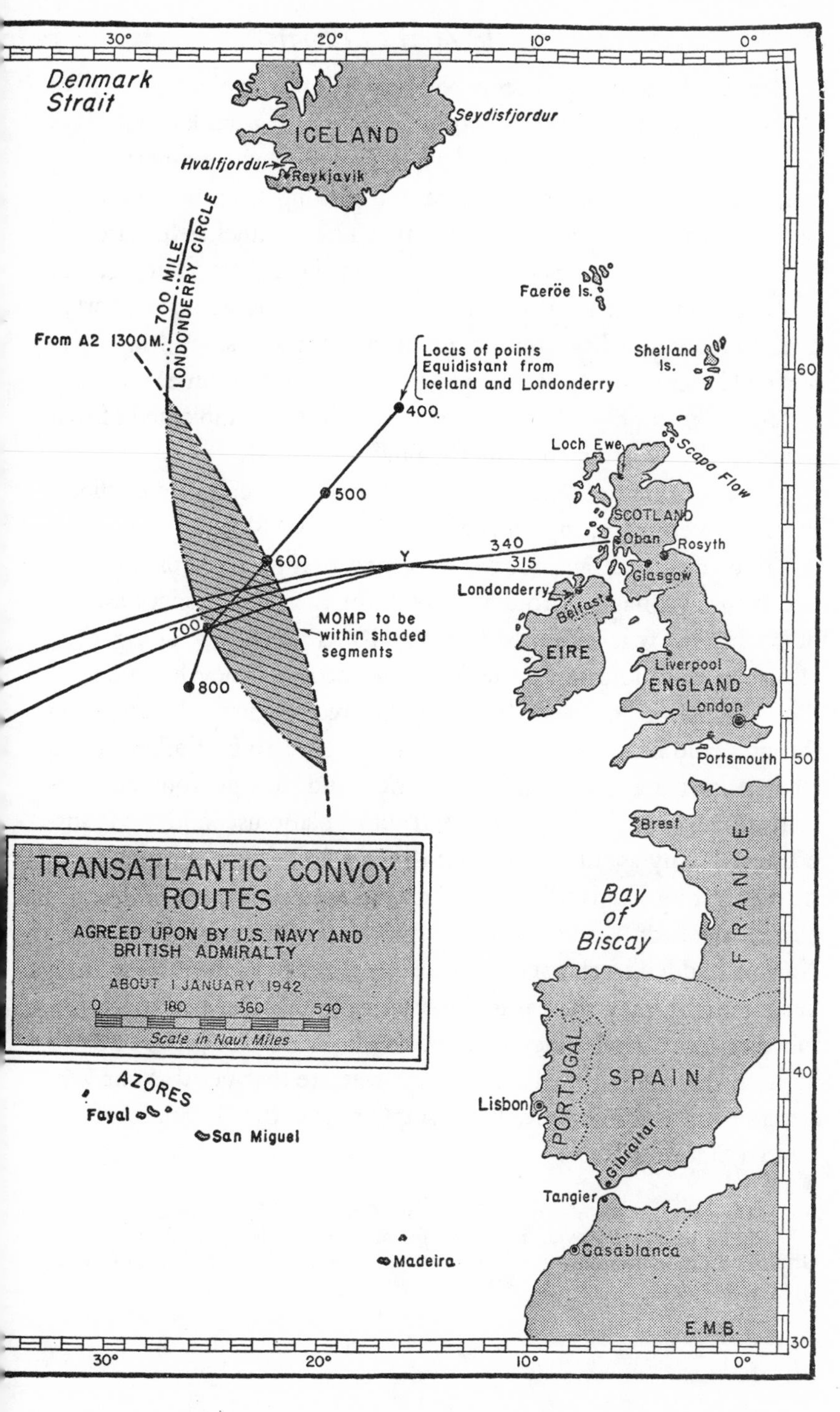

TRANSATLANTIC CONVOY ROUTES
AGREED UPON BY U.S. NAVY AND BRITISH ADMIRALTY
ABOUT 1 JANUARY 1942
0 180 360 540
Scale in Naut Miles
Denmark Strait
ICELAND
Seydisfjordur
Hvalfjordur
Reykjavik
700 MILE LONDONDERRY CIRCLE
From A2 1300 M.
Locus of points Equidistant from Iceland and Londonderry
400
500
600
700
800
Y
340
315
MOMP to be within shaded segments
Faeröe Is.
Shetland Is.
Loch Ewe
Scapa Flow
SCOTLAND
Oban
Rosyth
Glasgow
Londonderry
Belfast
EIRE
Liverpool
ENGLAND
London
Portsmouth
Brest
FRANCE
Bay of Biscay
PORTUGAL
SPAIN
Lisbon
Gibraltar
Tangier
Casablanca
Madeira
AZORES
Fayal
San Miguel
30°
20°
10°
0°
60
50
40
30
E.M.B.

week's overhaul at the Boston Navy Yard after dropping convoys off Newfoundland or Nova Scotia, followed by a week or ten days at the destroyer base in Casco Bay for training and gunnery practice, before returning to Argentia and picking up a new convoy. But the scarcity of escorts was such that a much quicker turnaround had to be made. Repairs took up the time allotted for training, and a destroyer was lucky if she had five days at Boston out of forty-five. "This vessel has fired no gunnery practices since May," reported Commander E. R. Durgin of U.S.S. *Niblack* on 23 November 1941; "insufficient liberty" had been so often complained of that it was hardly worth mentioning again.[30]

The strain was not only physical but psychological. These officers and men were enduring all the danger and hardship of war; yet it was not called war, and for the most part they were escorting ships under foreign flags. Forbidden to talk of their experiences ashore, or even to tell where they had been and what they were doing, their efforts were unknown to the American people. They had none of the satisfaction derived from public recognition. After going through cold hell at sea they would reach port, to find other young men making money in safe industries, and college football stars featured as heroes of the day. Barroom isolationists and (it is suspected) enemy agents worked on the men in Boston, taunting them with "fighting England's battles" and tempting them to desert. But our bluejackets had seen for themselves the new terrors that the Nazi had added to the perils and dangers of the deep. Few realized better than they the threat to America in this German strike for sea supremacy. And the fact that morale in the destroyers remained high, throughout this period of bitter warfare that yet was not war, attests to the intelligence, the discipline, and the fortitude of the United States Navy.[31]

[30] Letter with report of Escort Operations Convoy HX-156, Cinclant file.

[31] Life on board destroyers in the winter of 1941–1942 is depicted by Lt. Cdr. Griffith Coale USNR in *North Atlantic Patrol* (1942), and by Tom Lea in *Life* for 25 May 1942.

3. *Convoy Procedure and Early Lessons*

a. Procedure

A convoy is a beautiful thing, whether seen from a ship or viewed from the sky. The inner core of stolid merchantmen in column is never equally spaced, for each ship has individuality. Someone is always straggling or ranging ahead until the commodore becomes vexed and blinks angrily "Number So-and-so take station and keep station." Around the columns is thrown the screen like a loose-jointed necklace, the beads lunging to port or starboard and then snapping back as though pulled by a mighty elastic under the sea; each destroyer nervous and questing, all eyes topside looking, ears below waterline listening, and radar antennae like cats' whiskers feeling for the enemy. Yet a convoy is also impersonal: unless you are on board a weaving destroyer you never see a soul outside your own ship. At a thousand yards' distance, the usual spacing, the few hands topside a merchant ship look like robots through binoculars. On dark nights only a few shapes of ships a little darker than the black water can be discerned. One must consult that boon to seamen, the SG radar screen, to be convinced that the flock is all there. Coming on deck for the dawn watch, it is a recurrent wonder to see the same ships day after day, each in her appointed station, each with her characteristic top-hamper, bow wave, lift and dip; the inevitable straggler, the inveterate smoker, the vessel with an old shellback master who "knew more about shipping forty years ago than any goddam gold-braid in a tin can," and whose sullen fury at being convoyed translates itself into belated turns, unanswered signals and insolent comebacks. When air cover is furnished there are darting, swooping planes about the convoy; upon approaching port, the stately silver bubble of a blimp comes out, swaying in the breeze and blinking a cheery welcome.

There is nothing beautiful, however, about a night attack on a convoy (unless you see it from a periscope, and the convoy is Japanese). A successful attack is signaled by a flash and a great orange flare, followed by a muffled roar which tells that another ship has been hit. Guns crack at imaginary or too briefly glimpsed targets, star shell goes up, the rescue ship hurries to the scene of the sinking, and sailors in the other ships experience a helpless fury and dread. If the convoy has a weak escort it can only execute an emergency turn and trust that the rest of the wolf-pack will be thrown off or driven down; if the escort is sufficient a "killer group" peels off, searching relentlessly with radar and sonar, while everyone stands by hoping to feel underfoot the push of distant depth charges that tells of a fight with a submerged enemy.

The revised Escort-of-Convoy Instructions issued by Admiral King on 17 November 1941 left the distance and stationing of escorts from convoys flexible, to be decided by escort commanders according to circumstances; but "the guiding principle shall be that, whenever it is possible, escorts will be so disposed that no submarine can reach a successful firing position without being detected." In place of the earlier instructions that discouraged night patrolling, escorts were ordered to "patrol their assigned areas as far as may be practicable." This was a transition to the insistence on aggressive night patrolling that came in the summer of 1942. Zigzagging was advised for fast convoys, or for small ones with a narrow front; but large or slow convoys must follow a straight course, because zigzagging diminished the distance made good, caused confusion and straggling, and had proved ineffective in avoiding submarines. "Evasive courses" – changes of 20 degrees to 40 degrees on each side of the base course, persisted in for periods of two to six hours – were the recommended alternative for large, slow convoys.

Correspondence between Admiral Bristol's staff and Captain Wilder D. Baker, commanding Destroyer Squadron 31, in November–December 1941, indicates that Argentia then believed in a patrol distance of 3000 to 5000 yards from the convoy in daytime and less in darkness; while Captain Baker (whose interest in and grasp of the problem caused him to be selected to head the first anti-submarine warfare unit of the Navy) recommended that destroyer escorts patrol "out as much as 6000 yards" at night. That became doctrine in 1942.

Eight days prior to the sailing date, the Admiralty transmitted the proposed route to the Convoy and Routing section of the Chief of Naval Operations at Washington. "Opnav" concurred or recommended changes, and the route was agreed upon. It took the pattern of four or more ocean positions (designated by letter symbols) through which the convoy was ordered to steam, and a designated "Momp" south of Iceland, where the United States Navy escorts peeled off for Hvalfjordur with the Iceland-bound shipping.

Once the route had been decided, "Opnav" transmitted to the Admiralty, to Commander in Chief Atlantic Fleet ("Cinclant"), to the British Commander in Chief of the Western Approaches ("Cincwa"), to the commander of the task force that supplied the escort, to the British Commanding Officer Atlantic Coast ("Coac") at Halifax, to Canadian Naval Staff Headquarters ("Nshq") at Ottawa, to the Flag Officer Newfoundland Forces ("Fonf") at St. Johns, and to the Canadian port director concerned, the following data: ocean route positions, date and position of "Momp," standard route for stragglers. Cinclant or the commander of the task force concerned then informed Opnav and the port director concerned as to the designation and composition of the ocean escort.[32] At Halifax or Sydney the convoy commodore held a convoy conference on the morning of sailing day, attended by the local escort commander and the masters of the merchant ships sailing with him. There each master was given routing directions and cautioned about radio silence, darkening ship, holding station and straggling. At the Western Ocean meeting point ("Westomp") south of Newfoundland, the United States Navy ocean escort from Argentia or St. Johns met the convoy. Weather permitting, an Argentia-based naval patrol squadron assisted the escort in locating the convoy and furnished air protection to the limit of its endurance. But this area was very foggy, and through no fault of their own the patrol planes were unable to furnish much coverage during the winter of 1941–1942.

[32] This procedure is from a directive signed by Admiral King as Cominch 15 Jan. 1942, but it is believed that it represents a procedure already worked out in practice during 1941.

From "Westomp" to the agreed-upon "Momp," the convoy was under command of the ocean escort commander, who was controlled from Washington up to the "Chop" (Change of Operational Control) date, when the Admiralty took over. It was necessary that convoys be controlled either from Washington or from London in order to prevent them running afoul of each other; for at this period there were often five or six convoys crossing the North Atlantic at the same time. The escort commander had authority to divert the convoy anywhere within a forty-mile-wide belt. If he wished to proceed outside that belt, as occasionally he must in order to avoid ice or evade a waiting wolf-pack, he was empowered to so do, but must report the change of route to Washington or London. The Admiralty, moreover, frequently ordered changes in the prearranged course on the basis of late information about submarine movements received from the high-frequency direction-finders ashore.

b. Communications [33]

A system of communications that had been adequate for the needs of a small peacetime Navy with experienced radio operators became clogged to the point of strangulation with the increase in operational traffic brought on by war. During peace most messages to ships were transmitted in plain English on prearranged circuits. The watch radioman "rogered" (acknowledged receipt) for a message when he believed that he had received it correctly; if any part seemed doubtful, he could request a re-transmission. Thus, the originator was immediately assured that he had reached his addressee. But

[33] This section, prepared by Cdr. A. C. Brown USNR, and Lt. (jg) Albert Harkness Jr. USNR who were Communications officers before they joined the writer's staff, is based on their experience, on the writer's observations when on convoy duty, on gramophone-recorded testimony at the court of inquiry at Charlestown on losses in Convoy ONS–92 (May 1942), and on numerous Reports of escort commanders, such as that of Capt. W. K. Phillips on Convoy ON–41, Dec. 1941; Capt. M. Y. Cohen on Convoys HX–157 and ON–22 Oct.–Nov. 1941; Capt. M. L. Deyo on Convoy HX–152 Oct.–Nov. 1941; Commanding Officer H.M.C.S. *Primrose* on Convoy SC–94. Additional data in "Administrative History of the Atlantic Fleet" II 87–88.

when the threat of submarines made it hazardous to disclose the position of ships, since even the briefest transmission could provide enemy direction-finders with a fix, radio silence was imposed. Since it was imperative that at least one-way contact be maintained with commanders afloat, the Navy used a system known as the Fox Schedule broadcast.[34]

A naval dispatch is divided into two main and equally important parts, the heading and the text. The heading contains in cryptic abbreviation the name of the originator, the single or multiple addressees and various transmitting instructions. As the presence of a ship in certain waters would be disclosed to the enemy if the message were transmitted clear, coded call signs changing daily were used when addressing commands afloat. The text, like the contents of a package, was hidden from view by being encrypted—"wrapped up," as the communicators called it. Messages for ships were first sent by the originator to one of three main radio stations at Washington, San Francisco and Pearl Harbor, which assumed the responsibility of reaching the individual ship. At this station they were "put on the Fox,"[35] which consisted of powerful, long-range, very-low-frequency broadcasts, one dispatch following immediately on the heels of another, transmitted several times a day on a fixed schedule. The comparatively slow rate of 18 words per minute of Morse code was used, so that a moderately experienced operator could take it. But as the volume of traffic to be transmitted increased, the speed occasionally had to be increased, and Fox reached its saturation point with almost continuous broadcasts. A 24-hour guard of Fox was required on board all ships, and operators copied all headings. The operator had to copy the entire Fox, but give to the coding officer only what was addressed to his ship. Reception might be so poor or the operator so green that he could not copy a

[34] "Fox" had been actively employed for many years before the war, but many of the difficulties had heretofore not been foreseen. The volume of communications in the expanded Navy created new difficulties.

[35] A significant advantage of the system, in addition to the security value, was this: by transmitting most of the traffic on one circuit, fewer radio operators and receivers were needed. Small ships would usually have to guard only one or two task force circuits in addition to "Fox."

coded text with sufficient accuracy for the coding officer to decrypt into sensible "clear"; but there was no opportunity to get a repeat. And, in the absence of a specific acknowledgment as in the receipt system, the originator had to assume that messages were received intelligibly. "Degarbling" imperfect texts became an art, though one despised by its reluctant practitioners.

So that messages requiring immediate action could be sent out ahead of ordinary traffic, originators assigned rates of precedence in five classes, ranging from "urgent" to "deferred." A low-precedence message in process of transmission might be interrupted if an "urgent" or "operational priority" came in to be transmitted. But even this expedient was not infallible. Commanding officers and flag officers frequently abused their privilege by assigning a higher precedence than the importance of the message warranted, inflating the high-priority traffic and delaying more important messages from going out. And "urgent" messages that were not urgent came along so frequently that when a really urgent one arrived the harassed coding officer might finish his coffee before starting to decode it. Moreover, it was an old Navy custom (discouraged by Admiral King about mid-1942) for commanding officers who wanted to know everything that went on to require their coding boards to decrypt almost all traffic sent out on the "Fox" even though addressed to others. Since communications personnel were assigned to ships on the basis of anticipated traffic addressed specifically to them, this practice tended to overwork the men so that they fell hopelessly behind.

All traffic to United States Navy escorted convoys came over Fox. At all times United States ships had to guard Radio Washington; while on the European side of the Atlantic they had to guard as well Radio Whitehall, from which emergency diversions and comparable information could be obtained more promptly when convoys were under Admiralty control.

Even before the war it was realized that combined operations between the Royal and United States Navies would demand a common cryptographic language. Naturally, each Navy favored its own system. United States communicators felt that the code furnished by the Admiralty, cunningly devised to be unbreakable by the enemy, was so complicated that decoding of messages put too much strain on junior officers who were unfamiliar with the system, and who were not working in a quiet office ashore, but on a wildly rolling destroyer in mid-Atlantic.[36]

The principal information received by both Navies about the movements and whereabouts of enemy submarines came from shore-based high-frequency direction-finders (HF/DF), whose bearings were plotted at Washington and London and sent out on Fox in a secret daily bulletin giving estimated positions and directions of advance.[37] While these fixes were seldom accurate within 50 or 100 miles, if obtained in time they enabled an escort commander to order an evasive change of course, which had a fair chance of avoiding a wolf-pack. By Admiral Doenitz's admission these diversions from the course laid down before the convoy sailed frequently frustrated his wolf-packs. But sometimes the machinery became stalled. Many instances occurred in which the daily report of U-boat positions that threatened the safety of a convoy reached the escort commander after dark, when it was impossible to plan and execute an evasive change of course except by blinker, the use of which was forbidden at night. Nor were these conditions much better before the fall of 1942.[38]

[36] "I received some messages in the numbers cypher but as has been found by previous experience, I never really knew whether I had the sense of such a message or not. All escort destroyer officers have protested against this cypher ever since we have had any experience with it. Furthermore, the abominable practice of cluttering up the text of the message with routing memoranda for communication officers on shore adds a grievous burden to the work of coding officers in destroyers and corvettes. I invite the attention of our top-flight communicators to the problems which confront coding officers who are rolling and pitching in destroyers and corvettes." (Capt. John B. Heffernan Report on Escort Operations Convoy HX–178, 21 Mar. 1942.)

[37] See Chap. VI, Sec. 3f, for details of this device.

[38] For instance, in Aug. 1942 Convoy SC–95, which suffered severely, received nine reports of U-boats from Cominch, one from the Admiralty, and one from Cincwa. For the Cominch reports, from 2h. 24m. to 11h. 57m. were required from the time Washington received the information to the time the message was received aboard the escort. But Admiralty got its message through in 1h. 57m., and Cincwa's took only 35m. (Cdr. A/S W Unit Atlantic Fleet to Cinclant, Report on Convoy SC–95.)

Within the convoy itself, there were special communication difficulties. Messages could be sent by eight different methods: loud-hailer, semaphore or international code flags by day; colored lights by night; steam whistles, voice radio, ordinary radio, or blinking by day or night. Merchantmen, especially the foreigners, were inept at making and slow to read flag hoists and usually had no blinker guns; nor could trained personnel or equipment be spared by the Navies to help them. There was particular difficulty in communications between air and surface escort. On one occasion in October 1941, aircraft out of Argentia located a convoy for a destroyer steaming out to join it, but was incapable of informing her of its whereabouts, except by swooping in the right direction. By far the best method of intra-convoy communications was the TBS or voice radio.[39] Very-high-frequency waves are quickly absorbed by the globe, and the sky waves are ordinarily not reflected by the ionosphere; hence they are not generally effective for more than 30 miles from the transmitter, and could not be heard by U-boats; nor could the submarines' direction-finders obtain a fix on such frequencies, except on very rare occasions.[40] Each escort group adopted a simple voice code of its own to use over TBS, both for names of vessels in the convoy and escort, degrees when changing course, and for enemy contact. But the use of voice radio (or any radio), except after contact with an enemy vessel had been established, was discouraged; for intra-convoy conversations could be picked up by a near-by U-boat and might give away the convoy's position even if not understood. And, as using any sort of light signal was strictly forbidden under all circumstances at night, that left steam whistles and loud-hailer as the only permissible means of intra-convoy communication after dark. A situation sometimes occurred in which an escort commander, in receipt of vital information transmitted from

[39] Merchantmen never have been equipped with TBS, although a small portable voice radio set (TBY) was generally supplied in 1943.

[40] Because of the supposed security of this method, messages were often sent in plain language. Ships on the other side of the world occasionally would get the signals which by some freak had bounced off the ionosphere.

Transatlantic Convoys, February 1942, from a Cruiser's Float Plane

"TBS Confusion" – a cartoon by Nelson

U.S.S. *West Point*

shore stations thousands of miles away, was unable to get it out to ships of his own group.[41]

It was more important to get essential information to our own forces than to deny it to the enemy; but during the first year of the Atlantic war, the Navy Department laid such stress on the security of communications that they sometimes failed of their essential purpose to communicate.

c. The Fueling Problem

Escort experience before the declaration of war not only taught the tactical lessons already mentioned, but suggested many improvements in the armament and equipment of destroyers. The first problem was what to do with the "short-legged" 1200-tonners of low fuel capacity. These older vessels had been designed in the light of experience in World War I, when all that was expected of an escort was a 48-hour run outbound with a convoy, followed by a 12-hour shift to a new "Momp" and another 48-hour run inbound. But the necessities of escort duty in 1941–1942 were such that every United States destroyer had to cover the route Argentia–"Westomp"–"Momp"–Iceland, or the reverse, which required at least ten days' steaming. In fair weather on a straight run without a convoy to escort, a short-legged destroyer like U.S.S. *Ellis* expended only 25 gallons of fuel oil per mile made good. But the same vessel escorting a westbound convoy in October consumed nearly 50 gallons per mile made good. It was impossible for such ships, especially in winter weather, to conduct the active, aggressive patrolling enjoined on all by the fate of U.S.S. *Kearny* and *Reuben James*.

Typical was the experience of the destroyers escorting Convoy ON–41. The escort group departed Reykjavik 2 December 1941 to close this westbound convoy south of Iceland. The convoy, two

[41] U.S.S. *Ingraham* was lost with all hands but eleven, and U.S.S. *Buck* severely damaged by collision within a convoy on 27 Aug. 1942, when these destroyers were being used as messengers to deliver to merchant ships orders that, but for fear of enemy detection, might have been transmitted by searchlight blinker.

days late at "Momp," was finally picked up well to the eastward of it. In the meantime the short-legged destroyers of the escort had wasted two days' fuel; so, after providing only four days' protection to the convoy, they had to be released on 10 December to refuel at Iceland. This reduced the escort to two warships.[42] Under these circumstances it was impossible to shift transatlantic convoy routes well to the southward of the great-circle course, as winter weather and U-boat concentrations made desirable. Some of the short-leggers were fitted with new fuel tanks, at the expense of their boiler space, which somewhat reduced their speed but made them more serviceable for escort duty.

Subsequently, fueling of escorts at sea from a merchant tanker in the convoy was introduced. Fueling at sea is an old story in the United States Navy, but previous to the war it had been practised largely in calm weather, and only from battleships; merchant tankers had neither the gear, the personnel nor the seamanship to do it. By adopting and perfecting this method in transatlantic convoys, short-legged destroyers and even corvettes could cross the Atlantic and perform their duties effectively. It was first tried about June 1942, with the four-piper *Babbitt*. By fueling once or twice from a tanker in the convoy she was able to patrol actively and make long sweeps ahead of the convoy all the way from the United Kingdom to "Westomp," where she had more than enough fuel to make Boston at 20 knots. Thereafter, during every winter month of 1942–1943, escorts of this group fueled at least once on each crossing, and never had to break off early because of fuel shortage. On one voyage twenty fuelings were made by escorts, some of them four or five times, from four tankers that were rigged for ocean fueling alongside or astern.[43]

The scarcity of suitable escorts was perhaps the greatest handicap during this period. Coast Guard Cutter *Campbell* was employed as escort on Convoy HX–159 in November 1941, and proved so effec-

[42] Comdesdiv 60 (Cdr. John B. Heffernan) to Cinclant 17 Oct. 1941; Cdr. W. K. Phillips Report on Convoy ON–41.

[43] Information from Cdr. Knight Pryor, A/S W Unit Atlantic Fleet.

tive that most of her sister ships of the Treasury class were diverted to this duty. These big seagoing cutters had everything that a destroyer had except speed and torpedoes; and seldom does an opportunity to use torpedoes occur in escort-of-convoy. U.S.C.G.C. *Alexander Hamilton* was torpedoed and sunk ten miles off Iceland 29 January 1942, when towing a disabled storeship.[44] Destroyer *Stack* (Lieutenant Commander Isaiah Olch) made two depth-charge attacks which sent *U-132* home for repairs.

4. *The First American Convoy to the Orient, WS-12X* [45]

Unknown to the American public, their Navy began to make her weight felt in remote parts of the world even before the United States was formally at war. In the late summer and fall of 1941, the situation of Great Britain and her allies rapidly deteriorated. Russia was hard-pressed; Greece and Crete were overrun by the Nazis; Rommel wiped out all the recent British gains on the North African littoral; and it was freely predicted that before Christmas the Axis would be in possession of all three gates of the Mediterranean – the Straits, the Dardanelles and the Suez Canal. Reinforcement of British forces in the Near and Far East was imperative, but the Admiralty could not spare shipping for the long voyage around Africa, and the eastern Mediterranean had become *mare nostrum* to the Axis and *mare clausum* to Britannia.

The only force in a position to help was the United States Navy. After a conference between British, Canadian and United States naval representatives at Washington, the Navy agreed to contribute a task force composed of its largest transports and best escort vessels in order to convey a division of British troops, consisting of over 20,000 officers and men, from Halifax to the Near East. Subsistence of the British troops was paid for out of lend-lease funds, but all other expenses were on the American Navy. British troops were required to conform to United States naval regulations in such mat-

[44] N.O.B. Iceland War Diary.

[45] Navy Department Convoy and Routing section, file on Convoy WS-12X; Report in Operations file; conversations with officers who were in the convoy.

ters as berthing, fire drills, and absence of liquor on board ship. Unlike the earlier transatlantic convoys, this was an all-American affair except for the passengers.

Rear Admiral Arthur B. Cook, Commander Air Force Atlantic Fleet in aircraft carrier *Ranger*, commanded Convoy "William Sail" as it was commonly called from the official designation WS–124. Captain D. B. Beary in U.S.S. *Mount Vernon* was the convoy commodore. This ship and U.S.S. *Wakefield*, each measuring 24,289 tons gross, and U.S.S. *West Point*, over 2000 tons larger, had recently been converted to troop transports from the three largest ships in the American Merchant Marine: *Washington*, *Manhattan* and *America*.[46] The complete convoy composition is on page 111.

As the escort group bringing the British transports to Halifax was reported to be short of fuel, the United States destroyers were sent out to help escort the troopships into Halifax 8 November 1941. While the men were being transferred to the American transports the destroyers made a quick round trip to Casco Bay for refueling and provisioning to capacity. The entire convoy sailed from Halifax 10 November, and proceeded to Trinidad via the Mona Passage, where air coverage was furnished by VP–31 of the Navy, based at Borinquen Field, Puerto Rico.[47]

At Trinidad the task force refueled, but none of the destroyers had the capacity to perform escort duty for the long South Atlantic voyage of some six thousand miles. There was some talk of refueling at Recife, but that was too near Trinidad to do much good. Consequently the United States naval tanker *Cimarron* joined the convoy 19 November, and from her the destroyers refueled at sea, twice on the outward passage and twice on the homeward.

At approximately lat. 17° S, long. 20° W, the carrier *Ranger* broke off and returned home via Trinidad, escorted by *Trippe* and *Rhind*. Captain C. E. Battle in *Quincy* then relieved Admiral Cook. Transport *Leonard Wood* developed boiler trouble and proceeded independently from Trinidad. Through the ingenuity of her en-

[46] *West Point* during the war carried about 350,000 American troops to Europe.
[47] War Diary Caribbean Sea Frontier for 1942, Introduction para. 12.

TG 14.4, CONVOY WS–12X

Rear Admiral Arthur B. Cook, Commander, in *Ranger*

CV 4	RANGER	Capt. W. K. Harrill
CA 39	QUINCY	Capt. C. E. Battle Jr.
CA 44	VINCENNES	Capt. F. L. Riefkohl
AP 22	MOUNT VERNON	Capt. D. B. Beary
AP 25	LEONARD WOOD	Cdr. H. G. Bradbury USCG
AP 26	JOSEPH T. DICKMAN	Cdr. C. W. Harwood USCG
AP 24	ORIZABA	Capt. C. Gulbranson
AP 21	WAKEFIELD	Cdr. W. K. Scammell USCG
AP 23	WEST POINT	Capt. F. H. Kelley
AO 22	CIMARRON *	Cdr. H. J. Redfield

Screen

Destroyer Squadron 8, Capt. T. C. Kinkaid †

DD 419	WAINWRIGHT	Lt. Cdr. T. L. Lewis
DD 362	MOFFETT	Cdr. P. R. Heineman

Destroyer Division 17, Cdr. L. K. Swenson

DD 358	MCDOUGAL	Cdr. D. L. Madeira
DD 359	WINSLOW	Cdr. H. R. Holcomb

Destroyer Division 16, Cdr. T. V. Cooper

DD 402	MAYRANT	Lt. Cdr. E. A. Taylor
DD 404	RHIND	Cdr. H. T. Read
DD 405	ROWAN	Lt. Cdr. B. R. Harrison
DD 403	TRIPPE	Lt. Cdr. R. L. Campbell Jr.

* Joined convoy 19 Nov. 1941 at Trinidad.

† Capt. Kinkaid was detached at Trinidad, promoted Rear Admiral, and went to the Pacific as Comcrudiv 5. Cdr. L. K. Swenson shifted from *McDougal* to *Wainwright* and took over duties of screen commander.

gineer officer, portable blowers were rigged to produce forced draft and increase the combustion rate; and in two days' time she rejoined the main body. When the convoy was approaching Africa, a message was received from the Admiralty that at least four German U-boats were moving in its direction along the coast, accompanied by their own supply ship *Python*. Shortly after came the news that H.M.S. *Dorsetshire* had sunk *Python* in lat. 27°53′ S, on 1 December; she did not get the submarines, which probably had to turn back when deprived of their tender so far from home. A southeast gale on 6–8 December forced the convoy to slow down and change course, as the destroyers could not take the punishment; before that gale was over, Japan was at war with the United States and the British Empire. Convoy WS–12X arrived at Capetown, 8132 miles from Halifax, on 9 December 1941. Two days later Germany and Italy declared war on the United States.

According to the original agreement, this convoy was under Admiralty orders and protection after reaching Capetown, for the United States escort was urgently needed elsewhere.[48] The original destination of the transports was Basra, at the head of the Persian Gulf; but the new war situation determined the Admiralty to route them elsewhere. *Mount Vernon* landed her complement of troops at Singapore, whence she was ordered to Suez to transport Australian troops from Egypt to Colombo and Fremantle. In Australia she took on board a few refugees from Corregidor, survivors from the Battle of Java Sea and personnel being withdrawn from the Netherlands East Indies, and proceeded to San Francisco via Wellington, New Zealand, arriving in March 1942. The main convoy, now commanded by Captain F. H. Kelley in *West Point*, and escorted from off Durban by H.M.S. *Dorsetshire*, reached Bombay on 27 December. The ships were then routed to Singapore, where *Wakefield* was damaged by a Japanese air bomb which also killed everyone in the sick bay. She made temporary repairs at Bombay and returned to the United States via Capetown.

No serious trouble was caused by British troops being placed under United States naval regulations, although the Australians were very undisciplined according to our standards. But the handling of transport operations by British and colonial authorities gave the United States naval officers an impression of disintegration. British military commanders and local authorities appeared to be at loggerheads, and it was difficult to obtain clear directions for the employment and movements of the American ships.[49] Probably our

[48] It continued however until near Durban before reversing course.
[49] Dispatch of U. S. Naval Representative, Singapore (Capt. Dyer).

Allies would have had the same impression of us at the time of the fall of Manila.

As a long-scale convoy operation, more than covering the distance around the world, Convoy "William Sail" was successfully conducted so far as the United States Navy was concerned; it is doubtful whether any convoy had ever been escorted so far with so few mishaps.

CHAPTER VI

The German Submarine Offensive of 1942

January–July 1942

1. *Transatlantic Convoys, December 1941–June 1942*

THE CONGRESS of the United States declared war on Japan at 1610 December 8, 1941. From all available evidence, both the German and Italian governments were uninformed about the Japanese attack on Pearl Harbor until it actually occurred.[1] Nevertheless Hitler took this occasion to abandon his policy of avoiding open warfare with the New World, and on 11 December declared war on the United States. Mussolini obediently followed suit, and at 1530 the same day, the Congress declared war on Germany and Italy.

Transatlantic convoys in mid-November had reverted to the more northerly routes, passing close to Greenland and heading for a "Momp" much nearer Iceland than had been customary. This had the advantage of affording the convoys Iceland-based air coverage, but the winter weather was worse in the higher latitudes, and foul weather by rendering sound gear less effective favors the submarine.

Admiral King,[2] appointed Commander in Chief United States

[1] The German War Diary, Naval Staff (*Kriegstagebuch der Seekriegsleitung*), for 7 Dec. 1941 states that both the attacks on Pearl Harbor and on Singapore were a "complete surprise."

[2] See biographical details on p. 51 *n*. By Executive Order No. 9096, 12 Mar. 1942, President Roosevelt combined the duties of Cominch and Chief of Naval Operations, and on the 26th Admiral King relieved Admiral Stark as CNO. On the same date Vice Admiral F. J. Horne, who had served with Admiral King on the General Board, assumed duty as Vice Chief of Naval Operations.

Fleet (Cominch) on 20 December 1941 at the age of sixty-three, was relieved ten days later as Commander in Chief Atlantic Fleet (Cinclant) by Admiral Royal E. Ingersoll. He continued, nevertheless, to exercise many of his former functions – not from any desire to retain power, but because Cinclant as a floating command lacked the necessary communications and other facilities to direct so complicated a war as this was becoming in the Atlantic.

"A man of adamant," as Mahan described Sir John Jervis, exactly fits Ernest J. King. Tall, spare and taut, with piercing brown eyes, a powerful Roman nose and deeply cleft chin, he looked the part of Commander in Chief of the Fleet, and he filled the part. From the day he entered the Naval Academy in 1897 King impressed his fellows. He was a sailor's sailor who neither had nor wanted any life outside the Navy. He believed that what was good for the Navy was good for the United States, the Americas, and indeed the world. In that sense and that alone he was narrow. But he had a firm grasp of naval strategy and tactics, an encyclopedic knowledge of naval detail, an immense capacity for work, and complete integrity. He had exercised every variety of naval command during the forty-one years he had been in the service, and in every one had shown uncommon ability. Endowed with a superior intellect himself, he had no toleration for fools or weaklings; everyone in the Navy respected him, but he had the reputation of a "sundowner" and was more feared than loved. He hated publicity, did not lend himself to popular build-up, and was the despair of interviewers. Unlike Admiral Stark's, his decisions were made quickly and without much consultation; when anyone tried to argue with Admiral King beyond a certain point, a characteristic bleak look came over his countenance as a signal that his mind was made up and further discussion was useless.

Admiral King's vast knowledge and energy were in a sense his only weakness, for naval business accumulated faster than anyone could have anticipated, and the Admiral's office tended to become an administrative bottleneck. Not for long, however; he cleared the deck ruthlessly at frequent intervals. A hard, grim, determined man, King was well fitted to cope with the most difficult situation perhaps ever faced by a naval commander, and to rule efficiently and justly the greatest Navy in the world's history. With nothing of the courtier in his make-up, he yet acquired and retained the confidence and esteem of President Roosevelt. The two men were in a sense complementary. Each had what the other lacked, and in concert with General Marshall who shared the qualities of both, they formed a perfect winning team. The Republic has never had more efficient, selfless and upright servants than these three men.

Admiral King brought with him to Washington Rear Admiral Richard S. Edwards (formerly Commander Submarines Atlantic Fleet) as deputy chief of staff,[3] and made Rear Admiral Russell Willson,[4] then Superintendent of the Naval Academy, his chief of staff. Other members of his Atlantic Fleet staff whom he brought to Washington were his operations officer Captain F. S. Low and his flag secretary Commander G. L. Russell. As assistant chiefs of staff he appointed Rear Admirals Richmond K. Turner and Willis Augustus Lee, who were already in the Chief of Naval Operations organization. When Turner went to Guadalcanal he was relieved as assistant chief of staff for plans by Rear Admiral Charles M. ("Savvy") Cooke Jr.

Apart from these three key men, Edwards, Willson and Cooke, and Horne who was Vice Chief of Naval Operations, Admiral King kept a continuous turnover on his staff. Senior officers were constantly being brought in from the various theaters of war, retained on duty with Cominch for a few months or a year, and presently sent back to sea again. Thus the fighting Navy point of view was maintained at Washington.

* * *

[3] Chief of Staff from 1 Sept. 1942.

[4] Ordered to the Pacific Fleet in Aug. 1942 but found physically unqualified for sea duty; returned to Washington as Deputy Commander in Chief and from Nov. 1942 was the Navy member of the Joint Strategic Survey Committee of the Joint Chiefs of Staff. Detached as Deputy Cominch 1 Dec. 1942 but remained in practice as a member of Admiral King's staff.

Since escort-of-convoy was every day becoming more important, and required heavy communications facilities, Admiral King took the direction of it with him from Newport to Washington. Shortly after becoming Cominch, he exchanged views on the subject with the Admiralty.

Observing that the current convoy routes were "rapidly becoming untenable," owing to "difficulties of operation, . . . weather, and severe storm damage which may be expected to increase," and that the Argentia and Hvalfjordur bases were far from being secure havens; predicting an "imminent probability of submarine attack" on the Atlantic seaboard of the United States, to take advantage of the well-known "weakness of our coastal defense force"; he declared it to be essential (1) that transatlantic convoy routes be shifted southward, (2) that three task groups of short-legged Canadian destroyers be employed as local escorts from Halifax to the meridian of Cape Farewell, and (3) that six or seven groups of long-legged Canadian destroyers and corvettes escort them thence to a "Momp" at long. 22° W (about five hundred miles from Northern Ireland), where British escorts from the United Kingdom could take over, and the Canadians proceed to Londonderry to fuel.[5]

The Admiralty concurred. Fast HX convoys, it was further agreed, should be escorted by United States destroyers to "Momp," where they, too, would break off for Londonderry, refuel, and escort a fast ON convoy home. In order to avoid extended stays at Argentia and Hvalfjordur, the destroyers would visit Boston for upkeep and repairs between every round voyage. A shuttle system of escorts from Iceland to "Momp" would take care of Iceland traffic. And the fast convoys were given routes more southerly than the great-circle course from Cape Race to Malin Head, Ireland.

[5] Fuel consumption is far less for escorts proceeding directly at a normal cruising speed of 12–15 knots than for those patrolling station escorting a slow convoy. The Admiralty also proposed that the São Jorge Channel in the Azores be used for refueling from tankers, but Cominch rejected this, as too far from any possible "Momp."

To Commander Task Force 24 (Admiral Bristol), Admiral King delegated operational supervision and control of escorts for all merchant convoys in the United States' strategic area of the North Atlantic. And Admiral Ingersoll exercised complete responsibility for troop convoys.

Formal war with the Axis gave the United States Navy this new responsibility. For it was part of the war plan immediately to start transporting units of the Army to the United Kingdom for training, so that there would be no shortage of troop-lift, as in 1918, when the Army was ready to strike. The first to transport American soldiers to the United Kingdom, it is believed, was Convoy NA–1, consisting of two British transports and two Royal Navy escorts, which sailed from Halifax 10 January 1942, and arrived at Londonderry about two weeks later. And until the invasion of North Africa was launched in October, every American soldier sent overseas went by this northern transatlantic route.

In February 1942, after about six small NA convoys had been sent across (one only escorted by United States destroyers), the Navy organized a series known as combined NA and AT, with a larger number of transports and a heavy American escort.[6] For instance, Convoy AT–15 sailed from New York 30 April and Convoy NA–8 from Halifax 3 May, the two joining in or near Chedabucto Bay. The combined convoy consisted of 17 transports, one of which broke off for Argentia, and four for Iceland. It was escorted by the old United States battleship *New York*, light cruiser *Brooklyn*, and twelve United States destroyers. There were usually more escorts than transports in these troop convoys, and a considerable number of destroyers were tied to this important duty. Moreover, troop transports enjoyed all the blimp and airplane escort that was available at each end of the route. Heavy weather was often encountered, and an occasional sound contact on a submarine was made, but a speed of 12.5 to 14.5

[6] The first, AT–12, 15 transports and 18 escorts. sailed from New York 19 Feb. 1942

knots and the heavy escort afforded sufficient protection, and not a ship nor a soldier was lost.

United States destroyers, escorting both troop and merchant convoys, began in January 1942 to use the Londonderry base, which had been ready for several months. This change of the turn-around point from Iceland was most welcome. Londonderry, a stronghold of strict Irish Presbyterians, offered bluejackets slight recreation on the Sabbath, but seemed like Coney Island after Reykjavik; and the green Irish countryside was heaven compared with the barren wastes of Iceland. Repair facilities also were superior, since Londonderry was already an important base of the Royal Navy, and the main British center for anti-submarine training. The British "dome teacher," in which personnel were trained to the use of anti-aircraft guns in a sort of planetarium, was of immense value to American gunners, as were the British "tame submarines" on which escort vessels practised both day and night attacks. A destroyer's stay in port was so arranged that the last two days before sailing were given up to anti-submarine training. This system allowed time for upkeep and recreation and sent sailors out on escort duty with fresh knowledge of the actual sound and appearance of a submarine under various conditions.

During December 1941 and early January 1942, so few submarines were contacted, even by merchant convoy escorts, that the merchant seamen became careless about making smoke and showing lights.[7] Connections were often missed at "Momp" in heavy weather; air coverage amounted to little more than one or two planes which circled once or twice over the convoy (sometimes delaying recognition signals until fired upon), and then departed. There was a rapid improvement, however, in air coverage during the early spring. Commander P. R. Heineman reported that on Convoy HX–183, which crossed in early April of 1942, "Conduct of air escort on both ends of journey was very satisfac-

[7] "Smoke from this convoy was frequently visible over 30 miles after the weather cleared on 17 Mar." Cdr. R. W. Hungerford Report on Escort Operations Convoy HX–179.

tory. The Navy plane present off Newfoundland gave splendid assistance in locating the convoy as well as giving data as to ships, their course, speed and distance ahead and also visibility. On the eastern end, almost continuous air escort was present on 12, 13 and 14 April; plane challenge and reply, as well as signaling, were very prompt and effective."

Radio equipment was often wanting or not working owing to new and improper installation, or lack of practice by personnel. Fog, snow and heavy weather sometimes scattered a convoy before the United States escorts picked it up south of Newfoundland. For instance, in Convoy HX–166, which passed Christmas at sea, only 36 vessels out of 41 originally scheduled actually sailed from Halifax, and only 6 met the escort at "Westomp." After cruising about for over 24 hours, with the aid of a plane the escort rounded up 22 more (including the commodore), but never did find the other 8, which steamed across independently. During the course of the voyage, "Momp" was altered three times by radio from Washington, in order to make allowance for heavy weather; and a part of the screen had to break off for Iceland, owing to low fuel, before its relief appeared.

There was some difficulty obtaining smooth coöperation between escort commanders and convoy commodores. The senior officer of the escort is always commander of the entire convoy; but during this era, he was apt to be a two-and-a-half-striper without much convoy experience, and consequently would hesitate to assert himself against a retired rear admiral of the Royal Navy, who served as convoy commodore. And, as United States escorts picked up transatlantic convoys at sea, their commanders had no opportunity to attend the convoy conference before sailing, and get acquainted. Fortunately common sense and consideration prevailed on both sides; there was no unpleasantness between the two services, only occasional misunderstanding. Escort-of-convoy duty in the year 1941–1942 did more to cement good feeling among the three Navies concerned, and their merchant marines, than years of speechmaking and good-willing.

The only American-escorted convoy that lost heavily during the first four months of 1942 was ON–67 of 35 ships in eight columns which crossed westward during the full moon of February. The ocean escort, consisting of the United States destroyers *Edison, Nicholson, Lea* and *Bernadou*, under Commander A. C. Murdaugh USN, steamed south to join from Iceland. *Nicholson*, the only one whose radar was working, picked up the convoy about 24 hours after the set time for rendezvous. H.M.C.S. *Algoma*, of the British escort, stayed with the convoy, and stations were taken by the five escort vessels in a circular disposition about 4000 yards out. The rescue ship S.S. *Toward*,[8] equipped with a high-frequency direction-finder, picked up a submarine's signal at 1730 February 21. U.S.S. *Lea* searched out on the bearing, but returned in less than an hour without a contact, and what followed showed the unwisdom of making so brief an investigation. For at 0305 February 22, two ships were torpedoed and sunk, probably by one U-boat (neither sighted nor heard) from outside the screen. Survivors were rescued by *Toward* and *Nicholson* as the convoy continued its course. On the afternoon of the same day, two destroyers swept out to 15 miles abeam and 10 miles astern, the then limit of visibility, in order to keep the U-boats down. They found nothing and no attack developed that night. But in view of what happened the following night, it is clear that the convoy was being shadowed.

Between 0030 and 0645 February 24, four ships were torpedoed, and two sank. On the second attack, at 0230, the convoy made illumination by "snowflake," a brightly burning powder fired in a rocket from a projector, with the object of enabling a merchantman's gun crew, as well as the escorts, to sight any surfaced submarine inside the columns.

[8] S.S. *Toward* of the Clyde Shipping Company was the first of the specially designated convoy rescue ships; S.S. *Rathlin* the second. They were equipped with accommodations for several hundred survivors, a R.N. surgeon and a well-staffed sick bay. Much new rescue gear, including a big dip net for picking up waterlogged and oil-smeared survivors, was devised on board these vessels. (B.B.C. broadcast printed in *American Seamen* IV No. 3, Summer 1944, pp. 129–133.)

After a quiet forenoon watch, S.S. *Toward* reported two suspicious signals on her direction-finder. *Lea* and *Nicholson* promptly ran down the bearing, and the latter sighted two U-boats on the surface, distant respectively four and five miles, and fifteen to twenty miles from the convoy. In view of the enemy's persistent trailing, Commander Murdaugh sent a message to Washington recommending dispersal of the convoy or a drastic change of course. Almost seven hours elapsed before the Chief of Naval Operation's reply and consent were received. By that time (1850) it was dark, but the convoy executed a 68-degree change of course.[9] During the intervening hours the screen made wide sweeps and aggressive patrols, which continued all the following night. About an hour after the change of course, *Edison* made a sound contact on the starboard bow of the convoy and sighted a U-boat in the moonlight just as it was diving. Six depth-charge attacks were made, covering a period of four and one-half hours; but this submarine escaped. *Edison* had been back on station about two hours when she sighted another U-boat at a distance of 200 yards, which submerged before the main battery could be brought to bear. No sound contact was obtained, but *Edison* patrolled between the convoy and the point of submergence for about four hours, and no further attacks developed.

There is nothing like experience to improve technique, and the voyage of ON–67 taught several lessons. First, the value of radar for anti-submarine work. Second, the necessity of active and aggressive patrolling – "You've got to go out and run them down." [10] Most of all, the urgent need of a definite doctrine for depth-charge attacks, and better training in following up underwater sound contacts. Commander Murdaugh's group was splendidly aggressive; but his officers were very deficient in attack technique.

Transatlantic convoy history was uneventful in March and April 1942. Escort units, composed usually of two United States

[9] This showed the advisability of granting escort commanders more discretion in such matters, and shortly afterwards Cominch so directed.

[10] Capt. Wilder D. Baker, in conference with Capt. Murdaugh and Comdr. Keating of *Nicholson*, 4 March 1942.

destroyers and four Canadian corvettes, directed by such seasoned commanders as W. K. ("Sol") Phillips in *Mayo*, P. R. Heineman in *Benson*, H. C. Fitz in *Niblack*, John B. Heffernan in *Gleaves* and R. W. Hungerford in *Bristol*, were getting the ships across safely – but they were not getting any U-boats. When March came in like a lion, weather seemed more deadly than the submarine. A convoy cannot heave-to like a single steamship, because vessels act so differently hove-to that collisions and wide scattering would result. It has to keep going somewhere, somehow. Except for two ships sunk out of Convoy ON–68, the only casualties in March were caused by the weather. There were no accidents due to collision between ships or with ice, for convoy technique had improved with experience, as much as that of escorting.

The escort dispositions illustrated on page 89 are those of Commander H. C. Fitz in the spring of 1942, when the usual escort consisted of two destroyers and four corvettes. They were much used by other escort commanders. Note the development of active patrolling and wide sweeps that had taken place within a few months.

Lieutenant Commander E. H. Pierce, in a memorandum dated at sea 23 April 1942, remarked: "For the past several months our convoys have been practically undisturbed, due chiefly to the fact that the submarines have been otherwise occupied and have avoided the convoy routes. This should not be allowed to engender a false sense of security." Commander H. C. Fitz, after safely conducting Convoy HX–196 of 43 ships, including 21 tankers carrying some sixty million gallons of oil, with an escort consisting of two United States Coast Guard cutters and four Canadian corvettes, concluded: –

"It appears to be only a question of time before the enemy will realize the weakness of this group, owing to the lack of speed, with the result that a large number of ships is liable to be lost. Even if a submarine is sighted shadowing on the surface, there is no ship of this unit that can make any appreciable gain on a submarine if it takes its maximum surface speed. It is not possible to

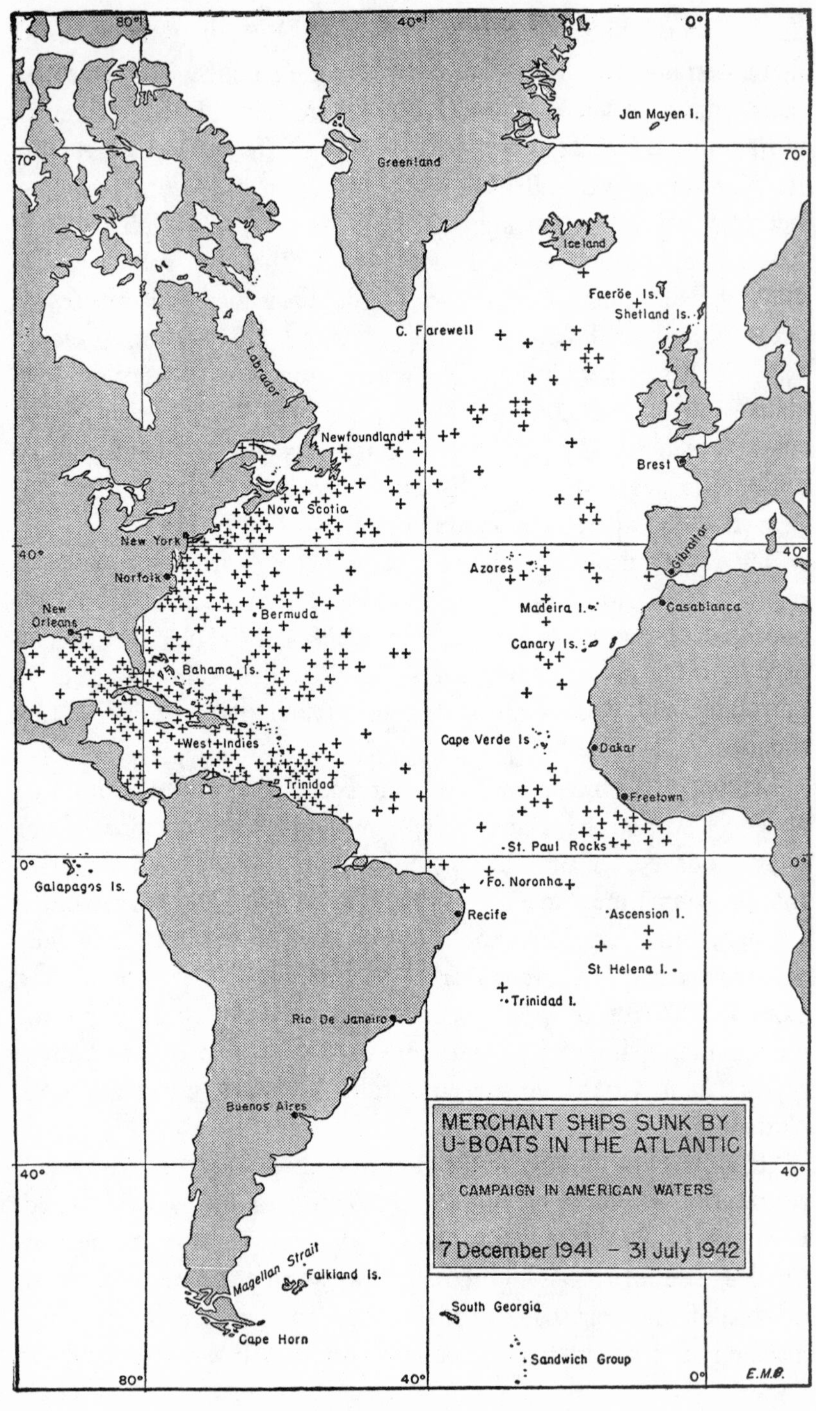

MERCHANT SHIPS SUNK BY U-BOATS IN THE ATLANTIC
CAMPAIGN IN AMERICAN WATERS
7 December 1941 – 31 July 1942
80°
40°
0°
70°
40°
Jan Mayen I.
Greenland
Iceland
Faeröe Is.
Shetland Is.
C. Farewell
Labrador
Newfoundland
Brest
Nova Scotia
New York
Norfolk
Azores
Gibraltar
Casablanca
Madeira I.
New Orleans
Bermuda
Canary Is.
Bahama Is.
West Indies
Cape Verde Is
Dakar
Trinidad
Freetown
St. Paul Rocks
Galapagos Is.
Fo. Noronha
Recife
Ascension I.
St. Helena I.
Trinidad I.
Rio De Janeiro
Buenos Aires
Magellan Strait
Falkland Is.
South Georgia
Cape Horn
Sandwich Group
E.M.B.

make proper sweep.[11]. . . It is strongly recommended that two destroyers be made available for this unit."

By this time the submarine offensive on coastal and Caribbean shipping had reached such proportions, and the troop convoys to the British Isles had become so numerous, that no United States destroyers could be spared for merchant convoys. Fortunate indeed for the convoys that the submarines were "otherwise occupied," but very unfortunate for unprotected shipping.

2. *The Assault on Coastal and Caribbean Shipping* [12]

a. From New England South

A prompt attack by U-boats on United States coastal shipping was to be expected, since that is what they had done during World War I. On that occasion, however, the German submarines caused more fright than they did damage. The six U-boats [13] which visited our coastal waters between April and November 1918 neither disrupted coastwise shipping nor caused the retention in home waters of any ships designated for duty in Europe.[14] Their operations were little more than nuisance raids, in which small, defenseless vessels were attacked, cables were cut, and mines laid off the coast and harbor entrances. Twenty-four ships ranging from 2000 to 10,000

[11] The Coast Guard cutters made 19 knots and the corvettes 14. The 500-ton U-boats could make 17.6 knots surfaced.

[12] Sources for this section: Lt. Cdr. J. T. Hardin "Study of the U-Boat Campaign" made for the A/S W Unit at Boston in July 1942; British Admiralty "The Battle of the Atlantic to May 1942"; Royal Canadian Naval Service Headquarters "Summary of Naval War Effort, 1 Jan.–1 Mar. 1942," 30 Apr.; O.N.I. Reports of merchant ship sinkings with accounts of survivors; and, in general, the files of the A/S W Unit of the Atlantic Fleet. Statistics of sinkings were confused in 1942 because some included U. S. and others all Allied vessels, some included sinkings from all causes and others only those by submarines. These quoted in this volume are compiled from figures in Fleet Operations Statistical Section, Navy Dept. dated June, July and Aug. 1945.

[13] Not counting the *Deutschland*, which made two visits in 1916 carrying cargo, and the *U-53*, which entered Newport 7 Oct. 1916 on a "good will" voyage, capturing and sinking five British and neutral steamers the very day she left.

[14] *German Submarine Activities on the Atlantic Coast of the United States and Canada*, Publication No. 1 of Office of Naval Records and Library, Historical Section Navy Department (1920).

tons and 76 smaller craft, mostly schooners and fishermen, were sunk by gunfire or torpedoes in our Atlantic sea frontiers. Admiral Tirpitz's coastal campaign of 1918 was a very faint taste of the foul dose that Admiral Doenitz administered in 1942.

Germany declared war on the United States 11 December 1941, but owing to Hitler's previous prohibition of submarine operations in the western Atlantic, no U-boats were then in position to raid the American coasts. The decision to send them thither was made at a conference between Admiral Raeder and Hitler on 12 December.[15] This operation was appropriately named *Paukenschlag* ("Roll of the Drums"). But Doenitz required a month to deploy his U-boats, and he had few to spare, owing to a great killing made by the Royal Navy and Air Force off Portugal and the Straits in November and December, and the desire of Hitler to render naval support to Rommel's current offensive in Africa.[16] Raeder believed that the attack by Japan would "relieve the Atlantic strain" by diverting United States warships to the Pacific, and he also guessed wrong as to our predetermined strategy of first concentrating against the European Axis partners. As both the Admiral and his Fuehrer were eager for a quick decision in North Africa, 25 U-boats were allocated to the Mediterranean, and only six 500-tonners to the Atlantic coast of the United States. However, Doenitz chose six of his best U-boat "aces" to command the initial submarine assault on American coastal shipping, and their success was both unprecedented and humiliating.

Fortunately the month's delay afforded minecraft of the Atlantic Fleet time to lay a protective mine field of 365 mines off the Capes of the Chesapeake, and to protect the harbors of New York and other Atlantic cities with nets and booms.

The first attack was delivered on 12 January 1942, when the British passenger steamer *Cyclops* was torpedoed and sunk about

[15] Assmann Diary.

[16] Eight U-boats were sunk in this area, and three (plus one Italian submarine) in the Mediterranean, mostly by British corvettes and sloops, in Nov.–Dec. 1941. It was not until July 1943 that the percentage of U-boats sunk to those at sea surpassed the ratio of Dec. 1941.

300 miles east of Cape Cod by *U-123*. In February, several others were sent over to augment these six, in an area where they could rend and tear their prey with impunity.

This area was the coastwise shipping lane that begins in the St. Lawrence River, debouches into the ocean by Cabot Strait, passes along the coast of Nova Scotia and outside the Georges and Nantucket Shoals to New York, where it is joined by vessels from New England ports that pass through the Cape Cod Canal and Long Island Sound. New York – with 50 arrivals and departures on the average each day of November 1941, and still more afterwards, all legitimate[17] prey – was the greatest port in the world. From New York the great coastal shipping lane passes south to Cape Hatteras, with important feeders up Chesapeake and Delaware Bays, and to Florida. Thence, one branch takes its way through the Straits of Florida to the Gulf of Mexico, and another, through the Old Bahama Channel to the Windward Passage, where it meets the merchant fleet southbound from New York to the Panama Canal. Many ships pass into the Caribbean through the Mona Passage, outward bound to the Lesser Antilles, Trinidad, the Guianas, and the important oil distilleries of the Dutch West Indies. In addition, there was a considerable traffic from New York to Cape San Roque, en route to Brazil, South Africa, and the River Plate; and the faster vessels from the West Indies to Britain had forsaken the convoyed routes since the fall, in order to save time and escape foul weather. Very little of this merchant shipping, except a part of the British, Dutch and Norwegian, was armed; and merchant ships' gun crews were almost never a match for U-boats. No more perfect set-up for rapid and ruthless destruction could have been offered the Nazi sea lords.

The massacre enjoyed by the U-boats along our Atlantic Coast in 1942 was as much a national disaster as if saboteurs had destroyed half a dozen of our biggest war plants. . . . If a submarine sinks two 6000-ton

[17] Early in 1942 Hitler declared the Atlantic Coast and Caribbean to be "blockaded" in order to justify sinking neutrals, and vessels of Sweden, the Argentine, and almost every neutral country trading with the United States except Spain, were among those sunk in the campaign.

ships and one 3000-ton tanker, here is a typical account of what we have totally lost: 42 tanks, 8 six-inch Howitzers, 88 twenty-five-pound guns, 40 two-pound guns, 24 armored cars, 50 Bren carriers, 5210 tons of ammunition, 600 rifles, 428 tons of tank supplies, 2000 tons of stores, and 1000 tanks of gasoline. Suppose the three ships had made port and the cargoes were dispersed. In order to knock out the same amount of equipment by air bombing, the enemy would have to make three thousand successful bombing sorties.[18]

Exactly how many U-boats were responsible for this merry massacre does not appear in the German records now available. According to Cominch and Admiralty estimates, there was a daily average of 19 U-boats operating in the United States Strategic Area (roughly, the western half of the Atlantic), in January 1942. This rose to an average of 28 in February–April, 35 in May, and 40 in June.[19] Probably the damage in the Eastern Sea Frontier was wrought by no more than 12 U-boats operating at any one time. And every month the Germans were building 20 or more new 740- and 500-tonners.

The U-boats were undoubtedly helped by enemy agents and clandestine radio transmissions from the United States, as well as by breaking codes. One of the German admirals who wrote an account of this campaign after the war was over said that they were successful in "busting" the code used by us and the British until about the middle of 1942 when we changed it so fast that the German cryptographers could not keep up. They were very clever at deceptive warfare too. The Canadian corvette *Spikenard* was torpedoed when sweeping ahead of a convoy, and after she went down a U-boat called plaintively, imitating the keying of her radio operator, and asking for a bearing of the convoy. The ruse worked, the bearing was furnished, and the convoy suffered more casualties. Two days later, on 12 February 1942, an American freighter off Block Island heard a broadcast ordering all ships

[18] *Training Manual* prepared by Airasdevlant, Naval Air Station, Quonset Point, R. I.

[19] Compare figures in Appendix I for the entire Alantic.

Photo LIFE

Admiral Giffen on bridge of *Wichita* off North Cape, Iceland

Winter convoy scene, North Atlantic

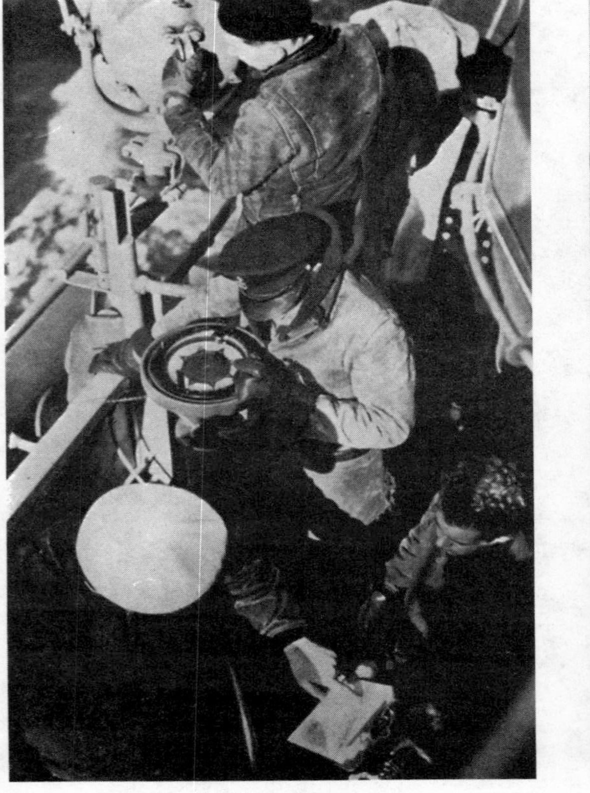

Messages are sent and received by blinker on bridge of U.S.S. *Greer*

Deck scene, U.S.S. *Greer*

into port; but when she entered Newport it was found that no such signal had been made by the Navy.[20]

One heard at the time a good deal of loose talk about U-boats fueling or provisioning secretly in American waters; but the 500-tonners had so great a cruising radius that this was unnecessary, and it is believed that it was seldom if ever done.[21] A few tanker-submarines – "milch cows" as we called them – were sent to American waters to supply fuel, and commercial tankers were sent out regularly from the Canary Islands to supply them.[22] The 500-tonners, which made up the great majority of enemy submarines operating along our coast, carried enough fuel for a cruise of at least 42 days. Allowing two weeks for the outward passage and the same for the homeward to a French port, they could spend at least two weeks in the Atlantic Coast shipping lanes. Each U-boat carried fourteen torpedoes, including two or three of the new electrically propelled type that show no air bubbles in the wake, and so cannot be sighted or dodged. In addition they carried guns of sufficient caliber to sink most merchant vessels by shellfire alone. Their usual tactics, in the early months of 1942, were to approach a shipping lane at periscope depth, lie in wait on the surface at night, and launch torpedoes from seaward against a vessel whose silhouette might be seen against shore lights.

One of the most reprehensible failures on our part was the neglect of local communities to dim their waterfront lights, or of military authorities to require them to do so, until three months after the submarine offensive started. When this obvious defense measure

[20] Memorandum signed by Vice Admiral F. J. Horne 15 Apr. 1942.

[21] The U-boats sometimes commandeered fresh fruit and similar supplies from native schooners in the Caribbean, but these were not operated by enemy agents and were a very small factor in their success. Mr. J. Edgar Hoover stated in *American Magazine* Oct. 1943 p. 110 that the F.B.I. between Jan. 1942 and 15 May 1943 investigated over 500 reports of refueling enemy subs on our shores, signaling to them, and the like; but "every report . . . was a false alarm."

[22] A German prisoner who had been on board the tanker *Charlotte Schliemann* in Puerto de la Luz, Las Palmas, testified that she refueled 18 U-boats in 1941 and Jan. 1942. Mr. Winfield Scott, U. S. Consul at Tenerife, reported a U-boat fueling at Santa Cruz on 2 Mar. 1942, and stated that the Spanish minelayer *Marte* and sailing ship *San Miguel* carried oil and supplies out to meet submarines at sea.

was first proposed, squawks went up all the way from Atlantic City to southern Florida that the "tourist season would be ruined." Miami and its luxurious suburbs threw up six miles of neon-light glow, against which the southbound shipping that hugged the reefs to avoid the Gulf Stream was silhouetted. Ships were sunk and seamen drowned in order that the citizenry might enjoy business and pleasure as usual. Finally, on 18 April 1942, the Eastern Sea Frontier ordered waterfront lights and sky signs doused, and the Eastern Defense Command of the Army ordered a stringent dim-out on 18 May.

If one or two torpedoes did not hole the attacked ship fatally, the submarine finished her off by shellfire. Later in the spring, when the nights became shorter and the ineffectiveness of our anti-submarine warfare had been demonstrated, the U-boats became bolder and attacked in broad daylight, even surfaced. Although they invariably attacked without warning, they commonly gave the crew a chance to get away before opening gunfire, and refrained from machine-gunning survivors in lifeboats, as had been done freely in the early part of the war.[23] Survivors were often questioned as to the identity of the ship and the nature of her cargo, were sometimes offered water, provisions or cigarettes and dismissed with a standardized joke about sending the bill to Roosevelt or Churchill. When daylight sinkings enabled survivors to observe the U-boat, it was usually reported as manned by young, healthy and sunburned Germans who appeared to be having a splendid time, and who took snapshots and moving pictures of the sinking. A few submarines in the Caribbean region and further south were believed to be Italian.

Two days after S.S. *Cyclops* went down, enemy submarines moved into the shipping bottleneck off Cape Hatteras. A large Panamanian tanker, S.S. *Norness*, was sunk on 14 January; the

[23] There were many exceptions to this rule, however. For instance, S.S. *Cardonia* and *Esso Bolivar*, hit in the Windward Passage 7 Mar. 1942, had lifeboats machine-gunned when being lowered; the latter, and S.S. *Oregon* (sunk 28 Feb. 1942, 150 miles N of Mona Passage) had men machine-gunned in the water. *Esso Bolivar* made port after fine damage control by merchant crew and Navy salvagers.

British tanker *Coimbra* on the 15th; the American tanker *Allan Jackson* on the 18th. Next day the U-boats sank one of the smart Canadian "Lady boats," the American cargo ship *City of Atlanta* and a small Latvian freighter. Then three tankers in succession were sunk and three more before the end of the month, in the coastal area between New York and Hatteras. In all, 13 vessels measuring 95,000 gross tons, 70 per cent of it tanker tonnage, in a little over two weeks.[24]

Such protection as the Navy could furnish to shipping, during this blitz, was pitifully inadequate. Admiral Adolphus Andrews, Commander Eastern Sea Frontier, which extended from the Canadian border to Jacksonville, Florida, had no naval planes at his disposal in December capable of searching far out to sea. Offshore air patrol was therefore undertaken by the Army Air Force. Three short-range bombers based at Westover, Massachusetts, three at Mitchell Field, Long Island, and three at Langley Field near Hampton Roads, made two daylight sweeps every 24 hours. That was all. By 1 April 1942 the anti-submarine patrol had been built up to 84 Army and 86 Navy planes at 19 bases between Bangor, Maine, and Jacksonville, Florida.[25] The exact number of surface craft available to Admiral Andrews when the U-boats struck in is difficult to ascertain; but by 1 April 1942 the total was only 23 large (90-foot up) and 42 small (75- and 83-foot) Coast Guard cutters, three 173-foot PCs, twelve old Eagle boats and converted yachts and fourteen British armed trawlers. The Royal Air Force refused to release to us some American-built bomber planes that were all ready to be flown across; but by way of compensation, the Royal Navy lent the United States Navy 22 converted trawlers, complete with officers and men, who had had much experience combating U-boats in British waters.[26] These rugged little coal-burners, manned with tough, aggressive former merchant seamen, were a great help in the Eastern and Gulf Sea Frontiers.

[24] Eastern Sea Frontier War Diary.
[25] Same.
[26] The trawlers arrived about 1 Mar.

The total score of Allied, American and neutral merchant vessels sunk in the North Atlantic in January 1942, between our coast and the Western Approaches to the British Isles,[27] was 58; only three of these were in transatlantic convoys. The tonnage lost was 307,059 gross, of which 132,348 tons consisted of tankers of 5000 to 12,000 tons each; the rest were mostly cargo vessels of 75 to 9626 tons each.[28] In February, the score was almost identical for the same area; but the sinkings in the Eastern Sea Frontier alone passed the 100,000 tons mark, and new danger zones were added: east coast of Florida, and, in the latter half of the month, the Caribbean. Off the coast between New York and Florida shipping was so plentiful in the first two months of 1942, and so defenseless, that U-boats were able to husband their torpedoes for selective shots, letting ships in ballast pass unscathed in favor of a heavily laden freighter or tanker. *U-578* had the good luck to sink the patrolling destroyer *Jacob Jones* off the Delaware Capes on the last day of February. She was hit by two enemy torpedoes when proceeding southward alone on a calm moonlight night, and sank almost immediately, taking down all her officers and the great majority of the crew.

Along the Eastern Sea Frontier a few of the defensive measures that will be described in Chapter X began to take effect about April 1942. Owing to the prevalence of night attacks by submarines, coastwise vessels were ordered to anchor overnight in Chesapeake or Delaware Bays, and a mined and protected anchorage was provided for them behind Cape Lookout. Charleston, South Carolina, lay within twelve hours' steaming distance from Cape Lookout; consequently, a vessel could make Jacksonville from New York in about four daylight runs; eastbound shipping from New York was routed by Long Island Sound and Cape Cod Canal. This "bucket brigade" system, as Admiral Andrews called it, re-

[27] Including Canadian Coastal Zone (12 ships), Eastern Sea Frontier (14), North Atlantic Convoy Areas (10) and Bermuda Area (9). See chart.

[28] Figures from Fleet Operations Statistical Section, Navy Department, dated June and July 1945. The Truman Committee Report, No. 10 part 18 p. 3 states that the prewar fleet of U. S. merchant tankers numbered 350.

duced the possible losses, but the aggregate loss increased: 28 vessels of 159,340 tons sunk in March by U-boats in the Eastern Sea Frontier alone; 15 more of 92,321 tons in the Gulf and Caribbean areas, with an aggregate of 86 vessels and almost half a million gross tons for the entire Atlantic. The coastline from Wilmington, North Carolina, to Norfolk continued to be the scene of numerous sinkings; submarines lay off Diamond Shoals buoy "pickin' 'em off"; at least three U-boats maintained a patrol off Cape Hatteras, lying on the bottom in shoal water by day and hunting at night. Of the total tonnage sunk in March in the coastal and Caribbean areas, 57 per cent were tankers.

Some of the details of these sinkings, especially of the tankers, are pitiful to relate: oil scum ignited by signal flares on life preservers, men knocked out by cork life preservers, attempting to swim in a heavy viscous layer of fuel oil, and ducking to avoid flames. Tanker *O. A. Knudsen* was attacked three times in twelve hours off Hole-in-the-Wall, Bahamas, and finally sunk by two U-boats without her radio distress signals having attracted a single rescue vessel or plane. The loaded tanker *Gulftrade* was torpedoed and sunk two miles off Barnegat, only 300 yards from a Coast Guard cutter. Chilean freighter *Tolten* was torpedoed and sunk 30 miles off Ambrose Channel, New York, and only one man survived. A tugboat and three barges, shelled by *U–574*, sank the night of 31 March–1 April off Cape Charles and there were only two survivors from the tug; the same night, tanker *Tiger* was sunk off Cape Henry when maneuvering to pick up a pilot; on the following night, between Cape Charles and Cape Henlopen, the unarmed collier *David H. Atwater* was sunk by a submarine's gunfire at a range of about 600 yards. Her crew of 27, given no opportunity to abandon ship, were riddled by machine-gun fire; only three men survived.[29]

[29] The *Atwater*, about which there was an unusual amount of "scuttlebutt," was sunk at 2122 Apr. 2; approximate position lat. 37°46′ N, long. 75°05′ W. Her master had disregarded instructions and sailed from the Chesapeake in the afternoon, hence could not make the run to the Delaware Capes by nightfall. Two patrolling destroyers arrived on the scene at 2400, but *U–552* had already steamed off.

In a few instances there is suspicion of collusive sinkings. S.S. *Hanseat* of Panama registry was sunk on 9 March near the Windward Passage. The crew abandoned ship at invitation of the *U–126* commander before the attack; German officers boarded her and obtained confidential communications; and the crew later admitted that this was the third ship lost by them in that manner. *U–126* had been accused of firing on lifeboats earlier.

Among the ineffective measures taken to protect shipping, because the newspapers were demanding that something must be done, and because Admiral Andrews wished to try it, was an attempt at anti-submarine patrol by destroyers. This method had proved to be futile in World War I, when President Wilson called it "hunting the hornets all over the farm." [30] It was revived in early February 1942, when Commander Eastern Sea Frontier asked for fifteen destroyers and got seven. A typical anti-submarine patrol was that of U.S.S. *Hambleton* and *Emmons*. At 2000 April 1 they sailed from New York southward, steaming about one or two miles to seaward of the shipping lanes. The following afternoon a Norwegian freighter in sight a few miles ahead signaled that she saw two submarines. The destroyers speeded up and were promptly fired on by the "squarehead" gun crew, who had mistaken them for U-boats. After dark the destroyers searched two suspicious-looking craft, which proved to be friendly. They received a submarine-sighting report from an American tanker and searched the area, but made no contacts. Next, they patrolled between Wimble Shoal and Cape Lookout, frequently hearing reports of U-boats and making futile searches. At 0208 April 5 they received a message that S.S. *Bidwell* had been torpedoed, reached the position in forty minutes, searched the area until daylight, but made no contact; for as yet no scientific method of search to regain sound contact with a submarine had been worked out. If visibility was good, any alert U-boat commander could sight a destroyer before

[30] Elting E. Morison *Admiral Sims* p. 361. The same method had been tried against raiders by the Royal Navy at the beginning of the present war, with almost equal lack of success. Naval vessels are proved to be many times as effective against submarines or raiders when on escort duty, as they are patrolling.

A few moments after the torpedo hit, before lowering lifeboats

The sinking vessel completely hidden by smoke from burning oil

Tanker Byron D. Benson, *Sunk off Cape Hatteras, 5 April 1942*

Dixie Arrow, broken amidships by torpedo hit, off Hatteras, 26 March 1942

Santore, holed by mine off Chesapeake capes, rolls over and sinks, 17 June 194

Sinking Tanker and Collier

her sound gear picked him up, and easily evade her, especially off Hatteras where deep water comes close to shore. United States destroyers were then so ill-fitted for search and so imperfectly trained for attack that to use them as a roving patrol was worse than useless; it resulted only in the loss of *Jacob Jones.*

b. Gulf Sea Frontier

The Gulf Sea Frontier,[31] organized 6 February 1942 with headquarters at Key West,[32] was responsible for the protection of the Florida Coast and Straits, most of the Bahamas, the entire Gulf of Mexico, the Yucatan Channel and most of Cuba. Available defense forces were the small converted yacht *Carnelian,* two 165-foot Coast Guard cutters (*Nike* and *Nemesis*), one 125-foot cutter (*Vigilant*), and, in emergency, the craft used for instruction at the Key West Sound School. Air protection consisted of nineteen unarmed Coast Guard planes at various stations, fourteen O–47 Army observation planes based at Miami, armed only with .30-caliber machine guns; and two old Army medium bombers (B–18s) at Miami that were "practically falling apart."

The first U-boat known to enter this frontier, *U–128,* signaled her presence on 19 February 1942 by sinking tanker *Pan Massachusetts* about forty miles SE of Cape Canaveral. Two more ships were sunk on the 21st by the *U–504,* also in the area, and one on the 22nd. But this was merely the beginning, unfortunately for the ill-

[31] Commander Gulf Sea Frontier was always same person as Commandant Seventh Naval District, the one being conceived as an operational and the other (as well as the Eighth Naval District in New Orleans) as an administrative command.

[32] Removed to Miami 17 June 1942. Capt. Russell S. Crenshaw, Commandant Seventh Naval District, was Commander Gulf Sea Frontier until 3 June when Rear Admiral James L. Kauffman was relieved from his Icelandic command to take charge of the Gulf Sea Frontier. Information here given on Gulf Sea Frontier was obtained at Miami in Feb. 1944, through the courtesy of the Commander, Rear Admiral William R. Munroe, Capt. F. R. Doyle, Chief of Staff, and the historian, Lt. (jg) John A. Reynolds USNR. Lt. Reynolds in his "History Gulf Sea Frontier" (of the "Administrative History" series) states that the frontier hardly existed as a command functioning independent of the Seventh Naval District until mid-May 1942.

prepared frontier. Estimates of the situation varied all the way from the comfortable belief that no submarines would venture within the Gulf, to the expectation of a commando raid by ten to twenty submarines to land saboteurs in some Gulf port. Key West was an unsuitable place for frontier headquarters, being connected to the mainland only by a bridge and causeway road which luckily no U-boat attempted to breach with gunfire. Communications were very bad. If a submarine was sighted off Palm Beach, and Commander Gulf Sea Frontier was notified at Key West, he had to communicate by commercial telephone with the Third Army Bomber Command at Charleston, South Carolina, and request the Army planes based at Miami to begin a search. Liaison was effected early in March with the Governor of the Bahamas, which brought a few Royal Air Force planes into the defense picture.

A large field of 3460 mines, laid between 24 April and 2 May 1942, surrounded the anchorage on the Gulf side of Key West, and afforded good protection to what later became a convoy assemblage point. But it had many disadvantages. Westbound shipping had to steam an additional 18 to 20 hours from south of Key West around Rebecca Shoals before making the mine field entrance, which was so difficult to navigate that during the first ten weeks of its operation U.S.S. *Sturtevant* and three merchantmen fouled mines and were sunk.[33]

A new type of U-boat activity which commenced in May off Newfoundland, and extended into the Eastern, Gulf and Caribbean Sea Frontiers, was the sowing of mines off seaports, in the hope of catching ships entering or departing.[34] The only serious casualties suffered from this cause were inflicted by some of the 15 mines laid by *U–701* in the ship channel to the Chesapeake Capes on 12 June 1942. An explosion under a tanker betrayed the presence of this field. Before the mines could be swept up, one tanker, one

[33] Lt. Reynolds "History Gulf Sea Frontier" I 227. *Sturtevant* was sunk 26 Apr. 1942 with loss of 30 men. Three merchant ships fouled mines and were sunk between 15 June and 2 July 1942.

[34] Information from Mine Warfare Operational Research Group, Navy Dept. See Table in Appendix IV.

coal barge and a British armed trawler had been sunk; destroyer *Bainbridge* and a second tanker slightly damaged.

Of the eleven enemy mine fields laid during 1942 one more called itself to our attention by sinking a tugboat; five were promptly discovered and swept up, before doing any damage, by "bird" class sweepers of Service Force Atlantic Fleet and small motor minesweepers attached to the naval districts;[35] and the four others were so badly laid, or the mines so ineffective, that their existence was first made known from German records at the end of the war. Whenever a mine field was discovered the neighboring harbors were closed and shipping was diverted until sweeping operations were completed. New York was closed only once for this reason during the entire war.[36]

The Germans apparently did not find this activity very profitable. Two of the minelaying submarines, *U-701* and *U-166*, were sunk by aircraft attack shortly after "laying eggs," and two others were caught by British forces within three months.[37] After 10 November, no more enemy mines were laid off the American coast until 1 June 1943, when a fresh offensive began.

The enemy did not move into the Gulf Sea Frontier in any force until Admiral Doenitz realized that the organization of coastal convoys along the Eastern Sea Frontier and other defense measures in that area made a southward shift of U-boats desirable. In May 1942, losses in the Gulf Sea Frontier jumped to 41 ships of 219,867 gross tons, almost double the Eastern Sea Frontier losses in April. Of this loss, 55 per cent was tanker tonnage,[38] which made it all the worse.

It would have been worse still but for the augmented defense

[35] The sweeper section base for the Chesapeake was at Little Creek, Virginia; this was occasionally helped by school ships of the Naval Mine Warfare school, Yorktown.

[36] Two days in Nov. 1942. The other closures in 1942 were Chesapeake Bay, three days; Jacksonville, Charleston and Savannah, three days; Wilmington and Charleston, eight days; Castries (St. Lucia), six days.

[37] See Appendix IV.

[38] Figures from Fleet Operations Statistical Section, Navy Department, dated June and July 1945.

forces at the disposal of the frontier commander. By 1 April 1942, in addition to the three Coast Guard cutters and *Carnelian*, the O–47s and the B–18s, the frontier had two more converted yachts (*Coral* and *Emerald*), two 125-foot-class cutters (*Boutwell* and *Woodbury*), four 165-foot cutters (*Triton, Pandora, Thetis, Galatea*), two 4-piper destroyers (*Semmes*[39] and *Dahlgren*), one Fleet Air Detachment located at Naval Air Station Miami and a few more Army aircraft there and at West Palm Beach. During the May–June blitz the frontier acquired sixteen 83-foot and other small Coast Guard cutters, five PCs and SCs, two motor minesweepers, former yacht *Onyx* and eleven "Yippies" (YPs), patrol craft converted from motor boats. From that time until 1944 the air and surface defenses of the frontier were steadily increased until they were more than adequate.

By traveling at night surfaced and submerging during daylight hours, the U-boats bucked the Stream through the Straits of Florida into the Gulf or else chose the Windward Passage – Yucatan Channel route. One of their most fruitful hunting grounds in May and June 1942 was right off the Passes of the Mississippi. S.S. *Alcoa Puritan*, carrying bauxite from Trinidad to Mobile, was only 75 miles SSE of the Passes and 100 miles from her destination on 6 May when torpedoed and sunk. The U-boat commander shouted to the survivors on their rafts, "Sorry I had to do it. Hope you make it in." With the help of *Boutwell*, they did. At the end of that day Cominch declared the Gulf and the Florida Straits to be a danger zone in which no merchant ships could steam unescorted. Tanker *Eastern Sun* dodged three torpedoes off the Passes, and after her Naval Armed Guard had fired one round, the U-boat made off. Near that spot on 13 May, tanker *Gulf Penn*, escorted by a patrol bomber, was sunk in two minutes. The submarine had lain in wait for her in a patch of muddy water. And a second tanker, *David McKelvey*, was sunk in the same area before midnight. At almost the same moment a Mexican tanker named

[39] Relieved by *Noa* 18 April. All three destroyers were attached to the Key West Sound school, but were frequently called upon for anti-submarine duty.

Portrero del Llano was torpedoed and sunk near Miami, eight miles SSE of Fowey Rocks. As Mexico was still neutral the *Portrero* was brilliantly illuminated and her flag spotlighted; but that did not save her, and only nine of her crew were rescued;[40] cutter *Nike*, three PCs and a number of patrol bombers searched for the submarine in vain. Tanker *Mercury Sun*, with a load of precious fuel oil for Pearl Harbor from Beaumont, Texas, was sunk by three torpedoes off Cape Corrientes, Cuba, on 19 May; the master and five others were killed. The Navy Section Base at Burwood, at the junction of the Passes, had nothing in the way of surface craft capable of driving a submarine down.

Before the Gulf blitz began, Admiral Ingersoll had sent two destroyers, *Noa* and *Dahlgren*, to patrol in the frontier, but they never had more than one chance to develop a contact properly, and their attack on that occasion was unsuccessful. They were dispatched hither and yon with the same desperate but futile zeal that attended the Eastern Sea Frontier patrol. For instance, the destroyer *Dallas*, released from Sound School duties for patrol when the blitz struck in, sighted a submarine off Miami on 7 May. She closed to attack with gunfire, and when the U-boat submerged, depth-charged it; but while still engaged in developing this contact she was diverted to help a plane keep down another submarine supposedly damaged the previous day, and lying on the bottom. That "contact" turned out to be a wreck.

It must not be supposed that the Navy sat with folded hands while these things went on. Every submarine spotted was hunted; but the hunters, few in number, had not yet acquired the necessary technique to kill. Between 8 and 10 May, the following measures were taken: A night patrol by a radar-equipped Catalina was established between Cape Canaveral and Fowey Rocks. A squadron of Hudson bombers was sent to base in Jacksonville, and six Mitchell patrol bombers (B–25s) were staged in to Miami. Merchantmen were routed from the Canal to New Orleans through the Old Bahama Channel, past Key West, and along the Florida West

[40] Mexico decided to declare war on Germany shortly after.

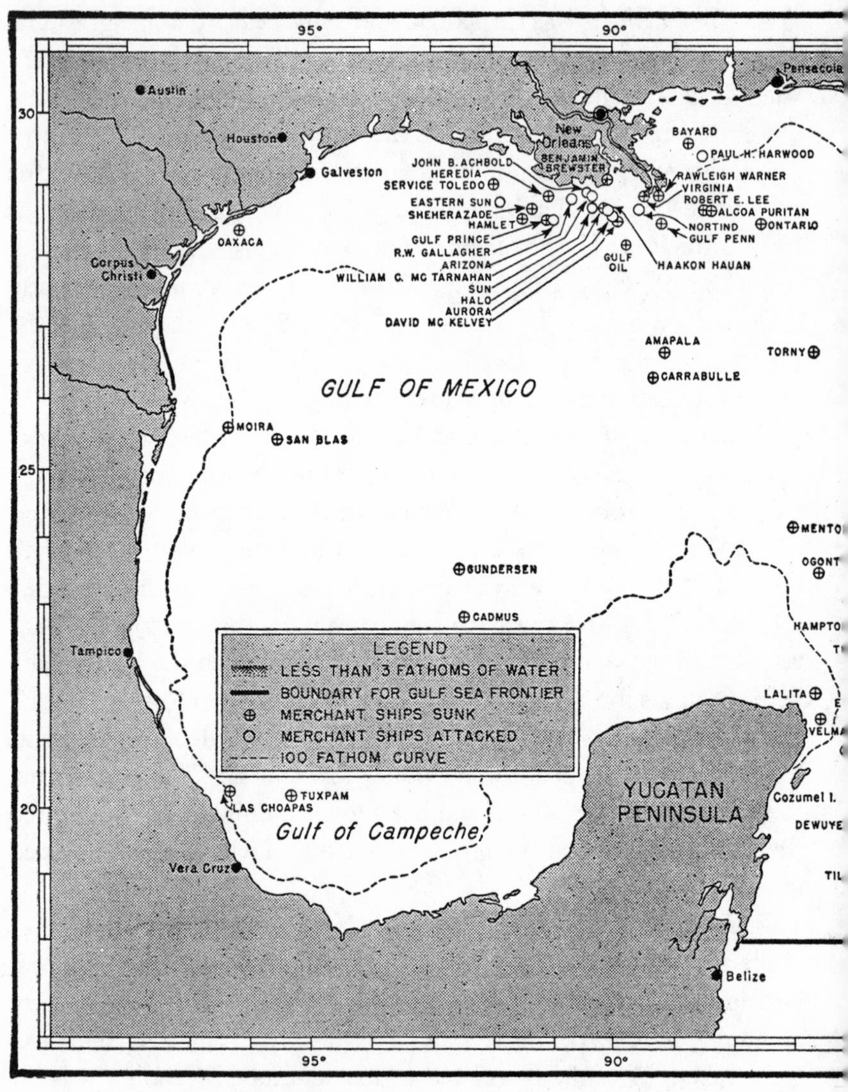

Coast; several of those sunk in the Yucatan Channel, or between there and the Passes, had disregarded routing orders. A detachment of B–25s was sent to Havana, to patrol the Yucatan Channel, and preparations were made to take over the San Julian airfield near Cape San Antonio and to build an airfield on Grand Cayman for

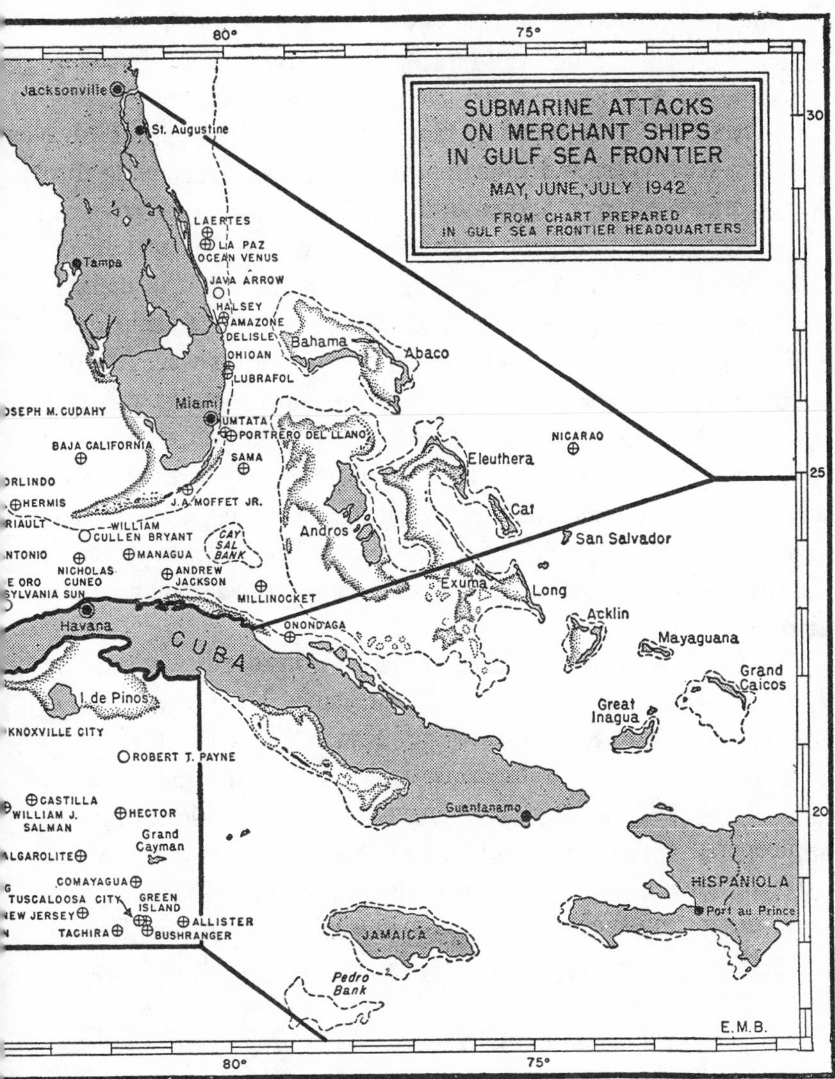

these and future anti-submarine planes to operate from. The Yucatan Channel patrol began on 21 May, and on the very next day the S.S. *Pablo*, pursued by a U-boat off Cozumel, received a plain message from San Julian that a bomber was coming to her assistance; the submarine apparently got the message too, for it broke off gunfire and disappeared. On 18 May, as we have seen, the dim-out was belatedly enforced along the Florida East Coast, where the bright lights and neon signs of the beach resorts had been competing unsuccessfully with burning tankers. The newly organized New York–Key West and Guantanamo convoys were passing through this area every day, and enjoying a relative immunity from attack.

Unescorted merchant shipping received the full weight of this U-boat blitz, which gave the Gulf Sea Frontier the melancholy distinction of having the most sinkings in May (41 ships, 219,867 gross tons) of any area in any month during this war. All this was wrought by not more than six submarines operating at one time; not more than two, most of the time; and the sad thing is that at least half these sinkings might have been prevented by the measures later adopted – coastal convoys for all merchantmen, and adequate air coverage. For at this period U-boats were in deathly fear of aircraft, and usually submerged at the sight of even a small unarmed Civil Air Patrol plane.

The Gulf Sea Frontier forces were considerably stimulated by the appointment of Rear Admiral James L. Kauffman as commander on 3 June 1942. "Reggie" Kauffman,[41] who had had plenty of experience with submarines in his Iceland command, believed that the best way to sink them was by organized killer groups of properly equipped ships and planes that would go out on any favorable contact and stick to it until they scored. He lost no time in organizing such a group from the frontier craft at his disposal, and between 10 and 13 June they enjoyed a memorable and successful hunt.[42]

It began with a report that the steamship *Hagan* had been torpedoed at lat. 22° N, long. 77°30′ W in the Old Bahama Channel

[41] James Laurence Kauffman, b. Miamisburg, Ohio 1887, Naval Academy '08. Served in destroyer *Barney* in World War I, Bureau of Engineering and staff duty 1920–26, member Naval Mission to Brazil, exec. U.S.S. *Texas* 1931, Naval War College course 1933–34, C.O. *Memphis* 1936, Captain Mare Island Navy Yard 1938, Comdesrons 30 and 7, 1940–41, Com N.O.B. Iceland 1 Nov. 1941; member Allied A/S Bd. Feb. 1943; Com DDs and Cruisers Pac. Fleet Jan.–Oct. 1944; Com Phil S. F. to end of war; Com Four 1946; ret. 1949.

[42] War Diary and files Gulf Sea Frontier; conversations with participants.

north of Cuba, on the night of 10 June. Within three hours of this event an Army radar-equipped B–18 out of Miami was patrolling over the spot. At 0628 June 11 it made contact, missed a surfaced U-boat with its bombs, and then returned to base to fuel. At 0755 a Pan American plane sighted the U-boat surfaced on a westerly course, four miles from the last attack position. Relief airplanes were soon patrolling this area.

In the meantime Admiral Kauffman with exemplary energy mobilized all available surface craft. He sent a group of PCs from Key West to form search line in the Nicholas Channel, another from Miami to form search line in the Santarem Channel, U.S.S. *Noa* to seek out the enemy in Old Bahama Channel, *Dahlgren* to patrol the southeast tip of Salt Cay Bank, and *Greer* to close the eastern entrance to Old Bahama Channel. Most of these ships were on station by the late afternoon of 11 June. Each was given constant daylight air coverage, except during a longish thunderstorm, and two radar-equipped B–18's were kept on night patrol. Yet *U–157*, the hunted submarine, succeeded in eluding everything and everybody by sneaking close along the Cuban shore. It was well on the way to a landfall on the Florida Keys when picked up by the radar of a B–18 at 2250 June 12 in lat. 23°36′ N, long. 81°27′ W. The plane attacked unsuccessfully and its radio conked out, so it had to return to base to make the contact report. But at 0200 June 13 another B–18 was dispatched to the predicted position of the U-boat (lat. 24° N, long. 81°40′ W), followed shortly by *Noa*, *Dahlgren* and several PCs. This plane sighted the submarine at the predicted position at 0305, and again at 0520; but it escaped by a prompt dive.

Four planes without radar relieved the B–18 at 0700 June 13. One, an Army A–29, sighted the periscope at 1330 and the *U–157* itself just under the surface at 1430. By this time the Key West surface killer group had reached the area and was searching. Cutter *Thetis*, Lieutenant (jg) N. C. McCormick USCG, made sound contact at 1550 and attacked with seven depth charges, and each of the other five ships made one or more attacks with three to eight depth charges each. Weather conditions were highly favorable and evidence of damage was recovered in the shape of two pairs of pants and an empty tube "Made in Germany." *Noa* arrived at 2015 June 13 to find these vessels milling around and making so much wake that sound contact was impossible. They were ordered to withdraw and form search line, while *Noa* made a sound sweep. No contact was obtained and the search was broken off next morning in confidence that a kill had been made.

Thetis actually did sink that submarine, the *U-157*. Everybody enjoyed the hunt and it paid dividends in training and morale; but the experiment was not repeated for two reasons. The large number of air and surface craft that could be employed on nothing else for several days left shipping unprotected, and it was believed that better results could be obtained, whenever enough escorts were available, by attaching support or killer groups to escort units. That was generally done on transatlantic convoys beginning in the spring of 1943.

c. Caribbean

On the sixteenth of February, U-boats began working the Caribbean – Operation "Neuland." It continued through September. With devilish economy, Admiral Doenitz concentrated on two particularly soft spots – the Dutch islands of Curaçao and Aruba, where over half a million barrels of gasoline and oil derivatives were produced daily; and Trinidad, through or by which most of our shipping to and from South America, and all the bauxite trade, had to pass. Thirty-one ships of 154,779 gross tons were sunk within the Caribbean Sea Frontier (west) in February and March 1942; 41 ships of 198,034 tons in April and May; 42 ships of 218,623 tons in June and July. During June, German submarines disposed of more shipping in the Gulf of Mexico, the Caribbean and their approaches than they had sunk the world over during any month previous to 1942.

Rear Admiral John H. Hoover, Commander Caribbean Sea

Frontier at San Juan, had to do the best he could with even less than most sea frontier commanders.[43] And he was burdened by the necessity of keeping constant watch on the French in Martinique and Guadeloupe. His sea frontier was very decentralized; the commandants at Guantanamo, Curaçao and Trinidad by necessity were given almost complete responsibility for defense in their respective areas.

U-boats showed the utmost insolence in the Caribbean, their happiest hunting ground. At Aruba, where one Dutch motor whaleboat, three 7½-inch coast defense guns and a few Army Air Force medium bombers defended the valuable oil industry with its radiating tankers, a submarine shelled a shore refinery on 16 February 1942. On the same day a determined and costly attack was made on the specially designed light-draft tankers that carried oil from Lake Maracaibo to the islands, and on seagoing tankers just departing; six in all were sunk. *U-161* entered Castries Harbor, St. Lucia, at night on 10 March, torpedoed the Canadian passenger steamer *Lady Nelson* and a cargo vessel that were lying, brilliantly lighted, alongside the dock; but fortunately failed to see a blacked-out American tanker in the same harbor. The same U-boat had sneaked into the Gulf of Paria on 18 February. That night *Kapitänleutnant* Albrecht Achilles torpedoed two big ships at anchor off Port of Spain. "Ajax," as this bold bantam-weight skipper was known, then steamed out fully surfaced and showing running lights.

A glance at the map will show the peculiar strategic importance of Trinidad, "Land of the Hummingbird." [44] It blocks off the Gulf of Paria, an inland sea which, if properly protected, becomes the ideal center for handling an immense flow of traffic between the Atlantic and Gulf ports of the United States and the Guianas, Brazil, the River Plate and Africa. Tanker traffic between the

[43] Destroyers *Blakeley* and *Barney*, two Eagle boats of World War I, three S-class submarines and 12 Catalinas of Patrol Squadron 12 with their tender *Lapwing*.

[44] Much of the data that follow were derived from local N.O.B. files and from conversations with various officers at Port of Spain, Trinidad, in Nov. and Dec. 1943, and from a memorandum "Establishment of the U. S. Naval Operating Base Trinidad," compiled 1 April 1943 by Lt. K. S. Wales.

Dutch West Indies and Europe or Africa passes the same way. Itself the seat of an oil industry, Trinidad also protects the oil fields of the San Juan River of Venezuela and acts as a clearing-house for bauxite, an ore essential for the manufacture of aluminum, and so for airplane construction. The bauxite mines in British and Dutch Guiana were situated up the Demerara, Berbice, Cottica and Surinam Rivers, at the mouths of which were bars that admitted a maximum draft of 17 feet. In order to augment the small fleet of British and Dutch bauxite ships, ore carriers from the Great Lakes were tied to this trade route; and as most of these could not load to capacity because of the river bars, it was economical for them to terminate their outward voyages at Port of Spain, where they filled their holds from smaller ships that maintained a shuttle service between Trinidad and the Guianas. Already important at the opening of the war in Europe, Trinidad gradually built up until in 1943 it was one of the world's greatest centers of sea traffic.

The right to establish ground facilities for naval, army and air bases in Trinidad had been ceded to the United States as part of the original destroyer-naval base deal of 2 September 1940. Rear Admiral J. W. Greenslade selected sites in January 1941; civil engineers of the Navy, headed by Lieutenant Commander C. P. Conrad USNR, arrived shortly; 99-year leases were signed in April and the work was under way in May 1941. The original plans provided only for a naval air station near Port of Spain and an Army base in the interior, but it was soon decided to expand the naval air station into a naval operating base for which additional land was acquired. N.O.B. Trinidad was commissioned 1 August 1941, with Captain A. W. Radford USN as commanding officer. Forests had to be cleared, swamps drained, and thousands of natives had to be moved off the land and relocated. A tremendous amount of work was accomplished in a short time. But on the date of Pearl Harbor, N.O.B. Trinidad was still almost undefended. For ships there were the 500-ton converted yachts *Opal* and *Turquoise*, two yard-patrol craft (*YP-63* and *-64*); for planes, four Catalinas of Squadron VP-31 with their seaplane tender and one utility transport; for personnel, one Marine officer, eleven naval officers, sixty bluejackets and about a hundred Marines. The local defense force, small, weak and inefficient, had accomplished very little to prepare the area for war.[45] The United States Army, however, was already present in considerable force. Its commanding officer, Brigadier General Ralph Talbot, outranked Captain Radford and so became head of the unified Trinidad Sector and Base Command.[46]

During the first few months of the war the chief concern of this command was to push construction. The seaplane ramp at Carenage, for instance, was not ready until 8 February 1942. Completion was delayed by enemy activities, such as the sinking of a freighter that was bringing two million dollars' worth of radio, telephone and telegraph equipment to Port of Spain. The establishment of proper communications was held up by this loss, and also by the old native custom of converting telephone wire to domestic uses.

Although the first sinking off Trinidad occurred practically in the harbor on the night of 18–19 February, almost two months passed before a protective mine field could be laid off Port of Spain, and the mining of the deep Bocas with their swift currents presented so many problems that they were not stopped up until June, 1943. Sea frontiers and naval districts nearer home naturally had the first call on such mines, planes and small craft as were available. Yet, with the two converted yachts, two "Yippies," and four Catalinas, N.O.B. Trinidad joined with the equally poverty-stricken section base at Curaçao in establishing convoys between these two vital points. The Army Air Force in June sent planes to base at Trinidad, on the Zandery airfield in Dutch Guiana, the Atkinson airfield in British Guiana and at Curaçao.[47] The arrival of a 110-foot subchaser (*SC-453*), first vessel of the "Humming-

[45] The writer speaks from experience. Three months after the war began in Europe he made landfall at Galeota Point in a sailing vessel, anchored for the night off the oil fields on the south coast of Trinidad, passed through the Boca de la Sierpe, and entered Port of Spain without being boarded, spoken, or even reported. Had he been a German raider he might have landed without opposition and destroyed the oil industry.

[46] Relieved by Maj. Gen. H. C. Pratt USA 12 Jan. 1942.

[47] Monthly Plane Availability Reports, Caribbean Sea Frontier.

bird Navy" to be equipped with sound gear, was an event comparable to the addition of an *Essex* class carrier to the Pacific Fleet.

Nowhere in the Navy was there a finer example of doing the best you could with the little you had than at N.O.B. Trinidad. Rear Admiral Jesse B. Oldendorf who, as commandant, arrived from Curaçao on 2 July,[48] proved a tower of strength. For chief of staff, he chose an Army officer of great tact, energy and ability, Brigadier General Charles F. Born USA. Between them they ironed out every incipient Army–Navy conflict, and ran military activities as one team, with flexibility and intelligence. "Oley" and "Charley" were an inspiration to their subordinates; and the naval personnel worked themselves ragged to "keep the ships sailing."

Until the Key West–Trinidad convoys were organized in July, the efforts of these few planes and ships were largely rescue operations. They brought in literally hundreds of survivors from torpedoed ships. Few planes or ships patrolling outside the Bocas failed to sight a burning or sinking merchantman. Seaplanes were often forced to expend their bombs before returning, in order to come down and rescue torpedoed seamen. *SC–453* and the yachts and "Yippies" would dash into Port of Spain, land survivors, take on fuel and water, and depart immediately on another patrol. The shore crews never refused a repair job, worked all night in the tropical summer, worked until their officers had to order them to lay off. At one time *YP–219* had been "robbed of all her engines except the blocks" to repair the others. There was no time to train, only to do.

d. Off the Canal Entrance[49]

The Panama Sea Frontier, the only one with a foot in each ocean, had a task baffling in its complexity. Relatively speaking,

[48] Relieving Capt. Thomas Moran USN.

[49] This account is based on a study of Panama Sea Frontier files and on conversations and correspondence with participants.

it was less well provided with means than the Eastern, the Gulf and the Caribbean frontiers. On the Pacific side it extended from the Mexico–Guatemala boundary and out around the Galapagos Islands to latitude 5° S on the West Coast of South America. On the Atlantic side, with which we are here concerned, this frontier included the coast from the Mexico–British Honduras boundary on the Yucatan Peninsula to Punta de Gallinas, Colombia, about 90 miles west of Aruba. The boundary between the Panama and Caribbean Sea Frontiers ran from the Yucatan Peninsula along latitude 18°05′ N to longitude 80°27′ W (a point about 85 miles SSE of the Grand Cayman) and thence to Punta de Gallinas. Thus, this frontier covered British Honduras, the Caribbean shores of Guatemala, Honduras, Nicaragua, Costa Rica, Panama and Colombia. And the prime, overriding and ruling responsibility of this sea frontier was defense of the Panama Canal.

That, too, was a responsibility of the United States Army, Panama Canal Command; and because the Army had supervised the digging of the Canal and administered the Canal Zone, the Commandant 15th Naval District and Commander Panama Sea Frontier (who since 15 April 1942 had been Rear Admiral Clifford E. Van Hook) was inferior in the chain of command to the Commanding General, Lieutenant General Frank Andrews. While the Army protected the Canal from sabotage or land and air attack, the Navy was charged with defense of the sea approaches in both oceans, and of merchant and combat shipping in either direction and in transit. Until about 1944, United States military and naval authorities estimated that the principal menace to the Canal would be Japanese. They were constantly on their guard against Japanese submarine or carrier raids on the Pacific end, and most of the few available naval forces were deployed in that direction. Moreover, an attack on the northern end of the Canal would require a deep penetration of the Caribbean by U-boats, a passage of the Lesser or Greater Antilles, and of the forces deployed by the Caribbean Sea Frontier; while the Pacific end had no such outer line of defense.

This sea frontier also had to cope with a difficult political and espionage situation. The Panama Canal naturally attracted a flock of enemy agents; and local posts of Franco's Falange, centers of Axis propaganda, were in every town. The pro-German president of the Republic of Panama, Dr. Anulfo Arias, who had been endeavoring to turn his country into a little brother to the Axis, had been replaced by the loyal President De la Guardia only a month before Pearl Harbor; but his party continued to plot for his return, and so for the enemy. German planters and storekeepers were spotted along the coastline, especially on the Gulf of Darien, and as traders and mahogany cutters among the Miskito and Jicaque Indians; Panama had wisely kept them out of the Gulf of San Blas. Guatemalan foreign trade was largely in the hands of a German bank. Italian naval officers had made a careful survey of every river, creek and estuary on the coast between the Bay Islands and Cape Gracias á Dios in the summer of 1939, and acquired the support of the local commandant at Puerto Castilla, Honduras. The governments of the Central American republics were officially friendly but still somewhat dubious as to who would win the war, and anxious not to offend the Axis irrevocably. In any case, they had no means to supervise their isolated coasts.[50] They had no navies or vessels capable of even inshore patrol; thus, except for sporadic help from the meager Honduran Air Force during the first eight months after Pearl Harbor, the entire burden of their defense fell on the United States Navy.

One of the Navy's most exasperating tasks in this frontier was the investigation of rumors that enemy submarines were using Central America for refueling. Stories were constantly coming in of local schooners taking drummed diesel oil out to U-boats; but not one is based on sufficient evidence for an historian (who requires much less evidence than a court of law) to credit; nor, so far, has evidence of it been found in German records. It is highly probable,

[50] The entire Caribbean coast of the Republic of Panama, outside the Canal Zone, in 1942 was served only by local roads and trails; in order to reach the coastal settlements it was necessary to go by sea, and in many of them nothing larger than a canoe could get across the bar. The same applies to the greater part of Costa Rica, Honduras, Nicaragua, and to Colombia west of Cartagena.

however, that local Germans or the descendants of buccaneers who inhabited the Bay Islands sent out fresh provisions to the U-boats in small craft. The frontier was constantly being needled on the subject of fueling from Washington; and it was necessary as a precaution to employ several small naval vessels in searching every river mouth, reef-protected anchorage or mangrove-lined creek where a U-boat might possibly hide out or procure drummed fuel.

Enemy submarines entered only the outer edges of this sea frontier before the second week of June 1942. That was a favorable moment for attack. Admiral Van Hook had at his disposal only one division of old four-stack destroyers, *Borie*, *Barry*, *Tattnall* and *Goff;* tugboat *Woodcock*, 6-inch gunboat *Erie*, two PCs, two small converted motor yachts for surface patrol and local escort on the Caribbean side, as well as Patrol Wing 3, consisting of 24 Catalinas with their tenders, for the air patrol of both coasts.[51] In view of the Japanese attacks on the Aleutians and Midway during the first week of June, the frontier had to expect a carrier or submarine raid at Balboa on the Pacific side, and its most watchful care was extended in that direction. Reinforcements for the Pacific Fleet were constantly passing through the Canal; on 10 June, for instance, an important task force comprising battleship *North Carolina*, carrier *Wasp*, cruisers *Quincy* and *San Juan* and seven destroyers.

Late in the night of 9 June S.S. *Merrimack* carrying military stores to the Isthmus was torpedoed and sunk by *U-68* south of Yucatan Channel, about 60 miles off Cozumel Island. Destroyer *Borie* was sent thither to recover survivors and search for the submarine. On the 10th and 11th two merchant vessels were torpedoed and sunk near Swan Island, three near Old Providence and St. Andrews Islands, and one within 85 miles of the Canal entrance at Colon, when under escort of gunboat *Erie*, which never made a contact. The submarine that did this damage was *U-159*. On these two days, *Erie* was the only combat vessel available for hunting

[51] Panama Sea Frontier Task Organization, 1 June 1942. Gunboat *Niagara* was detached 5 June, and *Borie* departed same day to escort two British ships to Key West. A fifth destroyer, *J. Fred Talbott*, was under overhaul.

U-boats, and she was completely unsuccessful. The four destroyers were on offshore patrol, but as they were not yet equipped with radar, the submarines had no trouble in evading them, as indeed had been the case with destroyer patrols along the Eastern Sea Frontier. *U-159* sank two more merchantmen right off the Canal on the 13th. *U-504*, *U-172* and *U-161* were also in the area.

Admiral Van Hook ordered the port of Cristobal closed to outbound traffic on 13 June, stationed all the small craft equipped with depth charges in the offshore patrol areas, and next day organized a "killer group" – composed of destroyer *Edison*, which had just escorted a naval tanker into Cristobal, destroyer *Barry* (just pulled in from patrol), three motor torpedo boats which were en route to the Pacific and sundry PBYs – to go get a submarine sighted by an Army plane about 80 miles north of Colon.

So fortuitous a collection of uncoördinated craft which had never been together before was a mere travesty of a killer group, but the best that the frontier could organize. *Edison*, even by bending on 35 knots, could not reach the position until several hours after the contact. One Army and two Navy planes flew out to help her, but were able to communicate only by arm signals and soon departed after dropping their bombs, apparently, on a cloud shadow. As the skipper of *U-159* reported to Admiral Doenitz, "increased air activity, unpractised."[52] *Barry* then closed and joined *Edison* in a box search without avail. Toward evening, however, they spoke the Colombian schooner *Resolute* carrying survivors of three merchant ships sunk that week off St. Andrews, and took them on board. Finally, just as the search had been called off by Sea Frontier Headquarters, the motor torpedo boats – a type of craft completely useless for submarine hunting – put in an appearance. To cap this tale of futility, when *Edison* arrived off Cristobal Harbor entrance at 0100 June 15, ship-to-shore communications failed and she had to jill around outside the net for four hours before obtaining permission to enter.[53]

All Catalinas of Patrol Wing 3 were now transferred to the Carib-

[52] German Commander Submarines (B.d.U.) War Logs, June 1942.
[53] Lt. Cdr. W. R. Headden (C.O. *Edison*) to Cominch, 22 June 1942.

bean side, ten planes of the VI Army Air Force were placed under Admiral Van Hook's operational command, and a convoy of transports for the Pacific, escorted by five destroyers, was seen safely through the Canal on 17 June. But on the same day a British tanker bringing diesel oil to Cristobal was shelled and sunk by two U-boats within 75 miles of her destination. Shortly after, two ships were sunk off Santa Marta, probably by these U-boats on their way out; and the schooner *Resolute* was shelled and sunk between St. Andrews and Old Providence on the 23rd. The U-boat machine-gunned women and children passengers at point-blank range; they were rescued by the timely arrival of a United States patrol plane 40 minutes after the U-boat left. On 2 July the redoubtable "Ajax" put into Puerto Limon, Costa Rica, where a steamer was loading at a dock, and sank it with two torpedoes, *U-161's* parting shots.

That was the end of this blitz on the Panama Canal approaches. Not more than five submarines had disposed of an average of a ship a day for two weeks, and retired without damage – without being attacked, indeed, except from the air. Many new precautionary and defense measures were now adopted. Puerto Limon was closed by a net. The formation of Canal Zone–Guantanamo convoys was hastened and the first one sailed on 10 July. Air patrol out of Coco Solo was reinforced with radar-equipped PBYs and so extended that any submarine contact could be followed night and day for 36 hours. Four Catalinas were stationed at Grand Cayman, two at Port Royal Bay, Jamaica, and a few short-range inshore patrol planes operated from Almirante in the Veraguas Province of Panama. The VI Army Air Force covered the Colombian Coast and Venezuela up to Curaçao. A seaplane base with tender *Matagorda* was set up at Puerto Castilla, Honduras, in July.

Before these measures were completed, a persistently followed contact and well-coördinated attack resulted in the Panama Sea Frontier's first kill. On 11 July the net tender *Mimosa*, returning from laying an anti-torpedo net at Puerto Castilla, was attacked about 60 miles off Almirante [54] by *U-153* with five torpedoes, some

[54] Lat. 10°18′ N, long. 81°45′ W; the *U-153* was sunk at 9°56′ N, 81°29′ W. Panama Sea Frontier War Diary; *Lansdowne* War Diary.

of which passed right under her keel. *PC-458* (also known as U.S.S. *Evelyn R.*) and a PBY were ordered to the position. The Catalina arrived first and at 0400, after a radar contact with the submarine, dropped flares and depth charges which probably damaged it. One B-18 and three P-39s of the VI Army Air Force and a second PBY joined the search after daylight, and searched the "hot spot" for over 24 hours, the planes being relieved when they had to return for gas. At 1013 July 13, *Evelyn R.* (Lieutenant M. V. Carson USNR) picked up the submarine's oil slick and dropped all her depth charges; the planes then took over and expended all they had. In the meantime, destroyer *Lansdowne* (Lieutenant Commander William R. Smedberg III) had arrived at Cristobal as escort to a convoy. Admiral Van Hook sent her out to relieve the patrol craft; and within 15 minutes of so doing, she made an excellent sound contact, dropped four 600-pound depth charges and sank *U-153* in a 1500-fathom deep. There were no survivors.[55]

3. *First Kills of U-Boats*

This was only the eighth kill of a German submarine by United States naval forces since we entered the war; not a very encouraging score. The first, of *U-656*, had been made on 1 March 1942 off Cape Race, Newfoundland, by Ensign William Tepuni USNR, when piloting a Lockheed-Hudson of Squadron VP-82 based on Argentia. Donald Francis Mason, Chief Aviation Machinist's Mate of the same squadron, has the credit of the second. This was not his famous "Sighted Sub Sank Same" affair of 28 January, as that particular submarine evaded his attack; but another one, *U-503*. On 15 March when searching for Convoy ON-72 near the southeast corner of the Grand Bank of Newfoundland, Mason sank this U-boat with two out of four Mark-17 depth bombs that he released from 50 feet altitude.[56] Shortly after, he was commissioned Ensign.

[55] *PC-460* accidentally rammed and sank *S-26* off the Canal on 25 January.
[56] Position lat. 45°50′ N, long. 48°50′ W.

The old destroyer *Roper* (Lieutenant Commander H. W. Howe) was the first United States naval vessel to make a kill. The story is amusing in the light of later events, as the destroyer's excessive caution was canceled by the U-boat's overconfidence. Steaming south from Norfolk at 18 knots on the night of 13–14 April, *Roper* had just passed Wimble Shoal light, when her radar screen showed a "blip" at a range of 2700 yards. Howe turned up a speed of 20 knots and overhauled the target, which constantly changed its bearing. A torpedo passed close aboard at a range of 700 yards; but it was not until the range had further closed to a mere 300 yards, and a searchlight had been turned on, that the target was positively identified as a submarine. *Roper* then opened fire with her main (3-inch) and machine-gun batteries, prevented the Germans from manning their gun, obtained a direct hit near the waterline as the boat began to submerge, and then depth-charged on sound contact. Next morning 29 bodies were recovered. They were from the 500-ton *U-85*, completed in June 1941, on its second cruise in American waters that year. It had already sunk two ships and had escaped four airplane attacks and two by a destroyer.

The new 500-ton *U-352* on her maiden war cruise was caught in comparatively shoal water off Cape Lookout by the sound equipment of the Coast Guard Cutter *Icarus* (Lieutenant Commander Maurice Jester USCG) at 1625 on 9 May 1942. After firing a torpedo, *U-352* ran aground and was so knocked about by the cutter's depth charges that the commander decided to abandon ship. He surfaced in order to allow the men to escape, and then scuttled.

The other two kills in the first half of 1942 were that of *U-157* June 13, victim of the killer hunt already described; and *U-158*, sunk off Bermuda on 30 June,[57] which will be related presently. The first two weeks of July brought a couple more. That of *U-153*, off Panama, we have already dealt with; the other was the work of an Army Air Force bomber.

U-701, a 500-tonner commanded by Horst Degen, sailed from

[57] The "probable kills" credited to Coast Guard Cutters *Nike* and *Northland* on 22 May and 18 June 1942 turned out to be misses.

Lorient 20 May and moved into an operational area between Chesapeake Light and a point 15 miles south of Cape Lookout. On 16 June it fired two torpedoes at a southbound freighter, but missed. During the next two days it escaped two small naval vessels, one the escort of a two-ship coastal convoy, that depth-charged inaccurately. About daybreak on 19 June, the submarine surfaced off Cape Hatteras very close to U.S.S. *YP–389* and opened fire. The patrol craft's 3-inch gun jammed, the depth charge she tossed out failed to explode (probably because of shoal water), and poor "Yippie" was sunk, losing six officers and men. During the next week *U–701* sighted two convoys and torpedoed a British tanker in one of them; an escort vessel depth-charged but inflicted very slight damage. At noon on 28 June, *U–701* made a crippling hit on the 14,000-ton tanker *William Rockefeller,* then under the escort of Coast Guard cutter No. 470 and one plane. They counterattacked so ineffectively that the submarine was able to surface that night and sink the tanker, which otherwise could have been salvaged. Nine days passed without contacts, but on the afternoon of 7 July the U-boat's number turned up. An Army Lockheed-Hudson of Squadron 59, piloted by 2nd Lieutenant Harry J. Kane USA, on anti-submarine patrol out of Cherry Point, North Carolina, caught it flatfooted about 30 miles off Diamond Shoals Lightship and dropped three Mark-17 depth charges from an altitude of 50 feet just as it was submerging. Water poured in and the tanks were blown, to no avail. Eighteen men escaped through the conning tower hatch at depths between 45 and 60 feet. Eleven of them drowned; the rest drifted 65 miles northward with the Gulf Stream in the next 50 hours. Finally they were sighted by a blimp that dropped them a rubber boat and a sack of provisions; and shortly after the seven survivors, including the commanding officer, were rescued by a Coast Guard seaplane.[58]

Eight kills in six and a half months — about as many new U-boats as were being produced every ten days. And in the meantime, in

[58] Interrogation of survivors *U–701;* Records of Court of Inquiry on loss of *YP–389.*

the areas where these submarines operated, over 360 merchant ships totaling about 2,250,000 gross tons had been sunk. An appalling rate of exchange for the Allies; one highly encouraging for the Axis. Admiral Doenitz was naturally delighted with the performance of his boys. On 15 June he reported to Hitler the gratifying number of sinkings compared with the small number of submarines employed, and predicted "vast possibilities through the rapid increase in number of U-boats and the use of supply submarines." He dwelt on the poor quality of American defenses, the heavy destruction of tankers and the failure of new construction to replace the Allies' shipping losses. If American anti-submarine warfare improved, so that coastal work no longer paid, he proposed to concentrate anew on the transatlantic convoys.[59] In an interview that he gave to a German war correspondent during the summer of 1942, Doenitz declared: "Our submarines are operating close inshore along the coast of the United States of America, so that bathers and sometimes entire coastal cities are witnesses to that drama of war, whose visual climaxes are constituted by the red glorioles of blazing tankers."[60]

No frantic boast, this; burning tankers were not infrequently sighted from fashionable Florida resorts, and on 15 June two large American freighters were torpedoed by a U-boat within full view of thousands of pleasure-seekers at Virginia Beach.

[59] Assmann Diary.

[60] Translation in *Monthly Report Army Air Forces A/S Command* (mimeographed pamphlet) Oct. 1942 p. 16.

CHAPTER VII

The North Russia Run[1]

December 1941–July 1942

1. *Conditions and Urgencies*

OF all the disagreeable and dangerous duties in the North Atlantic during the first seven months of the war, that of the North Russia convoys was easily the worst.

This run from Iceland past Spitsbergen into the Barents Sea was one of the vital lifelines that provided Russia with the means to fight. President Roosevelt promised aid to Russia when she was attacked by Germany in June 1941, the first token shipments under lend-lease were sent that fall, and the first protocol for a nine months' supply was signed at Moscow 1 October.[2]

There were three principal routes for sending cargoes from the United States to Russia under war conditions. The first, the transpacific, confined exclusively to Soviet bottoms after Pearl Harbor, took 46 per cent of the total cargoes shipped from 1 October 1941

[1] North Russia convoys, a British responsibility, were escorted by the Royal Navy; hence a complete story of them will not be found here. But the Admiralty has kindly allowed me to use its sources. Material on experiences of U. S. merchant ships and their naval gunners was obtained at the Naval Armed Guard "desk" under the Vice Chief of Naval Operations, by Lt. (jg) J. Willard Hurst USNR. Many equally interesting events are recorded in the files of the *Pilot,* organ of National Maritime Union, in 1942–1943; but as the ships concerned could not then be identified, this material has not been used. Capt. S. B. Frankel, Assistant U. S. Naval Attaché for Archangel and Murmansk, has answered many questions. A memorandum of 28 Oct. 1943 by Cdr. C. E. Ames USNR of Convoy and Routing Section Tenth Fleet was of great assistance. For German ship movements I have depended largely on the official publication *Operationen und Taktik, Auswertung wichtiger Ereignisse des Seekrieges.*

[2] E. R. Stettinius Jr. *Lend-Lease, Weapon for Victory* (1944) Chapters 11, 18, 19.

to 30 September 1943.[3] The Japanese left these ships alone, as part of the price of keeping the Soviet Army off their backs. The second route, whose eastern termini were the Persian Gulf ports of Hormuz and Basra, was exceedingly lengthy until the Mediterranean was reopened in June 1943. Shipping bound thither from American Atlantic ports was routed via the Cape of Good Hope, which required about 76 days for the 14,500-mile passage, or via Panama Canal and the Pacific, which was some 3200 miles longer. About 23 per cent of our shipments to Russia in 1942–1943 went to the Persian Gulf.

Much the shortest and easily the most dangerous route from the Atlantic Coast of the United States to Russia was the one with which we are immediately concerned: New York or Philadelphia via North Atlantic, Iceland and the Barents Sea to Murmansk on Kola Inlet, or Molotovsk or Archangel on the White Sea. This was the North Russia run. Murmansk is an ice-free port. The railway, having been cut off from Leningrad by the Germans in 1941, was connected by a hurriedly constructed branch to the Archangel–Moscow line. Archangel is generally ice-free only from 1 June to 1 December. The average length of a convoy voyage from Iceland to Murmansk was ten days; to Archangel, twelve days. Although the North Russia route was not used between 15 February and 30 September 1943, it carried 23 per cent of all shipments from the United States to Russia down to the latter date, and in addition, a very large proportion of the shipments from the United Kingdom to Russia. About 21 per cent of all cargoes sent by this route were lost, as against 8 per cent of the shipments to the Persian Gulf, and only minor marine casualties among those shipped in Soviet bottoms from the West Coast to Siberian ports.[4]

There was a regrettable wastage of shipping on both the Persian Gulf and the North Russia routes, owing to bottlenecks. The docks at Basra could not handle the cargoes sent there in 1942, and many

[3] Cargo statistics here are based on measurement (40 cubic feet to a ton) of actual cargoes, including casings, and are given in Cdr. C. E. Ames's Memorandum.

[4] Cdr. Ames's Memorandum, with figures supplied by the Lend-Lease Administration.

goods had to be discharged at Karachi, India. Similarly, ships waited months at Reykjavik for a North Russia convoy to come along, and were detained for months at Murmansk for a return convoy; some of the ships detained in Iceland finally discharged in Scotland. In February 1944, goods that left New York and Philadelphia in 1942 were still being sent into Russia from Karachi and from Scottish ports. The Navy protested against the shipping out of cargoes from the United States at periods of congestion, and the Royal Navy regarded the North Russia convoys as little better than suicide. But it had to be done in order to satisfy Russia that we were doing our best.

North Russia convoys, started by the British in August 1941, always remained a Royal Navy responsibility. The United States Navy participated in escort and covering duties at the toughest period, from April through July 1942; and American merchant ships carrying Naval Armed Guards, laden with high explosives and other war materiel, sailed in the convoys from December 1941.[5] The first American merchant ship to make the run with a Naval Armed Guard was the 3800-ton freighter *Larranga*. She sailed from Boston the day before Pearl Harbor, with a typically slender armament of the period – one 4-inch gun and eight .30-caliber machine guns, Ensign H. A. Axtell Jr. USNR and eight bluejackets – and joined Convoy PQ–8 at Iceland, sailing thence 8 January 1942. On the night of 17 January this convoy was attacked by a U-boat which hit but did not sink the flagship and an escorting British destroyer. The convoy reached Murmansk 19 January.

At that period of the war, most of the American ships destined for North Russia sailed from Philadelphia and at Halifax or Sydney joined a transatlantic convoy and stayed with it as far as the breaking-off point for Iceland. A British convoy, formed at Gare Loch or Loch Ewe on the west coast of Scotland, joined them at Hvalfjor-

[5] Further on in this volume will be found a description of Naval Armed Guards and the arming of merchant ships. Data on number of and sinkings of merchant vessels are taken from Cdr. Ames's Memorandum, not from the Armed Guard commanders' Reports, as they often were not in a position to know whether or not a ship torpedoed was sunk.

dur where a "PQ" convoy for Murmansk was formed, with an escort of British corvettes, destroyers and light cruisers. These convoys were routed through the mined channel in Denmark Strait, and as far north as ice conditions permitted. Eventually they had to head south for Kola Inlet, which brought them within a short bombing distance of the Luftwaffe bases in Norway and Finland. Russia-bound ships carried all manner of war materiel, such as explosives, munitions, oil, machinery, guns, vehicles, planes, and parts. On the southbound voyages they were not so heavily or dangerously laden, but carried appreciable quantities of chrome, potassium chloride, magnesite, furs and skins, wood products and even goose feathers to the United States.

Most of the ships of the German Navy larger than submarines were deployed in various Norwegian harbors and fjords during this period owing to Hitler's "inspired" conviction that the British would attempt a landing in Norway. The remaining big battleship *Tirpitz* was sent to Trondheim in January, pocket battleship *Scheer* in February, heavy cruiser *Hipper* in March, and pocket battleship *Lützow* in May, all with a certain number of destroyers.[6] This deployment afforded the German Navy a unique opportunity to raid convoys and tangle with the British and American covering forces; but it seldom rose to the occasion.

This "fleet in being" was the least anxiety of the North Russia convoys. They had to contend with high seas, ice, snow, fog, cold water and colder air; with U-boats painted polar white and served by air reconnaissance that they seldom enjoyed in other areas; and with Luftwaffe dive- and torpedo-bombers operating from bases in German-occupied Norway and Finland, guided to the convoys by long-range reconnaissance planes and aided by the perpetual summer daylight of the Arctic Circle. Here was submarine warfare to the Germans' taste; but the elements helped the hares as well as the hounds by providing fog cover at sundry crucial moments.

[6] *Operation und Taktik. Prinz Eugen* on her way to Norway with *Scheer* was torpedoed by a British submarine and had to return to Germany for repairs. *Scharnhorst* and *Gneisenau* were injured by mines during their spectacular dash through the English Channel in February. *Scharnhorst* went to Norway in 1943.

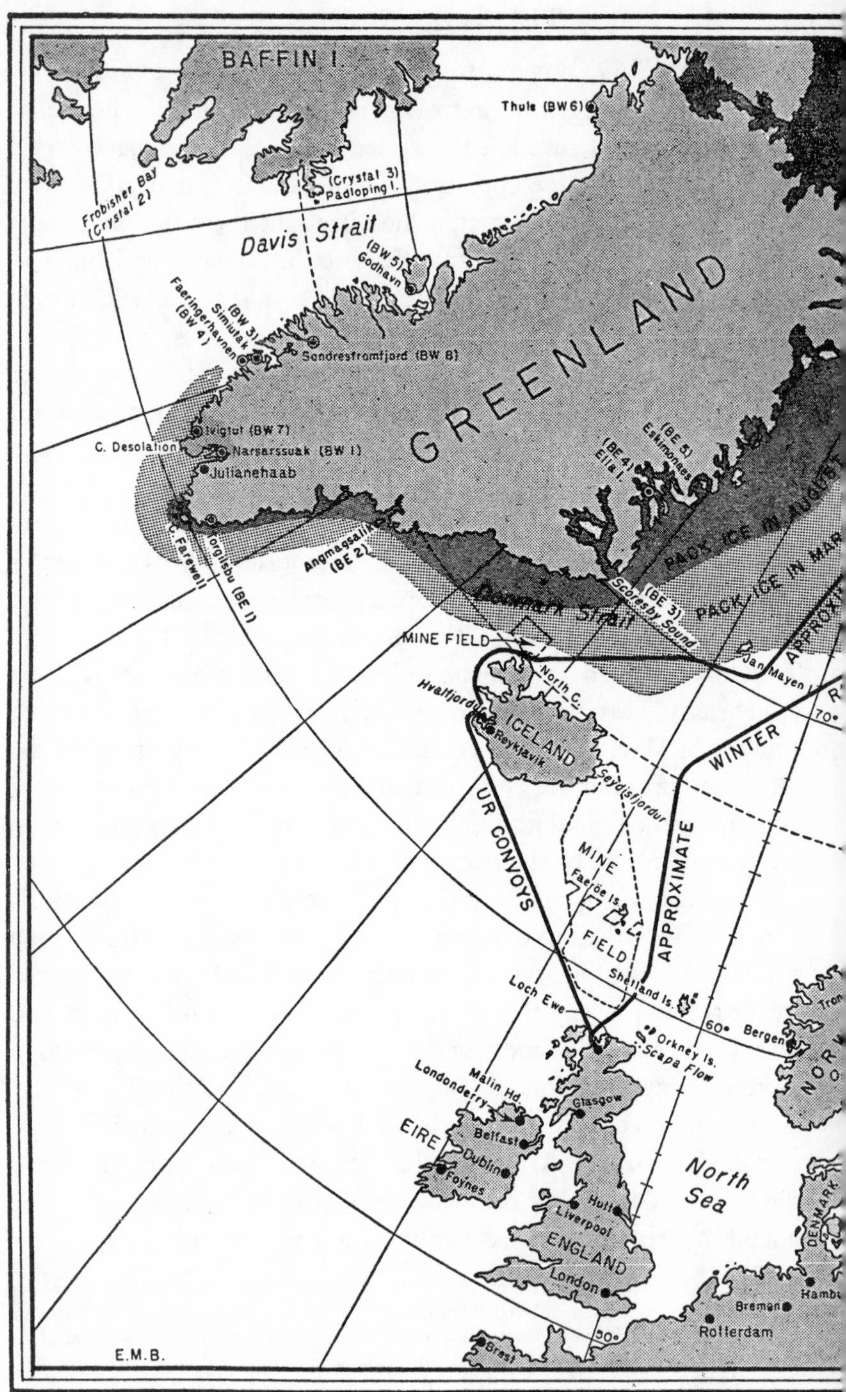

BAFFIN I.
Thule (BW6)
Frobisher Bay (Crystal 2)
(Crystal 3) Padloping I.
Davis Strait
(BW 5) Godhavn
Faeringerhavnen (BW 4)
(BW 3) Simiutak
Sondrestromfjord (BW 8)
GREENLAND
Ivigtut (BW 7)
C. Desolation
Narsarssuak (BW 1)
Julianehaab
C. Farewell
Torgilsbu (BE 1)
Angmagsalik (BE 2)
(BE 4) Ella I.
(BE 5) Eskimonaes
PACK ICE IN AUGUST
PACK ICE IN MAR
Denmark Strait
(BE 3) Scoresby Sound
MINE FIELD
Jan Mayen I.
North C.
Hvalfjordur
ICELAND
Reykjavik
70°
WINTER
Seydisfjordur
UR CONVOYS
MINE
Faeröe Is.
FIELD
APPROXIMATE
Shetland Is.
Loch Ewe
60°
Bergen
Orkney Is.
Scapa Flow
Malin Hd.
Londonderry
Glasgow
EIRE
Belfast
Dublin
Foynes
North Sea
Hull
Liverpool
ENGLAND
London
DENMARK
Bremen
Hamb
Rotterdam
50°
Brest
E.M.B.

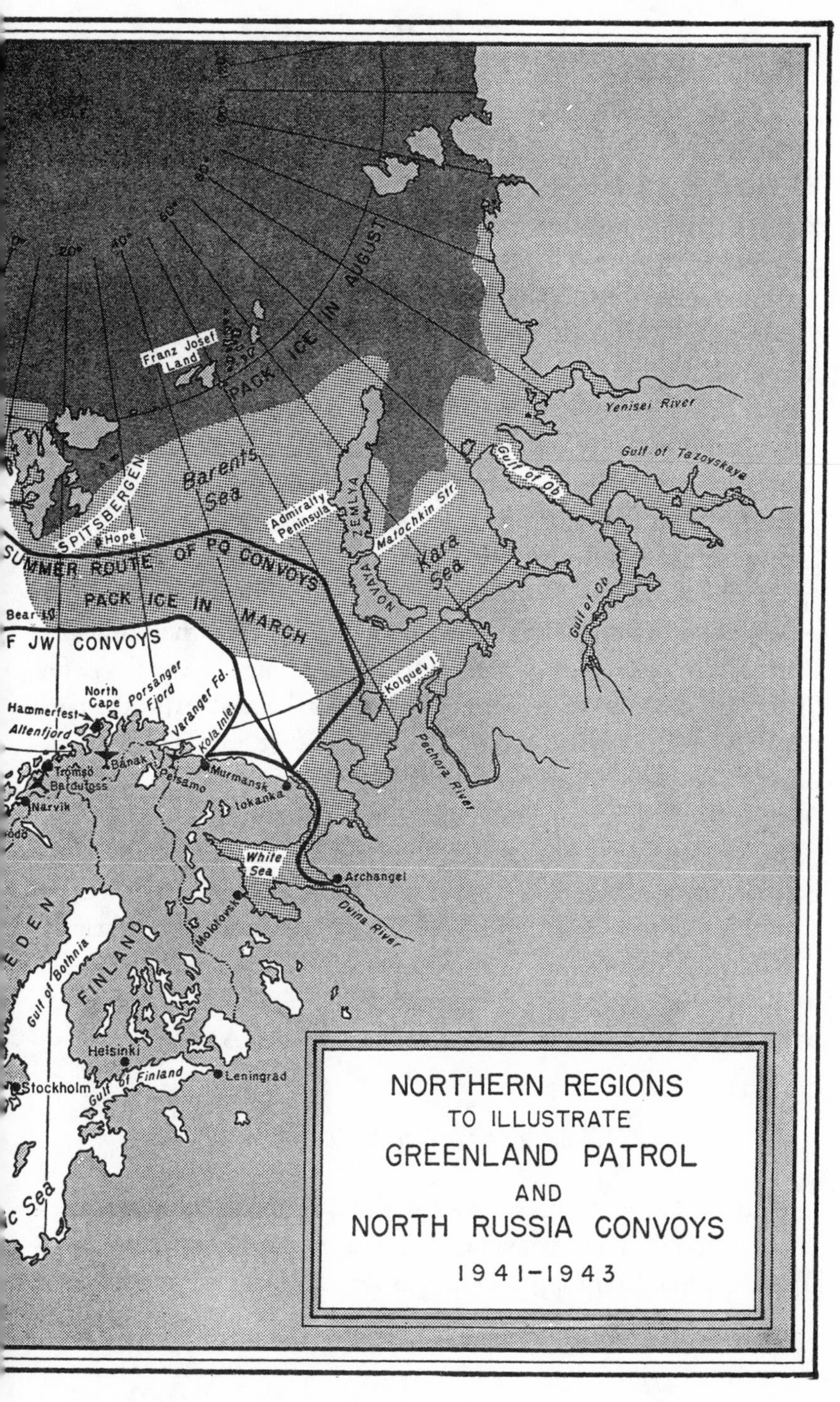
Franz Josef Land
PACK ICE IN AUGUST
Barents Sea
SPITSBERGEN
Hope I.
Admiralty Peninsula
NOVAYA ZEMLYA
Matochkin Str.
Kara Sea
Yenisei River
Gulf of Tazovskaya
Gulf of Ob
SUMMER ROUTE OF PQ CONVOYS
PACK ICE IN MARCH
Bear I.
F JW CONVOYS
North Cape
Porsanger Fjord
Varanger Fd.
Kola Inlet
Kolguev I.
Hammerfest
Altenfjord
Tromsö
Bardufoss
Banak
Petsamo
Murmansk
Iokanka
Narvik
Pechora River
White Sea
Archangel
Dvina River
Molotovsk
FINLAND
Gulf of Bothnia
Helsinki
Stockholm
Gulf of Finland
Leningrad
NORTHERN REGIONS
TO ILLUSTRATE
GREENLAND PATROL
AND
NORTH RUSSIA CONVOYS
1941–1943

Perils of the North Russia run were not confined to the high seas. Murmansk was only a few minutes' flying time from German-held airfields, and the hills that ringed the harbor made surprise easy. Machine guns had to be constantly manned in a port where only seconds might intervene between the sighting of a plane and the dropping of bombs.

Our seamen were highly impressed with the determination of the Russians and their eagerness to kill Germans, but they had no protection afloat from Russian planes and very little from the Russian Navy. The Soviet Army air force (they had no naval air arm) did not take easily to flying over water, and the offers of British and American aviators to indoctrinate their pilots were turned down. The Russians, for all their splendid fighting qualities, were still highly suspicious of their "capitalist" allies, forbade their people to fraternize with our bluejackets or merchant seamen, and made no public acknowledgment of the heroic efforts that they and the British were making to get the stuff through, until Admiral W. H. Standley's calculated indiscretion forced a belated expression of gratitude from Marshal Stalin. The British lost at least as many merchant ships as we on this run, and, in addition, two light cruisers, four destroyers, four minesweepers and one submarine, before 1943. The Russian Army, however, more than held its own against Axis ground forces deployed on this front. Admiral Doenitz has revealed that the German Navy "demanded" the conquest of Murmansk, Petsamo and the whole Fisher Peninsula. This "was never attained, as a result in particular of insurmountable difficulties of terrain," and, he might have added, because of the Russian Army.[7]

2. *The Tough Month of March*

Until halfway to the summer solstice of 1942, only one merchant ship out of 110 convoyed was lost on the North Russia run. Then, in three months, April–June 1942, 143 ships carrying 826,000

[7] Doenitz Essay, Sec. 86.

tons of cargo left United States ports for Russia, and 84 of them, carrying 522,000 tons, were routed by the North Cape to Murmansk. But only 44 of these, carrying 300,000 tons, reached their destinations. Of the rest, 23 were lost by enemy action or marine casualty, while 17 discharged their cargoes in Scotland, to await better conditions. By midsummer 1942, more than half the ships making the run were flying the American flag. And they experienced some of the toughest fighting in this war.

During the first week of March 1942, the German Navy muffed a good chance to wipe out the northbound Convoy PQ–12. Luftwaffe air patrols sighted it on the 5th – 15 ships escorted by a British cruiser and four destroyers or corvettes, about 70 miles south of Jan Mayen Island – when the passage had barely begun. Next day Admiral Raeder ordered *Tirpitz* and three destroyers to sortie and break it up; six U-boats were to lie in wait east of North Cape to finish off any ship that escaped. Vice Admiral Otto Ciliax, commanding the *Tirpitz* attack group, had little stomach for this operation, deeming it foolish to expose his mighty ship merely to destroy a little convoy; and since he felt that way it is not surprising that his sortie failed. The weather was overcast and the seas too rough for the battleship to launch planes, or for the Luftwaffe to take the air. After the not very glorious bag of one small unescorted Russian freighter sunk, the destroyers began to run low on oil, and it was too rough to fuel from *Tirpitz;* they had to be sent into Norwegian ports while *Tirpitz,* then south of Bear Island, steamed entirely unescorted for over 24 hours. Admiral Raeder ordered the operation broken off on the 8th.

In the meantime a formidable support force of the Royal Navy, Admiral Sir Jack Tovey in *King George V*, with two other battleships, carrier *Victorious* and nine destroyers, organized to cover Convoy PQ–12 and the southward-bound QP–8, was thwarted by the same foul weather in its efforts to come to grips with *Tirpitz.* Fighter planes from *Victorious* finally picked her up early on 9 March, when headed for Norway, and twelve Albacore torpedo planes attacked under favorable conditions; but every one missed and *Tirpitz* got into West Fjord unscathed. The two convoys, the objects of all this activity, enjoyed good fog cover all the way and escaped molestation.

Convoy PQ–13 had a very different story. This northbound convoy of 19 merchant ships escorted by H.M. cruiser *Trinidad* and three destroyers sailed from Reykjavik 20 March. Foul weather, culminating in a full gale 25 March, caused several ships to straggle. German air reconnaissance picked up this convoy, three destroyers were dispatched from Kirkenes to intercept and from 28 to 31 March the Germans "threw the book" at it, attacking with high-level and dive-bombers, submarines and destroyers, from a position about 85 miles north of North Cape up to the meridian of Murmansk. The American S.S. *Effingham* and a British merchantman were sunk; two Panamanian freighters disappeared on the 28th. Next morning at 0930,[8] the German destroyers attacked in conditions of very low visibility (150–200 yards) amid heavy recurrent snow squalls. Dirty weather probably saved the convoy; the enemy, never sighted, dropped salvoes among the merchant ships for about ten minutes without making a serious hit. A German destroyer tangled with H.M.S. *Trinidad* and was so badly damaged by shell-fire that she had to be sunk; not however before she had got a torpedo hit on the cruiser. *Trinidad*, though badly holed, managed to make port, and was quickly restored to duty. When escorting another PQ convoy in May, she was set afire by a dive-bombing attack, and finished off by torpedo-bombers which sneaked in while her crew were busy with damage control.[9]

Just before Convoy PQ–13 passed the Murmansk harbor nets, it was attacked by a submarine wolf-pack, yet evaded injury. The ships were received by the Luftwaffe with an air raid as they steamed into Kola Inlet, and this set the pattern of their stay in port, which lasted almost a month.

[8] Position lat. 72°07′ N, long. 32°15′ E, given by convoy commodore. Other details from *Operation und Taktik*.

[9] Information from former Commanding Officer H.M.S. *Trinidad* (Capt. Saunders RN).

3. *Task Force 39*

Before the next Murmansk convoy left Iceland,[10] the United States had furnished a strong covering and support force, including our two newest battleships, to help guard against another sortie by the *Tirpitz* to break up the North Russia run. The reasons for this force being in northern waters are somewhat involved but highly interesting as showing the essential unity of this global war.[11]

According to the best Allied intelligence, Japan was about to follow up her capture of Singapore (15 February) and most of the Netherlands East Indies by seizing Madagascar from the Vichy French, who were unable, even if willing, to defend it. A Japanese air-naval base in Madagascar would, in effect, slam the back door to the Mediterranean on the Allies, and render any passage into the Indian Ocean precarious. The British Chiefs of Staff had, therefore, decided to send an expeditionary force at once to take over Madagascar in the name of General de Gaulle. Mr. Churchill so informed Mr. Roosevelt on 14 March. He added that the expedition must have a strong naval covering force for which the only available group in the Royal Navy was Force "H" (H.M.S. *Malaya, Argus, Hermione* and several destroyers) then covering the western Mediterranean. He therefore requested the United States Navy to provide two battleships, a carrier and a few cruisers and destroyers to relieve Force "H" during April, May and June.

President Roosevelt passed along this request to Admiral King. Cominch was about to order to the Pacific our only two new battleships that were completed. He saw the point of the Madagascar operation at once and decided that U.S.S. *Washington* and *North Carolina* for the time being could better make their weight felt in the Atlantic. Owing to logistics difficulties of supplying an American task force at Gibraltar, he preferred that they relieve

[10] Convoy PQ–14, seven or eight merchant ships, included the American S.S. *Yaka* and *West Cheswald,* and entered Murmansk 19 Apr. with the loss of one ship.

[11] My information on this episode is from conversations with President Roosevelt.

British units in the Home Fleet, which could in turn relieve Force "H." So the Premier was informed by the President on 16 March, and so it was decided.

Accordingly Task Force 39, commanded by Rear Admiral John W. Wilcox Jr. in *Washington,* departed Casco Bay 25 March.[12] It comprised heavy cruisers *Wichita* and *Tuscaloosa* of the former "White" Patrol, aircraft carrier *Wasp* and Destroyer Squadron 8, commanded by Captain D. P. Moon in *Wainwright.* The task force ran into exceedingly thick and foul weather, so rough that *Wasp's* flight deck, 57 feet above the waterline, shipped green water. In the midst of this, at lat. 42°24′ N, long. 61°34′ W, Admiral Wilcox was swept overboard and lost, and a plane launched by *Wasp* to search for him, splashed and was also lost. Rear Admiral R. C. Giffen in *Wichita* then assumed command. H.M.S. *Edinburgh,* flying the flag of Rear Admiral S. S. Bonham-Carter RN and screened by four or five destroyers, met Task Force 39 on 3 April in a typical dirty North Atlantic dawn with a heavy sea running, about 50 miles west of Rockall, and accompanied into Scapa Flow this first heavy unit of the Atlantic Fleet to reach British waters since the declaration of war. *Washington* was exceedingly eager to swap punches with *Tirpitz,* but the Germans never afforded her the opportunity.

On 28 April this group less *Wasp,* combined in one covering force with H.M. carrier *Victorious,* light cruiser *Kenya,* five British destroyers, and H.M.S. *King George V* flying the flag of Admiral Sir Jack Tovey RN, Commander-in-Chief Home Fleet, departed Scapa in order to cover the North Russia convoys.

On the same day the American freighters *Dunboyne* and *Eldena* with eleven British and other merchantmen, organized as Convoy QP–11, departed Murmansk, escorted by H.M.S. *Edinburgh,* eight British destroyers, six corvettes and an armed trawler. No sailings from Murmansk could escape German observation, and Admiral Raeder at once deployed destroyers, U-boats and Luftwaffe to break up QP–11. On 30 April two U-boats severely damaged *Edinburgh.* May Day opened with an attack on the convoy by six Junker

[12] See next chapter for her missions to Malta.

torpedo planes. All torpedoes missed. At 1245 three German destroyers appeared. On account of peeling off escorts to stand by *Edinburgh*, Convoy QP–11 at this point was protected by only four destroyers, which at once made smoke and attacked the enemy at long range. According to the Germans' admission, the convoy was very skillfully handled, the British convoy commodore maneuvering his merchant ships behind an ice field. The German destroyers, unable to close, finally broke off after expending all their torpedoes and most of their ammunition on the British screen, to no purpose. Many shells landed among the merchant ships, but the only one sunk, a Russian freighter, was hit by a U-boat's torpedo.

Next day, 2 May, the three German destroyers located H.M.S. *Edinburgh*, almost dead in the water with four destroyers standing-by. Destroyer *Schoemann* made a torpedo run on the cruiser; she returned a 6-inch salvo which hit both engine rooms, so that the German crew had to abandon ship. But *Edinburgh*, too, was doomed; flooding could not be controlled and she went down.

Northbound Convoy PQ–15, which passed Convoy QP–11, was also covered by Task Force 99.[13] Its story can best be seen from the deck of S.S. *Expositor*, a 4959-ton American freighter loaded with a lethal cargo that included 5000 cases of TNT. As often had to happen in the early months of 1942, she was under-manned and under-gunned for a voyage of this nature, and crossed the Atlantic in March with one 4-inch 50-caliber gun, served by a Naval Armed Guard consisting of Ensign Robert B. Ricks USNR, four seamen and one signalman striker; and four .30-caliber machine guns manned by the merchant crew. *Expositor* proceeded to the Clyde, and, before sailing thence for Iceland, two 20-mm Oerlikon machine guns and one twin-mount Hotchkiss were added to her armament; but the slender gun crew was not augmented.

When Convoy PQ–15 departed Reykjavik 26 April, it comprised 23 merchant ships, including three American freighters, *Francis Scott Key*, *Deer Lodge* and *Expositor*, escorted by nine British destroyers and three armed trawlers, later augmented by two heavy

[13] Designation changed from TF39 about 25 April.

cruisers and a "flak ship" – a British anti-aircraft cruiser. The convoy encountered floating mines next day, but escaped injury. On 30 April a reconnaissance plane circled just outside firing range, but was driven off by long-range fire from the escorts. Next day the convoy was circled for hours at long range by two or more planes, one of which attempted three attacks and was knocked down on the last. The main attack developed 2 May, and for 48 hours the ships were at general quarters almost continuously. Aboard *Expositor*, Ensign Ricks notes that "the Armed Guard crew, because of the lack of men, and because of the alertness which had to be maintained at any cost, went without sleep and very little rest; and they can now be considered real fighting men." At about 0056 May 3, three to five planes were sighted on the starboard wing of the convoy and fire was immediately opened. At least one was shot down, but two got through the barrage and dropped torpedoes at ranges estimated to have been about 500 yards. Two merchant vessels and a British corvette were hit almost simultaneously. The British S.S. *Cape Corso*, loaded with explosives, and apparently set afire when a German plane crashed in flames just ahead of her, blew up and sank in a few seconds. The other two vessels sank less rapidly. Just after one of them went down, *Expositor's* after lookout: –

> . . . sighted the exposed part of a submarine's conning tower in the center of the convoy, and just a few yards off our starboard quarter. In fact, she was so close aboard that neither the 4-inch gun mounted on the stern nor the machine gun mounted on the poop deck were able to be brought to bear. Evidently realizing that we had sighted her, the submarine changed course and came across to the port quarter. When she was about twenty-five yards away from the ship, fire was opened with the 4-inch gun, the second shot struck her squarely on the conning tower. As the shell exploded, the top of the conning tower was blown off. As she appeared to sink, the water boiled up in a great froth of air and bubbles. After observing the spot where she sank, we saw an oil slick forming with occasional bubbles rising to the surface. At this point one of the gunners reported a torpedo track crossing our bow from port to starboard. The ship immediately backed at full speed and the torpedo missed us by a few feet.[14]

[14] Report of Ens. Ricks. The U-boat escaped.

Admiralty Photo

King George VI inspecting Marine Guard of U.S.S. *Washington*, 7 June 1942
Left to right: Admiral Giffen, the King, Admiral Stark, Captain Benson

Photo by Ensign Carraway

S.S. *Troubadour* working into Matochkin Strait, Novaya Zemlya, where S.S. *Ironclad* is anchored

M–3 tank with 37-mm gun used as anti-aircraft gun on S.S. *Troubadour*
H.M.S. *Ayrshire* in background

An aerial torpedo hit on a merchant vessel

Scenes on the North Russia Run

On the night of 3–4 May, two more torpedo-bombers attacked this convoy, but were driven off by heavy anti-aircraft fire without inflicting damage. The convoy arrived at Murmansk 5 May without further serious incident.

The *Edinburgh* was not the only warship lost from Task Force 99. When steaming through a thick fog on 1 May, at about lat. 67° N, long. 5° W, H.M.S. *King George V* cut H.M. destroyer *Punjabi* clean in two. U.S.S. *Washington*, steaming in column abaft the flagship, passed between the two halves of the destroyer just as the stern sank and the depth charges exploded directly under her. Subsequent examination showed very slight damage.

QP–12, a southbound, 14-ship convoy including nine American merchantmen,[15] departed Murmansk 21 May. During the first four days of the voyage it was protected by low visibility. The entire passage to Iceland was uneventful, as the Germans concentrated their efforts on ships bringing munitions to Russia.

Now the American factories working for Russia were in full production, which meant stepping up PQ convoys from a dozen or so ships to thirty and more. Yet the days were lengthening until there was sufficient daylight in those high latitudes for visual attack every hour of the twenty-four. Hitler seized the opportunity and reinforced his Luftwaffe at the northern Norwegian bases.

4. *Convoys PQ–16 and QP–13*

Convoy PQ–16 was the first big one to feel the weight of this enhanced air power. The 34 ships departed Reykjavik 20 May, protected by what the Rear Admiral in command referred to as a strong Royal Navy escort "of Mediterranean convoy caliber," including two cruisers of the *Dorsetshire* class, two of the *Southampton* class, two flak ships, six destroyers, six armed trawlers and two submarines. But the United States was still unable to provide ade-

[15] S.S. *Alcoa Rambler, Expositor, Francis Scott Key, Mormacrio, Paul Luckenbach, Seattle Spirit, Bayou Chico, Texas* and *Zebulon B. Vance*. S.S. *Seattle Spirit*, after joining a westbound transatlantic convoy, was sunk in a submarine attack.

quate armament or gun crews for all American cargo vessels. The most glaring instance was that of the 5035-ton merchantman *Alcoa Banner*, unarmed except for five little .30-caliber machine guns which were installed in Iceland. One apprentice seaman and one apprentice radioman, assigned to her as a communications liaison group, were the only naval personnel on board. Other ships with a more adequate armament lacked sufficient ammunition; S.S. *Mauna Kea*, for example, ran out of .50-caliber during the running attack on 27 May, and until she could borrow a supply from S.S. *John Randolph* (whose crew broke cargo to obtain it), she could man only her two .30-caliber machine guns. And any ships that arrived at Murmansk with shot in the locker had to fire it all off at German bombers over the harbor. The United States Naval Attaché in North Russia, Captain Frankel, recommended that every American merchant ship be assured 5000 rounds per gun on leaving Iceland. He had to beg .50-caliber ammunition from the Russians, so that S.S. *Eldena*, *Dunboyne* and *Mormacmar*, who had done "excellent work defending themselves and port against enemy bombers," might have something to fight with on the passage home.

The running attack on Convoy PQ–16 began 25 May and lasted until the ships entered Murmansk six days later. This battle was the most intense and sustained, and involved the greatest number of planes seen up to that time on the North Russia run. For six days and daylighted nights, the Germans attacked with submarines, high- and low-level bombers and torpedo planes, strafing, bombing and launching air torpedoes. Early on the morning of 26 May a U-boat surfaced near the two British submarines of the escort, which blanketed the fire from some ships and confused others; and in the *mêlée* the American freighter *Syros* was torpedoed and sunk.

One of the most hard-pressed vessels of this Convoy PQ–16 was the American freighter *City of Joliet*, a target of eight torpedo planes and 18 dive-bombers in four attacks on the first day of the battle. The enemy came in on the starboard beam at about 150 knots in line abreast, about 75 feet apart. Breaking formation, the bombers dove at a 50-degree angle and released three to five impact bombs, averaging 300 pounds each, from a height of 1000 feet. The torpedo planes attacked in two groups, coming in 30 to 50 feet above the water and releasing torpedoes simultaneously at about 3000 yards on the starboard side of the convoy. That day *City of Joliet* escaped with a severe shaking-up from near misses. Next day the attacks went wide of her; but on the 27th, the aërial assault reached a climax. There were ten separate attacks on her that day, around lat. 73°41′ N long. 21°58′ E. The Naval Armed Guard, reported their commander Lieutenant J. C. Grotenrath USNR, "composed of green and untried personnel, remained calm and cool while undergoing their first baptism of fire. The merchant crew also remained at their respective battle stations and greatly assisted the Armed Guard." She was not hit, but damage from several near misses caused *City of Joliet* to take in more water than her pumps could handle, and she was abandoned on 28 May without loss of life.

The Naval Armed Guard commander in the freighter *Michigan* gives a vivid picture of this battle of 27 May 1942, a day that no sailor who went through it will ever forget.

27 *May*, 0115. Very low ceiling overhead. Went to General Quarters just as flight of eight torpedo bombers appeared on horizon off starboard beam of convoy. Destroyers from the van and those on the starboard flank move out to meet the attack, but the planes hedgehopped into the clouds and then came down again to attack the convoy at point-blank range. Entire starboard side of convoy opened heavy fire but planes flew directly into it. As each plane dropped its torpedo, it banked sharply and circled the stern of the convoy. Torpedoes were dropped from a height of approximately 200 feet. Two ships were hit and dropped astern. Three planes returned to attack from the port quarter of the convoy, but one of the escort vessels screening that sector opened fire just as the planes emerged from the clouds. This fire coupled with the fire from the merchant ships in the vicinity forced the three planes to drop their torpedoes early and no hits were made on the convoy. Secured from General Quarters at 0200.

0255. Patrol plane which had been circling overhead in cloud bank came into range. Ships opened fire and drove plane back into cloud bank. Ships which had been struck by attack of 0115 have been able to make repairs and have now rejoined convoy.

0900. General Quarters. Perfect weather for air attack. Very light wind and unlimited visibility. 0930. Attack by flight of eight bombers from starboard quarter of convoy. Planes approached at between 15,000 and 20,000 feet, then dove on convoy, releasing bombs at about 1000 feet. Two ships in starboard columns were hit forward and burst into flames. One of these ships had been hit previously in the 0115 attack. Both fell rapidly astern.

1025. Attacked by wave of six bombers from the starboard beam of the convoy. Five of the planes passed directly overhead, but the sixth dove directly at the *Michigan.* Both guns opened fire as the plane began to dive. Four shells exploded directly ahead of plane, causing it to veer slightly toward bow of ship. When within 1000 feet of ship, plane released five bombs, then leveled out and strafed ship with machine-gun fire from after wing surfaces and from after gun pit. Bombs landed within 100 feet of bow and beam of ship. A very large quantity of heavy black oil floated on the surface where the bombs exploded in the water. This is evidently what caused all the ships so far to burst into flame immediately. No casualties.

1100. Attacked by several planes which dove at convoy from different directions. Planes strafed port side of convoy badly, but all bombs missed their targets.

1155. Attacked by formation of bombers that approached convoy from stern. One stick of two bombs landed within 100 feet of port gun platform. No casualties. Another stick of five bombs straddled destroyer patrolling port quarter. Fire started in forward turret, but was quickly extinguished. Near hit on ship in port column caused her to fall astern rapidly for about ten minutes, then she regained headway and caught up with convoy. Two of the destroyers and one corvette are not far astern, helping to fight fires on ships hit earlier in day. One has managed to get fire under control and seems to be making headway, but the other is still falling astern.

1245. Attacked by formation of six planes which approached from astern. S.S. *Empire Lawrence* hit by a stick of five bombs. Immediately listed heavily to port and began to sink. Port lifeboats were jammed in davits or blown away by bombs. Second attack followed immediately. One plane crashed into *Empire Lawrence* and ship sank immediately. Corvette circled to pick up survivors and was heavily attacked with bombs and machine guns.

1520. Attacked by wave of eight bombers from port bow. Commodore's ship hit by bombs forward. Number 1 hatch immediately caught fire and burned for some time but ship did not sink. Antiaircraft ship became new commodore. Another ship in starboard column hit heavily forward but did not sink. Continued to list by head, however.

1730. Combination torpedo-plane, dive-bomber and submarine attack. Formation of eight torpedo planes approached convoy from starboard beam. These planes sheered off to circle stern of convoy without firing torpedoes. At the same time destroyer which was screening port beam headed into convoy at full speed blowing "submarine sighted" signal. Other ships in port columns also sounded six blasts on whistle. Destroyer circled rapidly between columns 2 and 3 sounding the whistle continuously. Ship in next column to port struck amidships by torpedo. Abandoned immediately. Boats were lowered away successfully and rafts were held secure to ship's side by painters until full. An escort vessel picked up crew. At the same time a flight of eight dive bombers dove out of sun from port quarter of convoy. The ship whose regular position was astern of us had drawn up alongside our starboard side. One plane dove directly for us and dropped a stick of five bombs. The bombs cleared our ship but two landed on the forward part of the ship alongside to starboard. Number 1 and 2 hatches immediately spouted fire, and the crew abandoned the ship. The life rafts were not secured to the ship by painters and drifted rapidly astern, forcing the crew to swim a long distance to get on them. There were over twenty-five men swimming when the ship passed astern. The ship continued to burn for three hours before finally exploding. The planes continued to drop large sticks of bombs on all sides but made no direct hits. . . . Two stragglers were attacked at masthead height, but for some reason both planes dropped their bombs at least 1000 yards off the targets.

2200. Heavy ceiling covered convoy. Secured from General Quarters.

During this battle of 27 May, Convoy PQ-16 had only destroyers and armed trawlers as escorts. The cruisers had peeled off the day before, as it was then deemed suicidal to expose any combat ship larger than a destroyer to intensive land-based air attack. On the 28th, three Russian destroyers came out to help escort this battered convoy into Murmansk, and their anti-aircraft fire helped to keep subsequent air attacks at ineffective altitude. A fog-mull helped,

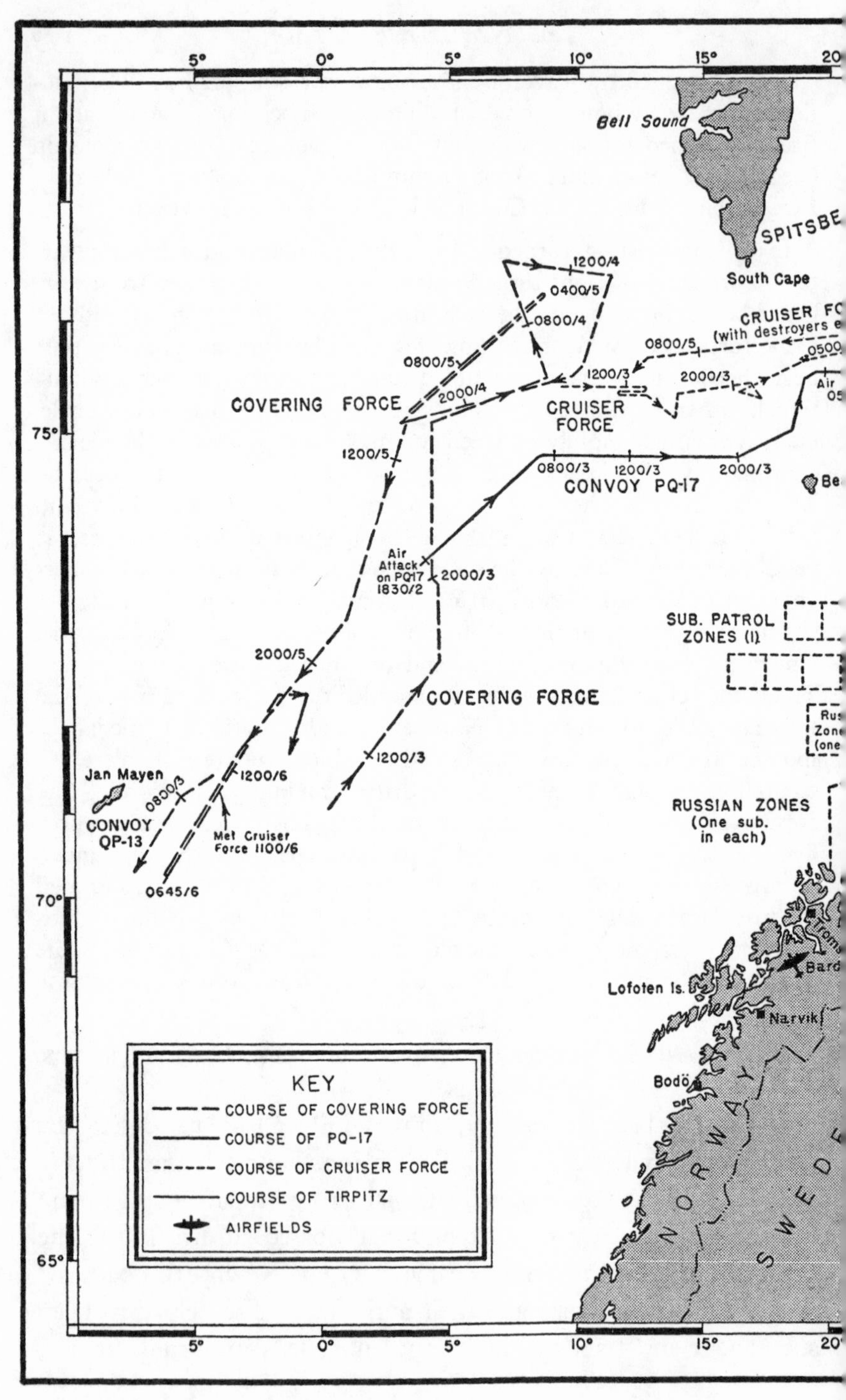

Bell Sound
SPITSBE
South Cape
CRUISER FC
(with destroyers e
COVERING FORCE
CRUISER FORCE
CONVOY PQ-17
Air Attack on PQ17 1830/2
SUB. PATROL ZONES (1)
COVERING FORCE
Jan Mayen
CONVOY QP-13
Met Cruiser Force 1100/6
RUSSIAN ZONES (One sub. in each)
Lofoten Is.
Narvik
Bodö
NORWAY
SWEDE
KEY
COURSE OF COVERING FORCE
COURSE OF PQ-17
COURSE OF CRUISER FORCE
COURSE OF TIRPITZ
AIRFIELDS

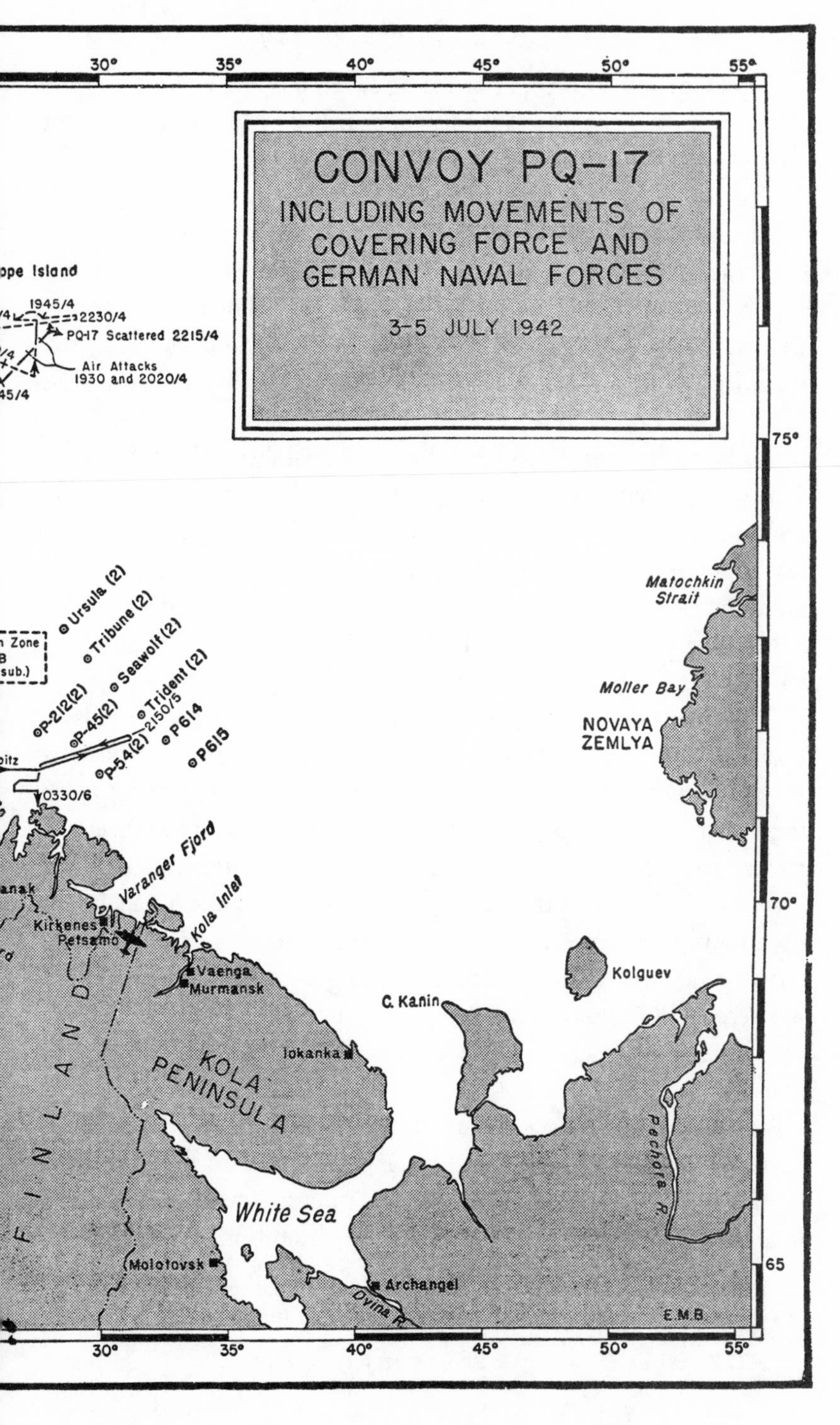

CONVOY PQ-17
INCLUDING MOVEMENTS OF COVERING FORCE AND GERMAN NAVAL FORCES
3-5 JULY 1942
30°
35°
40°
45°
50°
55°
75°
70°
65
1945/4
2230/4
PQ-17 Scattered 2215/4
Air Attacks 1930 and 2020/4
45/4
Ursula (2)
Tribune (2)
Seawolf (2)
Trident (2)
2150/5
P-212(2)
P-45(2)
P-54(2)
P614
P615
0330/6
Varanger Fjord
Kola Inlet
Kirkenes
Petsamo
Vaenga
Murmansk
FINLAND
KOLA PENINSULA
Iokanka
C. Kanin
Kolguev
Matochkin Strait
Moller Bay
NOVAYA ZEMLYA
Pechora R.
White Sea
Molotovsk
Archangel
Dvina R.
E.M.B.

too; and Convoy PQ–16, after losing seven merchant ships carrying 31,000 tons of cargo,[16] reached Murmansk 30 May and Archangel 1 June with the remaining 27 ships carrying 125,000 tons of cargo for Russia.

The next southbound convoy, QP–13, departed Archangel 26 June and picked up a section from Murmansk. Escorted by five British destroyers and nine smaller ships, it included the American merchantmen *Capira*, *Exterminator*, *John Randolph*, *Lancaster*, *Massmar*, *Mauna Kea*, *Michigan*, *Nemaha*, *R. H. Lee*, and 26 of other flags. There were several submarine alarms and shadowing planes were frequently sighted, but low visibility afforded protection through much of the voyage. On 5 July in a fog the convoy commodore made a mistaken landfall and blundered into a mine field that guarded the eastern entrance to Denmark Strait. Five ships including *Massmar* and *John Randolph* were lost. *John Randolph*, to be precise, was "two thirds lost," because her bow floated and was salvaged.[17] The rest reached Reykjavik 7 July.

This was the last southbound convoy to leave a North Russian port for three months. Losses on the North Russia run had been extremely heavy since 1 March; 16 out of 84 northbound ships, 11 out of 78 southbound ships, in four convoys each way. These were far greater than the losses on any other convoy route, nor do these figures include vessels damaged or sunk at Murmansk by air bombing and mines. Losses while in port were so serious, and the loss of berthing facilities by air bombing was so great, that Captain Frankel ordered all PQ convoys after 1 July to proceed to Archangel, and transferred all American ships thither that were detained at Murmansk.

Although the German surface fleet had proved far less dangerous than submarines or Luftwaffe, it was some relief to the Allies that no enemy sorties were made for two months after 2 May, when *Schoemann* was lost. The reason for this abstention, it subsequently

[16] American S.S. *City of Joliet*, *Mormacsul*, *Syros*, *Alamar*; British S.S. *Empire Purcell*, *Lowther Castle*, *Empire Lawrence*. Survivors to the number of 300 were brought in by the Polish destroyer *Garland*.

[17] N.O.B. Iceland to Convoy & Routing 31 July 1942.

appeared, was German shortage of fuel oil;[18] *Tirpitz* had consumed such enormous quantities by her spring cruise in the Land of the Midnight Sun that there had to be a logistics build-up before any capital ship could come out again. By the first of July she was ready again; and Convoy PQ–17 was the intended victim.

5. *The Ordeal of PQ–17*

Fighting through to North Russia worked up to a climax on 4 July 1942, when Convoy PQ–17, from Iceland bound to Archangel, was dispersed in the grimmest convoy battle of the entire war.[19]

Convoy PQ–17, 33 merchantmen in addition to three rescue vessels and a fleet oiler, sailed from Reykjavik 27 June 1942. It included 22 American merchantmen, several of which had been to Murmansk before. Others had left United States ports as long ago as March, and reached Iceland by way of an HX convoy and Loch Ewe, Scotland. The unusually large escort – six destroyers, two flak ships, two submarines and eleven corvettes, minesweepers and armed trawlers, H.M.S. *Keppel* (Commander John E. Broome RN) flagship – was supplemented, as we shall see, by powerful support and covering forces. There were more combat ships escorting or supporting this convoy than there were merchant ships to protect.

The German naval commander in northern waters, who had the appropriate name of Schniewind, was ordered from Berlin at the end of May to plan a combined air-surface-underwater operation to annihilate the next North Russia convoy. The German Ad-

[18] *Operation und Taktik.*

[19] See head of chapter for general sources. The captured *Kriegstagebuch der Seekriegsleitung* (War Diary of German Naval Staff), printed secret publication *Operationen u. Taktik, Auswertung wichtiger Ereignisse des Seekrieges* No. 13 Part I (Berlin, Aug. 1944), with chart, and Admiral Carls's Action Report on Operation "*Rösselsprung*," contain ample information from the German side. Action Reports and War Diaries of U. S. warships involved, especially those of *Wainwright* and of Comdesron 8 (Capt. D. P. Moon); conversations with Capt. H. E. Orem, executive officer of U.S.S. *Wichita*. Survivors' stories in *N. Y. Times* 23 Feb. 1945 are very inaccurate.

miralty was very well informed of the sailing date and composition of Convoy PQ–17,[20] and to this operation, which received the name *Rösselsprung* ("Knight's Gambit"), it assigned battleship *Tirpitz,* as well as *Scheer, Hipper* and seven destroyers.

Convoy PQ–17 was routed around the western and northern coasts of Iceland to long. 19° W, then northeast to lat. 75° N, passing along the eastern shore of Jan Mayen Island; then due east to well past Bear Island, next southeast, and finally south to the White Sea entrance. Fortunately the ammunition allowance for merchant ships engaged in Russian business had been doubled before this convoy sailed, but many of the ships were still pitifully underarmed. The Liberty ship *Benjamin Harrison,* for example, carried only two .50-caliber Browning and two .30-caliber Lewis machine guns, plus a twin Marlin .30-caliber put aboard in Scotland. Her Armed Guard commander reported that he saw bullets of both calibers bounce off the armor of attacking planes. Only three of the American merchantmen carried 3-inch anti-aircraft guns; the rest had nothing heavier than machine guns. The Panamanian *Troubadour* had one 4-inch 50-caliber. With the master's consent, Ensign H. E. Carraway USNR, the Naval Armed Guard officer, opened up two tanks carried as deck cargo, put their 37-mm guns in readiness, and broke out ammunition from the hold. These tank guns were used effectively and probably disabled one plane in the attacks of 4 July. Ensign Carraway was commended for having broached the ship's cargo to such good purpose; one of the rare instances in naval history when barratry has been rewarded by a decoration instead of a stretch in the "brig." [21]

Supporting Convoy PQ–17 was a cruiser task force commanded by Rear Admiral L. H. K. ("Turtle") Hamilton in H.M.S. *London,* comprising H.M.S. *Norfolk,* U.S.S. *Wichita* (Captain H. W. Hill) and U.S.S. *Tuscaloosa* (Captain N. C. Gillette). The screen included U.S.S. *Wainwright* and *Rowan* and seven British destroyers

[20] Assmann Diary, recording conference of Admiral Raeder with Hitler on 15 June.

[21] Office of Naval Records, Sound Archives Recordgraph No. 357, 26 Mar. 1945.

and corvettes.[22] This force sailed from Seidisfjord, Iceland, 1 July 1942. An even more formidable covering force, constituted in order to deal with the *Tirpitz* or other German capital ships, was commanded by Admiral Tovey (Commander-in-Chief Home Fleet) in H.M.S. *Duke of York*, and comprised U.S.S. *Washington* flying the flag of Rear Admiral Giffen, H.M. aircraft carrier *Victorious*, heavy cruiser *Cumberland*, and light cruisers *Nigeria* and *Manchester*, two U. S. destroyers (*Mayrant* and *Rhind*) and nine or more British destroyers and corvettes. The covering force sailed from Scapa Flow 29 June, but operated in waters between Iceland and Spitsbergen because it was also responsible for the safe return of a westbound convoy. In course of time, this force ceased to be in direct support of Convoy PQ–17, but its presence, reported by German aircraft, led to the *Tirpitz* being ordered to retire, since the German high command was not prepared to expose her to the danger of attack by carrier-borne aircraft.

Convoy PQ–17 sailed from Hvalfjordur 27 June, and in the Strait of Denmark encountered thick fog and heavy ice floes. One freighter ran aground and another was so damaged by ice that she had to put back. On 1 July, when about 200 miles west of Bear Island, the first German reconnaissance planes were sighted, and shadowed them. Next day the first submarine attack was delivered by six U-boats, but "frustrated by the destroyers." [23] The Germans were now very much muddled in their estimate of the convoy's position and the composition of the Support Force, although their submarines had been dogging it from a point 60 miles east of Jan Mayen. They were confused by the presence of the westbound convoy (QP–13) in the same area, and by their reconnaissance plane pilots, who reported *Wichita* and *Tuscaloosa* as aircraft carriers and H.M.S. *London* as a battleship. Nobody in Berlin or Narvik was able to figure out exactly what the Allies had up there; but they located PQ–17 all right, and "threw the book" at it on 2 July.

[22] Six of these joined 4 July.
[23] *Kriegstagebuch*. *U–367* and *U–253* are mentioned.

Just as *Rowan* was joining the convoy that day, eight torpedo planes attacked the convoy. She shot one down with no damage to the ships.[24] At 1500 July 3, twenty-six German planes launched a bombing attack which failed owing to low cloud ceiling. Shortly after the weather cleared, Admiral Hamilton's Support Force appeared, and continued to patrol within visible distance, but mostly on the north flank of the convoy, which afforded no anti-aircraft protection.

At 0300 July 4, a Heinkel 115 emerged from a fog bank on the convoy's starboard hand, and launched a torpedo that passed between *Samuel Chase* and *Carlton* in the outer column, heading for the midship section of the Liberty ship *Christopher Newport* in the eighth column. Her Naval Armed Guard officer ordered his .30-caliber machine-gun crew to open fire on the torpedo in an attempt to explode it before it reached the ship. As he tells the story: –

> . . . The merchant seamen acting as loaders and other merchant seamen near the gun turrets became panic-stricken. They yelled at Hugh P. Wright, Seaman First Class, to run for safety and scrambled down the ladder on the after end of the flying bridge, heading for the boats on the port side. Wright opened fire in the water just ahead of the torpedo wake. He continued firing and changing pans as fast as he emptied them. Realizing the complete uselessness of his .30-caliber, Wright still kept firing until the torpedo passed out of sight under the starboard boats which were swung out. Throughout the firing, Wright's fire was very accurate and his coolness was evidenced by the fact that he kept up a running stream of oaths directed at his "B–B gun." . . . He knew that 30 feet away he would be in comparative safety. When the torpedo exploded, Wright was blown off the flying bridge, down two decks to the boat deck, spraining his ankle and knocking him unconscious.

As the torpedo exploded in the engine room, destroying her power plant, *Christopher Newport* was abandoned and sunk by the guns of an escort.

Independence Day celebration had barely begun. The Fourth

[24] War Diary. She had just been detached from the Covering Force to join the PQ–17 Escort or Support Force.

opened overcast, if you can call it opening when darkness never closed in. The ceiling was 300 to 500 feet, just what the planes wanted; sea smooth as an undulating mirror, and light airs. Next on the German program was a bombing attack and a torpedo attack by Heinkel 111Ks. Three of them were shot down, one after S.S. *Washington's* gun had poured about 600 rounds of ammunition into her at point-blank range. Next, at 1915, came a torpedo attack by 25 Focke-Wulfs. Four ships were hit, but two subsequently rejoined the convoy. A feature of this battle was the gallant action of U.S.S. *Wainwright* (Lieutenant Commander R. H. Gibbs), flying the pennant of Captain D. P. Moon, Commander Support Force Screen. In mid-afternoon she proceeded to join the convoy, then about 18 miles away, in order to fuel from the British tanker *Aldersdale*. During her approach, at about 1647, she helped break up an attack by six torpedo planes in the starboard quarter of the convoy, and at 1700 drove off another torpedo plane. She delivered highly accurate long-range fire, which prevented the planes coming anywhere near dropping distance. The enemy, having recognized "Don" Moon's value to the convoy, paid him the compliment of singling *Wainwright* out for a brief dive-bombing attack by planes hidden in the 500-foot ceiling. She evaded them successfully by hard right rudder and turning up maximum speed; the bombs missed by 150 yards.

About two hours later, during a delusive and temporary quiet spell, the *Wainwright*, which had been at the head of the convoy, proceeded down its starboard flank to close the tanker from which she was to fuel. Then, at 1820, about 25 two-torpedo planes (Heinkel 111Ks) were sighted circling just above the southern horizon. As *Wainwright* turned left, the planes formed into two columns, one on the starboard quarter heading north in line abreast, and the other circling to the left to attack on her starboard bow. Captain Moon estimated this group as the more dangerous, because the convoy's advance meant an additional run for the torpedoes launched from his quarter. When the attack developed she had about cleared the convoy and was inside the screen. Bending on

32½ knots she passed outside the screen, aiming to meet the Heinkels and shoot them down beyond effective torpedo firing range. She opened at 10,000 yards on the planes coming in on the starboard quarter, and continued shooting until her fire became dangerous to the convoy, when she shifted attention to the more dangerous bow attack.

Captain Moon reports, "By the time the planes on the starboard bow were ready to launch torpedoes, the *Wainwright* had moved out to a position between 3000 and 4000 yards on the starboard bow of the convoy. Of this bow group of planes only one was observed to drop its torpedo inside the *Wainwright*." The others dropped at a range of 1000 to 1500 yards on the starboard bow of the destroyer. Their wakes were observed and the ship's course was changed hard right to "comb" their tracks. No torpedoes from the bow group of planes connected with a target, but several of those coming in from the starboard quarter, where there was no destroyer protection, scored. Liberty ship *William Hooper* was abandoned without orders by her crew and four of the Naval Armed Guard when hit in the engine room, and subsequently sunk by the escort. The Russian tanker *Azerbaidjan* was damaged but carried on. *Wainwright* was intensively strafed, but no one was injured, and three or four planes were damaged by her anti-aircraft fire. The whole action lasted only ten minutes. Despite the success of *Wainwright's* maneuver (and the German Staff War Diary admitted "unfortunately greater losses sustained by the attacking group"), Captain Moon had no illusions as to the threat presented by determined air attack: "With determined torpedo plane attacks carried right into a convoy and picking out individual targets by a large number of planes without regard to risk, it is believed that heavy losses to a convoy would always result. In this attack only one plane met this standard – a very brave man. The water looks cold 900 miles from the Pole. However, the other planes on the starboard quarter followed him into good firing range."

The worst was yet to come. At about 1900 July 4, Admiral Hamilton, on orders from the Admiralty, announced the withdrawal of his Support Force, and ordered the convoy to scatter.[25] Information had reached London that *Tirpitz, Scheer* and eight destroyers were on the warpath; consequently the Support Force withdrew to the westward in the hope that this might divert the enemy from the scattering convoy. No effort was made to head the enemy off, as in December 1943 when the *Scharnhorst* was caught, because air and surface strength was so heavily loaded in favor of the Germans that the risk was inacceptable. Admiral Tovey's Covering Force, including U.S.S. *Washington*, was at that time steaming west of South Cape, Spitsbergen, some 230 miles from the convoy and a good 400 miles from the *Tirpitz;* and so beyond any possibility of protecting the one or handling the other. Everyone from Admiral Hamilton down was distressed at the Admiralty's orders,[26] which were based on an overestimate of the enemy's aggressive intentions. *Tirpitz, Scheer, Hipper*, seven destroyers and three torpedo boats did indeed sortie from Altenfjord on 5 July with Admiral Carls in tactical command, but the German high command was so mystified by the conflicting reports of Luftwaffe pilots, and so intent on not losing its last remaining battlewagon, that the *Tirpitz* group steamed footlessly to the eastward about 25 miles off North Cape,[27] and then returned to Altenfjord without making a contact. The Admiralty also was in doubt, having information of German fleet sorties from Trondheim and Narvik. Although the screen was not included in the Admiralty's orders to withdraw, the escort commander "expected to see the cruisers open fire and the enemy's masts appear on the horizon at any moment." [28] He decided to pull his destroyers out to sup-

[25] War Diary 4 July at 1923 records it. The actual signals were, "Cruiser Force withdraw to westward at high speed. Owing to threat from surface ships, convoy is to disperse and proceed to Russian ports. Convoy is to scatter."

[26] "I know you will all be as distressed as I am at having to leave that fine collection of ships to find their own way to harbor" – message from the Admiral recorded in *Tuscaloosa* War Diary 0115 July 5.

[27] Admiral Giffen's War Diary reports receiving radio report at 1949 July 5 that *Tirpitz* & Co. were at lat. 71°25′ N, long. 23°40′ E, and that a Russian submarine claimed two hits on the big boy. This was a correct estimate of their position according to a German chart obtained after the war.

[28] Admiralty sources.

port the cruisers; this created a near panic among the armed trawlers and other weak escorts and they too scattered.

Convoy PQ–17, when dispersed, was 240 miles bearing 8° from North Cape. The merchantmen had over 450 miles to go before reaching whatever protection Novaya Zemlya might afford. Already near the edge of the ice pack, they could withdraw no further from the Norwegian coast, but had to steam along within range of enemy airfields.

That passage from the dispersal point on was a *via dolorosa* for every merchant ship. There has never been anything like it in our maritime history. The Barents Sea, named after the Netherlandish discoverer of Novaya Zemlya, whose crew made their way home in an open boat after their ship had been crushed in the ice, was known to very few of our mariners. They had ample opportunity to check on the experience of that old Dutchman: "The ice came so fast upon us that it made our haires stare upright upon our heades, it was so fearefull to behold."[29] But there were no U-boats or Luftwaffe in those days.

The tank-laden S.S. *Carlton*, steaming alone, was sunk by a U-boat on 5 July. Most of her crew were rescued by the submarine, and the skipper gave the Germans valuable information.[30] S.S. *Washington*, already leaking from previous attacks, proceeded when the convoy dispersed to lat. 79° N, where an ice floe barred her passage into the Barents Sea. She then steamed southeasterly, in company with two British merchantmen, hugging the ice floe and stacking the more explosive part of her cargo – 350 tons of TNT – on the port side, since torpedoes could only reach her from the starboard hand. Radio reports kept coming in of other ships being torpedoed. At 1500 on 5 July a Junkers 88 swooped down, sprayed the three vessels with machine-gun fire, and dropped bombs which near-missed; the plane got away, undamaged by

[29] Gerrit de Veer *Voyage of William Barents to the Arctic Regions 1594, 5, 6*, English trans. of 1609 (Hakluyt Society ed.) p. 195.

[30] *Kriegstagebuch* for 5 July. Prisoners from this ship, released after V–E day and returned to the United States, were responsible for some wild stories about the convoy.

Washington's .50-caliber fire. Three quarters of an hour later, nine more Junkers dove on the three merchantmen out of the clouds and sank them, every one.

Washington's crew of 46, including the naval unit, got away safely in two lifeboats. S.S. *Olopana* appeared in answer to her S O S, but the crew refused to board her, deeming their own boats safer; they were right, for *Olopana* was torpedoed and sunk next day. On 8 July the lifeboats ran into floating ice and a snowstorm that lasted six hours; another snowstorm almost as long overtook them next day. On the 11th they sighted the coast of Novaya Zemlya, and landed the 12th, suffering acutely from exposure and hunger. Ensign Charles M. Ulrich USNR, commander of the Armed Guard, shot a sea gull; others captured eight goslings, and soup was made. Having eaten, all hands returned to their boats in the hope of finding a settlement further along the coast. They did not have the luck of another torpedoed merchantman's crew, who made land hard by a camp of Soviet "pioneers," husky children who fed them well.[31] After two more days in their boats, *Washington's* men met four boatloads of survivors from S.S. *Paulus Potter*, the Dutch merchantman sunk in the same attack. All landed together on Novaya Zemlya, snared a hundred or more helldiver ducks, and made soup for over a hundred men, one third of whom, with frostbitten feet, could no longer walk. Next day, 15 July, they began rowing in the direction of the Russian mainland and encountered S.S. *Winston-Salem* grounded on a sand bar.[32] All hands boarded her for their first real meal and rest in ten days. A Russian whaling ship took them off and placed them on board the British S.S. *Empire Tide*, who had been chased by a German submarine into Matochkin Strait, the passage that divides the two large islands of Novaya Zemlya. This small steamer now had 240 men aboard. German observation planes constantly flew over and food ran short; so *Washington's* crew, excepting the Navy detail, took to

[31] Survivor's narrative in *N. Y. Daily Worker* 20 Sept. 1942.

[32] Capt. S. B. Frankel flew up to Novaya Zemlya in an antique Catalina to help get the *Winston-Salem* off, and she proceeded under her own steam to Molotovsk.

the boats again and camped on the shores of the Strait. On 20 July *Empire Tide* joined a remnant of the convoy which had been picked up again by escorts. Five days later this battered fleet, consisting of five merchant ships, one Fighting French corvette, two Russian destroyers and eight small British escorts, steamed into Archangel, where crew members who were in a bad way received good treatment in Russian hospitals.

The Liberty ship *Daniel Morgan* made a magnificent effort to carry her cargo through. Throughout the Fourth of July she remained within sight of her sister ship *Samuel Chase*, dogged by German patrol planes. At midnight a British flak ship paused long enough to blink the cheerful signal that the *Tirpitz* group were coming. For her part she proposed to seek safety in any bay that offered along the Novaya Zemlya coast, and advised *Chase* to do the same. The anti-aircraft ship then steamed off at 14 knots, which soon left 12-knot *Chase* well astern. *Morgan* laid a course for Admiralty Bay, Novaya Zemlya, maintaining a zigzag pattern. Early on 5 July she joined three other merchantmen from the scattered convoy. They proceeded in company towards the protection of a near-by fog bank. An enemy patrol plane kept them under observation. *Morgan's* Armed Guard officer, Lieutenant (jg) Morton E. Wolfson USNR, reports that "Just before entering the fog bank, this ship swung around, keeping the patrol plane ahead, and fired its 3-inch 50-caliber gun in a steady barrage, not allowing the plane to check the courses taken by the other merchant vessels as they entered the fog. This ship then stood off alone."

In the late afternoon when the fog lifted *Daniel Morgan* found herself near another lost sheep, the *Fairfield City*. Before long they were bombed by three Junkers 88s and the *Fairfield* was sunk. Shortly after, three more Junkers came in view and joined the others in an attack on *Morgan*. "Nine sticks of bombs were dropped on this ship during the next hour, resulting in no hits or near-misses," reported Lieutenant Wolfson. "The ship was kept swinging and all anti-aircraft guns firing; the forward gun at a rate of 30 per minute. The men were beginning to show signs of physical exhaustion and eyestrain, having been at quarters over 28 hours. . . . There was a short interval of 15 minutes between attacks, giving us time to load the ready boxes before another group of five Junkers 88s came into view. The planes circled and rose for position in the sun, and then individually, in succession, started their dives." The first plane, after releasing two bombs which missed, was hit by *Morgan's* 3-inch gun, and was last seen with flames coming out of his engine and the forward part afire. The second and fourth planes missed and pulled out. The third missed, was set afire by the 3-inch shells, and splashed three miles away. The fifth dropped two bombs close aboard which ruptured plates between Numbers 4 and 5 holds. After two more dives had been executed unsuccessfully, *Morgan's* 3-inch gun overheated and jammed. She was taking water fast, and her ammunition was nearly exhausted. Fortunately the three remaining Junkers retired.[33]

Morgan was now in a sinking condition, and the captain ordered his men to abandon ship. As they pulled away she was sunk by a torpedo from a submarine which surfaced, took snapshots, asked questions of the survivors, and gave them the course to the nearest land. The lifeboats at 0200 July 6 encountered the Soviet tanker *Donbass*, formerly of the convoy, which took the survivors on board. *Morgan's* Navy gun crew, though physically exhausted, at once volunteered to man the tanker's forward gun. This was fortunate both for them and for the Russians, as they scored a hit on a diving Junkers 88 that very day and drove off two more the next. They also repaired the after gun, manned by the Russian crew, who had neglected lubrication. *Donbass* came to anchor at Ioanka at 0130 July 8, ending a long continuous watch for the American gun crew. After a rest of six hours she proceeded under Russian escort into the White Sea and to Molotovsk. The Soviet government was so pleased with *Morgan's* Naval Armed Guard that they sent a high-ranking commissar out to thank them personally.

[33] This action took place in lat. 75°08′ N, long. 45°06′ E, about 140 miles due W of Admiralty Peninsula, Novaya Zemlya.

Samuel Chase in the meantime, constantly hearing by radio of the sinking of her friends, continued to flee before the reputed course of the German battle fleet. With three other American merchantmen she took refuge in Matochkin Strait on 6 July. With the British flak ship, the British S.S. *Ocean Freedom,* and other small escorts and merchantmen who were hiding there, she made up a convoy of six ships with ten escorts. Next day this pitiful remnant got under way, planning to run close along the shore of Novaya Zemlya to Ioanka. They encountered thick fog and heavy ice. S.S. *Benjamin Harrison* disappeared; the rest were dive-bombed continuously, except for one ten-minute interval, from 2200 July 9 to 0530 next day. Heavy anti-aircraft fire kept the planes from diving low, and of the nine ships only *Hoosier* and *El Capitán* had to be abandoned in a sinking condition. *Samuel Chase* was dive-bombed by six Junkers 88s, receiving six near misses which snapped all the steam lines, cut off the auxiliaries, and blew the compass out of the binnacle; but after a few hours of vigorous repairing she was able to proceed. Two planes were shot down in this action. That afternoon *Chase* was again attacked by Junkers, but the protective fire from two British sloops and an armed trawler kept them high, and no damage was done. During the evening Russian planes appeared overhead and a Russian pilot came aboard to guide them into the White Sea and up to Molotovsk.

Except for frostbitten feet, there were no casualties among these three splendid gun crews of S.S. *Washington, Daniel Morgan* and *Samuel Chase.* Their clothing was inadequate and their ammunition insufficient, but their fighting spirit never failed. And they were vigorously supported by the officers and men of the merchant ships whom they were protecting.

When S.S. *Benjamin Harrison* disappeared from this rump of a convoy, she had merely lost them in the fog. On 8 July she returned to Matochkin Strait, where she was joined by H.M. armed trawler *Ayrshire,* the Panamanian S.S. *Troubadour,* and two British merchantmen. Master George J. Salvesen of the *Troubadour* showed himself to be a fellow of infinite resource and cunning.

A veteran navigator of the Arctic, he had cast around in his mind for the best method of concealing his ship. An abundance of white paint was discovered in the paint locker, and when apprised of this, the commander of H.M.S. *Ayrshire* immediately approved his plan and ordered all ships in the group to paint their starboard sides white and spread bed and table linen over the hatches for Arctic camouflage. With all hands vigorously painting and the *Troubadour* (whose reinforced bow made her the logical choice) leading at her best icebreaking speed of 3½ knots, the column penetrated the ice for a distance of about 20 miles, turned their starboard sides seaward and waited until late in the afternoon of 6 July.[34]

These five ships in Matochkin Strait were now joined by two Russian freighters, a tanker and a trawler, all from Convoy PQ–17. They too adopted the Salvesen white camouflage doctrine, and moved inshore as far as the ice would permit, under the shadow of the Novaya Zemlya mountains. A low-flying enemy plane that entered the strait never sighted them. After a not uncomfortable sojourn of about two weeks, this group got under way and made Archangel on 25 July.

Of the 21 American merchantmen in this convoy carrying Naval Armed Guards, two thirds were lost.[35] On 4 August 1942 there were at Archangel and various places in the Kola Inlet about 1300

[34] Report of *Troubadour's* Armed Guard Officer, Ens. H. E. Carraway USNR, 5 Nov. 1942 and conversations with him in Mar. 1945.

[35] Summary of American (U. S. and Panama) merchantmen in Convoy PQ–17: (1) Sunk in convoy, *Christopher Newport* and *William Hooper*, both by torpedo planes. (2) Sunk after dispersal, traveling alone, *Alcoa Ranger, Honomu, John Witherspoon, Carlton* and *Olopana*, by U-boats; *Pan Atlantic* and *Pan-Kraft*, by dive-bombers. (3) Sunk in company with other merchantmen, unescorted, *Daniel Morgan, Fairfield City, Peter Kerr*, and *Washington*, all by dive-bombers (*Morgan* finished off by U-boat). (4) Sunk in rump convoy, *El Capitán* and *Hoosier*, by dive-bombers. Total sunk, 15. (5) Got through, *Samuel Chase, Ironclad, Silver Sword, Benjamin Harrison, Winston-Salem, Troubadour*, and *Bellingham*. British ships sunk were *River Afton, Navarino, Earlston, Empire Byron, Bolton Castle, Hartlebury*. Also Netherlands ship *Paulus Potter*. Two British and two Russian ships got through. Total merchant ships lost in this convoy, 22 out of 33, with 123,000 tons cargo out of 188,000 (Correspondence of Capt. Frankel and Memorandum of Cdr. Ames). This does not include the rescue ships: S.S. *Zaafaran* was sunk but her crew were rescued by the second, S.S. *Zamalek*, who got through, with the third, S.S. *Rathlin*. British fleet oiler *Aldersdale* was also sunk. Admiralty confirms these figures, except that it lists S.S. *Earlston* as Panamanian.

survivors, 581 of them Americans, whose ships had been sunk. Their fate demonstrated that unescorted merchant ships are helpless against land-based bombing planes, unless equipped with fairly large caliber guns and trained gun crews. The .30-caliber bullets could not make the range and the .50-caliber merely rattled off the Junkers; all the execution was done by 3-inch guns. As a result of this experience, the Navy issue of winter clothing was improved, and 20-mm, 3-inch AA and even 5-inch guns were shortly after installed on all merchant ships running "bomb alley" to North Russia, with sufficient naval personnel to man them properly.[36]

The Germans naturally were much elated over the result of "Operation Knight's Gambit." A not very exaggerated account of it, omitting the ignominious retirement of *Tirpitz,* was included in the pocket manual issued to the fleet, entitled "Convoy Slaughter in the Arctic Sea."

[36] Endorsement by "C.C.C." on Ens. Ulrich's Armed Guard Report.

CHAPTER VIII

Missions to Malta[1]

April–May 1942

THE gallant defense of the strafed, bombed and starved island of Malta has been well recounted elsewhere, and is in no need of further telling here.[2] But the United States Navy's part in relieving the besieged island fortress has a definite place in the history of American participation in the Battle of the Atlantic.

The trials of Malta began early when on 10 June 1940 Mussolini followed his "stab in the back" with the first bombing mission against the island; but the most acute period in its fight for survival occurred in the months of March and April 1942. Completely surrounded by Axis airfields in Sicily, Italy, Sardinia, Greece and Tripolitania, Malta was separated by nearly one thousand miles of sea from Gibraltar and over eight hundred miles from Alexandria, the nearest Allied base.

Some idea of the violence of the attacks which Malta sustained in 1942 may be gained by noting the weight of bombs dropped. In February it had not quite reached 1000 tons; in March it had increased to 2170, and in April to 6728 tons. The enemy was gaining local air superiority; and although Malta managed to continue its useful function of steppingstone for long-range aircraft proceeding from Great Britain to the Middle East, it was rapidly losing the ability to launch fighter planes to intercept bombing attacks. Air raids were so nearly continuous that an officer of the

[1] Commodore commanding Force "W" (Commo. C. S. Daniel RN) letters of 22 Apr. and 15 May 1942, enclosed in Comnaveu (Admiral Stark) "Reports of the Reinforcements of Malta by Spitfires Flown from U.S.S. *Wasp*" 26 June 1942; information from officers of *Wasp*.

[2] Ian Hay *Malta Epic* (1943); *The Air Battle of Malta; the Official Account of the R.A.F. in Malta, June 1940 to November 1942* (London, 1944).

Royal Artillery suggested that the British Broadcasting Company cut a long story short by reporting the number and duration of "all clears" during the month, instead of the attacks.

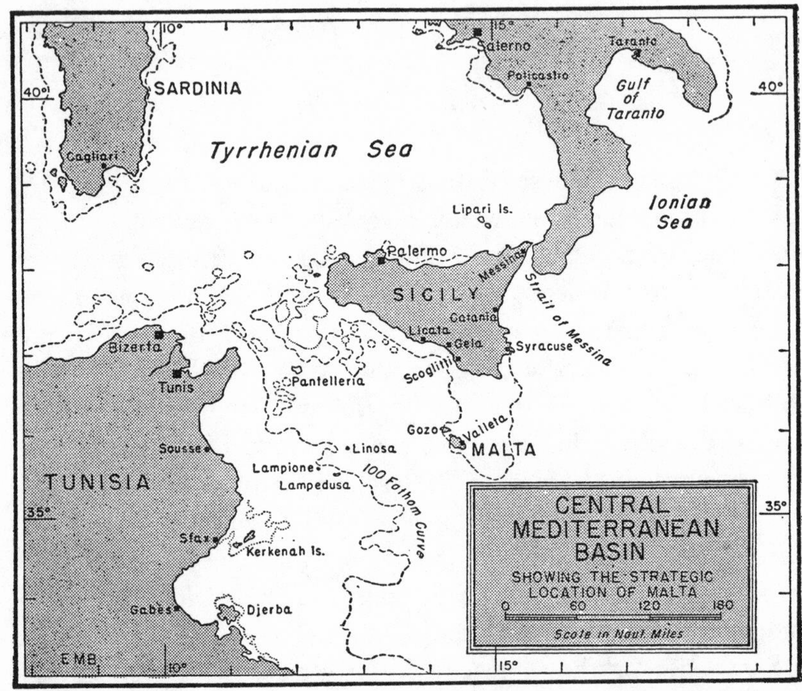

Malta's crying need was Spitfires with which to defend herself. These fighter planes did not possess sufficient range to fly the whole way from England via Gibraltar; they needed a lift. No British carrier that could transport enough planes to count was available. Consequently the Admiralty asked for and obtained the loan of U.S.S. *Wasp* (Captain J. W. Reeves Jr.) then operating in the North Sea. Admirals Ingersoll and King approved the assignment; *Wasp* sailed around Scotland through Pentland Firth and the Minches, called at Greenock and sailed right up the Clyde to Glasgow. Crowds on the riverbanks cheered madly as she stood up the stream; shipwrights at the John Brown yard even tossed their tools in the air by way of greeting. She took on board 47

Spitfires, together with their pilots and crewmen, at King George V Dock, turned in the artificial turning basin, and sailed on 14 April, escorted by Force "W" of the British Home Fleet, Commodore C. S. Daniel RN commanding in H.M. battle cruiser *Renown*. The screen, commanded by Captain W. W. Warlick USN, consisted of U.S.S. *Lang* and *Madison* and four British destroyers.

The passage south was uneventful; no Axis submarines bothered Force "W." It maneuvered so as to be out of sight of Cape Spartel at moonset 18 April, passed Europa Point abeam at 0200 on the 19th in order to avoid being sighted by Spaniards and Axis spotters, and headed eastward for the chosen launching position, about 50 miles north of Algiers.

At 0400 April 20, *Wasp* commenced launching planes "extremely quickly and with great precision,"[3] at a speed of 28 knots against a force 4 southwest wind. First eleven of her own fighter planes flew off for combat air patrol, the British-manned Spitfires followed, and all 58 planes were in the air by 0501. Such fast work was possible only because of special preparations. The Wildcats were readied topside while the Spitfires warmed up on the hangar deck. After the Wildcats were sliced off, each Spitfire rode up the elevator in eight seconds with engine running, found the takeoff flag already flying when reaching the flight deck, and took off immediately.[4]

Once the planes were on the way, Force "W" headed back for Gibraltar. At 1147 the welcome news arrived on board that all Spitfires had safely landed in Malta. Her mission accomplished, *Wasp* passed through the Straits during the night of 20–21 April and arrived at Scapa Flow on the 26th.

Unfortunately, the arrival of the Spitfires was immediately known to the enemy, who destroyed several of the planes on the ground before they could even be refueled and serviced. Although

[3] Force "W" letter, 22 April 1942.

[4] This system of launching, which had never been tried before, was necessary because the Spitfires had fixed, not folding, wings, so they could not be parked close on the flight deck prior to takeoff; and to take each one aloft in a slow and leisurely manner would have been far too hazardous for the *Wasp*. (Conversations with one of her officers.)

the others shot down about 40 Axis bombers in this attack, the situation in Malta became increasingly desperate during the last ten days of April. By the end of the month, the defenders had lost 23 Spitfires, with the rest so badly damaged that for days on end the air force was virtually grounded. It looked as though *Wasp's* reinforcements were "too little and too late."

Plans for sending out more planes were already under way, and on 7 May the island received the welcome news. Once more the *Wasp* provided transportation for 47 Spitfires, and again she accomplished her mission with exemplary skill and dispatch.

Escorted from the United Kingdom by U.S.S. *Lang* and *Sterett* and H.M.S. *Echo* and *Intrepid*, *Wasp* threaded the Straits for the third time on the night of 7 May. Off Europa Point she was joined by H.M. Carrier *Eagle*, transporting 17 planes from Gibraltar, and by the rest of Force "W." [5] Next day the task force made a detour to the northeastward, took departure from Formentera Light in the Balearics at 0200 May 9, and launched from about lat. 37°48′ N, long. 03°06′ E. This position was well within the 580-mile radius from Malta which had been laid down as the maximum range for Spitfires. *Wasp* sent off her first Malta-bound plane at 0638 and had launched the 47th and last 53 minutes later. One Spitfire accidentally dropped its belly tank and had to return to the carrier. "The pilot landed with considerable skill and immediately asked permission to fit a new tank, take off and proceed independently." [6] This was not granted, as the other planes then had too great a head start to be overtaken and the force was already steaming at 21 knots toward Gibraltar.

Wasp arrived at Scapa Flow on 15 May, and recovered the rest of her own planes. On the 18th she sailed for Hampton Roads. Thence she proceeded to the Pacific, where she soon met her end.

[5] *Eagle* was sunk by U-boats on 10 Aug. 1942 when escorting a Malta convoy.

[6] Force "W" Letter, 15 May 1942. Landing on the carrier was a difficult task, inasmuch as his plane had no hook. *Wasp* bent on all possible speed (30 knots), meanwhile issuing explicit instructions to the pilot. He made one feint and failed, and then took a one-wire landing, stopping only 10 feet from the forward edge of the flight deck.

Almost all the Spitfires staged in from *Wasp* and *Eagle* landed safely on Malta's pitted runways on 9 May. Reinforced by another flight over a week later, the R.A.F. was able first to hold its own and later to wrest the initiative from the Luftwaffe. Axis attempts to knock Malta out of the war became more numerous and more desperate. The siege and blockade of Malta continued through May, June and July of 1942 and several convoys were forced to turn back. A battle for supplies succeeded the battle of the air. But for the courage and resource of individual Maltese, the island would probably have fallen; aye, and would certainly have fallen but for the assistance afforded by U.S.S. *Wasp*, H.M.S. *Eagle* and other aircraft carriers which ferried in the planes to stave off defeat.

CHAPTER IX

Trends and Conclusions

January–June 1942

IF the reader will turn to the statistics in Appendix I at the end of this volume, he will obtain a conspectus of the ups and downs in anti-submarine warfare. The Eastern Sea Frontier, where the U-boats sank 82 ships of almost half a million gross tons during the first four months of 1942, had the unhappy distinction of being then the most dangerous area for shipping in the whole world; but afterwards it became comparatively safe. In Gulf Sea Frontier and Caribbean waters in May 1942 the Germans hung up a new record of 73 sinkings totaling over 350,000 tons. Particularly dangerous were three soft spots: off the Passes of the Mississippi, the East Coast of Florida, and the Yucatan Channel. The Gulf, the Caribbean and the eastern approaches to them were the most dangerous areas for shipping in June; the 69 ships sunk in these waters alone, amounting to 365,000 tons of shipping, were more than the entire world-wide loss by submarines in any month prior to February 1942.

These losses were serious enough in themselves, their repercussions were widespread and dangerous, their implications ominous. The only bright spots in the overall picture were the comparative immunity of transatlantic convoy routes since February, and the shipbuilding program. New construction had not yet replaced past losses, but in June it closely approached, and in July actually attained, the tonnage of total losses for that particular month. Since Admiral Doenitz's major objective was "to destroy more enemy tonnage than can be replaced by all Germany's enemies put together,"[1] the rise of new construction was cheering; but new ships

[1] From a press interview intercepted and translated at the time.

did not bring back lost cargoes or drowned sailors, and the number of submarines operating against our commerce was steadily rising as their skill increased. The submarine sailors had obtained experience rich with the realism of war, and attended by negligible losses. Some commanding officers were already on their third cruise in American waters. Their men had had ample opportunities for torpedo practice on live targets, for gunnery practice against unprotected merchantmen, and in eluding attacks by armed escorts. Admiral Doenitz had shown flexibility in his tactics and a strategy superior to that of Tirpitz in World War I; as soon as Allied build-up in one area brought diminishing returns, he pulled his packs off and sent them to a more promising spot, leaving one or two U-boats to patrol the convoyed area, seek targets of opportunity, and pin down ships and planes. Although he had been forced to lay off transatlantic convoys for the time being, he had seriously embarrassed American coastwise traffic and interrupted trade with Latin America.[2] Even Puerto Rico was suffering from inability to move crops or procure necessary food; one fifth of the tonnage employed in supplying that island and the armed forces stationed there had been lost by mid-June. Good neighbors to the southward were beginning to doubt the big neighbor's ability to win through. Sugar and coffee rationing were forced on the people of the United States, and tanker casualties — 3½ per cent per month of the tonnage employed — were so heavy that coastwise shipments of fuel oil for domestic purposes were stopped altogether. The available pool of oil derivatives was so diminished and the transport of them across seas, from the Dutch West Indies and the United States to Great Britain and to American bases in the Pacific, was so cut-into by the heavy loss of tankers, that impending military operations in Europe, Africa and the Far East were threatened. And, although the convoyed transatlantic lifeline

[2] Besides the heavy May–June sinkings in the two Caribbean and the Panama Canal areas, many of the 29 ships sunk in the mid-Atlantic area during those two months were plying between U. S. Atlantic ports and those of the East Coast of South America beyond the Amazon. In addition, there were five sinkings in the Brazilian area (see Chapter VI).

was still intact, it was rightly predicted in July that "because of our failure to devise an effective weapon to destroy submarines once they have been located, their concentrations in the North Atlantic are expected to continue to increase." [3] North Russia convoys were taking a terrible beating, and the still unprotected Cape route to the Middle and Far East was certain to be the object of attack before long.

During the first six months of 1942, losses of the American Merchant Marine from enemy action already surpassed those suffered during the entire course of World War I.

Another ominous development was the use of U-boats to land spies and saboteurs in the United States. *U–202*, which departed from Lorient 28 May with a party of saboteurs, landed them from a rubber boat at Amagansett, Long Island, on 16 June 1942, grounded but floated at high tide, refueled from another U-boat, and sank the Argentina freighter *Rio Tercero* on the homeward passage to Brest.[4] A second party of saboteurs was set ashore from the *U–584* on Ponte Vedra Beach, near Jacksonville, Florida, on 17 June. Both gangs were mopped up through vigilant work of the F.B.I. and Coast Guard.

This writer cannot avoid the conclusion that the United States Navy was woefully unprepared, materially and mentally, for the U-boat blitz on the Atlantic Coast that began in January 1942. He further believes that, apart from the want of air power which was due to prewar agreements with the Army, this unpreparedness was largely the Navy's own fault. Blame cannot justly be imputed to Congress, for Congress had never been asked to provide a fleet of subchasers and small escort vessels; nor to the people at large, because they looked to the Navy for leadership. Nor can it be shifted to President Roosevelt, who on sundry occasions prompted the Bureau of Ships and the General Board of the Navy to adopt

[3] Cdr. Hardin's Report p. 6.

[4] *U–202* was sunk off the Bay of Biscay 2 June 1943. From German sources it appears that the only other landing by a U-boat on American shores before 1944 was an agent placed on the southern shore of the Gaspé Peninsula, Quebec, on 9 Nov. 1942.

a small-craft program; but, as he once observed, "The Navy couldn't see any vessel under a thousand tons." In the end the Navy met the challenge, applied its energy and intelligence, came through magnificently and won; but this does not alter the fact that it had no plans ready for a reasonable protection to shipping when the submarines struck, and was unable to improvise them for several months.

Only once before, since the sixteenth century, had Anglo-American supremacy in the Atlantic been so seriously threatened as in the twelve months beginning in April 1942. That was exactly twenty-five years earlier. On that occasion, Lloyd George and Admiral Sims had persuaded the Admiralty to protect British shipping by convoys.[5] This time, the same remedy might prolong the patient's life by giving him temporary protection against the submarine bacteria, but he could not be cured unless those persistent and aggressive microbes were neutralized or killed. The attainment of that object, in conjunction with the two Royal Navies, was a task the magnitude of which was second only to defeating Japan; a task whose complexity goes far to condone our early setbacks.

[5] Elting E. Morison *Admiral Sims* p. 348.

CHAPTER X

The Organization of Anti-Submarine Warfare

1939–1942

1. *The Complex Problem*

HAVING described what the German U-boats accomplished during the first six months of declared war, we may now turn to the countermeasures initiated before the war began, and those adopted under the pressure of the emergency during 1942 and the first three months of 1943. Some were adopted promptly, others after several months' experiment, a few were tried and abandoned. The total effect, in this period of nine months, appeared to be little better than an even break with the U-boats. In April and May 1943, the quantity of escorts and quality of training began to tell; barring new factors, the German assault on shipping was definitely thwarted.

Anti-submarine warfare, even in the Atlantic, is difficult to isolate from other aspects of that total war. Every overseas operation that wrested bases from the Axis; every raid by United States Army and Royal Air Force bombers on German cities where submarines or their parts were made; every man on board ship or plane that harried a submarine or kept it down; every merchant seaman who did his duty and kept his mouth shut ashore; every fisherman who rescued a survivor from the ocean; every policeman or F.B.I. man who clamped down on a waterfront spy; every citizen who paid his taxes, bought war bonds, and restrained a desire to squawk over civilian inconveniences, helped to win the

Battle of the Atlantic. Nevertheless, in order to combat the U-boats, new organs of naval administration had to be set up, hundreds of new surface ships and thousands of new planes built, new technical devices developed by scientists in laboratories, schools to train naval personnel in anti-submarine warfare established, and officers trained to instruct in these schools. The history of the anti-submarine campaign would lose half its meaning if we did not know something of the organization and the special efforts and devices behind it.

In seeking a solution to the submarine problem a persistent delusion fostered by side-line strategists, and by certain naval officers too, was the notion that some one "answer" could be found; that the convoy system (or complete dispersal), building more and faster merchant vessels (or more and faster escorts), improving depth-charge procedure, replacing depth charges by ahead-firing devices, night illumination, replacing surface escorts by aircraft, improved sound devices and radar, better gunnery control, bombing the U-boat bases in France and the shipyards in Germany, and other less practicable methods, techniques or devices, would win the war against the U-boat. Actually the problem of combatting the submarine was like that of lifting an immense jellyfish. Grasping it with two hands accomplished nothing, but with hands-all-around and heaving together, one could really do something to the so-and-so. Progress was made against the submarine only by seven-rayed coöperation: between the United States, British, Canadian and Brazilian Navies, among different branches of the American armed forces and merchant marine, between all bureaus of the Navy Department, between naval officers specially detailed for anti-submarine work and the Operational Research Group of civilian scientists, between foreign policy and military operations, and between the armed forces and the public.

The amount of study, energy and expense necessary to combat a few hundred enemy submarines is appalling. Hanson Baldwin declared in September 1943 that the major naval effort of the United Nations had so far been employed in anti-submarine warfare.

In money terms alone, counting the sunken ships and cargoes, time lost at sea, and expense of operating naval vessels and planes to protect the seaways, the efforts of the American Republics and the British Empire amounted to some hundreds of billions of dollars; while the lives lost by submarine action reached tens of thousands.

Considered globally, submarine warfare was not one-sided. In the Pacific the United States submarines made an immense contribution to victory over Japan, which may be balanced against the losses in the Atlantic that the German and Italian submarines inflicted on us. But in the Atlantic the balance did not begin to tip our way until mid-1943. Beaten Nazis may take comfort in reflecting that no army, fleet or other unit in World War II, with the exception of their own people who dealt in organized torture, wrought such destruction and misery as the U-boats. They deserve a diabolic paraphrase of Winston Churchill's tribute to the Royal Air Force – "No one accomplished so much with so little."

Accordingly, the anti-submarine measures, procedures and devices adopted by the United States armed forces, from before the war to about April 1943, will now be described in the following order. First, administration; second, the training devices that were invented, and the schools and analysis-research units set up; third, the ships; and fourth, the air fleet. Next we take up a major achievement in organization, the development and perfection of the coastal convoy system; transatlantic convoys having already been described in the previous narrative. A chapter devoted to various stopgaps and more or less amateur efforts follows. Finally we take up the subject of merchant ship production and protection to replace losses.

All these aspects and branches of the struggle were in great measure interdependent. Coastal convoys were impossible without more escorts and patrol planes; ships were ineffective without proper detection devices and offensive weapons; these in turn needed operators trained in special schools; inevitable losses of merchant ships had to be replaced by new construction, and all merchantmen needed better protection. A separate description of each aspect of anti-submarine warfare involves considerable repetition and some distortion; but there seems to be no other way to bring the whole subject home to the reader.

2. *Administration and Sea Frontiers*

Anti-submarine warfare, by its multifarious nature, could not be waged under a single command. In Germany, Admiral Doenitz never had more than one officer between him and Hitler. He too experienced difficulties in training personnel and procuring materiel, but he had almost complete control over the U-boats' designs, movements, strategy and tactics. Moreover, submarine warfare made up over 90 per cent of the German Navy's activity; it was hardly 20 per cent of our naval activity, though it consumed the major part of our effort in the Atlantic. In the first half of 1942 the Navy Department debated whether this aspect of warfare could not, similarly, be placed under an "anti-submarine czar," a single head responsible to the Commander in Chief of the Fleet. It was considered impossible because most of the ships, personnel, bureaus and organizations engaged in anti-submarine warfare had other duties as well. At almost every stage in the Battle of the Atlantic, nobody under the Combined Chiefs of Staff could decide how much effort and materiel, how many ships and personnel, could be devoted to combating U-boats. For instance, the production of the new Destroyer Escort class was set back many months because new construction of merchant vessels and landing craft for amphibious operations in both oceans were given priority for steel and diesel engines.

There was no administrative center of the Navy's efforts against the U-boats until March 1942, when Admiral King designated Captain Wilder D. Baker, then head of an anti-submarine analysis unit in Boston,[1] to set up an anti-submarine section of his staff in

[1] See below, Sec. 3*c* of this chapter, for the history and composition of this unit.

Washington. Captain Baker's section took the Pacific within its cognizance. It was responsible for overall materiel, supply, development and personnel training;[2] while the Boston Anti-Submarine Unit, of which more anon, analyzed past attacks and conducted a special training course for anti-submarine "teachers."

An important step toward unified control of merchant shipping was taken on 15 May 1942, when the Convoy and Routing Section of the Chief of Naval Operations, headed by Rear Admiral M. K. Metcalf, became a section of Cominch headquarters. About 1 July "C. & R." assumed full responsibility for the routing and reporting of all merchant shipping in the United States strategic area, and for troop convoys. The Army simply informed "C. & R." how many troops it wanted transported where and when, and how many Army transports it could provide; the Navy did the rest. Commander in Chief Atlantic Fleet, Admiral Royal E. Ingersoll,[3] provided the escorts and the rest of the transports; "C. & R." organized the convoy, and, in conjunction with the Admiralty, laid down the route.

Until the Tenth Fleet was organized in May 1943, Admiral Ingersoll was the head of anti-submarine warfare. He was one of the most sagacious of our flag officers on active duty. Living on board his flagship U.S.S. *Vixen*, steaming from one Atlantic port to another as occasion required, he kept his finger on the U-boat pulse. The public knew nothing of him; even to most of the Atlantic Fleet,

[2] The Miami subchaser school, and the two preëxisting sound schools at Key West and San Diego, were supervised and "sparked" by Capt. Baker from Washington.

[3] Royal Eason Ingersoll, son of Rear Admiral Royal R. Ingersoll, b. Washington, D. C. 1883, Naval Academy '05, 4th in class (three ahead of Nimitz). Ensign on board U.S.S. *Connecticut* when flagship of Rear Admiral Robley D. Evans, and made the world cruise in her. Taught seamanship and English at Naval Academy 1911–1913. Flag lieut. to three successive commanders Asiatic Fleet, in the old *Saratoga* and exec. U.S.S. *Cincinnati* in same fleet. Duty in office of Chief of Naval Operations during World War I; exec. of *Connecticut* and *Arizona;* three years in Office of Naval Intelligence; C.O. survey ship *Nokomis* 1924; Naval War College senior course and staff duty; asst. chief of staff to Admiral W. V. Pratt when Commander Battle Fleet and U. S. Fleet. C.O. *Augusta;* fitted out and commanded U.S.S. *San Francisco;* War Plans Division Opnav 1935–1938; Comcrudiv 6 1938; asst. to C.N.O. 1940; Cinclant 1 Jan. 1942–Nov. 1944; Com West S.F. and Dep. C.N.O. to Apr. 1946, when retired as Admiral.

he remained a shadowy, almost a legendary figure. But to Admiral Ingersoll's sagacity and seasoned "sea-cunning," to use an Elizabethan phrase, the Allied nations owed in large measure their progress against the submarine in 1942–1943.

A large responsibility in anti-submarine warfare fell on the sea frontiers, by reason of their control of coastal convoys and defense of the waters adjacent to the continent and the West Indies. These new organizations were necessary because modern warfare raised problems and created burdens that could not be dealt with by the old Atlantic Coast naval districts. Created early in the century, the naval districts covered small areas; there were seven of them between Quoddy Head and Key West. To rely on them to defend our coasts against submarines would have been equivalent to depending on county police for protection against high-powered gangsters. Admiral H. R. Stark, as Chief of Naval Operations, ordered the establishment of the Sea Frontiers on 1 July 1941.

Territorially, a sea frontier is an area extending from a definite section of the coast of North America seaward, for a space of roughly two hundred miles. There are four sea frontiers, including the Canadian Coastal Zone, on the Atlantic; the Panama Sea Frontier straddles the Isthmus. The Eastern Sea Frontier was the parent sea frontier organization and the only one whose authority extended beyond its own limits. Commander Eastern Sea Frontier had complete operational control over all forces allocated to his frontier. Once Admiral Andrews got his clutches on a destroyer, she ceased for practical purposes to belong to the Atlantic Fleet; only Admiral King could take her away. And he exercised jurisdiction over a coastal convoy that originated in his frontier, throughout its entire voyage, in order to simplify control. He worked in close coöperation with the Army Air Force, whose liaison officers sat side by side with naval officers in the control rooms at frontier headquarters, 90 Church Street, New York City.

As regards transatlantic convoys, the sole responsibility of a sea frontier was that of furnishing air protection while the convoy was within its area. After Cominch's "C. & R." Section had made up the convoy on paper and determined its route, all details of logistics, drawing up the sailing schedule with the time each ship must pass through the net, and many other details were attended to by the port director's office at the harbor where the convoy originated.

Commander Eastern Sea Frontier until the closing months of 1943 was Vice Admiral Adolphus Andrews.[4] A sixty-two-year-old Texan, senatorial in port and speech, "Dolly" Andrews had been on the active list for 41 years, and was one of the best-known flag officers of the Navy. Presidents were one of his specialties; his friendship for President Roosevelt probably saved him from being the scapegoat for the burning of the *Normandie*, and certainly helped him to get things for his vital frontier. He was receptive to every new suggestion for combatting the submarine menace. His staff was exceptionally large but highly efficient, including Captain Thomas R. Kurtz (chief of staff), Captain S. B. Bunting (assistant chief of staff), Captain John T. G. Stapler (operations), Captains Harry E. Shoemaker and Stephan B. Robinson (convoy and routing), Captain Ralph Hungerford (anti-submarine warfare), Captain Henry M. Mullinnix (air), and Lieutenant Commander Harry H. Hess (submarine tracking).

Rear Admiral James L. Kauffman, who came to the Gulf from N.O.B. Iceland 30 May 1942, in the midst of the U-boat blitz, was another efficient sea frontier commander. With a very small staff, of which Captain G. B. Hoey was chief, and slender resources, he pulled things together in a remarkable manner. He also had much delicate liaison work to perform with Mexico and Cuba. The Cuban Republic, which had a small fleet of gunboats and patrol

[4] Adolphus Andrews, b. Galveston, Texas 1879, Naval Academy '01. Served on board Presidential yacht *Dolphin* in Theodore Roosevelt administration; during World War I exec. of *Mississippi* and C.O. of the old *Massachusetts;* Naval War College and asst. chief of staff to Cincus; C.O. Presidential yacht *Mayflower* in Harding administration; naval aid to President Coolidge; American representative at Geneva Conference, 1927; C.O. *Texas;* chief of staff to Cincus 1934; Chief of Bureau of Navigation 1938; Commander Scouting Force with rank of Vice Admiral, 1938; Commandant Third Naval District and Eastern Sea Frontier 10 Mar. 1941. Retired 11 Nov. 1943; Chairman Navy Manpower Survey Board to 1945; died 19 June 1948.

craft, was the most coöperative and helpful of all the Caribbean states. The Cuban Navy took care of its own coastal shipping and participated in escorting the seatrains from Port Everglades to Havana.

3. *Weapons and Devices*[5]

a. Anti-Submarine Weapons

At the conclusion of World War I, the United States Navy almost lost interest in the effects of submarine warfare on slow-moving merchant convoys. The British, well knowing that their very existence depended on keeping sea lanes open, were not quite so casual. As early as 1921 the Admiralty set up an anti-submarine warfare unit for study, experimentation and practice. Officers of the Royal Navy were encouraged to enroll and allotted extra pay if they did. Thus, when war broke out in 1939 the British were somewhat prepared to fight U-boats, and the Canadians had the benefit of their experience.[6]

During the years of peace, American naval planning had been based on the assumption of mighty fleet actions in the Pacific. Fast transpacific convoys were anticipated, composed largely of transports and fleet auxiliaries; but training to protect slow-moving merchant convoys was largely neglected until 1937, when the growing aggressiveness of Hirohito and Hitler suggested that history might repeat itself fairly soon. This training had been given to very few officers of the United States Navy by 1941. The majority of officers knew that if a lurking enemy were picked up by a de-

[5] Based largely on study at and files of the A/S W Unit and the Operational Training Command Atlantic Fleet, and on *OEG Report 51* (Operational Evaluations Group Office of Chief of Naval Operations, Anti-Submarine Warfare) Part 1, History; Part 2, Anti-Submarine Measures (1946).

[6] Canadian escort vessels also had their own Sound School at Halifax, and attack teachers and dome teachers at Sydney, Ottawa, St. Johns and elsewhere. The Canadians invented a special night escort teacher. Officers and men of the Canadian Navy when in U. S. ports had full access to our training facilities as well. There was a complete interchange of equipment, teaching devices, doctrine and publications between the U.S.N., R.N. and R.C.N. since early 1941.

stroyer's sound gear, it was not enough to head the ship for the submarine by "seaman's eye" and drop a couple of "ashcans" on the spot, for the U-boat, in the meantime, would have selected another spot. "Seaman's eye" needed spectacles, such as sound gear drills, attack training and anti-submarine practice. For several months after we entered the war, there were too few vessels and patrol planes to train or use against a submarine running below the surface. Not for want of courage or lethal weapons, but from sheer lack of ships to find and hit targets through the opaque medium of salt water, were our first efforts so meager and unproductive.

The most common and ancient anti-submarine weapon is the depth charge, tossed out over the submarine from a destroyer or other ship. The familiar 300-pound "ashcan" set to fire by hydrostatic (water) pressure down to a depth of 300 feet, was evolved during World War I; 600-pounders and the Y-gun to fire them were developed at the very end of that conflict. But by 1920 interest in depth charges had practically ceased. Most United States ships turned in what they had and dismantled their depth-charge racks and firing devices. Slight improvements in pistols, covers, and in the hydraulic release gear of depth-charge racks were made in 1921–1922, and 1938; these however were but details added to the depth-charge armament left over from the last war. The Royal Navy was no better off; their only depth charge was "in all essential particulars . . . the same as that in service in 1918." [7]

At the end of 1941, the Mark–1 depth-charge projector, commonly known as the "Y-gun," was ordered replaced by the new Mark–6 or "K-gun." This could lay better patterns than the Y-gun, owing to the fact that as many could be installed along a ship's topsides as circumstances warranted, and the ship's gear did not interfere with it.

There was much discussion and experimentation [8] before the

[7] Admiralty *A/S Report* Sept.–Dec. 1945 p. 50.

[8] The experiments in the United States were conducted by the old Bureau of Construction and Repair before World War II.

Wasp at Scapa Flow, April 1942. In the background are H.M.S. *King George* and *Victorious*, U.S.S. *Washington* and *Wichita*

Spitfire being warmed up on deck of *Wasp*. H.M.S. *Eagle* in background

Mission to Malta

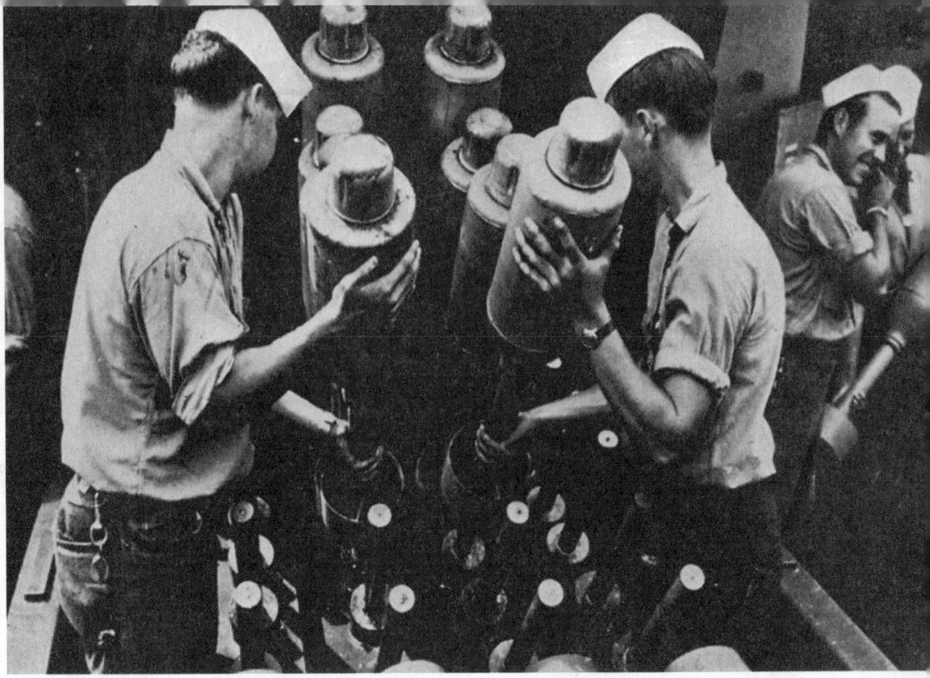

Hedgehog: projectiles being loaded on spigots

Mousetrap: loader raising retainers

"Mousetrap" and "Hedgehog"

war, both in England and the United States, as to how far a depth charge had to explode from a submarine's pressure hull in order to puncture it. In the instructions issued by the Atlantic Fleet at the end of 1942 it is stated that the Mark–6 (300-pound) charge is lethal within 21 feet, and the Mark–7 (600-pound) within 29 to 35 feet. This was probably too optimistic and, in any case, most lethal effects were produced by cumulative nonlethal damage from repeated attacks. By the middle of 1943 the Bureau of Ordnance had brought out a new 600-pound Mark–9 depth charge, streamlined so that it required only 8.6 seconds to sink 100 feet, and charged with Torpex which is half again as destructive as TNT.[9] But this was not available during the period now under review. The development of sonar echo-ranging, shortly to be described, changed depth-charge barrages from random patterns to an attempted saturation of a small area. No method of accurately determining the depth of a submarine was ever found, and the most perfect attack failed if the depth-charge setting was too high or too low.

In any depth-charge attack there is a necessary element of guess between the moments when sound contact on the target is broken and depth charges are released. Sound contact is always broken between 100 and 150 yards from the submarine, when it passes under the sound beam. If one could only shoot at the sub while still holding sound contact, it would be possible to aim a depth charge instead of tossing it out when you thought you were over the target. For that reason, ahead-thrown weapons were required in order to shoot when the enemy's position under water was certain.

Two ahead-thrown weapons were adopted by the United States Navy in 1942: "hedgehog" (Mark–10 and –11) and "mousetrap" (Mark–20 and –22). Hedgehog, adapted from a British design which Captain Paul Hammond USNR called to the attention of the

[9] The increased rapidity of sinking was of course extremely important in improved accuracy. The 250-lb. Torpex depth charge, the one commonly used by planes, was estimated after a series of experiments to be lethal only if it exploded within 10 or 11 feet of the hull.

Royal Navy,[10] consisted of a steel cradle from which project six rows of spigots firing 24 contact-fuzed projectiles. The charges fit over the spigots and are fired from them. As the ship is firing ahead before sound contact is broken, and as there is no disturbed water in case of a miss, she has a far better chance than in a depth-charge attack of inflicting damage and regaining contact.

The weight and severe recoil of the hedgehog projector precluded its use by PCs, SCs and smaller anti-submarine craft. For such vessels, and for destroyers which had no room for hedgehog on deck, the scientists developed "mousetrap." This device fires a pattern of four or eight small rocket projectiles. Since the projector is rigidly fastened to the deck, the ship herself must be aimed.

Perhaps because of better weather conditions, hedgehog was more successful in the Pacific than in the Atlantic, and mousetrap accounted for very few kills in either ocean. Neither replaced the depth charge, which was improved, as well as better employed, during the war. In 1945 the Royal Navy produced a new ahead-thrown weapon, the "squid," which proved very effective.

Together with these special weapons, anti-submarine ships mounted the usual types of naval ordnance according to their size. Machine guns proved to be useful in clearing a surfaced submarine's deck, but there is no record of any U-boat being sunk with a gun smaller than a 3-inch. The various 5-inch types were the most effective.

b. Sound Gear and Sound Schools[11]

The successful use of any weapon on an underwater target depends on detection devices installed on shipboard. Of these the oldest, developed by the Navy in 1916, was SC listening gear. This device, installed on the ship's bottom, conveyed to the operator's earphones the sound and direction of a U-boat's (or any

[10] Admiral Sir Geoffrey Blake RN informed the writer that Capt. Hammond, when on the U. S. Naval Attaché's staff in London early in 1942, "hotted up hedgehog" and persuaded the Royal Navy to experiment with it in the Clyde.

[11] Lt. Arthur L. Funk USNR "History of the Fleet Sonar School, Key West"; personal inspection of this school and the one at San Diego.

other ship's) propellers, but not the range. Experimentation for the improvement of sound gear was carried on by the United States and Royal Navies between the two wars. In order to provide range, both the British and ourselves invented a supersonic echo-ranging sound equipment which they called "asdic" and we named "sonar."[12] Housed in a streamlined retractable dome projected beneath the ship's bottom but operative only at moderate speeds owing to water noises,[13] sonar could be employed in two ways: listening for the U-boat's propeller noises, and echo-ranging with a sharp "ping" which the U-boat's hull returned, the time giving the range and the direction indicating the bearing. The echo reached the operator with varying degrees of pitch, depending on the nature and movements of the target. This variation in the pitch, known as the doppler effect, told a trained operator with a sensitive ear whether the target was a ship or a whale, whether it was stationary or moving, and its direction and speed.

In order to defeat sound search, German submarines were equipped with *Pillenwerfer*. This device shot out from a special tube a multitude of small, stationary gas bubbles, which returned an echo similar to that of a submarine. Trained sound operators could detect a submarine's echo from that returned by *Pillenwerfer* because the latter was stationary and hence gave no doppler effect.

But we are getting ahead of the game. Detecting doppler was but the first of many refinements which, together with sundry attachments, made sonar fairly effective in tracking submarines. An intensive course of training was necessary before a bluejacket could qualify to operate this device, or an officer use it intelligently. Experimental sonar was first installed on Destroyer Division 19 (U.S.S. *Rathburne*, flag, and *Waters*, *Talbot* and *Dent*), commanded by Commander James Cary Jones, Jr., and on two submarines, in 1936.[14] In 1939, when the Navy had sufficient funds

[12] I.e., "Sound-Navigation, Ranging." "Supersonic" means frequencies above the audible range of 16,000 to 15,000 vibrations per second.

[13] Up to 18 knots until about June 1943 when the design was improved.

[14] Information from Mr. Philip T. Russell, Sonar Installation Group, Electronics Division, Bureau of Ships.

and war seemed sufficiently close to recommission the old four-stack destroyers, it was decided to fit them out with sonar in order to make them effective anti-submarine vessels. About 60 old and new destroyers had been so equipped by September 1939; but by that time the Royal Navy had asdic on 165 destroyers and 54 other craft.

One or two ships of Division 20 were kept tied up at the San Diego destroyer base in 1939 in order to instruct sound operators of the newly fitted destroyers. Then a shore sound unit was set up at San Diego, and gradually the West Coast Sound School evolved.

The East Coast or Atlantic Fleet Sound School was established for the same reason and in the same way. It was first located at the submarine base at New London, where some of the shore personnel were already familiar with sound equipment, and where "tame" submarines could be borrowed to practise on. The first course opened on 15 November 1939 under Captain R. D. Edwards as commander, and Chief Radioman W. A. Braswell as instructor, to teach 16 men who had been assigned to four World War I destroyers of the Atlantic Squadron, U.S.S. *Ellis*, *Dupont*, *Cole* and *Bernadou*, first in the Atlantic to have sonar installed. They had no textbooks to study, no sound equipment to use, and only one day at sea; but they learned everything they could, and the top four men of the first class, who "graduated" in March 1940, were retained as permanent instructors. One of these, H. F. Rudowski (later commissioned Lieutenant), was identified with the Key West School throughout the war.

New students came in 1940, and the four above-mentioned destroyers gave them practice off New London until May 1940, when they were relieved by Destroyer Division 83 (*Lawrence*, *Humphreys* and *Sands*). The students, like all healthy young Americans, were delighted to handle a new piece of machinery. "Everybody in anti-submarine warfare at that time," recalled one of them, "was an inventor." But New London proved an unsatisfactory location for the Sound School on account of fog, shoal water, poor sound conditions, and other reasons. Consequently

Admiral King, when he became Commander in Chief Atlantic Fleet in September 1940, decided to transfer the School to Key West, where conditions were more favorable. There the School reopened in December under Commander Edward H. Jones with his Destroyer Division 54 (*Roper*, *Herbert*, *Jacob Jones* and *Dickerson*), three "tame" submarines of the S class, Lieutenant J. B. Swain as executive officer, three chief radiomen instructors, and a class of 61 enlisted sound operators. And at Key West the Atlantic Fleet Sound School remained. During 1941 its "output" was increased to 130 sound operators per month; and by Pearl Harbor, 170 United States destroyers exclusive of those allotted to the Royal Navy had had sonar installed.[15]

The Key West Sound School continued to enlarge until, during the first three months of 1943, 250 officers passed through the eight-weeks course, 1033 enlisted men began basic sound training and 969 were graduated. In addition, the Key West Sound School also trained 1016 officers and men of seven different foreign Navies[16] during the war. When it became too crowded, officers and men of the Atlantic Fleet were sent to the West Coast Sound School at San Diego, which kept up a steady enrollment of about 1200 students. To encourage men to seek this training, a sound film was shown at all "boot" training centers ashore to "sell sound," and recruits who volunteered were given a series of sound aptitude tests, devised by psychologists of the University of California, including the ability to distinguish doppler effects. Thus the Navy procured an intelligent and enthusiastic group of young men as operators. Not only at San Diego and Key West, but at Quonset, Bermuda, Guantanamo, Coco Solo, Trinidad and Recife, and several Pacific advanced naval bases, destroyers, naval planes and small anti-submarine craft were constantly practising attacks on "tame" submarines which stayed down for a period of six to

[15] Navy release above mentioned, p. 8.

[16] Including 615 British and 223 Brazilian. Cdr. E. H. Jones on 4 Jan. 1944 was relieved by Capt. J. S. Keating, who in turn was relieved by Capt. R. B. Nickerson on 10 Nov. 1944. All the earliest PCs, SCs, Coast Guard cutters and other escorts mentioned earlier in this volume were trained in sound-gear operation at Key West.

eight hours, matching their wits and evasive methods against the eager aggression of their surface and air "enemies."

Among the important devices to implement sonar that were adopted early in the war were the chemical recorder and the attack teacher, both British inventions. The former is a small metal box with a glass top, underneath which is a constantly moving roll of chemically treated paper. A small stylus moves back and forth over the paper, giving the range element on an underwater target. The recorder is attached to the vessel's sonar gear, and when an echo is received, a trace is made on the paper by the stylus. From the angle established by a series of these traces, an adjustable plotter bar indicates the rate at which the range is closing, and also gives the correct time to fire depth charges.

By the fall of 1941, the United States Navy had obtained from the Royal Navy several of these chemical recorders for installation at Argentia on destroyers engaged in transatlantic convoy. These were found to be so useful in depth-charge attacks that a contract for production of a similar device was awarded to the Sangamo Electric Company, whose first recorders built for the United States Navy were delivered 1 February 1942.[17]

While the chemical recorder is a practical device for installation on anti-submarine vessels, the attack teacher, also a British invention,[18] was a training device. In brief this was a large mechanical table on which anti-submarine attacks could be worked out in miniature and the results studied. A novice could thus learn how to direct his ship when confronted with a U-boat; an experienced officer who had bungled an attack could, by reproducing the conditions, learn wherein he had erred. United States Naval observers in England, seeing the possibilities of the British attack teacher, sent one for study to the Naval Research Laboratory in the summer of 1941, and in October it was installed at Portland, Maine, for the use of destroyer personnel. A second instrument was procured for

[17] Information obtained at A/S W Unit Atlantic Fleet.

[18] An American attack teacher was invented at the San Diego School, but did not prove satisfactory.

Argentia, where it was placed in charge of Lieutenant Commander A. G. W. McFadden, ordnance repair officer for Admiral Brainard's Support Force.[19] Another year elapsed before improved American versions of it were being produced in any appreciable numbers. The "Sangamo," first delivered 30 June 1942,[20] was the one mainly used in the two sound schools, and eventually installed at 15 or 20 naval bases at home and abroad which were frequented by anti-submarine craft. It projected the attacking vessel, the submarine, the sound echo and the depth-charge pattern [21] on a vertical screen visible to the "submarine crew," but not to the "destroyer crew" in the same room.

There were many pitfalls for inexperienced operators of sonar. Schools of blackfish, whales, wrecks, coral reefs, and even a layer of water of different temperature gave back echoes which could be distinguished from echoes on a steel hull only by an expert, and not always by him. Snapping shrimps on the ocean bottom made a curious crackling noise that disturbed sound-listeners. The *Anti-Submarine Warfare Bulletin* had to print special articles about the distribution and habits of these cetaceans and crustaceans in order to diminish false alarms.

Many seeds of future development in anti-submarine warfare were being sowed in Admiral Bristol's staff conferences at Argentia, and it was from his office that the suggestion came of a unit devoted exclusively to study and analysis of war against the submarines. On 27 January 1942 the Admiral, through Captain Carney his chief of staff, recommended "the establishment in Boston of an anti-submarine warfare unit, located where the dope can best be collected on the spot while it is hot, free from any other duties, working from practical experience, and furthering the aims of Cominch without further cluttering up Cominch's own staff. I feel sure that such a

[19] At that time all matters pertaining to anti-submarine warfare were under the cognizance of the Support Force Atlantic Fleet.

[20] This set went to the West Coast Sound School. (Information from Sangamo Electric Co.) Rear Admiral W. L. Ainsworth, when Comdespac, had one set up at Pearl Harbor in Aug. or Sept. 1942.

[21] The DC pattern, speaking strictly, is not projected but plotted by hand with a template.

unit commanded by the right officer would work in perfect harmony with Fleet Training, and at the same time furnish hot material for the Atlantic Fleet and its task forces daily engaged in anti-submarine warfare." [22]

c. The Anti-Submarine Warfare Unit

As a result of this letter a conference of destroyer officers and others was held on 5 February at the Boston Navy Yard. The Argentia proposal was adopted and further developed. Cominch and Cinclant promptly approved, and the Atlantic Fleet Anti-Submarine Warfare Unit was commissioned 2 March 1942 in Boston with Captain Wilder D. Baker, an experienced escort commander, as skipper. Captain Baker built up an able staff of assistants all of whom had experience and knowledge of anti-submarine warfare.[23] When detached to set up an anti-submarine section under Cominch at Washington in April 1942, he was relieved by Commander Thomas L. Lewis, another experienced destroyer officer. Closely articulated with the Boston organization was Asworg, the civilian scientists' Operational Research Group to be considered presently. They and the officers of the Unit produced valuable statistics, analyses and conclusions derived from or based on the attack information that flowed in from the Fleet. Collection and correlation of data, analysis and deduction were primary functions of the unit. A great volume of information was sifted, analyzed and published for the benefit of the Atlantic Fleet, and ultimately, for all United States and Allied fleets.

If the first function of this unit was study, the second was the training of instructors for the Key West Sound School, for the Subchaser School at Miami and for the various attack teachers

[22] Capt. R. B. Carney to Cdr. W. B. Moses, Gunnery Officer Atlantic Fleet, A/S W Unit files.

[23] Lt. Cdr. A. B. Vosseller, air activities; Lt. Cdr. McFadden, in charge of surface craft training; Lt. Cdr. J. T. Hardin, submarines; Lt. W. W. Strohbehn, communications; Lt. S. D. B. Merrill, materiel for surface craft; Lt. Richard Parmenter, Sea Frontiers' Liaison Officer; Maj. Cecil F. Reynolds, Army Air Liaison Officer; Chief Yeoman Francis C. Reynolds.

which were set up at naval bases from Iceland to Brazil. Thus the Boston Unit became a sort of teachers' college for anti-submarine warfare.[24]

Moreover, it had a salutary influence in standardizing anti-submarine doctrine.[25] Until it had been in operation a few months there was no standard procedure for sonar operators. A dozen different techniques in operating sonar were being followed in the summer of 1942. The study of doppler effect was largely neglected. The British were still far ahead of us in the use of asdic (as they called sonar); their sound operators on escort vessels were giving their officers more and better information than was supplied by ours. An American observer at the British Anti-Submarine School at Dunoon reported in June 1942 that lack of a specific, standard operating procedure for search and attack, such as the Royal Navy had had for some time, was the outstanding cause of our weakness in anti-submarine warfare.[26] The Boston Unit had, a month earlier, issued its first manual of standardized procedure; this was revised by the Key West Sound School, adopted by the Anti-Submarine Warfare Unit, and by it issued to the Atlantic Fleet on 2 August 1942. And a general manual on submarine warfare was issued by Cominch on 9 July. Doctrine was to evolve further until it became really standard; but even this early and imperfect systematization greatly increased the efficiency of anti-submarine instruction.

d. Scientists at Operational Level[27]

In every aspect of this planetary struggle, men of science have worked in laboratories inventing, developing and testing new

[24] Until the Subchaser School was established, the Boston Unit was the only school to which officers could be detailed from the Atlantic Fleet for a general anti-submarine warfare training, or to which newly commissioned officers could be sent for instruction in this specialized form of combat.

[25] "History of the Fleet Sonar School, Key West" pp. 12–13.

[26] Report of V. O. Knudsen to Dr. C. P. Haskins of the National Defense Research Committee, 23 June 1942, quoted in "History of Fleet Sonar School" p. 13.

[27] The Anti-Submarine Warfare Operations Research Group (Asworg) *Review of Activity* 1 Apr. 1942 to 31 Aug. 1944; *Summary Report to the Office of Field*

weapons, devices and military equipment in unheard-of quantities for the armed forces of the United States and her Allies. These indispensable means to victory worked in the background; some (like the David Taylor Experimental Model Basin) under the Navy; others (like the Harvard Sound Laboratory) in universities, and still others (like the famous Atomic Bomb enterprise) independently. These do not fall within the scope of a history of Naval Operations, and hence cannot be described in this work, despite their transcendent importance.

One organization of civilian scientists must however be included here because its members worked on the operational level, side by side with naval officers in advanced bases, in special groups like the Anti-Submarine Warfare Unit of the Atlantic Fleet, and even on board ships and in planes. This was the Anti-Submarine Warfare Operations Research Group (Asworg), an offshoot of the National Defense Research Committee whose chairman, since May 1941, had been James B. Conant, President of Harvard University. It was an integral part of the Navy, although its members remained civilians.

Conant with a number of fellow scientists visited England during the Battle for Britain and returned convinced that one of the main factors which saved England from destruction under the long sustained assaults of the Luftwaffe was a group of "operational" scientists. These men not only invented and developed, but aided and abetted, the operation of coastal aircraft-warning radar. The instruments, spotted along the coasts of the North Sea and the English Channel, picked up incoming waves of bombers at what then seemed an immense distance. Thus the Royal Air Force had sufficient time before a bombing attack to get the Spitfires on the backs of the German bombers. A small group of these scientists, organized by Professor Patrick M. S. Blackett of the University of Man-

---

Service, O.S.R.D. 1 Dec. 1945. These mimeographed books have been supplemented by conversations with members of Asworg, and by Jacinto Steinhardt "The Role of Operations Research in the Navy" *U. S. Naval Institute Proceedings* LXXII 649 (May 1946); by the Navy release of 6 Apr. 1946 "Location of Submerged Submarines"; and by James Phinney Baxter 3rd *Scientists Against Time* (1946), an outstanding book whose figures on A/S W are subject to correction.

chester, worked closely with the R.A.F. fighter command to coördinate coast warning radar with defending fighter planes. Results were so favorable that similar scientific groups were organized to help other branches of the R.A.F., including the Anti-Submarine Coastal Command. In an illuminating paper on "Scientists at the Operational Level," Professor Blackett asserted: "Relatively too much scientific effort has been expended hitherto in the *production* of new devices and too little in the *proper use* of what we have got." Men of science working with military staffs assemble data and acquire the operational outlook; to these data they apply scientific methods of analysis, and these analyses are of the utmost value, "especially in those aspects of operations into which probability considerations and the theory of errors enter." [28]

Anti-submarine warfare was preëminently such an aspect of warfare. What pattern of depth charge at what settings had the best (*a*) mathematical chance (*b*) probability, under the human factor, of killing a submarine? What sort of track should a ship steer to have best chance of regaining a lost underwater contact, or finding a submarine reported to have submerged at a given position after various lapses of time? How would this search plan be modified if two or more ships were available? How large an expanse of ocean, under varying atmospheric conditions, can (*a*) a ship, (*b*) a plane profitably patrol in one hour? What is the probability (*a*) of a submarine being there and (*b*) the lookout, radar or sound gear making contact if it is there? What disposition of escorts around a convoy gives optimum protection by (*a*) day, (*b*) night, (*c*) in low visibility? What type, weight and pattern of air bombs are most dangerous to submarines? Answers to these and a thousand other questions on anti-submarine warfare could not be left mere trial and error, or the Battle of the Atlantic might have been lost before the right answer was found. And it was not sufficient for scientists to invent a new radar set or sound device; they must observe its employment, collect and analyze data on which to base improvements both material and operational.

[28] Printed as Appendix B to *Review of Activity*.

Even after we had been fighting the U-boats for several months, no detailed quantitative analyses of methods, attacks or devices were being made anywhere in the United States Navy. Few naval officers had the scientific training to make such analyses, and none could be spared from urgent and pressing sea or staff duties. Accordingly Captain Wilder D. Baker on 16 March 1942, shortly after he had become head of the Anti-Submarine Warfare Unit Atlantic Fleet, wrote to Dr. John Torrence Tate,[29] Chief of the Subsurface Warfare Section of the National Defense Research Committee (a section engaged in materiel development only), requesting him to organize an *operational* research group to coöperate with the Boston Unit. As yet, he said, we had only British analyses of British methods, attacks and devices to work on. These had been "invaluable so far in expediting our preparations," but we must have similar analyses of our own forces, devices and methods engaged in fighting the U-boats. Following British experience, any such operational research group should be composed partly of men of the highest standing in the physical and chemical sciences, partly of mathematicians and actuaries skilled in analysis and the theory of errors. "The atmosphere required is that of a first class pure scientific research institution," said Captain Baker; but everyone in it should spend considerable time in close touch with sailors and aviators, on board ship or in advanced bases from which they operate.[30]

Dr. Tate responded immediately. Four days after Captain Baker's letter was written, he had a skeleton organization of Asworg and on 1 April Professor Philip M. Morse, sound physicist of the Massachusetts Institute of Technology, accepted the directorship.[31] They were attached to Captain Baker's Anti-Submarine Warfare Unit at Boston, and some of them followed him to Washington where he set up a similar section under Cominch. Soon Asworg was centered

[29] Professor of Physics University of Minnesota; his section was a part of Division C of the National Defense Research Committee, of which the head was then Dr. Frank B. Jewett, President of Bell Telephone Laboratories.

[30] Appendix A to *Review of Activity*.

[31] Dr. Morse, Ph.D. (Princeton) 1929, had directed the M.I.T. Sound Project for the Bureau of Ships in 1940–1942, and served on several committees on anti-submarine warfare.

at Washington, with subgroups in Boston, New York and Miami. Individual members were attached to the Naval Air Base, Norfolk; to the Army anti-submarine research and training station at Langley Field, Virginia; to N.O.B. Argentia; to headquarters of Eastern, Gulf, Caribbean and Moroccan Sea Frontiers; to Trinidad and Brazil; and at London in order to keep abreast of British developments. "By far the most important work done by the group during the first year of the existence was at the outlying bases." [32]

The work of Asworg may be broken down roughly into three categories, although the same scientist often worked on two or more. (1) The statistical part, collecting and analyzing operational data, especially the Action Reports of attacks on submarines. (2) The analytical part, combining a knowledge of past operations with that of the behavior of devices in order to determine, usually mathematically, the best tactics in a given situation. (3) The materiel part, a detailed study of apparatus in action, in order to indicate the most effective methods of employment, and also to improve the design or develop new equipment.

Although the aid of these scientists in analyzing and evaluating data was asked for by the Navy and highly appreciated by almost everyone responsible for anti-submarine warfare, there was a certain natural suspicion of "long-haired scientists" by "practical seamen" that had to be overcome. In the early days, the scientists probably heard quite as frequently as did the historian, "I'm too busy fightin' this war to talk to you." Dr. Morse was eminently successful in "selling" the services of his men, and those attached to fleet commands where the battle with the U-boat was being desperately waged in 1942–1943 won golden opinions. The principle laid down by Dr. Morse and inflexibly adhered to – that no scientist was to claim credit for anything, since he took no responsibility for the ultimate decision; that his duty was simply to help the fighting Navy to improve its anti-submarine technique – brought about the closest and most friendly relations between naval officers and civilian scientists.

[32] *Review of Activity* p. 11.

The mathematicians and analysts worked out a whole complex of search problems, including patterns of "box search" by surface ships, on Greek key patterns, for regaining underwater contacts with a submarine; they worked up data on the effective search speed, altitude and airborne time for patrol planes; they proved that three destroyers searching abreast were more than three times as effective as a single destroyer. Dr. R. F. Rinehart proved that an air "umbrella" over a convoy was far less potent a protection than a wide-ranging search on front and flanks; Dr. G. E. Kimball headed an investigation into fundamental principles of search; Dr. Jacinto Steinhardt worked out the continuous gambit tactics for aircraft, most fruitful in regained contacts, and also the famous Atlantic Narrows air patrol that caught several German blockade runners; Mr. J. R. Pellam's tests of the behavior of aircraft depth bombs had immediate repercussion on tactical air doctrine, and it was he who set up the Straits of Gibraltar patrol with the Magnetic Air Detector (MAD); Mr. L. A. Holloway carried out an extensive and important survey of convoy routing and control; Drs. Robert M. Elliott and Edwin A. Uehling, with others, organized countermeasures which stymied the German acoustic torpedo as soon as it appeared. The microwave air search radar (SCR–517 and –717, ASG and others), although primarily a laboratory product, was brought into successful operation as the anti-submarine device most feared by the enemy, and against which he never found any defense, partly by the work of several scientists in the field.

e. Radar in Anti-Submarine Applications

Radar, the radio-wave device that records on a luminous screen the range and bearing of any object on or above the surface, acted as the nighttime cat's eyes for anti-submarine vessels and planes. It enabled escorts to keep themselves constantly informed of the position of their convoy in thick weather or in darkness, to spot icebergs or derelicts and to pick up any surfaced submarine approaching to attack.

One of the first discoveries that led to the invention of radar was made by Dr. A. Hoyt Taylor and Mr. Leo C. Young, working at the Naval Aircraft Radio Laboratory in Anacostia, District of Columbia, in September 1922. On the basis of reports made by these two American scientists, the British started their own research, and in the following years, although working independently, arrived at frequencies and circuits similar to those developed in the United States.[33] Radar, as we have seen, helped to save Britain from the Luftwaffe in 1940–1941. Several of the ASV-type radar with wooden antennae, designed as aircraft sets, were sent over from England in the summer of 1941 and installed by the *Prairie* crew on three squadron flagships of the United States support force. The importance of radar was stressed in a preliminary study of anti-submarine warfare prepared by the Atlantic Fleet Division of Fleet Training in November 1941, and the use of it was described in the revised Escort-of-Convoy Instructions issued by Cinclant that month.

The first American-built radar sets were installed in the Fleet in October 1941, but by December not more than one escort vessel in each convoy had one. The installation was both heavy and complicated. From the outside an observer saw only the clumsy antennae on the superstructure, looking like gigantic broilers or bedsprings; but the gear below decks of these first radar sets took up so much space and weight that in some cases one gun had to be removed from a destroyer's main battery when radar was installed.[34] Many other important applications to warfare, such as providing more accurate gunnery control than that of optical range finders, were discovered. Here we shall consider only its uses in anti-submarine warfare.

Probably the first radar contact on a submarine in United States naval history was made in 1941 by U.S.S. *Leary* at 1540 November

[33] Navy Department Press Release of 23 May 1943. The British acknowledged their debt to us at a series of conferences held in Sept. 1940 between the British Technical Mission, the Navy Department and the Naval Research Laboratory.

[34] Cdr. W. K. Phillips's Report, as above; Capt. Louis E. Denfeld's Report on Convoy HX–156; conversations with Capt. Wilder D. Baker; Cdr. T. L. Lewis's Memo. No. 6 on radar equipment (A/S W Unit) 22 June 1942.

19, when escorting Convoy HX–160. By the summer of 1942 almost every combat ship in the Atlantic Fleet had been equipped with some form of radar, and an improved model designated SG, with greater range, accuracy and intensity of portrayal, had passed the test of experiment and was ready to be installed about 1 October.

For aircraft the value of radar was even greater, because it enabled planes to pick up a surfaced submarine far beyond visible distance, to deliver a surprise attack, and also to home on other planes and ships. The first sets installed in planes were on meter-wave. But the Germans invented a search receiver for this and began installing it on their U-boats in October 1942. This device reduced the usefulness of meter-wave radar as a detecting device, and the invention of a microwave plane radar to take its place became urgent. As a stopgap, fourteen 10-cm sets were built at the M.I.T. radiation laboratory and flown over to the British, to be used in R.A.F. planes patrolling the Bay of Biscay; production was rushed on a similar "S-band" set for United States Navy planes and on a model called SCR–517 for Army planes.[35] These did the trick, and as the German search receiver failed to detect them, the enemy was completely in the dark as to what was guiding our planes to the U-boats. Microwave radar made possible the large number of kills by aircraft in the spring and early summer of 1943. Hitler referred to it peevishly, in his New Year's 1944 address to his armed forces, as "one invention of our enemy" which had thwarted his submarine fleet; and even after the Germans caught onto it, they never could figure out a way to detect or jam the 10-cm radar waves.

f. The High-Frequency Direction-Finder [36]

A convoy is no better than its ears and eyes. Radar furnished the convoys with a cat's eyes, sonar with its ears, while the high-frequency direction-finders (HF/DF, pronounced "Huff-Duff"),

[35] *OEG Report 51*, A/S Warfare in World War II, Part I, p. 67

[36] This account is largely based on the OEG Reports and information obtained in conversations with Capt. P. R. Heineman.

picking up from land or ship the radio transmissions of U-boats at sea, acted as a highly sensitive and elongated cat's whiskers.

The Royal Navy was the first to adopt this method in its fight against submarines. The principle was simple enough. In place of the single loop-finder that fishermen and other vessels use to get cross-bearings on radio beams from known shore stations, you planted direction-finders along the coast in order to get cross-bearings on a submarine commander who was talking to another submarine or reporting to Admiral Doenitz. It did not matter that one could not tell what he was saying; the mere fact that he was transmitting served to fix his position. These bearings were sent in from the shore stations to the Admiralty, where specially trained men and women were able to plot the course of a submarine across the Atlantic.

The Canadians developed a device whereby the bearings were recorded semi-automatically. As a further improvement the United States Navy developed a machine which plotted the bearings geometrically. Sometimes as many as thirty bearings would be had on one submarine's transmission. But the HF/DF stations in England and Africa provided better fixes than those in Canada and the United States, because the American coastline is roughly parallel to the transatlantic convoy route that the U-boats traveled as well.

There is no better example of the effectiveness of the land-based high-frequency direction-finder than that of the submarine kill by Lieutenant Schreder's plane. About noon on 30 June 1942, high-frequency direction-finder ranges were obtained by the stations at Bermuda, Hartlant Point, Kingston and Georgetown. Operations officers at N.O.B. Bermuda plotted the bearings, which made a perfect fix, showing the submarine to be at lat. 33° N. long. 67°30′ W, about 130 miles WSW of St. Georges.[37] Lieutenant Richard E. Schreder USNR in a Mariner of Squadron VP–74, on patrol out of

[37] This kill was the more welcome because the forces at N.O.B. and N.A.S. Bermuda had hitherto drawn only blanks. Many ships were torpedoed within easy air range of Bermuda; Administrative History Atlantic Fleet Vol. V Appendix C lists 13 attacks on U-boats by planes and 11 by ships based at Bermuda in 1942; but Schreder's was the only successful one.

Bermuda, was about fifty miles away. Immediately notified, he laid his course accordingly and found *U–158* within ten miles of the predicted position, idling on the surface with about fifteen men sunning themselves on deck. He dropped two demolition bombs which missed, one depth charge which near-missed, and one which stuck to the superstructure and detonated as the submarine went down. It never came up, and there were no survivors.

Although the shore HF/DF stations were of inestimable value in locating submarines in time to divert the routing of convoys, or to warn them of the enemy's presence, the necessary delay in receiving their reports made it highly desirable to install HF/DF on escorts. In the summer of 1942, the Navy obtained three British shipborne sets from the Admiralty which were turned over to the Naval Research Laboratory, where a civilian scientist, Dr. Harry Goldstein, was largely responsible for the development of an American version. Captain P. R. Heineman, long an advocate of HF/DF, was particularly interested in the operational development. As early as June 1942, when escort commander of Convoy ONS–102, he made it the subject of a special report. Having seen it demonstrated by Canadian ships in his group, he wrote that "two of the HF/DF bearings reported by the *Restigouche* led to the sighting of two and possibly three submarines on the surface on 16 June."[38] About 1 October 1942, new type sets were installed in the Coast Guard Cutters *Spencer* and *Campbell* which Captain Heineman alternately rode as escort commander.

If only one ship in a convoy had HF/DF, she was made the rescue ship and sailed in the last place of the middle column. It was much better, however, to equip several ships with it in each convoy they disposed, so as to obtain cross-bearings on near-by submarines making transmissions. The Germans long ignored the danger of shipborne HF/DF; their U-boats continued to chatter among themselves and to Doenitz when closing on a convoy, which revealed their position to the screen.[39]

[38] Letter of 28 June 1942.
[39] *OEG Report 51* p. 68.

4. *The Anti-Submarine Fleet*[40]

a. Subchasers

Even before the war broke in Europe it was anticipated that the United States Navy would need many small vessels to locate, keep down and destroy enemy submarines. As a heritage from the last war we had only a dozen or so craft smaller than destroyers that were built and equipped for anti-submarine work. Eight of these were Eagle Boats (PEs) constructed around 1918–1919 by the Ford Motor Company. Square-built, slow, weak, lively and wet, the PEs were almost completely useless. For the rest, there were four or five wooden 110-foot Submarine Chasers (SCs), all that were left of the gallant mosquito fleet designed by Captain A. Loring Swasey USNR of the Bureau of Ships, and built during World War I.

In 1937, under an impulse from President Roosevelt, the Bureau of Ships held a competition for designs of motor torpedo boats[41] and for submarine chasers of two classes. The prize for wooden-hulled 110-footers was divided between the Luders Marine Construction Company and the Elco Company. Two boats were built, *SC–449* and *SC–450*, one from each design.[42] *SC–453*, designed by the Bureau of Ships, was completed early in 1941 and placed under the command of Lieutenant C. S. Kirkpatrick, who cruised some 15,000 miles to try her out. She was the first with the new General Motors "pancake" diesel engine, an immense improvement in marine engineering, which enabled her to turn up 22 knots as against 16 knots for the first two. *SC–453* became the prototype of the present fleet of SCs, wooden ships powered with pancake diesels. But only one managed to sink a submarine in World War II.

[40] This section is derived in part from conversations, especially with Rear Admiral Herbert S. Howard, director of the David W. Taylor Model Basin; with Capt. A. Loring Swasey of the Bureau of Ships, and with Lt. Cdr. C. S. Kirkpatrick.

[41] The origin of the motor torpedo boat (PTs) is told in Volume II.

[42] Originally designated *PC–449* and *–450*, but by 1942 the PC designation had been reserved for the 173-footers and the 110-footers were called SCs, so I have used the later designation consistently.

The competition for the larger class was won by a 165-foot vessel, *PC–451*, designed by Sydney A. Vincent of the Newport News Shipbuilding and Dry Dock Company, in collaboration with three other naval architects. While this competition was in progress the Bureau of Ships designed a 173-foot steel vessel known as the *PC–452* class. All but the prototype were diesel-powered, and *PC–451*, the first to be completed, reported to the Fleet before Pearl Harbor, and was found to be adequate. These five (*SC–449*, *–450*, *–453* and *PC–451*, *–471*) comprised the entire subchaser fleet when the U-boats struck in off the East Coast.[43] Orders for sixty PCs and SCs had already been placed, but they were not due for completion until the summer and fall of 1942.

The question has often been asked why the Navy was so unprepared with these indispensable small craft for anti-submarine warfare. One answer that the writer received appears to hit at least part of the truth: "We were just plugging along to find out what sort of anti-submarine craft we wanted in case we needed them, and then all of a sudden, by God, we were in the war!" Behind this excuse the real reason was the desperate concentration of the Navy on building destroyers and larger ships to fight an impending two-ocean war. Small craft were neglected because, it was believed, they could be improvised and rapidly produced in quantities at small shipbuilding yards. But if the President's wishes and recommendations had been followed, the Navy would have been better prepared to meet the U-boats.[44]

Small-craft advocates, however, made up for lost time very quickly. The great problem was to find competent builders of wooden vessels, a breed of men all but extinct. Captain Swasey traveled up and down the country begging boat and yacht yards to build SCs for the Navy, or to speed them up after their keels were laid. The PCs were less of a problem because steel shipbuilding can readily be learned. As the pancake diesel failed when mass produc-

[43] A sixth experimental 173-footer with steam turbines, *PC–452*, was in the water, but inoperative. They were "still working on her" in Feb. 1944.

[44] Compare Admiral Sir William James's statement of why the Royal Navy was similarly unprepared in 1939, quoted in note 19 to Chapter I, above.

SC–1037

Coast Guard Cutter *Ingham*

Photo by Autho

PCE–847, a 180-footer specially designed for escort duty, closes a Central Atla convoy to pick up a passenger for Bermuda

PC–574, a 173-footer, patrolling in the Caribbean

Two Types of Patrol Craft

tion started, it was decided to use a General Motors straight-eight diesel until the problem of mass-producing pancakes was solved, as solved it was by mid-1942. The slogan "sixty vessels in sixty days" was nailed to the mast in the second week of April 1942, and sixty-seven – 33 PCs and 34 SCs – actually came through by 4 May. A second 60–60 program was promptly under way. And in 120 days, 201 minesweepers, which made good emergency anti-submarine craft, were also completed.

The original PCs and SCs were not designed as escort vessels, but as harbor-based patrol craft which could be organized in killer groups to hunt a reported submarine. A few submarines were sunk by 173-foot PCs under favorable conditions, but SCs were too small for rough transatlantic escorting and their armament was too weak to make them effective submarine killers. Nevertheless both PCs and SCs had to be used on the convoy routes between New York and Brazil, and in the Mediterranean. Their crews drove them to tasks far beyond their planned capacity, and under conditions of acute personal discomfort. The Subchaser Training Center at Miami was especially set up to train young officers for this "Donald Duck Navy," as the SCs and PCs were nicknamed. Older men could not stand the strain.

Later in 1942 a new class of 180-foot patrol craft, designated PCE, began coming out. These proved to be suitable escorts for coastal convoys and many eventually were converted to small gunboats for amphibious warfare in the Pacific.

b. The Subchaser School at Miami [45]

As the subchasers were to be officered entirely by reservists it was necessary to provide a special training school for their crews; other naval training stations were already overtaxed, and nobody wanted responsibility for the "Donald Duck Navy." On 26 March 1942 the Submarine Chaser Training Center was commissioned at Miami,

[45] Based on a visit to the School in Feb. 1944, on conversations with sundry graduates thereof, and on an article by Sidney Shalett in *N. Y. Times Magazine* 13 Feb. 1944 p. 11.

Florida, for the special purpose of instructing officers and men how to handle PCs, SCs and other anti-submarine craft. About that time Lieutenant Commander E. F. McDaniel put into port after a strenuous tour of North Atlantic escort duty in U.S.S. *Livermore*. Someone in the Bureau of Personnel had the happy idea of appointing him commandant of this training center, and he took charge on 8 April. School opened with about 50 pupils. At that time McDaniel was told to prepare for a peak load of 150 officers and 650 bluejackets. By 1944 there were 2500 officers and 9000 enlisted men taking instruction, and 10,396 officers and 37,574 enlisted men had been trained for the United States Navy alone. These included the crews of 285 destroyer escorts, 213 PCs, 43 PCSs and PCEs, 397 SCs, 123 "crash boats," and 27 other craft; a total of 1088 vessels. All before 1944.

McDaniel, promoted Commander USN before being detached, was a lean, mean, thin-lipped officer whose eyes burned with hatred of the enemy and all his works, and whose heart glowed with devotion to the Navy, especially the anti-submarine part of it. Somewhat of the fanatical zeal of a seventeenth-century Scots Covenanter was in his make-up; but a sense of organization and a natural teaching ability were there too. With the aid of a few professional pedagogues from the University of Chicago he worked out courses and curricula. The "faculty," like the "student body," was constantly changing; for McDaniel would have for instructors none but officers who had actually hunted submarines, and back to sea they went after a few months. He operated the school on a seven-day-week basis. Despite indignant protests from the Miami Chamber of Commerce, he expanded the school over several piers of the waterfront, and into about ten hotels on Biscayne Boulevard. He maintained close relations with shipyards at Miami, to which he sent the half-finished craft "completed" by private builders to be fitted for sea duty.

About four fifths of the student officers were from indoctrination school. The remainder were experienced officers, untrained in handling destroyer escorts. About 250 new ones arrived every week, and a new course began every Monday. Instruction was imparted by lectures; examinations came weekly, and weeding-out was ruthless. Even after graduating from "McDaniel's Academy" the alumni were not through with the "Old Man." They were constantly calling him up for advice and support, as he encouraged them to do.

Before this Miami institution was many months old, the United States began to deliver subchasers under lend-lease to Allied European and American nations, and the task of training their crews was thrown on the Subchaser Training Center. Instructors speaking the necessary languages were found among the United States pupils. In 1942 and 1943, 360 officers and 1374 men were trained there for fourteen different foreign Navies. Some of these returned to their own countries for assignments, while others manned 49 American-built DEs, PCs, SCs and 83-foot cutters, delivered to their respective Navies. Norway, Russia, Brazil, France and several Latin American nations were represented. At the time the writer visited the school, classes for the Navies of France, the U.S.S.R., the Dominican Republic and Peru were under way; Uruguayans and Venezuelans were expected the following week.

c. Cutters, Gunboats and Destroyers

The taking-over of the United States Coast Guard by the Navy on 1 November 1941 made several types of Coast Guard cutters, manned by keen coastguardsmen, available for escort duty. The 1200-ton, 165-foot *Algonquin* class and smaller classes were used on one of the hardest assignments, the Greenland Patrol; larger ones were employed extensively on transatlantic and coastal convoys. Their performance was glorious; their casualties heavy. The new 2750-ton, 327-foot "Treasury" class,[46] built a few years before the war, capable of 20 knots and armed with four 5-inch 50-caliber guns, proved able and aggressive transatlantic escorts. In addition, four 240-cutters of the *Haida* class, fourteen large converted steam or diesel yachts, seventeen 165-foot cutters with classic names and

[46] So called because they are named after Secretaries of the Treasury.

thirty-two 125-foot cutters similar to the Navy SCs were available for anti-submarine and escort work by 30 June 1942.[47]

Some of the large PGs (gunboats), converted diesel yachts of 200 feet long and upward, such as U.S.S. *Plymouth* and *Zircon*, made excellent coastal convoy escorts. Many of the larger mine-sweepers had to be diverted to that duty. At times, anything and everything down to converted fishing draggers and yard craft was pressed into escort duty for short hauls; but whatever protection they could afford was of a moral rather than a physical nature.

The destroyers were the best escorts and the most efficient anti-submarine vessels until the destroyer escort came out. As such they were special objects of enemy attack, and 13 were lost in the years 1941–1943.[48] Consequently the production and training of new destroyers was a matter of extreme urgency for the whole anti-submarine campaign. In this matter, the production and manning record of the Navy yards and private yards was magnificent. The Navy went right ahead building destroyers of the *Fletcher* class (originally in the 1940–1941 program), 376½ feet long, displacing 2050 tons, designed speed 35½ knots, armed with five 21-inch torpedo tubes, and as many Oerlikon 20-mm and Bofors 40-mm anti-aircraft guns as could be accommodated. About 125 of these were added to the Fleet between 1 July 1942 and the close of 1943, and in the same period about 30 of the next oldest *Bristol* class were completed. Most of these operated in the screens of the growing Pacific Fleet, and not many were available for escort-of-convoy duty; but those that were had the chief responsibility for protection against submarines.

The following table of anti-submarine vessels, compiled for this work by the Bureau of Ships, includes everything in the United

[47] Figures supplied by Vice Admiral R. R. Waesche USCG, Commandant U. S. Coast Guard, 19 Apr. 1944. The list I have given above is not exhaustive, but I believe that it includes all classes of Coast Guard cutters commonly used for escort or anti-submarine warfare.

[48] Atlantic Fleet destroyers lost, which includes two by collision, one by grounding, one by explosion and one by foundering, are for each year as follows: 1941, one; 1942, four; 1943, eight; 1944, seven. From O.N.I. publication "Naval Losses of All Nations, 3 Sept. 1939 to 15 Aug. 1945."

DESCRIPTION AND AVAILABILITY OF U.S.N. AND U.S.C.G. VESSELS USED IN ANTI-SUBMARINE WARFARE AND ESCORT DUTY. WORLD-WIDE *

"On Hand" Columns based on "Ready to Report to Fleet" date

Symbol	*Type Vessel*	*Length feet*	*Complement o. and m.*	*Displacement tons*	*Maximum Speed*	*On Hand 6/30/41*	*On Hand 6/30/42*	*On Hand 6/30/43*
CVE	Escort Carriers	490–558	456–967	6730–14,000	16–20	1	2	17
DD	"4-stackers"	314–315	100–153	920–1190	30–35	83	73	61
DD	*Benson, Bristol,* classes	341–381	171–286	1365–1630	35–37	80	103	137
DD	*Porter, Craven* classes	381	225	1805–1850	35	13	13	12
DD	*Fletcher* class	376	272–340	2050	38	–	1	71
USCGC	"Treasury" class Cutters	327	243	2750	12	–	6	6
USCGC	*Haida* class Cutters	240	195	1955	10.2	–	4	4
USCGC	*Algonquin* class Cutters	165	99	1200	9.4	–	6	5
DE	Destroyer Escorts	289	198	1150	20	–	–	22
DE	Destroyer Escorts, large	306	194–208	1275–1400	20–24	–	–	13
DMS	High-Speed Minesweepers	314	122–134	1060–1190	33–38	17	18	18
AM	Minesweepers, Fleet	173–221	59–94	275–840	14–21	26	5	55
AM	Minesweepers, Convtd.	122–147	34	354–500	9–10	13	18	18
YMS	Motor Minesweepers	136	28	207	14	–	41	192
PCE	Patrol Craft, Escort	180	98	598	20	–	–	–
PC	Patrol Craft	173	61–67	261	22	1	41	154
PG	*Argo* class Cutters	165	75	350	11	–	17	17
PG	*Active* class Cutters	125	46	276	8	–	32	33
SC	Subchasers	110	26	75–85	16–22	13	54	306
PF	Frigates	301–305	88–191	1100	20	–	–	2
PG	Gunboats, old, new, & convtd.	205–333	65–287	785–3253	12–20	11	26	30
PG	Same, under Coast Guard	215–315	141–265	1860–3300	8–9	–	4	5
PY	Patrol Yachts, Convtd.	160–245	49–175	400–1100	11–26	14	24	19
PYc	Coastal Pat. Yts, Convtd.	20–198	4–88	20–627	9–17	9	27	45
PG	Miscellaneous Cutters	105–205	22–122	260–1200	7–9.5	–	12	19

* Navy data prepared for this work by Scheduling Division Buships, Cdr. Russell Keith and Mr. J. W. Rettew, Feb. 1944; Coast Guard data prepared in office of Commandant.

States Navy, from CVEs and destroyers down, that was available at any time for anti-submarine warfare, in either ocean, together with the number "on hand" each year. It does not include ships of the British and other Navies that were used in anti-submarine work in various parts of the Atlantic.

The "on hand" figures shown in this tabulation include all vessels which had reported to the Fleet before the date indicated, with no consideration given to their availability for active sea duty. They also include all vessels under repair or overhaul. Weeks or even months passed after reporting to the Fleet before some of the smaller vessels were ready for sea, owing to the shockingly incomplete condition in which they were delivered by the private yards where they were constructed. For instance, the two frigates listed as having reported before 30 June 1943 were not yet ready for sea duty on 22 February 1944. Some PCs were delivered to the base where their crew joined, with wiring hanging loose, equipment in wooden crates on deck, bulkheads not welded but only tacked up at the corners; some SCs were built on keels of green wood, full of knotholes that were puttied and painted over.[49] While this condition, to take a charitable view, may be attributed more to green shipyard workers and the desire of shipbuilding companies to make a quick turnover and hang up records, rather than to greed and rascality, the Navy is not without blame. It was constantly putting pressure on the builders to speed up production, and its own inspection service, which should have caught the culprits before the mischief was done, proved unequal to the strain of so great an expansion. About the middle of 1942, Vice Admiral Russell Willson (Admiral King's Chief of Staff) looked into the inspection service and "blew the roof" off the Bureau of Ships. A board of investigation was appointed, headed by Admiral Charles Snyder. This "Gestapo Board," as it was nicknamed, effected a complete shake-up of the Navy's inspection service in the late summer of

[49] Information from numerous naval officers and personal inspection of some of these "jobs." The complaint is by no means confined to small craft. The frigates however are an exceptional case; they were Maritime Commission hulls, originally designed as small freighters, but released to the Navy to make into combat vessels.

1942, and as a result ships were delivered in a condition more nearly approaching seaworthiness.

5. *Air Power and the Submarine*[50]

a. The Army Anti-Submarine Air Command

In World War I, the narrow seas around Britain were the most dangerous waters for merchant vessels; if once a ship got out into blue water, she was reasonably safe. In this war, on the contrary, the Coastal Command of the Royal Air Force and small anti-submarine craft were so successful in detecting U-boats and bombing and depth-charging them that they were forced to move out; by the time the United States entered the war, the Western Approaches to the British Isles were almost as safe as the Great Lakes. Since America is an air-minded nation, and the Atlantic Coast from Quoddy Head to Miami is not much longer than the periphery of the British Isles, one naturally inquires why the United States did not do as well.

One answer is given by geography. The American strategic area stretches for thousands of miles from Labrador to below the Brazilian bulge, with no "tight little island" where planes could operate from interior lines to any part of the circumference. Hence many times the number of bases and planes were needed to cover the sea frontiers effectively.

The other cause was largely a matter of organization. The Army Air Force, which controlled almost the entire supply of United States military land-based planes in 1941, did not expect to include anti-submarine warfare among its duties. Army pilots were not trained to fly over water, protect shipping or bomb small moving targets like submarines. And the Navy did not have the planes to fill the rôle so successfully assumed by the British Coastal Com-

[50] This section is based in part on interservice correspondence, in part on elucidatory conversations with Capt. A. B. Vosseller, Capt. E. W. Parish Jr. and Dr. Edward L. Bowles, expert consultant to the Secretary of War on anti-submarine problems. The conclusions are the writer's own.

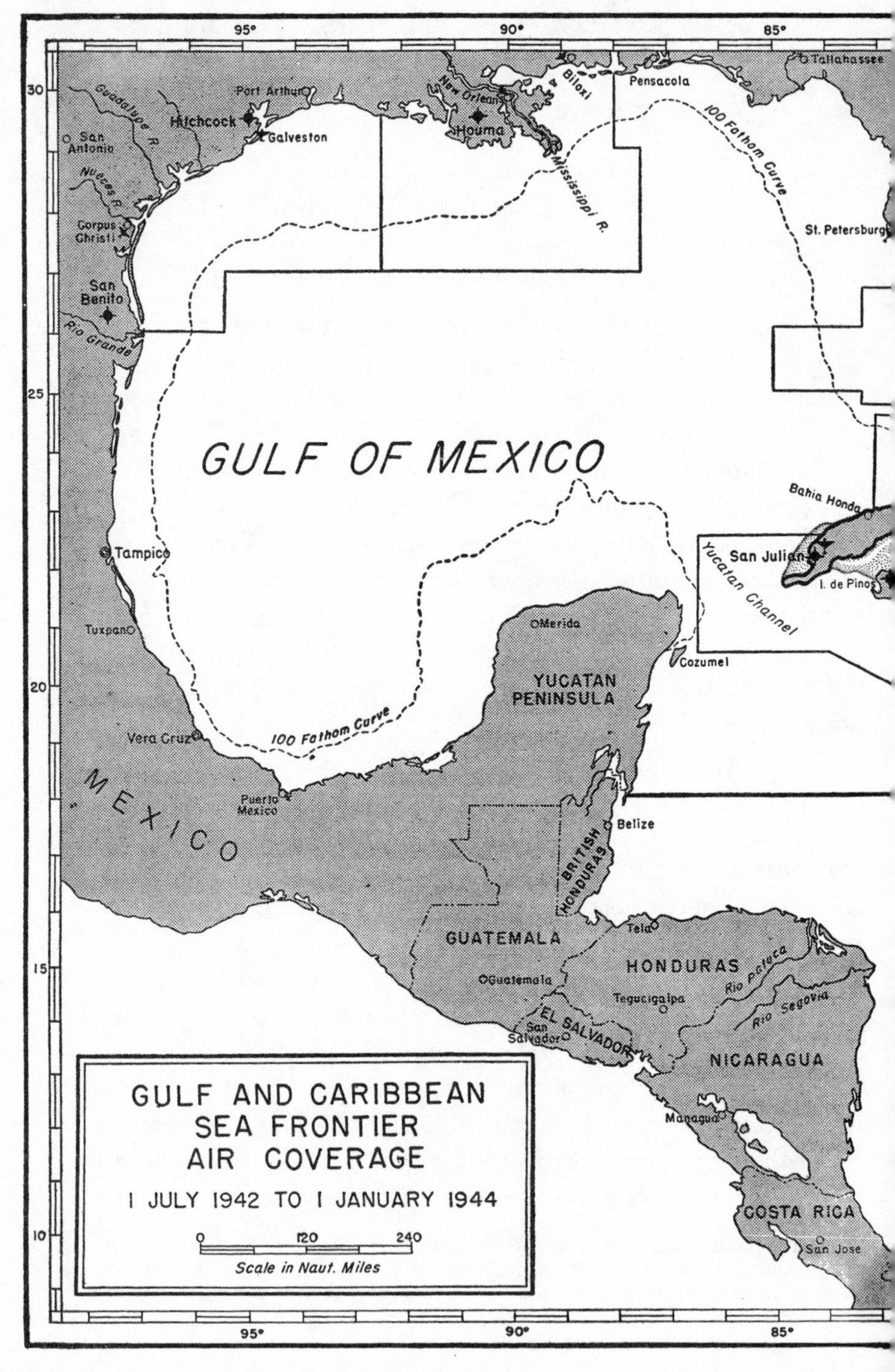
GULF OF MEXICO
GULF AND CARIBBEAN SEA FRONTIER AIR COVERAGE
1 JULY 1942 TO 1 JANUARY 1944
0
120
240
Scale in Naut. Miles
95°
90°
85°
30
25
20
15
10
Tallahassee
Pensacola
Biloxi
New Orleans
Houma
Port Arthur
Hitchcock
Galveston
San Antonio
Guadalupe R.
Nueces R.
Corpus Christi
San Benito
Rio Grande
Mississippi R.
100 Fathom Curve
St. Petersburg
Bahia Honda
San Julian
I. de Pinos
Yucatan Channel
Tampico
Tuxpan
Merida
Cozumel
YUCATAN PENINSULA
Vera Cruz
Puerto Mexico
MEXICO
Belize
BRITISH HONDURAS
GUATEMALA
Guatemala
Tela
HONDURAS
Tegucigalpa
Rio Patuca
Rio Segovia
EL SALVADOR
San Salvador
NICARAGUA
Managua
COSTA RICA
San Jose

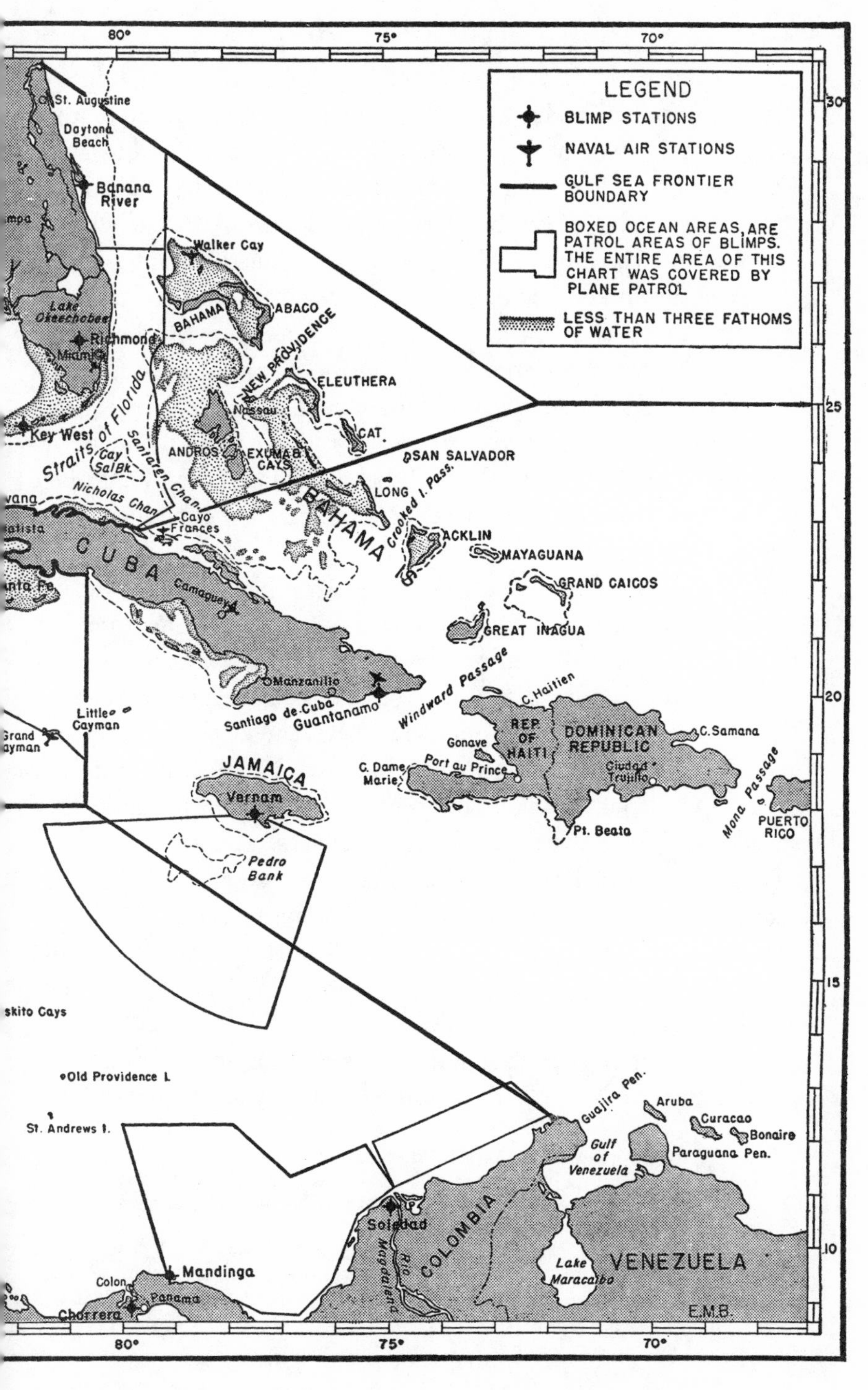

LEGEND
BLIMP STATIONS
NAVAL AIR STATIONS
GULF SEA FRONTIER BOUNDARY
BOXED OCEAN AREAS ARE PATROL AREAS OF BLIMPS. THE ENTIRE AREA OF THIS CHART WAS COVERED BY PLANE PATROL
LESS THAN THREE FATHOMS OF WATER
80°
75°
70°
30°
25
20
15
10
St. Augustine
Daytona Beach
Banana River
Walker Cay
BAHAMA
ABACO
Lake Okeechobee
Richmond
Miami
NEW PROVIDENCE
ELEUTHERA
Nassau
Key West
Straits of Florida
Santaren Chan.
Cay Sal Bk.
ANDROS
EXUMA CAYS
CAT
SAN SALVADOR
LONG
Crooked I. Pass.
Nicholas Chan.
Cayo Frances
BAHAMA IS.
ACKLIN
MAYAGUANA
CUBA
GRAND CAICOS
Camaguey
GREAT INAGUA
Manzanillo
Windward Passage
Santiago de Cuba
Guantanamo
C. Haitien
Little Cayman
Grand Cayman
REP OF HAITI
DOMINICAN REPUBLIC
C. Samana
Gonave
Port au Prince
Ciudad Trujillo
C. Dame Marie
JAMAICA
Vernam
Mona Passage
PUERTO RICO
Pt. Beata
Pedro Bank
skito Cays
Old Providence I.
Guajira Pen.
Aruba
Curacao
Bonaire
St. Andrews I.
Gulf of Venezuela
Paraguana Pen.
Soledad
COLOMBIA
Rio Magdalena
Lake Maracaibo
VENEZUELA
Mandinga
Colon
Panama
Chorrera
E.M.B.

mand. This was not due to lack of foresight, but to the principle first incorporated in the Army Appropriations Act of 1920 that the Army should control land-based and the Navy sea-based aviation. Consequently the Army received the entire American production of military land planes, except short-range scouting jobs (of which a few were delivered before October 1941); while the Navy received the entire production of military seaplanes. And the production of neither kind was adequate. When the experience of the British showed the value of large land-based bombers in anti-submarine warfare, the Army modified this agreement. On 7 July 1942, General Marshall consented to a reallocation of production that promised the Navy a fair share of Liberators and other long-range bomber types. But by that time the submarines had done their worst off the Atlantic Coast.

When they struck in January 1942, the Navy's few available squadrons of Catalina flying boats (PBYs), invaluable because they could be shifted with their tenders where the need was greatest and commence operations at once, had already been reduced to help the Pacific Fleet. There was one 12-plane squadron at Argentia, another at Norfolk, a third split between Jacksonville and Key West, and a fourth divided between San Juan and Trinidad. One squadron of the newer Mariners (PBM) was at Argentia, and one of Kingfishers at Bermuda. The first two were excellent long-range patrol planes but presented too large a target to a U-boat's machine guns, and were too slow to catch them napping.[51] The Navy badly wanted 4-engine land-based bombers for anti-submarine work.[52]

On 7 February 1942, Admiral Andrews reported that except for the Catalinas at Norfolk there were no planes in the Eastern Sea

[51] Lt. E. M. Morgan "The Patrol Plane Controversy" *U. S. Naval Institute Proceedings* LXIX 939 (July 1943). Also one squadron of Catalinas was in the Canal Zone 7 December and probably still there in January, and one squadron of PBOs was being activated at Norfolk.

[52] Specially equipped Liberators (called B-24 by the Army, PB4Y-1 by the Navy) did very well; the Privateer (PB4Y-2) was better, but the "perfect" plane for this work, the 2-engined Neptune (P2V), did not come out until the war was over.

Frontier capable of maintaining a constant patrol off shore and giving adequate protection to merchant shipping. The only naval planes attached to the districts were small single-engined OS2U–3 and SOC–3, which, when carrying depth bombs, could fly a little over three hours.[53]

In its dire need, the Navy called for help from the Army Air Force. The Army responded generously to the best of its ability. A directive of 26 March 1942 placed "all Army Air Force units allocated by defense commanders for operations over the sea, to protect shipping and conduct anti-submarine warfare," under the operational command of Admiral Andrews, Commander Eastern Sea Frontier. Lieutenant General Hugh A. Drum, Army Eastern Defense Commander, retained only administrative and training control. By that time aircraft available for sea patrol in the Eastern Sea Frontier had been built up to 84 Army planes, 83 Navy planes and four Navy blimps, based at 18 different fields between Bangor and Jacksonville. On 10 June 1942 Admiral King informed his sea frontier commanders that the War Department had reorganized the 1st Bomber Command "in order to employ it primarily as a unit to wage anti-submarine and related operations on the Eastern and Gulf Coasts." It was prepared to establish new bases and allot additional radar-equipped aircraft as rapidly as production permitted. Admiral King then estimated that 500 radar-equipped medium and heavy bombers would be required to give adequate protection to the Eastern, Gulf and Caribbean Sea Frontiers.[54]

By the end of July 1942, the Army had expanded its air force available for anti-submarine work in the Eastern Sea Frontier to 141 planes, while the naval air arm had grown to 178 planes and 7 blimps. These were spread among 26 fields along the coast from Argentia to Jacksonville.

This coverage was far from effective, partly because the Army

[53] Eastern Sea Frontier War Diary Feb. 1942. There were also 4 blimps at Lakehurst, N. J.

[54] Cominch to Commanders E.S.F. and G.S.F. 10 June 1942; Cominch to Chief of Staff U. S. Army same date (as quoted in E.S.F. War Diary). In the statistics that follow, Coast Guard planes are included with Navy planes.

and Navy had different communications systems, and partly because of a deficient command organization. Each sea frontier commander held fast to what he had, instead of sending planes where the need might be greater. General Marshall observed to Admiral King on 14 September 1942 that effective employment of aircraft against submarines demanded accurate and rapid communications, mobility "and freedom from the restrictions inherent in command systems based upon area responsibility." Hence he proposed to set up a special anti-submarine group, to absorb those elements of the 1st Bomber Command engaged in the war against the U-boats. They would remain under operational control of naval sea frontier commanders, but the allocation of planes would be controlled by the War Department in order to concentrate them in the most dangerous areas. Admiral King concurred, and the 1st Anti-Submarine Army Air Command was formed in October 1942, with Brigadier General Westside T. Larson as commander.

This new command established two air wings, the 25th and 26th, with headquarters at New York and Miami for the Eastern and Gulf Sea Frontiers respectively, and in the same buildings as the sea frontier commands. The 26th wing included seven squadrons based on fields from Lantana (Florida) to New Orleans. By 26 February 1943, when the command reached its top strength in the Eastern Sea Frontier, it had 124 planes operating from 20 bases between Brunswick (Maine) and Jacksonville. The Navy then had in the same area 174 planes and 17 blimps. In the Gulf Sea Frontier at the same date, 62 Army and 96 Navy planes were operating from 14 fields between Banana River (Florida) around the Gulf and to Grand Cayman Island. In the Caribbean Sea Frontier, on 7 December 1942, there were 134 Army, 87 Navy and 33 Marine Corps planes, besides a squadron of the Royal Air Force, operating from 17 bases between the Bahamas and the Guianas. But less than half these planes had sufficient range to fly out and effectively patrol waters where the submarines were.

From the first, there were many honest differences of opinion between higher echelons of the Anti-Submarine Army Air Command and the commanders of naval sea frontiers. The Navy wished to use planes primarily for anti-submarine patrol and convoy cover; for it had ascertained that the mere presence of aircraft near a convoy was often sufficient to keep U-boats down and discourage attack. The Army regarded routine patrols and convoy cover as useless drudgery in areas where Intelligence reported that no U-boats were operating. Morale of aviators could not stand up against the boredom of daily patrols for weeks on end without making a single submarine contact. The Army wished to organize anti-submarine planes in "killer groups" to go after any U-boat sighted or reported, believing that killer tactics would be a better deterrent than routine patrol, even if kills were few. They pointed out that the British Coastal Command employed more than half its available planes in "seek and strike" missions. The Navy retorted that air cover of convoys, including sweeps ahead of them, served the double purpose of protecting the ships and catching U-boats when nibbling at the convoy "bait." But, as yet, few Army pilots were sufficiently versed in navigation to find convoys readily,[55] their ship recognition training was defective; they were unable, for lack of a proper system of air-surface communications, to coöperate with ships in joint operations; and they were not trained to bomb a target so small and mobile as a surfaced submarine.

The War Department met these criticisms by establishing a training and research center for anti-submarine air warfare at Langley Field, Virginia.[56] But Admiral King had no intention of permanently sharing with the Army what he considered to be a naval responsibility, the protection of shipping. He had never conceived of Army participation in anti-submarine air warfare as any-

[55] Of 278 A.A.F. missions sent out to convoys up to 1 Oct. 1942, 72 failed to find the convoy. But some of these failures were due to lack of prompt dissemination of intelligence. The tendency, so often complained of within the Navy, for Intelligence to withhold valuable data until all value was lost was even more evident when it had to be passed from a Navy to an Army communications set.

[56] The research unit installed there in the summer of 1942, under the direction of Dr. Edward L. Bowles and before the 1st Bomber Command was reorganized, was called the Sea Search Attack and Development Unit. The training unit at Langley, commanded by Lt. Col. R. W. Finn USA, was set up a few months later.

thing but a temporary expedient. So, as fast as the Navy obtained land-based planes and trained pilots, they were moved into the sea frontiers until such time as they could relieve the Army Air Force of this special duty.

At that time the Royal Air Force Coastal Command wanted many more long-range planes to cover the Bay of Biscay, through which the U-boats based on the Brittany outports had to move, and which was too remote from English bases for most of the British anti-submarine planes. Accordingly, in November 1942, sixteen Liberators of the 1st Army Anti-Submarine Air Squadron under Lieutenant Colonel Jack Roberts USA, equipped with microwave search radar, were dispatched for duty in England. A few reached St. Eval, Cornwall, in time to take part in Operation "Torch."[57] Eleven of the twelve Liberators of the 2nd Army Anti-Submarine Air Squadron arrived in England in January 1943. Two months later, both squadrons, organized as the 480th Anti-Submarine Group A.A.F., were moved to Port Lyautey, Morocco, where they performed excellent patrol service in Mediterranean and North African waters; while the 479th Group relieved them in England. From time to time other detachments of the Army Anti-Submarine Command operated from Bermuda, Trinidad, Cuba and Ascension Island.

All through the latter half of 1942 and first half of 1943, when the German submarine threat was at its peak, this struggle for control and organization of the air aspects of anti-submarine warfare was going on. In an acute situation, where a prompt solution and close teamwork were imperative, neither the Joint Chiefs of Staff nor any other authority were able to find the one or impose the other.

Agreement was almost reached in May 1943 when the Tenth Fleet, the Navy anti-submarine command, was being set up.[58] It was

[57] Even before these anti-submarine planes arrived in England, the U. S. Army Air Force based there made a brave effort by raiding Lorient with Flying Fortresses and Liberators on 21 Oct. 1942, and St.-Nazaire on 9 Nov. Although considerable damage was done by well-placed bombs, no effect on U-boat operations could be discerned.

[58] The Tenth Fleet is described in Volume X 21–24.

then proposed that a general officer of the Army command all anti-submarine aviation as an integral part of the Tenth Fleet. His functions would be confined to training, administration and materiel readiness. For operations, air wings, groups or squadrons under their own commanders would be allocated to the Atlantic Fleet, to sea frontiers, or to special task forces under Army or Navy command. This would have meant an organization very similar to that of the British Coastal Command, which had worked beautifully. But agreement was not reached because the Army insisted that all naval commands in the Atlantic be reorganized in accordance with the Army principle of separating the command of aviation from that of other arms. That, to Admiral King, seemed equivalent to erecting a party wall between ships and planes. "I cannot assent to any such scheme," he wrote to General Marshall on 5 June 1943. There must be a close coördination, he observed, between training, doctrine and operation of both planes and ships in anti-submarine warfare; and inasmuch as the Navy was responsible for the defense of shipping, it "seems reasonable that the naval principles of command organization be followed."

The controversy was referred to the Joint Chiefs of Staff, which was unable to find a solution. General Marshall then decided, 10 June 1943, that the A.A.F. must pull out of anti-submarine work in the western part of the Atlantic; that the Navy as soon as possible must assume entire responsibility for air protection of the Atlantic coastal frontiers and the transatlantic convoy routes, to within bomber-plane distance from European bases. Accordingly, on 1 September 1943 the Army Anti-Submarine Air Command was disbanded.[59] At that time it possessed 266 planes, 187 of which were Liberators with special anti-submarine equipment. Many of these were turned over to the Navy in exchange for B–24s not so equipped, but the personnel stayed with the Army Air Force.[60] Thus the Navy acquired complete control of the aërial aspects of

[59] It actually operated in some areas into November, as the Navy was not yet ready to take over.

[60] The Army-Navy agreement to this effect was concluded 9 July 1943.

anti-submarine warfare, and of over-water patrolling in all Atlantic areas not covered by the Royal Air Force Coastal Command or the Royal Canadian Air Force.[61]

This contest between Army and Navy for control of anti-submarine air forces never ended. The underlying issue was one of power. Although General Marshall was against it, so many newly promoted "boy generals" of the Army Air Force were propagating the separate air force idea that the Navy feared it would lose its air arm, and also the war; the separate Luftwaffe, according to Admiral Doenitz, was a principal reason for Germany's defeat. Great Britain, to be sure, had a separate air force; but the English with their genius for compromise met the submarine problem through the special Coastal Command over which the Admiralty had the last word, and in which Army-Navy coöperation was excellent. Whether or not that particular form of organization was suitable for the United States, it is not to the credit of the two services that they wrestled over this problem of organization for eighteen of the most critical months of the war without reaching a solution. Their failure to do so, in the writer's opinion, was due more to conflicting personalities and service ambitions than to any inherent difficulty; and also to the fact that nobody under the President had the authority to impose an agreement. It seems significant to him that in certain areas remote from Washington, such as Trinidad and the Solomons, Army, Navy, Marine Corps, British and Australian Army aircraft coöperated very well with the Navy.

At the time of writing, this question of command is not yet settled. In view of the methods of unified control over ships and planes (both land-based and shipborne) in a specific anti-submarine operation, which were worked out by the Navy in the latter half of the war (and so not considered in this volume), it would seem logical to leave the Navy in charge. The Army, on the other hand, might procure specially designed and equipped anti-submarine

[61] The Brazilian Air Force was also a considerable factor, but it was largely (and wholly insofar as anti-submarine activity was concerned) under the operational control of Commander U. S. Fourth Fleet.

planes, train aviators to fly them efficiently, and coöperate with the Naval command, as was done in Great Britain. A decision and a plan are imperatively necessary; for, in view of the rapid development of submarine design late in the war, and the proved effect of atomic bombs and guided missiles on surface ships, it must be assumed that underwater warfare has a brilliant and devastating future. Defense against the submarine will require the closest coöperation at the tactical level between ships, shipborne planes, shore-based planes, and even submerged warships. A divided command over these various elements is a luxury that the country probably cannot afford again.

In the meantime, let us remember that the Army Air Force came to the Navy's assistance at a critical moment, stood by as long as it was needed, contributed to the technique of anti-submarine warfare,[62] and killed several submarines.[63] No sailor should forget that many an Army pilot lost his life protecting ships and sailors.

b. The Naval Air Patrol[64]

At the outset of the war the naval air arm of the Atlantic Fleet consisted almost entirely of amphibian Catalinas (PBY–5A), organized in seven patrol wings of four 12-plane squadrons each, with two others forming. These were intended to be mobile operational entities of the Fleet, each self contained with its own staff and tender. The only long-range bombers that the Navy could

[62] The Army Air Force received first delivery of the SCR–517 and SCR–717 microwave search radars (counterparts of the Navy "S-band") and the Langley Field research unit did excellent work getting them into service. This unit began other profitable experiments in fields later taken over by the Navy's Asdevlant unit at Quonset, which will be treated in Volume IX of this work.

[63] See Appendix II. Mr. Baxter's statement in *Scientists Against Time* (p. 42), that two B–18s commanded by Col. W. C. Dolan "sank their first U-boats on April 1 and May 1" 1942, is incorrect. The earliest A.A.F. kill was that of *U–701*, 7 July 1942.

[64] Lts. Jay DuVon and J. P. King USNR, "Air Task Organization in the Atlantic Ocean Area"; "History of Northern Air Group Eastern Sea Frontier," and "History of Fleet Airships Wing Two," Appendix B to "History Gulf Sea Frontier." These are in the Administrative and Type History series.

spare for the Atlantic were sent up to Iceland and Argentia before war was declared. Wartime exigencies resulted in sending some of the patrol wings to the Pacific while others were combined with land-based search and observation planes and with Coast Guard and lighter-than-air wings as air groups under sea frontier commanders. To go through all the successive reorganizations and regroupings would be tedious. Suffice it to say that between 6 July 1942 and 9 October 1943, Commander Eastern Sea Frontier had at his disposition the Northern, Narragansett, New York, Delaware, Chesapeake and Southern Air Groups operating from about 16 different airfields and stations between Bar Harbor and Jacksonville, together with a blimp airship group at Lakehurst, two inchoate fleet air wings and a special air escort group at Quonset for convoy coverage.[65] Gulf Sea Frontier at about the same period had one naval air task group whose components operated from various fields between Banana River, Florida, and San Julian, Cuba, and an emergency navy strike group composed largely of the planes at the naval air training stations, Pensacola and Corpus Christi. The Caribbean Sea Frontier similarly operated planes and blimps at Guantanamo and other eastern Cuba stations, at Puerto Rico, Antigua, Trinidad, Curaçao, Aruba, and the Guianas. The whole organizational set-up looks cumbrous and complicated, but actually was very flexible and, so far as aircraft were available, served the immediate purpose of regular air patrols over sea frontier waters, convoy coverage to the operational limit of aircraft, and air-sea rescue.

The naval air squadrons based at Argentia, under the successful command of Admirals Bristol and Brainard, were particularly useful in covering convoys during the critical moment of changing escort groups at "Westomp," and also in killing submarines. Squadron VP-82, based at Argentia from the beginning of the war, scored, as we have seen, the first two kills of submarines (*U-656* and *U-503*) made by the United States Navy in the Atlantic, and Lieutenant R. E. Schreder USNR of VP-74 based at Bermuda made

[65] Operation Plans quoted in "Air Task Organization" pp. 13-14.

the fifth kill, *U-158*, on 30 June. During the second half of 1942 the score was only slightly improved. Two planes of Squadron VS-9 based at Marine Corps Air Station, Cherry Point, piloted by Ensign Frank C. Lewis USNR and Ensign Charles D. Webb USNR, assisted the Naval Armed Guard of S.S. *Unicoi* to sink *U-576* off Diamond Shoals on 15 July; a Coast Guard J4F plane of U.S.C.G. Squadron 212 based at Houma, Louisiana, and piloted by Ensign Henry C. White USCG, killed *U-166* off the Passes of the Mississippi on 1 August; a PBY-5A of VP-73 piloted by Lieutenant (jg) R. B. Hopgood USNR sank *U-464* south of Iceland on 20 August when covering Convoy SN-73; another Catalina of VP-92 out of Guantanamo on 28 August blew *U-94* to the surface in the Windward Passage, where H.M.C.S. *Oakville* finished it off; Lieutenant R. C. Millard patrolling north of Iceland with a PB4Y of Squadron VP-84 sank *U-408* on 5 November, and Lieutenant (jg) H. L. Neff killed *U-611* some 350 miles south of Reykjavik on 10 December 1942.

The score of kills, however, far from exhausts the usefulness of planes in anti-submarine warfare. Their sightings, signaled ashore or to ships, resulted in numerous attacks by surface craft. Moreover, in 1942 German submarines were under orders to dive when they sighted a plane. Consequently air patrol over frontier waters or a convoy route was a constant embarrassment to the U-boats and indirectly protected shipping.

The amphibious "Cats" found a new sphere of usefulness in air-sea rescue work, and eventually PBYs were trained and equipped for that purpose alone. But in 1942, rescue duties fell on the standard patrol Catalinas. For instance, on 9 March a PBY under command of Ensign F. E. Pinter USNR, carrying two co-pilots and a crew of five, took off from San Juan bound for Guantanamo. En route a message was received: a patrol plane had sighted a raft with survivors on board, several miles off Port à l'Écu, Haiti. Forty-five minutes later, Ensign Pinter also sighted it; he brought his plane down alongside in a rough sea, and passed a line to the raft, which was then pulled to the bow of the plane. Seventeen men and one woman, survivors of the torpedoed American merchantman *Barbara,* and so weak from hunger and thirst that they could do little to help themselves, were dragged aboard and inside through the navigator's hatch. With this unusual pay load, the Catalina just managed to take off by "giving her the gas on the bounces," and it took her twenty minutes to climb to 500 feet.

An important if relatively ineffective component of the naval air arm was the lighter-than-air dirigible, the so-called blimp. Most naval officers, in view of the rapid development of planes, were very skeptical of these handsome sausage-shaped airships. But they had advocates who had been trained in their operation; the company that manufactured them was influential; and at a time when the U-boats looked like winners the Navy dared reject nothing that might contribute to eventual victory. Consequently the Fleet Airship Wings (as the blimp organizations were designated) were greatly expanded under the overall command of Rear Admiral C. E. Rosendahl. Their original home base at Lakehurst, handy for patrolling off New York, was supplemented by several others between South Weymouth (Mass.) and the Gulf. Captain W. E. Zimmerman's Airship Wing Two, commissioned at Richmond, Florida, on 1 March 1943, expanded into the Gulf of Mexico, to Jamaica and Trinidad, and eventually Brazil.

The blimps patrolled at 45 to 50 knots, with a maximum speed of 65. They were radar-equipped early in the war and armed with depth charges and machine guns. It was hoped that the slow rate of flight would enable them to spot surfaced submarines that escaped the lookouts in fast-flying planes, and that they could "hold down" a submarine once contacted, following it under water with some sort of magnetic device in order to coach in a ship or bomber plane for attack. These expectations proved to be largely unfounded. Rear Admiral J. L. Kauffman, Commander Gulf Sea Frontier, liked the blimps for patrol because of their endurance factor, and their ability to operate in foul weather and at night.[66]

[66] In reply to a query from Admiral King, about 1 Nov. 1943. ("History Gulf Sea Frontier" p. 117.)

But most naval officers regarded them as inferior to planes for area patrol and worse than useless in convoy coverage, because they could be sighted by a U-boat even further away than the most smoke-careless freighter. It is certain however that the blimps contributed to seagoing morale. Merchant seamen standing out of New York in a slow transatlantic convoy with every prospect of a nasty crossing, felt somewhat assured to see a stately blimp flying overhead. The crews of the bauxite shuttle ships between Trinidad and the Guianas, a route for which no surface escorts could at first be spared, are said to have threatened mutiny unless they were given protection; they were afforded blimp cover all the way and the men were satisfied.[67]

Air search and air attack, because of the delicate instruments and the mathematical and probability factors involved, were peculiarly subject to improvement through the efforts of the operational scientists. Some of these, as we have seen, were attached to the U. S. Army Anti-Submarine Command at Langley Field, and there effected important improvements in materiel, procedure and doctrine for over-water flyers. In anticipation of the dissolution of that unit, the Navy stepped into the breach by setting up early in 1943 the Anti-Submarine Development Detachment (Asdevlant) at Quonset Point, Rhode Island, to which the scientists formerly at Langley Field migrated.

The opening of this unit, and the administrative reorganization consequent to the appointment of Rear Admiral "Pat" Bellinger as Commander Air Atlantic Fleet in March 1943, opened a new and brilliant chapter for naval air in anti-submarine warfare. In particular, this era was marked by the equipping of naval search planes with a microwave search radar that the Germans could not detect and which both Hitler and Admiral Doenitz acknowledged to be the greatest single factor in defeating the U-boats.

[67] The writer has spent a good deal of time talking with lighter-than-air advocates in the Navy, and even went on one patrol out of South Weymouth to find out how they operated; his somewhat gloomy conclusions as to their usefulness were reluctantly reached after much cogitation.

6. *Coastal Convoys* [68]

a. Atlantic Coast Shipping Lanes

Trace a line from Cape Race, Newfoundland, about 250 miles off the Atlantic Shores of the New World, around the bulge of Brazil to Rio de Janeiro and the River Plate, including the Caribbean Sea and the Gulf of Mexico, and you have a belt of ocean which comprises some of the most congested sea lanes in world shipping. In time of peace these are vital arteries of commerce upon which nations depend to sustain industry and general well-being. In time of war they tap the most important world sources of coffee, cotton, sugar, oil, iron, steel and bauxite. These commodities, with the possible exception of coffee, are essential to a nation engaging in modern warfare; and, although the United States Navy might win a war without coffee, it hopes never to be forced to make the experiment.

The great industrial cities of the Eastern Seaboard were dependent on coastwise tankers, freighters and towed barges for a large proportion of their bulk commodities, such as oil, coal, iron, concrete, and lumber. Fuel was necessary for the heat and light of the civilian population during winter in the northern cities, as well as to run their war industries; for the development of water power in the New England and Middle States had been neglected in an era when the profit motive ruled and fuel was cheap. Only a small part of these heavy commodities could be diverted to the already overburdened railroads. Most of the sugar consumed in the Eastern States was shipped from Cuba and the West Indies;

[68] Information collected by Lt. (jg) Henry Salomon Jr. after conversations with many naval officers engaged in coastal convoy operations, and from the Eastern Sea Frontier files, especially the following documents: Capt. Harry E. Shoemaker Address Given at Eastern Sea Frontier Headquarters Mar. 1943; Capt. F. G. Reinicke "Brief History of the Port Director's Office; Calendar Years 1939 to 1942 Inclusive" 1 Jan. 1943; Vice Admiral Adolphus Andrews Abstract of Remarks at a Luncheon-conference with Radio Commentators at the Algonquin Hotel 21 July 1942; Capt. W. A. S. Macklin Address to Eastern Sea Frontier Officers Apr. 1943.

this source could not be replaced by the comparatively small production of Louisiana and of the beet sugar belt. Every pound of coffee had to come by sea. Bauxite, a vital ingredient for the aluminum used in airplanes, was obtained from the Guianas and Brazil.

Oil was carried to East Coast cities and to Great Britain from Curaçao and Aruba in the Netherlands West Indies, from the near-by Venezuelan oil fields, and from the American gulf ports of Corpus Christi, Houston and Port Arthur, Texas. The United Kingdom alone consumed in wartime approximately 1500 tanker loads of oil and petroleum products yearly, the equivalent of four tankers each day;[69] and the convoy system required more rather than fewer tankers because of the increased time necessary to complete a voyage. Only six round voyages a year were possible when operating in convoy between New York and the United Kingdom; only four voyages per year between the Gulf or Caribbean and the United Kingdom, if convoyed over the entire route via New York.[70]

Coastal routing preceded coastal convoys. This function of port directors' offices in the Atlantic seaports was immediately expanded after Pearl Harbor. "Verbal orders were received on the evening of 7 December 1941 to begin coastal routings. This was confirmed by dispatch, but written directives on the conduct of routing did not appear for some time. . . . The Department issued directives only after they were justified by experience." [71] Such was our first and feeble attempt to protect coastwise shipping.

For ocean-going vessels, only the Cape Cod and the Delaware-Chesapeake Canals were of advantage in shortening the coastal route and affording protection from enemy attack. Although in time of peace the sea-level Cape Cod Canal was not regularly used by vessels larger than coastwise steamers, the protection it afforded was such that all possible shipping was immediately diverted through it. From the southern entrance to the Cape Cod Canal, westbound

[69] The fuel oil used abroad consists of a mixture one half Venezuelan and one half U. S. oil. This is called "Admiralty Oil."

[70] Capt. Shoemaker's Address.

[71] "History of Port Director's Office."

vessels proceeded through the swept channel in the Buzzards Bay mine fields, along the coast through Narragansett Bay swept channel, and entered Long Island Sound at the Race. But deep-draft vessels had to skirt the south shore of Long Island instead of passing through the protected Sound. Between Sandy Hook and Cape May, shipping had to follow the exposed Jersey coast.[72] Vessels of 24-foot draft or less, proceeding from Philadelphia to Hampton Roads, were routed via the Chesapeake and Delaware Canal.

South of Cape Henry no inland waters were available except for extremely shoal-draft vessels. A system of dredged channels and canals parallels the coast all the way from Chesapeake Bay to Florida, and a considerable volume of tonnage was moved in it by small diesel freighters with a draft under ten feet.

b. "Bucket Brigades"

The assault on coastwise, Caribbean and South American shipping in February–April 1942 proved that the convoy system must be extended to those waters. But convoys mean escorts. And "when the U-boats hit our coast in January 1942, we were caught with our pants down through lack of anti-submarine vessels." [73] Knowing that a convoy without adequate protection is worse than none, Admiral Andrews decided that convoys were then inadvisable. But on 1 April a partial convoy system was inaugurated whereby ships were moved from anchorage to anchorage escorted by such local craft as were available in the various Naval Districts under the direction of Commander Eastern Sea Frontier.

This partial convoy system was aptly labeled the "Bucket Brigade" by Admiral Andrews. It was the best defensive measure that could be put into effect given the paucity of escort ships and planes. Ships steamed during daylight hours as close to shore as

[72] Unfortunately the once useful Delaware and Raritan lift-lock canal, which could have given shoal-draft passage between New York and Philadelphia, had long been abandoned by the railroad owning it, and plans to restore it were defeated by the Congress on 20 May 1942.

[73] Capt. W. A. S. Macklin Address to Eastern Sea Frontier Officers Apr. 1943.

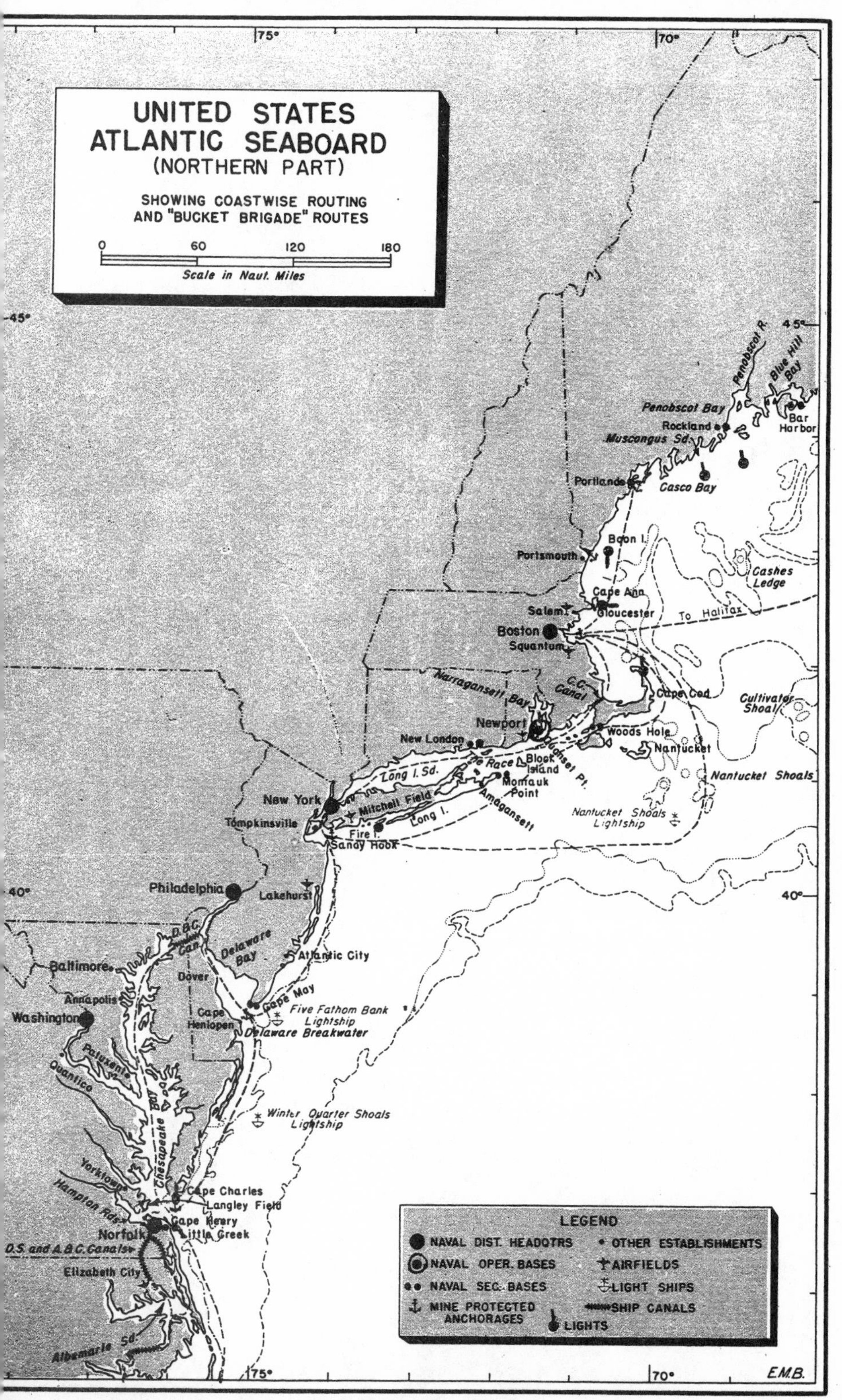

UNITED STATES
ATLANTIC SEABOARD
(NORTHERN PART)
SHOWING COASTWISE ROUTING
AND "BUCKET BRIGADE" ROUTES
0
60
120
180
Scale in Naut. Miles
75°
70°
45°
40°
Penobscot R.
Blue Hill Bay
Penobscot Bay
Rockland
Bar Harbor
Muscongus Sd.
Portland
Casco Bay
Boon I.
Portsmouth
Cashes Ledge
Cape Ann
Salem
Gloucester
To Halifax
Boston
Squantum
C.C. Canal
Cape Cod
Cultivator Shoal
Narragansett Bay
Newport
Woods Hole
Nantucket
New London
The Race
Block Island
Montauk Point
Nantucket Shoals
Long I. Sd.
Sakonnet Pt.
New York
Mitchell Field
Long I.
Amagansett
Nantucket Shoals Lightship
Tompkinsville
Fire I.
Sandy Hook
Philadelphia
Lakehurst
D.&C. Can.
Delaware Bay
Atlantic City
Baltimore
Dover
Cape May
Annapolis
Washington
Cape Henlopen
Five Fathom Bank Lightship
Delaware Breakwater
Patuxent
Quantico
Chesapeake Bay
Winter Quarter Shoals Lightship
Yorktown
Hampton Rds.
Cape Charles
Langley Field
Cape Henry
Norfolk
Little Creek
D.S. and A.&C. Canals
Elizabeth City
Albemarle Sd.
LEGEND
NAVAL DIST. HEADQTRS
NAVAL OPER. BASES
NAVAL SEC. BASES
MINE PROTECTED ANCHORAGES
OTHER ESTABLISHMENTS
AIRFIELDS
LIGHT SHIPS
SHIP CANALS
LIGHTS
E.M.B.

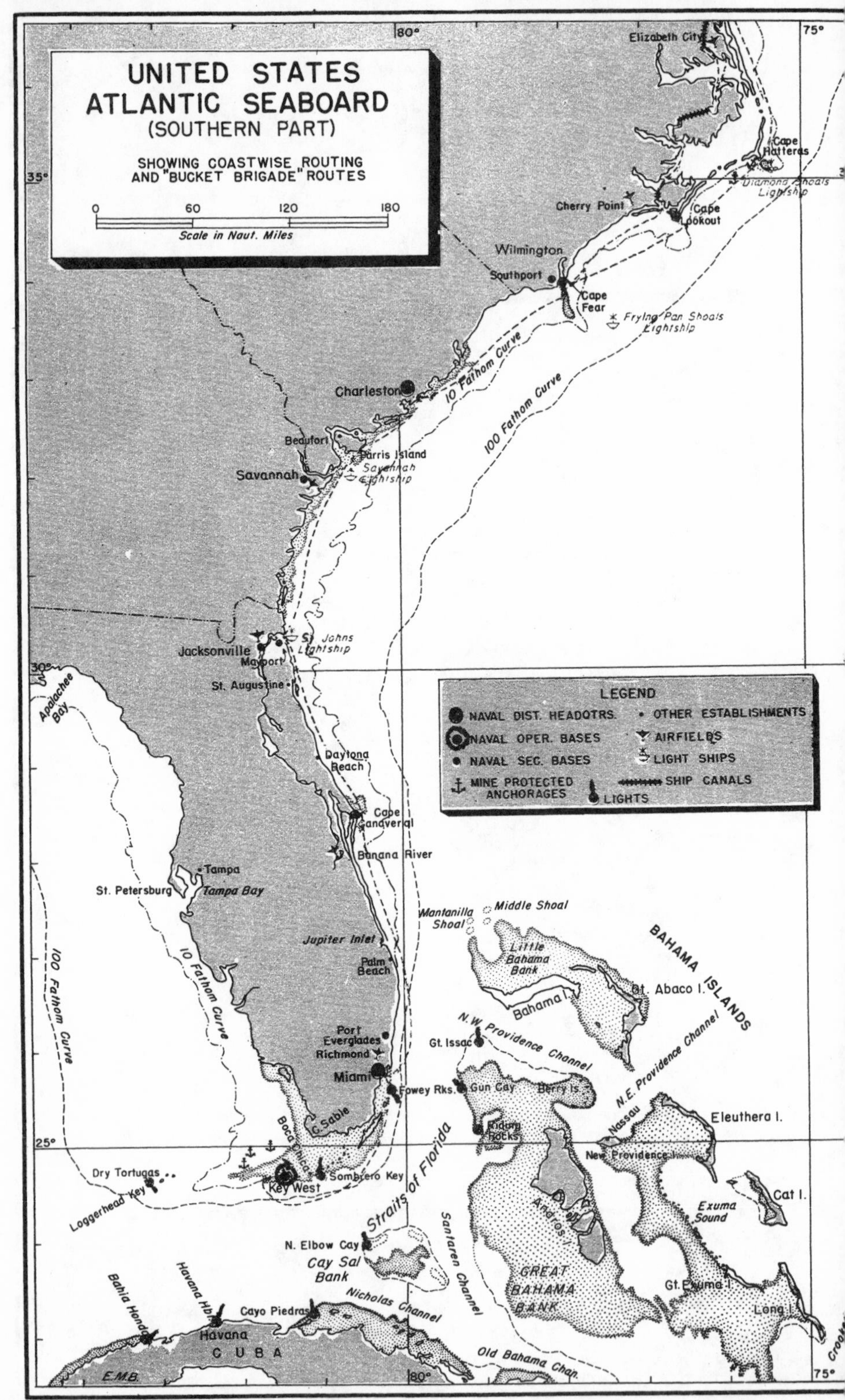
UNITED STATES
ATLANTIC SEABOARD
(SOUTHERN PART)
SHOWING COASTWISE ROUTING
AND "BUCKET BRIGADE" ROUTES
0 60 120 180
Scale in Naut. Miles
LEGEND
NAVAL DIST. HEADQTRS.
NAVAL OPER. BASES
NAVAL SEC. BASES
MINE PROTECTED ANCHORAGES
LIGHTS
OTHER ESTABLISHMENTS
AIRFIELDS
LIGHT SHIPS
SHIP CANALS
80°
75°
35°
30°
25°
Elizabeth City
Cape Hatteras
Diamond Shoals Lightship
Cherry Point
Cape Lookout
Wilmington
Southport
Cape Fear
Frying Pan Shoals Lightship
10 Fathom Curve
100 Fathom Curve
Charleston
Beaufort
Parris Island
Savannah
Savannah Lightship
St. Johns Lightship
Jacksonville
Mayport
St. Augustine
Apalachee Bay
Daytona Beach
Cape Canaveral
Banana River
Tampa
St. Petersburg
Tampa Bay
Mantanilla Shoal
Middle Shoal
Jupiter Inlet
Palm Beach
Little Bahama Bank
Bahama I.
Gt. Abaco I.
BAHAMA ISLANDS
N.W. Providence Channel
N.E. Providence Channel
Port Everglades
Richmond
Gt. Issac
Miami
Fowey Rks.
Gun Cay
Berry Is.
Nassau
Eleuthera I.
Boca Chica
C. Sable
Riding Rocks
New Providence I.
Dry Tortugas
Key West
Sombrero Key
Loggerhead Key
Straits of Florida
Santaren Channel
Andros I.
Cat I.
Exuma Sound
N. Elbow Cay
Cay Sal Bank
GREAT BAHAMA BANK
Gt. Exuma I.
Long I.
Bahia Honda
Havana Hbr.
Cayo Piedras
Nicholas Channel
Havana
CUBA
Old Bahama Chan.
E.M.B.

safely permitted, and at night took shelter in a protected anchorage. This system was practicable because the Atlantic Coast north of Hatteras is divided into approximately 120-mile stretches between good harbors, which is about the maximum run that a slow merchant ship can make during daylight. South of Cape Henry, where there were no adequate harbors of refuge, the Eastern Sea Frontier established net-protected anchorages about every 120 miles, the most important being under Cape Hatteras, and adjoining Cape Fear.[74] The next jump was to Charleston Harbor, and the next to Jacksonville. "There were each day between 120 and 130 ships requiring protection within the boundaries of the frontier," and "in all there were 28 surface vessels that could be used on convoy work, and should these ships be used on such duty, the harbor entrances and coastwise lanes would be practically stripped of protection." [75]

The U-boats' depredations soon made it evident that these protective measures were inadequate. During the first four months of 1942 the enemy sank 82 merchant ships of almost half a million gross tons in the Eastern Sea Frontier alone.

A thorough and comprehensive system of convoy was necessary before any real measure of protection against submarines could be attained.

c. Convoys Extended Coastwise [76]

Admiral King appointed an informal board, consisting of representatives of Cominch, Cinclant and commanders Eastern, Caribbean and Gulf Sea Frontiers, to lay plans for more extensive convoy operations. This board submitted recommendations on 27 March 1942 to Admiral King, who on 2 April wrote, "The principles enunciated and the general procedure suggested in this

[74] These anchorages were later protected by mine fields, but the Hatteras field of 2635 mines was not laid until 25 May. (War Diary Service Squadron 5.)

[75] Eastern Sea Frontier War Diary Feb. 1942.

[76] All north-south convoys along the eastern coast of the Americas were known as Coastal Convoys, although they originated in Canada and eventually extended to Rio de Janeiro.

excellent report are concurred in." [77] After making a few minor changes in the report, Cominch delegated to Commander Eastern Sea Frontier "all necessary authority to integrate this plan and to deal directly with agencies concerned."

This plan planted the seeds of what later grew into the great Interlocking Convoy System. It included detailed arrangements for ocean convoys between Guantanamo and Halifax, and for coastal convoys between New York and Key West, the only harbor along the Florida coast suitable for assembling, organizing and clearing large numbers of vessels. The board estimated that a 45-ship convoy would be required every three days on each of these routes, so heavy was the traffic along the Atlantic Coast.

These new convoy routes required for efficient operation a minimum of 31 destroyers and 47 corvettes or PCs or the equivalent, which was more than the Navy could then provide. Nevertheless, the naval officers concerned set about organizing what convoys they could with the limited number of escort vessels at their disposal. In commenting on this possibility, the board laid down excellent convoy doctrine, as follows: –

> While it is recognized that the strength of escorts may have to be meager, it should be borne in mind that effective convoying depends upon the escorts being in sufficient strength to permit their taking the offensive against attacking submarines, without their withdrawal for this purpose resulting in unduly exposing the convoy to other submarines while they are on this mission. Any protection less than this simply results in the convoy's becoming a convenient target for submarines. . . .
>
> As a result of experience in the North Atlantic it now appears that the minimum strength that will afford reasonable protection is five escorts per convoy of 40 to 50 ships, of which all should make 18 knots (the maximum at which sound gear is usable), and be equipped with sound and depth charges, and two should be destroyers to permit ranging to the flanks and astern and rejoining without waste of time.

Owing to the scarcity of suitable escorts, the old Bucket Brigade remained in effect between New York and Hampton Roads. Good

[77] Cominch to Vice Chief of Naval Operations 2 Apr. 1942.

air coverage was there available, and the run could be broken at the Delaware Bay mined anchorage.

After Admiral Ingersoll had assigned additional vessels to Commander Eastern Sea Frontier, these escorts were organized as six task units of seven ships each. A unit "usually consisted of two destroyers, two trawlers, and three miscellaneous. The senior destroyer was escort commander. Ships were assembled at Hampton Roads and Key West and the first southbound convoy sailed on 14 May; the first northbound convoy sailed 15 May." [78]

During May a northern link, New York–Halifax, was attached to the convoy chain. The first fleet to sail under the new system departed Execution Rock on 19 May, and at Woods Hole formed Convoy BX–19 (Boston–Halifax).[79] Thus, by the end of May, a merchant vessel could steam from Key West to Halifax, and return, with a large measure of protection.

The good effects of coastal convoy with increased air coverage were immediately apparent. Monthly sinkings in the Eastern Sea Frontier dropped off from 23 in April to 5 in May. In June they rose to 13, fell to 3 in July, and then to zero for the rest of 1942.[80]

In August, owing to enemy submarine activity off the Gulf Coast, a Galveston–Mississippi convoy was established for the protection of tankers. It was extended from the Passes to Key West a month later.

d. Caribbean Convoys

Axis submarines, always on the lookout for soft spots, commenced moving south when they found operating along the Eastern Sea Frontier increasingly difficult, and began to concentrate their efforts in the Caribbean Sea and the Gulf of Mexico. May through September of 1942 was the worst period of the war for shipping in these waters, which in our days of innocence were supposed to

[78] Capt. Macklin's Address.
[79] History of Port Director's Office.
[80] Statistics in Chapters IV and VI.

be protected from submarine attack by narrow passages, swift currents, and island barriers. Here, in five months, enemy submarines sank an average of 1½ ships *per day*, and destroyed *over one million gross tons of shipping.*

By the middle of 1942, Admiral Ingersoll could spare enough escorts to institute Caribbean convoys. The Royal and Canadian Navies helped by detaching a number of their battered destroyers and corvettes from the northern transatlantic route for this purpose (a welcome change for them); Cinclant rounded up a few small Dutch naval craft that were attached to Curaçao, and a number of PCs and SCs were attached, although the long runs in rough water ruined their engines and exhausted their personnel.[81] In July 1942, four new convoys were inaugurated: Halifax to the Dutch West Indies,[82] Panama Canal to Guantanamo, Trinidad–Aruba–Key West, and Trinidad eastward. The escorts of the Canal Zone–Guantanamo convoy [83] protected their merchant ships without any casualties for several months. In the 60 days during which the Trinidad–Aruba–Key West convoy (TAW–WAT) operated, 746 ships sailed this route in 34 convoys, with a loss of 15 ships by enemy action.[84] In September this convoy terminated at Guantanamo, and became one of the basic subsidiary routes in the Interlocking System.

Owing to a large number of sinkings in the ocean approaches to Trinidad, the Navy in July began to escort merchant ships and tankers about 200 miles to the eastward and southward of the island, the escort vessels returning to Trinidad from the ocean dispersal point. This proved costly, inasmuch as the U-boats soon learned to hide near the dispersal point and attack the ships as soon as their

[81] *SC-453*, detached from the local defense forces at Trinidad and used for escort duty, bounced about so much that no cooking could be done for as many as five days running, and the fresh-water supply allowed each man only one quart a day for all purposes. In Sept. 1942 most of the 110-foot SCs were replaced by 173-foot PCs.

[82] There were only four of these "AH–HA" (Aruba–Halifax) convoys: one in July, two in Aug., one in Sept., when they were discontinued as their function became absorbed in the Interlocking System.

[83] Originally known as PG–GP, later as GZ–ZG.

[84] Lt. Cdr. Charles Ames, Cominch Convoy and Routing Section.

Seaplane Tender *Pocomoke* enters Gulf of Paria, October 1942, followed by local escort

Photo by H. Salomon Jr.

United States Naval Section Base, Teteron Bay

Trinidad

Blimp at Edinburgh Field, Trinidad

U.S.S. *Zircon*. A converted yacht used as escort flagship

Air and Surface Escort in the Caribbean

former escorts were hull-down. During July, August and September, 17 of these TE (Trinidad Eastward) convoys, comprising 235 ships, were operated. By the end of the year enough escorts were available to organize fast tanker convoys for the entire crossing from Trinidad to Europe or North Africa, which increased in importance after the landings in Morocco and Algeria.

A welcome addition to the defense and anti-submarine forces at Trinidad was a squadron of the Royal Air Force Coastal Command, under Group Commander Comming, which arrived in August 1942. As the geographical set-up at Trinidad resembled that of England, part protected waters and part open sea, Coastal Command experience was pertinent to the problem. During the few months of his stay, Commander Comming did much to improve the communication and other techniques of the United States Army Air Force and Naval Air Arm. In particular, he supervised an efficient system of coast-watching stations.

The British Lockheed-Hudson bombers, because of their superior speed and white camouflage, proved to be the best planes for anti-submarine warfare in the Trinidad area, with the United States B–18As second. In the four months August–November 1942, each type made 16 attacks, but the B–18As flew 64 per cent more hours than the A–29s and made more sightings. The brave old Navy "Cats" (PBYs) flew even more hours than the Hudsons, but they were too slow to catch U-boats and managed to make only six attacks. During these same four months, 1360 ships arrived and 1462 departed from Port of Spain and other places in Trinidad or the Gulf of Paria, with a total loss of 53, amounting to about 270,000 tons, by enemy action. Of the departures, 1354 ships were in 119 different convoys and 108 unescorted. Yet of the 53 sinkings, only 11 ships, of 65,203 gross tons, were in convoy.[85] Few more impressive figures as to the efficiency of convoys have been adduced.

[85] "Statistical Report on the A/S Flying Effort in the Trinidad Sector of the Caribbean Sea Frontier from 9 August to 30 November 1942" prepared by Combat Intelligence and Statistical Section, N.O.B. Trinidad.

e. The Interlocking System

At the end of August 1942 a great change was effected in the organization of coastal convoys. After nine months at war, the Navy produced the ingenious and efficient Interlocking System, by which ships were run almost like trains.

The Interlocking System involved thousands of ships and scores of routes, yet is simple enough to understand if one bears in mind two central facts: (1) Northbound coastal convoys were timed to arrive at New York just before a transatlantic convoy sailed for Great Britain. (2) The two main convoys to which all others tied in were the Key West–New York and return (KN–NK) and the Guantanamo–New York and return (GN–NG). These two may be likened to express trains; the rest to local trains, feeding freight into two big southern termini, Key West and Guantanamo, on schedules so carefully worked out that lost shipping days were kept at a minimum. For, if a coastal convoy arrived a day late, ships destined for an express convoy would lie idle until the next one came through. The local convoys, run on ten-day intervals, usually met every other express convoy, since they were run on intervals of four or five days.

This reorganization of the Atlantic coastal convoys resulted from a conference of sea frontier representatives at Admiral King's headquarters on 1 August.[86] On 27 August the first New York–Guantanamo convoy (NG–300), and next day the first New York–Key West convoy (NK–500) sailed. The first convoy from Key West directly to New York (KN–136) arrived on 9 September, and the first express convoy from Guantanamo to arrive in New York was GN–1 on 12 September 1942.[87]

[86] "Atlantic Coastal Convoys," a Cominch document later attached to "Operations of Convoys–U. S. Navy" which is dated 20 June 1942 and was drawn up by the Convoy and Routing Section. This meeting at Cominch headquarters planned the Interlocking System and designed it for ships with speeds from 8 to 14.9 knots. Ships slower than this sailed inshore along the coast by the old "bucket brigade" method. However, by this time small district craft were available for the added protection of these ships. Ships over 14.9 knots were routed independently since their speed permitted them to outrun submarines.

[87] History of the Port Director's Office p. 46.

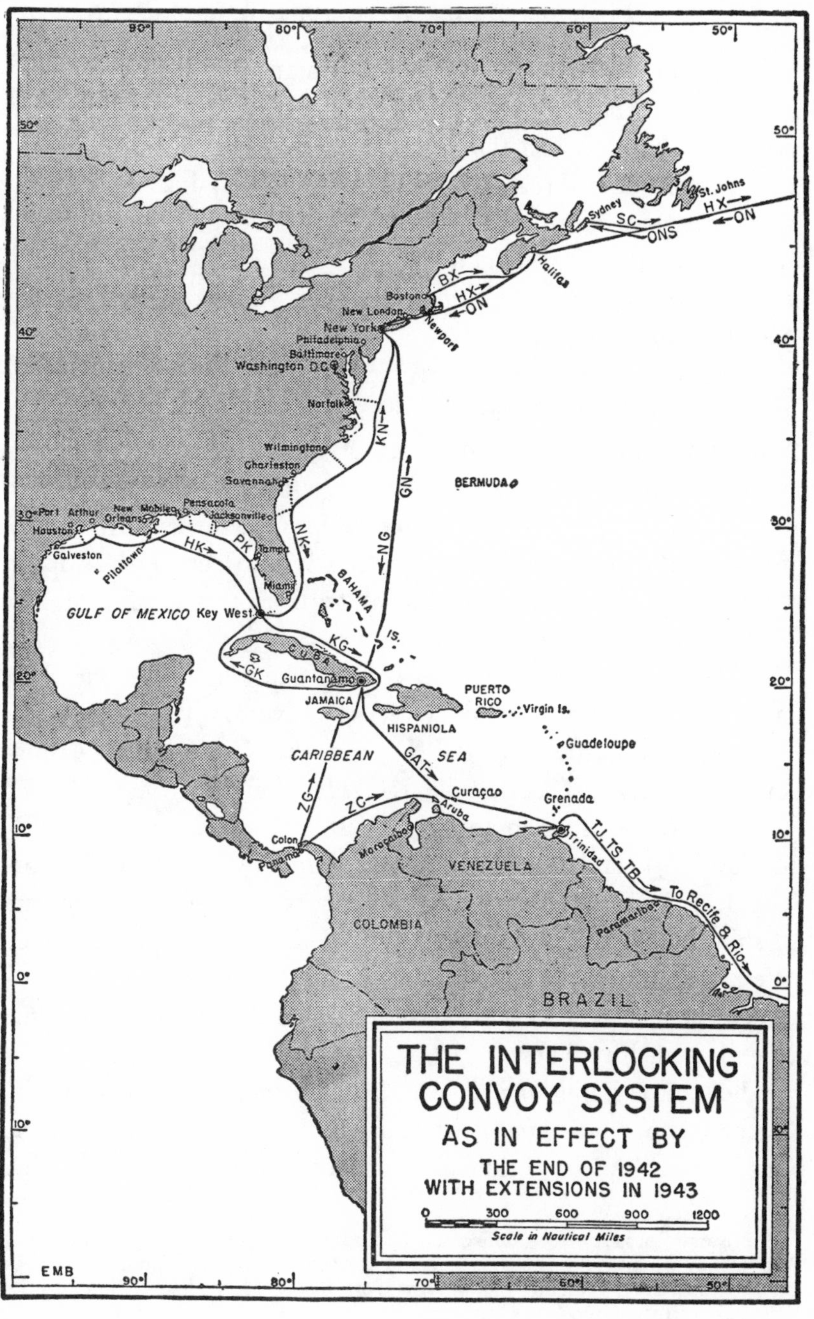

THE INTERLOCKING CONVOY SYSTEM
AS IN EFFECT BY
THE END OF 1942
WITH EXTENSIONS IN 1943
Scale in Nautical Miles
0 300 600 900 1200
GULF OF MEXICO
CARIBBEAN SEA
BERMUDA
BAHAMA IS.
CUBA
JAMAICA
HISPANIOLA
PUERTO RICO
Virgin Is.
Guadeloupe
Grenada
Trinidad
Curaçao
Aruba
Maracaibo
VENEZUELA
COLOMBIA
BRAZIL
Paramaribo
Colon
Panama
Guantanamo
Key West
Miami
Tampa
Pilottown
Galveston
Houston
Port Arthur
New Orleans
Mobile
Pensacola
Jacksonville
Savannah
Charleston
Wilmington
Norfolk
Washington D.C.
Baltimore
Philadelphia
New York
New London
Newport
Boston
Halifax
Sydney
St. Johns
HX
ON
SC
ONS
BX
KN
GN
NK
NG
HK
PK
KG
GK
GAT
ZG
ZC
TJ, TS, TB
To Recife & Rio
EMB

New York, already the northern terminus for all southern shipping, became the great entrepot between Atlantic coastal and transatlantic convoys when the HX–ON (fast) and SC–ONS (slow) convoys, which had formerly used Halifax and Sydney respectively as their termini, were shifted thither. So drastic a change had many ramifications, one of which was the suspension of the Boston–Halifax convoys. These during their short life had convoyed over 500 ships eastward.[88]

With the two new coastal trunk lines New York–Guantanamo and New York–Key West, and the new transatlantic convoy New York–Londonderry in mind, let us turn to the Gulf and Caribbean in September 1942. Here there was developed a network of local convoys whose purpose was to feed ships into the two trunk lines going north. In reverse, their function was to convoy in ships to their final destinations from the southern express termini of Key West and Guantanamo.

Of these subsidiary convoys feeding the trunk line, the three most important were the Key West–Galveston (KH–HK), the Key West–Pilottown (KP–PK) and the Guantanamo–Aruba–Trinidad (GAT–TAG). The KH–HK convoy brought loaded tankers from Galveston to Key West in time to catch the KN to New York, and took the "empties" from NK back to Galveston. The Key West–Pilottown (KP–PK) was organized to take care of ships bound to New Orleans and up the Mississippi, from Key West to Pilottown at the entrance to the Passes, and return.[89] Between them, HK–KH and KP–PK carried the bulk of the traffic to and from Key West.

The third important feeder hooked into the New York–Guantanamo trunk line at its Caribbean terminus. This was the Guantanamo–Aruba–Trinidad and return (GAT–TAG) which

[88] History Port Director's Office p. 47. This BX–XB convoy was reëstablished in March 1943 when traffic became too heavy for the Port of New York to bear. As before, ships sailed unescorted from New York through Long Island Sound to the approaches to the Cape Cod Canal.

[89] This convoy was given up in Jan. 1943 after the submarine menace in the Gulf had subsided.

carried the bulk of trade with South America, and the important tanker traffic originating in the Dutch West Indies. GAT–TAG took the place of WAT–TAW (Key West–Aruba–Trinidad), the northern terminus being shifted from Key West to Guantanamo to relieve congestion at the Florida roadstead. In order to link the southern termini of the two trunk convoys from New York, a shuttle convoy (GK–KG) was instituted at the same time between Guantanamo and Key West.

While the GAT–TAG convoy accounted for a large proportion of the ships fed into the Guantanamo–New York trunk line (NG–GN) there were other Caribbean convoys as well which brought traffic into Guantanamo: the Canal Zone one (GZ–ZG), which had existed since July, and a new Canal Zone–Curaçao convoy whose ships joined or peeled off from GAT–TAG at the near-by island of Aruba.

An extension of GAT–TAG southward, the Trinidad South (TS), started in October. Three TS convoys that month, comprising 47 merchant ships, went to Paramaribo or Rio de Janeiro. In November, six convoys with a total of 41 ships were dispatched eastward or southward from Trinidad – two to Freetown in Sierra Leone, two to Paramaribo, one to Rio and one to Recife. In the first week of December 1942, Rear Admiral Jonas H. Ingram, Commander South Atlantic Force, was directed to control all convoys sailing south from Trinidad, much as Admiral Andrews controlled those of the Eastern Sea Frontier. By arrangement with Brazil, the United States Navy provided escorts from Trinidad to Recife, where the Brazilian Navy took over; but Admiral Ingram retained operational control over the entire route. The first TB (Trinidad–Bahia) convoy left Port of Spain 15 December, and was dispersed off Bahia 1 January 1943.[90]

Such was the complete Interlocking System as it was put into effect in September 1942, and as it remained, with only minor

[90] This one was designated TS–1, the second was designated TR; thereafter they were known as TB–BT until July 1943, when they were permanently extended to Rio de Janeiro, at which time the designation was changed to TJ–JT. See Chap. VI Sec. 3.

changes, throughout the years 1943 and 1944, and until the war ended in Europe. A schedule for the whole system was worked out in order to make the convoys really interlock, yet avoid crowding the termini. In September 1942 the timetable was arranged as follows: –[91]

Days of Departure	*Northbound*	*Southbound*
Mondays	GK, ZG	GAT
Tuesdays	GN, KN, TAG	KG, PK
Thursdays	GK, KH	GAT, NG
Fridays	—	HK, KG, NK
Saturdays	GN, TAG	—
Sundays	KP	GZ, NG

As it would have been a waste of shipping time for through traffic to call at intermediate convoy termini, escorts were relieved off Key West and Guantanamo and the convoy changed its name, but merchant vessels bound through sailed on without entering port. In order to keep ships moving, special rendezvous for "joiners"[92] were designated off Norfolk, Curaçao, Port Arthur, Pilottown, Mobile and Pensacola; and breakoff points as well. Vessels outward bound from Norfolk to Guantanamo had the choice of proceeding coastwise to New York for inclusion in an NG convoy, which was routed too far off shore to admit "joiners," or hooking up with a New York–Key West convoy at a rendezvous off the Capes. Similarly, Guantanamo–New York convoys included vessels bound to all ports north of Cape Hatteras. These ships were not allowed to break off, but proceeded to New York for rerouting coastwise. If the master wished to eliminate backtracking, he could join a GK convoy to Key West and there pick up the KN, which was routed close enough to the coast to permit a safe breakoff.

The Interlocking System proved its worth immediately. During the last three months of 1942, the Eastern, Gulf and Panama Sea Frontiers suffered no loss from enemy submarines. But sinkings

[91] "Atlantic Coastal Convoys" document.

[92] "Joiners" were local shuttle convoys which were sailed when necessary and formed a link between a convoy route and a port along that route.

still continued in the Caribbean Sea Frontier, West, where thirty ships were sent to the bottom during these three months.

The very unfortunate sinking of the 2880-ton French submarine *Surcouf* occurred 18 February 1942 about 80 miles north of Cristobal. She was en route to Tahiti and in Bermuda had received onward-routing instructions to the Panama Canal. S.S. *Thompson Lykes*, steaming independently on a very dark night, reported striking and running down a partially submerged object which scraped along her side and keel. Her lookouts heard shouts from the water and she carefully searched the area, but found no survivors. Although the evidence is meager and entirely circumstantial, it seems certain that *Surcouf* was then rammed and sunk, for she disappeared about that time and place and none of her officers and men were ever heard from again.

Thirty-nine vessels sunk out of these convoys between 1 July and 7 December 1942 represent the total loss by enemy action to 527 convoys comprising 9064 sail of ships. In other words, less than one half of one per cent of the ships in coastal convoys were sunk. This was an even better record than that of the transatlantic convoys, the loss in which was 1.4 per cent from the time that the United States Navy began escort duty, to the first anniversary of Pearl Harbor.[93]

Despite excellent progress in protecting shipping there was a long way to go in the art of sinking U-boats before we could claim mastery of the sea. Until then, there would be use for convoys.

[93] "The Inauguration and Carrying Out of Convoy Operations and its Effect" prepared by Lt. Cdr. Charles Ames of Cominch Convoy & Routing Dec. 1942.

CHAPTER XI

Amateurs and Auxiliaries

1. *The Patrols*

a. Inshore

WHEN war broke out in Europe in 1939, the commandants of naval districts began planning to perform one of their primary duties, that of protecting the coastal waters within their commands. They were supposed to be aided in emergency by the Atlantic Fleet; but the Fleet had other and more urgent duties. It was up to locally based forces of small craft to do the work, in conjunction with Army, Navy and Coast Guard planes.

Out of early war plans there emerged the Inshore Patrol, which embraced all functions of local coastal defense other than coast artillery, minelaying and Army ground forces. In 1940 the Coast Guard and Navy began buying up motor yachts and converting them for use in this patrol. The command arrangements of Inshore Patrol were highly complicated until 16 June 1942, when an assistant commandant directly responsible for it was assigned in each naval district. But this assistant commandant had other duties as well. The one in the First Naval District (New England), for instance, commanded the following distinct groups: –

1. Local Defense Forces, comprising minesweepers, harbor patrol vessels, as well as harbor entrance control posts, loop receiving stations,[1] and section bases.

[1] Loop Receiving Stations, a development from World War I, were connected to cables which ran under a body of water. When ships ran over this cable the magnetic attraction was recorded on a flux meter in the station. If the ship was invisible, it was obviously a submarine. A large harbor would have several of these Loop Receiving Stations and their work was reported to the Harbor Entrance

2. Northern Ship Lane Patrol, consisting of large converted sailing yachts and other vessels capable of being used offensively against submarines at some distance off shore.
3. Northern Air Patrol, comprising aircraft of the Navy, Army Air Force and Civil Air Patrol.
4. Control Force, Cape Cod Canal.
5. Coastal Picket Patrol (to be described shortly).

Local Defense Forces were charged with enforcing the elaborate procedures regulating the examination of war and merchant vessels when entering port. Their patrol vessels operated for a few miles outside the 26 controlled harbors of the Atlantic Coast, Gulf, Caribbean and Canal Zone.

b. Ship Lane

The Ship Lane Patrol, operated by the Navy, was conceived as an offensive force to take an active part in anti-submarine warfare. Of that, it proved to be incapable; but it undoubtedly helped to protect shipping and keep U-boats down. Ship Lane Patrol provided flank coverage for convoys leaving terminal ports, escorts for stragglers, and offshore patrols in areas particularly important for shipping. The most satisfactory type for this service proved to be auxiliary schooner yachts such as *Migrant* and *Guinevere*, 200 feet or more long, armed with depth charges, one 3-inch 50-caliber and four 20-mm guns, and capable of remaining at sea for a week or ten days. After all available craft of this description had been procured, it was necessary to augment the Ship Lane Patrol by PCs, SCs and 83-foot Coast Guard cutters. The engines of these little cutters were a limiting factor in their usefulness; for each, if operated one day in every two, consumed about 20,000 gallons of gasoline per month. When the gasoline shortage on the East Coast became so acute as to threaten civilian morale, so large

---

Control Post which would take any necessary action. A submarine actually did cross a cable and get into Casco Bay in June 1942, but it escaped owing to the fact that the cable failed to record it on the way out.

a consumption of gasoline by the Coast Guard was deemed inadvisable. So, in order that civilians might enjoy a certain amount of pleasure driving, the 83-footers in September 1943 were ordered to cut out their motors and maintain a drifting patrol at sea. Thus gasoline consumption was reduced to 2300 gallons per month per ship.

c. Coastal Picket

Any vessel, friendly or hostile, approaching the Atlantic and Gulf Coasts of the United States during the war, would have to pass through the area of the Ship Lane Patrol first, and then encounter the Coastal Picket Patrol. This was a fleet of auxiliary [2] sailing yachts, motorboats, converted fishermen and small freighters. Most of the vessels were borrowed or requisitioned, not purchased; and the crews were of the most heterogeneous description, with a preponderance of amateur yachtsmen. Civilian in its origin and always informal, the C.P.P. was affectionately known to its personnel as the "Hooligan Navy"; the official Coast Guard title, "Corsair Fleet," was little used.

Prime mover in organizing this branch of naval defense was Alfred Stanford of New York, commodore of the Cruising Club of America. In the summer of 1941 he began the difficult task of convincing the Navy that pleasure boats and their owners might contribute to defense. On 5 March 1942, the Cruising Club offered the Eastern Sea Frontier the loan of thirty auxiliary sailing yachts between 50 and 90 feet long, with experienced skippers and skeleton crews. It suggested that this fleet be placed in commission immediately, and operated by the Navy as an experiment in patrol duty and anti-submarine warfare.

At that time, sinkings off the Atlantic Coast had reached alarming proportions, and the Navy was deluged with more or less crackpot anti-submarine devices. One, for instance, which obtained

[2] Auxiliary is here used in the yachting sense, a sailing yacht with an auxiliary engine, gas or diesel.

favorable publicity, was to anchor a chain of small boats five miles off shore, within hailing distance of one another, all the way from Maine to Florida. But the Cruising Club project had been worked out by experienced seamen. Yet on 27 April 1942, when the Club had lined up seventy seagoing yachts and one hundred smaller ones, it was informed by a sea frontier officer that the Navy's construction plans for small craft had been so accelerated that a yachting patrol was no longer wanted.[3] As this astonishing statement was made at a time when the Navy was notoriously short of small craft, before the "first sixty" SCs and PCs had even taken the water, and at a time when the U-boats were still numerous and deadly near our coasts, it provoked something like an explosion of indignation. Letters were written to Washington, editorials scoring the complacency of the Navy Department appeared in the press, and *post hoc*, if not *propter hoc*, the Navy changed policy. On 4 May 1942 Admiral King requested the Coast Guard Auxiliary to take over and organize this volunteer effort.

The Coast Guard Auxiliary had been formed many years before with the idea of training yachtsmen for coöperation with the Coast Guard's police and rescue work. At the outbreak of war it had a membership of some seven to eight thousand men, who among them owned two or three thousand boats. The greater part were small craft, unsuitable for offshore work. Congress in May 1942 amended the Coast Guard Auxiliary Act by authorizing the enlistment of suitable "web-footed" citizens in the Coast Guard Auxiliary for as short a period as thirty days, even though disqualified by age or minor physical defects from being bluejackets or coastguardsmen. Admiral King on 23 May ordered all sea frontier commanders "to expedite rigorous selection of craft for transfer from local defense forces to sea frontier forces . . . to which must be added measures to keep craft at sea at least two thirds of the time, whether for offensive action or rescue work."[4] A later directive

[3] *Cruising Club of America News* May 1942. The frontier was for the scheme; the statement was issued in order to "protect" it in case of rejection by Cominch.

[4] This and other operational orders are quoted from the copies in E.S.F. Coast Guard Operation Orders File.

defined the type of vessel wanted as those "capable of going to sea in good weather for a period of at least 48 hours at cruising speeds." They might be auxiliary sailing or motor yachts, fishermen, or other privately owned craft. They could be accepted as a loan, purchased, or requisitioned if the owners proved recalcitrant. They were to be equipped with "at least four 300-pound depth charges," at least one .50-caliber machine gun, and a radio set, preferably voice. Admiral King ordered the Coast Guard to organize these vessels, with others already in the Coast Guard Reserve, into operational groups, to be assigned by sea frontier commanders to restricted patrol stations established along the 50-fathom curve off the Atlantic and Gulf Coasts.

Thus was born the Coastal Picket Patrol (by Cruising Club out of Coast Guard), Cominch playing the somewhat unwilling rôle of midwife.

Rear Admiral R. R. Waesche, Commandant of the Coast Guard, then put the heat on his district officers and a wild scramble for yachts took place, each district officer trying to acquire as many as possible, regardless of size or condition.

The Eastern Sea Frontier's Operation Plan for Coastal Pickets was issued 14 July 1942. These vessels were organized in five task-group organizations – Northern, Narragansett, New York, Delaware, Chesapeake and Southern. Their duties were defined as "supplementing existing forces employed in anti-submarine, rescue and information duties." They "will be equipped with such armament and anti-submarine devices as is *practicable*." Each vessel was provided with an Army Interceptor Command grid chart, dividing the ocean for about two to three hundred miles off shore into sections fifteen nautical miles square. A normal operation was defined as patrolling one of these squares night and day, for a definite space of time. While so engaged, or whenever at sea, the little ship was instructed to "observe and report the actions and activities of all hostile submarine, surface and air forces," and to "attack and destroy enemy submarines when armament permits."

In and out and round about these dull events of organization, there played a crackling controversy as to the value of this force. Nobody questioned that able sailing yachts upward of 100 feet overall had been useful to the Navy in various capacities, but these queens of the pleasure fleet had already stowed the foul-anchor ensign, received a commission as U.S.S. Number So-and-So, and were doing duty as escorts, gunboats, or in the Ship Lane Patrol. Many fishing vessels, small steamers and diesel freighters had also been acquired by the Navy and Coast Guard. But the question, whether sailing yachts between 50 and 100 feet overall length could be any use in anti-submarine warfare, was debated in the Navy and the press, in waterfront taverns and along yacht club bars, and wherever two or more amateur admirals collided. The Navy was accused of shortsightedness and complacency in so long keeping at arm's length yachtsmen who were able and willing to help. The Dunkirk evacuation, in which numerous very small craft were employed, was frequently cited; and certain enthusiasts, fired by this example, appeared to believe that the American yachting fleet if properly armed and equipped, could alone cope with the submarine menace. Others scoffed at the notion of white-flanneled yachtsmen with fair-weather pleasure craft attempting to protect the seaboard against 500-ton submarines. It was predicted that they would at best be a mere suicide squadron which the U-boats could sink at will; at worst, a nuisance to the Navy, constantly getting in trouble, and, through yachtsmen's influence, obtaining equipment urgently needed for offensive forces. The Navy's decision to use these sailing yachts was based less on conviction than on hope; and it properly postponed the decision until it could furnish each boat with at least a transmitting radio. There was no sense sending yachts off shore merely to make faces at the submarines.

The first few months of operation proved that the truth lay between these extreme predictions. Auxiliary yachts proved to be useless for hunting submarines. They were too slow and vulnerable to take the offensive except by a very lucky break; and there were inadequate facilities for training their crews in the highly technical work of handling the most modern anti-submarine devices, even were these available for small craft in 1942.

But by definition "picket" implies guard duty, and that, the sailing yachts were well fitted to perform. They could radio-telephone to a shore station the position of any U-boat or aircraft sighted; and as most of them shipped a competent celestial navigator in their crews, the positions reported were not too wild. A sufficient number of radar-equipped planes and blimps, patrolling the sea approaches night and day, could have done a more thorough job; but these were not available in sufficient numbers in 1942. The personnel, even if experienced in deep-water yachting, needed training by the Coast Guard, especially in signaling. Many vessels were sent to sea under skeleton crews and patrolled all summer with no arms except pistols and rifles.

Each district had its peculiar problems. It is far more difficult to operate an offshore patrol between Cape Henry and Charleston than in the Gulf of Mexico or the Gulf of Maine; the easiest areas to patrol had the largest number of vessels, because they were the most attractive to yachtsmen. Generally speaking, no yachts but small motor cruisers were to be had between Cape Henry and Pensacola. Such boats cannot, even in midsummer, hold the sea off Hatteras, where protection was most needed. In July 1942 Commandant Fifth Naval District (Norfolk) had to transfer, from Coastal Picket Patrol to Inshore Patrol, six 42- to 90-foot diesel freighters and thirteen 40- to 60-foot motor cabin cruisers, which had found offshore patrol duty too arduous.

The First and Third Naval Districts, covering New England, New York and part of New Jersey, where blue-water yachtsmen flourished and the maritime tradition was strong, were naturally the forwardest in organizing this force. By 25 August 1942, the First District alone had in commission and on patrol fifty-one auxiliary sailing yachts from 50 to 75 feet overall length, including such handsome vessels as the yawl *Rose*, schooner *Blue Goose*, ketch *Tioga* and schooner *Grenadier*. Only the Seventh District

(New Orleans) had more pickets, and these for the most part were small motor fishermen, who patrolled for one week out of every four, fishing the other three. The Great Lakes were combed for suitable craft, and in September 1942 about fifty fast, powerful motorboats, 50 to 130 feet in overall length, were transferred from the inland seas to the Sixth Naval District (Charleston).

In many instances the yacht owner stayed on board, with the rating of chief boatswain's mate. A number of Great Lakes navigators placed themselves and their sextants at the disposition of the Coast Guard. College boys, adventurous lads of shore villages, Boy Scouts, beachcombers, ex-bootleggers and rum-runners – almost everyone who declared he could hand, reef and steer – and many who could not – were accepted by the personnel committees in the various naval districts, provided their loyalty was unquestioned and their appearance fairly rugged. Enlistments for the duration became the rule rather than the exception. Besides this "Hooligan" personnel, the Coast Guard assigned many of its original recruits to the Picket Patrol. By mid-1943 the force was largely manned by these men and officered by former yacht owners or sailing masters with chief petty officer ratings. Thus, the Coastal Picket as well as the Ship Lane Patrol became an excellent training school in fundamental seamanship, both for the Navy and the Coast Guard. Hundreds of Coastal Picket "graduates" were detached for duty in regular cutters, transports and landing craft, to the great profit of the service. This undesigned byproduct of the two patrols justified the effort and expense, whatever one may think of their main performance.

With few exceptions, the yachtsmen personnel proved keen, competent and rugged. A sailing picket squadron consisting mainly of the former Bermuda racers *Edlu II*, *Winfred*, *Sea Gypsy*, *Vema* and *Redhead*, each 70 feet or more overall, had the arduous task of patrolling areas around Nantucket Shoals, west to Shinnecock, and down to latitude 40° N. Some of the grids covered by these vessels were as much as one hundred miles from their base at Greenport, Long Island. They kept the sea for a week or more and took everything that Old Man Neptune uncorked. Another tough assignment was that of schooner *Primrose IV*, patrolling from Quoddy Roads out around Grand Manan and across the Bay of Fundy; and it was typical of the "Hooligan Navy" that she was commanded by a sixty-year-old Harvard professor who had been a naval reserve officer in the last war, but accepted the rating of chief boatswain's mate in this. The Navy expected to divert almost all Coastal Pickets from northern waters to the Gulf Stream in winter; but the Coast Guard believed that they could carry on and they did, through the unusually severe winter of 1942–1943.

The Coastal Picket Patrol met no conclusive test of its value, simply because the U-boats sheered off from the Eastern Sea Frontier before there were enough pickets to count. A few incidents will illustrate both the value and the limitations of this force. On 13 August 1942 the Army Air Base at Westover, Massachusetts, dispatched without notice a flight of ten airplanes to test the value of the Army's aircraft-warning system. This squadron swung across Cape Cod, south of Nantucket, and then headed west and south for Philadelphia. No naval vessel or shore station made contact with them by sight or radar; but four of the Coastal Picket Patrol reported the planes promptly and accurately.[5] *Edlu II*, patrolling south of Montauk Point in a light fog about 15 September 1942, sighted a U-boat less than a hundred yards distant. The former yacht was manned by a crew of tough hombres eager to close and kill; but they had no depth charges, and before the crew could man its machine gun the U-boat submerged. In the same area the following night, a former 53-foot motor cabin cruiser, equipped with depth charges, heard the motor of a surfaced submarine and sighted it distant 450 yards, when hove-to. As the picket boat started her engine the U-boat submerged. It was a calm night, and an excellent opening for attack; but the motorboat's owner-commander took fright, steamed away zigzagging, and even failed to report the position accurately.

[5] These were ketch *Sea Roamer*, schooner *Sea Gypsy*, power cruiser *Willidy II* and motor fisherman *Dorado*.

One can well understand why the U-boat submerged. United States submarines when operating in Japanese-controlled waters of the Pacific encountered auxiliary sampans that performed the same functions as our Coastal Picket Patrol, and found them very annoying. Not knowing how the sampan might be equipped, the submarine could not afford to remain surfaced in its vicinity, did not wish to give away its position by shelling, or to waste a torpedo. The U-boat reaction to our costal pickets was similar.

The attached table shows the development of the Coastal Picket Patrol on the Eastern and Gulf Sea Frontiers. It indicates the number of vessels on patrol, and in port between patrols, on that day of each week when the maximum number were on duty. The reduction of number in some districts is due to the transfer of vessels to others where few yachts were available. Transfers of this kind were not, however, practicable during the period of training. The personnel, recruited largely from the former yacht's own crew, and commanded in many instances by the owner or former sailing master, was familiar only with certain waters, and based on a definite home port. If sent to strange waters they would have been nearly useless for a long time. A Maine coast fisherman or yachtsman would rather take his small craft across the Atlantic than patrol off the coast of the Carolinas; a Gulf of Mexico fisherman would be wretched and helpless in Maine fogs.

In January 1943 Admiral King ordered a cut of 35 per cent in the picket force as a measure of economy,[6] and by that time 83-foot Coast Guard cutters were coming out in sufficient numbers to replace the auxiliaries. The process of returning them to their owners then began. A few of the larger and more efficient yachts, which were better fitted to keep the sea than the jumpy 83-footers, were retained. But the "Hooligan Navy" ceased to be on 1 October 1943. A much reduced patrol force carried on throughout the war with Coast Guard personnel and cutters.

The Coastal Picket Patrol is another of those things which should have been prepared before the war came to America. It would have

[6] Memorandum of Lt. Cdr. H. S. Browne Jr. USCG 5 Oct. 1943.

been slight protection against submarines, but might have saved many a merchant seaman's life at a time when survivors from torpedoed freighters and tankers drifted about for days within sight of the coast, unseen by aircraft or surface vessels. More of the Dunkirk spirit, "throw in everything you have," would not have been amiss in May and June 1942, when regattas were being held within Chesapeake Bay while hell was popping outside the Capes. The yachtsmen, or some of them, were eager to stick their necks out; but at the time of greatest need, the Navy could not see its way to use them. Eventually the Navy took in the little boats, and yachtsmen found their place in the war effort.

d. Civil Air[7]

Among the many civilian organizations which gave devoted service to the cause, the Civil Air Patrol held a unique place because it performed combat duty. This nation-wide organization of civilian airmen, formed on the initiative of private flyers a week before Pearl Harbor, performed a variety of tasks such as reconnaissance, fire patrol, rescue work, carrier and freighting service the country over. In anti-submarine warfare its coastal patrol squadrons were outstanding in quality and impressive in numbers.

The idea behind the Civil Air Patrol was much the same as that of the Coastal Picket Patrol, to mobilize amateurs with their planes for combat duty. Many, perhaps a majority of the 100,000 civilian pilots of the United States were ineligible for the armed forces by reason of age or physical disability. But they could fly even though some, veterans of the last war, had wooden legs; and they owned planes – some as small as 90-horsepower Stinson Voyagers.[8]

While the Coastal Picket Patrol was organized and operated by the Coast Guard, the C.A.P. organized itself and governed and

[7] O.W.I. Press Release on the C.A.P. for 25 June 1943; files of the C.A.P. at its headquarters, 500 Fifth Avenue, New York (Col. Harry H. Blee U.S.A. Commanding Officer); information obtained at individual bases.

[8] Some even smaller, but the Voyagers were the smallest used in anti-submarine patrol.

NUMBER OF COASTAL PICKET PATROL VESSELS ON DUTY AND IN PORT IN EACH NAVAL DISTRICT *

<table>
<tr><th>Week Ending</th><th colspan="2">First Naval Dist.</th><th colspan="2">Third Naval Dist.</th><th colspan="2">Fourth Naval Dist.</th><th colspan="2">Fifth Naval Dist.</th><th colspan="2">Sixth Naval Dist.</th><th colspan="2">Seventh Naval Dist.</th><th colspan="2">Eighth Naval Dist.</th></tr>
<tr><td>1942</td><td>Duty</td><td>Port</td><td>Duty</td><td>Port</td><td>Duty</td><td>Port</td><td>Duty</td><td>Port</td><td>Duty</td><td>Port</td><td>Duty</td><td>Port</td><td>Duty</td><td>Port</td></tr>
<tr><td>18 July</td><td colspan="2">25</td><td>14</td><td>12</td><td>2</td><td>0</td><td>2</td><td>26</td><td>4</td><td>4</td><td>3</td><td>0</td><td>12</td><td>8</td></tr>
<tr><td>14 August</td><td colspan="2">61</td><td>66</td><td>7</td><td>6</td><td>2</td><td>4</td><td>0</td><td>4</td><td>3</td><td>5</td><td>4</td><td>51</td><td>63</td></tr>
<tr><td>18 September</td><td>36</td><td>40</td><td>65</td><td>32</td><td>19</td><td>15</td><td>28</td><td>0</td><td>15</td><td>13</td><td>22</td><td>21</td><td>104</td><td>70</td></tr>
<tr><td>16 October</td><td>43</td><td>48</td><td>30</td><td>89</td><td>23</td><td>22</td><td>5</td><td>25</td><td>17</td><td>25</td><td>17</td><td>86</td><td>76</td><td>108</td></tr>
<tr><td>20 November</td><td>36</td><td>57</td><td>55</td><td>43</td><td>20</td><td>25</td><td>18</td><td>12</td><td>24</td><td>27</td><td>37</td><td>55</td><td>85</td><td>90</td></tr>
<tr><td>18 December</td><td>31</td><td>62</td><td>25</td><td>42</td><td>12</td><td>23</td><td>9</td><td>11</td><td>17</td><td>39</td><td>40</td><td>69</td><td>94</td><td>92</td></tr>
<tr><td>1943</td><td></td><td></td><td></td><td></td><td></td><td></td><td></td><td></td><td></td><td></td><td></td><td></td><td></td><td></td></tr>
<tr><td>15 January</td><td>38</td><td>50</td><td>32</td><td>101</td><td>10</td><td>22</td><td>3</td><td>15</td><td>15</td><td>40</td><td>65</td><td>35</td><td>156</td><td>96</td></tr>
<tr><td>19 February</td><td>40</td><td>32</td><td>41</td><td>66</td><td>6</td><td>24</td><td>6</td><td>11</td><td>22</td><td>39</td><td>68</td><td>37</td><td>183</td><td>75</td></tr>
<tr><td>19 March</td><td>39</td><td>23</td><td>33</td><td>52</td><td>5</td><td>8</td><td>8</td><td>8</td><td>23</td><td>38</td><td>68</td><td>40</td><td>58</td><td>190</td></tr>
<tr><td>16 April</td><td>38</td><td>24</td><td>34</td><td>50</td><td>4</td><td>9</td><td>5</td><td>11</td><td>29</td><td>33</td><td>67</td><td>37</td><td>20</td><td>58</td></tr>
<tr><td>14 May</td><td>42</td><td>20</td><td>39</td><td>45</td><td>4</td><td>9</td><td>8</td><td>7</td><td>31</td><td>30</td><td>78</td><td>37</td><td>38</td><td>40</td></tr>
<tr><td>18 June</td><td>37</td><td>24</td><td>40</td><td>45</td><td>3</td><td>10</td><td>9</td><td>6</td><td>24</td><td>36</td><td>79</td><td>37</td><td>33</td><td>30</td></tr>
<tr><td>16 July</td><td>37</td><td>24</td><td>36</td><td>49</td><td>3</td><td>9</td><td>4</td><td>11</td><td>25</td><td>35</td><td>67</td><td>45</td><td>21</td><td>42</td></tr>
<tr><td>20 August</td><td>38</td><td>23</td><td>41</td><td>44</td><td>3</td><td>9</td><td>4</td><td>11</td><td>26</td><td>34</td><td>62</td><td>59</td><td>26</td><td>36</td></tr>
<tr><td>17 September</td><td>33</td><td>28</td><td>38</td><td>47</td><td>3</td><td>9</td><td>4</td><td>11</td><td>24</td><td>36</td><td>53</td><td>61</td><td>0</td><td>61†</td></tr>
</table>

* From the Weekly Progress Reports graphs in E.S.F., and information from Gulf Sea Frontier.

† Hurricane.

disciplined itself. Eventually (29 April 1943) it was removed from the control of the Office of Civilian Defense and became an auxiliary of the Army Air Force; but the members were still civilians in uniform, and their planes remained private property.

When the German assault on coastal shipping began, the C.A.P. volunteered to establish a sea-lane air patrol base near Atlantic City. That was in late February 1942, when air coverage in the Eastern Sea Frontier was negligible. The C.A.P. had already done some intensive recruiting. A majority of the private flyers ineligible for armed services joined up, together with thousands of men and women, young and old, for mechanical, administrative or clerical work.[9] It was a rule of the organization that nobody should claim draft deferment; consequently every enrollment was an addition to the armed forces. Very few of the planes had room for more than a pilot, an observer and a small plane-to-shore radio set. At first they were completely unarmed, serving only for spotting submarines or survivors; but as time went on, the larger planes were equipped with one 325-lb. depth charge or two 100-lb. demolition bombs, and a simple homemade bomb sight. Their principal value, during the period of heavy sinkings along the Atlantic seaboard, was to sight disabled vessels or survivors in lifeboats, and to report strange or suspicious surface craft. The low speed and flying altitude of the C.A.P. planes enabled their pilots to observe many objects that escaped the notice of those in military planes. For instance, the survivors of the motor vessel *Gertrude*, sunk off Havana 15 July 1942, reported that they were spotted by two C.A.P. planes after eleven other aircraft had passed overhead without sighting their small boat.[10]

One of the outstanding qualities of the C.A.P. was its flexibility and freedom from red tape. If the Navy wanted anything from

[9] In June 1943, the total membership was over 75,000 of which 10 per cent were women. Casualties to that date on the Coastal Patrol alone were 26 flyers killed (ranging in age from 19 to 50), and 90 planes lost. C.A.P. men received no pay, only a subsistence allowance, and a mileage rental for their planes when on military missions.

[10] Miami *Herald* 28 July 1942.

blood plasma to a bomb sight to be flown anywhere in a hurry, or a message delivered to a ship at sea, the C.A.P. was always ready to take off. The energy of these flying civilians was amazing; their intrepidity beyond all praise. In foul weather that kept military planes grounded, they took off and searched for subs.

The second C.A.P. base to be established, and the first to begin patrol operations (5 March 1942) was at Rehoboth, near the Delaware Capes. The next to be set up on the Eastern Sea Frontier, in April and May, were those at Lantana, Florida; Parksley, Virginia; Flagler Beach, Florida; St. Simons Island, Georgia; Miami and Charleston. When U-boats began to penetrate the Gulf of Mexico the C.A.P. followed, establishing bases at Grand Isle, Louisiana; Beaumont and Brownsville, Texas; Pascagoula, Mississippi; Sarasota and Panama City, Florida; and Corpus Christi, Texas. During the late summer of 1942 two bases were established in Maine, at Portland and near Bar Harbor; two in North Carolina, at Manteo and Beaufort; one at Riverhead, Long Island; and one at Falmouth on Cape Cod.

Owing to their civilian status the members of the C.A.P. had infinite difficulties obtaining equipment, parts, and replacements. They had to buy their own gasoline, and in most states to pay the tax on it as well. They begged and borrowed equipment for bases and received many gifts from states, towns, counties, chambers of commerce, and individuals. But up to the middle of 1943 they had also spent about a million dollars of their own money on helping the anti-submarine air patrol.

A typical experience was that of the C.A.P. squadron at the Bar Harbor base. Thirty-five members with six planes arrived to take over that civilian airport on 24 August 1942. The one building available was a hangar with a dirt floor and a roof full of holes. No money was available. Few of the pilot owners had had any experience flying their fragile planes over salt water. Yet eleven days later this squadron began actively patrolling the area between Quoddy Head and Port Clyde. The members of this squadron came to fly, but they also had to dig, build, construct and assemble, between flights. Bar Harbor gave them an old stable; they dismantled it, hauled the lumber to the field in a borrowed truck, and put it together as their Operations Building. When winter set in they obtained a secondhand heating plant and built a false ceiling to the hangar; but before that was completed, mechanics were repairing planes in a temperature of 20 degrees below zero. A fire wiped out "Operations," consuming all the pilots' flying clothing and safety equipment; but operations were not interrupted, and new buildings were promptly erected. Patrolling went on right through that hard winter. These over-military-age pilots learned to make landings in a thick fog, and on unlighted fields, although none of them knew instrument flying. One plane crashed in the sea on 2 February and her crew of two (both over thirty, both married) were frozen to death before they could be rescued. Ten days later the squadron organized the rescue of a Navy pilot whose plane crashed in Blue Hill Bay and were just in time to save his life.

Throughout the winter, spring and summer of 1943, the C.A.P. at Bar Harbor, Portland and Falmouth (Cape Cod) were an integral part of air escort for Boston–Halifax convoys. None of the pilots at first knew anything but the most rudimentary navigation and meteorology; but they learned fast. An important byproduct of the C.A.P. was the training of young boys so that they could promptly qualify as pilots or aviation mechanics on reaching the proper age. In answer to a hurry call from the Ferry Command early in the war, one wing alone provided 50 trained pilots in three days.

There was nothing temporary or token about the C.A.P. In the Eastern and Gulf Sea Frontiers, the C.A.P. flew 64,000 plane hours during the first five months of 1943, as compared with 27,000 plane hours by the Army Air Force, and 72,000 plane hours by Navy planes.[11] If comparative statistics were available for 1942, they would show an even greater relative contribution by the amateurs.

[11] The total number of hours flown by C.A.P. on coastal patrol from 5 Mar. 1942 to Sept. 1943 was 244,000; total number of missions flown, 86,685, of which 5684 were convoy missions. It had reported the positions of 173 enemy submarines, reported 91 vessels in distress, and rafts or lifeboats containing 363 survivors.

Schooner *Aeolus* of the "Hooligan Navy"

Schooner *Guinevere* of the Ship Lane Patrol

Sailing Patrol Ships

A 20-mm machine-gun crew of *Campbell*

Campbell after ramming *U-606*, 22 February 1943

Coast Guard Cutter Campbell

In the summer of 1943, as Coast Guard cutters began replacing the "Hooligan Navy," the Navy took over all air aspects of antisubmarine warfare along the Atlantic Coast. The C.A.P. squadrons were relieved on 1 September, and sent to perform other duties. Fishermen, coastwise sailors and island dwellers were sorry to have them go; they missed the game little bright-colored one-engine jobs with the white pyramid mark, which they had learned to look for in daylight hours, however foul the weather, provided you could see above your masthead.

The C.A.P. and the Coastal Picket Patrol are outstanding American examples of that fusing of civilian with military effort for which the Russians are justly famous. They are the sort of thing we need more of, instead of inducing citizens to serve their country by swollen pay and enormous bonuses. Nor may we discount the devoted service of these two organizations on the ground that they consisted of wealthy sportsmen. They did not. At least 90 per cent of the personnel in both organizations consisted of men and women who had to earn their living, and who could have made big money in war industries or the merchant marine. But they were people who wanted to serve, not to gain; they proved that the call to work and sacrifice is stronger, and produces better service, than the lure of money.

2. *Mystery Ships*[12]

During World War I the so-called "Q" or Mystery Ships acquired a reputation for sinking submarines far in excess of their deserts, and inspired sundry thrillers and "now-it-can-be-told" yarns. The Q-ship was a heavily armed converted merchantman disguised as a peaceful trader in order to decoy U-boats, which were expected to approach surfaced in order to sink her by gunfire as an undefended vessel not worth the cost of a torpedo. The Q-ship's

[12] This section is largely taken from an account of the Q-ships written by Lt. E. E. Morison USNR, incorporated in Eastern Sea Frontier War Diary for Oct. 1943. Additional information from participants, and B.d.U. war diary.

naval crew in the meantime were at general quarters. At a given signal, camouflage nets were whisked off, gun ports popped open, and a bristling array of unmasked ordnance blew the unwary U-boat out of the water. At least, that is how this *ruse de guerre* was supposed to work; but it seldom did.[13] One unlucky Q-ship of the United States Navy in World War I, *Santee* by name, was torpedoed on her first mystery voyage.[14] The British used several in World War II, but they did not have much success and had given up by the end of 1941.

Unpromising as this expedient seemed, obsolescent as it proved to be, the submarine situation was so serious early in 1942 as to tempt the Navy to try anything; the fact that President Roosevelt proposed and Admiral King, not addicted to romantic methods, authorized mystery ships, proves how serious the situation was. On 20 January 1942 he ordered Commander Eastern Sea Frontier to give "immediate consideration" to the manning of Q-ships as an anti-submarine measure. Admiral Andrews replied that a disguised tanker, the then favorite target for U-boats, or a schooner so insignificant in appearance that on sighting it a submarine would not bother to submerge, would have "a reasonable chance of success," and was well worth trying. "Project LQ" was then set up under deep secrecy, to create the Q-ships.

Early in 1942 three vessels were selected to inaugurate the project: — U.S.S. *Eagle*, originally a diesel-powered Boston trawler named *Wave*, and S.S. *Carolyn* and *Evelyn*.[15] These two 3200-ton freighters, about thirty years old, were converted at the Portsmouth (N.H.) Navy Yard to U.S.S. *Atik* and *Asterion*, armed with four 4-inch 50-cal. guns, four .50-cal. machine guns, six depth-charge

13 Henry Newbolt *Naval Operations* (the continuation of Sir Julian Corbett's work) IV 334–37, 357–59, V 106–12. As a result of three Q-ships being sunk in one week of Aug. 1917 without getting a single U-boat, the type was discontinued.

14 Admiral W. S. Sims *The Victory at Sea* Chap. V.

15 On the Gulf Sea Frontier a schooner named *Alice* was converted to a mystery ship in Jacksonville and cruised in the Caribbean. I have only hearsay knowledge of her, but believe that she was decommissioned upon the discovery that the German agents set ashore from *U-584* in June 1942 at Ponte Vedra, Florida, were in possession of her conversion plans.

throwers, and sound gear. *Eagle* had similar equipment, gear and armament but only one 4-inch gun. She carried 5 officers and 42 enlisted men; the two old freighters carried 6 officers and 135 enlisted men each. *Eagle* was to preserve the appearance of a trawler innocently engaged in fishing; *Atik* and *Asterion*, that of unarmed merchantmen pursuing their lawful occasions. The unusual details of their conversion were observed and commented on by civilian workers in the Navy Yard, and it is probable that secrecy, the one essential condition for the success of Q-ships, was compromised before they sailed.

All three mystery ships, having the appearance of regularly commissioned armed vessels, sailed from New England ports on 23 March 1942. Once at sea they put on their various disguises, broke out false papers and painted new names, except that *Eagle* reverted ostensibly to her original character as trawler *Wave*.

Four days out, when cruising about 300 miles east of Norfolk, *Atik* (Lieutenant Commander Harry L. Hicks) was sunk in a fight with the *U-123*. *Kapitänleutnant* Hardegen, decoyed to attack at sunset, watched his first torpedo hit and the "panic party" take to the boats while a frantic SOS was radioed from the freighter. As the sub closed, *Atik* dropped false bulwarks, tossed out depth charges and opened fire, making several hits and killing one German. *U-123* escaped out of range but after dark sank the disabled *Atik* with a torpedo. Ten days later Berlin triumphantly broadcasted that this Q-ship had been sent to the bottom by a U-boat. There were no survivors.

Despite this radio revelation that the Germans were prepared to deal with Q-ships, "Project LQ" nevertheless was continued. Gathering intelligence, rescuing survivors and patrolling vigilantly, *Asterion* (Lieutenant Commander G. W. Legwen), had several good "nibbles" during six short cruises in the Eastern Sea Frontier, the Gulf of Mexico and the Caribbean without persuading a single U-boat to rise to the bait. Then a naval survey board reported her watertight integrity to be so weak that a single torpedo hit would be sufficient to sink her. Fitted with five transverse bulkheads, strengthened in her armament and otherwise altered and improved, *Asterion* was again ready for sea in October 1943. But the need for weather-reporting ships in the Atlantic was so urgent that she was diverted from the mystery business to the "rainmakers."

U.S.S. *Eagle* (Lieutenant Commander L. F. Rogers USNR), the ex-trawler, had an equally barren career. Her sister ship the *Foam* was sunk on 17 May 1942 off Nova Scotia by *U–432*, but *Eagle*, her name now changed to *Captor*, patrolled as a Q-ship unmolested. Her few sound contacts, in the light of enemy information received after the war, can only be evaluated as "non-submarine." This was a bitter disappointment to her skipper and her tough crew of 52.

The most formidable of the mystery ships was the ex-tanker *Gulf Dawn*, disguised as a fleet oiler at the Boston Navy Yard, given watertight integrity by thousands of sealed empty oil drums, and renamed *Big Horn*. Commander J. A. Gainard USNR, who had shown good judgment and daring early in the war as master of the *City of Flint*, was given the command; the total complement was 13 officers and 157 enlisted men. When ready for sea in September 1942, U.S.S. *Big Horn* was ordered to Trinidad, near which many ships had recently been sunk. She was directed to lag behind the escort of a TE convoy which conducted tankers and freighters to a dispersal point 200 miles east of Trinidad, in order to tempt a submarine to attack her as a "straggler." Unfortunately the U-boats were getting such good pickings from these inexpertly escorted convoys that they were not bothering with stragglers; so that when a pack of three submarines attacked this convoy off Galera Point, hitting two ships and sinking one, *Big Horn* was so far astern that she never got into the fight. On her next trip, she was lagging behind Convoy TAG–20 off Curaçao 12 November 1942, when the escorting gunboat *Erie* was torpedoed and subsequently lost; *Big Horn* was never able to fire a shot.

New mystery tactics were now put into effect. *Big Horn* was fitted with hedgehog, given two intensively trained PCs, Numbers *617* and *618*, as a deceptive escort, and the group was placed under the command of Commander Louis C. Farley USNR.[16] He was ordered to straggle from Convoy UGS–7A somewhere in Azorean waters, which U-boats were known to infest, the PCs staying over the horizon until a contact was made. In that character she delivered three hedgehog and several depth-charge attacks on a U-boat near lat. 29° N, long. 28°10′ W on 3 May 1943; but the submarine escaped both her and the PCs. On the way home she ran down several direction-finder contacts in the vain hope of meeting more U-boats. Following another overhaul she sailed in company with the PCs as part of Convoy UGS–13 on 27 July 1943. When trailing the convoy by about 50 miles she sighted a submarine; one of the PCs attacked with mousetrap but failed to connect; so once again the *Big Horn* group returned to New York empty-handed. A third and last cruise in November–December 1943 yielded one fight with a submarine, which escaped. *Big Horn* had spent so much time in waters known to be infested with U-boats, and yet had seen so very few as to suggest that the enemy knew all about her and had warned submarine commanders against exposing themselves to "straggling" oilers. So *Big Horn,* too, joined the weather-reporting fleet early in 1944.

The last United States mystery ship to be fitted out was the three-masted schooner *Irene Forsyte,* 156 feet long, built in Nova Scotia in 1920 and purchased for a moderate sum by the Navy. Commander Gerald Thompson supervised her conversion, and she was armed with one 4-inch gun, three automatic weapons, small arms, radar, mousetrap and sonar. She sailed from New London in late September 1943 in the character of an armed schooner, with Lieutenant Commander Richard Parmenter USNR as skipper and a volunteer Navy crew. When lying at anchor in Great Bight off Nantucket, the crew performed the entire work of concealing armament and altering both rig and profile so that she looked exactly like a certain fishing schooner of neutral registry. Thus *Irene* had a

[16] Naval Academy '05, a desdiv commander in World War I, and Operations Officer Eastern Sea Frontier in 1942.

very good chance of achieving the Q-ship's dream, complete surprise. Unfortunately, she put to sea in the hurricane season. In a heavy gale east of Bermuda her seams opened up and she narrowly escaped sinking by putting into Hamilton Sound. There repairs were effected, weights were lessened and tie rods installed. Mr. Parmenter requested permission to proceed, but Cinclant ordered her back to the States for decommissioning. A board of investigation reported on her condition to Admiral King who, completely disgusted with the project that he had been persuaded to launch, now issued orders that frontier commanders and district commandants would no longer enjoy "uncontrolled authority to implement projects of this nature."

So ended one of the least successful of all methods adopted to fight submarines. It had cost the lives of 141 officers and men, about one in four of the total personnel involved. Service in mystery ships proved to be more hazardous than in any other branch of the Navy; and the men deserve the highest commendation for their brave effort.

3. *Fishermen and Air Observers*

Compared with the information obtained by high-frequency direction-finder bearings, and through radar, visual or sound contacts by planes and naval vessels, all other methods of reporting submarines were unimportant. A few words will suffice to describe two of these methods which yielded meager returns compared with the effort expended. First, the Fishermen Observers.[17]

Fishermen have always been a peculiar maritime tribe, a law to themselves, mixing very little with other seafarers and uninterested in the Navy. A fisherman wants to fish; and fishing during the war was uncommonly lucrative. Any hand aboard a trawler or dragger from Down East, where profits are still shared on the old "lay"

[17] Information from Capt. Vincent Astor USNR and Lt. Cdr. Richard D. Sears Jr. USNR. Neither of these officers, however, is responsible for my somewhat gloomy conclusion as to the way this system worked out.

system, could make at least $500 a month; and when the meat shortage developed later in the war, the fishermen did even better; individual gains going into the five-figure income brackets became common. Your American fisherman argued with some cogency that catching fish for public consumption was highly important, and that he should continue to do what had taken him a long time to learn. Yet the scarcity of vessels suitable for patrol and escort was such that the Coast Guard and Navy requisitioned many fishing craft, without their crews, during the first half of 1942;[18] so many that the supply of fish in the markets was threatened. Consequently a directive was issued by the Navy early in July 1942, ordering district Coast Guard officers to go easy in this matter.[19] The great majority of American fishermen were loyal to the United States; and it seemed reasonable to assume that those who were too old to fight would be glad to help their country as observers of submarine movements. The Japanese Navy had been using fishermen for many years as gatherers of information and as spies on our naval movements.

Commander Vincent Astor USNR conceived a plan that was adopted by the Eastern Sea Frontier in early April 1942. It was simple enough: to equip every seagoing fishing vessel with two-way voice radio, frequencies sealed to those of the Radio Marine Company and Coast Guard; and to give the master or some other competent member of the crew a personal indicator number and a copy of the Army Interceptor Grid. By these means, upon sighting a submarine, plane, wreckage, or any suspicious object he could communicate with the Radio Marine Company, which had a special wire to the Army Interceptor Command, and that could relay the message to the proper Navy or Coast Guard headquarters.

Much patience and tact, numerous personal visits and elbow-crookings, were required to "sell" this idea to the fishermen, con-

[18] Including a Maine-built fleet of diesel-powered wooden trawlers. These were classified as AMcs (Coastal Minesweepers) and proved so useful as fleet auxiliaries that the Navy ordered many built for its own use in Down East Yards.

[19] Commandant Sixth Naval District Directive of 8 July 1942; Commander Eastern Sea Frontier to Commandants of Naval Districts 7 Aug. 1942. E.S.F. Files.

genitally suspicious of gold braid. But by 15 September 1942, some 625 fishing vessels on the Eastern Sea Frontier alone were carrying official observers. One year later the number in the same area had risen to 845, including every sort of fishing craft from Gulf of Maine mackerel seiners to Florida shrimpers.

As observers, the fishermen were naturally more competent than yachtsmen, and less likely to mistake a school of blackfish for a submarine. On the other hand, they had a strongly ingrained notion that reporting submarines was none of their business. Many consented to be enrolled as observers rather than incur a stigma of lacking patriotism, but that sort of spirit did not procure useful reports. Fishermen observers in the First Naval District, where scores of vessels were fishing well off shore every day, made only 105 pertinent reports in 13 months, and only 20 of these reports were of submarines. And this in spite of what happened to some of their fellows. Trawler *Foam* of Boston was sunk by *U-432's* gunfire 70 miles south of Halifax on 17 May 1942, and one of the crew was killed; trawler *Ebb* of Boston, steaming about 46 miles SE of Cape Sable on 28 July 1942, and carrying a fisherman observer, was fired on by a submarine that surfaced only 50 yards away; before the observer could even get to his microphone he and four other men were killed and seven wounded.[20] The *Ben and Josephine* and *Aeolus* of Gloucester, about four miles apart, were dragging the northeastern edge of Georges Bank on 2 June when a submarine fired a machine-gun burst at the *Ben's* pilothouse. Her crew abandoned ship under continued fire when the U-boat turned its attention to *Aeolus* and gave her a dose of the same. Both vessels were sunk by gunfire; and although the survivors in dories were over one hundred miles from the nearest land, no offer was made of provisions or water. Nevertheless all reached Mt. Desert Rock in safety.

With few exceptions, a fisherman who actually sighted a U-boat delayed so long making a report, fearing to be shot up if he used his

[20] It was rumored in waterfront circles that the *Ebb* "asked for it" because her master picked up his radio to report the sub; but that is not true. She was sunk cold-bloodedly, without warning, and before anyone was able to get at the radio signal.

radio, that his report was useless. Fishermen yield to no other seafarers for their courage in their own profession; but in spite of all efforts at Navy indoctrination they still believed, as one of them declared three centuries ago when reproached for lack of public spirit, "our main business is to catch fish."

The second group of amateur observers were on commercial planes.[21] In April 1941 the Navy first attempted to interest commercial aviators in reporting sightings of submarines. Two Pan American Airways officials drafted a simple code for radio reports to company headquarters, whence they were passed to Third Naval District headquarters. Matters continued on this informal basis until 10 July 1942, when Cominch ordered sea frontier commanders to take further action. Commander B. M. Baruch Jr. USNR, who had initiated the contacts with Pan American, was appointed staff officer at the Eastern Sea Frontier for commercial airplane reports. Procedure was laid down for identification of friendly vessels, rapid delivery of sighting reports, and indoctrination of the personnel. By 15 September 1942 the five principal airlines, the Naval Air Transport and the Army Air Transport Command had been brought into the picture, and in November the British transatlantic clippers operating from Baltimore joined up. Hence, by the end of 1942, the principal transatlantic routes, north and south, and the Atlantic Coast and Caribbean routes from Greenland were covered by these sighting reports.

For the most part, planes on these routes flew too high to observe surfaced U-boats. The record of each sighting by commercial aircraft, kept at Eastern Sea Frontier headquarters from April 1942 to the end of 1943, shows an average of ten to twelve reports monthly. Their value for detecting U-boats was insignificant, although possibly a shade better than that of the fishermen.

[21] Information from and files of Cdr. B. M. Baruch Jr. USNR, Eastern Sea Frontier headquarters.

CHAPTER XII

Merchant Ships and Their Armament

1. *Ship Production*[1]

AT THE HEIGHT of the submarine attack along the Atlantic Coast, in the early months of 1942, it was seriously urged by a few interested shipbuilders, and by others who should have known better, that the United States Merchant Marine retire from coastal waters and the country conduct its Atlantic coastwise commerce by a fleet of shoal-draft gasoline barges using the Intracoastal waterway. This counsel of despair was heeded to the extent of authorizing a $250,000,000 program of concrete barges, none of which were completed in time to relieve the bottleneck, and almost all of which were useless.[2] A similarly fantastic proposal for a transatlantic "bridge of ships" was that of the "Sea Otter." This 270-foot shoal-draft freighter of 1900 tons displacement, designed by an automobile engineer and a retired commander of the United States Navy, was to be propelled by sixteen 110-horsepower gasoline engines arranged radially and coupled hydraulically to four *vertical* shafts set in cylindrical wells. The ends of the shafts, projecting seven feet below the keel, were equipped with propellers geared at right angles like outboard motors, and could be hoisted up on deck. Torpedoes would pass harmlessly underneath these 10-foot-draft vessels

[1] The data and statistics in this section were furnished by Dr. H. L. Deimel Jr., head of the Division of Economics and Statistics of the U. S. Maritime Commission. Additional data from Truman Committee Additional Report No. 10 Parts 8 and 18, "Shipbuilding and Shipping" and "Merchant Shipping" 1943–1944; *The United States Merchant Marine at War*, Report of W.S.A. to the President 15 Jan. 1946.

[2] The story of these concrete barges, a major scandal of the war production, is told in above Additional Report 10 Part 8 pp. 17, 35–65.

and, so it was claimed, mass production would cost so little that each Sea Otter could be broken up at the end of her first voyage and the engines converted to military use overseas. Following experiments with an 80-foot model, the full-size *Sea Otter II* was completed during September 1941 at Orange, Texas. She proved to be dangerously crank and her draft was twice the amount predicted.[3] The 16 unmuffled gasoline engines made sufficient noise to alert any submarine within 50 miles, if not to permanently deafen the crew.

Although President Roosevelt still had faith in this design, to which both he and Secretary Knox had given initial encouragement,[4] the Bureau of Ships and the Maritime Commission were reluctant to divert vital materials and overtaxed shipbuilding resources to its production. Yet the Navy Trial Board was accused of prejudice in dropping Sea Otter, and the Senate Naval Affairs Sub-Committee was called on to investigate. Experienced shipbuilders agreed that the Navy and Maritime Commission "might have been hostile to the proposal, but their preconceived convictions seem to have been proven sound, not prejudiced." [5]

Fortunately the main efforts of the shipbuilding industry were directed along more constructive channels.

When the war broke in Europe the American Merchant Marine was in one of its frequently recurrent sick spells, and no fresh injections of mail contract subsidy could revive it. By the Merchant Marine Act of 1936 Congress created the Maritime Commission whose first wartime chairman was Rear Admiral Emory S. Land. With his able assistant Rear Admiral Howard L. Vickery, Admiral Land formed the most remarkable shipbuilding team in American history. Under his leadership the Maritime Commission undertook to provide merchant ship designs, to authorize construction and meet a good part of the cost, to allocate ships to private operators or

[3] Statements of Secretary Knox *N. Y. Times* 26 Feb. 1942.

[4] The President had been one of its staunchest promoters and announced at the press conference 10 Mar. 1942 that despite the discouraging preliminaries he had not lost faith in the Sea Otter. *N. Y. Times* 19 Sept. 1941 and 11 Mar. 1942.

[5] So stated by a naval architect who had been retained by the Navy Department to supervise construction. Eads Johnson "Result of the Sea Otter Trials" *Marine Engineering* May 1942 pp. 119–122.

to a government operating agency, and in many other ways to build up the merchant marine.[6] The Commission's modest goal was to provide the country with 500 new ships over a ten-year period. It adopted several designs for normal peacetime uses, of which the better known were the "C" classes of dry cargo freighters. The standard C–2, a five-hatch vessel 435 feet in length, was the most popular type, of which the first was delivered in July 1939.

Particulars and silhouettes of the principal ocean-going Maritime Commission designs are given below.[7]

The Maritime Commission got off to a slow start but in the right direction, its immediate purpose being to improve the quality rather than increase the quantity of American merchant ships. Only 82 vessels were constructed under its supervision in 1939 and 1940, in addition to 20 built under private supervision; and these meager figures include the production of all three seacoasts and the Great Lakes. By mid-1941 it was clear that this leisurely pace was not getting us far. War clouds were gathering and pressure was applied all along the line. Transfer from a peace to a war basis was signaled by the passage on 14 July 1941 of the Ship Warrants Act, which gave the Maritime Commission power to allot ship-construction priorities for national defense requirements. This was followed on 7 February 1942 by the creation of the War Shipping Administration, a wartime operating agency also headed by Admiral Land.

One of the mightiest of the many "miracles of production" by which American industry implemented the war effort was that of the shipbuilders. First it was necessary to design an emergency ship

6 "Construction differential subsidies" enabled shipowners to obtain new vessels built in American shipyards at the lower price of foreign shipyards, and "operating differential subsidies" covered the increased cost of American operation.

7 *Gross tonnage* is the entire internal cubic capacity of the ship expressed in tons of 100 cubic feet each. *Net tonnage* is derived by substracting from the gross tonnage the cubic capacity of certain internal spaces not available for carrying cargo such as machinery compartments, crew's and passengers' quarters, etc. *Deadweight tonnage* is the carrying capacity of a ship in long tons of 2240 pounds each – not, as many suppose, the avoirdupois weight of the ship itself. But the tonnage of warships *is* stated in terms of the vessel's weight, and is generally called *displacement*. Sinkings of merchant vessels in our statistics are expressed in gross tons. Deadweight tonnage (weight capacity) is roughly 50 per cent more than gross (cubic capacity) in freighters, even more in the case of tankers.

that could be built quickly and inexpensively in large numbers by modern assembly-line and mass-production methods. The similar need during World War I had given birth to the Hog Island freighters, some of which had survived to serve in World War II. But that program had been so slow in starting that the war was over

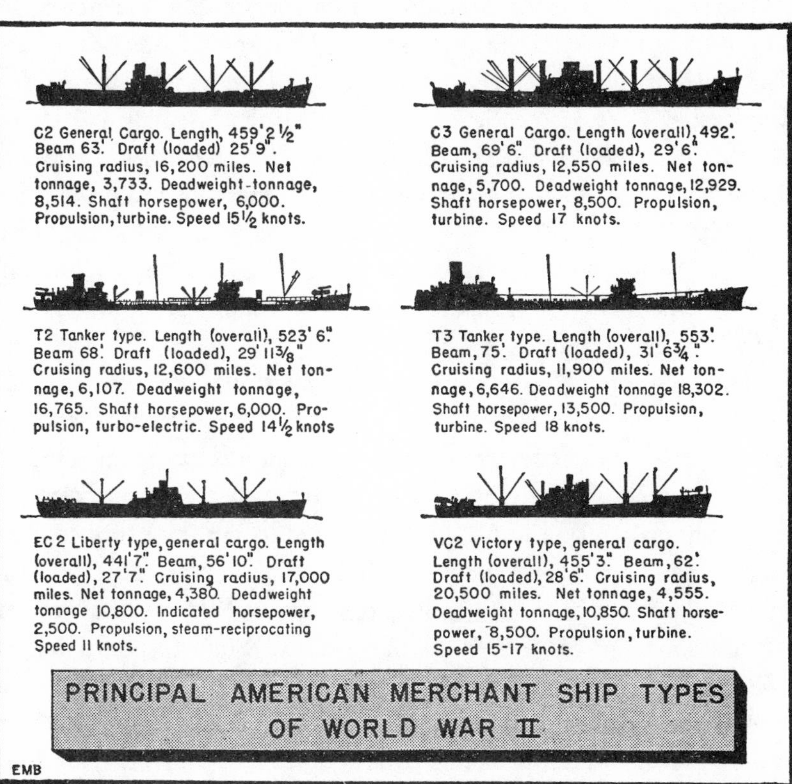

PRINCIPAL AMERICAN MERCHANT SHIP TYPES OF WORLD WAR II

before Hog Island began launching ships. In 1941 existing yards were working to full capacity on naval contracts. Hence the Maritime Commission had to establish new shipyards, each working on the same type of merchant vessel; friendly rivalry between them became an added spur to speedy construction. Eighteen new yards comprising 171 shipways, none of which existed before 1941, were being built and managed by the Maritime Commission at the end of that year.

The design finally selected as a standard emergency cargo vessel for World War II was the famous EC–2 or Liberty ship of 7176 tons gross and 10,500 tons deadweight, an adaptation of the British Sunderland-type tramp steamer but with welded hull construction. Old-style triple-expansion steam reciprocating engines, of only 2500 horsepower, simple to build and easily operated by inexperienced engineers, provided an average speed of 11 knots loaded. The first Liberty ship, appropriately named *Patrick Henry*, was launched 27 September 1941 at the Bethlehem-Fairfield Yards, Baltimore,[8] and delivered the last day of December. The slow speed of this type required the protection of escorts; but the engineering and production problems of getting out a 15-knot vessel were such that if the Maritime Commission had not stood firm for the 11-knot design, production of emergency types would have been reduced to about 25 per cent of what actually got built.[9]

Total figures of all types of merchant ships delivered in 1941 showed 100 per cent increase over 1940:[10] 103 ships of 805,424 deadweight tons under the Maritime Commission; 36 of 313,289 tons produced privately. But this step-up was far from sufficient. In 1942 ship production was further increased to 727 ships of 5,402,181 tons under Maritime; together with 89 ships of 732,796 tons constructed privately. In December 1942 alone there was a greater production than for the whole of 1941. The figures continued to rise during 1943, until in April the Maritime Commission had passed the goal of 140 ships of 1,000,000 deadweight tons *per month* – four times the *annual* production of 1939. And these tonnage figures were doubled again by December. At the end of 1943 almost a million and a half men and women were employed in ship construction.

[8] Altogether 2710 Liberty ships were produced by Maritime Commission Shipyards. The final one, *Albert M. Boe*, was delivered 30 Oct. 1945.

[9] Construction of a slightly larger emergency type with finer lines, the Victory ship (VC–2), with Lentz or turbine steam engines capable of 15 to 17 knots, began in 1943. The first completed was *United Victory*, delivered 29 Feb. 1944 by the Oregon Shipbuilding Corporation; 15 were afloat by 1 May 1944 and 82 by 1 Nov. Altogether 531 Victory ships were built.

[10] Figures from U.S.M.C. Official Construction Record 1939–1945.

During the last quarter of 1942, ship production for the first time topped ship destruction by enemy action and marine casualty. During the entire year there were constructed in the United States 646 freighters, of which 597 were Liberty ships,[11] together with 62 tankers and 33 of miscellaneous types. The only disappointing feature was the tanker production, which did not yet equal the destruction of this essential type by the enemy. Measures were then taken to step up tanker production, and 14 or 15 per month were being delivered by May 1943.

Only an amazing speed-up in shipbuilding made possible this vast production. Thus, *Patrick Henry* required 244 days' construction; but by 1944 the average time to build a Liberty ship was 42 days. The earlier world record attained in 1919, 724 ships of 3.3 million tons deadweight, was surpassed in the first six months alone of 1943, when 711 ships of 5.7 million tons deadweight were produced.

For the command and operation of this increasing fleet, the existing licensed and unlicensed personnel of the American Merchant Marine was inadequate. The War Shipping Administration undertook an intensive recruiting campaign for the merchant marine, set up training centers where ordinary seamen could be advanced to A.B. or ratings, and established wage schedules that were exceedingly attractive to young men of draft age. The training of officers was more difficult. The United States Merchant Marine Cadet Corps, established 15 March 1938 with one school and 99 cadets, expanded under the successive direction of the Coast Guard and the War Shipping Administration[12] to the three schools at San Mateo, California; Pass Christian, Mississippi; and Kings Point, Long Island. The cadets received basic training for nine months, served at sea in merchant ships for a year or more, and finally took an advanced training course of two years at Kings Point. By the beginning of 1944 over six thousand cadets had completed this course and received their commissions as Ensign Merchant Marine Reserve,

[11] Fifty-five of them for British account.

[12] Shifted from U.S.C.G. to W.S.A. 1 Sept. 1942.

USNR,[13] and were serving at sea in merchantmen or on active duty in the Navy. The War Shipping Administration also maintained three training schools to qualify merchant seamen for officers' tickets. There were many applicants for the four months' course but it was difficult to get merchant seamen through it; less than two thirds of those who enrolled managed to graduate.[14]

2. *Naval Armed Guards* [15]

Although the Navy did not build the merchant ships it was responsible for protecting them; and although escort-of-convoy was by far the best protection, that sort could not always be furnished. Many merchantmen had to proceed alone through infested waters, and even on such heavily escorted routes as the North Russia run a vessel's own armament manned by a Naval Armed Guard was an exceedingly valuable defense.

As soon as the sinking of the *Robin Moor* made it clear that United States ships were not to be exempt from destruction, even when completely defenseless and sailing within the noncombat zones to which they had been limited by the Neutrality Acts, the arming of merchant vessels came up for discussion. Owing it seems to the curious notion that protective measures against aggression would further provoke the aggressors, this essential step for the defense of American rights on the high seas was delayed until 17 November 1941. On that date Congress repealed those clauses of the Neutrality Acts that outlawed armed merchantmen and authorized the President to provide the necessary guns and men.[16]

13 Information from Bulletin of W.S.A. Training Organization U. S. Merchant Marine Cadet Corps. There were also five state schools (U.S.S. *Nantucket* in Massachusetts; Maine, New York, Pennsylvania and California), that trained young men as Merchant Marine officers.

14 The total number of merchant seamen in training, 1 September 1942, was 1427; by 31 December 1943, 10,590 more arrived for training; total number of graduates was 6628; 2856 were disenrolled and 2533 were still in training at end of 1943. Maritime Commission Training Div. letter of 18 Dec. 1947 to writer.

15 Data for this section were obtained by Lt. (jg) J. Willard Hurst USNR from the files of Cdr. Edward C. Cleave USNR, who had charge of the Arming Merchant Vessels desk under the Vice Chief of Naval Operations. See also Appendix III.

16 Public Law 294, 77th Cong. 1st Sess., Chap. 473.

In simpler days of naval warfare it had been enough to authorize shipowners to arm vessels at their own expense, the guns to be served by merchant seamen. Under modern conditions it was up to the Navy to provide and install the guns, and train naval personnel to serve them. Passage of the Act of 17 November found the Navy Department ready with a plan which next day, on oral instructions from the President, it put into effect. The Navy had in fact already placed defensive installations on a few American-owned ships of Panama registry; the flag of the Republic of Panama serving in this respect, as in many others, as a convenient means of by-passing inconvenient laws of the United States.

At that time, and until February 1942, only enough materiel was available, and personnel could only be trained fast enough, to arm a maximum of one hundred vessels a month. Not only American vessels, but Norwegian, Danish, Dutch, Polish, Greek and other ships flying the flags of Germany's victims, were demanding American guns; and as the merchant seamen of these nations were serving the common cause bravely and effectively, the arming of their ships was a matter of extreme urgency. Consequently, on 24 January 1942, the Secretary of the Navy, with the approval of the Chairman of the Maritime Commission, authorized the arming of not over forty foreign flag ships per month. None except the Panamanians were at first provided with United States Naval Armed Guards. In April 1942 the Navy decided to furnish them to the large French and British passenger ships that were carrying United States troops.

The commander of a Naval Armed Guard was usually an ensign or junior grade lieutenant of the Reserve. These lads had an unusually difficult task. They had to train the men to become a well-knit gun crew and maintain naval discipline in the unbuttoned atmosphere of a merchant ship, without any superior officer to support them or C.P.O. to help them. They had to achieve a working relationship with the master and officers of the vessel, and at the same time prove a "good guy" to the merchant seamen in order to obtain their assistance in passing ammunition, or as substitutes for bluejackets in case of casualty. As every other branch of the Navy was crying for officers it was decided on 17 February 1942 to place petty officers in command of the smaller Armed Guard units of six men or under. This meant that about half the ships then arming had no commissioned naval officers aboard. Here, too, as in every other type of naval vessel or activity that the writer has sailed in or visited, the rapidly expanding naval program required frequent drafts of officers and men to other ships whose need seemed more urgent to the Bureau of Personnel. The Armed Guards became a happy hunting ground for the harassed Bureau when called upon to officer and man the new class of Destroyer Escorts in 1943.

Relations between the Navy and the merchant marine have always been somewhat delicate, and the presence of the Naval Armed Guards on merchant vessels created a new point of friction. The National Maritime Union, most powerful of the seamen's unions, had recently been struggling for better wages and conditions on board merchant ships. Joseph Curran, its president, nailed the slogan "Keep 'Em Sailing" to the masthead of his journal, the *Pilot*, prevented strikes by his men in wartime, did his best to get rid of "performers" (drunkards, troublemakers, etc.) and displayed the most ardent patriotism. This union also showed a good example to the Navy, which it did not follow, in abolishing the color line and encouraging Negroes in every way.[17] But it was unduly concerned lest the government or the shipowners put something over. At the outbreak of the war, Mr. Curran repeatedly demanded the protection of naval gunners; but when this was being granted as fast as possible, he began a campaign to have the gun crews composed of merchant seamen, with only a Naval ensign and gunner's mate over them.[18]

Actually the Navy did its best to persuade merchant seamen to learn how to handle guns. Before Pearl Harbor centers of gunnery instruction for them were set up at principal Atlantic ports; but very few could be induced to attend. Later, the Navy endeavored to provide gunnery instruction in various merchant marine training

[17] The *Pilot* 17 Sept. 1943 p. 8 states that 20 per cent of all American merchant seamen are Negroes.

[18] The *Pilot*, 6 Mar., 10 July, 27 Nov., 4 Dec. 1942; 19 Feb. 1943.

centers; but that ran into difficulties. In the summer of 1942, there were organized three mobile units of guns on trucks manned by bluejackets, in order to bring instruction right to the docks; yet few of the civilian crews cared to take time out between voyages to receive this training. It was a case of using bluejackets to man the guns or having no trained men to serve them.

At the beginning of the war, trouble or friction with merchant seamen on board was reported by about 30 per cent of the Naval Armed Guard officers. Naturally the presence on board ship of military personnel who were neither under union control nor interested in pay, bonuses and overtime [19] was galling to many of the seamen and their union officials. Relations gradually improved; by the fall of 1943 "incidents" had become rare; and the ships' crews very generally coöperated by passing ammunition or otherwise helping to serve the guns. Nor were the licensed personnel (the ships' officers) uniformly coöperative. In the merchant marine there is a sturdy independence which in time of war becomes a fault; certain masters and mates were resentful of gold braid, although given the right to wear a uniform almost indistinguishable from that of the Navy. Proper orders of an Armed Guard officer in the interest of security – matters such as blowing tubes and dumping garbage after dark – were sometimes ignored because they disturbed the master's routine, or disobeyed because he regarded them as unnecessary.

The trouble between naval seamen and merchant seamen had its root in totally different attitudes. Any ship in which a bluejacket serves is his ship, his country's ship, to be defended with his life if

[19] The Navy bluejackets' pay started at $50 per month; the merchant seaman's at $100 for a 44-hour week (85 cents for every hour over that), plus $100 war bonus in the Atlantic, plus various sums around $100 for each different combat area entered. On 15 Mar. 1943 this last bonus, greatly to the indignation of the National Maritime Union, was commuted to a flat rate of $125 per man for every air raid occurring when the ship was in port, whether or not the ship was hit. Although the merchant seaman was not paid when on the beach, continuous employment was guaranteed during the war. He did not, of course, receive the family allowances and retirement pay of the naval seaman. Some very erroneous figures of "average wages" of merchant seamen, based apparently on their loafing half the year, were given out. The *Pilot* on 17 Sept. 1943 began agitating for a 40-hour week and overtime for all work on Saturdays, Sundays and holidays.

need be. But to the union-indoctrinated merchant seaman the ship is the owner's ship, his class enemies' ship, to whom he owes nothing, and from which he is morally entitled to squeeze all he can. The Navy principle "Don't Give Up the Ship" did not appeal to merchant seamen.

Into this large and controversial subject, it is impossible to enter at length; but the writer, after giving it considerable study and doing his best by conversations and by reading the *Pilot* to understand the merchant marine point of view, wishes to express his emphatic opinion that if and when another war occurs, the merchant marine should either be absorbed by the Navy or made an auxiliary service under military discipline, like the Naval Construction Battalions, the famous Seabees. Certain high-ranking officers of the Navy recommended this about 1 February 1942, but it was not done.[20] The cost to the war effort involved in antagonizing a powerful group of unions had to be weighed against the immediate advantage of safe and efficient seafaring. It proved to be difficult to keep the expanding United States Merchant Marine manned, even with enormous wages and bonuses; and the War Shipping Administration's program of 1943 for training 75,000 new seamen was violently attacked by Mr. Curran as a scheme to flood the industry "with thousands of non-union-minded personnel." [21]

Many old union men responded nobly to the call for service, hardship and sacrifice in the Seabees under Naval discipline. Would not the same incentives have served to man merchant ships? It was, to be sure, easier to create a new body like the Seabees than to militarize one that was already under union leadership and inspiration. But the country at large, *and the merchant seamen in particular*,

[20] The *Pilot* 6 Feb. 1942. The same paper on 13 Feb. said that "Stork Club Admirals, Hearst and Fr. Coughlin" wanted the Navy to take over the merchant marine. It carried on a steady campaign of ridicule and abuse against Rear Admiral Emory S. Land, head of the National Maritime Commission.

[21] The *Pilot* 2 Apr. 1943 p. 2. Robert Carse in *Lifeline* p. 90 declares that "over 2000 old-timers" responded to a government call to return to the sea early in the war; but Mr. Curran stated in the *Pilot* 2 Apr. 1943 that 23,000 skilled seamen were ashore in New York State alone; and on 22 Feb. 1944, according to the *Pilot*, a broadcast appeal was issued to an estimated 42,000 merchant seamen who had gone on the beach during or just before hostilities began.

paid heavily in lives lost and ships sunk for the privilege of preserving union rules during a desperate naval war.

Owing to their low speed, lack of armor and few watertight bulkheads, merchant ships are highly vulnerable to attack from the air. Hence an effort was made to increase their anti-aircraft armament, especially on ships on the North Russia, Mediterranean, Indian Ocean and Persian Gulf runs. This meant equipment with relatively large and complicated guns, such as 3-inch 50-caliber anti-aircraft, 5-inch 38-caliber dual-purpose, and 5-inch 51-caliber single-purpose, in addition to the standard 20-mm machine guns; and that meant more and better-trained men. One 5-inch 38 alone required a petty officer, a gunner's mate and four enlisted men, besides five of the merchant crew to help as loaders and ammunition passers. But the supply of guns and ammunition available for merchant vessels was woefully inadequate in 1942. Priority had to be given to vessels sailing in the most dangerous areas. The first installations of the dual-purpose 5-inch began about September 1942, on new ships of over 10,000 deadweight tons. As late as 19 August 1942 the shortage of all broadside guns was still so acute that the Vice Chief of Naval Operations had to issue the following directive: –

> The question has arisen as to the Navy Department's policy relative to ships sailing unarmed. Ships sailing independently should be armed. Ships sailing in regularly made-up convoys, *other than ships bound to North Russia or tankers en route to the United Kingdom*, may sail unarmed if the urgency of delivery of their cargo warrants it.

He recommended that anti-aircraft guns be removed from ships then in port and transferred to outbound ships, immediately.

Besides the allocation and mounting of guns, the Navy had to provide merchant ships with ammunition, stowage space, splinter protection for bridge and radio shack; it had to make necessary installations for darkening ship, to install sky lookout stations, and facilities for berthing and messing the Armed Guard.

Even with the fullest extension that the convoy system reached in the Atlantic in May 1943, 17½ per cent of all United Nations' merchant ships at sea in the United States Strategic Area, including all those capable of a speed of 14½ knots or better, were sailing independently without escort.[22] These ships depended exclusively on their own guns and Naval Armed Guards to defend them against enemy surface raiders, submarines, and aircraft. Heavy responsibility for the protection of American lives, cargoes and military supplies on the high seas fell on these Armed Guards. The story of their exploits could easily fill a large volume; in this History we shall have to be content with but a small selection of them, on the most dangerous routes.

[22] The average number of unescorted M/Vs daily at sea in the Atlantic areas in May was only 133.1; average number of convoyed M/Vs, 631.8. The areas in which there were more unescorted than escorted M/Vs were the Gulf of Mexico, Panama Sea Frontier (Caribbean side), the mid-ocean areas south of lat. 25° N, and east of the West Indies.

CHAPTER XIII

Examples, Errors and Lessons

January–June 1942

SO FAR AS the public knew, the answer to submarine warfare was more convoys and more escort ships to protect them; but the Navy was equally concerned with its failure to get at the heart of the business by killing U-boats. Our score of six enemy submarines sunk in the Atlantic in the first half of 1942 was not creditable. Naval officers who were in touch with the problem knew that the sudden drop of sinkings in the Eastern Sea Frontier from twenty-three in April to five in May and three in August, following the coastal convoy set-up, meant little more than driving the submarines from one area to another. As one officer remarked in the summer of 1942, "We are just like a housewife flapping her apron to chase the chickens out of the kitchen." We had scared them off the transatlantic routes and the coastal shipping, but every month they were growing more numerous, more hungry, and more expert.

The ineffectiveness of the Navy's efforts to kill submarines in 1942 may be attributed to faulty technique and lack of experience. As a British admiral remarked, you can't learn how to shoot birds in a shootin' school – you have to get out where birds are flyin'. Lack of persistence, abandoning a search within an hour or so after making a sound contact or unsuccessful depth-charge attack, was perhaps the most frequent fault. In part, this was due to lack of definite doctrine. Most officers working on the problem ashore believed that, once contact was made in convoy, one or more escorts should be detached to hunt the submarine for hours on end. Many officers at sea agreed that this should be done, if there were enough escorts left to protect the convoy. A good early example of persistence was that of U.S.S. *Niblack*. On 25 March 1942, escorting Convoy

ON–77, she regained contact by dint of searching one hour and three quarters after dark, and thus foiled the U-boat's efforts to attack or summon the wolf-pack of which it was the reconnaissance unit. *Niblack* did not get the submarine, but the convoy was not again molested.

Examples to the contrary were only too numerous. Most errors were committed by PCs or small patrol craft, whose personnel was green and excitable; but many too were made by experienced destroyers. U.S.S. *Rodman*, proceeding alone to join a convoy 19 June 1942, made two depth-charge attacks on a submarine, but discontinued search "in order to rendezvous with convoy and to preserve sufficient depth charges to carry out mission." She might have protected the convoy better by continuing to search, and the expenditure of every "ashcan" in her locker would have been justified if it had resulted in killing or even damaging the U-boat. A submarine would have no difficulty in regaining contact of a slow convoy the same day, if kept down for only an hour or two.

It was not that the officers of these destroyers were cautious; they simply did not know what to do, and authorities ashore had come to no agreement. The Anti-Submarine Warfare Unit of the Atlantic Fleet argued repeatedly that the best defense was offense, here as in other aspects of warfare; and that the risk involved in diminishing the convoy's protection by detaching an escort for the hunt was well worth the chance of killing the enemy, or even of keeping him down long enough so that he would not be a nuisance again on that voyage. But while Boston was intoning variations on Danton's *toujours de l'audace*, Argentia, nearer the scene of action, preached caution. Admiral Brainard warned escort commanders against exposing a slenderly escorted convoy by detaching ships for a possible kill. This warning was as much needed as the pep-talks. For, about mid-1942, wolf-packs began the practice of employing one or two U-boats as decoys, which retired at full speed in order to draw off escort units. so that the main pack would find less resistance when it was ready to attack.

Until more escorts could be provided no hard-and-fast attack doctrine could be laid down; a large measure of independent judgment always had to be given the escort commander. Nor must it be supposed that this difference of opinion was one between armchair strategists and practical seamen; for the Anti-Submarine Warfare Unit was composed of experienced submarine, aviation and destroyer officers.

The history of Convoy ONS–102 in June 1942 showed that sufficient escorts and aggressive patrolling in itself could not protect a slow convoy, if search and attack technique were faulty. There were 63 ships in eleven columns, protected by nine escorts – U.S.S. *Leary*, three big Coast Guard cutters (*Campbell*, *Ingham*, and *Duane*), one Canadian destroyer, and four Canadian corvettes. Commander P. R. Heineman was escort commander in *Campbell*. Speed of advance was 8 knots. At 0725 on 16 June, two contacts were made on high-frequency direction-finders, and one destroyer with one corvette was detached to run them down. At 0836 destroyer *Restigouche* sighted a U-boat on the horizon twenty miles from the convoy. Half an hour later, when the distance had closed to seven miles, the U-boat dove. *Restigouche* made an unsuccessful depth-charge attack. *Campbell* now joined the hunt, formed a scouting line with the two Canadians, and at 1300 sighted the U-boat on the surface about thirteen miles from its previous position, and 43 miles from the convoy. Her depth-charge attack was unsuccessful. *Ingham* in the meantime, while still searching on the early morning direction-finder bearing at 1330, flushed another U-boat on the surface and opened fire unsuccessfully at 13,000 yards. Thus, four escorts out of nine were employed in persistent pursuit of definite contacts. The convoy was left at peace that night, but not the next.

On the following day (17 June) extensive sweeping was employed. H.M.C.S. *Collingwood* and *Rosthern* patrolled all day 15 to 18 miles out on each flank of the convoy, H.M.C.S. *Mayflower* swept 15 miles astern of it in the late afternoon and U.S.S. *Leary* steamed 20 miles ahead at 1642 to investigate a direction-finder bearing. No firm contact was made. That night, although the convoy's van was covered by three escorts, two U-boats managed to make their way between the columns. Half an hour after midnight the first was sighted by a ship in the third column. She passed the word to H.M.C.S. *Agassiz*, which swept both flanks of the column, but made no sound contact owing to interference by the vessels' wakes. At 0125 June 18 the second ship in the eleventh column was torpedoed, and subsequently sank. A few minutes later *Campbell*, patrolling 5300 yards ahead, sighted a submarine headed for the convoy and distant 500 yards. This U-boat submerged and was depth-charged, unsuccessfully. Twenty-four hours later several torpedo wakes were sighted, the swirl of a diving submarine was seen, and several fruitless depth-charge attacks were delivered.

Admiral Brainard at Argentia, realizing the dangers surrounding Convoy ONS–102 as well as ON–103 which was steaming a day or two astern, organized a striking force of four Canadian corvettes to sweep at a considerable distance around the first. This striking force, as well as the western local escort group that was shortly to relieve the ocean escort, was in the vicinity of the convoy during the foggy night of 20–21 June. The local escort was trying to contact the convoy by voice radio; the ocean escorts were patrolling only 4000 yards out. One of them, H.M.C.S. *Agassiz*, sighted a U-boat about a mile ahead at 2242. It dove, and *Agassiz* attacked with depth charges, one of which made such a terrific explosion that several merchantmen thought themselves torpedoed, and fired star-shell rockets; one even secured engines in preparation for abandoning ship. The resulting illumination revealed a submarine right in the midst of the first column. The nearest merchant ship attacked it with machine-gun fire, and it submerged. Several escorts dashed about the now brightly illuminated convoy throwing depth charges to no purpose. The radar, with which every escort but one was equipped, broke down.

Convoy ONS–102 was lucky to get through with the loss of but one ship.[1] And all the attacking submarines escaped. The tactical

[1] Report by Cdr. P. R. Heineman 24 Aug. 1942, with comment by A/S W Unit, Boston. One merchant ship was torpedoed and sunk, one straggled in fog but got into port, one straggled and had not been heard from when the report was written.

errors which prevented these and other less aggressive escorts from making a kill may be summarized as follows. (1) A tendency to drop depth charges too early in the attack, corresponding to the common failure of anti-aircraft guns to give sufficient "lead." Although mostly due to overeagerness, several cases were explained by failure to correct relative speed on a last-minute turn by the target or the attacker, or an acceleration of speed by the attacker. (2) Sound operators sometimes failed to "sweep" the target or to inform the conning officer from which edge of it they were reading the bearing. (3) There was a tendency to economize on depth charges and not throw a large enough pattern. (4) Attackers were often baffled by a standard submarine escape-tactic of getting inside the turning circle of the attacker in such manner as to force her sound operator to take ranges on its wake rather than its hull, or on "knuckles" in the water caused by the sudden turn-up of the U-boat's propellers. (5) Although a ship has only one chance out of fifteen to catch a submarine after it has dived, the mathematically determined search course which would give her that one chance in fifteen of regaining contact was not always followed. (6) The old jinx of communications continued to hamper anti-submarine warfare even more than other branches of warfare, because of the imperative need for promptness. There was continued improvement in ship-to-ship and ship-to-shore communications; but as aircraft took an increasing share in anti-submarine warfare, infinite trouble developed in plane-to-ship communications.

Yet, over and above all these difficulties, the want of a definite anti-submarine doctrine for escort vessels was the greatest fault, which explains more than any other factor this lack of success in killing U-boats. This does not mean that the ships should (or could) have been told exactly *what* to do on every contact. That had to be left to the judgment of the skipper or the escort commander. But they wanted definite doctrine *how* to hunt a submerged U-boat in order to make best use of sound gear and the weapons available. Destroyer officers were given different attack instructions in each of the four destroyer training centers of the Atlantic Fleet; there were the Key West system, the Miami system, the Staten Island system and the Boston system. Many smaller escorts had no instruction whatever.

A good beginning was made by the issuance on 9 July 1942 of a Cominch information bulletin on anti-submarine warfare, the result of an intensive study by officers of the Anti-Submarine Warfare Unit and their attached scientists, extending over the six months of our participation in the war, and covering British experience as well. In clear, precise language it described the German submarine and its capabilities, and laid down rules and methods for escort-of-convoy and patrol operations, sound, sight and radar searching; surface, air and coördinated attacks. This manual became standard doctrine for all Navy ships, planes, shore installations and schools. It was of course superseded as more data were obtained and as new procedures and devices were developed.

Looking backward, this uniform doctrine, and the training and analysis systems set up, together with plain hard experience, seem to be the most important contributions during that woeful year 1942 toward controlling the U-boat menace. Convoys, patrols and the like, were only defensive; they decreased sinkings, but did not get at the root of the problem. Ship construction, both of merchant vessels and escorts, merely kept us ahead in the score; how little ahead was proved by the U-boat blitzes of 1943. Improved radar and sound gear were a definite help. But in the last analysis, the problem was human. All these devices and methods and gadgets would have been so much junk without proper knowledge of how to use them; and that is what doctrine, training and experience accomplished.

This period of anti-submarine warfare may well be closed with an exchange of memoranda on the subject between General Marshall and Admiral King. The General wrote on 19 June 1942:

> The losses by submarines off our Atlantic seaboard and in the Caribbean now threaten our entire war effort. The following statistics bearing on the subject have been brought to my attention.
>
> Of the 74 ships allocated to the Army for July by the War Shipping Administration, 17 have already been sunk. Twenty-two per cent of the Bauxite fleet has already been destroyed. Twenty per cent of the

Puerto Rican fleet has been lost. Tanker sinkings have been 3.5 per cent per month of tonnage in use.

We are all aware of the limited number of escort craft available, but has every conceivable improvised means been brought to bear on this situation? I am fearful that another month or two of this will so cripple our means of transport that we will be unable to bring sufficient men and planes to bear against the enemy in critical theatres to exercise a determining influence on the war.

To which Admiral King replied on 21 June:

1. I have long been aware, of course, of the implications of the submarine situation as pointed out in your memorandum of 19 June. I have employed – and will continue to employ – not only regular forces but also such improvised means as give any promise of usefulness. However, it is obvious that the German effort is expanding more rapidly than our defense, and if we are to avoid disaster not only the Navy itself but also all other agencies concerned must continue to intensify the anti-submarine effort.

2. As you are aware, we had very little in the way of anti-submarine forces in the Atlantic at the outbreak of the war except the fleet destroyers which were committed to troop escort duty and other services that made them unavailable for the protection of shipping in general. We had to improvise rapidly and on a large scale. We took over all pleasure craft that could be used and sent them out with makeshift armament and untrained crews. We employed for patrol purposes aircraft that could not carry bombs, and planes flown from school fields by student pilots. We armed our merchant ships as rapidly as possible. We employed fishing boats as volunteer lookouts. The Army helped in the campaign of extemporization by taking on the civil aviation patrol. These measures were worth something, but the heavy losses that occurred up to the middle of May on our east coast give abundant proof, if proof were needed, that they were not an answer to our problem.

3. Concurrently with these extemporized operations we were building up our regular and reserve forces. Shortly after the war started our anti-submarine building program began to produce a trickle of submarine chasers. We also obtained some suitable vessels by borrowing from the British and also – I regret to say – by robbing the ocean escort groups. With these increments we were able to establish on 15 May a coastwise escort system between Key West and northern ports. At about the same time your valuable contribution to the cause – the First Bomber Command – became effective. Since 15 May our east coast

waters have enjoyed a high degree of security. It should not be assumed, however, that this state of security will continue. We made it pretty hot for the Germans and they spread out to areas where the going was easier, but our east coast convoy system is still far from invulnerable and we may expect the Germans to return to this area whenever they feel inclined to accept a not-too-heavy risk.

4. Though we are still suffering heavy losses outside the east coast convoy zone the situation is not hopeless. We know that a reasonable degree of security can be obtained by suitable escort and air coverage. The submarines can be stopped only by wiping out the German building yards and bases – a matter which I have been pressing with the British, so far with only moderate success. But if all shipping can be brought under escort and air cover our losses will be reduced to an acceptable figure. I might say in this connection that escort is not just *one* way of handling the submarine menace; it is the *only* way that gives any promise of success. The so-called patrol and hunting operations have time and again proved futile. We have adopted the "Killer" system whereby contact with a submarine is followed up continuously and relentlessly – this requires suitable vessels and planes which we do not have in sufficient numbers. Large numbers of small local patrol craft are required to prevent mining of harbor entrances, to keep lookout and to reinforce escorts at focal points, but no system of patrol will give security to unescorted vessels. We must get every ship that sails the seas under constant close protection.

5. It is not easy to create an adequate and comprehensive escort system. Our coastal sea lanes, in which I include the Caribbean and Panama routes, total 7,000 miles in length. To this must be added the ocean convoy system to Great Britain and Iceland (which is already in effect) and extensions which should be made to protect traffic to the east coast of South America (and perhaps to the Cape of Good Hope), not to mention our Pacific Ocean commitments. An enormous number of seagoing vessels is required, as well as very large air forces. Aviation for ocean coverage must be taken along in auxiliary carriers. For convoys moving close to land the air should operate from shore bases. While observation planes can be used for certain limited missions, the bulk of the shore-based aviation should be of the patrol or medium bomber type. Land type planes are essential in freezing weather because sea planes ice up on the water. All planes must have radar. All must have crews specially trained in the technique of anti-submarine operations and must be able to operate at night as well as by day.

CHAPTER XIV

Ten Months' Incessant Battle

July 1942–April 1943

1. *Trends*

AFTER describing in some detail the measures adopted, methods devised, and organization created to combat the submarine menace, we may now return to the progress of this important aspect of the war during the ten months that followed the middle of 1942.

June of 1942 was no turning point in anti-submarine warfare. It simply marks the beginning of a period when the trees so laboriously cultivated in the spring of the year began to flower; more time elapsed before they bore fruit. Escort vessels of the Navy and Coast Guard, patrol planes of the Navy and Army, killed an occasional U-boat, though as yet not enough to counteract the increasing production of enemy submarines. The widening scope of convoys left no "soft spots" in the North Atlantic, so Admiral Doenitz sent his U-boats to the Caribbean and the South Atlantic. The occupation of North Africa, our first overseas operation in the Atlantic, required a large number of troop convoys in the last three months of 1942 and drew off so many destroyers that the protection of northern transatlantic merchant convoys was almost completely turned over to the Royal Navies. Admiral Doenitz intensified his efforts to break up this transatlantic lifeline by echelons of wolf-packs, but with diminishing success. By the end of the year merchant ship sinkings had considerably decreased while those of U-boats had more than tripled – 64 in the second half of 1942 as against 21 in the first half.[1]

[1] United States forces, however, killed only 11 U-boats in the second half as compared with 6 in the first half.

In January 1943, for the first time since we entered the war, merchant vessel sinkings in all Atlantic areas fell below one a day, and below 200,000 tons a month. Then came a sharp upturn of U-boat activity, concentrated in the North Atlantic convoy routes and the Mediterranean, with a corresponding rise in sinkings to over three a day and over 500,000 tons in the month of March. That blitz brought about a new organization of anti-submarine warfare by the United States; the first of May, 1943, logically concludes this phase of the Battle of the Atlantic.

In connection with the charts of sinkings and attacks, Table 4 in Appendix I[2] shows the trends clearly enough. In July 1942 the enemy sheered off because, as Admiral Assmann confided to his diary, "Defense measures on the American coast have improved." There were only three sinkings in that area in July, and none for the rest of the year; only two unsuccessful attacks. In July the most lethal area for merchant shipping was the Iceland–North Russia convoy route; the figures on sinkings by submarines tell only part of the story as most of the losses there were due to air attack. In August the enemy intensified his attacks in the Caribbean and the transatlantic convoy route, as the increased number of U-boats permitted; he concentrated on the mid-Atlantic as the area where convoys had no air coverage. "Superior radar equipment of English aircraft has caused U-boat losses," said Assmann; "air attacks in the Bay of Biscay are serious."[3] The acoustic torpedo was being perfected, anti-aircraft armament of U-boats strengthened, and by the fall of 1942 Admiral Doenitz was operating large supply submarines in the vicinity of the Azores. These "milch cows," as our Navy called the 1600-tonners, delivered fuel, provisions, fresh water and torpedoes. Supply submarines practically doubled the effectiveness

[2] Compiled by the Intelligence Group of the Office of Chief of Naval Operations under Captain A. V. S. Pickhardt.

[3] Diary for 26 Aug. 1942. U-boat losses to aircraft at that period were not, however, notably great – 19 U-boats and 6 Italian submarines sunk between 1 July and 22 Aug. 1942; three of these were sunk by British aircraft, five by United States aircraft, one by a Czechoslovak plane, and the rest by British and Canadian ships. It is possible however that a number of the boats sunk by ships had been reported by radar-equipped planes.

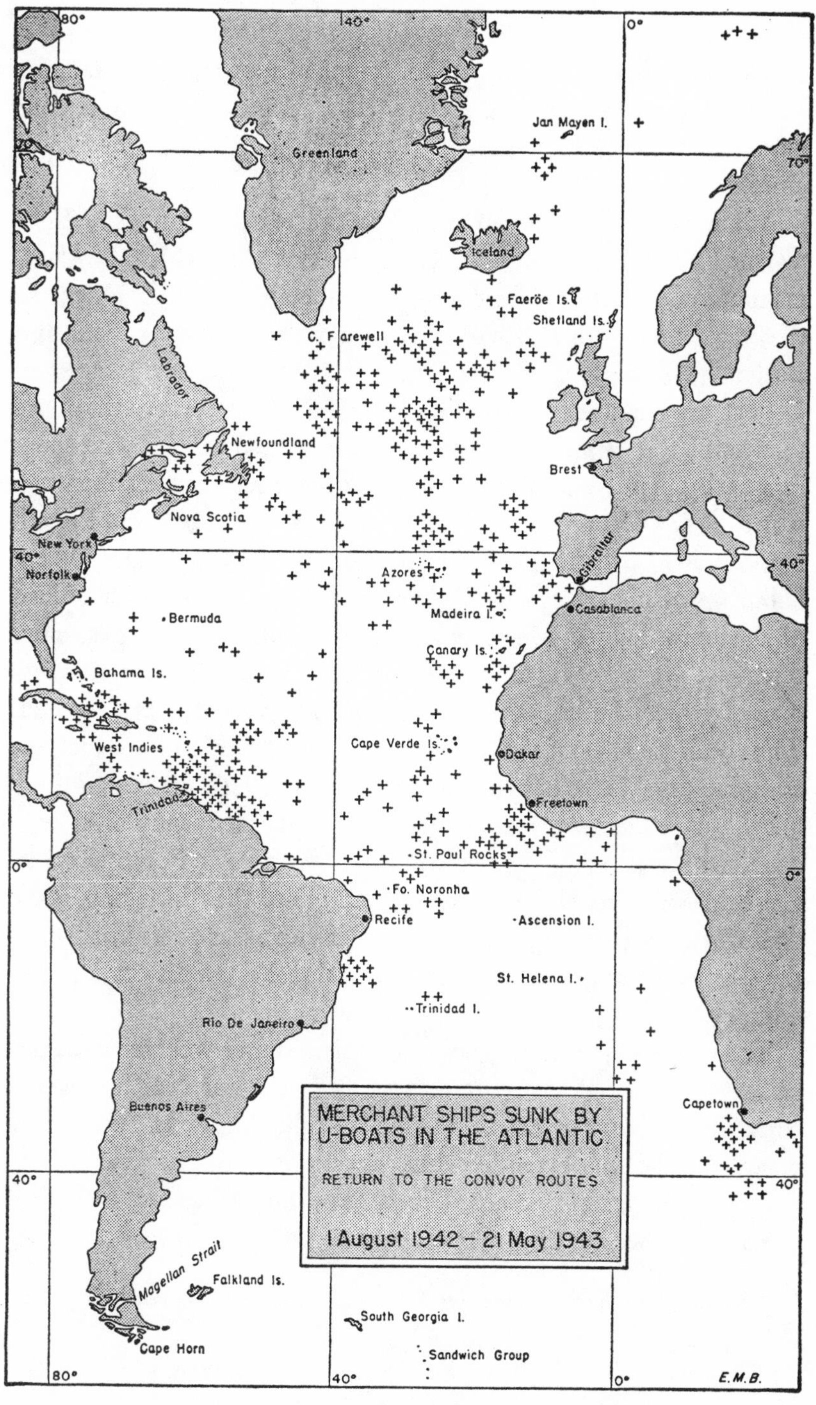
MERCHANT SHIPS SUNK BY U-BOATS IN THE ATLANTIC
RETURN TO THE CONVOY ROUTES
1 August 1942 – 21 May 1943
Greenland
Jan Mayen I.
Iceland
Faeröe Is.
Shetland Is.
C. Farewell
Labrador
Newfoundland
Nova Scotia
New York
Norfolk
Brest
Gibraltar
Azores
Madeira I.
Casablanca
Bermuda
Canary Is.
Bahama Is.
West Indies
Cape Verde Is.
Dakar
Freetown
Trinidad
St. Paul Rocks
Fo. Noronha
Recife
Ascension I.
St. Helena I.
Trinidad I.
Rio De Janeiro
Capetown
Buenos Aires
Magellan Strait
Falkland Is.
South Georgia I.
Cape Horn
Sandwich Group
80°
40°
0°
70°
E.M.B.

of the 500-tonners, enabling them to spend months in the combat area where before they had spent weeks;[4] war cruises of over four months by 500-tonners are on record, although that length was unusual.

Admiral Doenitz enjoyed almost complete autonomy. The Submarine Fleet was practically a separate Navy, over which the Commander in Chief of the German Navy had no jurisdiction.[5] Doenitz's command post until February 1943 was shifted between Paris and Lorient. He made a practice of personally greeting successful U-boat commanders when they returned from cruises; the more successful, the "aces," were invited to dinner and treated with great familiarity. And he took very good care of his men in port. Between war cruises a U-boat laid up for 28 days at one of the five French bases, Brest, Lorient, St.-Nazaire, La Pallice, and Bordeaux, where bomb-proof concrete-roofed pens protected the boats. One third of the crew lodged ashore, where hotels, brothels and a country resthouse were provided, while one third went on leave to Germany by special train, and one third worked at repairs and upkeep. Thus each member of the crew had nine days' work, nine days' rest and nine days' leave between cruises. Air bombing attacks on these bases, which were carried out with increasing frequency after July 1942, with the aid of the United States Army Air Force based in England, failed to do any essential damage to the U-boats or their operations; and although the town of Lorient was pretty badly hit the Germans simply moved their recreational activities out into the country.

The most sinister development of this summer was yet to come. In August the U-boats resumed working over our North Atlantic convoys with a new technique that brought results. In September, when the U-boats extended their operations into the Gulf of St. Lawrence, losses in this area became even more serious, averaging one a day. The Trinidad area showed no improvement; there was a

[4] The A/S W Operations Research Group reported that the average length of cruise of over forty 500- and 740-tonners, whose logs were known, was 4½ weeks if no fueling occurred and 9 weeks if fueled.

[5] Gladisch and Assmann, V. 8.

blitz in the Windward Passage and approaches that took about ten ships out of our coastal convoys. There were 15 sinkings off the Gulf of Guinea.[6] The total sinkings in all Atlantic areas, however, were 18 per cent less numerous than in August. In October total Atlantic sinkings were about the same (88 ships, 585,510 tons) as in September, but in the North Atlantic convoy route they reached a new high level of almost one a day which was maintained through November. The Cape of Good Hope was second most dangerous area in October and November, with the Caribbean third, and the Trinidad area showed little improvement.[7] November was the worst month of the war in the Atlantic for sinkings by U-boats, and the last month when the number sunk surpassed one hundred. The transatlantic convoy areas were still very bad; and another group of U-boats worked the Atlantic Narrows between Africa and South America, sinking nine merchant vessels in the vicinity of the St. Paul Rocks alone. In these waters off the bulge of Brazil sinkings went up during December, but in all other areas they declined.

Down to the first anniversary of Pearl Harbor, in December 1942, the United States Navy took part in escorting 9481 merchant ships in 250 different transatlantic convoys, with a total loss of 132 ships — 1.4 per cent.[8]

January 1943, the safest month in two years for North Atlantic traffic, brought few losses, except four ships to a convoy off Paramaribo, and seven to an African convoy about halfway between the Azores and the Cape Verde Islands. There were, in addition, a dozen sinkings in the Mediterranean, mostly by enemy aircraft. But February was the worst month ever for the North Atlantic convoy route, and March worse still; losses averaged four ships every three days.

[6] Sinking Chart, Intelligence Group of Opnav. These were split between Freetown and SE Atlantic Areas, and so do not show in Table 4, Appendix I.

[7] As the area within 200 miles of Trinidad crosses the Caribbean West and Caribbean East areas, it does not register well in the tables; but most of the 25 sinkings in November in the two Caribbean areas were within 300 miles of Trinidad.

[8] "The Inauguration and Carrying Out of Convoy Operations and its Effect," document prepared by Lt. Cdr. Charles Ames of Cominch C & R December 1942. Later cumulative figures by Cdr. Ames.

The end of January marks an important change in German naval policy and command. By the new year Hitler had become exasperated with the upkeep cost and ineffectiveness of his capital ships, most of them hiding in Norwegian fjords to escape the R.A.F. In one of his tirades he told Admiral Raeder that the main batteries should be removed from battleships and cruisers to be mounted on land for coastal defense. And on 30 January 1943 he promoted Doenitz to the topmost rank of Grand Admiral and made him Commander in Chief, Navy, in place of Raeder.[9]

This had the immediate effect of concentrating all German warship construction on submarines and putting Doenitz one step nearer the dictator's throne that he finally ascended after Hitler's death. He promptly moved his command post to Berlin in order to be near his Fuehrer.

In his first conference with Hitler as Commander in Chief, Doenitz spoke depressingly of the "surprising progress in the enemy's use of radar location, the failure of the Luftwaffe to help the submarines by air reconnaissance, which forced the U-boats to hunt their own prey and consigned many of them to fruitless cruises." Owing to Hitler's disregard of operational scientists, the Germans never produced a jamming device suitable for U-boats until very late in the war; and, unless on the North Russia run, Goering never gave Doenitz what he wanted in the way of air reconnaissance. He managed to invoke Hitler's authority to stop the drafting of submarine builders into the Army, but failed to solve the problem of finding trained personnel for the greatly increased U-boat fleet. By stopping work on the bigger ships and laying up some of the completed ones in ordinary, Doenitz acquired about 250 officers, 8000 men and 1300 shipyard workers; but that was not enough.[10]

Admirals Gladisch and Assmann, in their postwar report, observe bitterly that Doenitz succeeded in weeding out of the German Navy almost every flag officer senior to himself. They declare that

[9] Raeder became Inspector General of the Navy, a purely face-saving post.
[10] Assmann Diary Jan. and Feb. 1943.

his "unshakable belief in the U-boat men" showed "lack of objectivity," and remark with a certain *Schadenfreude* that his appointment to the top naval command came too late to do any good – the initiative had passed to the opponent.[11] But neither they nor anyone else has shown how Doenitz could have done better with the means he had. Germany, as Hanson Baldwin has said, was compelled "to wage an unlimited war with limited means." By 1943, it is now clear, Germany was fighting a war that she could never win unless by a breach among her enemies. Yet by the notions of the Nazi state it had to go on to the bitter end.

Nevertheless, Doenitz smelled forthcoming victory during the first two months of his new command. Looking backward after the war was lost, he considered the months January through March 1943 the peak of submarine achievement. "The number of U-boats was constantly increasing, losses were slight," the radius of all boats was extended by the "milch cows," and even a few tankers got through to the South Atlantic and Indian Ocean to fuel, service and supply with new torpedoes the submarines on extended patrols. The U-boat pens in the French outposts had been made virtually impregnable to bombing attacks, the German bureau of ordnance was about to launch the acoustic torpedo, the *Schnorchel* breathing device would soon (he then hoped) be ready to install on all submarines, and production of the new electric-drive Type XXI with a speed submerged of 17 to 18 knots was hoped for before the end of 1943 – actually it never got to sea until 1945. The only factors that then worried Doenitz were the increasing effectiveness of Allied aircraft in anti-submarine warfare, especially in their radar.[12]

2. *Transatlantic Convoys*

a. Daylight Attacks

The long immunity from attack that these convoys enjoyed (only one ship, a straggler, sunk in July) was rudely broken in

[11] Gladisch and Assmann p. 206.
[12] Doenitz Essay, Secs. 100–102, 119–121.

early August 1942 with an invigorated form of submarine warfare. Echelons of wolf-packs, preceded by U-boats whose sole duty was reconnaissance, attacked in daylight as well as by night. No doubt these tactics had long been planned by Admiral Doenitz. Now for the first time, owing to a marked increase in U-boat production, and Allied failure to make kills, he had the wherewithal. He concentrated on the transatlantic route, because the central part of it was the only area where plenty of targets could be found without air coverage.[13] By mid-1942 the Eastern Sea Frontier as well as the Western Approaches, the Straits and the Newfoundland–Iceland area were so well covered by aircraft that it had become difficult for a U-boat to escape detection, although it still remained fairly easy to evade destruction. But as yet no such air coverage was possible in mid-Atlantic. The Allied Navies could not spare large carriers for anything but troop convoys. Escort carriers as yet were only building, and neither Great Britain nor the United States had sufficient very-long-range planes to operate effectively from Newfoundland and Iceland.

The transatlantic convoy system in effect during the second half of 1942 differed very little from that already described. But, about 1 June, the Royal and Canadian Navies supplied the majority of vessels for escort duty in order to free United States destroyers for the troop convoys that were building up forces in the United Kingdom for the invasion of Europe and North Africa, and for coastal convoys and the Pacific war. "Fast" 9-knot HX convoys sailed from Halifax for Londonderry every seven days, followed three or four days later by a 6½-knot SC convoy, which sailed from Sydney except from December through April when that harbor was apt to be frozen. The reverse of the HX and SC were still designated ON and ONS respectively. Both convoys were fed at the American end by Boston–Halifax convoys, designated BX and XB, which received ships from the various coastal routes and formed up in Cape Cod Bay or Boston Harbor.

[13] Assmann Diary, 28 Sept. 1942.

For escort purposes, the North Atlantic was divided into three areas, with escort groups designated as follows: –[14]

1. *Western Local Area,* between Cape Cod and longitude 52° W. Eight escort units assigned, formed from British and Canadian destroyers, and Canadian corvettes or converted trawlers under Canadian command, based on Boston. These escorted eastbound convoys as far as Western ocean meeting point ("Westomp") on or about long. 52° W,[15] where they were relieved by escorts of the Mid-ocean group, and picked up a westbound convoy, which they conducted to Halifax. Thence they served as escorts of Boston-bound convoys. Air coverage for this area was furnished by (*a*) U. S. Army, Navy and Civil Air Patrol planes based on New England airfields, and by R.C.A.F. planes based on Yarmouth, Halifax and Sydney, (*b*) United States Navy planes based on Argentia. These took care of convoys up to lat. 48° N and long. 55° W.

2. *Mid-ocean Area,* between longitudes 52° and 22° W. Fourteen escort units (later reduced to eleven) were assigned, based on Argentia and St. Johns, Newfoundland, where they were under the supervision and command of Vice Admiral R. M. Brainard. Three of these fourteen units, under United States naval command, were formed from United States destroyers and Royal or Canadian Navy corvettes. Seven units under British command consisted of Royal Navy destroyers and Canadian destroyers and corvettes, two Polish destroyers named *Blyskawica* and *Burza,* and a few Fighting French corvettes.[16] Mid-ocean escort groups picked up eastbound convoys at "Westomp" and convoyed them to an East Ocean Meeting Point

[14] "Operations of Convoys, U.S.N.," document issued by Rear Admiral M. K. Metcalf, Director of Convoy and Routing Division of Cominch; CTF 4 (Vice Admiral Brainard) Memo. for Admiral Stark (Comnaveu) 21 May 1942, quoted in "Administrative History of the Atlantic Fleet" II 141–42.

[15] Changed from 45° W about 1 June to about 52° W for westbound and 50° W for eastbound convoys. Brainard Memo.

[16] The R.N. and R.C.N. units were under Commander in Chief Western Approaches to the United Kingdom (Cincwa) and Flag Officer St. Johns, Newfoundland (Fonf) respectively.

("Eastomp") near long. 22° W. There they were reinforced or relieved by escorts of Group 3, and proceeded to Londonderry to refuel. Returning, they picked up convoys at "Eastomp," escorted them to "Westomp," and proceeded to Argentia.

Air coverage was furnished by (*a*) United States Navy planes based on Argentia, (*b*) R.C.A.F. planes based at Torbay and Gander Lake, Newfoundland, which covered the area north of lat. 48° N and to the limit of their endurance east of Newfoundland; and (*c*) United States Navy planes based on Iceland.

3. *Eastern Local Area,* between long. 22° W and the British Isles. The escort units for this area, all British, were responsible for both east and westbound convoys, although they might be reinforced by Mid-ocean units going to or returning from Londonderry. Air coverage was by R.A.F. out of Irish and Scottish fields.

4. *Iceland Shuttle,* escorts for shipping to and from Iceland. One or more units of United States destroyers, based on Hvalfjordur, were assigned to escort ships from SC and ON convoys to and from a designated Mid-ocean meeting point. Air coverage was furnished by the Navy squadrons based on Iceland.

While the United States Navy continued to exercise a general strategic control over the western half of the Atlantic,[17] the Admiralty had complete control over the eastern half. Operational control of convoys shifted from Cominch to the Admiralty at "Chop" (Change of Operational Control), the predicted date when the convoy would cross that line of demarcation.

Towards the end of 1942 the air coverage over transatlantic convoys was gradually extended until the Allied air forces were able to cover an area extending 400 miles east of Newfoundland, 500 miles south of Iceland, and 700 miles west of the British Isles. This left a large mid-ocean area north of the Azores without air protection. The Navy hoped to receive permission to establish bases in the

[17] Starting at lat. 65° N, long. 10° W, the line went southwesterly to lat. 57° N, long. 26° W, then along long. 26° W, to lat. 43° N; westward along that parallel to long. 40° W, then south along that meridian to lat. 20° N, then east to long. 26° W, thence south along that meridian.

Azores to provide air coverage for this dangerous pocket of water in which submarines could cruise unmolested, and in which the enemy's big "milch cows" were believed to be operating. Negotiations looking to this desirable end were being slowly conducted by the British government with that of Portugal. Eventually very-long-range planes and escort carriers were available to the Allies to reduce this black spot, but in the period covered by this chapter, complete air cover for transatlantic convoys was not possible, even under the most favorable weather conditions.

The convoy system just described was an improvement over the one in vogue during the winter of 1941–1942, doing away with escorts hanging about "Momp" for late convoys to join. Moreover, improved fueling of escorts at sea had solved the problem of "short-legged" destroyers or corvettes. But the system was not good enough to cope with the German offensive which began in August 1942.

Convoy ON–115, crossing in July and August, was the first merchant convoy on this route to be attacked in months.[18] This westbound convoy of 41 ships under Canadian escort (H.M.C.S. *Saguenay*, flagship) was sighted and reported by submarine *U–210* when about halfway across. Screening vessels attacked on sound contact without result. *U–210*, on reporting to Admiral Doenitz, was instructed to shadow the convoy but not to attack until other U-boats had joined her. By 31 July, four submarines were dogging this slow convoy, and four or five more were being coached in to assist in the expected big kill, which never came off, owing to aggressive tactics by the escorting ships, two of which, H.M.C.S. *Wetaskiwin* and *Skeena*, killed *U–588*.

The pack lost contact with Convoy ON–115 during a Grand Bank fog on 4 August. Two days later Admiral Doenitz ordered them to go after Convoy SC–94, a slow eastbound convoy of 33 ships escorted by another Canadian unit.[19] H.M.C.S. *Assiniboine*

[18] Escort Commander's Report; Admiralty and A/S W Unit evaluations.

[19] Report of Commanding Officer H.M.C.S. *Assiniboine* to Captain (Destroyers) St. Johns Newfoundland 10 Aug. 1942; evaluation by Cdr. T. L. Lewis, A/S W Unit, Boston.

of the screen sank *U-210* on 6 August. Shortly after noon 8 August, in a calm sea, moderate wind and perfect visibility, Convoy SC-94 was suddenly flushed by a waiting wolf-pack, and lost three ships. H.M.S. *Dianthus*, after a hunt lasting three and a half hours, depth-charged to the surface *U-379*, and promptly rammed and sank it, recovering five survivors.

Admiral Doenitz now had echelons of wolf-packs strung across all probable transatlantic convoy routes between Iceland and the Azores, especially in areas where planes would not pester them, together with reconnaissance submarines posted a few hundred miles from the convoy termini in order to coach the packs. These were tactics exceedingly difficult to beat; and, as we shall see, they were not beaten for eight months. Only the improved technique of a painfully inadequate number of escorts prevented a summer holocaust. Not one transatlantic merchant convoy escaped attack in August 1942. In September there was a drop in total Atlantic sinkings, but they were still dangerously high – 88 ships, 454,548 tons. The U-boats showed great enterprise in penetrating the Gulf and River of St. Lawrence, where they sank seven ships out of Sydney–Quebec convoys. In the broad ocean, aggressive escorts were responsible for most of the convoys getting safely through the echelons of wolf-packs. Convoy SC-100, which was scattered by an equinoctial storm, lost four out of 24 merchant ships to submarine attack; the escorts (including U.S.C.G.C. *Spencer* and *Campbell*) sighted seven U-boats on the surface, but could not overtake them; one submarine attack was made in a 40-mile gale, and several sound contacts were foiled by *Pillenwerfer*.[20] ON-127, which was attacked for several days running, lost seven ships, although the enemy claimed 19 in an enthusiastic broadcast. But no exploit of the month received such acclaim in German propaganda as the supposed massacre of an "American troop convoy" composed of "large luxury liners" after a "fierce battle."

The true story is this. The British Ministry of War Transpor-

[20] Report of Capt. P. R. Heineman (escort commander) with endorsement by Admiral Brainard and evaluation by Cdr. T. L. Lewis.

tation had purchased eleven of our shoal-draft Long Island Sound and Chesapeake Bay passenger steamers. Eight were formed up at St. Johns into Convoy RB–1, which sailed under the escort of two British destroyers for Londonderry on 21 September. Four days out the convoy was badly worried by a wolf-pack around lat. 55° N, long. 18° 27′ W. The *Boston*, *New York* and *Yorktown* together with one of the escorts, H.M.S. *Veteran*, were sunk with a loss of 119 lives; but no troops of any kind were carried in those steamers.[21] The old Norfolk-Washington steamboats *Northland* and *Southland*, taken over by the U. S. Navy in 1943, survived to take part in the invasion of Normandy.

U-boats were gradually being moved southward. During September, 14 vessels were sunk by submarines in the area of the Gulf of Guinea, and in October the Southeast Atlantic area around the Cape of Good Hope suddenly jumped into second place as a danger spot, with 25 sinkings totaling 181,000 tons. In neither area were merchant vessels convoyed at that time.

Despite a new eight-day cycle for eastbound convoys,[22] which made for economy in escorts, the North Atlantic Convoy route still held first place for danger. Convoy SC–104 lost eight ships torpedoed in two night attacks along lat 54°–55° N below Cape Farewell; HX–212 lost five in four attacks on successive days;[23] and sinkings along this route as a whole reached a new high in October — 27 ships of almost 189,000 tons.[24]

These sinkings could have been even greater but for the fact that in late October and early November Admiral Doenitz deployed a large proportion of his U-boats among the Western Islands and off the Straits of Gibraltar. The German high command knew that an

[21] Information furnished by Director Naval Intelligence Canadian Naval Service Headquarters; article in *Washington Sunday Star* 20 May 1945. The others in the convoy were *President Warfield*, *Naushon* and *New Bedford*. Of the other three, one burned before sailing and two were eliminated by structural defects and did not attempt to cross. *Naushon* became a Royal Navy hospital ship and was used in the Normandy invasion in June 1944, in which *Northland* figured as U.S.S. *Leydon*.

[22] Started October 10 and 18. (Admiralty Notes.)

[23] Convoy Report by Cdr. T. L. Lewis, seen on board U.S.C.G.C. *Campbell*.

[24] This includes one sinking from a transatlantic convoy in the Canadian Coastal Zone.

Allied attack on Africa was pending, but fortunately was ignorant of the exact objective. The high-speed Task Force 34 of 101 ships that effected the landings in Morocco on 8 November successfully eluded attack, as did the convoys from Great Britain until they had passed the Straits.[25] But this new disposition of the U-boats made all ocean areas off the bulge of Africa highly dangerous for merchant ships. The British convoy SL–125 lost seven ships off Madeira and four more off Tenerife in October; nine other ships were sunk off the Straits in November.

In that month the total losses of merchant vessels by torpedoings in the Atlantic for the first and only time surpassed 600,000 tons. In addition several Army transports not counted in merchant ship losses were torpedoed and sunk in the African operation, after they had discharged their troops. Losses on the North Atlantic Convoy Route ran almost as high as in October. Convoy SC–107 suffered the greatest loss of any up to that time – 15 ships torpedoed and sunk in an action which started about midnight 1–2 November and lasted until the evening of the 4th. The enemy resumed activity in the area around Curaçao, where three Trinidad–Aruba–Guantanamo convoys lost eight ships; and he continued to infest the approaches to Trinidad but with slightly less success than in the summer. Now that Brazil had entered the war, U-boats began patrolling about the St. Paul Rocks off Cape San Roque, and made an appreciable kill of nine unescorted ships. The Capetown area seems to have profited most by the enemy's interest in North Africa; sinkings there were very few in November and nil in December.

The year 1942 closed with a hopeful drop in total Atlantic sinkings to 54 ships of 287,730 tons in December, less than half the tonnage lost in November. As the enemy was now operating more U-boats than ever before, 90 to 100 on the average in the Atlantic, this gave the Allied nations an unwarranted expectation of better things to come. The explanation of this drop in sinkings seems to be that Admiral Doenitz was concentrating on the troop and supply convoys approaching Africa, which proved to be too fast and

[25] See Volume II for these convoys.

cagey for his wolves to catch. Convoy ON–154, which suffered the heaviest loss of this month, 14 ships out of 44, was following a southern route and encountered a wolf-pack that was laying for the troop transports.

b. The Midwinter Blitz

The fast eastbound convoys HX–217, –218 and –219 fought their way across in December through heavily infested waters with slight losses. HX–217 was taken care of by an escort group composed of ships manned by three United Nations: H.M.S. *Fame* and *Vervain;* H.Nor.M.S. *Rose*, *Eglantine* and *Potentilla;* and the Polish destroyer *Burza*. They had worked together for several months, and this was their fourth U-boat blitz. Ably supported by Canadian, American and British aircraft, from bases in Newfoundland, Iceland and Northern Ireland, the 33 ships and 6 escorts plowed through successive wolf-packs with a loss of only two merchant ships; and the covering aircraft sank two submarines, *U–254* and *U–611*.

The first of these kills, on 8 December 1942, was by Liberator "H" of British Squadron 120 about 550 miles SW of Iceland. This squadron had been furnishing air cover up to 800 miles from its Icelandic base, and so continued until United States Navy Squadron VP–84 relieved it, 600 miles from Londonderry. On 10 December a Liberator of VP–84, piloted by Lt. (jg) H. L. Neff, sank *U–611* about 500 miles from the Irish coast.[26]

Dash of individual escorts, directed teamwork, and excellent use made of high-frequency direction-finder bearings to locate submarines and attack before they came within torpedo range, helped this convoy to get through. The U-boats followed the technique of working ahead of the convoy every day to obtain a favorable position for night attack. For the first time after generous air cover had been provided, the U-boats hung on instead of re-

[26] Both attacks were assessed as "probables," but the kills were proved from German records.

tiring; this persistence was what cost the pack two of its members. The appended chart of HX–217 will give some faint notion of the sort of life one led in a transatlantic convoy during the winter of 1942–1943.

Convoy HX–218 had a similar experience. H.M.S. *Hesperus* and *Vanessa*, escorting HX–219, killed *U–357* the day after Christmas in the vicinity of Rockall, after ten depth-charge attacks, a gunfire surface action and ramming. Most of January's attacks were confined to Convoy TM–1, consisting of nine tankers and four British corvettes, bound from Trinidad to Gibraltar, which had the bad luck to cross the track of homeward and outward bound U-boats. As it did so, four boats were ordered by Doenitz to join a nearby wolf-pack, which then outnumbered the escorts more than two to one. In four days' fighting between 3 and 10 January, Convoy TM–1 lost seven tankers. This was the highest percentage of loss inflicted by enemy U-boat action during the war. Cominch promptly shifted two long-range anti-submarine plane squadrons to North African fields to provide air cover over this dangerous area. In February the hungry wolf-packs returned and in that month and the next destroyed more shipping than in any earlier period of the war – 36 vessels of 227,109 tons in February, and 49 vessels of 295,970 tons in March. These sinkings, occurring at the worst season in the tempestuous North Atlantic, when the temperature of sea water hovers around 30° Fahrenheit, were accompanied by heavy loss of valuable lives. Hundreds of merchant seamen were blown up, drowned or frozen to death "getting the stuff across."

c. Troop Convoys

Throughout this period the United States Army continued to build up forces in Great Britain, ready to be thrown into Africa or Europe as higher strategy might dictate. From 7 July to the end of 1942, Task Force 37, Rear Admiral Lyle A. Davidson commanding, comprising U.S.S. *Philadelphia* and *New York*,[27] with

[27] *Texas* in July. This Task Force was designated 35 in December. The convoys were designated AT or NA.

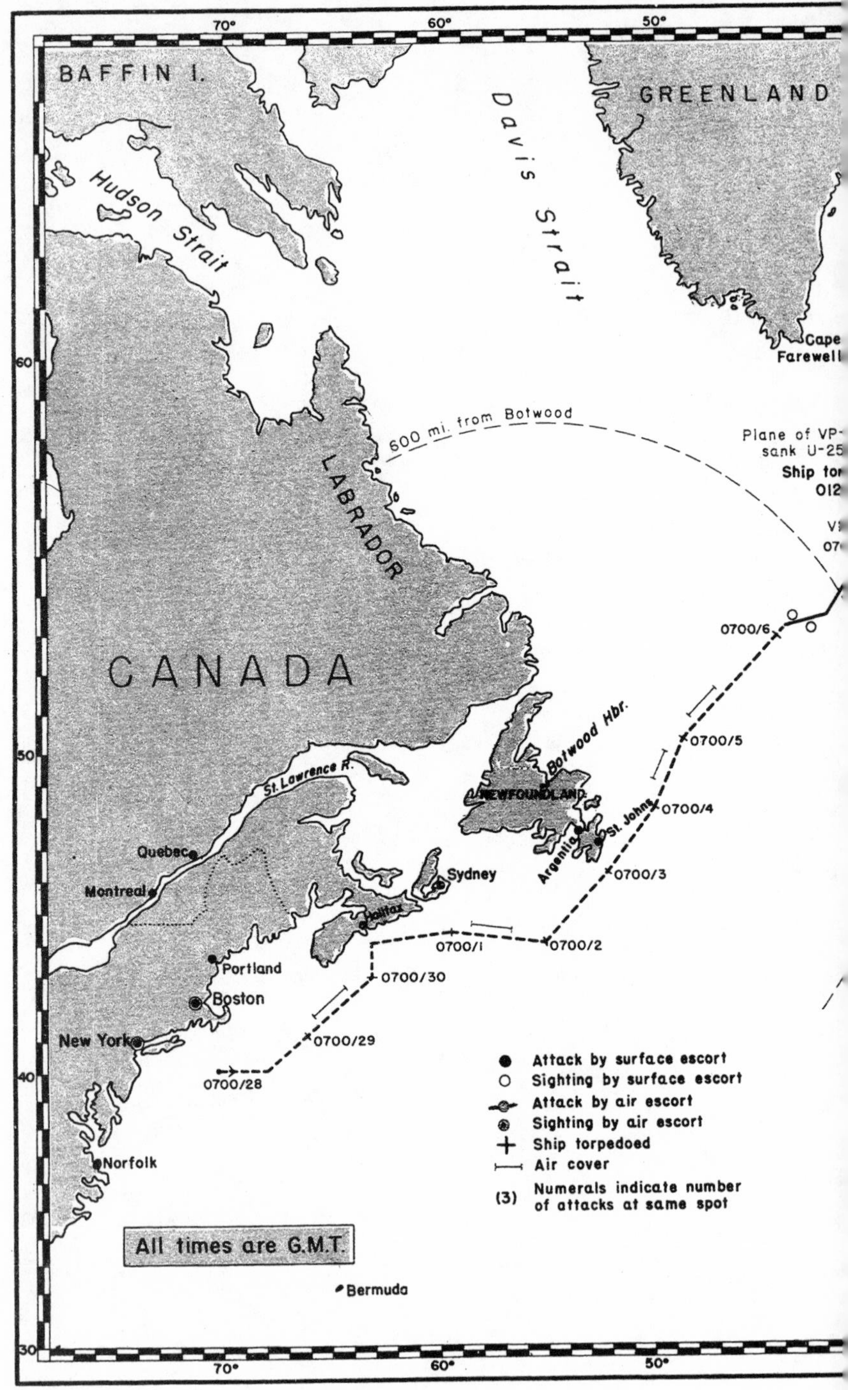

70°
60°
50°
BAFFIN I.
GREENLAND
Davis Strait
Hudson Strait
Cape
Farewell
60
600 mi. from Botwood
LABRADOR
CANADA
0700/6
0700/5
0700/4
0700/3
0700/2
0700/1
0700/30
0700/29
0700/28
Botwood Hbr.
NEWFOUNDLAND
St. Johns
Argentia
50
St. Lawrence R.
Quebec
Montreal
Sydney
Halifax
Portland
Boston
New York
40
Norfolk
Attack by surface escort
Sighting by surface escort
Attack by air escort
Sighting by air escort
Ship torpedoed
Air cover
(3) Numerals indicate number of attacks at same spot
All times are G.M.T.
Bermuda
30

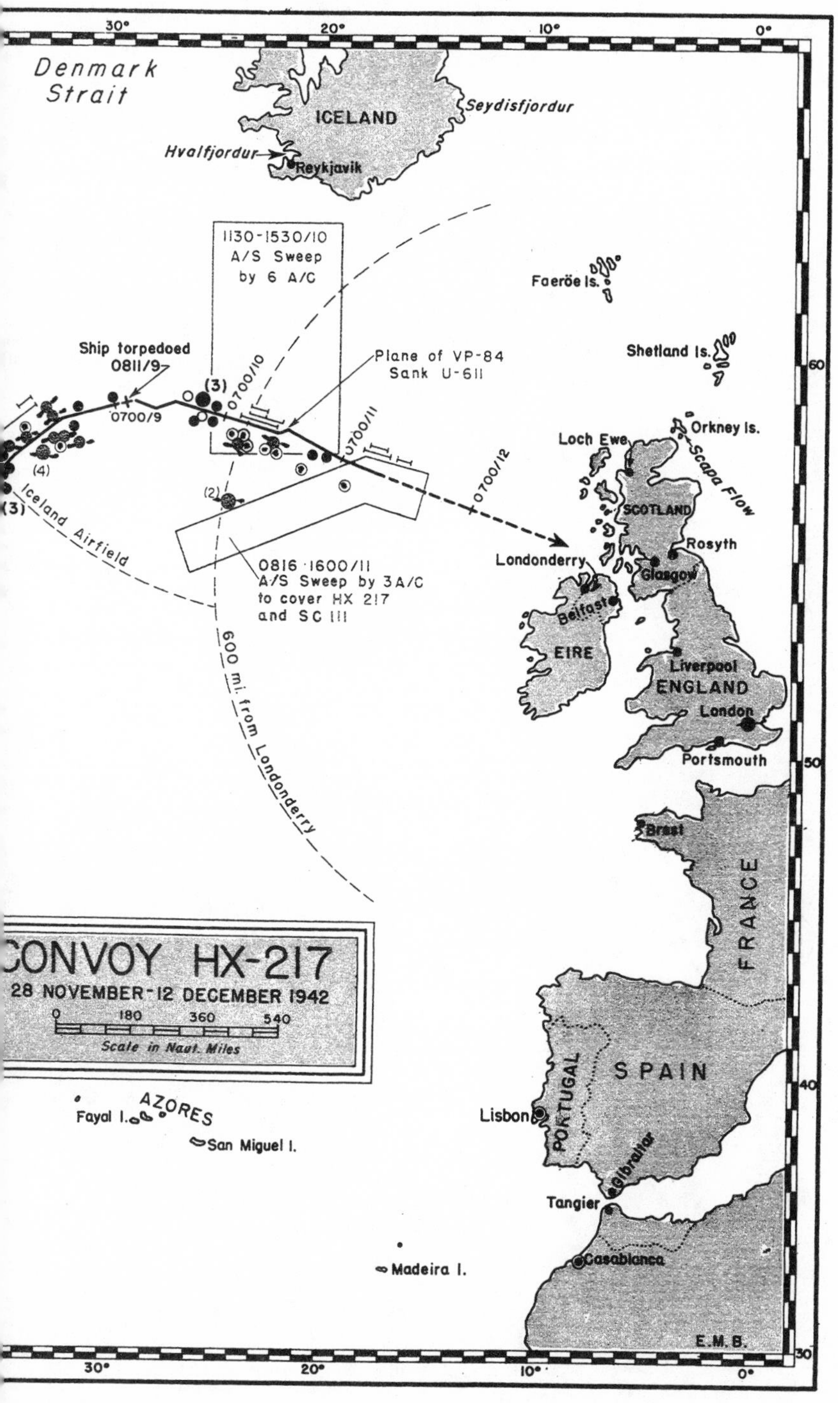

Denmark Strait
ICELAND
Seydisfjordur
Hvalfjordur
Reykjavik
1130-1530/10
A/S Sweep
by 6 A/C
Faeröe Is.
Shetland Is.
Ship torpedoed
0811/9
Plane of VP-84
Sank U-611
0700/9
0700/10
0700/11
0700/12
(3)
(4)
(2)
Iceland Airfield
Orkney Is.
Loch Ewe
Scapa Flow
SCOTLAND
Rosyth
Londonderry
Glasgow
0816-1600/11
A/S Sweep by 3 A/C
to cover HX 217
and SC 111
Belfast
EIRE
600 mi. from Londonderry
Liverpool
ENGLAND
London
Portsmouth
Brest
FRANCE
CONVOY HX-217
28 NOVEMBER-12 DECEMBER 1942
Scale in Naut. Miles
PORTUGAL
SPAIN
Lisbon
Gibraltar
AZORES
Fayal I.
San Miguel I.
Tangier
Casablanca
Madeira I.
E.M.B.

six to twelve destroyers; and Task Force 38, Captain C. F. Bryant Jr. commanding, comprising U.S.S. *Arkansas, Brooklyn* and seven to eleven destroyers, escorted troop convoys from New York and Halifax to Lough Foyle, the Clyde and the Mersey.[28] These convoys comprised from 8 to 15 transports or troopships, some of which broke off at "Momp" for Iceland. They were taken through without a single casualty to the troops, or, so far as is known to the writer, a single attack; but there was a bad accident to Convoy AT–20 in a mid-August fog off Nova Scotia. U.S.S. *Buck* had her fantail knocked off when trying to cross the bows of a merchant vessel; U.S.S. *Ingraham*, sent by the escort commander to investigate, was rammed by a tanker and blown up with the loss of all but eleven men of her crew.

On one of the return convoys (TA–18) the transport *Wakefield* (ex-*Manhattan*), Commander H. G. Bradbury USCG, carrying hundreds of civilian workers from construction camps in the United Kingdom, caught fire on 3 September 1942. By this time the Navy was well skilled in the technique of rescuing survivors from the water. Thought had been given to the problem of handling a major disaster to one of these great troops transports, which might involve caring for thousands instead of merely scores of men. Before leaving New York, Captain F. C. Denebrink, commanding U.S.S. *Brooklyn*, had his ship designated rescue vessel in case of such disaster. His staff drew up an elaborate survivors' bill, assigning specific duties to every member of his crew in the event of rescue operations, and providing for the handling and care of survivors from the time they were received on board to their eventual debarkation. Every detail for routing survivors to these prearranged stations, for guarding, bedding and feeding them, for temporary lavatories, medical attention, and eventual debarkation, was thought out beforehand; and the *Brooklyn's* crew was so well drilled in these novel exercises that when the time came every man knew exactly what to do.

[28] Task Force 38 took one convoy to Casablanca in November. (See Volume II.)

When the fire started *Wakefield* was the foremost ship in the port column; *Brooklyn* the second and rear ship in the second column. As soon as she obtained the necessary permission from Captain Bryant, the convoy commander, *Brooklyn* left position and proceeded full speed to assist the transport, screened by destroyer *Hilary P. Jones* against possible submarine attack. At the same time destroyer *Mayo*, patrolling the station nearest *Wakefield*, obtained permission to close her bow, where hundreds of men were cut off by flames from the stern. At about 1900 *Mayo* came alongside and seven minutes later *Brooklyn* had three lines out from her forward deck to the after deck of the burning vessel. The sea was calm, with a slight ground swell, and the two ships lay comfortably board to board. *Wakefield* already had her abandon-ship ladders over the side; these were hauled aboard *Brooklyn* and *Mayo* and the men came over easily and promptly. At 1917 *Mayo* cast off, having taken about 247 men, and ten minutes later *Brooklyn* cast off with about 800 passengers. Commander Bradbury wished to retain on board *Wakefield* the balance of about 450 men, mostly crew members, in order to fight the fire.

After *Brooklyn* had started to rejoin the convoy, flames were noticed leaping from the transport's superstructure as high as the stacks. Captain Denebrink then decided to stand by, and two destroyers peeled off to screen the two large ships, *Mayo* rejoining the convoy. At 1947 *Wakefield* signaled *Brooklyn* "come alongside same place," and the rescuing maneuver was repeated. In the meantime the burning vessel had cast a number of life rafts adrift, and launched 14 lifeboats, some partially manned, but most of them empty. Destroyer *Madison* now placed herself about 50 yards off *Wakefield's* port bow, and picked up 80 survivors from the lifeboats. At 2015 *Wakefield* hauled down her colors, and all hands transferred to *Brooklyn* by rope ladders, the Captain leaving last at 2032. A total of 1173 men had been taken in by the cruiser. They were conducted to their assigned positions in 120 different compartments below, without the slightest hitch or confusion. Every man was given a bunk and three hot meals were served before the *Brooklyn* reached New York, 22½ hours later; disembarkation was effected there in 22 minutes. The *Wakefield's* entire complement of 1500 men was saved, without a single serious injury either to the men or to the rescuing vessels.

Two ocean-going tugs arrived from New York about 24 hours later and took *Wakefield* in tow. A Navy fire-fighting team under Commander Harold J. Burke USNR was flown out from Quonset in a float plane; it made a landing alongside, put portable gear on board and with its new "fog" nozzles sufficiently controlled the fires so that the ship could be towed to Halifax and beached.[29] She burned there for eight days before the fire was extinguished. Fortunately it was largely confined to the superstructure and the vessel could be salvaged. Temporary repairs were made at Halifax, whence *Wakefield* was towed to the drydock at South Boston and practically rebuilt. By May 1944 this great transport was once more in service under Coast Guard command.

Beginning 2 August, the Navy and Admiralty put into effect a method tried and proved in the last war, the employment of big, fast, luxury liners to carry troops without an escort. The French S.S. *Pasteur*, Canadian *Empress of Scotland*, British *Queen Mary* (81,000 tons) and *Queen Elizabeth* (85,000 tons) were among those so used. All except the American S.S. *Mariposa* were operated by the British. "Mary" and "Lizzie" were able to steam an average of 26.5 knots for the entire voyage and to make a British port in less than five days from New York; the others too were fast enough to baffle the U-boats, whose anxiety to catch them may be gauged by frequent German claims that they had been sunk. These ships made ten eastbound voyages heavily loaded with American and Canadian troops, and twenty more during the first six months of 1943. Except in coastal waters and in the Western Approaches where they were given air and surface escort, the big liners made the crossing unattended, and did not lose a man. It was twice as

[29] Navy Press Release 8 Sept. 1945. Cdr. Burke had been head of the Marine Division New York City Fire Department, and he was the protagonist of the new "fog" nozzle which, with great improvement in fire-fighting efficiency, replaced solid streams of water.

expeditious a method of transporting troops as the fastest convoy, and far more pleasant for the troops.

Troop convoys to Iceland and Greenland were not so fortunate. The first American troopship loss of the war was that of U. S. Army Transport *Chatham* in the Strait of Belle Isle on 27 August 1942. She was in one of the "SG" Greenland convoys, which were the poor relations of the whole system. They were given the slowest and worst equipped escorts, under Coast Guard officers and crews who had been given slight training in escort duty or anti-submarine work; and it was only by guess, by guts and by God that some of them were not completely wiped out by the U-boats.

Convoy SG–6 departed Sydney, Cape Breton, on 25 August in two groups, a fast and a slow. The first consisted of U.S.C.G.C. *Mojave* escorting the Army transport *Chatham*, which was capable of a speed of 13 knots. The slow group consisted of cutters *Algonquin* and *Mohawk*, escorting three merchant ships, Navy oiler *Laramie*, and U.S.S. *Harjurand*, a coal-burning auxiliary whose maximum speed was 7 knots. This division into two parts, contrary to escort-of-convoy doctrine, only succeeded in weakening each. Both groups were routed through the Gulf of St. Lawrence and the Strait of Belle Isle. Air coverage was provided the night of 25 August and all next day, but there was none at 0915 on the clear, calm morning of the 27th when *Chatham* was torpedoed as she was making 9 knots. Half an hour later she lay on the bottom in 65 fathoms. *Mojave* searched the area for two hours, but made no contact, either before or after the attack. She then commenced rescue operations which were efficiently conducted with the aid of two planes that spotted survivors, and of a small Canadian patrol vessel. The sinking took place some 20 or 30 miles off shore, which many of the survivors reached, and almost the entire ship's company of 139 men and 430 American and Canadian soldiers were saved.[30]

Mojave continued searching until 1700, when she returned to Sydney with survivors, but without notifying anyone of the sink-

[30] Total losses, 9 or 10 killed in the explosion, 16 or 17 missing.

ing or even of meeting a submarine. Meantime the slow group of convoy SC–6 was steaming through the Strait, headed for disaster. At 2132 in bright moonlight, very near the spot where *Chatham* had gone down,[31] U.S.S. *Laramie* and S.S. *Arlyn* were torpedoed. *Laramie* stayed afloat and was salvaged; the merchantman went down amid scenes approaching panic, for she was carrying 400 tons of explosives. The crew rushed to the boats, leaving the Naval Armed Guard to swim. Passenger Roger McGrath, a Navy photographer, "took command of a very chaotic situation, restored order, bolstered morale and thereby saved the lives of many who otherwise would have been lost." [32]

Although the quality of escorts on the Greenland run had been improved by the time SG–19 departed St. Johns for Skovfjord on 29 January 1943, their equipment and training were still woefully inadequate, and heavy loss of life was incurred. This convoy consisted of two merchant ships and the 5252-ton Army transport *Dorchester*, carrying about 1000 tons of cargo, a crew of 130 men of the merchant marine, an Armed Guard of 23, and 751 passengers, mostly United States Army reinforcements for Greenland. They were escorted by a Coast Guard unit comprising cutters *Tampa*, *Escanaba*,[33] and *Comanche*. The flagship was capable of 14½ knots but the others could not do better than 11½, a speed too meager to give effective anti-submarine protection. The weakness of these ships had long been known to Task Force 24, but nothing could be done about it, as the demand for escorts was so heavy and pressing. Coast Guard cutters were equipped with radar if and when they had an overhaul, but not otherwise.

The convoy ran at once into very cold and dirty weather. *Escanaba* and *Comanche* had difficulty in keeping up, owing to the reduction to their speed by icing. At times they had to heave-to and

[31] Lat. 51°53′ N, long. 55°58′ W.

[32] Report of District Intelligence Office First Naval District 9 September 1942. The Armed Guard was picked up the next day by *Harjurand*.

[33] *Escanaba* was later sunk 13 June 1943, after being blown to bits by an explosion of undetermined cause. The entire complement of officers and men were lost with the exception of two boatswains mates, who were picked up by U.S.C.G.C. *Raritan*, and they had no idea what caused the disaster.

remove ice with live steam; guns, depth charges and mousetraps were sealed tight by thick ice, and excessive water noises rendered sound gear of little value.

The convoy was sailing in the following formation: –

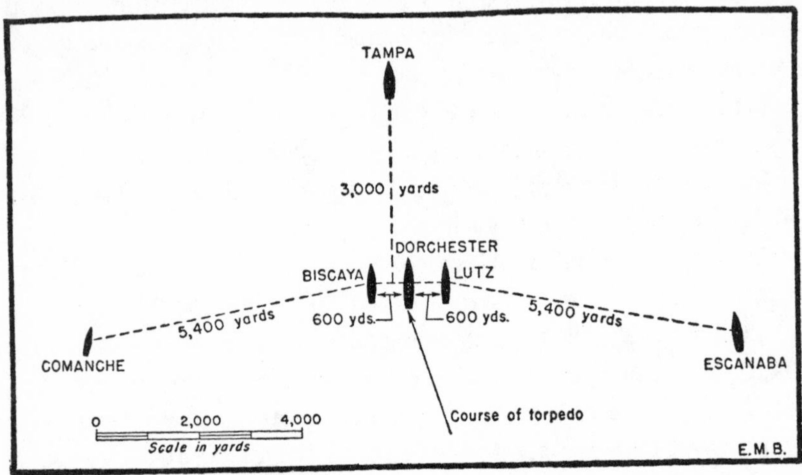

This formation followed one of the plans for convoys of this size and nature, as given out by the Convoy and Routing Section of Cominch.

On 2 February when the weather had moderated somewhat, Cominch advised that the presence of a U-boat in the vicinity had been indicated by direction-finder. The escort commander, Captain Joseph Greenspun USCG, so informed the convoy, and a warning was issued over the public-address system of *Dorchester*. Upon receipt of this warning *Tampa* made a sweep ten miles ahead and five miles on the flanks at her best speed of 14½ knots and returned to her patrol area at dark. The low speed of the other two escorts precluded their being used for sweeping. The convoy was sailing on evasive courses but not zigzagging. Half an hour after midnight, the course was altered 36 degrees to starboard.

The convoy was steaming at 10 knots and had reached a point about 150 miles from Cape Farewell[34] at 0355 February 3 when

[34] D.R. position 59°22′ N, 48°42′ W.

Dorchester was torpedoed without warning on her starboard side. *U-456*, approaching on that quarter, had taken full advantage of the blind spot caused by the lack of radar on *Escanaba*, and the torpedo hit a lethal spot. At 0358 the master ordered Abandon Ship, and *Dorchester* sank rapidly by the bow. No radio distress signal was sent out, for all power was lost at once; in the confusion no one remembered to send up a rocket or flares; and in a pitch-black night the escort remained unaware of anything wrong until after the transport had sunk. Both discipline and seamanship were wanting in abandoning ship. A terrific list kept most port lifeboats from being launched, others were lowered but capsized through overcrowding, fouling the releasing gear or poor handling in the water. Rafts were dropped so hastily as to hit men swimming in the icy water. Some soldiers refused to abandon ship. The Naval Armed Guard officer, Lieutenant (jg) William H. Arpaia USNR and two of his men, Winfield McCoy and W. J. McMinn, released one of the remaining rafts and lowered themselves into the water, only to find the raft already taken over by passengers. Without an order or a word from the lieutenant, the two enlisted men climbed back on board and found another raft on which they saved themselves. Four Army chaplains, Rabbi Alexander Goode, Father John P. Washington, Reverend George L. Fox and Reverend Clark V. Poling, gave up their lifebelts to soldiers and went down with the ship.

Some passengers did not hear the abandon-ship signal, which was only partially completed as there was not enough steam to blow all six blasts. While *Tampa* escorted the other two merchant ships to Skovfjord *Comanche* and *Escanaba* conducted a fruitless sweep for the submarine, returning later to pick up survivors.[35] It was still dark, recovery was difficult, and only men of high vitality were still alive – the temperature of the water was 34° and that of the air 36° Fahrenheit. Almost all survivors were so stiff from cold that they could not even grasp the cargo nets on the rescuing vessels, much less pull themselves up; coastguardsmen

[35] *Tampa* was escorting the other two merchant ships, and delivered them at the entrance of Skovfjord at 1714.

of *Comanche* and *Escanaba* entered the freezing water in order to tow life rafts to the cutters and help survivors on board. Of the 906 men aboard *Dorchester*, only 229 were saved.[36]

In the morning of 3 February, the United States seaplane tender *Sandpiper*, then completing a rescue mission in Arsuk Fjord, Greenland,[37] received a message to proceed to the area of the sinking and recover survivors from *Dorchester*. But the fjord had frozen up and she could not get out until a cutter came to break the ice; so she was unable to reach the scene of the sinking until the morning of 4 February. Three vessels of the Greenland Patrol were already there, and hundreds of dead bodies were seen floating on the water, kept up by their life jackets.

Anyone inclined to blame the *Dorchester* disaster on these slow and ill-equipped Coast Guard cutters will be more tolerant when he finds that Convoy SC–118 lost a troopship three days later in spite of a fair number of escorts and ample air protection.

This large, slow convoy sailed from New York 24 January, and at "Westomp" on the 31st was picked up by an escort group of seven British and Canadian corvettes. Next day U.S.C.G.C. *Bibb* joined them from St. Johns with a number of merchant ships that brought the total up to 64. Just before dawn 4 February 1943, as

[36] Of the 677 lost, 404 were U. S. Army.

[37] *Sandpiper's* rescue mission illustrates the versatility of bluejackets. A Navy Catalina with a crew of seven had left Narsarssuak for Ivigtut 27 January 1943, to sweep for a convoy ahead. It was cutting across the icecap in thick weather returning to base when it accidentally grounded, and sank into the crust that forms over the ice. The crew radioed Narsarssuak; some Army planes flew to the spot and dropped food, clothing, and spare parts. But installing new parts proved to be of no avail as the weight of the plane forced it further into the snow, and after a couple of days, a rescue party was organized of eight soldiers and Mr. Sinclair Adams, a civilian worker in the cryolite mines who was familiar with the peculiarities of icecaps. *Sandpiper* carried them to Arsuk Fjord, the nearest landing place to the PBY's position. Their equipment included two large motor toboggans and materials to construct a base camp. A difficult landing was effected on a small beach at the head of the estuary, whence rocky cliffs rose almost vertically, with occasional ledges wide enough to allow storage of materiel. As the rescue party was struggling ineffectively with the problem of getting equipment up to the plateau from the beach, Lt. H. T. E. Anderson, skipper of *Sandpiper*, detailed thirty members of his crew to help. The men made a human chain up the side of the cliff and passed up the equipment, including the two motor toboggans, hand-to-hand. The rescue party then completed its mission successfully.

convoy SC–118 was passing south of Greenland, some thick-headed individual on a foreign merchant ship set off snowflake illumination by accident. This gave away the convoy to *U–187*, scouting for a wolf-pack. But it paid heavily for the information. H.M.S. *Beverley* (an old U.S.N. four-piper) sighted the U-boat 15 miles ahead of the convoy at 1110, but could not get "on" with her main battery because the target appeared only occasionally when both it and the destroyer were on the crests of waves. H.M.S. *Vimy* picked it up on her asdic at 1235, and within the next hour delivered three attacks with depth charges and one with hedgehog, while *Beverley* circled dropping depth charges. The submarine could not take it, but surfaced. Both destroyers attacked with gunfire and sank *U–187*, recovering a number of survivors.

That evening, the three port columns of the convoy failed to hear a whistle signal for an emergency turn, and in consequence the convoy was split in two parts about 15 miles apart, with stragglers in between. This was a lovely opening for the shadowing submarines, but aggressive attacks by the escorts on every sound or surface contact prevented any torpedoings that night. A straggler was torpedoed the following noon, when *Beverley* and *Vimy* were attacking two submarines some 15 miles on the starboard quarter of the reunited convoy. That night nothing happened, and the escort was reinforced by the arrival of cutter *Ingham* with U.S.S. *Babbitt* and *Schenck* from Iceland, whence air cover of Liberators arrived overhead at 0900, February 6. All that day the planes were busy investigating high-frequency direction-finder bearings. They made eight sightings of U-boats, and delivered four attacks unsuccessfully; *Bibb* also made a hedgehog attack with negative results. *Vimy* attacked one U-boat 25 miles astern of the convoy at nightfall; *Lobelia* on the port beam made four attacks on another after 2000.

"The situation was now one to inspire sober confidence in the outcome of the battle," reports the Admiralty's analyst. "The first shadower had been sunk, a classic start. The following night, with the convoy split, had been an anxious one, but the U-boats had missed their opportunity. Again, on the next night they had kept their distance. And then, on the 6th, the aircraft arrived and the surface escort was reinforced by three more United States ships. Throughout this period, encounters and attacks on U-boats had been satisfactorily frequent, and the high-frequency direction-finder in the rescue ship *Toward* had been invaluable."

Yet, in spite of all this, and an escort of twelve ships, half of them destroyers, the enemy regained the initiative and torpedoed seven ships in the darkness before dawn of 7 February, at a time when air cover availed naught. One submarine thrust inside the columns; three were detected within a few miles of the convoy, and several others at a greater range. The Fighting French corvette *Lobelia* sank one of the submarines, *U-609*, but the others escaped for the time being. Loss of life was heavy, especially as the rescue vessel *Toward* was the first to be torpedoed; and it was heaviest from S.S. *Henry R. Mallory*, 6442 tons, carrying 384 United States troops and bluejackets to Iceland.[38] She had a merchant crew of 77 and a Naval Armed Guard of 34, who never had a chance to open fire as the submarine was not sighted. Wind and sea were moderate, and the *Mallory* stayed afloat for thirty minutes; but she lacked compartmentation: progressive flooding took charge and she sank stern first. No general alarm was sounded, no orders were issued from the bridge, according to some, but other survivors indicated that morale was good and abandonment was orderly. Nine out of ten lifeboats got into the water but they capsized or were overloaded. As a result, 60 per cent of the ship's company were lost.[39] Both the *Dorchester* and the *Mallory* were fortunately the only instances of what could happen to any troop transport torpedoed at night in mid-Atlantic during winter weather.[40]

Except for a collision the following night, which cost one more

[38] Her inclusion was explained because of the shuttle arrangement for Iceland-bound shipping.

[39] Summary of survivors' statements prepared by Op-16-B-5, 6 Mar. 1943, and reports of *Bibb* and *Ingham*, files A/S W Unit Atlantic Fleet.

[40] The Navy type "doughnut" life rafts proved worse than useless, as they subjected survivors to such constant ducking in freezing water that many died of exposure before being picked up.

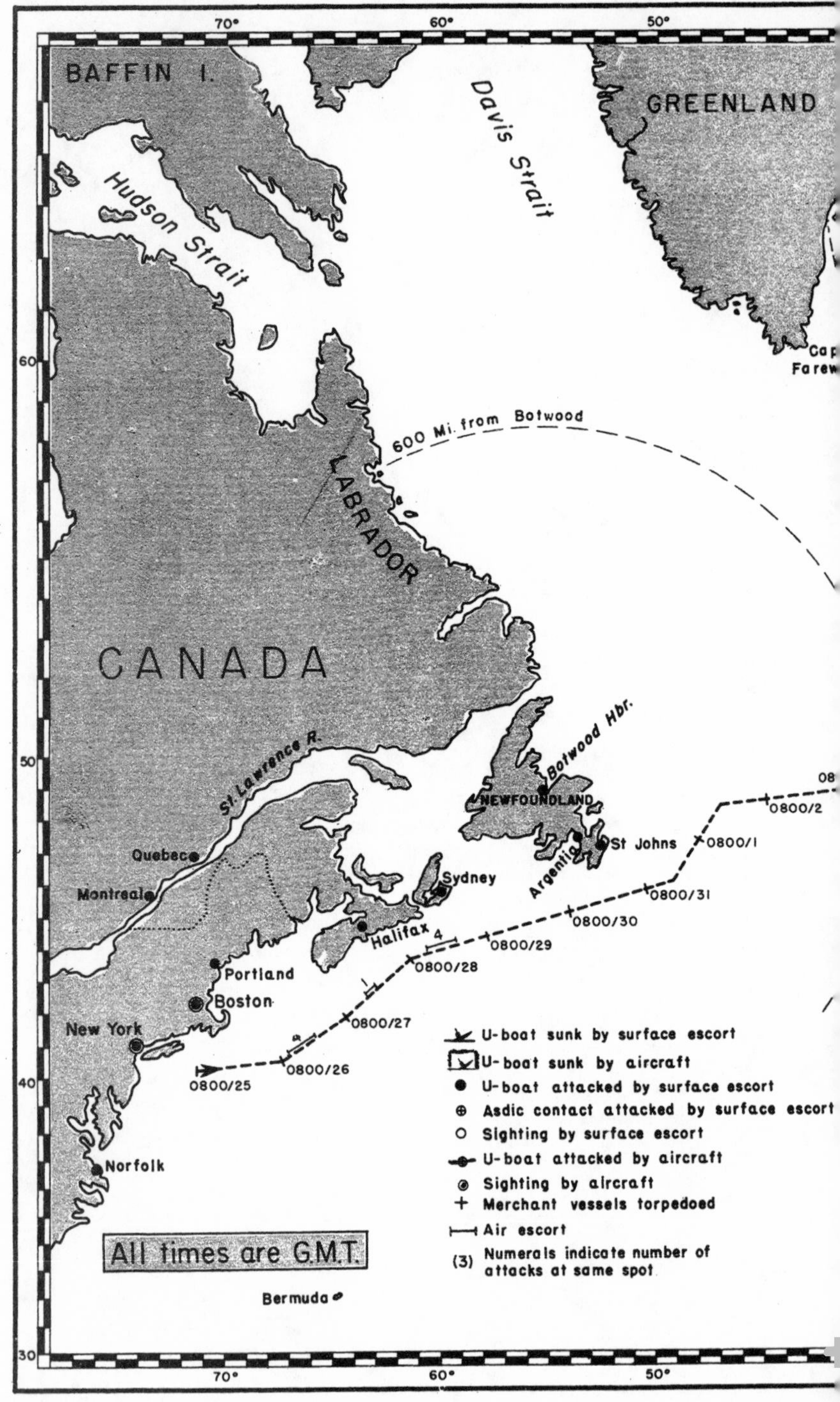

70°
60°
50°
BAFFIN I.
GREENLAND
Davis Strait
Hudson Strait
60
Cap
Farew
600 Mi. from Botwood
LABRADOR
CANADA
St. Lawrence R.
Botwood Hbr.
50
NEWFOUNDLAND
Quebec
Montreal
St Johns
Argentia
Sydney
Halifax
Portland
Boston
New York
0800/2
0800/1
0800/31
0800/30
0800/29
0800/28
0800/27
0800/26
0800/25
4
40
Norfolk
U-boat sunk by surface escort
U-boat sunk by aircraft
U-boat attacked by surface escort
Asdic contact attacked by surface escort
Sighting by surface escort
U-boat attacked by aircraft
Sighting by aircraft
Merchant vessels torpedoed
Air escort
(3) Numerals indicate number of attacks at same spot
All times are G.M.T.
Bermuda
30

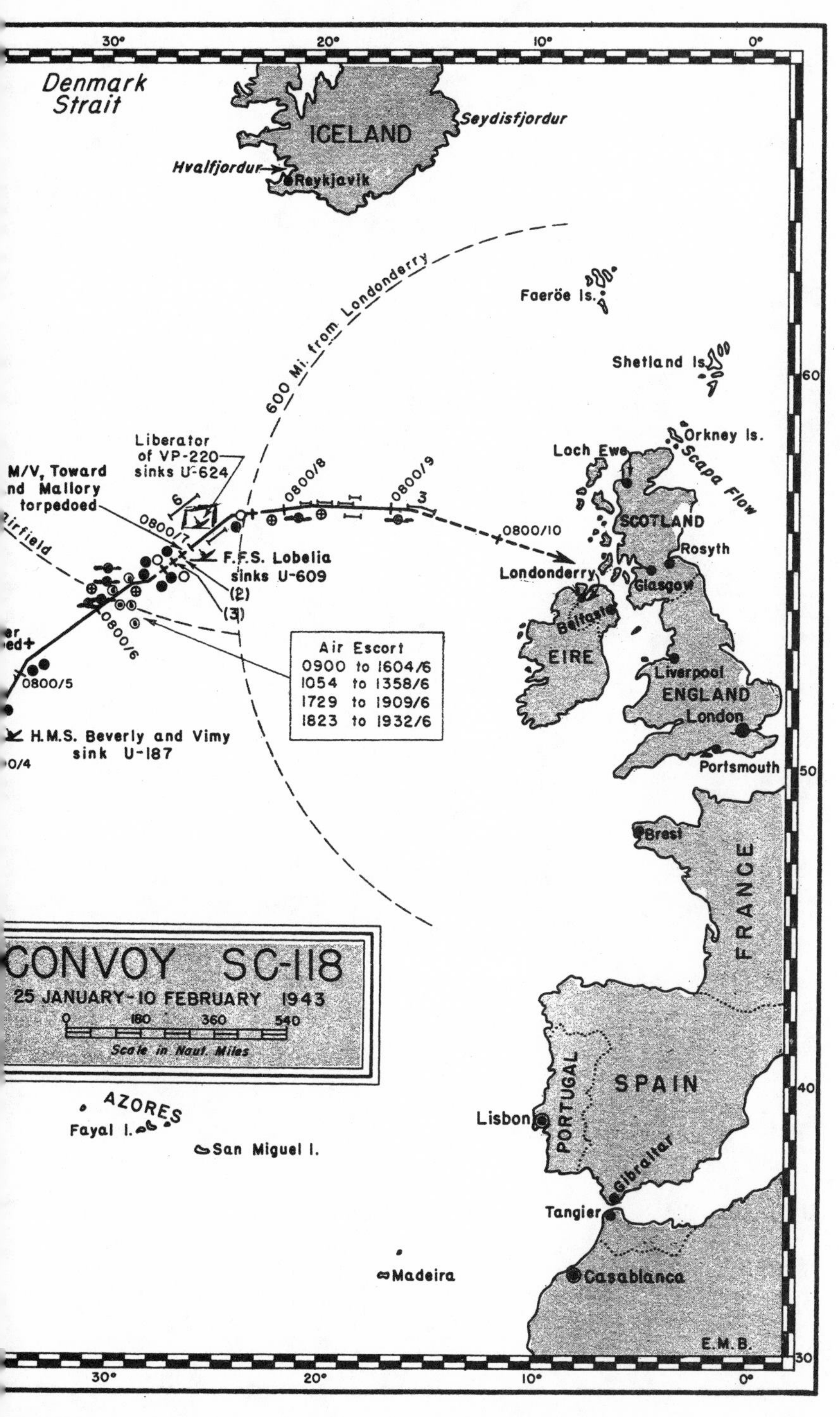
Denmark Strait
ICELAND
Seydisfjordur
Hvalfjordur
Reykjavik
600 Mi. from Londonderry
Faeröe Is.
Shetland Is.
Orkney Is.
Scapa Flow
Loch Ewe
SCOTLAND
Rosyth
Glasgow
Londonderry
Belfast
EIRE
Liverpool
ENGLAND
London
Portsmouth
Brest
FRANCE
SPAIN
PORTUGAL
Lisbon
Gibraltar
Tangier
Casablanca
Madeira
AZORES
Fayal I.
San Miguel I.
Liberator of VP-220 sinks U-624
M/V, Toward and Mallory torpedoed
F.F.S. Lobelia sinks U-609
H.M.S. Beverly and Vimy sink U-187
0800/4
0800/5
0800/6
0800/7
0800/8
0800/9
0800/10
Air Escort
0900 to 1604/6
1054 to 1358/6
1729 to 1909/6
1823 to 1932/6
CONVOY SC-118
25 JANUARY-10 FEBRUARY 1943
Scale in Naut. Miles
E.M.B.

ship, this convoy suffered no further casualties. Two more submarines that approached were kept down by the air cover, and one, *U–624*, was sunk by an R.A.F. Liberator out of Ireland. But the score was distinctly disappointing, and ominous.

d. Heineman's Harriers

One of the worst winters on record was lashing the Western Ocean. Heavy gales were almost continuous; seas broke continuously over vessels' bows, icing their superstructures in the high latitudes; hardly a day passed without snow squalls or bone-chilling rain. Although these conditions made submarine operations difficult, they were even worse for merchant ships that could not lie low, or even lie-to when in convoy. During the majority of the winter days weather was so foul that long-range land-based planes could not fly, and several of those that did never returned. Merchant ship losses, by marine casualty alone, for the five months November 1942–March 1943 reached the enormous and unprecedented figure of 166 vessels (over one a day) and 337,852 tons.[41]

Ocean Escort Unit A–3, commanded by Captain P. R. Heineman USN, was truly international, comprising United States Coast Guard cutters *Spencer* and *Campbell*, H.M. Corvette *Dianthus*, four Canadian corvettes (*Chilliwack, Rosthern, Trillium*,[42] *Dauphin*), and, later, the Polish destroyer *Burza*. This group took over the 63 merchant ships of westbound Convoy ON–166 at about noon of 12 February 1943 at "Eastomp." They found tough going; northwesterly gales persisted during the first three days of the voyage and the convoy averaged only four knots' advance. Despite foul weather there were only two stragglers at the end of the first week, and escorts were fueled from three tankers in the convoy on nine days out of fourteen, even during a 50-knot wind. High-frequency direction-finder bearings revealed submarine activity on

[41] Of these losses 92 occurred in the Atlantic. See Appendix I, Table 2.

[42] The C.O. of *Trillium*, Lt. Philip C. Evans RCNR, was a retired U. S. Naval officer who joined the R.C.N. and helped instruct it in fueling at sea.

18 February, but it was thought that the enemy was preparing to attack another convoy near by. On the 21st there was a large pack of U-boats in the vicinity of the convoy. *Spencer* and *Campbell* ran down two fixes from high-frequency direction-finder bearings, and *Campbell* made several attacks as a result of sound contacts, with no apparent success. She was about to rejoin the convoy when an "S S S" was reported from a straggler from another convoy fifteen miles to the rear, and she went to assist. On investigation, she found no trace of this ship and started to rejoin Convoy ON-166 at 1750. In the meantime, *Spencer* and *Dianthus* went to assist a plane that was attacking three submarines ten miles away on the convoy's starboard quarter, and helped it to drive them down. *Spencer* sighted another submarine at 2014 and attacked with gunfire and depth charges. She had to break off contact to rejoin the convoy, owing to the absence of other escorts, but it subsequently appeared that this attack had finished *U-225*. *Rosthern* made radar contacts with two submarines and gave chase, but they retired at high speed. Most German submarines were faster than a corvette when surfaced.

The real trouble had not yet begun. During the next three days Convoy ON-166 underwent six separate attacks, yet managed to give Admiral Doenitz's boats one mortal wound and several serious ones. Up to now the convoy had been well protected by excellent teamwork of the escort vessels, and by R.A.F. Liberators that operated up to one thousand miles from bases in the United Kingdom. On the evening of 21 February the convoy lost this protection; and, since very-long-range planes were not yet available on the western side of the Atlantic, ON-166 received no more air cover until the night of 24 February. In the meantime the wolf-packs got in their dirty work.

The next attack came 21 February at 2135 at lat. 49°07′ N, long. 28°52′ W. Probably seven submarines were involved.[43] After six had been driven off, the seventh made a torpedo attack and hit

[43] Analysis of ON-166 prepared by Lt. Cdr. Folger at A/S W Unit Atlantic Fleet.

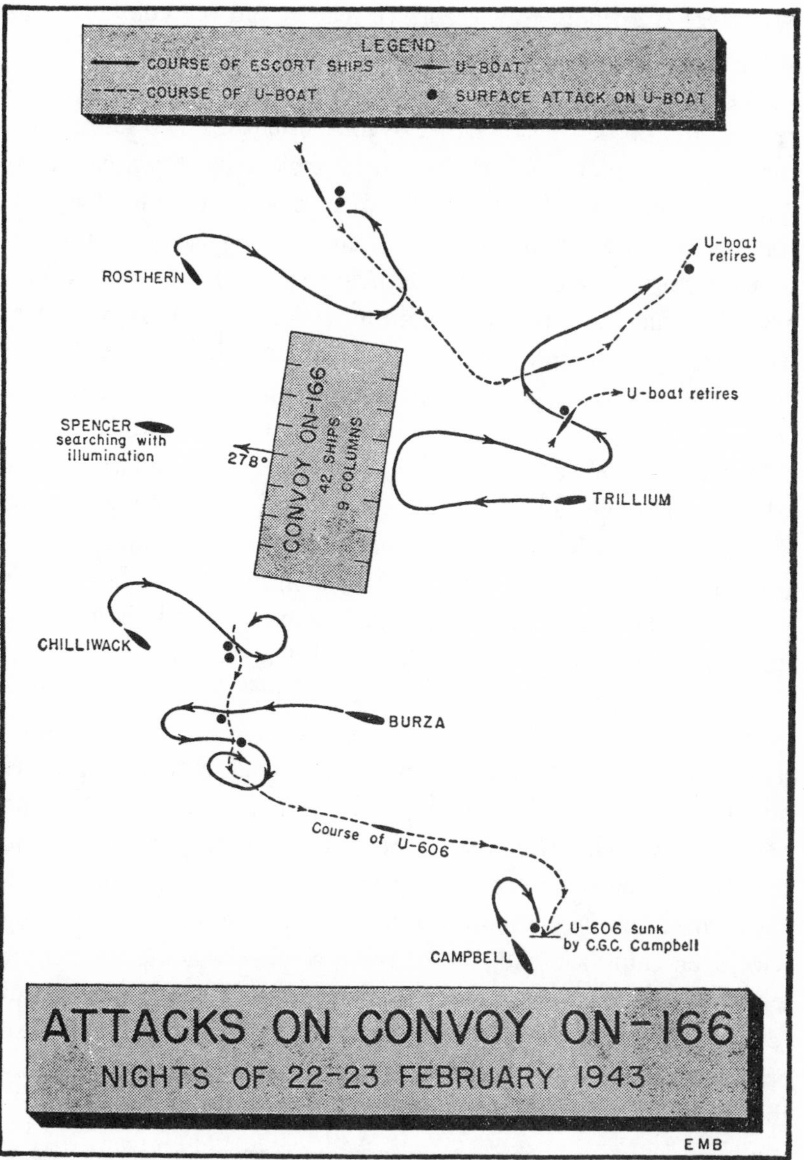

ATTACKS ON CONVOY ON-166
NIGHTS OF 22-23 FEBRUARY 1943

S.S. *Empire Trader*, leading ship in the second column.[44] At this time there were only four escort vessels around the convoy [45] and no U-boat was detected by them.

This attack was followed up about six hours later by the torpedoing of another freighter. At 0730 February 22 two submarines were sighted astern of the convoy, attacked by *Campbell* with depth charges and by *Dianthus* with hedgehog. The harassed convoy, now consisting of 42 ships and making 9 knots, was left alone during the day, but it was being trailed by *U-606*, which had been fueled and provisioned at sea only eight days before. At 2125, an hour and a half after sunset and 30 minutes before moonrise, *U-606* torpedoed three ships on the left flank of the convoy. *Chilliwack* sighted it when retiring and delivered a depth-charge attack, but failed to regain contact. *U-606* shifted rudder after submerging, and was then picked up by the sound gear of *Burza*, the Polish destroyer which had just joined the convoy. *Burza* (described by *Campbell's* men as "the fightin'est ship they'd ever seen") closed fast and depth-charged twice. The submarine dove to 130 fathoms, where it was ascertained that the pressure hull was ruptured; and, on the statement of the engineering officer that it could not float another half hour, all tanks were blown. *U-606* then surfaced at a steep angle. Badly damaged and running blind on the surface, it was sighted by *Campbell*, whose commanding officer set a collision course to ram. The German turned just in time for its hydroplanes to strike the cutter a glancing blow which cut a large hole in the hull. *Campbell* in the meantime was firing with everything she had, the German skipper was killed, and the senior officer on deck ordered abandon ship. Twelve men out of 48 were rescued by boats from *Burza* and *Campbell*. The United States cutter lay dead in the water for several hours, screened by the Pole, but finally made port.[46]

[44] *Empire Trader* did not sink right away and *Dauphin* was to escort her to the British Isles. Later orders from the Admiralty caused her to be abandoned and sunk.

[45] *Spencer*, *Campbell* and *Dianthus* had not yet returned from their mission with the plane; *Burza* had not yet joined.

[46] "The Cruise of the *Campbell*," article beautifully illustrated by Lt. Cdr. Anton Otto Fischer USCG in *Life* 5 July 1943. A curious circumstance of this attack was

The wolf-pack was not yet through with ON–166. At about three hours before sunrise 23 February, two or three U-boats came in on the other flank of the convoy, but depth-charge attacks by *Rosthern* and *Trillium* drove them away.

It was too rough for fueling at sea, and H.M.S. *Dianthus* was now so short of oil that she peeled off before midnight 23 February in order not to be an encumbrance. Two days later, reported her commander, the men "emptied 120 gallons of Admiralty Compound into Number 6 tank, also all gunnery oil, paint mixing oil, and two drums of special mineral oil. This increased fuel remaining by approximately half a ton, and eventually enabled me to get in." Apparently only the castor oil in the sick bay was overlooked. *Dianthus* coasted into Harvey's Wharf, St. Johns, with every tank bone-dry.

Three more U-boats came in on ON–166 before dawn 24 February, and sank one ship. The sixth and last attack came two hours before sunrise on the 25th, and cost one more merchant vessel. During these final attacks, *Spencer* thrice avoided torpedoes. All U-boats approached the convoy surfaced under cover of darkness, but were detected by radar. Considering the small number of high-speed escorts for so large a convoy, Captain Heineman's unit did exceptionally well; it lost seven merchant ships but killed two U-boats. And its success in anticipating attacks by high-frequency direction-finder bearings encouraged the further development and use of that device.

Plucky Escort Unit A–3 had barely tasted the uneasy shelter afforded by Argentia Harbor when it was ordered to sortie and take charge of Convoy SC–121. March is usually the worst month for wind in the North Atlantic, and this was no exception. Continuous westerly gales for nine days, frequent snow and hail squalls, with intermittent high and low visibility, made operations hazardous and signaling difficult. The British convoy commodore, who lost his life, had formed the 56 ships into 14 columns, making a front

---

the denial by survivors of any collision. The probable explanation is that *U–606* was getting so banged-about that a mere collision did not strike the crew as being anything different from a depth charge.

seven miles long, which added to the difficulties of patrolling; and it was too rough to attempt to close up.[47] There was constant straggling owing to the heavy weather, and every night the ships became widely scattered. Captain Heineman's escort unit was feeling the strain of constant service in winter weather. Half the ships' radars were out of commission, and three had defective sound gear; the steering gear of H.M.C.S. *Dauphin* broke down so that she fell out of the screen, and the flagship's communication system conked out during an attack. The Navy Liberator squadron based on Iceland bravely flew out air coverage daily, but the U-boats evaded. Three times between midnight 6–7 March and midnight 9–10 March, on the stretch between the meridians of Cape Farewell and eastern Iceland, this unfortunate convoy was set upon by wolf-packs; [48] at least seven ships were torpedoed and all but one sunk, with unusually heavy loss of life.[49] The sea was so rough that even the veteran personnel of U.S.S. *Greer* on one occasion could not pick up survivors from lifeboats and rafts, and had to let them go. The merchant crew of the American S.S. *Malantic*, one of those torpedoed in the first attack, "behaved with extraordinary calmness and executed orders splendidly; the Armed Guard commander displayed courage, efficiency, and a willingness to coöperate of outstanding quality. The second cook lost his life after holding his lifeboat to the rescue ship until all were aboard; then, too exhausted to climb the net, he fell back into the sea and was lost." [50]

Several wolf-packs were concerned in these assaults on Convoy SC–121. Their success was well earned. They attacked at night from periscope depth, to avoid radar contact, and from two or three directions at once. Decoy submarines were used to lure

[47] In ON–166 the number of columns had been reduced by the Commodore from 12 to 9 on 22 Feb., and later to 7.

[48] In addition to the daylight torpedoing of a single "romper" (a vessel that forges ahead, the opposite of a straggler).

[49] From 6 of the ships there were 76 survivors and 199 lost, including the convoy commodore. One of the ships lost was the escort oiler.

[50] Lt. (jg) Robert G. Fulton Intelligence Report on Survivors, filed with SC–121 papers A/S W Unit Atlantic Fleet.

away the escorts by high-frequency direction-finder transmissions; and on one occasion a German broke into their voice-radio circuit with a bogus message. Captain Heineman had five escorts (*Spencer*, *Greer* and three Canadian corvettes) at the time of the first attack, seven during the others (*Bibb* and *Ingham* having joined from Iceland); and it is to their credit that following these four days of danger and discouragement their aggressive counterattacks pulled the rest of the convoy through additional danger without further loss.

Both in this and the next SC convoy (122), which lost nine ships, and in HX–229 which lost 11 ships on 8–10 March,[51] there were numerous acts of heroism and self-sacrifice on the part of merchant seamen as well as coastguardsmen and bluejackets. But it is sad to find instances of the same neglect, indiscipline and carelessness on board merchant ships that had been losing lives needlessly for four years. Lifeboats capsized and their painters parted, boats and rafts were cast off before the torpedoed ship stopped, tillers were missing, insufficient lifelines were rigged, rafts were not equipped with a heaving line to rescue men afloat, expensive lifesaving suits were abandoned, life jackets lacked straps or handles to help a rescuer to pull an oiled-up survivor from the water. The sole survivor of 38 merchant seamen and 24 Naval Armed Guards of the American S.S. *Puerto Rican*, torpedoed and sunk north of Iceland on 9 March, owed his life to going below and putting on his rubber lifesaving suit before abandoning ship. Not far away at the time was the American S.S. *Richard Bland*, a straggler from the convoy, which had been torpedoed. She received her death blow from another submarine only 35 miles off the coast of Iceland on 10 March; over half her crew and Naval Armed Guard managed to reach shore safely.[52] Both these vessels were on the North Russia, not the transatlantic, convoy route; their loss is here mentioned in

[51] A curious thing happened in this convoy. The officers and crew of S.S. *Mathew Luckenbach* were so disgusted at the convoy's not changing course after 5 ships had been torpedoed that they held a meeting and decided to straggle. But the U-boats got her just the same.

[52] Survivor Files A/S W Unit Atlantic Fleet.

order to emphasize what a winter's harvest the U-boats were reaping in a single area of the North Atlantic.

Nobody outside the Navies and merchant marines concerned knew how serious the situation was in March 1943. The U-boats, in this and other areas, sank 41 ships in the first 10 days, and another 44 ships in the second 10 days of March. Over 500,000 tons of shipping gone in 20 days; and 68 per cent of it in convoy. The only compensation was one submarine, *U-633*, sunk by a Liberator of British Squadron 220 out of Iceland on 7 March. So many escorts were under repair that the group organization was in danger of disintegrating. So many U-boats were out (an average of 116 operating daily in the North Atlantic) that evasive routing was futile; a convoy avoided one concentration of wolf-packs only to fall in with another. The enemy never came so near to disrupting communications between the New World and the Old as in the first twenty days of March 1943.[53] Clearly we could not go on losing ships and men at that rate. When convoy after convoy came in with six to a dozen ships missing, the morale of seamen who had to make the next voyage was impaired. The patriotism, the energy, and the sheer guts that kept these men of the merchant service, and of the three escorting Navies, to their allotted task is beyond all praise.

By 21 March, one may say, the crisis had passed. Losses were cut during the rest of the month, and in April there was a distinct improvement.

The most eventful eastbound convoy that month was HX-233, composed of 57 ships in eleven columns, escorted over the Mid-ocean sector by the same experienced unit commanded by Captain P. R. Heineman in *Spencer*. The escort, eight in number, joined the convoy from St. Johns on 12 April. On the 16th *Spencer* attacked on a sound contact without apparent result, and the route was altered to elude a closing wolf-pack. Next day a support force of four British destroyers joined the escort. The convoy had reached the meridian of Reykjavik and the height of Ushant when

[53] Admiralty *Monthly A/S Report* (Red Book) Dec. 1943 p. 3.

General Quarters!

Coast Guard Photos

Depth charge flying from K-gun

Depth charge explodes

U–175 blown to surface

Attack of Spencer *on* U–175, *17 April 1943*

U–175 under gunfire attack . . .

Coast Guard Ph

. . . sinking

German survivors. Stripped of wet clothing, wrapped in blankets, receiving coffee and cigarettes

Burial at sea. J. T. Petrella, RM3 battle casualty. Commander H. S. Bc dine USCG reads service; Captain P. Heineman stands at right

Attack of Spencer, *Gunfire Phase*

Spencer "sighted dark object well ahead." She and H.M.S. *Dianthus* commenced a lively hunt as the day broke fair with a moderate northeast breeze, good visibility, smooth sea accompanied by heavy swell. About sunrise, when the two escorts were still running down their sound contacts about ten miles astern, a freighter was torpedoed. Around noon, when *Spencer* was back patrolling her regular station, she made sound contact on the 750-tonner *U-175*, which was approaching to launch a torpedo attack from within the screen. The cutter made two urgent attacks, dropping two patterns of eleven depth charges each. *U-175* in the meantime had submerged to 38 fathoms. *Spencer* stood down between columns of the convoy, maintaining sound contact, firing mousetrap, and coaching in her sister ship *Duane* among the merchantmen. The submarine, severely damaged by the depth charges, broached 48 minutes after the first contact, about a mile from *Spencer* and *Duane* and in the rear of the convoy. The Naval Armed Guards on the merchant ships and both cutters opened fire with everything they had, and the cutters headed full speed for the enemy. *U-175*, steaming slowly in a circle, returned fire for a short time and fatally wounded one of *Spencer's* crew; but the cutters' fire was so accurate and devastating that before *Spencer* could carry out her intention to ram, the German crew abandoned ship. While H.M.S. *Dianthus* screened them, the cutters recovered 41 survivors, several of whom were hysterical; and *Spencer* sent away a boarding party which had a good look-around before the *U-175* sank.[54]

The position was 600 miles from Lands End, yet within a very few hours plane cover from England arrived over the convoy, and stayed with it day and night. This proved of inestimable value in spotting submarines on the surface, in driving them down and keeping them down. At 0055 April 18, one of the escorting planes reported by voice radio a U-boat submerging about three and a

[54] Position given by Action Report as lat. 47°59′ N, long. 21°12′ W; by Navy press release of 27 June 1946 on enemy submarine losses as lat. 48°50′ N, long. 21°20′ W. The boarding party had been specially trained by Lt. Cdr. John B. Oren USCG for almost a year in order to obtain information from enemy subs and if possible to salvage them.

half miles ahead of the convoy. *Spencer* searched out on the bearing with negative results, and then steamed at full speed between the columns, from one flank of the convoy to the other, dropping depth charges en route; other escorts also dropped charges. This procedure undoubtedly prevented an attack from the submarine approaching from ahead. It was also significant of the training and discipline of these "Treasury" class cutters. A year earlier, no escort commander would have dared dash up and down convoy columns at night, for fear of collision. And, as another result of long sea experience, the ocean escorts fueled 17 times from four different tankers in Convoy HX–233 at the speed of advance, without any damage to their gear. Discipline within the convoy was not so good; two American merchant vessels collided in broad daylight and the crew of one abandoned ship, leaving her to be towed in by a very disgusted Royal Navy tugboat.

3. *Gulf and Caribbean*

The Atlantic and Gulf Coasts of the United States, where over a ship a day had been sunk during the first half of 1942, were relatively free from U-boat attacks after July.[55] The Gulf of Mexico blitz accounted for 16 ships of 65,924 tons in July, some around the Passes of the Mississippi and others in the Straits of Florida; an occasional transatlantic wolf-pack penetrated the Gulf of St. Lawrence and fouled up coastal convoys; but, by and large, sailing along the East Coast in convoy after 1 August 1942 was no longer dangerous. The principal hazards to shipping were convoy collisions and accidental bombing by aviators insufficiently trained in ship recognition; small Navy craft can easily be mistaken for enemy submarines.

An uncommonly saucy U-boat gave Gulf Sea Frontier a final kick in the teeth on 12 August. It attacked a small Key West–

[55] In Canadian Coastal Zone, Eastern and Gulf Sea Frontiers, 201 ships were sunk 1 Jan.–30 June; 50 between 1 July and 31 Dec. 1942; and 5 in the first half of 1943. Cf. Appendix I.

Havana convoy, escorted by two PCs, seven miles south of Sand Key Light. Two Cuban merchantmen were torpedoed and sank immediately, their smoke being visible from the windows of the Key West Sound School. Destroyer *Dahlgren* and other school ships, which were just steaming out for their daily exercises, were promptly organized as a killer group.[56] Thirteen to fourteen ships and numerous planes took part in the hunt, which extended for three days and two nights; but they never made contact with the U-boat.

Optimists who predicted that convoys were "the" answer to submarine activity were themselves answered by what happened in the Caribbean during the second half of 1942. In July, August and September 1942, submarines sank 75 ships, the majority of them under escort, in these waters.

The two principal sore spots were Trinidad and the Windward Passage. In August four or five U-boats conducted a ten-day blitz along the eastern approaches to Trinidad, which resulted in a very serious destruction of tankers on passage between Curaçao and Great Britain, Gibraltar or Capetown. That same month there were 35 sinkings of merchant ships within 250 miles of a rhumb line between Trinidad and Freetown, West Africa.

The experiences of *U-162* in this area are illuminating. This 500-tonner, operating east of Trinidad on an earlier cruise in May 1942, expended all its torpedoes and sank nine unescorted ships. *U-162* then returned to Lorient for the usual month's lay-up, sailed again 7 July, was depth-charged by a British plane in the Bay of Biscay, but effected the Atlantic crossing before 1 August. Off Trinidad it was attacked by Army aircraft of the First Bomber Squadron; no damage. In August off the Bocas and northeast of Trinidad, *U-162* sank three tankers and one freighter, and on the last day of the month fueled from a sister U-boat about to return home. It had a favorite soft spot, a shoal off Tobago, where it lay on the bottom occasionally to give the men a chance to catch up with their sleep. Near dusk on 3 September, when about 50 miles

[56] War Diary *Dahlgren;* conversation with Lt. Thomas W. Nazro, a participant.

to the southward of Barbados,[57] *U–162* made the mistake of taking a crack at H.M.S. *Pathfinder*, who with two other destroyers, H.M.S. *Quentin* and *Vimy*, was proceeding to Port of Spain to pick up a convoy. The torpedo broached and missed. Under these conditions, one U-boat against three well-equipped destroyers having no other duties to distract them, there should have been a sure kill, and there was. Three depth-charge patterns, averaging ten each, spread over a space of five hours, so damaged the submarine that it had to surface, and when *Vimy* turned her searchlight on, the skipper abandoned ship. All but two men were rescued.

There was always close correlation between sinkings and the number of U-boats operating, no matter how great the protection. But anti-submarine measures were a major influence on the number operating, because as soon as they became effective in a given area, Admiral Doenitz pulled his boats out. Thus, the estimated average number of nine enemy submarines operating daily in the Trinidad sector, in September 1942, accounted for 24 sinkings; eight in October got one each; five in December, the same. By January 1943 the estimated number of U-boats operating daily had dropped to three, and there was only one attack that month.[58]

While the east- and southbound tankers were being attacked around Trinidad, those bound to and from New York from Trinidad, Venezuela and Aruba were catching it between Haiti and Cuba. During August 1942, the approaches to this Windward Passage were as dangerous for shipping as any part of the ocean. Ten ships were sunk out of Trinidad–Aruba–Key West convoys that month; but Admiral Doenitz lost one of his veteran U-boats and skippers, *U–94* commanded by Oberleutnant Otto Ites, on its tenth war cruise.

Convoy TAW–15, consisting of 21 ships in seven columns,[59]

[57] Lat. 12°21′ N, long. 59°29′ W. It will be observed that *U–162* spent at least five weeks in its operational area.

[58] "Statistical Report on the A/S Flying Effort in the Trinidad Sector of the Caribbean Sea Frontier 9 August to 30 November 1942," prepared by Combat Intelligence and Statistical Section N.O.B. Trinidad.

[59] Files of TAW–15 at A/S W Unit Atlantic Fleet.

was steaming from Trinidad to Key West. The escort group, typical of that route, consisted of the United States destroyer *Lea*, flying the pennant of Commander J. F. Walsh; the Netherlands armed minelayer *Jan Van Brakel;* Canadian corvettes *Oakville, Halifax* and *Snowberry;* one PC and three SCs of our "Donald Duck Navy." At 2200 August 27, on a clear bright moonlight night with a fresh trade blowing, the convoy was steering north by west in order to round Cape Tiburon, Haiti, and enter the Windward Passage. *U–94* had been waiting there for a week for something to turn up, and had spent all day 27 August dodging Navy flying boats. At last it was about to be rewarded. Convoy TAW–15, a fleet of juicy tankers, came steaming across the path of the moon and Oberleutnant Ites had just maneuvered his boat unobserved inside the screen when a night patrolling Catalina out of Guantanamo, piloted by Lieutenant Gordon R. Fiss, caught him from the rear. The Catalina dropped four 650-lb. depth charges from an altitude of 50 feet, and a flare which revealed the position of *U–94* to the nearest escort, H.M.C.S. *Oakville* (Lieutenant Commander Clarence A. King RCNR). Ites crash-dived as soon as he observed the PBY, but the depth charges blew his bow hydroplanes off, brought him to the surface, and made it impossible to submerge. *Oakville* attacked ferociously with everything she had and on top of that rammed the target three times. U.S.S. *Lea* came in fast and happy, but the game little Canadian neither wanted nor needed assistance. Ites fought back, but after the third ramming found his engines so damaged that there was no chance of escape, and ordered abandon ship – *Alle Männer aus dem Boot.* Commander King then laid *Oakville* alongside and sent a boarding party away. They shot two Germans who acted ugly, and had a good look-around before *U–94* sank. Twenty-six of the survivors were rescued and taken to Guantanamo by *Oakville*, too heavily damaged by the ramming to rejoin the convoy. While this fight was going on, another U-boat that nobody sighted or even contacted sank two ships and damaged two more out of the convoy. But the Catalina and the corvette had shown how to make a coördinated air-surface attack.

The first kill off the Guianas was *U-512*, a 750-tonner, on 2 October 1942. This new submarine was on its first war cruise. Sailing on 15 August from Kristiansand, Norway, it entered the Atlantic between Iceland and the Faeroes, passed the Azores, and on 12 September sank the unescorted 11,000-ton tanker *Patrick J. Hurley* at about lat. 26° N, long. 46° W. On 2 October, when proceeding on the surface about 50 miles north of Cayenne, *U-512* was surprised by a Trinidad-based Douglas B-18A of the 99th United States Army Bombing Squadron, which dropped four bombs and made two direct hits. The boat blew all tanks but settled rapidly and hit the bottom at a depth of 23 fathoms. The crew collapsed from the effects of chlorine gas and high pressure. Three men escaped by the torpedo loading hatch, but only one reached the rubber raft dropped by the plane; he was picked up by U.S.S. *Ellis* ten days later.

One U-boat in this area was literally hounded to death in a series of actions which offer a beautiful example of an efficient radar-equipped air patrol, combined with surface ships and good intelligence.[60] On the evening of 2 March 1943 Convoy TG-4 outbound from Trinidad to Guantanamo was pounding along at five knots down wind, just clear of the Bocas. About 30 miles in its rear a Douglas Army Air Force bomber, returning to base at an altitude of 2000 feet from a protective sweep over this convoy, made a radar contact at 17 miles' range. The pilot changed course to run it down, and at a point about 15 miles north of the Paria Peninsula, and 20 miles from the Bocas, sighted in the afterglow a surfaced U-boat chasing the convoy at 10 knots. He turned back and released two depth bombs from an altitude of 100 feet just as the conning tower went under, circled the area for ten minutes, and then, being low on gas, returned to Trinidad. An hour and a half later, at 2040, a second Douglas bomber arrived to take up the hunt, and made a radar contact at 8 miles, near the position

[60] "Statistical Report on the A/S Flying Effort in the Trinidad Sector" 1-31 Mar. 1943, prepared by C. I. & S. Section Joint Operation Center N.O.B. Trinidad 7 Apr. 1943.

of the first attack. Approaching with landing lights on to help identify the target, this B–18B drew the enemy's fire, and was obliged to evade, thus losing contact. The pilot then began a box search, and at 2310 made another radar contact at 11 miles' range, about the same distance from the last attack. He ran in on the target, but in the dark of the moon could not gauge his glide with sufficient accuracy to release bombs. On a fourth run, however, two depth bombs were released from an altitude of about 200 feet on the surfaced sub, which was then making 15 knots. They straddled its stern, but no evidence of damage was observed. The submarine when last sighted was heading for home, away from the westbound convoy.

At 1600 the following day, 3 March, U.S.S. *Nelson*, escorting Convoy TO–1 about 60 miles NE of Tobago,[61] heard torpedo propeller noises. She instituted a box search, made a good sound contact at 1700, attacked with a nine-charge pattern; and shortly after a heavy diesel-oil slick appeared on the surface, where the depth is over 1000 fathoms. Three more contacts were made and three more depth-charge attacks delivered; the search was abandoned at 2000.

Intensive air and surface sweeps were now sent out from Trinidad, but no further contact was made until 8 March. Shortly after noon a Navy Catalina of Squadron VP–53 was just returning from the extreme limit of its sweep at a position 340 miles due east of Barbados,[62] altitude 4500 feet, speed 115 knots and excellent visibility. It sighted a fully surfaced submarine eight miles away, proceeding on an easterly course. This was *U–156*, probably the same boat that had been attacked five and six days earlier. By clever maneuvering behind clouds the Catalina was able to pull a complete surprise on the submarine; some of its men were caught sunning themselves on deck. Diving at a 45-degree angle from 1200 feet, and flattening out to 30 degrees, the plane released

[61] Lat. 11°37′ N, long. 59°21′ W. This was about 150 miles from the last attack.

[62] Lat. 12°38′ N, long. 54°39′ W. This was 400 miles NE of the Naval Air Station, Trinidad, and 275 miles ENE of the scene of *Nelson's* attack.

from an altitude of 100 feet four 350-pound Torpex bombs in salvo, two of which straddled the conning tower. *U-156* broke into three sections and sank at once. Eleven men were seen to be clinging to wreckage, the plane dropped emergency rations and a life raft, and at least five of the crew were seen to reach it. Although the Navy searched for them assiduously for several days, these survivors were never recovered.

4. *Central Transatlantic Convoys*

The 8th of November 1942 was D-day for Operation "Torch," when American troops landed on the Atlantic coast of Morocco, and also in the Mediterranean.[63] All shores and seaports of the French Empire in Africa west of Tunis, including Casablanca and Dakar, the only two harbors between Gibraltar and the Gulf of Guinea, were in Allied hands by mid-November.

This North African campaign affected the anti-submarine war in several ways. The concentration of Royal Navy ships in and R.A.F. planes over the Mediterranean, to cover the Center and Eastern Task Forces which invaded North Africa at Oran and Algiers, resulted in the loss of six U-boats in the Mediterranean in November. The newly won air bases at Agadir, Casablanca and Port Lyautey, where both Army and Navy began basing bombers as early as 10 November, and naval control of Casablanca, enabled British and American patrol craft and planes to push submarines away from the West Coast of Africa.[64] During the American landings, German U-boats operated as close inshore as they could find sufficient water, and two of them did considerable damage among anchored transports. *U-173*, the submarine that sank transport *Joseph Hewes* and torpedoed destroyer *Hambleton* and tanker *Winooski* on 11 November, was itself sunk by destroyers off Casablanca five days later; but *U-130*, which sank three United States

[63] See Volume II of this History.

[64] Later the French took charge of surface coverage and coastal convoys along this frontier.

Transports on the 12th, escaped for the time being.[65] After air cover had been provided in the shape of Liberators, Catalinas and medium-range Army bombers, there were no more sinkings within 200 miles of the coast, and the Moroccan Sea Frontier became relatively safe. Allied control of the Straits also made it possible, in 1943, to establish a Liberator patrol of planes equipped with the magnetic airborne detector (MAD), which almost closed the Straits to enemy submarines.

On the other hand, as the Mediterranean had now become the seat of offensive land operations, enormous additional quantities of war materiel and oil derivatives had to be transported thither across the Atlantic or from the United Kingdom. These operations took the best escorts, and a large part of our diminished tanker fleet. So much oil and gas were consumed by Army vehicles in North Africa, and by Allied ships and planes in the Mediterranean, that the oil stocks in the United Kingdom became dangerously depleted. Consequently, in December 1942 plans were made for establishing a new set of transatlantic tanker convoys from America to Great Britain and Gibraltar. Mr. Churchill considered the subject so important that he transmitted this proposal directly to President Roosevelt on 12 December 1942.[66]

The Premier's proposal was to institute direct tanker convoys every twenty days between Curaçao or Aruba and the United Kingdom, "by which we should hope to improve our imports by 100,000 tons a month." He recommended that fast tankers be sent unescorted from New York to Casablanca, and insisted that the normal carriage of oil from the United States Navy pool in New York to the United Kingdom must be maintained.

All this and more was accomplished. Three new transatlantic convoy routes were instituted in January 1943 particularly to protect tankers – (1) Curaçao–Aruba to United Kingdom and return (CU–UC); (2) "Oil-Torch" (OT–TO)[67] between Curaçao–

[65] See Vol. II of this History.

[66] Prime Minister to President of U. S., No. 234.

[67] This designation was originally used for Aruba–Trinidad convoys, but discontinued 1 July 1942.

Aruba and Casablanca–Gibraltar; and (3) New York or Norfolk to Casablanca and return (USG–GUS). On 20 March northern transatlantic convoys were placed on a ten-day cycle in order to release escorts for these southern ones. Thus three new Central Transatlantic convoy routes were added to the two much battered northern ones that had been going for four years. The Royal Navy coöperated in escorting the first, but the other two were under the complete control of the United States Navy.

The new transatlantic convoys were highly successful in getting the oil across. The only one that suffered loss during the first three months of 1943 was Convoy UC–1 from the Bristol Channel to Curaçao, consisting of 33 ships, mostly tankers in ballast, escorted by six British sloops or corvettes, together with a support group of four United States destroyers, *Madison*, *Charles F. Hughes*, *Hilary P. Jones*, and *Lansdale*. Speed of advance was ten knots. This convoy had reached a point beyond air protection, about halfway between Tenerife and the Azores, when five tankers were torpedoed during the night of 23–24 February 1943. Fortunately a tanker in ballast is difficult to sink, and one Britisher and one Dutchman managed to stay with the convoy; but the American *Esso Baton Rouge* and two others went down.

Next day the convoy heard from London that direction-finder bearings indicated as many as ten submarines were estimated to be in its vicinity. At nightfall the escort took positions according to this diagram. *Hilary P. Jones* sighted a U-boat's conning tower about 75 yards abeam and dropped a full pattern as it dived, but missed. Later the same night she opened fire on a second submarine at 1600 yards' range, but again missed, and then made a third attack, on radar contact. Although the sea was smooth and conditions almost ideal for the submarines, the aggressive escorts drove the U-boats off, and convoy UC–1 reached Curaçao without further damage. That losses were kept so low was due largely to the excellence of the American-type radar, and to the fine work of the American destroyers – "No escort group has ever been better supported," said the British escort commander.

From the last week of October 1942, a stream of troop convoys including merchant vessels capable of 14 knots or over left Hampton Roads for Casablanca and the Mediterranean. No damage was done to any one of them. Convoy GUS–3, a fast convoy returning from Casablanca, consisted of 24 ships in seven columns, escorted by U.S.S. *Philadelphia*, *New York* and several destroyers. By 3

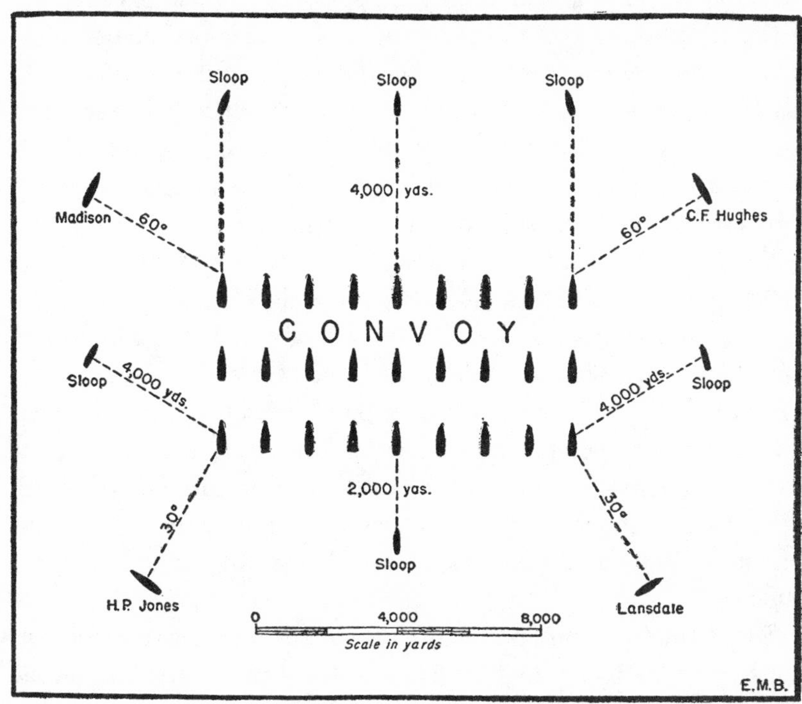

January 1943 it had reached mid-ocean. Sea was calm and the night clear. U.S.S. *Earle*, whose skipper, Commander H. W. Howe, had made one of the earliest kills of the war as captain of U.S.S. *Roper*, picked up a submarine on radar contact, opened gunfire on searchlight illumination, and claimed at least two hits before the target dove. *Earle* and *Parker* depth-charged and hung on for as much as ten hours, when they had to retire in order to catch up with the convoy. That submarine, which undoubtedly escaped, was probably an Italian; but the following night *Earle's* sorrow was turned to joy when she spotted on her SG radar screen an object at 8700 yards that turned out to be a German U-boat.

The action that followed was described by Rear Admiral Deyo, Commander Destroyers Atlantic Fleet, as "a classic example of aggressive action in which radar control was used to best advantage." [68] *Earle* verified the contact and commenced tracking at once. Searchlight and all gun-mounts were placed in automatic. Computer solution showed target to have a speed of 14 knots on course 200°; convoy course was 275°. At 2355, having closed to 3300 yards, *Earle* turned to starboard in order to unmask her port battery, and when steady on the new course turned on a large searchlight. It revealed a clear silhouette of a large surfaced submarine, turning left. Fire was opened immediately by main and machine-gun batteries, and, after ten seconds, one torpedo was fired, aimed at the conning tower and set for 30-foot depth and 46 knots. By midnight, when cease-firing was ordered, 34 rounds of 5-inch, three of 40-mm and 360 of 20-mm ammunition had been expended, and at least twelve 5-inch hits were observed around the sub's conning tower. The FD radar operator was able to follow the 5-inch shots right to the target. Just before gunfire ceased the submarine disappeared. Shortly after it surfaced momentarily, and then apparently disintegrated under a torpedo hit. Nevertheless this submarine, too, escaped.[69]

Submarines seldom approach dangerously near a troop convoy, but there were plenty of slow convoys for them to attend to on the North Africa route. Yet surprisingly little damage was inflicted. S.S. *City of Flint,*[70] *Julia Ward Howe* and *Charles Cotesworth Pinckney*, stragglers from Convoy UGS-4 (United States-Casa-

[68] Comdeslant to Cominch, 18 May 1943, recommending a reassessment of this attack, which had been evaluated as only "probably damaged." The employment of radar so increased that six months after this attack it was a commonplace for escorts to open fire on radar contact alone.

[69] The writer when first recording this action believed that an injustice had been done to *Earle* by Cominch's assessment "probably damaged," for the commanding officer of a transport in the convoy believed he saw the submarine disintegrating under the torpedo hit, and the *Earle's* illumination revealed wreckage. But German records indicate no submarine sunk at that time and place.

[70] This terminated the career of that old Hog Island freighter, famous for her participation in a diplomatic incident early in the war. On 9 October 1939, while

blanca) were sunk by a wolf-pack on 27 January 1943 when 300 miles from the Azores; the captain of one U-boat boasted that the *Julia* was his thirtieth victim. The Naval Armed Guard on the *Pinckney* opened fire and forced one submarine to dive, but another got her.[71] The survivors were picked up by a Portuguese destroyer and taken to Ponta Delgada, whence they were returned to the United States.

These central transatlantic convoys had the pick of available escorts, task forces made up of United States destroyers, including many that had taken part in the North African operation. Slow eastbound convoy UGS–6, consisting of 45 ships laden with valuable strategic materials, with an all-destroyer escort (U.S.S. *Wainwright, Trippe, Champlin, Rowan, Mayrant, Rhind, Hobby*) commanded by Captain Charles Wellborn Jr., reached the vicinity of the Azores on 12 March depleted by two ships as a result of collision.[72] All these destroyers were equipped with three types of radar (SG, SC and FD), and at least one QC projector. None had high-frequency direction-finders, but the cross-bearings obtained by such instruments made it possible for Cominch to send out fairly accurate reports of shadowing U-boats. As a result of the first of these reports, and on orders of the Commander in Chief, course was changed on 12 March in order to pass to the northward of the Azores. Other evasive course changes were frequently employed. The destroyers made frequent high-speed sweeps away from the

---

on a voyage from New York to the United Kingdom, she was seized by a German cruiser who alleged she was carrying contraband and placed a prize crew on board. Instead of proceeding directly to a German port, the *Flint* was taken to Murmansk because of unspecified sea damage. The Soviet authorities made no effort to restore the ship to her American owners and she sailed under the German crew. She called at a Norwegian fjord on the way south to Germany and there the Norwegian authorities properly interned the German prize crew and returned the command to the American master on 3 November. Joseph A. Gainard, *Yankee Skipper: the Life Story of the Captain of the City of Flint* (1940), describes this eventful voyage.

71 Ens. L. Z. Carey USNR, Armed Guard Officer, displayed "exemplary courage," and William Bohn, ship's radioman, carried his radio over the side and supported it in the water for 45 minutes before being picked up; this radio sent messages to the Portuguese destroyer that rescued the survivors.

72 An unescorted Norwegian freighter fouled the convoy, sinking herself, damaging one of the ships in convoy, and taking out a second which remained to rescue survivors.

convoy to break submarine contacts. Convoy discipline was excellent, and the speed of advance was nine knots; yet, lacking air cover,[73] the convoy was constantly shadowed from 12 to 18 March. More and more U-boats moved up to intercept, four torpedo attacks were made, and four ships (one a straggler) were sunk. Several times the escort protected the convoy by attacking on radar or sighting contact, but on every occasion but one the enemy escaped; at that occasion *Champlin* sank *U-130*,[74] the submarine that had sunk U.S. transports *Edward Rutledge*, *Tasker H. Bliss* and *Hugh L. Scott* exactly four months earlier, on 12 March. The U-boat tactics were to make a high-speed approach submerged, fire torpedoes from periscope depth about sunset, retire at high speed submerged and recharge on the surface during darkness. The escort commander justly observed that, unless air cover from the Azores, or an escort carrier, or more destroyers could be provided for these New York–Casablanca convoys, losses could hardly be avoided.

Conditions for abandoning ship and rescue were infinitely better, along this southern transatlantic route, than in northern waters. Instead of gale-force westerlies, high-breaking seas and ice-cold water, you had horse-latitude calms and light trade winds, moderate seas, and water in which a man could live for several days. Many of the sinkings, moreover, took place so near the friendly Azores and local shipping that survivors had a good chance. From Convoy UGS–6, only 6 men were lost out of 268 in the three vessels sunk.

5. *North Russia Convoys*

a. *Tuscaloosa's* Mission[75]

After the sad experience of Convoy PQ–17 in July 1942, the British Admiralty refused to route another convoy to North Russia

[73] Continuous air cover was provided from just before sundown 17 March, a few minutes before the last enemy attack.

[74] Position lat. 37°10′ N, long. 40°21′ W. For the earlier exploits of *U-130* see Volume II of this History.

[75] Report by Captain Gillette on Operation E–U, CTF 99 to Commander in Chief Home Fleet 31 August 1942; conversations with Captain Gillette.

until September, when days were shorter. In the meantime "Uncle Joe" sent an urgent plea to Uncle Sam for food, materiel, planes and munitions that the Russian Army could not do without. So the United States Navy came through with the goods. A task force composed of heavy cruiser *Tuscaloosa* commanded by Captain Norman C. ("Shorty") Gillette, screened by destroyers *Emmons* and *Rodman*, played merchantmen and did the trick. This was called Operation "Easy-Unit."

At Greenock on the Clyde on 12 August, *Tuscaloosa* loaded 300 tons of cargo for Russia, including ammunition, pyrotechnics, radar equipment, medical supplies, dry stores, provisions and 36 torpedoes. Seven British naval officers, four officers of the Royal Air Force and 167 ratings of the two services shipped as passengers. Each destroyer took on board 20 tons of R.A.F. provisions and 19 tons of general supplies.

The task group sailed 13 August, called at Scapa Flow, arrived at Seidisfjordur in Eastern Iceland 19 August, and departed the same evening for Kola Inlet, with H.M. destroyers *Onslaught*, *Martin* and *Marne* added to the screen. A German reconnaissance plane sighted the group on the evening of 20 August and apparently reported its position. Course was changed and poor visibility helped concealment. *Tuscaloosa* broke radio silence to report the sighting to Commander in Chief Home Fleet, hoping that this would be interpreted by the enemy as routine patrol procedure. And, as Captain Gillette remarked, "God sent a fog" which concealed the ships for the rest of this anxious voyage. Two British and one Soviet destroyer met the group outside Kola Inlet, and escorted them into Vaenga Bay on 23 August. Their arrival had been timed to allow for unloading and fueling during that period of the day when the Luftwaffe was generally grounded, and fortunately it kept schedule. Excellent arrangements had been made by local Soviet authorities and British liaison officers for discharging cargo and all hands turned to with a will to get their lethal load on the beach. This was accomplished by 0700 next morning, 24 August, and at 0749 Group "Easy-Unit" departed, after taking some 240 convoy survivors on board *Tuscaloosa* and another 300 men, including four Russian diplomats, in the five destroyers.

On the return passage, the three British destroyers peeled off to intercept a German minelayer, and sank her. The rest of the group was shadowed by reconnaissance planes, but no attack developed; and all arrived safely at Seidisfjordur 28 August 1942.

A neat mission, well executed.

b. Convoy PQ–18

By September the Admiralty felt it safe to resume regular North Russia convoys. Convoy PQ–18 of 33 merchantmen escorted by five destroyers and five armed trawlers was made up at Loch Ewe and departed 2 September. The Admiralty had learned a lesson from PQ–17, and this time incorporated all the combat ships it could spare in the escort itself. So on 7 September off Iceland the escort was considerably augmented until it comprised H.M. escort carrier *Avenger* (Commander A. P. Colthurst RN) with about 15 planes on board, anti-aircraft cruiser *Scylla* (the flagship of Rear Admiral Burnett), 24 destroyers, two submarines and a number of smaller craft.[76] Two oilers accompanied the convoy and two more were stationed at Lowe Sound, Spitsbergen, to assist. There were several alarms of aircraft and submarines, but the first definite contact was made by a German patrol plane on 12 September.

Two ships were sunk by a submarine's torpedoes next morning. The first major air attack came that afternoon, 13 September, when the convoy was west of the southern cape of Spitsbergen. A number of high-level planes attacked ineffectively. These were followed at an hour's interval by 30 to 40 low-flying torpedo planes, Junkers 88s and Heinkel 111s, which split into three sections when approaching line abreast like "a huge flight of nightmare locusts." The escort threw up heavy anti-aircraft fire – apparently a surprise to the

[76] Cdr. Colthurst Action Report. H.M. escort carrier *Audacity* had performed similar duty the previous autumn but was sunk escorting a Halifax–Greenland convoy in December 1941.

enemy; this was the first time he had encountered a convoy whose armament was really adequate to the task. Such planes as penetrated the barrage came in to suicidally close ranges, even to 40 feet it was reported, before dropping torpedoes. The attack might have been met more successfully had the carrier planes not been still chasing the earlier flight of high-level bombers, for Hurricanes had proved to be one of the convoy's best defenses. Lieutenant (jg) Wesley N. Miller USNR, commanding the Armed Guard on board S.S. *St. Olaf*, reported: –

> The ring of destroyers, the flak cruisers and the merchant ships gave them everything they had from a thousand guns. The noise was deafening. The aircraft carrier was trying desperately to get in position for the Hurricanes to take off into the wind. On and on came the torpedo planes in an unending line. They darted up, then down, to confuse the aim of our gunners. Some of the typical torpedo planes were painted solid black with the tips of their wings painted orange or green. They were weird and awful to behold. . . .

The convoy commander's signal for an emergency 45-degree turn was not heard by the two starboard columns and the enemy planes concentrated on them, sinking 8 ships in the outer column. Late afternoon brought another but unsuccessful attack by a few Heinkel 115s. The Germans lost 8 torpedo planes in the three attacks.

A tanker was torpedoed by a submarine about 0300 September 14, and had to be sunk. Warning of approaching planes was given by the convoy commodore about 1300 that afternoon. The carrier with two destroyers crossed from the starboard to the port front of the convoy, to launch her Hurricanes, and a fierce action ensued, which is vividly described by Lieutenant (jg) R. M. Billings USNR, commanding Naval Armed Guard of S.S. *Nathanael Greene:* –[77]

> At 1337 upwards of 25 torpedo planes attacked the port flank of the convoy and some of them went for the aircraft carrier. At about 1355 a swarm of torpedo planes were sighted near the water in front of the convoy, on the starboard side. We fired an eight-second fuse-

[77] Other good reports from the same convoy are by Lt. (jg) B. B. Upchurch of S.S. *White Clover*, and by Lt. (jg) J. L. Laird USNR of S.S. *Virginia Dare*.

nosed projectile at them from the 3-inch gun. Luck was sitting in the pointer's seat for we got a direct hit on the leading plane and it blew up. The planes circled and came in directly at us, and we opened fire with everything we had. The planes split up right off our port bow and some of them passed ahead of us at not more than 100 feet, and the rest went down the port side. One plane crossing our bow received a direct hit from our 3-inch gun and crashed in the water. Two more planes were shot down by our machine-gun fire as they went down the port side, and another plane was shot down on the starboard side. . . . The planes were so close you couldn't miss with a machine gun. A parachute was dropped off our port side by one of the planes. At that time the ship experienced a terrific explosion. My helmet and phones were blown off and much debris was dropping all over the ship. I had seen four torpedoes dropped by planes off the bow and thought we had been torpedoed. Boat stations was sounded by the Captain. The wounded and injured were brought to the boats. The Second Mate ordered my men to let go the two forward life rafts, which they did. The engines had been stopped by the Master. The First Assistant Engineer came up from below and said that everything was all right in the engine room. I ordered my men back to their guns. Two had been wounded, five of the merchant crew had received injuries, and one was lost overboard. The British destroyer *Onslaught* came alongside and took off the injured. Several of my men had small wounds which were treated aboard ship. We then resumed the place in convoy that we had temporarily vacated. The Captain, George A. Vickers, should be commended for his ship handling and coolness during the attacks and explosion. He dodged four torpedoes that I saw and never gave order to abandon ship. . . .

We discovered upon returning to the convoy that the S.S. *Mary Luckenbach* had blown up about 200 yards off our starboard quarter. I believe that this explosion plus the object on the parachute exploding was responsible for all our damage. All the cargo boxes on deck were smashed by the concussion. About ten doors and some bulkheads were blown down and smashed. . . . The cast-iron ventilators buckled. Shrapnel and scraps were covering the deck. A piece of angle iron penetrated my starboard 4-inch ready box and went through a shell, missing the primer by less than an eighth of an inch. Glass ports were smashed. The hospital aft was practically demolished. The compasses were all out of adjustment. The pointer's platform on the 4-inch gun had completely disappeared, and the pointer's sight was nearly ruined. A side plate about two feet square was found on deck. Bullets were picked up all over the deck – both tank ammunition from the *Luckenbach* and bullets fired at us by the planes. Every splinter shield on the ship had bullet marks on it. Every gun station had been marked by shrapnel and bullets. The ship's hull held up; and as far as we now know, no leaks were sprung. Why everyone topside was not killed or injured seriously, I don't know. It is impossible to put into words the force of the explosion or the amount of debris that hit the ship. . . .

The ship and the crew, including my Navy men, held up 100 per cent. If we had abandoned ship, I believe that the planes would have come back to finish us off, as they had been doing to others. My men never showed the least sign of cowardice. Although scared stiff (and who wasn't?), they obeyed my orders to the letter and kept fighting. No man could be more proud of a group of men than I am of the Navy men and those who were assisting them at their gun stations.

On the morning of 15 September, the British convoy commodore signaled to *Nathanael Greene*, "Reverences to your gunners; you are at the top of the class." He credited the ship with shooting down five planes.

That same morning, a submarine wolf-pack tried unsuccessfully to decoy the screen out of position in order to leave a hole. Afternoon brought a high-level bombing attack. Hurricanes from *Avenger* went up to meet it, ships' anti-aircraft accounted for several, and the convoy suffered no loss. Submarine alarms, with dropping of depth charges, marked 16 September. When darkness fell, the larger escorts peeled off to pick up a southbound convoy, leaving PQ–18 with about ten warships to protect it. This offered the enemy a clear opportunity for attack from his air bases less than 300 miles away. It was an anxious period for the ships.

The convoy was scouted by the enemy as it entered the White Sea on the morning of 18 September, and medium-altitude bombers attacked it ineffectually. Later in the day twelve Heinkel 111s came in and one more ship was sunk by an aërial torpedo. Despite the withdrawal of the carrier and other anti-aircraft protection the German planes were not so daring as before; and four Russian destroyers which joined on the 17th and 18th gave great assistance in discouraging them. The ships reached the Dvina bar off Archangel on 19 September, but their troubles were not yet over; for on that day and the next two they were subjected to high-level bombing attacks which scored many near misses. Finally on 21 September they arrived at Molotovsk. Out of 40 merchant ships the convoy lost 13, ten of them by air attack, and eight of these American.[78]

PQ–18 was the most heavily armed convoy that had made the North Russia run, and it was subjected to the worst air attack suffered on that route. Some merchant ships had as many as eight 20-mm guns in addition to a 3-inch 50-caliber, and they needed every one. Over a hundred torpedo planes and almost the same number of bombers were counted on the three critical days 13–15 September; 24 more torpedo planes and at least as many bombers attacked on 18–20 September. This was the greatest effort the Luftwaffe had made to date, and they paid for the ships they sank at the rate of more than four to one. *Nathaniel Greene* was but one of many merchant ships that turned in a first-rate gunnery performance. Lieutenant Miller, commanding Naval Armed Guard S.S. *St. Olaf*, noted on 15 September: –

I have not slept longer than two hours at night for the past three nights. My food is brought to the bridge. I do not leave even to visit the head. And so it went with the majority of the ship's crew, including the merchant crew. It was 21 hours' duty out of every 24, if one wanted to live. There is 19 hours continuous daylight. The rubber suits are torturing our weary bodies, but they must be endured as the water is cold and ships must be abandoned too quickly to take time to put them on later . . .

Lieutenant (jg) Blake Hughes USNR, Armed Guard commander in the original Liberty ship *Patrick Henry*, laden with high explosives, recorded a gallant message from his men: –

I want to preface the report of our return voyage from Archangel with a tribute to the 23 men under my command, none of whom, with

[78] S.S. *Oliver Ellsworth*, *John Penn* (not to be confused with the transport of that name), *Wacosta*, *Africander*, *Oregonian*, *Mary Luckenbach*, *Kentucky*, and Panamanian *Macbeth*.

the exception of the coxswain, had ever been to sea before, and none of whom had previously been in action . . . At the close of the first day of attack (September 13), when 25 per cent of our ships had been destroyed by submarines and 60 to 70 Heinkel and Focke-Wulf planes, and while we were still at general quarters, I received the following message by phone at my station on the flying bridge: *All the men would like you to know, sir, that their spirits are high and that they are ready for the enemy*. With the picture of a near-by ship completely pulverized in a horrible explosion a few minutes before still before me, I thought those were the most courageous words I ever heard.

c. "Trickle" and Renewed Convoys

Southbound Convoy QP–14, consisting of fifteen merchantmen (two of them American), departed Archangel 13 September 1942 and was picked up off shore by the same escort group that had taken care of PQ–18. Admiral Burnett routed it up the west coast of Spitsbergen, as the state of ice permitted. That took the convoy out of enemy air range, but a pack of U-boats had the enterprise to follow it up, and the anti-submarine air patrol from H.M.S. *Avenger* was unable to keep them down. On 20–22 September they sank a British minesweeper and destroyer (H.M.S. *Somali*), two American merchant ships (*Bellingham* and *Silver Sword*), one British merchantman and a British fleet oiler. None of the guilty U-boats was sunk, although Admiral Burnett's destroyers had reduced the number of the pack just before it struck.[79]

The last North Russia convoys had taken such a beating, and the demand for escorts for Operation "Torch" was so insistent, that the advocates of independent routing, both in the Admiralty and in the Navy Department, obtained a hearing; and what was called the "Trickle" movement was tried out in the late fall, when nights were long. Five American and five British merchantmen were dispatched unescorted from Reykjavik to North Russia, two every day, between 29 October and 2 November 1942. Their only protection

[79] *U-88* sunk by H.M.S. *Onslow* 14 Sept. and *U-457* by H.M.S. *Impulsive* 16 Sept. One submarine, *U-435*, claimed to have sunk five of the six ships lost by this convoy.

consisted of a few trawlers "spaced along the route for lifesaving." Of the four American ships whose reports are on file, one was sunk by a submarine, two survived aërial attacks and got through, and one made the voyage without incident. Out of ten ships of various flags routed northward, four were sunk and one was wrecked. Although of some 30 ships which "trickled" home from Russia between the end of October and 24 January 1943, only one was lost,[80] this experiment was not considered a success; North Russia convoys, redesignated JW and QP, were revived at the period of minimum daylight.[81]

The first northbound convoy of the new series, JW–51A, 16 merchant ships with an escort of eight British destroyers, departed Loch Ewe 15 December 1942. The twelve American ships in this convoy were greatly astonished to have an uneventful voyage. Old Man Winter was the seaman's friend; the Luftwaffe had either been pulled out of Lapland, or had not caught on. Convoy JW–51A delivered over 100,000 tons of cargo at Murmansk and Molotovsk on 25 and 27 December.

Convoy JW–51B, 14 ships escorted by about 15 British destroyers and corvettes, which, with H.M.S. *Sheffield* and *Jamaica* in support, departed Loch Ewe 22 December, was not so fortunate. On the last day of the year, when it had reached a position about 100 miles southeast of Bear Island [82] but before the Support Force had cleared, this convoy was attacked at long range by a German task force consisting of heavy cruisers *Hipper* and *Lützow* and three destroyers. In a confused *mêlée* under the feeble twilight from a sun that never rose above the horizon, with overcast and snow squalls, the British destroyers of the escort stood off the two German cruisers, losing two of their number; but a German destroyer, through mistaking H.M.S. *Sheffield* of the Support Force for

[80] Records in Convoy & Routing Admiralty gives slightly different figures.

[81] The new designation was given because the North Russia convoys no longer called at Reykjavik. American merchantmen destined for Russia crossed in HX or ON convoys to Scotland, and formed up at Loch Ewe. Southbound Russian convoys were designated RA commencing 30 December.

[82] Lat. 74°03′ N, long. 29°38′ E.

Hipper, was sunk with all hands. All the merchant ships arrived safely, except for a Panamanian freighter that ran aground entering Kola Inlet.[83]

A tabulation of the North Russia convoys from their inception in August 1941 through 1942 gives the following figures: in 21 northbound convoys 301 ships sailed, 248 arrived, 53 were lost. In 16 southbound convoys 232 ships sailed, 216 arrived, 16 were lost. About half the merchant ships lost were American; but the Royal Navy paid heavily, losing two light cruisers, four destroyers, four minesweepers and a submarine.[84]

On New Year's Day 1943, Convoy JW–52 was on its way north with 13 merchant ships (five of them American) escorted by seven or eight British destroyers, two corvettes, a minesweeper and two trawlers, later augmented by six more destroyers. This convoy passed safely through floating mines on 20–22 January 1943. Next day it was scouted by an enemy patrol plane, herald of an air attack which developed on the 24th. At 1230 three Heinkel 115 torpedo-bombers, flying in and out of the low-lying clouds, appeared on the horizon. Crossing the rear of the convoy from starboard to port, the enemy apparently picked what they regarded as a hole in the screen and came through in column formation. Lieutenant Richard Stone, commanding the Naval Armed Guard on board S.S. *Cornelius Hartnett*, gives a vivid account of what followed: –

At this time we opened up with the 5-inch 38 at a 6-seconds fuse setting, with the object of keeping them well off if possible. At the same time the escorts opened with a crossfire of what looked like 20-mm. The 3-inch 50 also opened up at this time with an 8-second fuse setting, and followed the leading plane in with 4.8, 4.4, 3.2 and 2.1-seconds fuse settings, a total of 13 rounds, while the 5-inch 38 expended a total of three more 6-seconds fuse settings, with the idea of keeping off the other two planes which were further out.

All the planes came through the escorts safely, and we opened up with the four port 20-mm at a range of between 1400 and 1700 yards.

[83] Admiralty Files; German records of the engagement, translated by British Naval Intelligence Division, 14 Jan. 1946.

[84] Admiralty Files.

At outside 1000 yards the leading plane veered to its left, and there was a definite bluish-white flame on its pontoon. Obviously it had been hit. . . . When the leading plane was broad off our port bow, the 3-inch 50 scored a direct hit at a one-second fuse setting to burst at 750 yards. Marko Jurasevich was gun captain. The plane burst into flames, passed in front of our column leader, and hit the water forward and to the left of column two. It floated down between columns one and two with only its tail showing.

The second plane came in broad on our port beam within 500 to 700 yards into a barrage of 20-mm, and then banked sharply to its left, when it was definitely hit on its fuselage and wings by at least 9 to 12 rounds from the No. 6 20-mm on the flying bridge aft, with Wilbert J. Warren BM 1c firing. Just after it banked, it dropped one or two torpedoes which went ahead of our bow towards ships Nos. 11 and 21, then out ahead of the convoy and slightly to the right, where two destroyers fired at it. It then appeared to go into a snow squall. The plane was smoking when off our port bow. The third plane veered to its right when about 1300 yards out, flew abeam of ship No. 13, and circled to the stern of the convoy, where shots were heard.

This last plane was taken under fire by several other ships and was seen to crash. No damage was suffered by the convoy. From the first sighting of the enemy until the last shot, the action lasted less than 20 minutes. It will be observed that *Cornelius Hartnett* was very heavily armed for a merchant ship, and that her naval gun crew was well trained. Except for one brief and ineffective attack upon a destroyer by a lone enemy bomber on 25 January, the remainder of this voyage was uneventful, and the convoy entered Kola Inlet 27 January without losing a ship.

Convoy JW–53 of 22 ships, eight of them American, escorted by a British cruiser and 20 other warships including eleven destroyers, sailed from Loch Ewe 15 February 1943. It was scouted by patrol planes on the 23d and 24th, and next day an air attack developed. After about four planes had repeatedly circled and crossed the convoy at high altitudes, without dropping bombs, ten or twelve JU–88s or 89s in two waves dive-bombed the convoy. Out of respect for the ships' fire power they pulled out of their dives at 1500 feet altitude or higher, and no damage was done. At about noon 26

February, two waves of six or seven planes flew in and out of the clouds which dotted the sky, and eventually attacked; again the convoy escaped damage. Following the two-section procedure, this convoy reached Kola Inlet 27 February and Molotovsk 2 March. The American ore carrier *City of Omaha* and tanker *Beacon Hill*, which were in JW–53, made several round trips safely between Murmansk and Molotovsk or Archangel, during the months March through August 1943. Russian icebreakers kept the Gorlo Inlet and a channel to Molotovsk open, but the inlet where Archangel is situated froze solid.

The only southbound North Russia convoy of this period that found the going really tough was RA–53, which departed Murmansk 1 March 1943. It consisted of 30 merchantmen, eleven of them American, with about 25 Royal Navy escorts, including three cruisers and eleven destroyers. On the 5th it was subjected to a well-coördinated submarine and air bombing attack, at about lat. 72°45′ N, long. 11°40′ E. Early in the morning reconnaissance planes appeared; about 0930 S.S. *Richard Bland* and *Executive* were torpedoed by a U-boat; the *Executive* was sunk but the *Bland* carried on. Then, at 1430, twelve Heinkel 111s attacked in shallow dives. The convoy threw up a terrific barrage which caused them to drop their bombs ineffectively.

Convoy RA–53 now ran into such heavy weather that it became separated. Twenty-one ships managed to get together and reached Loch Ewe on 14 March, but the *Richard Bland* while proceeding alone was torpedoed by a submarine on the 10th, about 35 miles off Langanes. She floated until three hours later when a second torpedo struck her. In the heavy seas it was impossible to sight the submarine in time for an effective counterattack. Over half the ship's crew of 41 were saved, but 15 members of the Naval Armed Guard of 27, including the commanding officer Ensign E. S. Neely, were lost. Another casualty among the stragglers was the S.S. *Puerto Rican*, sunk 9 March by a U-boat about 287 miles north of Iceland. She went down in 20 minutes; and out of a crew of 38 and a Naval Armed Guard of 24, only one survived to tell the story. Owing to severe weather and ice coating, three of the four ship's boats were frozen in and completely useless. When the fourth reached the water, its after fall could not be released, due to ice coating, and the boat capsized. Eight men swam to a cork life raft and six of them later transferred to a larger raft; but all except one either froze to death or were washed overboard. The sole survivor, a fireman, was rescued 12 March 1943 by H.M.S. *Elistin* and taken to the base hospital at Reykjavik. Both his feet were frozen and had to be amputated.

Liberty ship *J.L.M. Curry*, a casualty of the sea, was the final loss from this trouble-ridden convoy. Pivoted on a huge wave, she broke her back, and had to be abandoned and sunk by the guns of an escort. All hands were saved.

RA–53 was the last southbound convoy to leave North Russia that season, and no northbound convoy arrived after 2 March 1943. Lengthening days were bringing back hazardous conditions. Even before the Germans were cleaned out of Tunisia in April, Allied control of the Mediterranean was well enough secured so that the Gibraltar–Suez–Persian Gulf route from the United States to Russia was preferred. Eight American merchant ships and about the same number of British spent the spring and summer at North Russian ports, and had to await the resumption of North Russia convoys at the close of 1943. At that time a Murmansk-bound convoy could get through with comparative ease.

d. American Seamen in North Russia Ports

Limited port facilities, slow unloading, long waits for the arrival of suitable escorts, and unfavorable weather, were some of the reasons why American and other freighters were forced to lie at North Russian anchorages for weeks and even months before returning south. The Americans did not find the climate particularly severe; Murmansk is in the same winter temperature belt as Chicago. Foul weather, inadequate food and fuel, boredom unrelieved by satisfactory recreation facilities, were the least things against which the bluejackets and merchant seamen had to contend.

The port – noted one Armed Guard commander around January 1943 –

> . . . berths from twelve to thirteen large merchant ships at one time, has many good anchorages; and although its actual technical facilities for unloading are poor, its railways and rolling stock are excellent. These rail lines extend out on every major dock. Cargoes are unloaded from ships into near-by large freight cars by the ship's own winches. Heavy deck cargoes were . . . taken off by the British S.S. *Empire Meteor*, a ship especially fitted out with heavy cranes for lifting tanks. Bomb damage to the docks and shipping facilities, including the Murmansk–Leningrad Railway, has been slight. Several of the docks were badly hit during the summer months, but this damage has been almost completely repaired by Red Army soldiers on leave. The sheds on most of the docks have been demolished, but those that were of vital use have been rebuilt.

Unloading was done by Soviet soldiers on leave, by Russian women, and (with doubtful efficiency) by political prisoners.[85]

The nearest German airfield was about 35 miles away, only seven to ten minutes' flying time, which reduced the amount of advance warning even under the most favorable conditions, and facilitated repeated attacks by small units. Both high-level and dive-bombing were done at night, incendiaries being dropped first in order to start fires as guides. Enemy daytime air activity was largely limited to photography missions and "sneak" dive-bombing. It was an easy matter for enemy aircraft to glide in over the hills and under the Russians' anti-aircraft barrage; there was no time for fighter planes to intercept. Lieutenant Laughlin reported that firing was useless unless Naval gunners waited literally with finger on trigger, for dive-bombers glided in silently at 250 m.p.h., dropped their deadly loads, gunned their engines and pulled out. The American S.S. *El*

[85] Report of Lt. (jg) Herbert L. Laughlin, commanding Armed Guard S.S. *Beauregard*.

Oriente caught it 27 February 1943, and had four casualties in her Naval Armed Guard.

Docks and railroad facilities rather than ships were the principal points of aim, but there were enough direct attacks on anchored ships and vessels discharging to create a feeling of constantly impending death and destruction. S.S. *Dunboyne* manned her anti-aircraft guns 58 times in one month of 1942 at Murmansk. S.S. *Yaka*, during nine days in April, experienced 156 air raid alarms, 48 of which materialized, and in five of which planes attacked her directly and dropped some 50 bombs. She was hit twice, fired about 2500 rounds of .50 caliber, 400 rounds of .30 caliber and a few rounds from her 3-inch gun.[86] S.S. *Capira*, during the 53 days of May and June that she lay off Murmansk, went to general quarters 125 times, and sighted enemy planes during 66 of these alerts. There were 16 bombing attacks in the two days 23–24 June. By that time, half Murmansk was uninhabitable.[87] Even in the short winter days, S.S. *Dynastic* experienced 65 alerts from Christmas Day 1942 to the end of January.

Mines dropped from enemy planes created an additional hazard. On 21 June 1942, S.S. *Alcoa Cadet* was sunk by a mine when at anchor at Kola Inlet, after having discharged her cargo; and S.S. *Steel Worker* was sunk by another 3 June while standing out.

The best course of action for the ships at night was to keep quiet and take it, since the chance of hitting an enemy plane was scant, and a ship's fire revealed her position. Conservation of ammunition and desire to avoid hitting Russian interceptors, which closely resembled German planes, were reasons for not opening fire in the daytime unless a ship were singled out for direct attack.

Owing to the official Soviet attitude of suspicion, so many obstacles were placed in the way of the R.A.F. squadron which the *Tuscaloosa* helped to stage in that they finally pulled out. Owing to Soviet regulations, American bluejackets and merchant seamen were not allowed to assist unloading, no matter how great the con-

[86] Report of Ens. George T. Smith USNR (commanding Armed Guard of *Yaka*)
[87] Capt. Frankel's dispatches of those dates.

gestion. One ship's company, which had been waiting over a month to discharge, met the situation by landing their cargo on an ice floe. As one of them told the writer, "The Russians got *that* stuff onto the beach pretty goddam quick!" The Russian people were grateful, friendly, and hospitable with what they had; but the government tried to canalize personal relations into official channels. Americans invited to private houses had to enter through the cellar bulkhead, and sailors who got themselves girls ashore were chased out periodically by the secret police. The Soviet government maintained clubs at Murmansk, Archangel and Molotovsk for the English and Americans, where they could dance with a corps of interpreter girls of impeccable conduct who were sent up from Moscow. American ships were not allowed to use short-wave radio in port and so were dependent on the Russians for news. Officers were not allowed to travel, even if their ships were detained for months; but the American ambassador to the U.S.S.R., Admiral W. H. Standley, managed after protracted negotiations to bring the detained shipmasters and Armed Guard commanders up to Moscow as his guests.

About the only solace for the rougher elements among detained seamen was vodka, which the local people obtained in great quantities and readily exchanged for food and clothing from merchant ships' storerooms and slop chests. Captain S. B. Frankel, the United States Navy representative in North Russia, did his best to assist shipmasters in keeping rudimentary discipline. "This office," he informed the Navy Department on 30 August 1942, "has intervened in an alarming number of cases of crew troubles beyond the limited capacity of ships' masters to handle. Some of the serious offenses have been refusal to work, absence from ship for several days, theft of food and lifeboat rations for illicit sale ashore, and threatening the lives of officers. . . . Soviet Government extremely loath to arrest foreigners but, upon my insistence and acceptance of full responsibility, have placed crew members of S.S. *Troubadour* and *Ironclad* in 'protective custody.' "

Conversely, the concern expressed in some American quarters lest our seamen become Communists was unnecessary. The Russians made no attempt to propagandize them. An officer of a ship detained there eight months said that he had never heard one seaman, bluejacket or officer evince the slightest interest in the Soviet system; the poverty and drabness of life in North Russia were a sufficient deterrent. Merchant seamen, as on less dangerous routes, were getting increases in their pay and bonuses, which were enormous. In addition to the base pay of $100 per month for a 44-hour week, war bonus of the same amount, and overtime for work on Saturday and Sunday, a common seaman drew $5.00 a day for each day's detention in North Russia, $125 for every air raid to which he was subjected after March 1943, a 17 per cent bonus for handling ammunition, and, on top of that, a $100 bonus from the Soviet government – until "Uncle Joe" got on to the fact that he was tipping marine plutocrats, and stopped it. For one round voyage that included several months' detention in North Russia, the least pay anyone received on a certain American merchantman was $3200.

The National Maritime Union went all out for taking lend-lease goods to Russia, and tried everything possible to induce merchant seamen to see them through; which, though safer waters offered the same lavish pay, most of them did. It must be remembered that no merchant seaman, if sober, shipped for Russia unknowingly; nor could he be ordered to do it, like a Naval Armed Guard. Yet many who did could not, or would not, take it.[88] S.S. *Campfire*, for instance, ran aground in the channel to Archangel 20 September 1942, and her engines were rendered useless by sand clogging the condenser. The master, over the protest of the reserve ensign commanding the Naval Armed Guard, ordered all hands ashore for fear of air bombing. Master, Armed Guard and seven volunteers returned to the ship, the bluejackets manning winches to unload the explosive cargo. When that dangerous duty was over the rest of the crew reported, as they had no desire to remain in Russia.

Fortunately there were many incidents of a different sort. Inadequate port facilities at Murmansk called for the exercise of old-fashioned seamanship, recalling the days when any competent

[88] At least two ships were lost by premature abandoning in PQ-18.

Royal Canadian Navy Photos

H.M.C.S. *Oakville*

H.M.C.S. *Restigouche* seen from *Skeena*

Royal Canadian Navy Photos

shipmaster was capable of heaving down his vessel on a lonely beach and effecting repairs. The American freighter *Deer Lodge* was dive-bombed by six enemy planes while at anchor in Kola Inlet. A near miss aft hove the stern bodily out of water and subjected the hull to a series of violent buckling movements. Prompt action by the Chief, closing the watertight bulkhead to the shaft alley, saved the ship that time. Shifted to an anchorage in shoal water, she was dive-bombed again by seven German planes. Still taking water heavily, and no drydock being available, she was helped by a Russian diver to locate a shoal – where she was safely grounded by filling Number 1 hold and forepeak with water, in order to bring her to a trim parallel to the harbor bottom. There, despite more dive-bombing, repairs were completed by 27 July 1942. "Without the excellent spirit of coöperation and bravery of the ship's complement and Armed Guard," reported Captain Frankel, "she would have remained an abandoned hulk at Murmansk." [89]

In these North Russia ports, British and American seamen were thrown together and, despite the usual exchange of detraction and flourishing of fists, the association was a good thing for Anglo-American relations. "Upon arriving at Archangel," reported Lieutenant (jg) Blake Hughes, "I heard one seaman exclaim, 'If I ever hear anyone knock the Limey navy, I'd knock his block off!' – a sentiment shared by all the men on my ship. The bang-up courageous job done by our British escort has instilled in our men who participated in this convoy a deep respect for the British Navy. As a result of common experiences, relations between American and British men and officers were the most cordial I have ever seen. After a grueling engagement with enemy planes, British destroyers on several occasions steamed up and down our columns, and our men and theirs shouted words of encouragement to one another, waving, wisecracking, making the 'V' and 'Thumbs up' sign. There was something in that which bolstered morale all around."

[89] Report attached to that of Ensign T. E. Delate USNR, commander Naval Armed Guard.

CHAPTER XV

"Deus É Brasileiro"[1]

September 1941–April 1943

BRAZIL'S entry into the war on 22 August 1942 was an event of great importance in naval history. Brazil was the largest and most populous of the South American Republics. Her territorial waters extended from lat. 5° N to lat. 32° S, and she had an excellent small Navy, including several modern minelayers and planes which only needed modern equipment and training to be suitable for escorts. Cape San Roque approaches so close to the bulge of Africa that in unfriendly hands it would have been a serious handicap to the American cause. With Brazil as an ally, and Uruguay friendly, we only needed French North Africa in the Allied camp to bring the Allied nations' influence down to the River Plate in America, and to Cape Agulhas in Africa. It would then be possible to establish a patrol across the "Atlantic Narrows" to catch the German and Japanese blockade-runners.

The background to a happy coöperation between the Brazilian and United States Navies was laid as far back as 1914. On the request of the government a United States Naval Mission was sent to Rio de Janeiro, and Admiral Caperton, an admirable ambassador, arrived in command of a fleet. The functions of this naval mission, which continued with only one short break, were both diplomatic

[1] "God is a Brazilian," a saying in that country to account for the extraordinary good fortune that has attended the Republic. This chapter profits by conversations of Lt. (jg) Salomon with Vice Admiral Ingram and officers of his staff, with Capt. W. S. Macaulay, Chief of U. S. Naval Mission, Rio; Capt. C. J. Rend, U. S. Naval Attaché; Capt. Harold Dodd, Commandant of N.O.B., Rio; and officers on their respective staffs. Files in Recife and Rio were used extensively. Much of the material on the Brazilian Navy was furnished by Capitão de Fragata Olavo de Aranjo at the Ministério de Marinha, Rio de Janeiro. Prof. C. E. Nowell's Vol. XI "Commander South Atlantic Force," in "Administrative History Atlantic Fleet," has also been drawn upon.

and professional; "to cultivate friendly relations between the Brazilian government and ours, based on the mutual interests of the two Navies," and "to increase the efficiency of the Brazilian Fleet so that Brazil could provide effective naval combat assistance in the protection of the Western Hemisphere."[2] Lack of funds prevented much increase of the Brazilian Navy, but the Mission performed its diplomatic function so well that the Navy, in contrast to the Army, was pro-United States from the beginning of hostilities.

Although Brazil was a valuable ally, she was also highly vulnerable. If the Axis, with the collaboration of Pétain and Laval, could control the Atlantic Narrows between Cape San Roque and the Cape Verde Islands, it would be able to cut off the foreign and much of the domestic trade of Brazil. For the interior of that country was still largely undeveloped; civilization and culture were largely concentrated in isolated centers along the coast, between which the only communication was by sea or air. Except in the State of São Paolo, Brazilian railroads were local networks built to serve a single port. Following the 4000-mile coastline south from the Amazon, there was no railway connection between Belem and São Luiz, between São Luiz and Fortaleza, between Fortaleza and Natal, between Recife and Bahia, or between Bahia and Vitoria; and the considerable port of Florianopolis was served by no railroad whatsoever. The dependence of Brazil on coastwise shipping recalled that of the United States before 1850.

South Atlantic Force (later Fourth Fleet) United States Navy evolved from the South Atlantic patrol of 1941. Rear Admiral Jonas H. Ingram, commanding Task Force 3 comprising the four old light cruisers *Memphis*, *Cincinnati*, *Omaha* and *Milwaukee* and five destroyers (*Somers*, *Jouett*, *Davis*, *Winslow*, *Moffett*), sailed from Newport 24 April 1941 to patrol the big triangle of ocean comprised between Trinidad, Cape San Roque and the Cape Verde Islands. For this patrol, which steamed over 81,000 miles in four

[2] Memorandum "Background of Naval Mission Functions," seen at Naval Mission headquarters in Rio.

months, Recife[3] was the natural port of call and replenishment. "This port," wrote Admiral Ingram on 4 September 1941, "is strategically well located for operations off Cape San Roque, which is the most vital strategic point in the South American area. The harbor of Recife cannot be compared with Bahia. In fact Bahia is far superior to Recife as a naval base in every respect, *except position.* The four hundred miles increase in distance makes a great difference."[4] Both ports were promptly made available to the United States Fleet for refreshment, upkeep, fueling and supplies, without any 24-hour limit, which made the somewhat uneventful South Atlantic patrol easier and more effective.

The Brazilian Navy in October 1941 commenced training merchant ships to sail in convoy with their new *Carioca* class minelayers, and sent the *Camaquam* to patrol the northeast coast. She was being relieved by *Camocim* when Pearl Harbor was attacked. Brazil immediately broke diplomatic relations with the Axis and ordered *Camocim*, together with a cruiser, a destroyer and three other minelayers, to patrol the whole coast from Belem (Para) to Santos (São Paolo), with orders to repress any activities in ports or territorial waters, whether by Axis elements or Brazilians, contrary to the interests of the United States.

Natal was chosen as the principal air base in Brazil owing to its strategic location and favorable winds. On 11 December 1941 United States Naval Air Squadron VP–52, consisting of six Catalinas (PBY–5s), arrived and was cordially welcomed by the Brazilian Army Air Force. VP–52 finally grew into Fleet Airwing 16, but the development of the Naval air arm and its fields in Brazil was a long, difficult and delicate task.

Before the war three European companies, Air France, the German Condor and the Italian Lati, controlled all airlines between Brazil and the Old World, as well as airways within Brazil. After the outbreak of war in Europe the Germans and Italians used their

[3] Formerly called Pernambuco.

[4] "Report on Equatorial Area" 29 July and 5 Sept. 1941. In the same report Admiral Ingram tells of unsuccessful attempts of Axis agents to instigate ill feeling between the populace at Recife and our liberty parties.

lines to fly contraband, propaganda and spies between Europe and South America. As airways were very important for a country with so few communications as Brazil, the government refused to suppress these activities. Consequently Pan American Airways formed a subsidiary, the Airport Development Project, which contracted with the Brazilian government to build airfields under the supervision of the United States Army Engineer Corps. It was agreed that Pan American would use them during the war, and turn them over to Brazil six months after it was over; Brazil furnished the land and the United States the funds. But until Pan American was ready to provide air transportation, the German and Italian lines were allowed to operate, and with American gasoline at that. It was a hard bargain; but we had to have air bases in Brazil both for antisubmarine warfare and as links in the shortest air route from America to Africa, India, the Far East, and the Pacific.[5]

Fortunately the Germans were much too busy in the North Atlantic and Caribbean during the first three months of 1942 to send U-boats into the South Atlantic. In the meantime, work on the airfields of Belem, Fortaleza, Recife, Natal, and Bahia was progressing, and on 1 April 1942 Lieutenant Commander Sperry Clark arrived at Natal with land-based Navy Catalinas (PBY–5As) to relieve Squadron VP–52. After the second section of this new squadron, VP–83, had arrived on 13 June, it was able to patrol the entire coast of Brazil in some fashion; but most of the 475 officers and men of the squadron were occupied with base construction throughout the summer and fall of 1942.

In the South Atlantic, 1200 miles east of Recife, lies lonely Ascension Island, a British possession. It had been written off as a possible air base in time of peace, owing to an exceedingly rugged surface; but its strategic position, only 840 miles from the West African coast and athwart the direct air route from the United States to

[5] Lati and Air France ceased operations in June 1940; Condor on 24 Dec. 1941; by the end of Jan. 1942 Condor was nationalized by the Brazilian government and became Serviços Aéreos Cruzeiro do Sul on 21 Nov. 1942. William A. M. Burden *The Struggle for Airways in Latin America* (1943), issued by the Council on Foreign Relations.

South Africa, made the subject worth looking into. Accordingly, U.S.S. *Omaha* and *Sands* visited Ascension in December 1941 with four United States Army officers to make a survey. They reported the construction of a landing field to be feasible, and the 38th Engineer General Service Regiment United States Army was sent thither in two Army transports, escorted by *Memphis*, *Cincinnati* and four destroyers. They arrived 30 March 1942. Landing conditions, exceedingly difficult at best, were rendered almost impossible by foul weather, and by the attitude of the transports' merchant seamen, who refused to work overtime and regarded the bluejackets sent aboard to do their work as "finks." Naval energy and resourcefulness were largely responsible for getting the bulky bulldozers and other materiel ashore;[6] the Army Engineers then turned-to, surmounted every difficulty of construction and had the Ascension field operational by July 1942. It was used primarily as a staging point for planes between the United States and Africa, but eventually played a part in anti-submarine warfare.

Listeners on short-wave radio were grieved to hear from an Italian broadcast on 22 May 1942 that one of their submarines had sunk "an American battleship of the *Maryland* class" off the island of Fernando Noronha; and this was followed up (7 October) by the sad news that the same submarine *Barbarigo* had sunk another "of the *Mississippi* type" with four torpedoes, at lat. 2°15′ N, long. 14°25′ W. No such battlewagons ever were with Admiral Ingram's force, or in these waters; the reports were a complete fabrication. On the strength of them the Italian submarine commander and his crew were received at Bordeaux by the Italian ambassador and lavishly entertained by the Germans.

Enemy submarines sank six ships of 36,000 gross tons during April and May 1942 in waters within 1200 miles of the coast of Brazil. The Brazilian Lloyd steamer *Commandante Lyra*, torpedoed, abandoned and left burning off Cape San Roque on 18 May, was boarded by a salvage party from U.S.S. *Omaha* and towed into Fortaleza by seaplane tender *Thrush*. Although the guilty U-boat

[6] "Administrative History Atlantic Fleet" X 152–53.

evaded every attack delivered by ship or plane, this seamanlike rescue and salvage operation won golden opinions for the Navy in Brazil and, incidentally, a donation of $50,000 from the *Lyra's* owners to the Navy Relief Society.[7]

Hitler decided at a conference with Admiral Raeder on 15 June 1942 to launch a real U-boat blitz against Brazil. A group composed of eight 500-tonners and two 700-tonners was dispatched from the French outports early in July. At a designated point off the northeast coast of Brazil they met a "milch cow," *U-460*, and fueled; then took up stations close to the Brazilian coast.[8] The first week of August was a favorable moment for them to operate in the South Atlantic because Convoy AS-4, escorted by ships of Task Force 3 and carrying the General Sherman tanks that later figured in the victory of El Alamein, was then passing along the coast of Brazil. It even made a forty-hour call at Recife. The Germans knew its whereabouts all right; one of their broadcasts beamed at Brazil so stated and threatened its destruction.[9] But apparently no submarine managed to reach an attack position.

The ten U-boats then carried out their mission against Brazilian shipping, and made another powerful enemy for their country. Between 14 and 17 August, five vessels of the Brazilian Merchant Marine, with a total tonnage of 14,822 gross, were torpedoed and sunk, not far off shore. One ship was carrying about 300 men of the Brazilian Army, most of whom were drowned. A plane of Squadron VP-83 found and attacked one of the U-boats, but it escaped.

When the news of these sinkings was released, anti-Axis demonstrations and rioting took place all over Brazil. The government immediately reacted to public opinion, and on 22 August 1942 declared war on Germany and Italy.

Unfortunately the next reaction of the Brazilian government was to clap an embargo on every harbor, and to order into port every merchant ship then at sea. At this point there took place a profitable

[7] "Administrative History" IV 61-63.
[8] German Admiralty minutes of the Fuehrer's Conferences.
[9] *History U. S. Naval Operations* II 13; "Administrative History" IV 65-67.

intervention by Vice Admiral Jonas H. Ingram, Commander South Atlantic Force.[10] During the course of frequent calls at Recife and trips to Rio during the past fifteen months, the Admiral had established close personal relations with President Vargas and ranking officers of the Brazilian Navy and Air Force. A distinguished flag officer well before the war, Admiral Ingram [11] had the right combination of tact, energy and firmness to get things done; and he comported himself with a native vigor and a certain magnificence that both pleased and impressed our new allies. A few days before the Brazilian declaration of war, he shifted his flag from U.S.S. *Memphis* to *Patoka*, the versatile old Navy oiler then moored at Recife,[12] in order to release the cruiser for sea duty. Immediately after he flew to Rio and persuaded President Vargas that sailings must be resumed. The embargo would gravely embarrass United States war industries, and would be fatal to the internal economy of Brazil. The Admiral offered more protection in the shape of escorts; and, implementing military need with political pressure, managed to obtain several PCs and PGs of the former Canadian "flower" class from Admiral Ingersoll. President Vargas was sufficiently impressed to lift the ban on shipping; and although two more ships were sunk in the Brazilian area in August, two in September and one in October, the situation was greatly eased.

Admiral Dodsworth Martins, the able and distinguished Commander in Chief of the Brazilian Navy, now reorganized it into two groups for better coöperation with the South Atlantic Force: (1) Grupo Patrulha Sul (Commander Ernesto de Araujo) based on a southern port of Brazil, and (2) Fôrça Naval do Nordeste,

[10] TF 3 was so designated 16 Sept. 1942; on 1 Mar. 1943 it became the Fourth Fleet.

[11] Jonas H. Ingram, born Indiana 1886, Naval Academy '07, was a great football player and coached the Academy teams for several years. During World War I he served in U.S.S. *New York*. Received his first command, of a destroyer, in 1924; exec. of the *Pennsylvania* 1930; public relations officer of the Navy 1933; Comdesron 6 1936; C.O. *Tennessee* 1940; Comcrudiv 2 Jan. 1941; Com Fourth Fleet Sept. 1942; Cinclant 15 Nov. 1944–Sept. 1946; ret. as Admiral 1947; died 10 Sept. 1952.

[12] *Patoka* was known as the "triple threat," since she combined the functions of tender, oiler, and supply ship, and in addition mounted a mooring mast for blimps. The Admiral's later flagships were *Melville* (1 March 1943) and *Perseverance*.

commanded by Rear Admiral Alfredo Soares Dutra, with headquarters at Recife. The second force was placed under the operational control of Admiral Ingram. Similarly, Brigadier General Gomes, commander of the Fôrça Aerea Brasileira (Army Air Force) accepted a combined plan dividing all United States and Brazilian planes and tenders into (1) an "Orange" task group to patrol and operate striking forces between Belem and Rio, and (2) a "Blue" task group for similar service between Fortaleza and Maceió. Admiral Martins accepted after some hesitation a plan for combined inshore patrol, consisting of Brazilian and United States ships and planes.[13]

Before long the Brazilian Navy began to send officers to the Key West and Miami schools for indoctrination in anti-submarine warfare. Admiral Ingram obtained an attack teacher for Recife to carry on instruction there for both Navies. Two PCs were presented by the United States to the Brazilian Navy in September, the first installment of successive donations which amounted to eight PCs and eight SCs by the end of 1943.

Rear Admiral Pegram RN, who exercised the British Naval command in West Africa, flew to Recife on 3 September for a conference with Admiral Ingram. There, arrangements were made for mutual communications and combined operations if desirable against Axis ships trying to pass the Atlantic Narrows. And it turned out that one of the most important and successful tasks of the South Atlantic Force was the destruction of German blockade-runners. Two more were caught late in 1942. Rear Admiral O. M. Read in command of Task Group 23.2 of the South Atlantic Force (U.S.S. *Milwaukee, Cincinnati, Somers*), when conducting a routine search, was apprised that two enemy runners were expected to attempt to run the Narrows about 20 November.[14] Thus Admiral Ingram was able to dispose his forces, with the aid of a group from the Royal Air Force in

[13] "Administrative History" IV 58–59.

[14] Admiral Read relieved Admiral Ingram as Comcrudiv 2 in October, as Ingram now had too many duties to continue his sea command.

West Africa, so as to comb the ocean area thoroughly. Early in the morning of 21 November *Milwaukee* and *Somers* encountered a strange ship under Norwegian colors, which replied to their challenge with call letters assigned to a certain Norwegian merchant vessel. At 0655 (Greenwich) *Somers* sent away an armed boat party to board. One minute later three heavy explosions were observed, blowing debris several hundred feet into the air. The Norwegian ensign was lowered and the Nazi flag raised, lifeboats were lowered, and the ship began to sink rapidly by the stern. Notwithstanding, a boat party laid her aboard and ascertained that she was the German 5000-ton freighter *Anneliese Essberger*, 16 days out from Bordeaux and returning to Japan to load rubber. She carried a small token cargo and a motor torpedo boat. All 62 hands were recovered. They were a scrubby lot – "the worst batch of prisoners yet captured in this war." [15]

Milwaukee and *Cincinnati* departed to search for *Kota Nopan*, the other suspected blockade-runner. This search proved fruitless, but about four months later the same task group caught up with her. Admiral Read, flying his flag in cruiser *Savannah*, accompanied by escort carrier *Santee* to give air coverage and destroyers *Eberle* and *Livermore*, was patrolling an assigned area when on 10 March 1943, about 650 miles east of Recife, a carrier plane sighted a ship flying the Netherlands flag, about 17 miles from the formation. *Savannah* and *Eberle* at once peeled off to investigate, went to general quarters, and closed at 31 knots. The ship was recognized from her specially painted masts. Admiral Read directed *Eberle:* "Never mind Dutch flag, pile in there, this is a runner." Warning shots were fired, but the Germans began at once to abandon ship, and before *Eberle's* boat party was able to lay her aboard, the runner was burning briskly. No sooner had the boarding party begun to search than demolition charges exploded, as a result of which eight bluejackets were killed and she sank. The ship was identified as the 7300-ton blockade-runner *Karin*,

[15] Comcrudiv 2 Action Report, 27 Nov. 1942. The sinking took place at 0°54′ N, 22°34′ W.

ex-Dutch S.S. *Kota Nopan.* She had sailed from Malaya 4 February 1943 with a cargo of tin and rubber for Germany.[16]

These Atlantic Narrows became a dangerous place for blockade-runners after the Fourth Fleet and the British West Africa Command had established this patrol. *Karin* had already made a round voyage from Germany to Yokohama. Only two out of eighteen runners that departed Japan for French ports after 1 September 1942 with cargoes destined for Germany actually delivered the goods. But earlier runs had been so successful that during the entire war about half the cargoes from Japan arrived safely in France or Germany.[17]

In spite of the increased protection and better organization brought about by Brazilian belligerency and the South Atlantic Force, November and December 1942 were the worst months for sinkings in that part of the Atlantic which extends about 1200 miles off the coast of Brazil. Nine merchant ships were sunk in November and twelve in December, which knocked 118,000 tons off the Allied merchant marines, and in the Freetown and Southeast Atlantic areas, nearer Africa than Brazil, there were respectively ten sinkings of 49,000 tons and twenty-five of 127,000 tons. This was another case of Admiral Doenitz's success in finding soft spots. Owing to lack of convoys in this great stretch of ocean, the U-boats hung about the St. Paul Rocks, Fernando Noronha, in the doldrums between Cape San Roque and Cape Verde, and off the Cape of Good Hope, in order to catch through traffic. Once more the ineffectiveness of anti-submarine surface patrolling as compared with convoying was demonstrated.

[16] Same, and CTG 23.1 (Admiral Read) Action Report 14 Mar. 1943.

[17] A British Intelligence Report "Blockade-running between Japan and Germany" made after the war from German sources states that in the years 1941–1944 21 runners left French ports with 69,300 tons of cargo for Japan and 15 with 57,000 tons got through. In reverse, 35 ships with 257,000 tons cargo left East Asia ports for France, and 16 with 111,490 tons got through. Admiral P. W. Wennecker (German Naval Attaché at Tokyo) in a report made to 441st Counter Intelligence Corps Detachment U. S. Army at Karuizawa 20 March 1946 lists all runners from Japan to France (37 in all) by name, and states that only 16 got through, with about 53 per cent of total cargoes. The successful period of blockade-running westward was 1940–1942. There was also a minor trickle of supplies carried by U-boats and Japanese submarines.

Air patrol was somewhat more effective. Beginning 12 December daily patrols of six to eight planes were sent out from Natal and the other naval air bases; several sightings were made and attacks delivered. Squadron VP-83 made a well-deserved kill of *U-164* about 80 miles northeast of Fortaleza on 6 January 1943. The submarine was seen to break in two, and survivors were recovered in a rubber raft dropped by the plane's pilot, Lieutenant William Ford USNR.

This new blitz in the South Atlantic hastened the formation of Trinidad-Brazil convoys, which had been urgent for many months but postponed for lack of escort vessels. The first regularly scheduled Trinidad-Bahia convoy left Port of Spain 15 December 1942, and was dispersed off Bahia on New Year's Day. These convoys included ships of any Allied nation with a speed from 8 to 14½ knots and destinations in South Africa, the Red Sea, or South America below Santos. Faster vessels for the same destinations were routed independently via the Panama Canal and Cape Horn.[18]

In these Trinidad-Bahia convoys, designated TB-BT, an escort group of the United States Navy, consisting largely of PCs and ex-Canadian "flower" class corvettes, conducted merchant vessels over the long leg from Port of Spain to a position off Recife. There a Brazilian Navy escort group relieved them for the short leg to Bahia. After Squadron VP-94 of 12 amphibious Catalinas commanded by Lieutenant Joseph Tibbets USNR arrived at Natal 21 January 1943, to help out VP-83 and VP-74, the Navy was able to furnish day coverage to shipping from Belem at the mouth of the Para, to Bahia. At that time we had no adequate bases for these planes, which had to follow the convoys for over 2000 miles, fueling and resting overnight at emergency fields along the coast. Squadrons VP-83 and VP-94 were reviewed by President Vargas and President Roosevelt (returning from Casablanca) on 28 January 1943. In mid-February these squadrons were formed into Fleet Air Wing 16 under command of Captain R. D. Lyon, with headquarters at Natal; but they continued to enjoy a high

[18] South Atlantic Force War Diary 7 Jan. 1943.

degree of autonomy owing to the immense distances involved.

Convoy TB–1, third of the Trinidad–Bahia convoys,[19] which sailed 5 January 1943, lost four out of twelve ships by submarine attack off Surinam in January, and took refuge in the Para River for five days before proceeding. During the next six weeks only a few unescorted ships were lost off Brazil and the Guianas. But in March 1943 Convoy BT–6 ran into trouble.[20]

That northbound convoy consisted of 29 vessels, some of which had come from the Indies via Capetown, and many of which had had no convoy experience. It included five Liberty ships, whose 11-knot speed was cramped in an 8-knot convoy. Security, survivors asserted, was very slightly observed at Bahia, where "Torpedo Annie," a handsome redhead who consorted with nobody under the rank of master, was suspected of passing along to the Nazis such confidences as she was able to extort during hours of amorous dalliance. This *belle dame sans merci* owed her unromantic sobriquet to the observed fact that her lovers, shortly after parting, were apt to go down with their ships.

One Liberty ship out of Convoy BT–6 was lost by a torpedo hit on the run from Bahia to Recife, when the convoy was escorted by the Brazilian warships *Carioca, Caravelas* and *Rio Branco.* The principal losses, however, occurred after the Brazilian escort had been relieved off Recife by a United States Navy group, consisting of the 1920-vintage destroyer *Borie,* PGs *Courage* and *Tenacity,*[21] *PC–575,* and *PC–592.* After nightfall 3 March one of the merchant ships reported the sighting of a submarine to the commodore, who executed an emergency turn to starboard by light signals, as he possessed neither green Very stars nor voice radio. The whole port side of the convoy turned on running lights and great confusion reigned.[22] Fortunately no attack developed.

[19] Numbered 1 because the two earlier ones had been designated TS and TR.

[20] Files of Convoy BT–6 at A/S W Unit Atlantic Fleet, supplemented by those in Tenth Fleet files, Washington.

[21] *PG–70* and *PG–71,* each armed with one 4-inch 50-caliber, and four 3-inch 50-caliber.

[22] Report of escort commander in U.S.S. *Borie* 12 Mar. 1943.

Shortly after midnight 5 March, Convoy TB–6, which had been routed to pass 20 miles to port, was sighted dead ahead. The escort commander of BT–6 made rocket signal for an emergency turn, "which was not obeyed by the convoy, except by two ships who almost rammed each other," and the southbound convoy passed dangerously close in the darkness.

Convoy BT–6 continued its undisciplined voyage around Cape San Roque and the Amazon mouths, frequently getting fouled up, showing lights, tooting whistles, sending up flares and even firing rockets, until the escort commander threatened to fire on any vessel that broke the blackout. A neutral Swede in the convoy was so very careless as to be suspected of coaching in a submarine which attacked at 0210 March 9, when the convoy was about one hundred miles north of Cayenne.[23] This U-boat should have been avoided, as a sighting report of its position had been received. One Liberty ship (*James K. Polk*) sank immediately, and three others and a British freighter were torpedoed, but subsequently were towed into port. Offensive but badly coördinated sweeps were made by all escorts, and two of them were detailed to hang on for two hours, but not a single contact with the U-boat was made. On 10 March around noon an Army plane reported a "disappearing target" twelve miles ahead, but an evasive course avoided this enemy, and the rest of the vessels were delivered safely at Georgetown in British Guiana and Port of Spain, Trinidad.

"It is apparent," concluded the Atlantic Fleet's analyst, with almost British understatement, "that the passage of Convoy BT–6 was not a well-regulated operation." That officer, Captain P. R. Heineman, made the suggestion that each escort commander of a coastal convoy should be relieved from command of a ship, as had been the practice in American escort groups with transatlantic convoys, in order that he might devote himself to training and coördinating his escort group.[24] This suggestion was adopted by June or July; and in the meantime Admiral Ingram had seen to

[23] Lat. 7°11′ N, long. 52°30′ W.
[24] Analysis Report dated 13 May 1943.

Martin Mariners over Rio

Showing the Flag in the South Atlantic

it that the larger escort vessels on this route were provided with voice radio, and all with Very stars.

It should be remembered in defense of the harassed escorts of BT–6 that poor sound conditions generally prevail off the Orinoco and the Amazon, where the great volume of fresh water, flowing into the ocean, makes layers that reflect sound echoes.[25] But the main trouble on this route was the lack of fast escort vessels, such as destroyers or DEs. Although classed as a coastal convoy route, the long leg of the Trinidad–Bahia run, from the Paria Bocas to a point off Recife, was actually several hundred miles longer than the transatlantic route from Cape Race to Londonderry; and although sea and weather conditions were easier here than in the North Atlantic, they were too tough for converted gunboats and 173-foot PCs.

Originally the Navy had two organizations in Rio, the Mission attached to the Brazilian Navy, and the Naval Attaché at the Embassy. Rear Admiral Augustin T. Beauregard exercised both functions. With increased naval activity in southern Brazil, this dual organization became inadequate. On 2 December 1942, a United States Naval Operating Base, corresponding to those at Iceland, Bermuda and Trinidad, was commissioned at Rio de Janeiro with Admiral Beauregard as commandant[26] and Admiral Ingram in overall command. Preparations began at once to extend the TB convoys to Rio, but it required some time for the Brazilian Navy to train crews to handle the SCs and PCs lent by the United States Navy for escort duty along the southern part of this route. The first regularly scheduled Trinidad–Rio convoy, TJ–1, sailed from Port of Spain 3 July 1943.

Daily five-plane barrier sweeps out of Natal commenced 10 April 1943, in the hope of picking up blockade-runners. This sweep,

[25] Evaluation of attack by U.S.S. *Saucy* 22–23 Mar. 1943. Files of Convoy TB–8 at A/S W Unit, Boston. This attack failed because *Saucy* made eleven false contacts on tide-rips off the mouth of the Amazon, chased them all night, and was damaged by her own depth charges. A submarine was present, but escaped.

[26] Letter from Vice Admiral Ingram to the writer 21 Apr. 1944. Admiral Beauregard was relieved as Commandant N.O.B. Rio by Captain H. Dodd on 8 May 1943. The U. S. Naval base at Recife was known as a "Naval Operating Facility."

the details of which were worked out by an Asworg scientist attached to Admiral Ingram's staff, was maintained by planes of VP–83 and VP–94 for seventeen days. In the course of it a plane piloted by Ensign Robertson, which had been airborne for ten hours, sighted the Italian submarine *Archimede* about 350 miles east of Natal on 15 April. The enemy immediately opened fire and Robertson maneuvered his plane to make a dive-bombing attack, which succeeded in preventing the submarine from submerging. Having no more bombs, Ensign Robertson made two strafing attacks. Within an hour, a plane piloted by Lieutenant (jg) G. Bradford Jr. arrived on the scene, overwhelmed *Archimede* with a perfect straddle, and, during the eight minutes that elapsed before the submarine sank, made a strafing run in face of fire. About twenty-five survivors were counted in the water, but only one managed to reach shore, and that after a life-raft voyage of twenty-nine days.

Thus, an excellent beginning had been made by the South Atlantic Force, or Fourth Fleet as it had been renamed 15 March,[27] in conjunction with the Brazilian Navy. The convoy system and airplane sweeps were offering considerable though far from complete protection against submarines on the American side of the South Atlantic. The Brazilian public was reassured, and their pride in their own Navy had been enhanced by its active participation

[27] At that date United States ships in the Fourth Fleet comprised: –

LIGHT CRUISERS

Cincinnati	Capt. E. M. Senn
Marblehead	Capt. E. W. Morris
Memphis	Capt. H. Y. McCown
Milwaukee	Capt. J. H. Jacobson
Omaha	Capt. C. D. Leffler

DESTROYER SQUADRON 9, Cdr. A. H. Oswald

Davis, Moffett, Winslow, Jouett, Somers

GUNBOATS

Courage, Saucy, Surprise, Tenacity

SMALL CONVERTED YACHTS

Carnelian, Siren

OLD DESTROYERS

Barry, Borie, Goff

AUXILIARIES

Humboldt, Patoka, Melville

MINESWEEPERS

Flicker, Linnet, Spry, Thrush

15 PCs, 1 floating drydock, 2 YMSs, 1 YO, 1 tug

in warfare. To the saying *Deus é Brasileiro* – "God is a Brazilian" – they now added, *e o seu filho é oficial da Marinha* – "and His son is an officer of the Navy."

They certainly needed divine assistance in the South Atlantic. Tough going lay ahead.

CHAPTER XVI

Unescorted Ships with Armed Guards[1]

UNESCORTED vessels were given substantial protection by the mere presence of Naval Armed Guards. This was demonstrated by the fact that in most torpedoings the submarine remained submerged or at periscope depth until the ship had been abandoned. Although the greater number of Armed Guards were thus deprived of the satisfaction of hitting back, such attacks called for the most selfless devotion to duty. Their General Instructions were terse and explicit: –

> There shall be no surrender and no abandoning ship so long as the guns can be fought. In case of casualty to members of the gun crew the remaining men shall continue to serve the gun. The Navy Department considers that so long as there remains a chance to save the ship, the Armed Guard should remain thereon and take every opportunity that may present itself to destroy the submarine.

There were many instances of Armed Guards serving their guns until the guns would no longer fire, or standing by until the ship fell away under their feet.

S.S. *Arriaga*, a Panamanian tanker, was sunk on 23 June 1942, while en route from Baltimore to Aruba in water ballast. "The submarine surfaced 700 yards from the ship and two gunners fired the 6-pounder after gun at the submarine with no results and abandoned ship when the gun was awash." The U-boat promptly submerged and did not reappear until the tanker had gone down.

Freighter *Deer Lodge*, after returning safely from her North Russian ordeal, was independently routed from Baltimore to Suez

[1] Data obtained by Lt. (jg) J. Willard Hurst USNR from the citation file at the Armed Guard office, Cominch.

via Durban, South Africa, with a general cargo of 6250 tons and a deck cargo of four locomotives and tenders and three trucks. At 0209 on 17 February 1943, a submarine was sighted about 20 yards on the starboard beam. The general alarm was sounded and all stations were manned. The ship tried to zigzag, but her steering gear broke down. The report of Ensign J. K. Malo, Armed Guard commander, notes: –

> At exactly 0252 ship's time, the first torpedo hit on the port side in No. 2 hold . . . The ship listed sharply to port but righted herself considerably and went down by the bows somewhat. I ordered the gun trained to a bearing of 300°, and myself and my crew made every effort to spot the submarine. But it was too dark, all we could see were many shadows on the heavy swells. By this time the ship was completely out of control; the crew were abandoning ship, but the ship still had some headway. About 15 minutes after the first torpedo hit, I gave the order, through the battle phones, for the 20-mm gunners to abandon ship; the rest of us remained aboard waiting for the submarine to show itself. About forty minutes after the first attack the second torpedo hit in practically the same place on the port side. This time she listed heavily to port but didn't come back and was settling well down forward; I gave the order to abandon ship as it appeared she was going under. My coxswain and pointer threw the small doughnut raft, that we had ordered left behind for us, off the poop deck, and we all went over the side. We were subsequently picked up by one of the lifeboats just as dawn was breaking. The ship went down, bow first, a few minutes later. We were in the lifeboat about 32 hours and were picked up by a fishing trawler and taken into Port Elizabeth.

An old Lake steamer named *Jack* was proceeding from Ponce (Puerto Rico) to New Orleans with a cargo of sugar on 27 May 1942, when she was torpedoed after moonset. In the brief four minutes before she sank, the Naval Armed Guard swept the darkness with machine-gun fire in a circular range hoping that the tracer bullets would illuminate the submarine for their 4-inch gun. But the U-boat was not sighted. The gun crews, consisting of eight bluejackets and four soldiers, manned their guns until the platforms were awash and they could shoot no longer. Two survivors with several of the ship's crew were picked up after thirty-two days on a raft.

There are no more striking instances of stubborn sticking to the guns than on board steamships *M. F. Elliott* and *Warrior.* The former, a 6940-ton tanker, was torpedoed in daylight 3 June 1942, when proceeding from Newport News to Venezuela, and went down in six minutes. "The crew abandoned ship immediately, having first sent a distress signal to the Navy plane which was patrolling the area. The Navy Armed Guard stood by until the gun muzzle was in the water, but never sighted the enemy." S.S. *Warrior,* a 7500-ton freighter carrying a cargo for Russia to Bandarshahpur, was torpedoed about 55 miles out of Trinidad in daylight 1 July 1942, and sank in five minutes. Members of the Armed Guard stationed at the forward 3-inch gun went into action within four seconds after the first explosion. Ensign Alfred W. Anderson ran from the bridge to the forward gun platform, helped four seamen to fire a few rounds, and then ordered his men to abandon ship; but he and a bluejacket named Abasta refused to leave. These two continued to fire the 3-inch gun right up to the moment when the *Warrior* upended and slipped under. At the last moment, when the deck had assumed a 90-degree angle to the water, Ensign Anderson fell from the gun platform, striking a hatch and sliding into the water, while seaman Abasta struck the foremast, hung for a moment and then dropped. Both were lost.[2]

Against a determined enemy, the Armed Guard's best hope was to inflict a retaliatory injury. But there were instances in which steady gunfire drove off an attacker. Five shots from S.S. *Atenas* apparently scored hits on a submarine shortly after the vessel cleared the Passes of the Mississippi at noon 26 May 1942. The U-boat pursued, and attacked by shellfire at 2209. It made seven hits, but *Atenas's* gunners drove it down and she escaped. A member of the naval gun crew on watch in motor vessel *Blenheim,* en route New Orleans to Mobile 14 May, sighted a submarine beginning to surface. Fire was opened promptly and several shots were

[2] Survivors' Report by O.N.I. Two others of the Armed Guard were also lost.

observed to hit close to the periscope. Planes appeared shortly after and nothing further was seen of that U-boat.

Freighter *Columbian,* en route New York to Basra with goods for Russia, was saved by her officers' skill in plotting evasive courses and maneuvering during a night encounter marked by rapid and accurate fire by the naval gun crew. Just before dark 16 June 1942, five days out of Trinidad and 700 miles off the coast of Brazil, she spotted a surfaced submarine. The master, Edwin E. Johnson, changed course twice before dark and twice after; and although he did not shake off the enemy, his evasive courses prevented the U-boat from reaching a position to make an attack. Just after the last course change at midnight, the chief officer, who had taken station topside wheelhouse as the best vantage point, shouted "Hard right! There she is!" Mr. Johnson gave the order immediately, and the submarine barely missed fouling the stern of his ship. It promptly opened fire, *Columbian* replied with her 4-inch stern chaser, and the first shot was a direct hit at point-blank range. There was a blinding flash from the sub, and a great volume of orange flame lit up both ships. Two of the *Columbian's* 20-mm machine guns opened up, the 4-inch made another hit, and the submarine ceased to fight. "The last I could see of him," reported the master, "he was lying still at right angles to our course, and seemed to be getting low in the water." He escaped destruction, however. Ensign Merrill R. Stone Jr. observed that "coöperation between officers and crew of the *Columbian* and the Armed Guard unit was the chief factor in the success of this engagement, because, by the proper maneuvering of the ship, we were able to get a good range on the submarine."

The Armed Guard of S.S. *Unicoi,* commanded by Ensign M. K. Ames USNR, helped sink a submarine on 15 July 1942. *Unicoi* was in a Hampton Roads–Key West convoy steaming south off Diamond Shoals, and provided with air cover. Submarine *U–576,* which had already suffered some damage in sinking three ships, surfaced at daylight in the middle of the convoy about a hundred yards astern of *Unicoi,* whose 5-inch gun promptly scored a hit. Two

Army planes then straddled the conning tower with depth bombs, and *U-576* went down for keeps.

As an example of what merchant ships experienced, take this story of a six months' round voyage of the steamer *Alcoa Prospector*. She departed New York 12 September 1942 for Port Sudan by the Cape route with no other escort than a Navy blimp that saw her safely out of sight of land. Reaching Egypt without incident, she discharged cargo and was chartered by the Admiralty together with two British freighters and one other American freighter to carry relief to Malta. These four merchantmen, after passing through the Suez Canal 1 December, received a Royal Navy escort whose strength was a tribute to Axis sea power in the Eastern Mediterranean; it comprised a cruiser of the *Ajax* class, ten destroyers, a fast minelayer and one other ship. Day and night air cover by four to six Hurricanes was provided from shore bases. On 3 December this convoy was joined by a tanker with two more destroyers; and on the 4th the escort was augmented by four more (making 16 destroyers in all) and three anti-aircraft cruisers of the *Dido* class. Both on the outward passage to Malta and the homeward one to Port Said, the convoy was attacked by enemy planes and motor torpedo boats, but the escorts never let plane or boat come within range of the merchant ships. It was a merchantman's dream of a proper escort.

Alcoa Prospector departed Port Said 23 December 1942 and proceeded via Mombasa and Capetown to Buenos Aires and Montevideo, without incident. Owing to submarine activity in the South Atlantic, she was routed from the River Plate to New York by the Straits of Magellan and the Panama Canal, later joining a coastal convoy off Florida. Ensign C. O. Tritchler, commanding her Naval Armed Guard, reported "There has not been one instance of friction between the unlicensed merchant seamen and the men under my command. The courage and coöperation of all members of the ship's company under the rather trying conditions of the operation to Malta deserve the highest praise."

There were several instances of ships surviving a torpedo attack because the enterprise of the Armed Guard prevented a U-boat from following it up. Tanker *Gulf Belle* en route Belem to Aruba was hit by a torpedo 21 miles north of Tobago on 3 July 1942. The U-boat surfaced for about five minutes and crossed her stern, whereupon the gun crew fired one round from the 5-inch gun at 300 yards. They overshot and the submarine submerged. The master's order to stand-by was misunderstood and the merchant crew abandoned ship, but the Armed Guard stayed on board. The merchant crew later returned and next day the tanker was taken in tow by a British warship and brought safely to Port of Spain.

The story of the tanker *Brilliant* begins in convoy, but the outstanding efforts of a naval "jg" and a young merchant mariner saved her. A 9000-ton motorship of Socony fleet, *Brilliant* was torpedoed in convoy on 18 November 1942 en route New York to Belfast. The torpedo exploded with great force directly abaft the bridge, kindling an intense fire. A report from the port captain for Socony-Vacuum, as related by the Naval officer to whom it was given orally, embellishes it with more detail than the official report allows: –

The Master, first, second and third mates, also the cook and the steward, abandoned ship in a lifeboat. This prompt action of the Master and the others struck the Armed Guard officer, Lieutenant (jg) J. R. Borum who was observing it, so humorously that the fourth officer, Mr. Cameron, checked himself on going overside and decided to wait awhile. The Armed Guard officer asked him why he didn't try to put out the fire, so the fourth officer, who remembered the layout of the Lux fire-fighting system from recent study, turned on the system.

Meanwhile bridge communications were resumed and engineers ordered to charge firemains and start steam-smothering system. This brought the fire under control. Muster of crew showed 9 missing.

The fourth officer thereafter relied on the Armed Guard officer. Neither claims to be proficient in navigation, but between them they managed to bring the ship, at 3 knots, back to the Newfoundland coast, and finally located themselves after stormy weather in Bonavista

Harbor, where they anchored. The day following the ship got underway again, and on 24 November was safely brought into Saint Johns.

It is sad to relate that both Lieutenant Borum and Mr. Cameron lost their lives when *Brilliant* broke up and sank on 20 January 1943, while under tow from St. Johns to Halifax.

Merchantmen with Naval Armed Guards also distinguished themselves in two engagements with large German raiders. The American freighter *Stephen Hopkins* (Paul Buck, master) had an old-time sea battle with two German ships that recalls the War of 1812.

On the morning of 27 September 1942 this 7818-ton Liberty ship was proceeding from Capetown toward Paramaribo.[8] Two enemy motorships, the 5000-ton Raider "J" (ex-*Cairo*) and the 7800-ton blockade-runner *Tannenfels*, were sighted at noon in hazy weather. Both attacked promptly. Mr. Buck swung *Stephen Hopkins* to bring her 4-inch gun to bear on the raider, which was the more heavily armed of the two Germans. Ensign Kenneth M. Willett USNR of the Naval Armed Guard, although seriously wounded in the stomach by flying shrapnel, took charge of the stern gun and, at 1000 yards' range or under, fired thirty-five 4-inch shells, most of which hit the raider along the waterline. When an enemy shell exploded his magazine, Ensign Willett went down on deck to help cast loose life rafts.

The conduct of the merchant officers and crew of *Stephen Hopkins* was outstanding. After the explosion, Edwin O'Hara, 19, the ship's cadet, shot the five remaining 4-inch shells at the *Tannenfels*.

The second mate, Joseph E. Lehman, who was in charge of the two 37-mm guns forward, put round after round into the larger raider, until his ammunition handlers were killed and the gun platform wrecked. . . . The chief mate, Richard Maczkowski, who was shot high in the chest and in the left forearm, continued to direct and rally his men and to advise the master to keep the ship turning with her stern bearing on the enemy, although he was losing considerable blood due to his great activity. He continued to rally his men from a reclining

[8] Position 28°08′ S, 20°01′ W.

position on the deck and then got on his feet again with the aid of an ordinary seaman, so as to be better able to discharge his duties.[4]

There could be only one end to this unequal engagement. Raider "J" was armed with one 3-inch and six 5.9-inch guns mounted in turrets or behind shields, with a central fire-control system. *Tannenfels* carried no heavy guns forward and limited herself to pouring machine-gun fire into the *Hopkins*, who in turn swept her decks at close range with plenty of the same kind. A shell from the raider penetrated one of *Hopkins's* boilers, reducing her speed to one knot; two more hit the radio mast, destroying the aërial. The steering engine room was struck and incendiary shells set fire to the main deckhouse. *Stephen Hopkins*, after fighting gloriously for almost three hours, riddled with shellfire and aflame from stem to stern, plunged with colors flying into a 2200-fathom deep.

Raider "J" was also aflame, and had to be abandoned in a sinking condition. *Tannenfels* took off her crew and, although damaged, made Bordeaux.[5]

Twenty minutes before *Stephen Hopkins* went down, all hands abandoned ship on the master's orders in a high wind and heavy sea, the able-bodied assisting the wounded. Ensign Willett was last seen covered with blood as he helped his men to cut away their life rafts. The only undamaged lifeboat, lowered by the second assistant engineer and the steward, picked up survivors; and without charts or navigating instruments made a safe landing on the coast of Brazil, after a voyage of 31 days, with 15 men still alive. They were the only survivors; 42 were lost.[6]

[4] O.N.I. Survivors' Report, signed by Lieut. N. V. Stebbins USNR.

[5] British Admiralty W.I.R. No. 181, Raider Supplement No. 3.

[6] *Stephen Hopkins* file EO 2 at Armed Guard office Cominch, including Mr. G. D. Cronk's log of lifeboat voyage; article in Washington *Post* 10 Dec. 1942; Report of Intell. Div. Opnav. 28 Oct. 1943 p. 77.

CHAPTER XVII

Analysis and Conclusion

April 1943

1. *The Situation from the German Point of View* [1]

WE MAY now venture a few conclusions on this ten-months period of the Battle of the Atlantic, and analyze the situation as it appeared to both sides about the end of April 1943.

If the high naval commanders of the United States and Great Britain had been able to listen in on conferences at Hitler's headquarters, or to read the thoughts of Admiral Doenitz, their picture of the anti-submarine situation in April 1943 would have been far brighter than it was. Hitler had lost the strategic initiative, our counter-weapons had begun to take effect, and the German high command was at its wits' end what to do. For them the world situation was very black. An expensive all-out attempt to capture Stalingrad had been definitely liquidated on 3 February when the German army there surrendered. The German Black Sea Fleet was fighting a losing battle for the supply of the Kuban bridgehead. With Operation "Torch" almost over, the Axis was making desperate effort to evacuate the last of its troops from North Africa. Pressure on the Suez "lifeline" had been removed, once and for all. Allied forces were massing for an invasion of the European Continent. No consolation for the Axis was to be found in the Pacific; it must have been clear to German intelligence that Japanese power

[1] This section is based on the Doenitz Essay, on the U. S. Navy publication of translation from German Naval Archives entitled *Fuehrer Conferences on Matters Dealing with the German Navy, 1943* (1946), and on Admirals Walter Gladisch and Kurt Assmann, "Report to Office of British Commander-in-Chief, Germany, 10 Feb. 1946," translated by Lt. Cdr. H. D. Reck USNR.

began ebbing fast after Midway and Guadalcanal, and that a mighty offensive by the United States Pacific Fleet would start presently.

At his conference with Hitler on 11 April 1943, Doenitz expressed discomfort at the rising losses of U-boats. Forty had been sunk since the beginning of the year, together with six or seven Italian submarines; the Admiral would have been still more distressed could he have anticipated the loss of 41 in May alone. "I fear," he said, "that the submarine war will be a failure if we do not sink more ships than the enemy is able to build." He urged, and Hitler accepted, an accelerated program of submarine construction.[2] But U-boat prospects waned as spring turned into summer. The Germans knew, at least in a general way, about the rapid increase of escort vessels in the United States. They knew that the escort carriers were coming out, and greatly feared their effect. For, as Gladisch and Assmann well expressed in their Report, carrier planes broadened the protection of a convoy, as though it were passing through coastal waters within reach of land-based planes. The rapid increase of very-long-range plane coverage from Iceland, Newfoundland, the British Isles and North Africa, to which the Azores would presently be added, alarmed the German Navy; and "of even greater consequence," wrote Doenitz after the war ended, "was the fact that the U-boats could be located at a great distance by the enemy's radar, apparently on short wave, without previous warning on their own receivers, and were then heavily attacked by destroyers and aircraft carriers without even seeing the enemy. . . . The U-boat losses, which previously had been 13 per cent of all the boats at sea, rose rapidly to 30 and 50 per cent. . . . These losses were not only suffered in enemy attacks, but everywhere at sea. There was no part of the Atlantic where the boats were safe from being located day and night by aircraft."[3]

It was even seriously considered whether the submarine campaign should be given up altogether, since the U-boats were no longer

[2] *Fuehrer Conferences 1943* p. 20.
[3] Doenitz Essay, Secs. 116, 117.

paying their cost in terms of shipping sunk.[4] Nevertheless, the German high command decided to continue it for two very good reasons. Submarines, even if not directly profitable, pinned down for the protection of shipping hundreds of combat ships, over a thousand planes, and a very large component of Allied production and military effort which otherwise might be employed for the invasion of Europe. And Doenitz promised a renewal of submarine victories as soon as the new mass-produced prefabricated Types XXI and XXIII were in production. The first and larger of these was a very formidable threat. It was an electric-drive submarine displacing 1600 tons on the surface (as compared with 708 tons for the so-called 500-tonners), 251 feet long (as against 220 feet) with scientifically determined lines and heavy power that promised a *submerged* speed of 17 to 18 knots, as against 7.6 knots for the 500-tonners.[5]

Although Doenitz was now in a good position to put the heat on Armaments Minister Speer for prompt production of these new types, they could not be promised before 1944, and actually did not appear before 1945. So the high command decided as an interim strategy to make radical alterations to the existing U-boats in order to increase their effectiveness. These improvements took the form of an increase in anti-aircraft armament and the *Schnorchel* or breather which enabled the boats to stay under water indefinitely. The first took effect in April 1943. U-boats with the increased anti-aircraft armament were ordered to stay surfaced and fight it out with planes instead of submerging whenever they sighted aircraft.[6] But no *Schnorchel* appeared before 1944.

Thus, from the German point of view, the period from 1 May 1943 until the spring of 1945 was a holding operation, during which the U-boats destroyed as much shipping as possible, and

[4] Gladisch and Assmann Report p. 163.

[5] Data from U-boat Characteristics Chart in O.N.I. Operational Intelligence Section.

[6] Doenitz Essay, Sec. 118–120. In this Essay Doenitz does not mention the new acoustic torpedo of which he expected great things in mid-1943, because, owing to prompt development of countermeasures, it proved a dud.

pinned down Allied forces protecting shipping, until new types, increased production and revised tactics regained superiority. In that sense it was comparable to the first period of our war with Japan in the Pacific; but the results were very different, because the German total power and production were permanently declining in relation to those of their enemies.

2. *The Situation from the Allied Point of View*[7]

From the Allied point of view, victory was not even in sight; the most one could say, in Winston Churchill's phrase, was that this period, from July 1942 to April 1943, marked "the end of the beginning."

On the part of the American public, the ill-informed optimism which greeted the first U-boat blitz of 1942 had given place to an unwarranted pessimism. Navy news releases dwelt on losses and difficulties rather than on achievements. Military operations in Tunisia were disappointingly slow; Guadalcanal, secured at great cost in early February, seemed a very long way from Japan. And some exaggerated statistics on shipping losses were given out.[8]

The prospect of increased merchant tonnage, however, was fairly bright. There had been a loss of almost two million deadweight tons during the year 1942, but during the last quarter there had been a net gain of 738,000 deadweight tons of new construction over total losses by enemy action and marine casualty. Deliveries of Liberty ships and T–3 (tanker) hulls had been greater even than optimistic predictions.[9] As more of the weaker, smaller and slower

[7] I have decided to leave this section exactly as I wrote it in the early summer of 1943, except for revision of statistics, because it represents the feeling and estimates in U. S. Navy circles at that time.

[8] Notably in the Truman Committee Report, 78th Cong. 1st Sess. (1943), Senate Report No. 10, Part 8 p. 23, which said that an average of about a million tons of merchant shipping was sunk *monthly* in 1942.

[9] Available deadweight tonnage of all Allied Nations, 1 January 1942: 44,390,000; 1 January 1943: 42,421,000; estimated for 1 January 1944: 51,505,000. C.C.S. "Measures for Counteracting," Summary of Appendices. For rough equivalents in gross tonnage, reduce these figures 33 per cent.

prewar ships were knocked off, the merchant fleet became more efficient, and the average speed of convoys increased. Admiral Doenitz warned his Fuehrer on 11 April, "The war on shipping will fail if we don't sink more ships than the enemy can build."

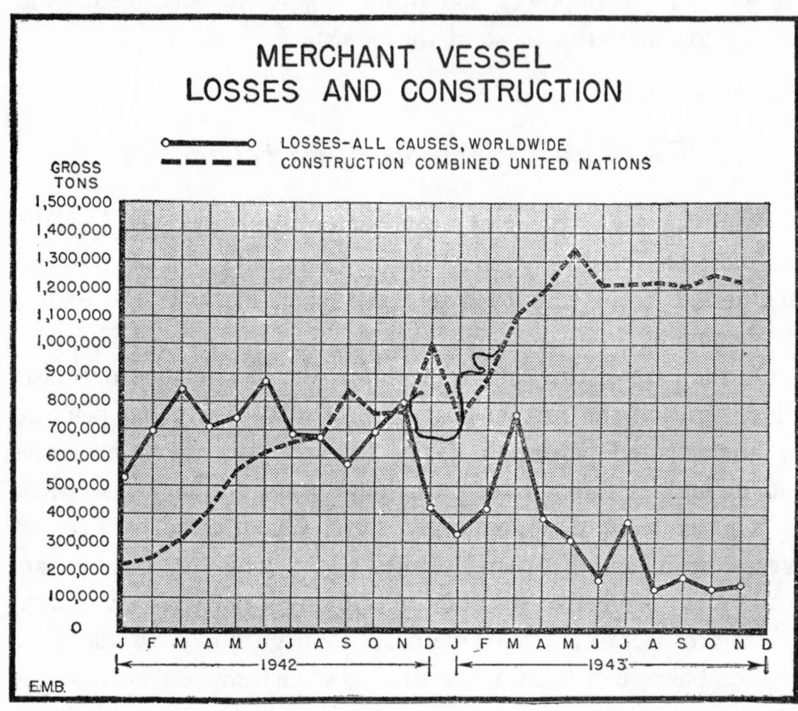

The convoy system had been extended as far as possible with available escorts, and now covered most of the shipping routes in the Atlantic. There were still many unescorted vessels, but convoys from North America went as far as Bahia on the Brazilian coast, and those from the United Kingdom to Freetown in West Africa.

The following table shows the development which the convoy system had attained in the United States strategic area alone in April 1943, the number of unescorted merchantmen in each area, and the estimated number of underwater enemies.

Thus, every day on the American half of the North Atlantic convoy route, there were five or six convoys at sea, making all

AVERAGE NUMBER MERCHANT VESSELS, CONVOYS, ESCORTS, AND (ESTIMATED) U-BOATS AT SEA DAILY IN U. S. STRATEGIC AREA, APRIL 1943 [10]

	Number Merchant Vessels		*Number of Convoys*	*Number Escort Vessels*	*Number U-boats Operating Daily*
North Atlantic Convoy Area	Indep.	1.1	5.6	38.0	49.0
	Conv.	206.3			
Mid-Atlantic Area and Caribbean Sea Frontier	Ind.	9.2	3.8	31.8	3.6
	Conv.	108.3			
Eastern Sea Frontier and Canadian Coastal Zone	Ind.	34.4	8.5	25.7	1.8
	Conv.	190.1			
Gulf Sea Frontier	Ind.	27.7	4.3	12.3	0.7
	Conv.	33.9			
Panama Sea Frontier and Caribbean Sea Frontier, West	Ind.	13.2	7.4	28.8	1.9
	Conv.	98.8			
Brazilian and South Atlantic Areas	Ind.	34.8	1.8	8.7	1.6
	Conv.	35.3			
Total:		793.1	31.4	145.3	58.6

together 206 ships and 38 escorts, and 49 U-boats after them. Every day in coastal waters between Quebec and Jacksonville, there were 205 ships, 190 of them with 26 escorts in eight or nine convoys. In the Gulf of Mexico and Caribbean, besides 41 unescorted vessels, there would be 133 ships with 41 escorts in twelve convoys. The small daily averages of U-boats in these areas do not mean much, because when there were any at all, there were several; for most of that month there were none.

Impressive as these figures of merchant ships are, they do not include any ships in the British strategic area (roughly, the eastern half of the Atlantic); or any troop convoys, anywhere. One may, at a guess, double them to cover the whole Atlantic, and figure on 120 ships unescorted, 1350 in convoy, at sea every day.

Although the number of ships at sea increased encouragingly, there was still a shortage of escort vessels to protect them. Troop convoys took the pick, and an increasing proportion of the total; with new convoy routes being established, and the average number of merchant vessels per convoy rising, the production of new

[10] Cf. above, Chap. X, 6.

escort vessels fell behind the demand. It is significant that, in 16 North Atlantic convoys which lost four or more ships each by torpedoing from November 1942 through May 1943, the number of U-boats attacking the convoy at the height of the attack exceeded the number of escorts present. In order to give a convoy a break it should have at least 50 per cent more escorts than the maximum number of attacking submarines. In order to give it an edge, there should be at least two destroyers or DEs that could peel off as a killer group, and yet leave sufficient protection for the convoy.

While the escort program was no longer impeded by priorities in other construction, the long-promised destroyer escorts and escort carriers were not yet ready, and the Navy was using more 178-foot PCs, converted yachts, minesweepers and even SCs for escort purposes than was safe or desirable. The Combined Chiefs of Staff planning committee figured out in January 1943 that 566 escort vessels of 200 feet length or over would be needed that year in the Atlantic. On 15 February, 449 were actually available, after counting those of the Royal Navies, and the French, Norwegian, Brazilian and Netherlands contributions. Deficiencies were greatest along the East Coast of the United States. But the progress of naval shipbuilding assured us that these deficiencies would be slowly made up, and that 800 sizable escorts would be available by 1944.

Nor was the escort problem merely a matter of numbers and equipment; upkeep, training and teamwork were to be considered. In mid-1943 escorts were still being overworked, so that anti-submarine and other equipment frequently gave out when most needed. If a ship performed escort duty for several months without a fight, officers and key men became stale and needed refresher training. Teamwork was also essential for success against submarines; yet many escort groups had to be broken up as soon as they began working well together, because some of the ships were needed for new convoys or in new danger areas.

The number of U-boats killed by forces of the Allied nations was still too small, and of that number those credited to United States' forces were a minority.[11] There was indeed an increase since June 1942, a monthly average of 13 German and Italian submarines sunk in the second half of 1942 as compared with 4.7 during the first half; but the average monthly kill remained 13 during the first four months of 1943. Hitler was still building 'em faster than we could sink 'em; 18 to 23 new ones a month.[12] The average number of enemy submarines daily at sea in the Atlantic mounted steadily from 48 in March 1942 to 105 in October and to over 110 in March 1943. Total strength of the German and Italian submarine fleets had more than doubled in 1942, and had passed 400 in number on 1 January 1943. These were principally 500-tonners but included a considerable number of 740-tonners, and some of the 1600-ton supply submarines or "milch cows" which had materially increased the operating range of the smaller U-boats. Of this total under-surface fleet, about 135 were training in the Baltic, 110 operating in the Atlantic, the rest in port for repairs and upkeep. If the hares had become more numerous, so had the hounds.

The average bag made by U-boats had steadily declined from its high point 1 May 1942, just before coastal convoys were set up. For that month, every U-boat at sea sank on the average 12,000 tons. By April 1943 the average kill per U-boat at sea had sunk to 2000 tons. This might be interesting as a sort of sporting score, but the number of U-boats operating had so greatly increased that it was of little significance in solving the problem. When Daniel Boone, who shot fifty bears a year, was replaced by fifty hunters who averaged one each, the bears saw no occasion to celebrate the decline in human marksmanship.

The Combined Staff Planners, who made an intensive study of the submarine and shipping situation in April 1943, predicted that Germany would retain her strategic initiative in submarine warfare

[11] See Appendix III.

[12] See Appendix I. The actual average construction Jan.–May 1943 was 21 per month.

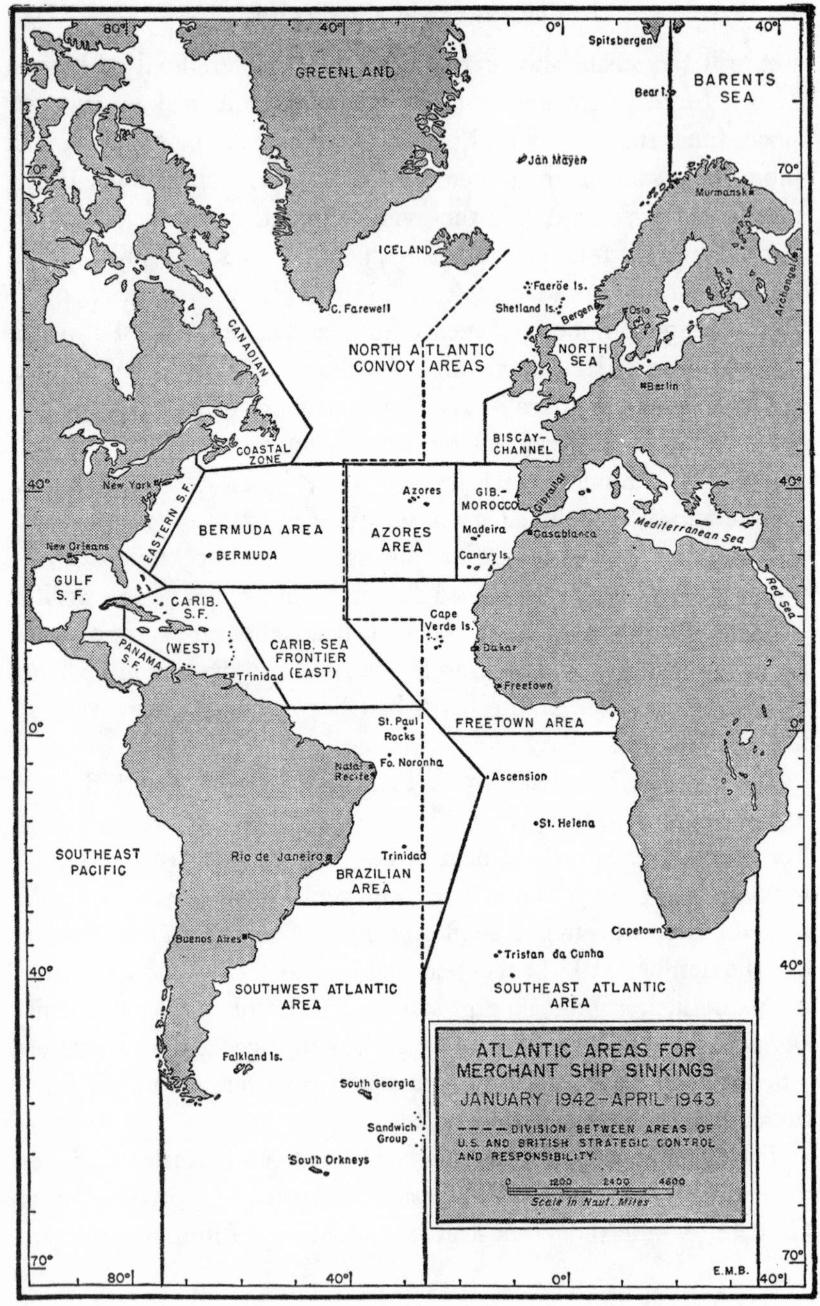

GREENLAND
BARENTS SEA
Spitsbergen
Bear I.
Jan Mayen
Murmansk
Archangel
ICELAND
Faeröe Is.
Shetland Is.
Bergen
Oslo
C. Farewell
CANADIAN
NORTH ATLANTIC CONVOY AREAS
NORTH SEA
Berlin
BISCAY-CHANNEL
COASTAL ZONE
New York
EASTERN S.F.
BERMUDA AREA
BERMUDA
Azores
AZORES AREA
GIB.-MOROCCO
Gibraltar
Madeira
Casablanca
Canary Is.
Mediterranean Sea
Red Sea
New Orleans
GULF S.F.
CARIB. S.F. (WEST)
PANAMA S.F.
CARIB. SEA FRONTIER (EAST)
Trinidad
Cape Verde Is.
Dakar
Freetown
FREETOWN AREA
St. Paul Rocks
Fo. Noronha
Natal
Recife
Ascension
St. Helena
SOUTHEAST PACIFIC
Rio de Janeiro
Trinidad
BRAZILIAN AREA
Capetown
Buenos Aires
Tristan da Cunha
SOUTHWEST ATLANTIC AREA
SOUTHEAST ATLANTIC AREA
Falkland Is.
South Georgia
Sandwich Group
South Orkneys
ATLANTIC AREAS FOR MERCHANT SHIP SINKINGS
JANUARY 1942–APRIL 1943
– – – – DIVISION BETWEEN AREAS OF U.S. AND BRITISH STRATEGIC CONTROL AND RESPONSIBILITY
0 1200 2400 4800
Scale in Naut. Miles
E.M.B.

until adequate countermeasures had been developed by the United Nations. In the endeavor to overtake the dangerous German lead, many measures had been improvised with air and naval forces inadequate for the task, with a consequent failure to reduce shipping losses below half a million tons a month as recently as March. These heavy losses caused grave anxiety in the American and British high command, and helped to bring about both a new organization (the Tenth Fleet) and a salutary improvement in antisubmarine warfare.

Thus, the Navy was anything but complacent about the submarine situation in April 1943. But it had earned the right to be proud. The Navy and Merchant Marine had "kept 'em sailing," and delivered indispensable supplies to the United Kingdom and to Russia, enabling England and the Soviet Union to implement the valor of their armed forces and the determination of their people. The Navy had escorted some two million American troops to Europe and Africa, together with the immense mass of materiel and supplies needed in modern warfare, without losing a single loaded troopship.[13] The Navy had been a principal factor in securing the alliance of Latin America down to the River Plate, and especially in Brazil. And all this when fighting another first-class war in the Pacific.

Looking backwards, we can see that the peak of enemy success came exactly halfway between the winter and the summer solstices of 1942–43. More danger lay ahead, but the darkest days were over. More of everything – of very-long-range planes, of escort carriers, destroyers, destroyer escorts, sloops and frigates – better training and doctrine, better weapons and devices, were to reap a notable harvest of 41 U-boats in May; and although Doenitz still had a number of tricks up his sleeve, he was destined never to recover the initiative.

[13] The three mentioned earlier in this volume were destined for Greenland and Iceland.

APPENDIX I

Losses of Merchant Shipping

1. *Allied and Neutral Merchant Vessels Lost by Submarine Attack,*[1] *Compared with U-Boats Built and Operating*[2]

a. All Atlantic and Arctic Areas

	NUMBER OF SHIPS	GROSS TONS	DAILY AVERAGE OF U-BOATS AT SEA IN ATLANTIC	NEW U-BOATS CONSTRUCTED
1942				
January	46	270,348		20
February	72	427,733		18
March	88	507,502	47.7	19
April	65	388,182	48.8	23
May	120[3]	586,149	61.1	20
June	115	603,402	59.2	23
July	83	425,864	69.6	18
August	102	526,329	86.4	20
September	88	454,548	99.7	17
October	88	585,510	105.4	23
November	106	636,907	94.9	17
December	54	287,730		26
1943				
January	29	181,767	91.5	18
February	50	312,004	116	19
March	95	567,401	116	23
April	44	276,790	111	23
May	41	211,929	118	22

[1] Figures from Fleet Operations Statistical Section, Navy Department.

[2] German U-boat Command (B.d.U.) War Diary; U. S. Strategic Bombing Survey, German Submarine Industry Report, Exhibit B–2.

[3] Of these 40 were American, and this was the highest loss of U. S. merchant vessels by submarines in any one month. Of the 571 allied vessels sunk, Mar.–July, 150 were American.

b. Other Areas[4]

1942	Mediterranean and Red Sea No.	Gr. Tons	Indian Ocean No.	Gr. Tons	North, Central and South Pacific No.	Gr. Tons	Southwest Pacific No.	Gr. Tons
January	0	0	8	31,081	0	0	6	19,481
February	0	0	4	13,072	0	0	6	29,331
March	0	0	5	23,583	0	0	1	913
April	2	7,379	5	32,404	1	1,435	0	0
May	1	4,216	0	0	3	16,582	0	0
June	6	10,348	15	69,366	1	3,286	3	13,692
July	3	5,885	4	17,050	2	11,949	3	15,301
August	3	12,321	1	5,237	0	0	2	523
September	3	774	6	30,052	0	0	0	0
October	0	0	3	15,103	2	13,691	0	0
November	5	44,527	5	30,446	0	0	0	0
December	4	33,981	4	22,161	0	0	0	0
1943								
January	4	12,049	0	0	1	7,176	1	2,051
February	9	27,973	0	0	2	7,363	2	11,988
March	11	45,667	2	14,309	0	0	0	0
April	5	13,934	1	5,047	1	7,176	5	24,996
May	1	5,979	3	13,472	3	28,113	2	5,359

2. *Allied and Neutral Merchant Vessels Lost by Other Causes in All Parts of the World*

1942	Aircraft No.	Gr. Tons	Surface Ships No.	Gr. Tons	Enemy Mines No.	Gr. Tons	Other or Unknown Enemy Action No.	Gr. Tons	Marine Casualty No.	Gr. Tons
January	15	50,786	1	3,275	11	10,079	9	19,920	48	103,663
February	29	138,498	1	983	2	7,242	17	36,640	18	53,006
March	12	48,501	9	21,521	5	16,862	105	168,980[5]	32	53,778
April	16	82,273	25	131,188	8	14,934	3	6,237	18	28,219
May	13	58,995	3	19,363	5	18,786	2	312	15	26,075
June	11	54,769	7	48,474	6	19,930	1	242	14	32,535
July	18	74,313	11	54,358	2	8,905	0	0	26	81,937
August	6	60,532	8	59,432	0	0	0	0	15	21,744
September	12	57,526	4	24,388	0	0	0	0	30	38,747

[4] Also two ships of 6,447 tons Jan. 1942 and two ships of 8,256 tons Apr. 1942; place of sinking unknown.

[5] This heavy loss occurred almost entirely in the Southwest Pacific, and includes Allied vessels scuttled or captured in the abandonment of Malaya and the Dutch East Indies.

	AIRCRAFT		SURFACE SHIPS		ENEMY MINES		OTHER OR UNKNOWN ENEMY ACTION		MARINE CASUALTY	
	No.	*Gr. Tons*	*No.*	*Gr. Tons*	*No.*	*Gr. Tons*	*No.*	*Gr. Tons*	*No.*	*Gr. Tons*
1942										
October	1	5,683	3	7,576	2	5,114	0	0	22	58,190
November	7	61,793	5	10,484	1	992	0	0	28	56,715
December	2	4,156	8	19,352	3	344	0	0	36	65,657
1943										
January	5	25,503	0	0	5	18,745	0	0	46	110,512
February	1	75	1	4,858	7	34,153	0	0	27	27,388
March	9	61,806	0	0	1	868	0	0	29	77,580
April	1	2,996	1	1,742	4	11,956	0	0	15	33,286
May	5	20,942	0	0	1	1,568	2	12,066	14	29,503

3. *Allied and Neutral Merchant Vessel Gross Tonnage Lost Monthly*

	BY SUBMARINE ATLANTIC–ARCTIC	BY SUBMARINE OTHER AREAS	BY ALL OTHER CAUSES (AIR ATTACK, WEATHER, ETC.)	TOTAL
1942				
January	270,348	57,009	194,023	521,380
February	427,733	42,403	236,369	706,505
March	511,552	20,446	309,642	841,640
April	388,182	49,474	263,301	700,957
May	586,149	21,098	125,531	730,778
June	603,402	96,692	155,950	856,044
July	425,864	50,185	219,513	695,562
August	526,329	18,081	141,937	686,347
September	454,548	30,826	120,661	606,035
October	585,510	28,794	76,563	690,867
November	636,907	74,973	151,820	863,700
December	287,730	56,142	89,571	433,443
Grand Total		8,333,258		
Monthly Average		694,438		
1943				
January	181,767	21,276	161,703	364,746
February	312,004	47,324	71,122	430,450
March	567,401	59,976	140,254	767,631
April	276,790	51,153	49,980	377,923
May	211,929	52,923	64,079	328,931
Grand Total		2,269,681		
Monthly Average		453,936		

4. *Atlantic Areas of Most Severe Losses by Submarine Attack*[6]

		SHIPS	GROSS TONS
1942			
January	1. Eastern Sea Frontier	14	95,670
	2. Canadian Coastal Zone	12	49,866
	3. North Atlantic Convoy Areas[7]	10	62,731
	4. Bermuda Area	9	56,608
February	1. Eastern Sea Frontier	17	102,846
	2. Caribbean Sea Frontier, West	19	88,679
	3. North Atlantic Convoy Areas	12	78,105
	4. Bermuda Area	9	58,663
March	1. Eastern Sea Frontier	28	159,340
	2. Bermuda Area	19	109,216
	3. Caribbean Sea Frontier, West	12	66,100
	4. Freetown Area	9	52,857
	5. Caribbean Sea Frontier, East	7	50,133
April	1. Eastern Sea Frontier	23	133,184
	2. Bermuda Area	18	112,442
	3. Caribbean Sea Frontier, West	11	67,928
May	1. Gulf Sea Frontier	41	219,867
	2. Caribbean Sea Frontier, West	30	130,106
	3. Bermuda Area	15	83,082
	4. North Atlantic Convoy Areas	8	42,475
	5. Caribbean Sea Frontier, East	8	37,021
	6. Canadian Coastal Zone	6	22,613
	7. Eastern Sea Frontier	5	23,326
June	1. Caribbean Sea Frontier, West	25	146,489
	2. Gulf Sea Frontier	21	91,277
	3. Bermuda Area	14	77,579
	4. North Atlantic Convoy Areas	14	63,371
	5. Eastern Sea Frontier	13	73,585
	6. Panama Sea Frontier (Atlantic)	13	63,061
	7. Caribbean Sea Frontier, East	10	64,288
July	1. Azores and Freetown Area	17	121,424
	2. Caribbean Sea Frontier, West	17	72,134
	3. Gulf Sea Frontier	16	65,924
	4. Barents Sea	10	62,058
	5. Canadian Coastal Zone	7	21,664

[6] Figures from Fleet Operations Statistical Section, Navy Dept., dated June-Aug. 1945. With two exceptions, I have included only areas with seven or more sinkings per month.

[7] Includes a part of the North Russia convoy route, but few of its casualties figure here because the majority of them were caused by air attack.

		SHIPS	GROSS TONS
1942			
August	1. Caribbean Sea Frontier, West	33	167,404
	2. North Atlantic Convoy Areas [8]	25	130,089
	3. Azores and Freetown Area	13	86,338
	4. Caribbean Sea Frontier, East	13	75,401
	5. Brazilian Area	7	18,132
September	1. North Atlantic Convoy Areas	28	151,411
	2. Caribbean Sea Frontier, West	25	115,234
	3. Canadian Coastal Zone	10	38,615
October	1. North Atlantic Convoy Areas	26	184,843
	2. Southeast Atlantic	25	181,240
	3. Gibraltar–Morocco Area	11	72,300
	4. Caribbean Sea Frontier, West	8	26,918
	5. Caribbean Sea Frontier, East	7	41,251
November	1. North Atlantic Convoy Areas	29	163,247
	2. Southeast Atlantic	23	127,363
	3. Caribbean Sea Frontier, West	18	111,192
	4. Azores and Freetown Area	10	48,812
	5. Brazilian Area	9	58,858
	6. Caribbean Sea Frontier, East	7	38,940
December	1. North Atlantic Convoy Areas	23	122,368
	2. Brazilian Area	12	59,596
1943			
January	1. Azores and Freetown Area	11	80,047
February	1. North Atlantic Convoy Areas	36	227,109
March	1. North Atlantic Convoy Areas	49	295,970
	2. Southeast Atlantic	11	80,802
	3. Azores and Freetown Area	9	53,771
April	1. North Atlantic Convoy Areas	21	130,026
	2. Freetown Area	10	57,666
May	1. North Atlantic Convoy Areas	17	87,935
	2. Azores and Freetown Area	10	53,318
	3. Southeast Atlantic	7	41,105

[8] Some northern transatlantic convoys suffered losses in the Canadian Coastal Zone, while some losses in North Atlantic Convoy Areas were suffered by southbound traffic.

APPENDIX II

Monthly Sinkings of German and Italian Submarines[1]

Figures in parentheses represent the Cominch-Admiralty assessments made during the war, when different from actual sinkings.

	Ger.	Ital.	KILLS BY U. S. FORCES
1942			
January	3	2	none
February	2	0 (1)	none
March	6 (4)	3	*U-656* and *U-503* by VP-82 on 1st and 2nd
April	3 (2)	0	*U-85* by *Roper* on 14th
May	4 (5)	0	*U-352* by *Icarus* on 9th
June	3 (5)	2	*U-157* by *Thetis* on 13th
			U-158 by VP-74 on 30th
July	11 (9)	3	*U-701* by Army Bombron 396 on 7th
			U-153 by *Lansdowne, PC-458* and Bombron 59 on 13th
			U-576 by VS-9 and S.S. *Unicoi* on 15th
August	9 (12)	3 (5)	*U-166* by Coast Guard Squadron 212 on 1st
			U-464 by VP-73 on 20th
			U-654 by Army Bombron 45 on 22nd
			U-94 by VP-92 and H.M.C.S. *Oakville* on 28th
September	10 (8)	1 (0)	none
October	16 (13)	0	*U-512* by Army Bombron 99 on 2nd
November	13 (14)	3 (1)	*U-408* by VP-84 on 5th
			Sciesa by Army plane on 7th
December	5 (3)	4	*U-611* by VP-84 on 10th
1943			
January	6 (4)	3	*U-164* and *U-507* by VP-83 on 6th and 13th
February	19 (13)	3	*U-519* by Army A/S'ron 2 on 10th
			U-225 by *Spencer* on 21st
			U-606 by *Campbell* and Polish *Burza* on 22nd
March	15 (10)	1 (0)	*U-156* by VP-53 on 8th
			U-130 by *Champlin* on 12th
			U-524 by Army A/S'ron 1 on 22nd
April	15 (16)	1	*Archimede* by VP-83 on 15th
			U-175 by *Spencer* on 17th
			U-174 by VB-125 on 27th

[1] "German, Japanese and Italian Submarine Losses, World War II," Navy Press Release 26 June 1946.

APPENDIX III

Arming of Merchant Vessels

The following cumulative table, of the number of merchant vessels that had been armed by the United States Navy at a succession of dates to 31 March 1943, was compiled from the records by Lieutenant (jg) J. Willard Hurst USNR.

Those in the second column were mostly of Panamanian registry.

As of	U. S. FLAG	U. S. OWNED, FOREIGN FLAG
1941		
31 Dec.	14	*41
1942		
27 Jan.	71,[1] plus *25	*41
26 Feb.	176, plus *44	8, plus *54
28 Mar.	323, plus *74	43, plus *56
27 Apr.	499	74
31 May	722	94
30 June	924	140
31 July	1080	159
31 Aug.	1236	175
30 Sept.	1328	185
31 Oct.	1436	192
30 Nov.	1518	205
31 Dec.	1607	206
1943		
31 Jan.	1697	221
28 Feb.	1804	225
31 Mar.	1933	227

* Armament furnished but no Armed Guard.

[1] Nine of these received a U. S. Army Armed Guard.

APPENDIX IV

Mine Fields Laid by U-Boats in Western Atlantic, 1942[1]

	DATE LAID	LAID BY	NO. LAID	DISCOVERED BY	SHIP CASUALTIES
	1942				
St. Johns, Newfoundland	14 May	*U-213*[2]	15	undiscovered	None
Boston	12 June	*U-87*	6	undiscovered	None
Delaware	11 June	*U-373*	15	sweeper	Tug *J. R. Williams*
Chesapeake	12 June	*U-701*[3]	15	ship	S.S. *Robert C. Tuttle*,[4] H.M. trawler *Kingston Ceylonite*, coal barge *Santore*, sunk. S.S. *Esso Augusta*, U.S.S. *Bainbridge*, slightly damaged
Castries, St. Lucia	20 July	*U-66*	6	ship	U.S.C.G. launch destroyed; British MTB slightly damaged
Mississippi Passes	24–25 July	*U-166*[3]	9	undiscovered	None
Charleston	end July	*U-751*	12	undiscovered	None
Jacksonville	8 Aug.	*U-98*[5]	12	sweeper	None
Chesapeake	10 Sept.	*U-69*	12	sweeper	None
Charleston	18 Sept.	*U-455*	12	sweeper	None
New York	10 Nov.	*U-608*	10	sweeper	None

[1] Mine Warfare Operational Research Group, Navy Dept. "Undiscovered" means that its existence only became known from enemy sources at the end of the war.

[2] Sunk 31 July in Eastern Atlantic by H.M.S. *Erne*.

[3] See Appendix II for fate.

[4] This tanker was later salvaged.

[5] Sunk off Straits 19 Nov. by R.A.F. planes.

APPENDIX V

The Support Force Atlantic Fleet

18 March 1941[1]

SUPPORT FORCE

Rear Admiral Arthur LeR. Bristol Jr., Commander, in *Prairie*

Destroyer Squadron 7, Capt. J. L. Kauffman

DD 431	PLUNKETT	Lt. Cdr. P. G. Hale (Comdesdiv 13, Cdr. Dennis L. Ryan)
DD 424	NIBLACK	Lt. Cdr. E. R. Durgin
DD 421	BENSON	Lt. Cdr. A. L. Pleasants Jr.
DD 423	GLEAVES	Lt. Cdr. E. H. Pierce
DD 422	MAYO	Lt. Cdr. C. D. Emory
DD 425	MADISON	(Comdesdiv 14, Cdr. F. D. Kirtland) Lt. Cdr. T. E. Boyce
DD 426	LANSDALE	Lt. Cdr. John Connor
DD 427	HILARY P. JONES	Lt. Cdr. S. R. Clark
DD 428	CHARLES F. HUGHES	Lt. Cdr. G. L. Menocal

Destroyer Squadron 30, Capt. M. Y. Cohen

DD 199	DALLAS	Lt. Cdr. H. B. Bell Jr.
DD 154	ELLIS	(Comdesdiv 60, Cdr. J. B. Heffernan) Lt. Cdr. J. M. Kennaday
DD 153	BERNADOU	Lt. Cdr. G. C. Wright
DD 155	COLE	Lt. Cdr. W. L. Dyer
DD 152	DUPONT	Lt. Cdr. E. M. Waldron
DD 145	GREER	(Comdesdiv 61, Cdr. C. W. Brewington) Lt. Cdr. Forrest Close
DD 142	TARBELL	Lt. Cdr. S. D. Willingham
DD 144	UPSHUR	Lt. Cdr. W. K. Romoser
DD 118	LEA	Lt. Cdr. C. Broussard

Destroyer Squadron 31, Capt. Wilder D. Baker

DD 220	MACLEISH	Lt. Cdr. A. C. Wood
DD 246	BAINBRIDGE	(Comdesdiv 62, Cdr. J. R. Davis) Lt. Cdr. E. P. Creehan
DD 239	OVERTON	Lt. Cdr. J. B. Stefanac
DD 240	STURTEVANT	Lt. Cdr. W. S. Howard Jr.
DD 245	REUBEN JAMES	Lt. Cdr. H. L. Edwards
DD 223	MCCORMICK	(Comdesdiv 63, Cdr. T. V. Cooper) Lt. Cdr. J. H. Lewis
DD 210	BROOME	Lt. Cdr. T. E. Fraser
DD 221	SIMPSON	Lt. Alexander MacIntyre
DD 229	TRUXTUN	Lt. Cdr. H. B. Heneberger

[1] Cinclant Operation Order 2-41; Commanding Officers obtained, verified, by the Ships' Logs Unit and the Ships' Rosters Section, Bureau of Naval Personnel.

APPENDIX VI

The Atlantic Fleet of the United States Navy

5 August 1942

Vice Admiral Royal E. Ingersoll, Commander in Chief
Flagship: Heavy Cruiser AUGUSTA, Capt. Gordon Hutchins
Relief flagships: Gunboat VIXEN, Lt. Cdr. J. G. Blanche
Frigate CONSTELLATION, Lt. Cdr. John Davis

BATTLESHIPS, Rear Admiral Alexander Sharp

Batdiv 5, Rear Admiral Sharp: NEW YORK, Capt. Scott Umstead; ARKANSAS, Capt. C. F. Bryant; TEXAS, Capt. L. W. Comstock.

Batdiv 7: SOUTH DAKOTA, Capt. T. L. Gatch; INDIANA, Capt. A. S. Merrill; MASSACHUSETTS, Capt. F. E. M. Whiting; WASHINGTON, Capt. G. B. Davis.

CRUISERS

Crudiv 2, Vice Admiral J. H. Ingram: Light Cruisers MEMPHIS, Capt. C. E. Braine; MILWAUKEE, Capt. F. B. Royal; CINCINNATI, Capt. E. M. Senn; OMAHA, Capt. T. E. Chandler; MARBLEHEAD, Capt. E. W. Morris.

Crudiv 7, Rear Admiral R. C. Giffen: Heavy Cruisers WICHITA, Capt. H. W. Hill; TUSCALOOSA, Capt. N. C. Gillette; AUGUSTA, Capt. Hutchins.

Crudiv 8, Rear Admiral L. A. Davidson: Light Cruisers PHILADELPHIA, Capt. C. J. Moore; BROOKLYN, Capt. F. C. Denebrink; SAVANNAH, Capt. L. S. Fiske; JUNEAU, Capt. L. K. Swenson.

CARRIERS, Rear Admiral E. D. McWhorter

RANGER, Capt. C. T. Durgin; Escort Carriers CORE, Capt. M. R. Greer; NASSAU, Capt. A. K. Doyle; BARNES, Capt. C. D. Glover; BLOCK ISLAND, Capt. L. C. Ramsey; CROATAN, Capt. J. B. Lyon; SANTEE, Capt. W. D. Sample; CHARGER, Capt. T. L. Sprague.

Seaplane Tenders: GEORGE E. BADGER, BELKNAP, OSMOND INGRAM, GREENE.

PATROL WINGS, Rear Admiral A. D. Bernhard

Patwing 3, Cdr. G. L. Compo; 5, Cdr. G. R. Owen; 7, Cdr. F. L. Baker; 9, Cdr. O. A. Weller; 11, Cdr. S. J. Michael.

These were divided into the following *Patrol Squadrons*, each composed of 12 Catalinas (PBY-5) and 2 obsolete seaplanes:

VP-31, Lt. Cdr. A. Smith; VP-32, Lt. Cdr. B. C. McCaffree; VP-33, Lt. Cdr. H. D. Hale; VP-34, Lt. Cdr. R. S. Calderhead; VP-52, Lt. Cdr. F. M. Hammitt;

VP-53, Lt. Cdr. F. M. Nichols; VP-73, Lt. Cdr. J. E. Leeper; VP-74,[1] Lt. Cdr. W. A. Thorn; VP-81, Lt. Cdr. T. B. Haley; VP-82,[2] Lt. Cdr. J. D. Greer; VP-83, Lt. Cdr. R. S. Clarke; VP-84, Lt. Cdr. J. J. Underhill; VP-92, Lt. Cdr. C. M. Heberton; VP-93, Lt. Cdr. C. W. Haman; VP-94, Lt. Cdr. D. W. Shafer.

Seaplane Tenders: ALBEMARLE, POCOMOKE, CHANDELEUR, CLEMSON, GOLDSBOROUGH, LAPWING, THRUSH, SANDPIPER, BARNEGAT, BISCAYNE, HUMBOLDT, MATAGORDA, ROCKAWAY, SAN PABLO, UNIMAK.

DESTROYERS, Rear Admiral O. C. Badger [3]

Destroyer Tenders: DENEBOLA, MELVILLE, ALTAIR, PRAIRIE, HAMUL.

Destroyers: DAHLGREN, NOA.

Desron 7, Cdr. S. R. Clark: NIBLACK, PLUNKETT, BENSON, GLEAVES, MAYO, MADISON, LANSDALE, HILARY P. JONES, CHARLES F. HUGHES.

Desron 8, Capt. D. P. Moon: WAINWRIGHT, Lt. Cdr. R. H. Gibbs; MAYRANT (Cdr. C. C. Hartman),[4] Cdr. E. A. Taylor; TRIPPE, Lt. Cdr. C. M. Dalton; RHIND, Lt. Cdr. H. T. Read; ROWAN, Lt. Cdr. B. R. Harrison.

Desron 9, Capt. J. D. H. Kane: DAVIS, Lt. Cdr. M. R. Peterson; MCDOUGAL, Lt. Cdr. G. C. Wright; WINSLOW, Lt. Cdr. W. P. Mowatt; MOFFETT, Lt. Cdr. J. C. Sowell; JOUETT, Lt. Cdr. F. L. Tedder; SOMERS, Lt. Cdr. A. C. Wood.

Desron 10, Cdr. J. L. Holloway: ELLYSON, Lt. Cdr. J. B. Rooney; HAMBLETON (Cdr. C. Wellborn), Lt. Cdr. F. Close; RODMAN, Lt. Cdr. W. G. Michelet; EMMONS, Lt. Cdr. T. C. Ragan; MACOMB, Lt. Cdr. W. H. Duvall; FORREST (Cdr. T. L. Wattles), Lt. Cdr. M. Van Metre; FITCH, Lt. Cdr. H. Crommelin; CORRY, Lt. Cdr. E. C. Burchett; HOBSON, Lt. Cdr. R. N. McFarlane.

Desron 11, Capt. J. S. Roberts: ROE, Lt. Cdr. J. N. Opie; LIVERMORE (Cdr. D. L. Madeira), Lt. Cdr. V. Huber; EBERLE, Lt. Cdr. K. F. Poehlmann; KEARNY, Lt. Cdr. A. H. Oswald; ERICSSON, Lt. Cdr. C. M. Jensen.

Desron 13, Capt. J. B. Heffernan: BUCK, Cdr. H. C. Robison; WOOLSEY, Lt. Cdr. B. L. Austin; LUDLOW, Cdr. C. H. Bennett; EDISON, Lt. Cdr. W. R. Headden; BRISTOL, Lt. Cdr. C. C. Wood; WILKES (Cdr. E. R. Durgin), Lt. Cdr. J. B. McLean; NICHOLSON, Cdr. J. S. Keating; SWANSON, Lt. Cdr. M. P. Kingsley; INGRAHAM, Cdr. W. M. Haynsworth.

Desron 15: [5] DAVISON, Lt. Cdr. W. C. Winn; MERVINE, Lt. Cdr. S. D. Willingham; QUICK, Lt. Cdr. R. B. Nickerson; BEATTY, Lt. Cdr. F. C. Stelter; TILLMAN, Lt. Cdr. F. D. McCorkle; COWIE, Lt. Cdr. C. J. Whiting; KNIGHT, Lt. Cdr. R. B. Levin; DORAN, Lt. Cdr. H. W. Gordon; EARLE, Lt. Cdr. H. W. Howe.

Desron 27: DECATUR, Lt. Cdr. D. C. E. Hamberger; BADGER, Lt. Cdr. J. W. Schmidt; BABBITT, Lt. Cdr. V. Havard; LEARY, Lt. Cdr. J. E. Kyes; SCHENCK, Lt. B. Taylor; ROPER, Lt. Cdr. J. B. Gragg; DICKERSON, Lt. F. E. Wilson; HERBERT, Lt. Cdr. J. A. E. Hindman.

Desron 30, Cdr. G. W. Johnson: DALLAS, Lt. Cdr. R. Brodie; ELLIS, Lt. Cdr. L. R. Lampman; BERNADOU, Lt. Cdr. R. E. Braddy; COLE, Lt. G. G. Palmer; DUPONT, Lt. Cdr. F. M. Adamson; GREER, Lt. Cdr. L. H. Frost; TARBELL, Lt. Cdr. W. N. Foster; UPSHUR, Lt. Cdr. L. Ensey; LEA, Lt. Cdr. J. F. Walsh.

[1] This Patron was composed of 12 Mariners (PBM-1) and 2 obsolete planes.

[2] This Patron was composed of 15 Hudsons (PBO-1) and 2 obsolete planes.

[3] Destroyers' commanding officers not given if they are the same as in the Support Force, Appendix V.

[4] Names in parentheses are those of division commanders on board ships indicated.

[5] Cdr. C. C. Hartman became C. O. of Desron 15 in Sept. 1942, but he is already in this list under Desron 8.

Desron 31, Cdr. W. K. Phillips; MACLEISH, Lt. Cdr. W. R. Caruthers; BAINBRIDGE, Lt. Cdr. L. W. Creighton; OVERTON, Lt. Cdr. L. C. Quiggle; MCCORMICK, Lt. Cdr. E. S. Sarsfield; BROOME, Lt. Cdr. G. C. Seay; SIMPSON, Lt. Cdr. E. J. Burke.

GREENLAND PATROL

Coast Guard Vessels AIVIK, AKLAK, ALATOK, ALGONQUIN, AMAROK, ARLUK, ARUNDEL, ARVEK, ATAK, COMANCHE, ESCANABA, MODOC, MOHAWK, MOJAVE, NANOK, NATSEK, NOGAK, NORTHLAND, NORTH STAR, RARITAN, STORIS, TAHOMA, TAMPA, ACTIVE, BIBB, CAMPBELL, DUANE, FAUNCE, FREDERICK LEE, INGHAM, SPENCER, TRAVIS; *SC-527, -528, -688, -689, -704, -705.*

SUBMARINES, Rear Admiral F. A. Daubin

Subron 1 (based at New London), Capt. E. F. Cutts: *O-2* (Cdr. R. M. Peacher), Lt. W. T. Griffith; *O-3*, Lt. A. G. Schnable; *O-4*, Lt. K. E. Montross; *O-6*, Lt. W. J. Germershausen; *O-7*, Lt. V. B. McCrea; *O-8*, Lt. W. T. Kinsella; *O-10*, Lt. J. F. Enright; PORPOISE, Lt. Cdr. J. A. Callaghan; PIKE, Lt. Cdr. W. A. New; auxiliary SEMMES (Lt. Cdr. S. P. Moseley), Lt. Cdr. W. L. Pryor; *S-16*, Lt. O. E. Hagberg; *S-17*, Lt. B. J. Harral; *S-20*, Lt. S. D. Dealey; *S-48*, Lt. F. Connaway; MACKEREL, Lt. F. N. Wahlig; MARLIN, Lt. Cdr. G. A. Sharp; Rescue Vessel FALCON.

Subron 3 (based at Coco Solo), Capt. T. J. Doyle: BARRACUDA (Cdr. W. L. Hoffheins), Lt. M. J. Hamilton; BASS, Lt. A. H. Dropp; BONITA, Lt. Cdr. S. G. Nichols; *S-11*, Lt. Cdr. S. G. Barchet; *S-12*, Lt. F. McMaster; *S-13*, Lt. Cdr. D. L. Whelchel; *S-14*, Lt. C. E. Loughlin; *S-15*, Lt. F. C. Acker; *S-21* (Cdr. C. F. Erck), Lt. R. H. Crane; *S-24*, Lt. Cdr. J. Corbus; Tender ANTAEUS, Rescue Vessel MALLARD.

Subron 7, Cdr. J. B. Longstaff: *R-2* (Cdr. W. A. Gorry), Lt. D. T. Hammond; *R-4*, Lt. P. W. Garnett; *R-10*, Lt. B. E. Lewellen; *R-11*, Lt. Cdr. E. C. Folger; *R-13*, *R-14*, Lt. G. W. Kehl; *R-20*, Lt. Cdr. C. B. Stevens; *R-1* (Cdr. P. G. Nichols), Lt. W. R. Laughon; *R-5*, Lt. A. C. House; *R-6*, Lt. J. B. Grady; *R-7*, Lt. Cdr. C. L. Murphy; *R-9*, Lt. R. R. Williams; *R-12* (Cdr. R. A. Knapp), Lt. E. E. Shelby; *R-15*, Lt. J. C. Titus; *R-16*, Lt. Cdr. J. M. Clement; *R-18*, Lt. J. S. Coye; Tender BEAVER; Rescue Vessel CHEWINK.

AMPHIBIOUS FORCE, Rear Admiral H. K. Hewitt

Transports, Capt. R. R. M. Emmet: LEONARD WOOD, CALVERT; Hospital Ship RIXEY.

Transdiv 1, Capt. Emmet: JOSEPH T. DICKMAN, JOHN PENN, JOSEPH HEWES; Cargo Ships ARCTURUS, TITANIA.

Transdiv 3, Capt. R. G. Coman: WILLIAM P. BIDDLE, CHARLES CARROLL, GEORGE CLYMER, EDWARD RUTLEDGE; Cargo Ship OBERON.

Transdiv 5, Capt. L. F. Reifsnider: SAMUEL CHASE, THOMAS STONE, THOMAS JEFFERSON, HARRY LEE; Cargo Ship ELECTRA.

AMPHIBIOUS CORPS, Maj. Gen. Holland M. Smith USMC

9th Army Division, Brig. Gen. M. S. Eddy USA, and various Army units attached.

SERVICE FORCE, Vice Admiral F. L. Reichmuth

In addition to various subchasers, repair ships, hospital ships, oceangoing tugboats and miscellaneous auxiliaries, this included: –

Minron 6: Minelayers PILOT, PIONEER, PORTENT, PREVAIL, SEER, SENTINEL, STAFF, SKILL, SPEED, STRIVE, STEADY, SUSTAIN, SWAY, SWERVE, SWIFT, SYMBOL, THREAT, TIDE.

Minron 7, Cdr. A. G. Cook: Destroyer Minesweepers HOGAN, HAMILTON,

HOWARD, PALMER, STANSBURY; Minelayers RAVEN, OSPREY, AUK, BROADBILL, CHICKADEE, NUTHATCH, PHEASANT.

Minron 8: Minelayers DASH, DESPITE, DIRECT, DYNAMIC, EFFECTIVE, ENGAGE, EXCEL, EXPLOIT, FIDELITY, FIERCE, FIRM, FORCE.

Minron 9, Lt. Cdr. W. R. McCaleb: Minelayers GOLDFINCH, GRACKLE, GULL, KITE, ALBATROSS, BLUEBIRD, FLICKER, LINNET.

Servron 7, Vice Admiral Reichmuth: Ammunition Ships NITRO, KILAUEA; Storeships YUKON, POLARIS, TARAZED, URANUS, PASTORES, PONTIAC, MERAK, ARIEL; Cargo Vessels SATURN, POLLUX; Oilers MAUMEE, PATOKA, SAPELO, KAWEAH, LARAMIE, MATTOLE, RAPIDAN, SALINAS, SALAMONIE, CHEMUNG, CHICOPEE, HOUSATONIC, KENNEBEC, MERRIMACK, WINOOSKI, MATTAPONI, WABASH, SUSQUEHANNA.

Index

Names of Combat Ships, except Numbered Vessels, in SMALL CAPITALS
Names of Merchant Ships and Numbered Vessels in *Italics*

Abbreviations

A/S = Anti-Submarine; M/V = Merchant Vessel; N.A.S. = Naval Air Station; N.O.B. = Naval Operating Base

C

S

T

U